A New Reference Grammar of Modern Spanish

FOURTH EDITION

JOHN BUTT, PH.D.   CARMEN BENJAMIN

McGraw·Hill

New York   Chicago   San Francisco   Lisbon   London   Madrid   Mexico City
Milan   New Delhi   San Juan   Seoul   Singapore   Sydney   Toronto

Originally published by Hodder Education, part of Hachette Livre UK,
338 Euston Road, London NW1 3BH.

ISBN 978-0-07-144049-3

Contents

Preface to the fourth edition

The aim of this book is to collect under one cover, in a format designed for easy reference, most of what English-speaking students can reasonably be expected to know about the syntax and morphology of the Spanish of Spain and Latin America as it is spoken and written at the beginning of the twenty-first century.

Spanish is the main, usually the only, official language of twenty-one countries[1] and this vast geographical and political extension inevitably means that the language is subject to regional variations. This causes problems for any textbook which, like this one, tries to do justice to both the European and Latin-American varieties of modern Spanish.

The differences between the Spanish of Spain and of any *one* Spanish-speaking Latin-American country are probably about the same as between British and American English, i.e. obvious but not really problematic. The evident differences of pronunciations do not really hinder understanding as long as one avoids local dialect; the variations in syntax cause little confusion; but the divergences in the vocabulary can sometimes, especially at the colloquial and popular level, give rise to misunderstandings.

But there is a fundamental difference between English and Spanish. North-American English is amazingly unified, at least as far as vocabulary and grammar are concerned, and the regional accents are much less diverse than in Britain, so it is therefore possible to treat American English as a single language for the purpose of comparison with other types of English. But Latin-American Spanish varies from country to country and region to region, above all in its colloquial vocabulary, and to a lesser extent in syntax and pronunciation. The everyday, informal spoken Spanish of, for example, Mexico, is probably not much less different from that of Argentina, Peru or Colombia than it is from that of Spain, and these divergences appear to varying degrees wherever we look in the Hispanic world. There is therefore no single 'Latin-American Spanish' language about which one can make many useful generalizations, and no simple answer to the question 'what is the relationship between Latin-American and European Spanish?'

The international unity of English is also to a large extent ensured by the constant Americanization of vocabulary and even syntax that affects British and other varieties of English: linguists have often noted this creeping homogenization of

---

1   Argentina, Bolivia, Chile, Colombia, Costa Rica, Cuba, the Dominican Republic, Ecuador, Equatorial Guinea (on the African Atlantic coast between Gabon and Cameroon), Guatemala, Honduras, Mexico, Nicaragua, Panama, Paraguay, Peru, Puerto Rico, El Salvador, Spain, Uruguay and Venezuela.

English. But the language of no single Hispanic country is consciously or unconsciously imitated by all the others, and no country or region can (or should) claim to speak or write the 'best' Spanish. This raises the problem, acute for books like this one, that it is often impossible to say definitively what constitutes 'correct' or 'normal' Spanish, especially now that the edicts of the Royal Spanish Academy are not taken seriously. For example, the spelling reforms solemnly decreed in the Academy's *Nuevas normas de ortografía y prosodia* of 1959 are still deliberately ignored by many prestigious publishers and even by some grammarians.

What, for example, is the 'correct' Spanish for 'pavement' or 'sidewalk'? Educated, literary usage fluctuates between *acera* (Sp.), *vereda* (Arg., Ch., Pe.), *banqueta* (Mex.) and *andén* (Col., Central America), and there are probably other local words. Is *adentro de* for *dentro de* 'wrong' when it is preferred by the more than 85% of Spanish-speakers who live outside Spain? Is *se los dije* for 'I told them' to be condemned as 'illiterate' simply because Spaniards vehemently insist on *se lo dije*? *Se los dije* is now widespread in spoken Latin-American Spanish, even among educated speakers.

These and many similar questions constantly trouble grammarians and lexicographers of Spanish, and dictionaries and grammars that try to reflect the variety of living Spanish are inevitably packed with a disconcerting number of alternatives.

In this grammar we have tried to do justice to the international character of Spanish by providing examples from many different countries, these examples being chosen because, unless we state otherwise, they also represent normal language in Spain and therefore presumably reflect international Spanish usage. Where Latin-American language differs from Spain we comment on it, try to state where it is most prevalent, and show the Peninsular equivalent. We hope that this gives a broad and fair picture of living Spanish and that it will satisfy North-American students and those in the Southern Hemisphere who generally learn a Latin-American variety, and British students, who usually study Peninsular Spanish. However, since the native language of one of the authors and the dialect familiar to the other is Peninsular Spanish, the unattributed examples will inevitably reflect European usage and may sometimes sound strange to Latin Americans. We should not need to add that we do not imagine that the Spanish of Spain is in some way superior to the Latin-American varieties. The various kinds of Spanish spoken today are all the legitimate heirs of a language that was spoken five hundred years ago, and no one modern version can claim to be more 'grammatical' or faithful to its parent than any other.

As far as possible, our examples are of the Spanish spoken and written in the last thirty years: problems of space obliged us to omit historical questions. We also concentrate on syntactic and morphological questions. Lexical issues such as word formation (except diminutive and other similar suffixes) are barely discussed, mainly because of lack of space, but also because teaching foreigners how to coin new words encourages badly-formed vocabulary. Questions of pronunciation have also been omitted as numerous guides to the sound system of Spanish are already in print.

We assume that readers have a native knowledge of English, so our explanations have been shortened by reference to English whenever the languages seem to coincide. Since interference from French and occasionally Italian and Portuguese is a constant problem for teachers of Spanish, sporadic mention of these languages is made in order to emphasize some peculiarity of Spanish.

For this fourth edition of 'B&B' we have benefited from a reading of the Royal Spanish Academy's latest grammar, the three-volume, 5300-page *Gramática descriptiva de la lengua española* (Madrid: Espasa Calpe, 1999), which appeared just after the third edition of our book went to press. Its more than seventy contributors describe in great detail the syntax and morphology of the Spanish written, and above all spoken, in many different regions and countries, and their accounts are so detailed that in some cases they note discrepancies of usage between places only a few miles apart, e.g. between the use of *le/les* and *lo/la/los/las* in the Spanish cities of Toledo and Madrid.

The *GDLE* will dismay all but linguistic specialists. It is written in dauntingly technical language for academics who already speak Spanish fluently. It also creates a picture of a language splintered into countless varieties, but foreign learners can be assured that, as far as pronunciation and, probably, syntax are concerned (but not colloquial vocabulary), Spanish is more unified than international English. The *GDLE* aims to be rigorously descriptive, and carefully abstains from declaring some linguistic forms to be more 'correct' than others. The next prescriptive Academy grammar of Spanish is promised for late 2004 and it will reportedly attempt to lay down linguistic 'norms' for both Spain and Latin America. Until such norms are universally adopted (if they are), the problem of deciding what constitutes 'correct' Spanish will not disappear.

In view of the large number of books in print that quote extensively from 'B & B', we have not significantly altered the section numbers or the order in which material is presented in this new edition, even though these sometimes need improvement.

In response to constant pleas from students and teachers we have included a glossary of grammatical terms and have made renewed efforts to simplify, clarify and, where possible, shorten our explanations. Sometimes we sacrifice scientific rigour to brevity or clarity (as we see it). This is particularly so in the case of our refusal to use the International Phonetic Alphabet, and of our persistent use of words like 'delete', 'omit' and 'replace'. But despite these simplifications, we must emphasize that this book is not really intended for beginners.

Acknowledgements

We have availed ourselves of the labours of Andrés Bello, María Moliner, Ramsey and Spaulding and of other eminent grammarians and lexicographers, especially Manuel Seco: one disregards his recommendations about Spanish usage at one's peril. We are indebted to the numerous authors of the *GDLE* for many fresh insights about or confirmations of our statements, but there was no room to mention individual contributors. Of the works listed in the bibliography we are particularly indebted to E. García (1975), to C. E. Kany (Chicago, 1945, reprinted and translated into Spanish) and George DeMello's numerous published statistical analyses of educated spoken usage.

We are deeply indebted to a large number of Spanish-speakers who have helped us over the years: they are acknowledged in the prefaces to previous editions. Antonia Moreira Rodríguez of King's College, London, has again contributed to this, as to every edition, with her enthusiasm and innumerable valuable suggestions. Nick Cowan generously helped with the proofs. We are also indebted to the recommendations and criticisms of reviewers and readers, most of which we have tried to incorporate. But we alone are responsible for the omissions and mistakes that our book surely contains.

John Butt
Carmen Benjamin
London, 2004

Conventions, spelling and abbreviations

El mujer: a preceding asterisk marks a form that is not Spanish. It is occasionally also used for forms that may be heard but are very aberrant.

A preceding uninverted question mark –?*se puso detrás mío*, ?*adentro de*– shows that a form is not accepted by all speakers.

'Colloquial' describes forms that are acceptable in spontaneous educated speech but are usually avoided in formal speech or writing.

'Familiar' describes forms that are frequently heard in spontaneous speech but should be avoided in formal situations and treated with caution by foreigners.

'Popular' describes commonly-heard forms that may be stigmatized by some speakers as uneducated.

Forms separated by / are alternatives, either alternatives that have different meanings but use the same construction, e.g. *yo sé*/*él sabe* 'I know'/'he knows', or alternative ways of saying the same thing, e.g. *antes de que*/*antes que* 'before'. Words in round brackets may be optionally deleted with no or only slight effect on meaning or style, e.g. *con tal (de) que* 'provided that'.

Except where indicated, all examples represent usage worthy of imitation by foreigners, and the Latin-American quotations are also good European Spanish unless we state otherwise.

Words that represent the speech of fictional characters are marked 'dialogue' to avoid their language being attributed to their author.

The spelling of Spanish words observes the Academy's rules laid down in the *Nuevas normas de prosodia y ortografía* of 1959, although we indicate general usage where this remains at odds with the Academy's decrees, e.g. in the case of the demonstrative pronouns *éste*, *ése* and *aquél* and of *sólo* 'only', although to judge by the *GDLE* even the Academy has abandoned its preference for *solo* over *sólo*. The spellings *México*, *mexicano* are used throughout instead of *Méjico*, *mejicano*, on the grounds that Mexicans request everyone to use them, and the prestigious Spanish daily *El País* prefers them.

The English spelling is British, but American alternatives are usually shown except for 'preterite' and 'judgement', which are used throughout. In some constantly occurring cases, like 'col(o)ur', 'neighbo(u)r', readers who use US spelling can mentally delete the bracketed letter. The format used for dates is the British one: *dd-mm-yy(yy)*.

The term 'Latin American' is used throughout in preference to 'Spanish American', since the latter can annoy Spanish-speaking Latin Americans as much as 'British American' would no doubt irritate most citizens of the· USA. 'Latin

American' is linguistically inaccurate, but it should be obvious that we are not talking about Brazilian Portuguese or Caribbean French.

Spanish verbs and pronouns can be very ambiguous out of context. The temptation to translate Spanish sentences like *le dio un libro* always as '*he* gave *him* a book' is therefore misleading and may indicate a sexual bias, so we use the ugly forms '(s)he', 'him/her', 'his/her' in the translations: *fuma* = '(s)he smokes' (it could also mean 'it smokes' or 'you [*usted*] smoke', but we do not systematically note these possibilities). In earlier editions we often arbitrarily put 'she' rather than 'he' in the translations to recall that speakers of Spanish do not automatically conjure up a mental image of a man in the absence of a separate pronoun. We have abandoned this practice since it adds information absent in the original, and some readers found it very confusing.

Abbreviations

Esbozo	Real Academia Española, *Esbozo de una nueva gramática de la lengua española* (Madrid, 1973)
lit.	'literally', 'literal translation'
Nuevas normas	*Nuevas normas de prosodia y ortografía. Nuevo texto definitivo* (Madrid, 1959)
Lat. Am.	Latin America(n)
GDLE	*Gramática descriptiva de la lengua española*, Ignacio Bosque and Violeta Demonte eds, 3 vols, Colección Nebrija y Bello de la Real Academia Española (Madrid: Espasa Calpe, 1999)

Arg. Argentina	Cu. Cuba	Pe. Peru
Bol. Bolivia	Ec. Ecuador	Sp. Spain
Ch. Chile	Mex. Mexico	Ur. Uruguay
Col. Colombia	Par. Paraguay	Ve. Venezuela

The other countries are spelled in full.

1

Gender of nouns

This chapter deals with:

- The gender of nouns referring to human beings and a few other well-known animals (Section 1.2)
- The gender of nouns referring to other animals (Section 1.3)
- The gender of words referring to non-living things and to plants (Section 1.4)

1.1 General

Nouns in Spanish are either masculine or feminine in gender, except for a few nouns of undecided gender (see 1.4.13). The question of the gender of Spanish nouns is easier to understand if we divide them into two groups:

(A) Nouns referring to human beings, domesticated animals and a few wild animals: see 1.2.

(B) Nouns referring to lifeless things, to plants and to the animals not included in group A: see 1.3, 1.4.

1.2 Group A: Gender of nouns referring to human beings, domesticated animals and a few wild animals

Nouns referring to males are almost all masculine, nouns referring to females are almost all feminine. This rules applies to human beings, but only to a few domesticated and wild animals, most of them listed in 1.2.1. Other animals are discussed at 1.3.

The gender of these nouns is more biological in Spanish than in French, where the masculine nouns *le professeur* or *le docteur* can refer to a woman, or in German, where a girl (*ein Mädchen*) is neuter, or Italian where a policeman, *una guardia*, is feminine (*una guardia* = 'policewoman' in Spanish). Forms like *la recluta* 'recruit', *la centinela* 'sentinel' used to be applied to men in Golden-Age Spanish, but one now says *el recluta* for a male recruit, *la recluta* for a female. However, a few Spanish nouns of fixed gender, e.g. *la víctima*, *la celebridad*, may refer to both males and females: see 1.2.11 for a selection.

1.2.1 Special forms for male and female

Some nouns in group A have special forms for the male or female which must be learned separately. The following list is not exhaustive:

el abad/la abadesa abbot/abbess
el actor/la actriz actor/actress
el barón/la baronesa baron/baroness
el caballo/la yegua stallion/mare
el león/la leona lion/lioness
el macho/la cabra* billy-goat/goat
el carnero/la oveja* ram/ewe (sheep)
el conde/la condesa count/countess
el duque/la duquesa duke/duchess
el elefante/la elefanta elephant
el emperador/la emperatriz emperor/
   empress
el gallo/la gallina* cockerel/hen
   (or chicken)
el héroe/la heroína hero/heroine
   (or heroin)

el hombre/la mujer man/woman (or wife, in
   Spain)
el jabalí/la jabalina wild boar
el marido/la mujer husband/wife (or woman)
el padre/la madre father/mother
el príncipe/la princesa prince/princess
el rey/la reina king/queen
el sacerdote/la sacerdotisa priest/priestess
el toro/la vaca* bull/cow
el yerno/la nuera son/daughter
   -in-law (la yerna is heard in
   parts of Lat. Am.)
el varón (human) or el macho (animals)/la
   hembra male/female

NB: In Latin America *la esposa* is used for 'wife' and *la mujer* for 'woman'; *mujer* means both things in Spain.

(i) Asterisks mark a feminine form which is also used for the species in general: *las ovejas* = 'sheep' as well as 'ewes'. Normally the masculine is also the generic form, e.g. *los padres* means 'parents' as well as 'fathers'. See 1.2.8.

(ii) A number of animals make their feminine by changing the final *–o* to *–a*, e.g. *el cerdo* 'pig' (Sp.), *el chancho* 'pig' (Lat. Am.), *el ciervo* 'deer', *el ganso* 'goose', *el gato* 'cat', *el lobo* 'wolf', *el mono* 'monkey', *el oso* 'bear', *el pato* 'duck', *el pavo* 'turkey', *el perro* dog, *el puerco* 'pig', (Lat. Am.). So *la perra* = 'bitch' and *la cerda* = 'sow', etc.

1.2.2 Feminine of nouns in group A whose masculine form ends in -o

Nearly all of these make their feminine in *-a*:

el abuelo/la abuela grandfather/
   grandmother
el amigo/la amiga friend
el candidato/la candidata candidate

el hermano/la hermana brother/sister
el novio/la novia boyfriend/girlfriend
el tío/la tía uncle/aunt

But a few that refer to professions or activities are invariable in form and the sex of the person is shown by an article, as in *un soldado* 'a soldier', *una soldado israelí* 'an Israeli woman soldier'; or by an adjective, as in *el modelo* 'male model', *modelos francesas* 'female French models'. Other examples:

el/la árbitro referee
el/la piloto pilot/racing driver
el/la reo accused (in court)

el/la soprano soprano
el/la testigo witness (*la testiga* is popular
   Spanish)

A few words, e.g. *el médico/la médica* 'doctor', are controversial. See 1.2.7.

1.2.3 Feminine of nouns in Group A whose masculine form ends in -or, -ón, -ín, -és

These add *–a*, and any accent written on the last vowel disappears:

el asesor/la asesora adviser/consultant
el anfitrión/la anfitriona host/hostess
el bailarín/la bailarina dancer
el burgués/la burguesa bourgeois
el campeón/la campeona champion

el doctor/la doctora doctor
el león/la leona lion/lioness
el profesor/la profesora teacher
el programador/la programadora programmer

For adjectives like *cortés, preguntón, pillín* see 4.2.1.

NB: *El/la peatón* 'pedestrian' seems to be the only noun ending in *–ón* that does not add *–a* for the feminine: *la peatón recibió graves heridas…* (*La Voz de Galicia*, Sp.) 'the female pedestrian received severe injuries'.

1.2.4 Feminine of nouns in Group A whose masculine form ends in -*a*

These do not change:

el/la artista artist	*el/la colega* colleague/	*el/la guía* guide (*la guía*
el/la astronauta astronaut	workmate	also 'guidebook')
el/la atleta athlete	*el/la guardia* policeman/	*el/la pianista* pianist
	policewoman	

El modisto 'male fashion designer' is an unusual masculine form, common in Spain: *todo las separa, los lazos de sangre, el destino, e incluso los modistos* (*El Mundo*, Sp.) 'everything stands between them: blood ties, fate and even fashion designers'. Manuel Seco (1998), 299, and *El País* recommend *el modista* for males and *la modista* for females. *La modista* also means 'dressmaker'.

1.2.5 Feminine of nouns in Group A whose masculine ends in -*nte*

The majority do not change:

el/la adolescente adolescent	*el/la cantante* singer	*el/la transeúnte* passer-by
el/la agente police officer/	*el/la representante*	
agent	representative	
el/la amante lover		

But a few feminine forms in -*nta* are in use, at least in Spain; they may be unacceptable in parts of Latin America:

el acompañante/la acompañanta companion/escort	*el dependiente/la dependienta* shop assistant/US sales clerk	*el principiante/la principianta* beginner (young Peninsular informants preferred
el asistente/la asistenta batman (military)/ daily help (or 'cleaner')	*el pariente/la parienta* relative	*la principiante*)
el comediante/la comedianta actor/actress		*el sirviente/la sirvienta* servant

NB: *Comediante* and *comedianta* tend to be derogatory in Spain, particularly the feminine: *¡qué comediante/a eres!* 'what an act you put on!' Polite forms are *el actor cómico/la actriz cómica* 'comic actor'.

In the following two cases the invariable form is more formal: *el/la asistente social* 'social worker', also *la asistenta social*; *el/la presidente* 'president', also *la presidenta*, recommended by Seco (1998), 354, and now very widespread.

Forms like **la estudianta* for *la estudiante* are considered substandard. But a few popular nouns/adjectives form a feminine in -*nta*: *el golfante/la golfanta* 'lout'/ 'good-for-nothing', *el atorrante/la atorranta* (Lat. Am.) 'tramp'/'slacker'/US 'bum', *dominanta* 'bossy'/'pushy' (applied to women).

1.2.6 Feminine of other nouns in Group A whose masculine form ends in -*e* or in a consonant

Apart from those mentioned in the preceding section, these do not change:

el/la alférez subaltern	*el/la intérprete* interpreter	*el/la rehén* hostage
el/la barman (Sp.) barman/	*el/la líder* (political) leader	*el/la mártir* martyr
barmaid	*el/la joven* young man/	*el/la tigre* (or *la tigresa*)
el/la enlace representative/	woman	tiger
(Brit.) shop steward		

Exceptions: *el huésped/la huéspeda* 'guest' (also *la huésped*), *el monje/la monja* 'monk' / 'nun', *el sastre/la sastra* 'tailor'. For *la jefa* see 1.2.7.

1.2.7 Feminine forms of nouns referring to professions

Until the 1960s feminine forms of professional or educational titles sometimes had insulting or comic overtones or denoted the wife of the male, cf. *el bachiller* = someone who has passed the equivalent of the baccalaureate or pre-university examination, *la bachillera* 'bluestocking', i.e. a woman sneered at for being too educated; *el sargento/la sargenta* 'sergeant' / 'battleaxe', i.e. a fierce woman – the word is still used; *el general/la generala* 'general' / 'the general's wife'. In some places, especially in Spain, a stigma still attaches to some of these feminine forms of words referring to professions, so formal language shows respect by using masculine form with a feminine article, e.g. *el/la abogado* 'lawyer' / 'legal counsel' (*la abogada*, originally 'intercessionary saint', is however now widespread for a woman lawyer).

The following should be noted:

El/la juez 'judge': *El País* insists on *la juez* and in the Spanish countryside *la jueza* may still mean 'the judge's wife'. The Latin-American press sometimes uses *la jueza*, but often *la juez*.

El/la médico 'doctor': *la médica* is normal in much of Latin America, cf. *una médica blanca sudafricana* (*Granma*, Cuba) 'a white South-African female doctor'. *El País* approves of *la médica*, but it is thought disrespectful by many speakers of European Spanish. *Doctora* is used to address a woman doctor.

El/la miembro 'member' (of clubs); also, more commonly *el socio/la socia*.

El/la ministro 'minister', but *la ministra* is increasingly acceptable. *El País* and Manuel Seco both recommend *la primera ministra* over *la primer ministro*, although it logically means 'the first female minister'.

El/la jefe: *la jefa* is accepted by *El País* as the feminine of *el/la jefe* 'boss', but it sounds too familiar for some people. García Márquez (Col.) writes *Maruja había sido. . .jefe de relaciones públicas* 'Maruja had been head of public relations'.

Other nouns in *-o* may be regular: *el arquitecto/la arquitecta* 'architect', *el biólogo/la bióloga* 'biologist', *el catedrático/la catedrática* 'professor' (European meaning), *el filósofo/la filósofa* 'philosopher', *el letrado/la letrada* 'counsel' / 'legal representative', *el político/la política* 'politician', *el sociólogo/la socióloga* 'sociologist', etc. Nevertheless, forms like *la arquitecto*, *la filósofo*, *la letrado* may be preferred in Spain. *La magistrada* 'judge' (higher in rank than a British magistrate) is now usual.

Feminine forms are frequently used when the woman in question is not present: *¿qué tal te llevas con la nueva jefa?* 'how are you getting on with your new woman boss?', but *me han dicho que usted es la jefe del departamento* 'they tell me that you are the head of the department'; *ha llegado otra clienta* 'another woman customer has come', but in her presence *atiende a esta cliente* 'serve this customer'.

1.2.8 Nouns referring to mixed groups of males and females

With the rare exceptions noted at 1.2.1, the masculine plural is used either for a group of males, or a mixed group of males and females. In fact the masculine plural is usually assumed, out of context, to refer to both sexes, which confuses English-speakers. The instinctive answer to *¿tienes hermanos?* might be *tengo dos hermanos y una hermana* 'I've got two brothers and one sister'. Likewise *hoy vienen los padres de los niños* = 'the children's **parents** are coming today'. 'The children's fathers are coming' would have to be clarified by *vienen los padres de los niños—los padres solos* = 'the fathers on their own'. Further examples:

los hijos children/sons	*los perros* dogs/male dogs
los ingleses the English/Englishmen	*los reyes* the King and the Queen/
los niños children/little boys	kings and queens/kings
los profesores teachers/male teachers	

Feminine nouns refer only to females, so one must use the masculine in sentences like *no tengo más amigos que mujeres* 'the only friends I have are women' or *todos los profesores son mujeres* 'all the teachers are women'. **No tengo más amigas que mujeres* means 'the only female friends I have are women'! *Tú eres la más inteligente de tod**os*** 'you're the most intelligent of all' is a nicer compliment to a woman than *...de tod**as*** since the masculine includes males and females. But a sentence like *María es la mejor profesora del instituto* 'Maria's the best teacher in the school' is ambiguous: it may or may not include males. *Emilia Pardo Bazán es la mejor intérprete de la vida rural de toda la literatura española del siglo XIX* 'Emilia Pardo Bazán is the best interpreter of rural life in the whole of 19th-century Spanish literature' is assumed by convention *not* to mean that she is the best female interpreter of rural life, which would be *intérprete femenina*.

Care must be taken with words like *uno, otro*. If a woman from Madrid says *todos los madrileños me caen gordos* 'all Madrid people get on my nerves' one could reply *¡pero tú eres uno de ellos!* 'but you're one of them!', but not *...una de ellos*, since *madrileños* includes both males and females (*¡pero tú también eres madrileña!* avoids the problem). Compare also *Ana es una de las profesor**as*** 'Ana is one of the women teachers' and *Ana es uno de los profesores* 'Ana is one of the teachers'.

In a few cases usage seems uncertain. A woman might say either *unos están a favor y otros en contra. Yo soy de las que están a favor* or *...de los que están a favor* 'some are for, others are against. I'm one of those who are for it'.

1.2.9 Gender of nouns denoting non-living things when they are applied to humans

Feminine nouns that usually apply to lifeless things can sometimes be applied to human males. In this case the noun usually acquires masculine gender:

		applied to a male	
una bala perdida	stray bullet	*un bala perdida*	ne'er-do-well/waster
la cámara	camera	*el cámara*	cameraman
la piel	skin	*el piel roja*	redskin
la primera clase	first class	*un primera clase*	someone first-class
la superventa	top sale	*el superventa*	top seller
la trompeta	trumpet	*el trompeta*	trumpet-player
etc.			

The reverse case is better avoided: *la que toca la trompeta* 'the woman playing the trumpet', not *la trompeta*, which is the instrument.

1.2.10 Gender of names applied across sex boundaries

A female's name applied to a male acquires masculine gender: *tú eres **un** Margaret Thatcher* 'you're a Margaret Thatcher' (said to a man of his right-wing political ideas). But men's names usually remain masculine : *María, tú eres **un** Hitler con faldas* 'Maria, you're a female Hitler', lit. 'Hitler with skirts'.

1.2.11 Nouns of invariable gender applied to either sex

Some common words applied to human beings do not change their gender. One says *el bebé está enfermo* 'the baby is ill', whatever its sex. Similar words are:

el ángel angel	*el genio* genius	*el personaje* character
la calamidad 'calamity'	*la lumbrera* as in *M. no*	(in novels, etc.)
la celebridad celebrity	*es una lumbrera* 'M.'s	(*eres*) *un sol* you're
el desastre 'disaster'	no genius'	wonderful/an angel
el esperpento 'fright'/	*el ligue* 'date'/casual	*la víctima* victim
weird-looking person	boy or girlfriend	
la estrella star (TV, etc.)	*la persona* person	

and a few other masculine nouns referring to women, most involving sexual innuendo or comparisons with objects, cf. *el pendón* 'trollop' (lit. 'pennant'), *el marimacho* 'tomboy', etc.

Titles like *Alteza* 'Highness', *Excelencia*, *Ilustrísima* 'Grace' (title of bishops) and *Majestad* 'Majesty' are feminine, but the person addressed keeps his/her gender: *Su Majestad estará cansado* (to a king), 'Your Majesty must be tired'.

1.3 Nouns referring to animals not included under 1.2.1–11

Nouns referring to the animals not included in the preceding sections—i.e. to most wild animals—are of fixed, arbitrary gender and must be learned separately:

el asno ass	*el leopardo* leopard	*la araña* spider
el canguro kangaroo	*el panda* panda	*la ballena* whale
el castor beaver	*el puma* puma	*la mula* mule
el cisne swan	*el sapo* toad	*la rana* frog

and many others. If sex must be distinguished, the male is denoted by adding *macho* 'male' and the female by adding *hembra* 'female': *la ardilla macho* 'male squirrel', *el cangrejo hembra* 'female crab', etc. In good Spanish adjectives agree with the noun, not with the animal: *la rana macho está muerta* 'the male frog is dead', *un cisne hembra blanco* 'a white female swan'. Neither *macho* nor *hembra* agrees in gender or number: *las cebras macho* 'male zebras', *los gavilanes hembra* 'female sparrowhawks'.

Familiar language may give such nouns biological gender: *el/la gorila* 'he-gorilla' and 'she-gorilla' (properly invariably *el gorila*), *el/la jirafa* 'giraffe' (*la jirafa* is properly invariably feminine).

NB: *La canguro* ('she-kangaroo') is used in Spain for a female childminder.

1.4 Group B: Gender of nouns referring to non-living things

The gender of nouns referring to non-living things, to plants, and to the animals mentioned in 1.3 must be learned for each noun. It has no sexual implications and it occasionally varies from place to place (cf *la sauna* 'sauna' in Spain, *el sauna* in Latin America), or century to century (cf. Golden Age *la puente*, modern *el puente* 'bridge').

There are few infallible rules, and we quote only those which in our view do not encourage false generalizations. Other Romance languages are unreliable guides to Spanish genders, cf. *un oasis*, Fr. *une oasis*; *el límite*, Fr. *la limite*; *el calor*, Fr. *la chaleur*; *el período*, Fr. *la période*; *el paisaje*, Port. *a paisagem; la flor*, It. *il fiore*; and many more.

1.4.1 Masculine by meaning

Many nouns acquire the gender of an underlying or implied noun (metonymic gender). The following are typical:

(**a**) Rivers (*el río*): *el Amazonas* 'the Amazon', *el Jarama*, *el Manzanares*, *el Plata* 'the River Plate', *el Sena* 'the Seine', *el Támesis* 'the Thames', *el Volga*. Locally some rivers may be feminine, but outsiders rarely know this and the masculine is always correct.

(**b**) Mountains, oceans, seas and lakes (*el monte, el océano, el mar, el lago*): *el Etna*, *el Everest*, *el Himalaya* (singular), *el Pacífico*, *el Caribe* 'Caribbean', *el Windermere*.

(**c**) The names of cars, boats and aircraft (*el coche, el barco, el avión*): *un Toyota*, *un Mercedes*, *el caza* 'fighter plane', *el Queen Elisabeth*, *el Marie Celeste*, *un DC10*, *un F11*. But small boats (*la barca*) are usually feminine, as are light aircraft because of the underlying noun *la avioneta*, e.g. *una Cessna*.

(**d**) Months and days of the week (*los meses y los días de la semana*): *enero/abril pasado*, *el lunes* 'Monday', *un viernes frío* 'a cold Friday'.

(**e**) Wines (*el vino*): *el Borgoña* 'Burgundy', *el Chianti*, *un Rioja*, *el champaña* 'champagne', usually *el champán* in spoken Spanish, but often *la champaña* in Lat. Am. *El cava* is often used in Spain to refer to Spanish champagne.

(**f**) Pictures (*el cuadro*) by named artists: *un Constable*, *un Leonardo*, *un Rembrandt*, *un Riley*.

(**g**) Sports teams (*el equipo*): *el Barça* 'Barcelona FC' (pronounced [bársa]), *el Betis* (one of Seville's soccer teams), *el España*, *el Bilbao*, etc.

(**h**) All infinitives, and all quoted words: *el fumar* 'smoking', *el escupir* 'spitting', *el "cama" no se lee* 'you can't read the word "bed"', *no viene la señal, el "siga" que él esperaba* (E. Poniatowska, Mex.) 'the signal doesn't come, the "go on" that he was expecting'.

(**i**) Any adverb, interjection or other genderless word used as a noun: *el más allá* 'the Beyond', *un algo* 'a "something"', *tiene un no sabe uno qué que gusta* (L. Rafael Sánchez, Puerto Rico, dialogue) 'she's got something nice about her'.

(j) Numbers (*el número*): *un seis, un 5, la Generación del 98* the 'Generation of '98', *el dos por ciento* 'two per cent'.

(k) Musical notes: *el fa, el la* (underlying noun unclear).

(l) Colo(u)rs (*el color*): *el azul* 'blue', *el ocre* 'ochre'; *se amplía el naranja del horizonte* 'the orange on the horizon is spreading' (A. Gala, Sp.), *...sus uñas de un discretísimo rosa pálido* (M. Benedetti, Ur.) '...her nails, painted a very discreet pale pink'.

(m) Certain trees (*el árbol*) whose fruit (*la fruta*) is feminine, e.g.

el almendro: *la almendra* almond	*el guindo*: *la guinda* morello cherry
el avellano: *la avellana*: hazel	*el mandarino*: *la mandarina* tangerine
el castaño: *la castaña* chestnut	*el manzano*: *la manzana* apple
el cerezo: *la cereza* cherry	*el naranjo*: *la naranja* orange
el ciruelo: *la ciruela* plum	*el nogal*: *la nuez* walnut (also simply 'nut')
el granado: *la granada* pomegranate	*el papayo*: *la papaya* papaya
el guayabo: *la guayaba* guava	*el peral*: *la pera* pear

NB: In Spain *nuez de California* is sometimes used to specify 'walnut'.

But some fruits are masculine: *el limón* 'lemon', *el aguacate* 'avocado' (*la palta* in southern Latin America), *el melón* 'melon', *el albaricoque* 'apricot', *el higo* 'fig', etc. 'A banana' is *una banana* for many Latin Americans, but *un plátano* in Spain and parts of Lat. Am. The latter also means 'plane-tree' in Spain, so banana tree is *el plátano bananero*.

1.4.2 Masculine by form

(a) Nouns ending in *-o*: *el eco* 'echo', *el tiro* 'shot'. Exceptions:

la dinamo dynamo (also	*la magneto* magneto (masc.	*la moto* motorbike
el dínamo)	in Latin America)	*la nao* ship (archaic)
la foto photo	*la mano* hand (dim. *la*	*la polio* polio
la Gestapo the Gestapo	*manita* (Sp.), *la manito*	*la porno* porn(ography),
la libido libido	(Lat. Am.))	i.e. *la pornografía*

La radio 'radio' is feminine in Spain and in the Southern Cone, but in Mexico, Cuba and Central America and sporadically in northern parts of South America it is *el radio*. In some places *el radio* is 'radio set' and *la radio* is 'radio station'. *El radio* also everywhere means 'radius' and 'radium'. In Gabriel García Márquez's *Noticia de un secuestro* (Col., 1996) *el radio* and *la radio* appear with about equal frequency.

(b) Words ending in *-aje, -or, -án, -ambre* or a stressed vowel:

el equipaje luggage	*el valor* value	*Canadá* (masc.) Canada
el paisaje landscape	*el mazapán* marzipan	*el sofá* sofa/couch
el amor love	*el refrán* proverb	*el champú* shampoo
el calor heat	*el calambre* spasm/twinge	*el tisú* tissue (Kleenex)
el color colo(u)r	*el enjambre* swarm	*el rubí* ruby

But *la labor* 'labour', *la flor*, 'flower'. *El hambre* 'hunger' is also feminine: see 3.1.2 for explanation of the *el*. The forms *la calor* and *la color* for *el calor* 'heat' and *el color* 'colo(u)r' are heard in dialect and rural speech in Spain and in parts of Latin America. *La televisor* for *el televisor* 'television set' and one or two other unusual genders are also found in local Latin-American dialects.

1.4.3 Common masculine nouns ending in -*a*

There is no rule that says that Spanish nouns ending in –*a* are feminine. Many nouns ending in -*ma*, and several others ending in -*a* are masculine:

(a) Masculine nouns ending in –*a* (for masculine nouns ending in -*ma* see list **b**)

el aleluya alleluia (*la aleluya* is 'doggerel'/
  'jingle')
el alerta alert (*el alerta rojo* 'red alert';
  la alerta is now very common)
el bocata familiar in Sp. for 'sandwich'
  (*bocadillo*)
el busca bleeper/pager
el caza fighter plane
el cometa comet (*la cometa* = 'kite', the toy)
el día day
el escucha listening device/electronic 'bug'
el extra extra, extra payment
el gorila gorilla
el guardarropa wardrobe (all such
  compounds are masculine)
el Himalaya the Himalayas

el insecticida insecticide (and all
  chemicals ending in -*icida*)
el lempira Honduran unit of currency
el mañana the morrow/tomorrow
  (*la mañana* = 'morning')
el mapa map
el mediodía noon
el nirvana Nirvana
el panda panda
el planeta planet
el Sáhara or *el Sahara* the Sahara Desert
el telesilla ski-lift
el tranvía tram
el tequila tequila. (Also *la tequila*)
el vodka vodka
el yoga yoga

(b) Masculine nouns ending in -*ma*

These words are masculine, in most cases because the Greek words that they are derived from are neuter:

el anagrama anagram	*el dogma* dogma	*el plasma* plasma
el anatema anathema	*el drama* drama	*el poema* poem
el aroma aroma	*el eccema/el eczema* eczema	*el prisma* prism
el cisma schism	*el emblema* emblem	*el problema* problem
el clima climate	*el enigma* enigma	*el programa* program(me)
el coma coma (*la coma* =	*el esquema* scheme	*el puma* puma (not Greek)
'comma')	*el estigma* stigma	*el radiograma* radiogram
el crisma holy oil (but *te*	*el fantasma* ghost	*el reúma* rheumatism
rompo la crisma 'I'll	*el fonema* phoneme	(occasionally *reuma*)
knock your block off')	*el holograma* hologram	*el síntoma* symptom
el crucigrama crossword	*el lema* slogan/watchword	*el sistema* system
puzzle	*el magma* magma	*el telegrama* telegram
el diagrama diagram	*el miasma* miasma	*el tema* theme/topic/
el dilema dilemma	*el panorama* panorama	subject
el diploma diploma	*el pijama* pyjamas/US	*el trauma* trauma
	pajamas	

and most other scientific or technical words ending in -*ma*. But *la estratagema* 'stratagem', *el asma* 'asthma' (see 3.1.2 for the masculine article) and *la flema* 'phlegm' are feminine even though they are neuter in Greek. *La amalgama* 'amalgam' is feminine. For other feminine words ending in -*ma* see 1.4.6.

A few masculine words ending in –*ma* are made feminine in popular speech, dialects and pre-nineteenth-century texts, especially *problema*, *clima*, *miasma* and *fantasma*, cf. *pobre fantasma soñadora* in Lorca's *El maleficio de la mariposa*.

NB: 'Pyjamas'/'pajamas' is *la pijama* or *la piyama* in Lat. Am. The word is not Greek.

1.4.4 Feminine by meaning

The following are feminine, usually because of an underlying feminine noun:

(**a**) Companies (*la compañía, la firma*): *la IBM, la Seat, la Hertz, la Volkswagen, la Ford*.

(**b**) Letters of the alphabet (*la letra*): *una b, una c, una h, la delta, la omega*. But note *el delta* 'river delta'.

(**c**) Islands (*la isla*): *las Azores, las Baleares, las Antillas* 'West Indies', *las Canarias*, etc.

(**d**) Roads (*la carretera* 'road' or *la autopista* 'motorway'/US 'freeway'): *la N11, la M4*.

(**e**) Many fruits. See 1.4.1(m) for a list.

1.4.5 Feminine by form

Nouns ending in *–ez, -eza, -ción, -ía, -sión, -dad, -tad, -tud, -umbre, -ie, -nza, -cia, -sis, -itis*

la niñez, childhood	*la versión* version	*la crisis* crisis
la doblez duplicity	*la verdad* truth	*la tesis* thesis
la vez 'time' (as in two times')	*la libertad* freedom	*la diagnosis* diagnosis
la pez 'pitch' (i.e. 'tar')	*la virtud* virtue	*la parálisis* paralysis
la pereza laziness	*la cumbre* summit	*la bronquitis* bronchitis
la acción action	*la serie* series	
la tontería foolishness (but *el día*, 'day')	*la superficie* surface	
	la esperanza hope	
	la presencia presence	

But the following are masculine:

el análisis analysis	*el éxtasis* ecstasy	*el pez* fish
el apocalipsis apocalypse	*el paréntesis* bracket	
el énfasis emphasis/ pomposity of style	*el doblez* fold/crease	
	el fez fez	

1.4.6 Common feminine nouns ending in *-ma*

Most nouns ending in *-ma* are masculine (see 1.4.3), but many are feminine. The following are common examples of feminine nouns ending in *–ma* (asterisked forms require the article *el* for reasons explained at 3.1.2, but their gender is feminine):

la alarma alarm	*el arma** weapon	*la calma* calm
*el alma** soul	*el asma** asthma	*la cama* bed
la amalgama amalgam	*la broma* joke	*la cima* summit
la crema cream	*la firma* firm/signature	*la paloma* dove
la Cuaresma Lent	*la flema* phlegm	*la pantomima* pantomime
la chusma rabble	*la forma* shape	*la pamema* unnecessary fuss
la diadema diadem/tiara	*la gama* selection/range	*la prima* female cousin; bonus/prize
la doma breaking-in/ taming (= *la domadura*)	*la goma* rubber	*la quema* burning
la dracma drachma	*la lágrima* tear (teardrop)	*la rama* branch
la enzima enzyme	*la lima* file (for nails, wood)/lime (fruit)	*la rima* rhyme
la escama scale (fish)	*la llama* flame/llama	

la esgrima fencing (with swords)	*la loma* hillock	*la sima* chasm/abyss
la/el esperma sperm	*la marisma* marsh	*la suma* sum
la estima esteem	*la máxima* maxim	*la toma* taking
la estratagema stratagem	*la merma* decrease	*la trama* plot (of novel)
la fama fame	*la norma* norm	*la yema* egg yolk/fingertip
	la palma palm	

1.4.7 Gender of countries, provinces, regions

Countries, provinces, states or regions ending in unstressed *-a* are feminine, e.g.

la España/Francia/Argentina de hoy	Spain/France/Argentina today
la conservadora Gran Bretaña	conservative Britain
la Alemania que yo conocía	the Germany I knew

The rest are masculine: (*el*) *Perú*, (*el*) *Paraguay*, (*el*) *Canadá*; *Aragón, Devon, Tennessee* (all masculine). Some place names include the definite article and may exceptionally be feminine, cf. *las Hurdes* (near Salamanca, Spain). For use of the article with countries and place names, see 3.2.17. *El Sáhara* is masculine, pronounced [sáxara]; x as ch of 'loch'; alternatively *el Sahara*, pronounced [s(a)ára].

But constructions such as *todo Colombia lo sabe* 'all Colombia knows it' are normal and correct, especially with the adjectives *todo, medio, mismo*, etc., probably because the underlying noun is *pueblo* 'people'. Cf. *todo Piura está muerta* 'the whole of Piura is dead' (M. Vargas Llosa, Pe., dialogue). Compare the following, which refers to a place, not to people: *toda Argentina está inundada de obras mías* (Vargas Llosa) 'the whole of Argentina is full of books of mine'.

1.4.8 Gender of cities, towns and villages

Cities ending in unstressed *-a* are usually feminine, the rest are masculine:

la Barcelona de ayer	the Barcelona of yesterday
el Moscú turístico	the tourist's Moscow
...un imaginario Buenos Aires	...an imaginary Buenos Aires
(J. L. Borges, Arg.)	

But there are exceptions like *Nueva York* (but *Nueva York está lleno de ventanas*, J. Aldecoa, Sp., 'New York is full of windows'), *la antigua Cartago, Nueva Orleans, ...vieja Delhi, fétida Delhi...*(Octavio Paz, Mex.) 'old Delhi, fetid Delhi', and spontaneous language often make cities feminine because of the influence of *la ciudad* 'city': *Bogotá, antes de ser remodelada...* (Colombian press) 'Bogota, before it was refashioned'. Some cities include the definite article (written with a capital letter) in their name: *El Cairo, La Habana* 'Havana', *La Haya* 'The Hague'.

Villages are usually masculine even when they end in *-a*, because of underlying *el pueblo* 'village'.

For *todo Barcelona habla de ello* 'all Barcelona's talking about it' see 1.4.7.

1.4.9 Gender of compound nouns

Compound nouns consisting of a verb plus a noun (frequent) are masculine:

el cazamariposas butterfly net	*el paraguas* umbrella
el cuentarrevoluciones rev-counter	*el sacacorchos* corkscrew
el lanzallamas flame-thrower	*el saltamontes* grasshopper

NB: See 2.1.7a for two exceptions.

Compound nouns consisting of two nouns have the gender of the first noun: *el año luz* 'light year', *un perro policía* 'police dog'. See 2.1.7(b). The gender of other compound nouns should be learned separately.

1.4.10 Gender of foreign words

A large number of foreign, especially English words, are in daily use, often with unexpected meanings or pronunciations.

Words that refer to human beings will be feminine or masculine according to the gender of the person referred to: *los yuppies, el recordman* 'record-holder' (borrowed from French), but *la nanny*. Foreign words referring to non-living things may be feminine if they resemble a feminine Spanish noun in form or meaning or, occasionally, because they are feminine in the original language. Examples:

> *la chance* 'chance' (Lat. Am. only, sometimes masc.), *la élite* 'elite' (usually pronounced as three syllables), *la Guinness* because of *la cerveza* 'beer'. *la hi-fi* because of *la alta fidelidad*, *la NASA* because of *la agencia, la opus* in music (cf. *la obra*), but *El Opus* = 'Opus Dei', *la pizza, la roulot(te)* 'caravan'/US 'trailer', *la sauna* 'sauna' (masc. in Lat. Am.), *la suite* (all meanings).

But if the word is un-Spanish in spelling or ending, or is not clearly associated with a feminine Spanish noun, it will be masculine. The majority of foreign-looking words are therefore masculine regardless of their gender in the original language:

> *el (e)spray* 'aerosol', *el affaire* 'affair' (usually political; fem. in French), *el after-shave*, *el airbag* (pronounced [ayrβá]), *el best-seller, el boom* financial, cultural 'boom', *el chalet* 'detached house', i.e. a house built on its own land, *el chándal* 'track-suit' (French), *el Christmas* 'Christmas card', *el echarpe* (light) 'scarf' (fem. in French; pronounced as a Spanish word), *el escalextric* 'spaghetti junction', *el eslogan/los eslóganes* 'advertising slogan', *el fax, el footing* 'jogging' (from French), *el hardware* (colloquially *el hard*; the Academy prefers *el soporte físico*), *el iceberg* 'iceberg' (pronounced in Spain as [iθeβér], as in English in Lat. Am.), *el jazz, el karaoke, el lifting* 'facelift', *el módem, el office* 'pantry'/'utility room', *el poster, el pub* (in Spain, a smart bar with music), *el puenting* 'bungee-jumping', *el quark, el ranking, el slip* 'men's underpants'/US 'shorts', *el software* (colloquially *el soft*; the Academy prefers *el soporte lógico*), *el standing* 'rank'/'prestige', *el vodka* 'vodka', *el yoga* 'yoga', *los boxes* 'pits' (in motor racing, more correctly *el taller*), *los panties* 'tights' (Sp.).

NB: for the phonetic transcription used in this section see the introduction to Chapter 39.

The formation of the plural of foreign words is discussed at 2.1.5. There is wide variation between the various Hispanic countries as to the source and number of recent loanwords, so no universally valid list can be drawn up.

(i) Usage in Spanish and Latin-American webpages reveals that the gender of *Internet* is still in flux: *El País* advocates masculine. *Internet* is often used without the article: *lo puedes buscar en Internet* 'you can look for it on the Internet'. *Web* is usually feminine, but sometimes masculine. *La Telaraña* 'spider's web' is used for the Web in some Latin-American countries. 'Webpage' is *página web*, 'homepage' is *la portada*. *La web* is often also used for 'website'. 'Browser' is *un navegador*.

1.4.11 Gender of abbreviations

This is determined by the gender of the main noun:

la ONU UN	*la UVI (Unidad de*	*la CIA*
la OTAN NATO	*Vigilancia Intensiva)*	*el OVNI (objeto volante*
las FF.AA. (Fuerzas	Intensive Care Unit	*no identificado)* UFO
Armadas) Armed Forces	*el ADN (el ácido…)* DNA	

If the gender of the underlying noun is unknown the abbreviation is masculine unless there is a good reason otherwise: *el IRA* 'the IRA (Irish Republican Army)' (*la ira* = 'anger'); but *la RAF, la USAF* (*las* *fuerzas aéreas* 'air force'), etc. Note however that *ETA*, the Basque separatist organization, is feminine in Castilian, genderless in Basque.

NB: Abbreviated plurals are shown by double letters: *los EE.UU. los Estados Unidos, las CC.OO. las Comisiones Obreras* (one of Spain's trade unions), *los SS.SS.: los santísimos sacramentos* 'the Holy Sacraments'.

1.4.12 Gender acquired from underlying noun (metonymic gender)

Many of the examples in previous sections illustrate cases of a noun acquiring the gender of another noun that has been deleted. This creates apparent gender errors in informal speech:

> *la Carlos tercero = la universidad Carlos III* in Madrid
> *la Modelo = la Cárcel Modelo* 'Model Jail'
> *Radio Nacional de España, la número uno* (RNE, 11-1-92, *la emisora* 'broadcasting station' omitted) 'National Radio of Spain, the number one (station)'
> *la setenta y tres = la habitación número setenta y tres* 'room seventy-three'

1.4.13 Doubtful genders

The gender of a few words is undecided, one of the oddest being *el azúcar* 'sugar' which is masculine, despite the fact that a following adjective may be of either gender: *azúcar moreno/morena* 'brown sugar'. In the following list the more common gender comes first. If only one gender is given, the other is uncommon in Peninsular usage, and probably elsewhere as well:

el acne or *el acné* acne, both genders valid	*el lente* lens (*las lentillas* = 'contact
el calor heat (*la calor* is rustic)	lenses')
la/el cochambre dirt	*la linde* boundary
el color colo(u)r (*la color* is rustic)	*la pelambre* thick hair
la/el dote dowry/gifts (but always *las dotes*	*la pringue* fat/grease/sticky dirt
personales 'personal qualities')	(*esto está pringoso* 'this is sticky')
la/el duermevela snooze/nap/light sleep	*la sartén* (see 1.4.15)
los herpes herpes	*la tilde* the sign over an *ñ*
el hojaldre puff pastry (Lat. Am. *la*	*el/la tizne* soot/black smear or stain
hojaldra)	*la/el tortícolis* stiff neck
el/la interrogante question	*el trípode* tripod

Pre-twentieth-century texts may contain now obsolete genders, e.g. *la puente* 'bridge', *la fin* 'end', *la análisis* 'analysis', etc. For *Internet* and *Web* see 1.4.10(i).

1.4.14 Gender of *mar* 'sea'

Masculine, except in poetry, the speech of sailors and fishermen, in weather forecasts and in nautical terms (*la pleamar/la bajamar* 'high/low tide', *la mar llana/ picada* 'calm/choppy sea', *hacerse a la mar* 'to put to sea', *en alta mar* 'on the high seas', etc.), and whenever the word is used as a colloquial intensifier: *la mar de tonto* 'absolutely stupid', *la mar de gente* '"heaps" of people'.

1.4.15 Some Latin-American genders

Some words are given different genders in provincial Spain and/or some parts of Latin America. Examples current in educated usage and writing in some (but not all) Latin-American countries are: *el bombillo* (Sp. *la bombilla*) 'light bulb', *el cerillo* (Sp. *la cerilla*) 'match' (for making fire), *el llamado* (Sp. *la llamada*) 'call', *el vuelto* (Sp. *la vuelta*) 'change' (money), *el protesto* (Sp. *la protesta*) 'protest'. *Sartén* 'frying-pan' is variable: it is feminine in Spain and Argentina and masculine in Mexico and Bilbao. Students should enquire locally about its gender in other places.

1.4.16 Words with two genders

A number of common words have meanings differentiated solely by their gender. Well-known examples are:

busca (m.) bleeper/pager (f.) search
cometa (m.) comet (f.) kite (toy)
coma (m.) coma (f.) comma
consonante (m.) rhyming word (f.)
   consonant
cólera (m.) cholera (f.) wrath/anger
corte (m.) cut (f.) the Court/'Madrid'
capital (m.) capital (money) (f.) capital
   (city)
cura (m.) priest (f.) cure
delta (m.) river delta (f.) delta (Greek
   letter)
doblez (m.) fold/crease (f.) duplicity
editorial (m.) editorial (f.) publishing
   house
escucha (m.) electronic 'bug' (f.)
   listening/monitoring
final (m.) end (f.) final (race, in sports)
frente (m.) front (military) (f.) forehead
guardia (m.) policeman (f.) guard

génesis (m.) genesis (=birth) (f.) Genesis
   (Bible)
mañana (m.) tomorrow/morrow (f.)
   morning
margen (m.) margin (f.) riverbank
moral (m.) mulberry tree (f.)
   morals/morale
orden (m.) order (opposite of disorder)
   (f.) command or religious order
ordenanza (m.) messenger/orderly
   (f.) decree/ordinance
parte (m.) official bulletin (f.) part
pendiente (m.) earring (f.) slope
pez (m.) fish (f.) pitch (i.e. tar)
policía (m.) policeman (f.) police force
radio (m.) radius/radium/spoke (f.)
   radio
terminal (m.) terminal (computers)
   (f.) terminus/terminal (electrical)
vocal (m.) member of a board (f.) vowel

Arte 'art' is usually masculine in the singular, but feminine in the plural: *el arte español* 'Spanish art', *las bellas artes* 'fine arts'. But note the set phrase *el arte poética* 'treatise on poetry'. Seco (1998), 60, notes that a phrase like *esta nueva arte* 'this new art-form' is not incorrect, and **los** *artes de pesca* 'fishing gear' (of a trawler) is standard usage, although *las artes* is also used: …*temiendo que un lobo marino o un delfín se hubiera introducido en las artes* (*El País*, Ur.) '…fearing that a seal (Sp. *una foca*) or dolphin had got into the tackle'.

NB: For the gender of *radio* 'radio' see 1.4.2a.

2

Plural of nouns

This chapter discusses:

- How to form the plural of Spanish nouns (Sections 2.1.1–8)
- Mass nouns and count nouns in Spanish and English (Section 2.2)
- Agreement rules governing plural nouns (Section 2.3)

NB: for abbreviated plurals like *EE.UU., FF.AA.*, see 1.4.11

2.1 Formation of the plural of nouns

2.1.1 Summary of rules

The vast majority of Spanish nouns form their plurals in one of the following three ways:

Method	Main type of noun	Example
Add –*s* (Section 2.1.2)	(1) Nouns ending with an unstressed vowel (2) Many foreign words ending with a consonant (3) Nouns ending in *é, ó* & several nouns ending in *á, ú*	*la casa-las casas* *el chalet-los chalets* *el jersey-los jerseys* *el café-los cafés, el capó-los capós, el sofá-los sofás, el menú-los menús*
Add –*es* (Section 2.1.3)	(1) Spanish nouns ending with a consonant other than –*s* (2) Nouns ending with a stressed vowel + *s* (3) Many nouns ending with *ú* or *í*	*la flor-las flores* *el inglés-los ingleses* *el tabú-los tabúes* *el iraní-los iraníes*
No change (Sections 2.1.4–6)	(1) Nouns ending with an unstressed vowel + -*s* (2) Families of people or things (3) Some foreign nouns	*la crisis-las crisis* *el virus-los virus* *los Blanco, los Ford* *el déficit-los déficit*

2.1.2 Plural in -*s*

(a) Nouns ending in an unstressed vowel (numerous!):

    la cama-las camas bed   *la serie-las series* series
    el huevo-los huevos egg   *la tribu-las tribus* tribe

(b) Nouns ending in *-é*, and words of one syllable ending in *-e*:

>*el café-los cafés* coffee/café   *el té-los tés* tea
>*el pie-los pies* foot/feet

(c) Nouns of more than one syllable ending with *-ó* (rare):

>*el dominó-los dominós* domino   *el buró-los burós* roll-top desk

(d) Many foreign words ending in a consonant, e.g. *el club-los clubs*. See 2.1.5.

2.1.3 Plural in -es

When *–es* is added, any accent written on the last vowel of the singular disappears: *la revolución-las revoluciones* 'revolution', *el rehén-los rehenes* 'hostage'. But the accent is retained in the combinations *aí* or *aú* to show that the second vowel is pronounced separately and not 'y' or 'w', as in *el país-los países* 'country', *la raíz-las raíces* 'root'.

If *-es* is added to a final *z*, the *z* becomes *c* in spelling: *la cruz-las cruces* 'cross', *la voz-las voces* 'voice'.

The following words make their plural by adding *–es*:

(a) Native (or nativized) nouns ending in a consonant other than *–s* (numerous!):

>*el avión-los aviones* aeroplane/airplane   *la verdad-las verdades* truth
>*el bar-los bares* bar (i.e. 'café')   *el rey-los reyes* king
>*el baúl-los baúles* trunk/large suitcase   *la vez-las veces* time (as in 'three times')
>*el color-los colores* colo(u)r

(b) Nouns ending in a stressed vowel plus *s*:

>*el autobús-los autobuses*   *el dios-los dioses* god   *la tos-las toses* cough
>   bus   *el mes-los meses* month
>*el francés-los franceses*   *el país-los países* country
>   Frenchman   *la res-las reses* farm animal

NB: Exception: *el mentís-los mentís* 'denial' (literary styles).

(c) Nouns ending in *-í*, *-ú* or *–á* :

The following plural forms are used in formal, especially written language:

>*el bisturí-los bisturíes* scalpel   *el zulú-los zulúes* Zulu
>*la i-las íes* the letter *i*   *el tabú-los tabúes* taboo
>*iraquí-iraquíes* Iraqi   *el jacarandá-los jacarandaes* jacaranda tree

(i) If the singular ends in *-á* the accent disappears in the plural, as in *jacaranda*es.

(ii) Several common words simply add *-s*: *papá-papás* 'father'/'dad', *mamá-mamás* 'mother', 'mum'/'mom', *el sofá-los sofás* 'sofa'/'couch', *el menú-los menús* 'menu' (usually 'set menu' in Sp.; *la carta* = 'menu'), *el tisú-los tisús* '(paper) tissues', *el champú-los champús* 'shampoo'.

Moreover, nouns ending in *-í*, *-ú* or *-á* generally simply add *-s* in familiar speech: *los iranís* 'Iranians' (properly *los iraníes*), *los jabalís* (for *jabalíes*) 'wild boars', *los jacarandás*, *los rubís*, *los tabús*, *los zahorís* 'clairvoyants'/'water diviners'. A literary plural form of a truly popular word like *la gachí*, e.g. '*las gachíes*' instead of *las gachís* (Spanish slang for 'woman'–'women') would sound ridiculous.

(iii) The Latin-American words *el ají* 'chilli/chilli sauce', and *el maní* 'peanut' (Spain *el cacahuete*) often form the plurals *los ajises, los manises* in speech, although *ajíes, maníes* are used in writing.

(iv) Words ending in *-en* (but *not -én*) require an accent in the plural to preserve the position of the stress. Since they are constantly spelled wrongly, the following forms should be studied: *el carmen-los cármenes* 'villa with a garden' (in Andalusia), *el crimen-los crímenes* 'crime', *el germen-los gérmenes* 'germ', *la imagen-las imágenes* 'image', *el/la margen-los/las márgenes* 'margin' (masc.)/'river bank' (fem.), *el origen-los orígenes* 'origin', *la virgen-las vírgenes* 'virgin'.

NB: This also affects the word *el mitin-los mítines* 'political meeting' (an ordinary meeting, e.g. family, business, is *una reunión*. A 'reunion' is *un reencuentro*).

2.1.4 No change in the plural (quite common)

(**a**) Words ending in an unstressed vowel plus *s*:

el-los análisis analysis	*el-los croquis* sketch	*el-los mecenas* patron of
el-los atlas atlas	*la-las dosis* dose	the arts
el-los campus campus	*el-los lunes* Monday	*el-los paréntesis* bracket
el-los cactus cactus	(similarly all weekdays)	*la-las tesis* thesis
la-las crisis crisis		*el-los virus* virus

If the word contains only one vowel, the plural ends in *-es*, e.g. *el mes-los meses*; see 2.1.3b.

(**b**) Words ending in *-x*, e.g. *el/los dúplex* US 'duplex apartment', British 'split-level flat', *el/los Kleenex* '(paper) tissue', *el/los fax* 'fax' (or *faxes*): *no bajamos de tres o cuatro fax por día* (interview in *Cambio16*, Sp.) 'we don't send fewer than three or four faxes a day'.

(**c**) Latin words ending in *-t* and *–um* (at least in careful language) and a few other foreign words:

los altos déficit presupuestarios (El País, Sp.)	*e/losl accésit* second prize
'high budgetary deficits'	*el/los láser* laser
el/los CD-ROM the CD-ROM(s)	*el/los quórum* quorum

In everyday language Latin words ending in *-um* tend to form their plural in *–ums*: *el memorándum-los memorándums, el referéndum-los referéndums, el ultimátum-los ultimátums, el currículum vitae-los currículums vitae*. *El País* prefers *memorandos, referendos, ultimatos* and *currículos*, but these are not widely used. The singular forms *el memorando, el referendo, el ultimato* are Academy recommendations that have not caught on. *El currículo* 'curriculum' has recently spread in Spain, and possibly also elsewhere.

Spanish speakers do not try to impress by using Latin plurals, cf. our 'cacti' for 'cactuses' or our (incorrect) 'referenda' for 'referendums'.

(**d**) Words whose singular ends in a consonant plus *-s*: *los bíceps, los fórceps*.

2.1.5 Plural of foreign words ending in a consonant

The tendency is to treat them all like English words and simply add *-s* (but see 2.1.4c for Latin words). This often produces words ending in two consonants which are unnatural in Spanish and annoy the grammarians.

If a word ends in *b, c, f, g, k, m, p, t, v,* or *w,* or in two or more consonants, it is almost certainly a foreign word and will make its plural in *-s* unless it ends with a *s, sh* or *ch* sound, cf. *el kibutz* 'kibbutz', *el flash, el lunch, el sketch*; in this case it will probably be invariable in spontaneous speech. Well-informed speakers may use foreign plurals like *los flashes, los kibutzim, los sketches.* Some common examples:

el boicot-los boicots boycott	*el hobby-los hobbys* hobby-hobbies
el bug-los bugs 'bug' (in computing)	*el iceberg-los icebergs* iceberg
el complot-los complots (political) plot	*el kart-los karts* go-kart
el chalet-los chalets detached house	*el módem-los módems* modem
el gay-los gays gay (i.e. homosexual)	*el penalty-los penaltys* (in soccer)
el hit-los hits hit (song, film, etc.)	

El sándwich (made with sliced bread unlike *un bocadillo,* made from a baguette, in familiar Peninsular language *un bocata*), makes the plural *los sándwiches* in educated usage, but *los sándwich* is common, usually pronounced [sángwich]. The Academy's recommendation for sandwich, *el emparedado,* never found favour. A common Latin-American form is *sángüiche,* which is more pronounceable.

Some modern loanwords are treated as Spanish words and add *-es.* This happens most readily when the word ends in *-l, -n* or *-r*:

el bar-los bares bar	*el escáner-los escáneres* scanner/scanning
el dólar-los dólares dollar	(also *el scanner/los scanners*)
el electrón-los electrones electron	*el gol-los goles* goal (in sport)
	el hotel-los hoteles hotel

(i) 'Academy' plurals like *los cócteles* 'cocktail', *los córneres* 'corner' (in soccer), *los fraques* (for *los fracs*) 'dress-coat'/'tails', etc. are not generally used: *-s* alone is added. However *los filmes* 'films' is not uncommon and is recommended by *El País* (the everyday word is *la película*), and *los clubes* 'club' is normal in Latin America for *los clubs,* usual in Spain: *El País* prefers *clubes. Los álbumes* is generally preferred in writing and educated speech to *los álbums* 'albums'. *Los eslóganes* is heard as well as *los eslógans* '(publicity) slogan'.

(ii) Some writers and editors treat foreign words ending in a consonant like Latin words (see 2.1.4c), so forms like *los módem, los láser* are seen; *El País* recommends these two forms. Such zero plural forms are often given to foreign words in spontaneous speech.

(iii) *El País, Libro de estilo* 2002, 9.23, says that abbreviations should not be pluralized: *las ONG = organizaciones no gubernamentales,* i.e. NGOs or 'non-governmental organizations', not *las ONGs.*

2.1.6 Proper names

If a proper name refers to members of a family, it has no plural form: *los Franco, los Mallol, los Pérez; en casa de los Riba hay una niña que amaré toda la vida* (E. Poniatowska, Mex., dialogue) 'in the Ribas' house there's a girl whom I'll love for the whole of my life'. A group of individuals who merely happen to have the same name will be pluralized according to the usual rules, although names in *–és* and *-z* are almost always invariable:

> *Este pueblo está lleno de Morenos,*   This village is full of Morenos,
>   *Blancos y Péreces/Pérez*   Blancos and Perezes
> *no todos los Juan Pérez del mundo*   not all the Juan Perezes in the world
>   (J. Donoso, Ch.)

The same principle also applies to objects that form families: *los Ford* 'Ford cars', *los Chevrolet, los Renault*.

Royal houses are considered to be successive individuals: *los Borbones* 'the Bourbons', *los Habsburgos* 'the Hapsburgs'.

2.1.7 Compound nouns

(**a**) Those (the most common) consisting of a verb plus a plural noun do not change in the plural:

el-los abrelatas tin-opener	*el-los portaaviones* aircraft carrier
el-los cumpleaños birthday	*la-las quitanieves* snowplough/
el-los elevalunas automatic window	US snowplow. Seco (1998), 378,
opener (in a car)	gives the gender as feminine
el-los guardaespaldas bodyguard	*la-las tragaperras* gaming machine-
el-los lanzamisiles missile-launcher	gambling machine/ Brit. fruit machine;
el-los limpiabotas shoeshine	masculine gender is also used

(**b**) There is a growing class of compounds consisting of two nouns. Normally only the first noun is pluralized. The following forms have been noted from various written sources:

el arco iris-los arcos iris rainbow	*el hombre rana-los hombres rana* frogman
el bebé probeta-los bebés probeta	*el perro policía/los perros policía* police dog
test-tube baby	*la hora punta/las horas punta* rush hour
el año luz-los años luz light-year	(lit. 'point hour')

But always *el país miembro-los países miembros* 'member country', *la tierra virgen-las tierras vírgenes* 'virgin land'. Pluralization of the second noun robs it of its adjectival force: *los hombres ranas* sounds like 'men who are frogs'; compare *las ediciones pirata* 'pirate editions' and *los editores piratas* 'pirate publishers', *los niños modelo* 'model children' and *los niños modelos* 'child models'.

In Spanish the descriptive noun follows: *un hombre rana* is a frog-like man, not a man-like frog. *La ciencia ficción* 'science fiction' is an exception, borrowed from English.

These compounds are very common in phrases like *módem WAP, página web*; in abbreviated notices, e.g. *camisetas niño* 'children's T-shirts', *nueces California* 'walnuts' (Sp.); and in trade descriptions: *champú anticaspa* 'anti-dandruff shampoo', *un pc IBM*, etc. But their use is limited in ordinary language: *un bocata jamón* is substandard for *un bocata de jamón*, itself familiar in Spain for *un bocadillo de jamón* 'ham sandwich'.

(**c**) The following compound nouns are invariable in the plural:

el sin casa	*los sin casa*	homeless person
el-la sinvergüenza	*los-las sinvergüenza*	scoundrel, good-for-nothing
el hazmerreír	*los hazmerreír*	laughing-stock
el vivalavirgen	*los vivalavirgen*	fun-lover/laid-back/someone who
		couldn't give a damn

(**d**) Other compound nouns are treated as single words with regular plurals:

el altavoz-los altavoces loudspeaker
  (Lat. Am. *el altoparlante*)
la bocacalle-las bocacalles side street
el correveidile-los correveidiles tell-tale
los dimes y diretes gossip
el hidalgo los hidalgos nobleman
  (the old plural was *hijosdalgo*)
el parabién-los parabienes congratulations
el pésame-los pésames condolences

el quehacer-los quehaceres task
el rapapolvo-los rapapolvos telling-off/
  dressing-down
el sordomudo-los sordomudos deaf-mute
el tentempié-los tentempiés snack
el todoterreno-los todoterrenos four-wheel-
  drive vehicle
el vaivén-los vaivenes ups-and-downs,
  swaying motion

2.1.8 Irregular plurals

Only four irregular plurals are in common use.

(**a**) Three common nouns shift their stress in the plural: *el carácter-los caracteres* 'character (**not** *los carácteres!), *el espécimen-los especímenes* 'specimen' and *el régimen-los regímenes* 'regime'.

(**b**) *El lord* (British)'lord' has the plural *los lores* : *la Cámara de los Lores* 'the House of Lords'.

2.2 Peculiarities of Spanish plural nouns

2.2.1 Mass nouns and count nouns in Spanish and English

A count noun refers to countable items, 'egg'-'two eggs'. Mass or uncountable nouns denote non-countable items: 'justice', 'bread', but not * 'two justices', * 'two breads'. In both English and Spanish, mass or uncountable nouns can often be pluralized to mean different varieties of the thing in question: 'her fear'/'her fears', 'my love'/'my loves', 'I love French wine'/'I love French wines', 'the water of Finland'/'the waters of Finland'. This device is far more frequent in Spanish than in English, and idiomatic translation of the resulting plural noun may require thought, e.g.:

Para nosotros existen dos urgencias
  (interview in *Cambio16*, Sp.)
Ejercía diversas soberbias (J. L. Borges,
  Arg.)
La sociedad argentina reclama mayor
  transparencia en las conductas de los
  hombres políticos (*La Nación*, Arg.)

For us there are two urgent issues (lit.
  'urgencies')
He practised/US practiced various kinds
  of arrogance
Argentine society demands greater
  openness in the behavio(u)r of
  politicians

A number of Spanish nouns can be pluralized in this way whereas their English translation cannot, e.g.

la amistad	friendship	las amistades	friends
la atención	attention	las atenciones	acts of kindness
la bondad	goodness	las bondades	good acts
la carne	meat/flesh	las carnes	fleshy parts
el consejo	advice	los consejos	pieces of advice
la crueldad	cruelty	las crueldades	cruel acts
la información	information	las informaciones	news items
el negocio	business	los negocios	business affairs

el pan	bread	*los panes*	loaves of bread
el progreso	progress	*los progresos*	advances
la tostada	toast	*las tostadas*	slices of toast
la tristeza	sadness	*las tristezas*	sorrows
el trueno	thunder	*los truenos*	thunderclaps

Both languages may use counters or quantifiers to pluralize uncountable nouns: *tres pastillas de jabón* 'three bars of soap', *briznas de hierba* 'blades of grass', *dientes de ajo* 'cloves of garlic', *parcelas de terreno* 'plots of land', *trozos/hojas de papel* 'pieces/sheets of paper', *barras de tiza* 'sticks of chalk', *terrones de azúcar* 'lumps of sugar', *motas de polvo* 'specks of dust', etc.

2.2.2 Nouns denoting symmetrical objects

As in English, these nouns are usually invariably plural ('a pair of' is *unos/unas* before such nouns):

los auriculares earphones   *los gemelos* binoculars/   *las tijeras* scissors
las gafas glasses (Lat. Am.   cuff-links/twins
     los anteojos)   *las pinzas* tweezers

But colloquially the singular may be used in some regions, as in *¿podría prestarme una tijera?* (E. Poniatowska, Mex., dialogue) 'could you lend me some scissors?'. The more usual form in Spain comes first:

los alicates/el alicate pliers/pincer   *las pinzas/la pinza* peg/pincers/
los calzoncillos/un calzoncillo men's   tweezers/dart (in sewing)
   underpants/US shorts   *el pantalón/los pantalones* trousers/
las murallas/ la muralla city walls   US pants: sing. & plur. equally
la nariz/las narices nose (both used)   common in Spanish

NB: *Las escaleras* = 'stairs', *la escalera* = 'ladder'.

2.2.3 Nouns always plural in Spanish

As happens in English, some nouns or phrases are normally found only in the plural. The following list is by no means exhaustive:

las afueras outskirts   *buenas tardes* good afternoon
las agujetas aches and pains (in joints)   *los celos* jealousy
los alrededores surroundings   *las cosquillas* tickling
los altos (Lat. Am.) upstairs flat/apartment   *los cimientos* foundations
los bajos (Lat. Am.) downstairs flat/   *las ganas* urge/desire
   apartment   *(tener muchas) ínfulas* to be conceited
los bártulos (colloquial) belongings/'gear'   *los prismáticos* binoculars
los bienes goods, provisions   *los restos* remains
buenos días good morning   *las tinieblas* darkness
buenas noches good night (greeting or   *los víveres* provisions/supplies
   goodbye)   *las vacaciones* holiday/vacation

2.2.4 Singular for objects of which a person has only one

The English sentence 'they cut their knees' is ambiguous: one knee or both? Spanish normally clarifies the issue by using the singular if only one each is implied or if only one thing is possessed:

Les cortaron la cabeza	They cut off their heads
Se quitaron el sombrero	They took off their hats
Todos tenían novia	All had girlfriends (one each)
tres israelíes con pasaporte alemán (*Cambio16*, Sp.)	three Israelis with German passports
La cara de Antonio no refleja el mismo entusiasmo. Ni la de sus cuñados tampoco (Carmen Rico-Godoy, Sp.)	Antonio's face doesn't reflect the same enthusiasm. Nor do those (lit. 'nor does that') of his brothers and sisters-in-law

This rule is sometimes ignored in Latin-American speech: *nos hemos mojado las cabezas* (Bol., quoted Kany, 26) 'we've wet our heads', *lo hacían para que no les viéramos las caras* (L. Spota, Mex., dialogue) 'they were doing it so we wouldn't see their faces'. The plural can sometimes remove ambiguity, as in *los extranjeros felicitaban al maquinista por su gran pericia para lograr el descarrilamiento en el lugar preciso donde sus vidas corrieran peligro* (*La Época*, Ch.) 'the foreigners congratulated the engine-driver for his great skill in managing to cause a derailment exactly at the spot where their lives would be at risk', where the singular *su vida* might be taken to refer only to the train-driver.

The rule is often ignored in Spain with articles of clothing and possessions: *quítense el sombrero/los sombreros* 'take off your hats', *podéis dejar la chaqueta/las chaquetas aquí* 'you can leave your jackets here'.

2.2.5 Singular for plural

Singular nouns may sometimes be used to represent large numbers after words like *mucho*, *tanto*, etc., often, but not exclusively, with an ironic tone:

También había mucha estudiante con vaqueros y camiseta (J. Marías, Sp.)	There were also a lot of girl students in jeans and T-shirts
Se emocionó de ver tanto libro junto (L. Sepúlveda, Ch.)	He was moved to see so many books together
. . . y allí había mucho alumno (A. Bryce Echenique, Pe.)	. . . and there were a lot of students there

The *GDLE*, 1.2.3.5, notes that on entering a packed car park *hay mucho coche* sounds more pessimistic than *hay muchos coches* 'there are a lot of cars'.

2.3 Number agreement rules

This section covers various aspects of number agreement, mainly with nouns. For further remarks on the agreement of adjectives see 4.7. For the agreement of possessive adjectives, see 8.3.2. For agreement with *cuyo* see 35.7. For tense agreement see 16.16.

2.3.1 Number agreement with collective nouns

(**a**) Adjectives that modify a collective noun (i.e. a noun referring to a group of persons or things) are singular and the verb is singular when it immediately follows the noun. In other words, Spanish always says *la policía británica busca* 'the British police "is" seeking', *la gente dice* 'people "says"'..., never *'buscan'*, *'dicen'*. English —especially British English—tends to use the plural after collective nouns:

El gobierno considera . . .	The government consider(s)...
La tripulación está a su disposición	The crew are/is at your disposal
El resto de mis bienes es ya vuestro (A. Gala, Sp.)	The rest of my goods is yours now
La gran mayoría de los chilenos quiere resolver sus problemas concretos (*La Época*, Ch.)	The great majority of Chileans want to solve their specific problems

(**b**) When a collective noun is linked to a plural noun, usually by *de*, the safest option is to make the adjective or verb plural: *un grupo de vecinos airados* 'a group of angry neighbours', *una mayoría de españoles creen que...* 'a majority of Spaniards think that...', *un mínimo de 13 presos habían sido asistidos de heridas* (*El País*, Sp.) 'a minimum of 13 prisoners had been treated for injuries'.

But singular agreement is possible: *el resto de los presentes soportaba con estoicismo la elevada temperatura* (L. Sepúlveda, Ch.) 'the rest of those present were bearing the high temperature stoically', and the question of agreement in such cases is controversial. Seco (1998), 126, advocates the plural, but *El País* recommends the singular wherever possible. Seco's is the best advice for foreigners, since it will avoid nonsense like **un grupo de mujeres embarazado* ***'a pregnant group of women' for *un grupo de mujeres embarazadas* 'a group of pregnant women'.

When collective nouns are separated from the verb by intervening words, plural agreement is much more common: *cuando la policía llegó al apartamento, se encontraron con la cómica, aunque desagradable escena...* (*La Vanguardia*, Sp., quoted *GDLE* 1.4.4) 'when the police reached the apartment they found the comical but disagreeable spectacle...'

Native speakers sometimes hesitate over agreement with collective nouns: *una pareja amiga que se llama/llaman Mario y Ana* 'a couple who are friends of ours and are called Mario and Ana'.

NB: For constructions like *la mayoría* **son** *españoles, el comité* **son** *unos mentirosos*, see 2.3.3.

2.3.2 Plural noun after *tipo de*, etc.

After *tipo de* and similar phrases (e.g. *clase de, género de...*), countable nouns are usually made plural:

¿Por qué hacen los hombres este tipo de cosas? (C. Rico-Godoy, Sp.)	Why do men do this kind of thing?
Ese tipo de rostros es frecuente en los países sudamericanos (E. Sábato, Arg.)	That type of face is frequent in South-American countries

2.3.3 *Esto son lentejas, todo son problemas*, etc.

When *ser* (and a few other verbs like *volverse*) has a singular subject and a plural noun for its predicate (as in 'everything **is** problems'), it agrees in number with the predicate, in this case 'problems': *todo* **son** *problemas*. This most commonly occurs after neuter pronouns like *lo que...* 'what...', *todo* 'everything...', *esto* 'this...', etc. A similar phenomenon is found in French and German, which say 'it are lies': *ce sont des mensonges, es sind Lügen*:

El escrito eran sus 'condiciones' (*Cambio16*, Sp.)	The document was his 'conditions'
Primero todo fueron bromas (E. Poniatowska, Mex.)	At first it was all jokes
Lo demás fueron un par de detalles burocráticos (A. Bryce Echenique, Pe.)	The rest was a couple of bureaucratic details
Su morada más común son las ruinas (J. L. Borges, Arg.)	Their most usual dwelling-place is (in) ruins
Lo importante en sus relatos no eran las personas (P. Armando Fernández, Cu.)	The important thing in his stories wasn't people

This rule is not always applied in Latin America: *lo único que no falta es cigarrillos* (M. Vargas Llosa, Pe., for *son cigarrillos*) 'the only thing that isn't lacking is cigarettes', *lo primero que vi fue policías* (A. Bryce Echenique, Pe.) 'the first thing I saw was policemen', *lo que mejor se ve es las casas de enfrente* (M. Puig, Arg., dialogue) 'what you can see best is the houses opposite'.

For the rule to be applied, the predicate must literally refer to a collection of different things. In the following example María is really only one complex person: *María es en realidad muchas personas diferentes* 'Maria is really a lot of different people'.

2.3.4 Agreement with nouns linked by y, o and phrases meaning 'as well as'

(**a**) Nouns linked by *y* require plural agreement unless they form, or are felt to form, a single concept. Compare *su padre y su madre estaban preocupados* 'his father and mother were worried' (different people) and *Ángela era su mujer y secretaria* 'Angela was his wife and secretary' (one person, so obviously not *sus*).

When several things can optionally be viewed as one, either singular or plural agreement is in fact usually possible:

El derrumbe del socialismo y la desaparición de la URSS causó el mayor daño (Fidel Castro, Cu.; or *causaron*)	The collapse of socialism and the disappearance of the Soviet Union caused the greatest damage
Podemos pensar que en el juicio de Lope pesaba la rivalidad, el sentimiento, y la cercanía (E. Sábato, Arg.; or *pesaban*)	We can assume that rivalry, emotion and closeness to the events played their part in Lope's judgement (Lope de Vega allegedly called *Don Quijote* the worst book he had read)

(**b**) With *o*, agreement is optional if the verb comes first, but the singular stresses the idea of 'one or the other' more than the plural: *viene(n) Mario o Antonia* 'Mario or Antonia is/are coming'; but *Mario o Antonio vendrán*. Singular agreement is usual when the nouns represent a single idea: *la depresión o tristeza que afecta(n)...* 'the depression or sadness that affect(s)...'.

(**c**) Agreement after phrases that mean 'as well as', 'likewise', etc., seems to be optional, although the plural is more common: *tanto Mario como María pensaba(n) que* 'both Mario and Maria thought that...'.

3

Articles

This chapter discusses:

- The forms and uses of the definite article (*el*/*la*/*los*/*las*) (Section 3.1–2)
- The forms and uses of the indefinite article (*un*/*una*/*unos*/*unas*) (Section 3.3)
- The uses of *unos*/*unas* (Section 3.4)

For the use of the definite article to replace a possessive adjective, e.g. *se ha roto el brazo* '(s)he's broken his/her arm', *me dejé la cartera en casa* 'I left my wallet at home', see 8.3.5. For the definite article in sentences like 'the most interesting book' see 5.3. For the 'neuter article' *lo* see 7.2.

3.1 Forms of the definite article

3.1.1 Masculine and feminine definite articles

	Masculine	Feminine
Singular	*el*	*la*
Plural	*los*	*las*

La is not shortened to *l'* in modern Spanish: compare *la artista* 'woman artist' with Italian *l'artista*, French *l'artiste*. Nor is the *a* of *la* dropped in pronunciation before words beginning with a vowel other than *a*: *la emisora* 'radio station' is pronounced [laemisóra], not [lemisóra].

3.1.2 Use of *el* and *un* before certain feminine nouns

El and the indefinite article *un* are used immediately before singular feminine nouns beginning with stressed *a-* or *ha-*: this does not affect their gender. Common examples:

el/*un abra* mountain pass (Lat. Am.; Sp. *el puerto*)
el África de hoy Africa today
el/*un águila* eagle
el/*un alba* dawn
el/*un alma* soul
el/*un alza* rise/increase

el/*un ancla* anchor
el/*un área* area
el/*un arma* weapon
el/*un arpa* harp
el Asia de hoy Asia today
el asma asthma
el/*un aula* lecture room
el/*un haba* bean

el/*un habla* speech-form
el/*un hacha* axe/US ax
el/*un hada* fairy
el/*un hambre* hunger
el hampa the criminal underworld
el/*un haya* beech-tree

NB: Exceptions: *la a, la hache* a, h (letters of the alphabet); *la Ángela, la Ana* and other women's names; *la aya* children's governess, *La Haya* 'the Hague', *la/una haz* 'surface/face'; *la árabe* 'Arab woman'; *la ácrata* 'anarchist woman'; abbreviations: *la AUF Asociación Uruguaya de Fútbol.*

The plural is always with *las/unas*: *las águilas* 'eagles', *las hachas* 'axes' and adjectives are feminine in form: *un aula oscura* 'a dark lecture hall'. The feminine article must also be used if any word intervenes between the article and the noun: *una peligrosa arma* 'a dangerous weapon', *la misma agua* 'the same water'. Compare the following words which do not begin with a stressed *a*:

la/una amnistía amnesty	*la arena* sand	*la/una hacienda* ranch
la/una apertura opening	*la/una arroba* at-sign: @	*la/una hamaca* hammock

One often sees and hears mistakes like ?*habrá que encontrar otro aula* 'we'll have to find another lecture room' (for *otra aula*) or ?*a raíz del último alza del petróleo* (*Abc*, Sp., quoted Seco 1998, 176, properly *la última alza*) '...following the latest rise in oil prices'; and ?*tengo un hambre bárbaro* 'I'm starving hungry' or ?*tengo mucho hambre* 'I'm very hungry' are heard in relaxed speech on both continents. Such forms are banned from careful language.

(i) This construction is used only before nouns, not before adjectives:

una amplia estancia (F. Umbral, Sp.)	wide room
una amplia panorámica (M. Benedetti, Ur.)	a broad view
una alta mujer (J. L. Borges, Arg.)	a tall woman

(ii) for *alguna* 'some' before such nouns see 9.4.1a. For *ninguna* 'no' see 23.5.5. For the colloquial use of *este* 'this', *ese* and *aquel* 'that', before these nouns, see 6.1 note (iii).

(iii) The construction should also be used before those feminine compound nouns whose first element would have begun with a stressed *a* had it stood alone: *el aguamarina* 'aquamarine', *el aguanieve* 'sleet', *un avemaría* 'an Ave Maria'.

(iv) The use in written Spanish of *un* before these nouns is a recent development in Spanish: the Academy's Dictionary adopted it only after 1970 (see DeMello, 2000 (3)). Forms like *una alma* for *un alma* 'a soul' are therefore often found in premodern texts.

3.1.3 *Del* and *al*

De plus *el* is shortened to *del* 'of the', and *a* plus *el* is shortened to *al* 'to the'. *De él* 'of him' and *a él* 'to him' are not abbreviated in modern Spanish. The abbreviated forms are not used, at least in writing, if the article is part of a proper name:

la primera página de El Comercio	page one of *El Comercio*
Viajaron a El Cairo	They journeyed to Cairo
en el último número de El Vocero Cristiano	in the latest number of *The Christian*
(J. J. Arreola, Mex.)	*Spokesman*

3.2 Uses and omission of the definite article

3.2.1 General remarks on the use of the definite article

Article usage, especially use of the definite article, is notoriously difficult to define: why *does* one say *en* **la** *práctica* 'in practice' but *en teoría* 'in theory'? Use of the articles also varies slightly from region to region, so the rules given here must be supplemented by careful study of good writing and educated speech. The following pages should make it clear to readers who know French that, despite many similarities, the Spanish definite article is less used than its French counterpart, and apparently less than fifty years ago.

3.2.2 The French and Spanish definite articles

The following summary of the main differences and similarities may be useful.

The definite article in French and Spanish

French	Spanish
Used with unqualified names of countries, regions: *l'Espagne est un beau pays, vive l'Espagne!, la Normandie*, etc.	Not used (with some exceptions shown at 3.2.17): *España es un hermoso país, ¡viva España!, Normandía*, etc.
Used when addressing people: *salut les gars!, oui, monsieur le Président*	Not used: *¡hola muchachos!, sí, señor Presidente*
No preposition with numerous time words: *le soir* 'in the evening', *le matin* 'in the morning', *le lendemain* 'on the next day', *le mardi* 'on Tuesday'	Preposition often required: *por la tarde, por la mañana, al día siguiente*, but *el año pasado*, 'last year', *el martes* 'on Tuesday', etc.
Not used in time expressions of the type *il est huit heures*	Used: *son las ocho*
Used with generic nouns: *le vin est mauvais pour le foie* 'wine is bad for the liver'	Very similar, but not identical (see 3.2.6–10): *el vino es malo para el hígado*
Replaces possessives with parts of body: *il ferme les yeux, il lui caresse les cheveux, il a les yeux bleus*, etc.	Similar, but also with clothing and personal possessions: *cierra los ojos, le acaricia el pelo, he perdido el pasaporte* 'I've lost my passport', *te he aparcado el coche* 'I've parked your car', etc. See 8.3.4
Double article in superlatives when adjective follows noun: *le livre le plus intéressant*	Only one article, *el libro más interesante*. See 5.3
Used with superlative adverbs: *c'est lui qui chante le mieux*	Not used: *él es quien mejor canta*; see 5.4
Used in phrases like *cinq euros le kilo*	Same: *cinco euros el kilo*
De used before partitive nouns (i.e. to express 'some'): *il boit de l'eau, il y avait de la neige*	No article or preposition: *bebe agua, había nieve*, or *unos* used: *unas monedas*

3.2.3 A useful generalization about the Spanish definite article

With two important exceptions, if the definite article is used in English it is also used in Spanish:

la caída del gobierno   the fall of the government
El rey habló con los ministros The King spoke with the ministers

Exceptions:

(a) Ordinal numbers with kings, popes, etc.: *Fernando séptimo* 'Ferdinand the Seventh', *Carlos quinto* 'Charles the Fifth', *Juan XXIII* (*Juan veintitrés*).

(b) Some set phrases in Spanish have no article whereas in English they usually do.

a corto/largo plazo in the short/long run	*a título de* in the capacity of
a gusto de to the liking of	*a voluntad de* at the discretion of
cuesta abajo down (the) hill	*de plantilla* on the payroll/staff
cuesta arriba up (the) hill	*en alta mar* on the high seas
hacia oriente, etc. towards the east	*en dicho mes* in the said month
(*hacia el este*, etc.)	*en manos de* at/in the hands of
	en nombre de in the name of

This applies only to set adverbial phrases: compare *en las manos de Julia* 'in Julia's hands'. Note also *a fuerza de* 'by dint/means of', and *a la fuerza/por fuerza* 'by force'.

3.2.4 Definite article with more than one noun

Two or more nouns should each have their own definite article if they refer to different things (see 3.2.7 for further remarks on lists of nouns). Spanish thus differs from English, which omits the second determiner (see glossary) in phrases like 'the sun and moon', 'a dog and cat', 'my brother and sister', 'those men and women'. Spanish says *el sol y la luna, un perro y un gato, mi hermano y mi hermana, esos hombres y esas mujeres.* ?*El gato y perro* suggests a cross between a dog and a cat and **mis hermano y hermana* 'my brother and sister' is definitely not Spanish:

el padre y la madre	the father and mother
entre el hotel y la playa	between the hotel and beach
El desorden callejero y las piedras son	Street disorders and stones are
contrarios a la democracia (Época, Ch.)	contrary to democracy

But if the nouns are felt to form a single complex idea (often the case when they are joined by *o* 'or'), all but the first article may be omitted, especially in writing:

el misterio o enigma del origen... (O. Paz, Mex.)	the mystery or enigma of the origin...
El procedimiento y consecuencias son semejantes (M. Vargas Llosa, Pe.)	The procedure and consequences are similar
...los laboratorios, equipos, bibliotecas, aulas, sistemas audiovisuales indispensables para cumplir con su trabajo... (ibid.)	...the laboratories, equipment, libraries, lecture rooms, audio-visual systems indispensable for it to do its work

(i) Nouns may represent similar things in one context and not in another. One says *voy a comprar un libro y una revista* 'I'm going to buy a book and a magazine' (two different things), but *los libros y (las) revistas están en el estante de arriba* 'the books and magazines are on the top shelf' (books and magazines seen as aspects of one thing, 'publications').

(ii) Pairs of animals of different sex both require the article: *el toro y la vaca* 'the bull and (the) cow', *el abuelo y la abuela* 'grandfather and grandmother', never **el toro y vaca, *el abuelo y abuela*.

(iii) Articles cannot be joined with *y*, so **los y las estudiantes* is not allowed for *los estudiantes y las estudiantes* '(the) male and female students'.

3.2.5 Omission of articles in proverbs

Articles, definite and indefinite, are often dropped in proverbs and in remarks that are meant to sound like proverbial wisdom:

Gato escaldado del agua fría huye	A scalded cat runs from cold water
Virtudes y defectos van unidos	Virtues and defects go together
Oveja que bala, bocado que pierde	A bleating sheep misses a nibble (i.e. you miss out if you talk too much)
Turista que se enoja, no regresa (Luis Spota, Mex., dialogue. *Enojarse = enfadarse* in Spain)	An angry tourist doesn't come back

3.2.6 Definite article with generic nouns

With the exceptions noted at 3.2.10, the definite article is required before generic nouns, i.e. nouns that refer to something in general. These are typically:

(**a**) Abstract nouns referring to a concept in general:

la democracia	democracy
el catolicismo español/la sociedad cubana	Spanish Catholicism/Cuban society
Mi relato será fiel a la realidad (J. L. Borges, Arg.)	My story will be true to reality
El debate conceptual sobre la cultura, los derechos y la autonomía indígena (*La Reforma*, Mex.)	The conceptual debate about culture, rights and Native American autonomy

Colo(u)r nouns belong to this class of noun and require the article: *el azul* 'blue', *el negro* 'black', *el amarillo no me gusta* 'I don't like yellow'. A sentence like *¿te gusta el rojo?* is therefore ambiguous: 'do you like the red **one**' or 'do you like red?' Illnesses are also treated as abstract nouns: *el SIDA* 'AIDS', *la diabetes* 'diabetes', *el sarampión* 'measles'.

(**b**) Substances in general:

El salvado es bueno para la digestión	Bran is good for the digestion
El acero inoxidable es carísimo	Stainless steel is extremely expensive
La sangre no tiene precio	Blood has no price

(**c**) Countable nouns which refer to all the members of their class:

Los belgas beben mucha cerveza	Belgians (in general) drink a lot of beer
Los automovilistas debían contentarse con escuchar la radio (*La Nación*, Arg.; refers to all the drivers involved in the jam)	Car-drivers had to make do with listening to their radios
El tigre es un animal peligroso	The tiger is a dangerous animal
El periodista escribe para el olvido (J. L. Borges, Arg., dialogue)	Journalists (lit. 'the journalist') write for oblivion

Sentences like **franceses comen más ajo que noruegos* 'the French eat more garlic than Norwegians' are not Spanish: *los franceses comen más ajo que los noruegos.*

(i) These rules apply especially when the noun is the subject of a verb. The article cannot be omitted in the following sentences (but see 3.2.7. for the omission of the article from lists of two or more generic nouns): *no me gusta **la** manzanilla* 'I don't like camomile', ***el** azúcar es malo para los dientes* 'sugar is bad for the teeth'. But when the generic noun is the object of a verb or is preceded by a preposition, the definite article is sometimes omitted. See 3.2.10 for examples.

(ii) Sentences like *me gusta el vino, me gustan las cerezas* are ambiguous out of context: 'I like *the* wine/*the* cherries' or 'I like wine/cherries'. Context or intonation makes the meaning clear, or a demonstrative—*este vino* 'this wine', *estas cerezas* 'these cherries'—can be used for the first meaning.

(iii) Use of a singular count noun with a generic meaning is more frequent in Spanish than in English, where it may sound old-fashioned: *el español, cuando está de vacaciones, come mucho marisco* 'Spaniards, when they're on holiday, eat a lot of shellfish', rather than 'the Spaniard, when on holiday, eats...'.

NB: See 3.2.8b and 3.4.2 for sentences like *expertos americanos dicen...* 'American experts say' in which the noun is probably not generic.

3.2.7 Omission of the definite article in lists

When two or more generic nouns follow one another, all the articles may be omitted, especially, but not exclusively, in literary style. One must say *los hombres se exaltan al escucharlo* '(the) men get worked up listening to him', but one can say *hombres y mujeres se exaltan al escucharlo* (E. Poniatowska, Mex.) 'men and women get excited...'. Compare also *Darwin descubrió la idea **del** orden* 'Darwin discovered the idea of order' and *...descubrió las ideas de orden y estructura* '...discovered the ideas of order and structure'. Further examples:

Debilidad y falta de autoridad no son garantía de seriedad negociadora (El Tiempo, Col.)	Weakness and lack of authority are no guarantee of seriousness in negotiating
Tanto tripulación como oficialía se habían convertido en sus amigos (S. Galindo, Mex.)	Both crew and officers had become his friends

3.2.8 Omission of the definite article before partitive nouns (see Glossary)

The article is not used before nouns that refer to part of something or some members of a set, i.e.:

(a) before partitive mass (uncountable) nouns, e.g. substances and abstractions:

Quiero cerveza	I want (some) beer
Eso necesita valor	That needs courage
No hay agua	There isn't any water/There's no water
Dame paciencia	Give me patience

But the difference between generic and partitive mass nouns (see Glossary) is not always obvious, as in the sentence *como carne* 'I eat meat', where *carne* apparently refers to meat in general. See 3.2.10 for further comments on the subject.

(b) Before partitive count nouns, i.e. countable nouns that in English could normally be preceded by 'some':

No se te olvide traer clavos	Don't forget to bring (some) nails
Incluso nos dieron flores	They even gave us (some) flowers
Llevan armas	They're carrying weapons

Unqualified partitive nouns rarely appear before the verb of which they are the subject: *caían bombas por todas partes* (not *?bombas caían por todas partes*) 'bombs were falling everywhere', *salían malas hierbas entre las flores* 'weeds were emerging among the flowers', *ahora pasan taxis* 'there are some taxis going past now'. But partitive nouns modified by an adjective or by some expression like *como ése/ese* 'like that one' may appear in front of the verb: *cosas como ésas/esas sólo/solo te pasan a ti* (from María Moliner) 'things like that only happen to you', *hombres como él no se encuentran a menudo* 'one doesn't often find men like him'. For *expertos americanos dicen que. . .* 'American experts say that' see 3.4.2.

French and Italian regularly use *de* or *di* before partitive nouns: *il a des roses rouges/ha delle rose rosse = tiene rosas rojas* '(s)he's got some red roses'. *De* is not used in this way Spanish, although it may occasionally appear before words meaning 'this' or 'that' to make it clear that 'some of' rather than 'all of' is meant. Compare *tráenos de ese vino tan bueno que nos serviste ayer* 'bring us some of that really good wine you served us yesterday', and *tráenos ese vino tan bueno que nos serviste ayer* 'bring us that really good wine you served us yesterday'.

3.2.9 Definite article required before nouns modified by a qualifier

As in English, a noun that does not require the definite article when it stands alone usually requires it when it is qualified by a following word or phrase. Compare

Estamos hablando de religión	We're talking (about) religion
Está hecho de oro	It's made of gold
and	
*Estamos hablando de **la** religión de los antiguos persas*	We're talking about the religion of the ancient Persians
*Está hecho **del** oro que trajeron de las Indias*	It's made from the gold they brought from the Indies

This rule must be understood to override any of the rules of article omission that follow. However, a qualifier does not always make a noun specific: the resulting noun phrase may still be generic in its own right and have no definite article, and these nouns can only be learned by practice:

Está hecho de oro macizo	It's made of solid gold
Estamos hablando de religión antigua	We're talking about ancient religion
No hablo con traidores de su patria	I don't talk to traitors to their own country

3.2.10 Apparent exceptions to the rules outlined in 3.2.6

The general rule given at 3.2.6—that generic nouns require the definite article—has exceptions. For example, in *yo como carne* 'I eat meat', *carne* seems to be generic since it refers to all meat, but the definite article is not used. These exceptions usually occur in the following contexts:

(a) After prepositions. Nouns following prepositions very often really only denote a part or an aspect of the thing they refer to. If this is the case, they take no definite article:

Le gusta salir con ingleses (one or a few at a time, not the whole species)	(S)he likes going out with English people
Ella siempre acaba hablando de sexo (S. Puértolas, Sp., dialogue)	She always ends up talking about sex
. . .las polémicas sobre diálogos regionales con la guerrilla (*El Tiempo*, Col.)	. . .arguments about regional dialogues with the guerrilla forces

Omission or retention of the definite article with abstract and mass nouns after a preposition like *de* or *sobre* often depends on the point of view of the speaker. One can say either *publicó tres artículos sobre poesía* '(s)he published three articles on poetry' or *. . .sobre la poesía* 'on Poetry'. The latter implies the universal concept 'Poetry'; the former implies 'aspects of poetry'. The difference is slight and the strong modern tendency is to avoid using the article, although with nouns referring to more abstract concepts the article is more likely, as in *una conferencia sobre la libertad* 'a lecture on Freedom'. For further details about omission after the preposition *de*, see 3.2.11.

NB: Spanish usage differs from French with respect to the names of ministers and ministries: *el ministro de agricultura/le ministre de l'agriculture, el Ministerio de Defensa/le Ministère de **la** Défense*, etc.

(b) After certain verbs, e.g. of consuming, desiring, producing:

Los lagartos comen moscas	Lizards eat flies
Escribo novelas de ciencia ficción	I write science-fiction novels
Claro que uso jabón	Of course I use soap
Queremos paz	We want peace

But if the verb really affects the whole of its object in general—usually the case with verbs of human emotion like 'love', 'hate', 'admire', 'criticize', 'censure', 'reject', etc.—then the article is required:

Odio las novelas de ciencia ficción	I hate science-fiction novels
Me encanta el helado de vainilla	I love vanilla ice cream
Hay que combatir el terrorismo	Terrorism must be fought

(c) In many adverbial phrases

The article is not used in numerous adverbial phrases involving a preposition plus a noun:

la confusión por antonomasia	confusion personified/par excellence
a cántaros	in pitcherfuls
por avión	by plane
en tren/coche	by train/car
Estamos aquí de observadores	We're here as observers
De niña yo sólo/solo hablaba catalán	As a little girl I only spoke Catalan

3.2.11 The definite article after *de*

When two nouns are joined by *de* to express what is a new concept, the article is not used before the second noun. Compare *la rueda **del** coche* 'the wheel of/from the car', and *una rueda **de** coche* 'a car wheel':

la carne de la vaca	the meat of the cow
la carne de vaca	beef
los sombreros de las mujeres	the women's hats
los sombreros de mujer	women's hats

el dolor de muelas	toothache
la Edad de Piedra	the Stone Age
un tren de mercancías	a freight train
...la tristeza de flor de cementerio que dan	...the cemetery-flower sadness that
los lirios (M. Puig, Arg., dialogue)	irises give off

English often expresses these combinations by a compound noun: compare *la noche de la fiesta* 'the night of the party' with *la noche de fiesta* 'party night'.

Latin-American Spanish, particularly the press, uses *de* constructions without the article that are rejected in Spain, cf. *el problema de orden público es cada día más grave* (*El Tiempo*, Col.; Sp. *el problema del orden público*).

3.2.12 Use of the definite article after *haber* ('there is'/'there are')

Spanish does not normally allow the definite article to appear after *haber*: *hay agua* 'there's water', *hubo una tormenta* 'there was a storm', but *está el cartero* 'there's the postman'/ 'the postman's arrived'. See 30.2.1 (iii).

3.2.13 Omission of the definite articles in titles of books, films, etc.

In titles of books and films, etc., the definite article is often omitted before nouns that are not felt to be unique entities (for the non-use of capital letters in book titles, see 39.3.2d):

Política y estado bajo el régimen de Franco	Politics and the State under the Franco Regime
Casa de campo, de José Donoso	The Country House, by José Donoso
Selección de poemas	Selected Poems

But with unique entities or proper names the article is retained:

La casa verde, de Mario Vargas Llosa	The Green House, by Mario Vargas Llosa
La Iglesia en España ayer y mañana	The Church in Spain yesterday and tomorrow

3.2.14 Omission of definite articles in headlines

In Spain the grammar of headlines is fairly normal, but Latin-American headlines often follow the English practice of omitting articles (for the word order of these Latin-American headlines see 37.5.1 iii):

Abren proceso disciplinario contra fiscal de la Nación (*El Comercio*, Pe.)	Disciplinary proceedings initiated against National Prosecutor
Causa de deslizamiento verán expertos (idem)	Experts to investigate cause of landslide
Afirma divorcios producen temblor (*Última Hora*, Dominican Republic)	'Divorces cause Earthquakes' Claim

3.2.15 The definite article with names of unique entities

Use of the definite article with unique entities (things of which there is only one) is more or less the same as in English, e.g. *la Casa Blanca* 'the White House', *el Atlántico* 'the Atlantic', *la Virgen* 'the Virgin', *el Camino de Santiago* 'the Milky Way' (lit. 'St James's Way'), *la estratosfera* 'the stratosphere', *el Sol* 'the Sun'; but, as in

English, no article with names of planets: *Marte* 'Mars', *Júpiter* 'Jupiter', *Venus* 'Venus'. For the article with names of languages and countries, see 3.2.16 and 3.2.17.

But Spanish uses the definite article with mountains, volcanoes, Heaven and Hell: *el Infierno* 'Hell', *el Cielo/el Paraíso* 'Heaven'/'Paradise', *el Everest, el Vesubio.*

As in English, the definite article is not used with personal names as opposed to epithets, titles or nicknames: *Dios* 'God', *Cristo* 'Christ' (rarely *el Cristo*), *Jesucristo* 'Jesus Christ', *Satanás* 'Satan', but *el Salvador* 'the Saviour', *la Inmaculada* 'the Blessed Virgin', *'el Che'* '"Che" Guevara'. For the article before ordinary personal names see 3.2.21 below.

3.2.16 Definite article with names of languages

Usage is capricious and departures from the following rules may occur:

(**a**) no article after *en*, or, usually, after *saber, aprender, hablar*:

en español, en inglés	in Spanish, in English
Sé quechua	I know Quechua
Aprendo alemán/Habla griego	I'm learning German/(S)he speaks Greek

But when the verb is modified by an adverb the article is used: *habla correctamente el francés* '(s)he speaks French fluently', *hablaba bien el italiano* (J. L. Borges, Arg.). This also applies to the following section (**b**).

(**b**) Optional article after *entender* 'understand', *escribir* 'write', *estudiar* 'study':

Entiendo (el) inglés	I understand English
Escribe (el) italiano	(S)he writes Italian

(**c**) After prepositions, the article is used:

traducir del español al francés	to translate from Spanish to French
una palabra del griego	a word from Greek
Comparado con el ruso, el español parece poco complicado	Compared with Russian, Spanish seems uncomplicated

(**d**) After *de* meaning 'of', the article is used only if the whole language is meant: *curso de español* 'Spanish course' (really only 'aspects of Spanish'), but *dificultades del español* 'difficulties of Spanish' (in general), *las sutilezas del japonés* 'the subtleties of Japanese'.

(**e**) After *dominar* 'master', *chapurrear* 'speak badly', *destrozar* 'murder' and other verbs not discussed above, the article is used: *domina perfectamente el portugués* '(s)he's a complete master of Portuguese', *chapurrea el inglés* '(s)he speaks broken English'.

(**f**) If the language is the subject of a verb it requires the article: *el francés es difícil* 'French is difficult', *el español es una lengua hermosa* 'Spanish is a beautiful language'.

(**g**) If the language is qualified by a following word or phrase, the article is required: *el español de Colombia* 'the Spanish of Colombia', *el inglés que se habla en Tennessee* 'the English spoken in Tennessee'.

3.2.17 Definite article with names of countries

This is problematic since spoken usage varies and is often out of line with modern written styles. Unless the article is part of the name (as in *El Salvador*), *El País* (*Libro de estilo*, 2002, 8.27) orders its journalists to write all countries without the article except *la India, el Reino Unido* 'the United Kingdom' and *los Países Bajos* 'the Low Countries'. One even sees *en Reino Unido* in advertisements. The rules of everyday spoken language seem to be:

(**a**) Obligatory: *la India, El Salvador* (capital *E* because the *El* is part of the name), *el Reino Unido* 'the United Kingdom', *La República Dominicana* (the article is part of the name).

(**b**) Optional but usual: *el Camerún* Cameroon, *el Líbano* Lebanon, *la China, el Oriente Medio* 'The Middle East', *el Senegal, el Sudán, la Somalia, el Yemen*.

(**c**) Optional: *(la) Arabia Saudita, (la) Argentina* (article always used in Argentina), *(el) Brasil, (el) Canadá, (el) Ecuador, (las) Filipinas* 'the Philippines', *(el) Irak, (el) Irán, (el) Japón, (el) Nepal, (el) Pakistán, (el) Paraguay, (el) Perú, (el) Tibet, (el) Uruguay, (el) Vietnam*.

Other countries do not take the article: *tres años en Australia/Egipto/Noruega/Europa Oriental/África del Sur* 'three years in Australia/Egypt/Norway/Eastern Europe/ South Africa'.

(i) 'The United States' is either *los Estados Unidos*, plural agreement or, much more usually, *Estados Unidos*, singular agreement, no article – the only form allowed in *El País* (Sp.). *Gran Bretaña* 'Great Britain' does not take the article, but *el Reino Unido* 'the United Kingdom' does.

(ii) In older texts, particularly in solemn diplomatic language, names of countries occasionally appear with the article: *la Francia, la Inglaterra*, etc.

(iii) All place names require the article when they are qualified or restricted by a following adjective, phrase or clause, unless the qualifying word is part of an official name: *la España contemporánea* 'contemporary Spain', *la Suecia que yo conocía* 'the Sweden I knew'; but *en Australia Occidental* 'in Western Australia', *en Irlanda del Norte* 'in Northern Ireland'.

Names of some well-known regions, as opposed to countries, tend to be variable: *(la) Europa Central, (la) América del Sur*, the article being less usual nowadays.

3.2.18 Definite article with provinces, regions, cities and towns

Some place names include the article as an inseparable feature:

Los Ángeles	*La Haya* the Hague	*La Paz*
El Cairo	*la Mancha*	*la Plata*
La Coruña	*La Meca* Mecca	*la Rioja*

Otherwise the article is not used, unless 3.2.9 applies, as happens in *el Buenos Aires de hoy* 'Buenos Aires today', *la Roma de Cicerón* 'Cicero's Rome', etc.

(i) The article is usually written with a capital letter only in the case of cities (Seco 1998, 177). This is the practice recommended by *El País* (Sp.) and followed here.

3.2.19 Definite article before names of streets, roads, squares, etc.

The definite article is used before roads, squares, avenues, lanes, alleys and similar places:

> *Vive en la plaza/la calle de la Independencia*   (S)he lives in Independence Square/Street
> *la Embajada de los EE.UU., en la avenida*   the US Embassy on Wilson Avenue
> *Wilson (Caretas, Pe.)*

3.2.20 Definite articles with days of the week, months and years

(a) The definite article appears with days of the week:

> *Llegan el martes*   They're arriving on Tuesday
> *cerrado los viernes*   closed on Friday(s)
> *Los domingos las calles están casi vacías*   On Sundays the streets are nearly empty
>   *(M. Benedetti, Ur., dialogue)*
> *Odio los lunes*   I hate Mondays
> *El miércoles es cuando habrá menos*   Wednesday's the day there'll be least
> *a partir del domingo*   after Sunday/from Sunday on

The article is not used when the day is the predicate of *ser* 'to be', as in *hoy es lunes*. But if *ser* means 'to happen', the article appears: *fue el sábado por la tarde* 'it was/happened on Saturday afternoon'.

When the day of the week is preceded by *de* when it means 'of', the article is used: *ocurrió en la noche del viernes* 'it happened on Friday night'. Compare *trabajo de lunes a jueves* 'I work from Mondays to Thursdays'.

The article is not used in dates: *martes 23 de marzo de 1943* 'Tuesday 23 March 1943'.

(b) The definite article is not used with the names of months, but it is used with the words *mes* 'month', *año* 'year', *mañana* 'morning', *tarde* 'afternoon/evening', *noche* 'night', and *madrugada* 'dawn', except in phrases like *a finales de mes* 'at the end of the month', *a principios de año* 'at the beginning of the year':

> *Se casan en enero*   They're getting married in January
> *Empezarás el mes que viene*   You start next month
> *El próximo año iremos a Cuba*   We'll go to Cuba next year
> *¿Dónde estaba usted la mañana/tarde*   Where were you on Monday
>   */noche del lunes?*   morning/afternoon/night?

3.2.21 Definite article with personal names

The definite article sometimes appears before the surname of very famous women: *la Loren, la Callas, la Pardo Bazán, tengo que estar en Nueva York para el funeral de la Garbo* (Terenci Moix, Sp., dialogue) 'I have to be in New York for Greta Garbo's funeral'. But it is not used in this way before men's surnames.

Use of the article before first names, e.g. *la María, la Josefa, el Mario*, is considered substandard or regional, unless the name is qualified, as in *la simpática Inés* 'the kindly Inés'. The definite article usually appears before nicknames: *el Che nunca fue derrotado* '"Che" (Guevara) was never defeated' (*Cuba Internacional*, Cu.), *detuvieron a Ramón Pérez "el Duque"* 'they arrested Ramón Perez "the Duke"' (in Spain notorious criminals are usually known by their aliases).

In the Spanish spoken in Chile and Catalonia, use of the article before first names is normal, even in educated speech (DeMello, 1992, 3, shows it is much used in Santiago de Chile), but foreign learners should avoid this since it may suggest notoriety. Students of Portuguese should not use the article in Spanish: *o António quer um café = Antonio quiere un café.*

3.2.22 Definite article with sports teams

The masculine article is used before sports teams: *el Granada* 'Granada FC', *el Manchester United, el Argentina.*

3.2.23 Definite article before nouns of family relationship

Abuelo/abuela takes the article: *el abuelo no parecía dispuesto a soltarme* (S. Puértolas, Sp.) 'grandfather didn't seem inclined to let me go', *la abuelita llamó a un sacerdote* (A. Mastretta, Mex., dialogue) 'grandma called a priest'.

Tío/tía 'uncle / aunt' also takes the article: *el tío Enrique casi da un manotazo sobre la mesa* (S. Puértolas, Sp.) 'uncle Enrique nearly slapped the table with his hand'. But the article is not used by everyone when referring to their own relatives: *le di un beso a tía Julia* 'I kissed aunt Julia' (but *a la tía* is common). Latin-American usage also seems to be uncertain, although it overwhelmingly favours use of the article: *La tía Julia y el escribidor* (title of novel by M. Vargas Llosa, Pe.) 'Aunt Julia and the Scriptwriter', *la tía Verónica era una niña de ojos profundos y labios delgados* (A. Mastretta, Mex.) 'Aunt Veronica was a girl with deep eyes and thin lips'. In rural areas *tío/tía* may be used before the first names of local worthies: *el tío José/la tía Paca* 'old José' / 'old Paca'.

The article is not normally used with *papá, mamá*: *dale un beso a papá* 'give daddy a kiss' (not *al papá*).

3.2.24 Definite article with personal titles

The definite article is used before the title of a person being talked about: *el señor Moreira, el profesor Smith, el general Rodríguez, el presidente Belaúnde, el doctor Fleming, el padre Blanco* 'Father Blanco'. It is also used to refer to a couple: *los señores de Barral* 'Mr and Mrs Barral'. But it is not used if the person is directly spoken to: *pase usted, señor Sender/señor Presidente/padre Blanco* 'come in Mr Sender / Mr President / Father Blanco'.

The definite article is not used before *don, doña, fray, san, santa, sor,* or before foreign titles like *míster, monsieur, herr*: *don Miguel, fray Bentos, santa Teresa, sor Juana, míster Smith,* etc. Note that these titles are not written with capital letters.

For the military forms of address *mi general* 'General', *mi coronel* 'Colonel' see 8.3.3.

NB: *Don/doña* are sometimes used before the first names, or the first name followed by one or both surnames, of older persons to show respect, and on envelopes (less now than formerly): *señor don Miguel Ramírez, doña Josefa, don Miguel.* The first name must be included after *don,* so not simply **don Ramírez.*

3.2.25 Definite article in apposition

The definite article is usually absent in apposition (see glossary) when the following phrase is non-restrictive—i.e. it explains but does not limit the meaning of the previous phrase:

Madrid, capital de España	Madrid, the capital of Spain
Lázaro Conesal, propietario del hotel (V. Montalbán, Sp.)	Lázaro Conesal, the owner of the hotel
Buenos Aires, ciudad que no me atrae (J. L. Borges, Arg., dialogue)	Buenos Aires, a city that doesn't attract me
Ahora, a buscar un digno sustituto de Pedro, tarea nada fácil (J. J. Arreola, Mex., dialogue)	Now let's start looking for a worthy substitute for Pedro; not an easy task

But it is retained:

(**a**) if the following phrase is restrictive, i.e. it is used to remove a possible confusion of identity: *Miró, el autor* 'Miró the author' (not the painter); *Córdoba, la ciudad argentina* 'Cordoba, the Argentine city' (not the Spanish one);

(**b**) if the following phrase is a comparative or superlative: *Cervantes, el mayor novelista español* 'Cervantes, the greatest Spanish novelist', *Alma Pondal, la mejor novelista ama de casa* (M. Vázquez Montalbán, Sp.) 'Alma Pondal, the best of the "housewife" novelists';

(**c**) if the apposition is qualified by a following word or phrase: *Javier Marcos, el arquitecto que diseñó las dos fuentes* 'Javier Marcos, the architect who designed the two fountains'.

3.2.26 Definite article with numbered nouns

Unlike English, nouns identified by a number take the article:

Vivo en el piso (Lat. Am. *el apartamento/el departamento*) *38* (*piso* = 'ground' in Lat. Am.)	I live in apartment 38
Vive en la calle Serrano, en el 23/en el 23 de la calle Serrano/(but *vive en Serrano 23*)	(S)he lives at 23 Serrano Street
una disposición del artículo 277 de la Constitución	a provision of Art. 277 of the Constitution
unas fotos del 93	some photos from 1993
el diez por ciento de los peruanos	ten per cent of Peruvians

3.2.27 Definite article in phrases denoting place

The following require the definite article in Spanish whereas their English equivalents do not:

a/en/de la cama to/in/from bed	*en el escenario* on stage
a/en/de la iglesia to/in/from church	*en la televisión* on television
al/en el/del cielo/infierno to/in/from Heaven/Hell	*en el espacio* in space
al/en el/del hospital to/in/from hospital/ *en la cárcel/en la iglesia/en el colegio/ en el trabajo* in prison/at church/ at school/at work	*en el mar* at sea, on/in the sea
	debajo de la tierra (but *bajo tierra*) underground

Many other phrases resemble English, e.g. *sobre cubierta* 'on deck', *en contexto* 'in context', *salir de prisión* 'to get out of prison', *en/a clase* 'in/to class', *a misa* 'to Mass'. *A/en/de casa* 'at/in/from home' are often expressed by *a/en/de la casa* in Latin America.

Many speakers differentiate *en cama* 'in bed sick' and *en la cama* 'in bed resting', but the distinction is not universal.

3.2.28 Definite article after the verb *jugar*

Jugar takes the article in Spain: *jugar a la pelota* 'to play ball/with a ball', *jugar al ajedrez/a las cartas/al escondite* 'to play chess/cards/hide-and-seek'. It often appears without the article in Latin America: *mi padre no juega golf y mi madre no juega bridch* (L. Otero, Cu., dialogue; the usual spelling is *bridge*) 'my father doesn't play golf and my mother doesn't play bridge', *jugar tenis con él era como un consejo de ministros* (G. García Márquez, Col., dialogue) 'playing tennis with him was like (being at) a Cabinet Meeting'. But compare *ya sea fumando una pipa o jugando al ajedrez...* (M. Puig, Arg., dialogue) 'either smoking a pipe or playing chess'.

3.2.29 Definite article with personal pronouns

The definite article is required after first- and second-person plural pronouns in phrases like the following: *ustedes los uruguayos* 'you Uruguayans', *nosotros los pobres* 'we poor people', *vosotras las españolas* 'you Spanish women...' It is also used when the pronoun is not present:

Los ingleses siempre ocultáis vuestras emociones	You English always hide your emotions
Las mujeres de los mineros siempre estamos en vilo pensando en los hombres (A. López Salinas, Sp., dialogue)	We miners' wives are always on tenterhooks thinking about the men

3.2.30 Colloquial use of *la de*

In familiar language, *la de* may mean 'lots of' :

...con la de números de abogado que vienen en la guía...	...with all the dozens of lawyers' numbers there are in the phone book...
...la de veces que han dicho eso	...the number of times they've said that!
...la de lágrimas que solté (L. Sepúlveda, Ch., dialogue)	...the amount of tears I shed...

3.3 The indefinite article

This section covers the uses of the Spanish words *un, una* when they mean 'a/'an'.

3.3.1 Forms of the Spanish indefinite article

	Masculine	Feminine
Singular	*un*	*una*
Plural	*unos*	*unas*

Un is used before feminine nouns beginning with a stressed *a*, e.g. *un arma*. See 3.1.2.

3.3.2 Use of the indefinite article: general

In general terms, use of the indefinite article in Spanish corresponds to the use of 'a'/'an' in English, but there are two important differences:

(**a**) it is not used before singular countable nouns in certain contexts described below at 3.3.6–12, e.g. *tengo coche* 'I've got a car', *Mario es ingeniero* 'Mario's an engineer', *lo abrió sin llave* '(s)he opened it without a key', *es mentira* 'it's a lie'.

(**b**) It can appear in the plural: *unos pantalones* 'a pair of trousers', *son unos genios incomprendidos* 'they're misunderstood geniuses'. See 3.4 for details.

(i) *Un* 'a' must be carefully distinguished from *uno* 'one' when a masculine singular noun or adjective is involved. Compare *un verde* 'a Green' (i.e. 'ecologist') and *uno verde* 'a green one'; *un parecido* 'a resemblance', *uno parecido* 'a similar one'. The difference is not made in the feminine or in the plural: *una verde* = 'a female "Green" (ecologist)' or 'a green one'.

3.3.3 The indefinite article in French and Spanish

The French and Spanish indefinite articles compared

French	Spanish
The plural indefinite article is *des*, cf. *des gants, ce sont des clowns, je lui ai donné des roses*	The plural is *unos/unas: unos guantes, son unos payasos*, but omitted in many cases: *le di (unas) rosas*. See 3.2.8
De used in the negative: *elle ne porte pas de casque, je n'ai pas de crayon*	No article: *no lleva casco, no tengo lápiz*
Not used after 'to be' before professions: *je suis professeur*, but used after other verbs, e.g. *il a une femme*	Same: *soy profesor*, and omitted in many other cases, e.g. *tiene mujer*. See 3.3.7–8
Usually required before each noun: *un homme et **une** femme*	Same: see next section

3.3.4 Indefinite article before more than one noun

When more than one noun occurs in a sequence, the indefinite article is necessary before each noun, whereas English often omits the second article: *un hombre y **una** mujer* 'a man and (a) woman' (**un hombre y mujer* would be a cross between a man and a woman!):

> Compré una máquina de escribir y una papelera para mi despacho — I bought a typewriter and wastepaper basket for my office

However, omission is necessary when the nouns refer to the same thing or to different aspects of the same thing:

> *una actriz y cantante* — an actress and singer (same woman)
> *un cuchillo y abrelatas* — a combined knife and tin-opener
> *Este libro está escrito con una maestría y delicadeza insólitas* — This novel is written with unusual skill and delicacy

3.3.5 Omission before singular nouns: general

Un/una is often omitted before singular count nouns. This happens whenever the generic or universal features of the noun are being emphasized. Compare *Pepe tiene secretaria* 'Pepe's got a secretary' (like many bosses) and *Pepe tiene una secretaria que habla chino* 'Pepe's got a Chinese-speaking secretary'. Section 3.3.6–9 covers some of the cases in which this type of omission occurs.

3.3.6 Not used before professions, occupations, social status, sex

This is a common case of the phenomenon described in 3.3.7: *un/una* is not used before nouns which describe profession, occupation, social status, and it is often omitted before nouns denoting sex. In this case the noun can be thought of as a sort of adjective that simply indicates a general type:

Soy piloto/Son buzos	I'm a pilot/They're divers
Es soltero/Es casada (compare *está casada* 'she's married'; see 29.4.1a)	He's a bachelor/She's a married woman
Se hizo detective	(S)he became a detective
...y aunque Alejandra era mujer... (E. Sábato, Arg.)	...and although Alejandra was a woman...

But nouns denoting personal qualities rather than membership of a profession or other group require the article: compare *es negrero* 'he is a slave-trader' and *es un negrero* 'he's a "slave-driver"' (i.e. makes you work too hard); *es carnicero* 'he's a butcher (by trade)', *es un carnicero* 'he's a butcher (i.e. murderous)'; *es Supermán* 'he is Superman', *es un supermán* 'he's a superman'; *el sargento se decía: "No es un ladrón. Es un loco"* (M. Vargas Llosa, Pe.) 'the sergeant said to himself "he's no thief. He's a madman."'

If a noun of the type discussed above is qualified, it usually become particularized (non-generic) and therefore requires the article. Compare *es actor* 'he's an actor' and *es un actor que nunca encuentra trabajo* 'he's an actor who never finds work'; *me han dicho que usted es un hombre que se ha quedado solo* (A. Bryce Echenique, Pe., dialogue) 'they tell me that you are a man who has found himself alone'. But the resulting noun phrase may still be a recognized profession or generic type, so no article will be used: *soy profesor de español*. See 3.3.9 for discussion.

The article is used if it means 'one of...': —*¿Quién es ese que ha saludado?* —*Es un profesor* '"Who was that who said hello?" "He's one of the teachers"'.

3.3.7 Omission of the indefinite article with *ser* and nouns not included in 3.3.6

Omission of the indefinite article after *ser* is frequent (**a**) in certain common phrases, (**b**) in literary styles: a rare English counterpart is the optional omission of 'a' with 'part': 'this is (a) part of our heritage' *esto es (una) parte de nuestro patrimonio*. Omission is more common in negative sentences and apparently more frequent in Peninsular Spanish than in Latin-American. In the following phrases omission seems to be optional, and it produces a slightly more literary style:

Es (una) coincidencia	It's a coincidence
Es (una) cuestión de dinero	It's a question of money
Es (una) víctima de las circunstancias	(S)he's a victim of circumstances

However, no clear rule can be formulated since the article is retained in other common phrases like *es una lata* (colloquial) 'it's a nuisance', *es una pena* 'it's a pity', *es un problema* 'it's a problem', *es un desastre* 'it/(s)he's a disaster', *ha sido un éxito* 'it was a success'. Omission may occur after a negative verb even though it is not usual after the positive verb:

No es molestia/problema	It's no bother/problem
No es exageración	It's no exaggeration
No es desventaja	It's not a disadvantage

In other cases, omission often, but not always, produces a literary effect:

La codorniz es # ave tiernísima (M. Delibes, Sp.)	The quail is an extremely tender bird (to eat)
Es # mar de veras (M. Vargas Llosa, Pe. dialogue)	It's (a) real sea
¡Ésta/Esta es # cuestión que a ustedes no les importa! (J. Ibargüengoitia, Mex., dialogue)	This is an affair that has nothing to do with you!

In all the above examples the appropriate gender of *un* or *una* could have been used at the points marked with #, but the original texts do not use the article.

(i) If the following noun is not generic but merely implies the possession of certain qualities *un/una* must be used: *el hombre es **un** lobo para el hombre* 'man is a wolf to man' (but not a member of the wolf species), *Mercedes es **un** terremoto* 'Mercedes is an earthquake' (i.e. a hell-raiser), *está hecho una foca* 'he's got really fat' (*la foca* = 'seal'—the animal).

(ii) Omission of the indefinite article before a qualified noun tends to produce an archaic or heavily literary effect (or it makes the sentence sound like stage instructions), as in *entra una señora con sombrero verde con plumas de avestruz* 'a lady with a green hat with ostrich feathers comes in', where *un sombrero verde* would nowadays be much more normal. Where Unamuno wrote, in the early 20th century, *era un viejecillo[...]con levitón de largos bolsillos* 'he was a little old man in a large frockcoat with deep pockets', a modern writer might prefer *un levitón*.

NB: In formal literary styles, omission of *un/una* is normal in definitions when the subject comes first: *novela es toda obra de ficción que...* 'a novel is any work of fiction that...'.

3.3.8 Omission of *un/una* after other verbs

Spanish does not use *un/una* after a number of verbs such as *tener* 'to have', *comprar* 'to buy', *sacar* 'to take/draw out' (with cinema tickets, etc. 'to buy' or 'to book'), *buscar* 'to look for', *llevar* 'to wear', when their direct object is a noun referring to things of which one would normally have or carry only one: umbrella, pen, spoon, nanny, valet, cook, hat, etc.

Pepe ya tiene secretaria	Pepe's got a secretary now
¿Tenías idea de lo que serías capaz de hacer?	Did you have any idea of what you'd be able to do?
Ya he sacado entrada	I've already got a ticket
Vamos a buscarle novia	Let's look for a girlfriend for him
Siempre lleva anillo	(S)he always wears a ring

Barcelona tiene puerto y parque y tranvía y metro y autobús y cine (L. Goytisolo, Spain)	Barcelona has a port, park, tramway, metro, buses and cinema(s)
Hubo quien se ofendió y sacó pistola (M. Vargas Llosa, Pe.)	One person took offence/US offense and pulled a gun

NB: For the various Spanish equivalents of 'ticket', see 39.1.5.

(i) The indefinite article is used if the object has special characteristics: *llevaba una falda blanca'* she was wearing a white skirt', *tenía [...] una carita de chico pecoso...* (F. Umbral, Sp.) 'she had a cute face like a freckled boy's'.

(ii) Use of *un/una* with unqualified nouns may hint at some suppressed comment: *tiene un coche/una casa...* 'you should see his car/house...', *tiene unos ojos...* 'you should see his/her eyes...'. This may sound admiring or insinuating when applied to people, e.g. *marido* 'husband', *novio* 'boyfriend', *novia* 'girlfriend', e.g. *tiene una mujer...* 'he's got a wife (and is she...)'.

(iii) If it would be normal to have more than one of the things denoted, or if the idea of 'one' is relevant, the indefinite article must be used: *tiene mujer y **un** hijo* (E. Poniatowska, Mex., dialogue) 'he's got a wife and one child', *¿tienes un hermano?* (not *¿tienes hermano?*) 'do you have a brother?', *¿tienes un dólar?* 'have you got a dollar?', *tiene un novio en Burgos y otro en Huelva* 'she's got one boyfriend in Burgos and another in Huelva'.

3.3.9 Retention of indefinite article before qualified nouns

When nouns are modified by a clause, phrase or adjective, they become specific and the article is obligatory: *tengo padre* 'I've got a father' but *tengo un padre que es inaguantable* 'I've got an unbearable father', *era un hombre de costumbres cuidadosas* (A. Mastretta, Mex.) 'he was a man of prudent customs', *han organizado unas manifestaciones pacíficas* 'they've organized peaceful demonstrations'. But if the resulting noun phrase is still generic the article may still be omitted: *tú eres (un) hombre respetable* 'you're a respectable man', *es pastor protestante* 'he's a Protestant vicar', *el doctor Urdino es hombre serio, además de buen gerente, y persona curtida en asuntos económicos* (*El Tiempo*, Col.) 'Doctor Urdino is a serious man as well as a good manager, and a person well-versed in economic matters'.

The rule also applies in the plural: *es un ejemplo/son unos ejemplos que hemos encontrado en tu novela* 'it's an example/they're examples we found in your novel', *en seguida me llené de unos celos juveniles hacia él* (F. Umbral, Sp.) 'I was immediately filled with juvenile jealousy towards him', *nos convidó unas galletas de agua con queso fresco* (M. Vargas Llosa, Pe.; in Spain *convidó a unas...*) 'he offered us some water biscuits/US crackers with fresh cheese'.

3.3.10 Omission of indefinite article in apposition

The indefinite article is not normally used in apposition (see Glossary), at least in literary language:

El Español de hoy, lengua en ebullición	*Spanish today, a Language in Ferment* (book title)

Estuvimos quince días en Acapulco, lugar que nunca olvidaré a orillas del Huisne, arroyo de apariencia tranquila... (J. L. Borges, Arg.)	We spent two weeks in Acapulco, a place I'll never forget on the banks of the Huisne, a seemingly tranquil stream...

But in informal language, or if the noun in apposition is qualified by an adjective or clause, the article may be retained: *...el Coronel Gaddafi de Libia, un ardiente admirador del ayatollah Jomeini* (Cambio16, Sp.) '...Colonel Gaddafi of Libya, a fervent admirer of Ayatollah Khomeini'.

3.3.11 Indefinite article to distinguish nouns from adjectives

Many Spanish nouns are indistinguishable in form from adjectives: use of *un/una* indicates that the noun is meant:

Juan es cobarde/Juan es un cobarde	John is cowardly/John is a coward
Papá es (un) fascista	Father is a fascist
Soy extranjero/un extranjero	I'm foreign/I'm a foreigner

Use of the article often implies a more far-reaching or more negative value judgement. *Eres cutre* (Sp., colloquial = *tacaño, avaro*) = 'you're mean', *eres un cutre* = 'you're a mean person'; *eres tonto* 'you're silly', *eres un tonto* 'you're a fool'; *es vaga* (Sp. colloquial = *perezosa*) 'she's lazy', *es una vaga* 'she's a lazy person'.

The indefinite article is also used in the plural to retain the distinction: *son desgraciados* 'they're unhappy', *son unos desgraciados* 'they're wretches' (the meaning changes and is quite strong: *un desgraciado* = 'a wretch', 'a "creep"').

3.3.12 Omission after *como*, *a modo/manera de*, *por*, *sin*, *con*

(a) The indefinite article is not used after *a manera de*, *a modo de* and after *como* when it means 'in the capacity of' or 'by way of':

a manera de prólogo	by way of a prologue
a modo de bastón	as/like a walking stick
como ejemplo	as an example
Utilicé mi zapato como martillo	I used my shoe as a hammer
Vino como ayudante	(S)he came as an assistant

(b) It is not used after *por* when it means 'instead of', 'in place of' or 'for' in phrases like: *por respuesta le dio un beso* '(s)he gave him/her a kiss as a reply', *por toda comida me dieron un plato de arroz* 'for a meal they gave me a plate of rice' (i.e. 'all I got for a meal was...').

(c) It is not usually used after *sin* without:

No lo vas a poder cortar sin cuchillo/No vas a poder cortarlo sin cuchillo	You won't be able to cut it without a knife
Ha venido sin camisa	(S)he's come without a shirt on
un gato sin cola	a cat without a tail

But if the idea of 'one' is emphasized, or, in most cases, if the noun is qualified by an adjective or clause, the article is required: *sin un céntimo* 'without a (single) cent', *sin un amigo a quien contar sus problemas* 'without a friend to tell his problems to'.

(**d**) It is not used after *con* when it means 'wearing', 'equipped with', and in many other adverbial phrases:

Siempre va con abrigo	(S)he always wears an overcoat
una casa con jardín	a house with a garden
La Esfinge es un león con cabeza de hombre (J. L. Borges, Arg.)	The Sphinx is a lion with a man's head
Lo escribí con lápiz	I wrote it with a pencil

3.3.13 Omission in exclamations, after qué, and before *tal*, *medio*, *cierto*, *otro*

The following constructions differ from English:

¡Extraña coincidencia!	What a strange coincidence!
¡Qué cantidad!/¡qué ruido!/¡qué pena!	What a quantity/noise/pity!
¿Cómo ha podido hacer tal/semejante cosa? (colloquially *una cosa así*)	How could (s)he have done such a thing?
media pinta/medio kilo	half a pint/kilo
cierta mujer/otra cerveza	a certain woman/another beer

See 9.7 for *cierto* and 9.13 for *otro*.

3.4 Unos/Unas

Despite the fact that it derives from the Latin word for 'one', the Spanish indefinite article can be used in the plural with a variety of meanings (for a comparison of *algunos* and *unos*, which may sometimes both mean 'some', see 9.4.2. For the pronoun *uno* see 9.3 note iv and 28.7.1).

3.4.1 Uses of *unos/unas*

(**a**) before numbers, 'approximately':

El terremoto duró unos 25 segundos	The earthquake lasted some twenty-five seconds
. . .y unos cinco minutos después se detuvo (G. García Márquez, Col.)	. . .and about five minutes later it stopped

(**b**) before plural nouns, 'some' or 'a few', or sometimes 'a set of':

Tomamos unas cervezas	We had some beers
Todavía tenía unos restos de fe	(S)he still had some vestiges of faith
Sonreí. . .pero fue peor: unos dientes amarillos aparecieron (C. Rico-Godoy, Sp.)	I smiled, but it was worse: a set of yellow teeth appeared (or 'some yellow teeth appeared')
La compañía anunció unos resultados mucho peores de lo que esperaban los inversores (El País, Sp.)	The company announced a set of results much worse than investors expected
En unas horas vuelve a su casa (G. García Márquez, Col., dialogue. In Spain, usually *dentro de unas horas*)	You'll be going back home in a couple of hours

When used thus it may simply moderate the force of a following noun. It can therefore add a modest note:

Mira estas fotos—son unas vistas tomadas *en Guadalajara*	Look at these photos—they're a couple of shots taken in Guadalajara
Se sintió viejo, triste, inútil, y con unos *deseos de llorar tan urgentes que no pudo* *hablar más* (G. García Márquez, Col.)	He felt old, sad, useless, and with an urge to weep that was so urgent that he could speak no more

But sometimes use of *unos* makes little difference: *el pacifismo debería traducirse en unos comportamientos políticos que no tuviesen ninguna indulgencia con los violentos* (*La Vanguardia*, Sp., *unos* optional) 'pacifism ought to be translated into (a set of) patterns of political behaviour which show no indulgence towards the violent'.

(**c**) Before nouns that only appear in the plural, *unos* shows that only one is meant. If the noun denotes a symmetrical object like trousers, binoculars, scissors, *unos/unas* means 'a pair of':

Me caí por unas escaleras/por una escalera	I fell down some/a flight of stairs
Voy a tomarme unas vacaciones	I'm going to have a holiday/vacation
unos pantalones/unas gafas/unas cortinas	a pair of trousers/US pants/glasses/ curtains
Se quedó mirándolo con unos ojos azules *totalmente idos* (M. Vargas Llosa, Pe.)	He stood looking at him with totally vacant blue eyes (i.e. a pair of eyes)

(**d**) Use of *unos/unas* may show that the plural noun following is not being used generically:

Son payasos	They're (circus) clowns
Son unos payasos	They're (acting like) clowns
Son zorros	They're foxes (species)
Son unos zorros	They're really cunning/like foxes

(**e**) *Unos/unas* may be needed to show that the following noun is a noun and not an adjective or noun used as an adjective. See 3.3.11 for examples.

3.4.2 Omission of *unos/unas*

There is a widespread tendency in written Spanish, especially in newspapers, to avoid the use of *unos* (and of *algunos*) in sentences of the kind *expertos americanos afirman que...* 'American experts claim that...' This is no doubt a journalistic trick to hide the fact that only one or two experts were actually consulted. Spoken Spanish requires *los* if the meaning is 'all American experts', *algunos* if the meaning is 'some', and *unos* if 'a few' is intended.

In other cases omission produces a literary effect: *eléctricas letras verdes intermitentes anunciaron la salida del vuelo* (M. Vázquez Montalbán, Sp.) 'flashing green electric lights announced the departure of the flight', where *unas letras verdes* would have been more usual. Also *días después, una noche, luces verdes parpadearon en los cristales de mis balcones* (J. Madrid, Sp.) 'one night a few days later green lights flickered in my balcony windows'.

4

Adjectives

The main points discussed in this chapter are:

- The forms of adjectives (Section 4.2)
- Compound adjectives like 'light blue', 'socio-political' (Sections 4.3, 4.5)
- Shortened adjectives (e.g. *buen* for *bueno*) (Section 4.6)
- Agreement of adjectives (Section 4.7)
- Adjectives of place (Section 4.8)
- The suffix *–ísimo* (Section 4.9)
- The position of adjectives (Section 4.11)
- Relational adjectives (see glossary) (4.12)

4.1 General remarks about Spanish adjectives

(**a**) Nearly all Spanish adjectives agree with nouns and pronouns in number, and many also agree in gender. They therefore either have two forms, e.g. *natural/ naturales*, or four, e.g. *bueno/buena/buenos/buenas*. A few, e.g. *macho* 'male', *violeta* 'violet', are invariable in form.

(**b**) The position of adjectives is a subtle problem, the difference between *un problema difícil* and *un difícil problema* 'a difficult problem' being virtually untranslatable in English.

(**c**) It is necessary to distinguish 'descriptive' adjectives, e.g. 'a *big* book', 'a *blonde* girl' from 'relational' adjectives, e.g. 'a *nuclear* power-station', 'a *pedestrian* crossing' (the latter were called 'attributive' adjectives in previous editions of this book). See Glossary for definitions.

(**d**) As in other Romance languages, Spanish adjectives often become nouns if a determiner is added: *inglés* / *el inglés* 'English' / 'the Englishman', *joven/estas jóvenes* 'young' / 'these young women'; see 4.10b. Nouns can also occasionally be used like adjectives, as in *ella es más mujer que Ana* 'she's more (of a) woman than Ana' (or 'more feminine'); see 4.10a.

Although adjectives can usually serve as nouns, adjectives are nevertheless formed in unpredictable ways *from* nouns, e.g. *automóvil-automovilístico*, *legislación-legislativo*, *leche-lechero*, *lechoso* and *lácteo*, all of which mean different things.

(**e**) Some adjectives can be used with object pronouns and the verb *ser*: *me es importante* 'it's important to me', *nos son imprescindibles* 'they're indispensable to us'; but most cannot. See 11.9 (Pronouns) for discussion.

(f) Adjectival participles ending in *-ante, -iente*, e.g. *vinculante* 'binding', *preocupante* 'worrying', are discussed under participles at 19.4.

(g) The gerund in *-ndo* is a verbal form and must not therefore be used as an adjective: *una muñeca que anda* 'a walking doll', not *una muñeca andando* 'a doll walking'. For two exceptions to this rule, see 4.4. For a discussion of the Gerund see Chapter 20.

(h) Spanish adverbs are invariable in form, even when they look like adjectives: *los teléfonos están fatal* 'the phones are in a dreadful state', *estamos mejor* 'we're better'. See 31.3.3. for discussion.

4.2 Forms of adjectives

There are three types of Spanish adjectives:

- Type 1 agree in number and gender with the noun or pronoun. (4.2.1)
- Type 2 adjectives agree in number but not gender (4.2.2)
- Type 3 adjectives are invariable in form (not very numerous) (4.2.3 & 4)

4.2.1 Type 1 adjectives (agree in number and gender)

These include adjectives that end with: *-o, -án, -és , -ín, -ón, -or* (with the exceptions like *inferior* listed below), *-ote* and *-ete*.

NB: For *macho, modelo, oro* see 4.2.3–4; for *cortés, descortés, montés, afín* and *marrón* see 4.2.2.

How to form the feminine singular of type 1 adjectives

Masculine singular	Feminine singular	
ends with a vowel	change the vowel to *-a*	*bueno – buena* 'good'
ends with a consonant	add *–a*	*hablador – habladora* 'talkative'

How to form the plural of type 1 adjectives

Masculine singular	Masculine plural	Feminine plural
Ends with a vowel	Add -s: *bueno–buenos*	Add -s: *buena – buenas* *habladora – habladoras*
Ends with a consonant	Add *–es: hablador – habladores*	

In writing, a final -z is replaced by *c* before *e*, and any accent on the final vowel of the masculine singular disappears, as in the cases of *inglés, musulmán, pillín* in the chart:

Further examples of type 1 adjectives (agreeing in number and gender)

Singular		Plural		
Masculine	Feminine	Masculine	Feminine	
redondo	*redonda*	*redondos*	*redondas*	round
inglés	*inglesa*	*ingleses*	*inglesas*	English
musulmán	*musulmana*	*musulmanes*	*musulmanas*	Muslim
pillín	*pillina*	*pillines*	*pillinas*	mischievous
regordete	*regordeta*	*regordetes*	*regordetas*	plump/chubby
español	*española*	*españoles*	*españolas*	Spanish
andaluz	*andaluza*	*andaluces*	*andaluzas*	Andalusian

NB: Type 1 adjectives like *español*, *andaluz* or *gandul* (colloquial Peninsular Spanish 'slacker'/'layabout'), are unusual in that they end in a consonant other than *-és* and nevertheless have a feminine in *-a*.

Eleven adjectives that end with *-or* and have a comparative meaning are type 2, i.e. they have no separate feminine form. These are (singular-plural):

anterior-anteriores previous
exterior-exteriores outer
inferior-inferiores lower/inferior
interior-interiores inner/interior
mayor-mayores greater/older
mejor-mejores better

menor-menores minor/smaller/younger
peor-peores worse
posterior-posteriores later/subsequent
superior-superiores upper/superior
ulterior-ulteriores later/further

NB: Exception: *la madre superiora* 'mother superior' (of a religious order).

Cortés, 'courteous' and *descortés* 'discourteous' are type 2 adjectives, i.e. they have no feminine form. *Montés* 'wild' (i.e. not domesticated) is also usually type 2: *la cabra montés* 'wild goat'. These are the only adjectives ending in *-és* that have no separate feminine form.

Marrón 'brown' and *afín* 'related'/'similar' are type 2 (no feminine form): *una camisa marrón*, 'a brown shirt', *ideas afines* 'related ideas'.

4.2.2 Type 2 adjectives (no separate feminine form)

No difference between masculine and feminine. This class includes: (a) all adjectives whose masculine singular ends with a consonant, except those ending in *-ín*, *-án*, *-ón*, *-or*, *-és*, which are nearly all type 1; (b) adjectives whose singular ends with *-a*, *-e*, *-ú*, *-í*.

The plural is formed: (a) if the adjective ends in a consonant or *-í* or *-ú*, by adding *-es*. In writing, a final *-z* is replaced by *c* before *e*; (b) in all other cases, by adding *-s*.

Singular and plural of type 2 adjectives

Singular	Plural		Singular	Plural	
socialista	*socialistas*	socialist	*azul*	*azules*	blue
grande	*grandes*	big	*gris*	*grises*	grey/gray
imponente	*imponentes*	imposing	*feliz*	*felices*	happy
iraní	*iraníes*	Iranian	*feroz*	*feroces*	fierce
hindú	*hindúes*	Hindu/Indian	*ruin*	*ruines*	despicable
cortés	*corteses*	courteous	*inútil*	*inútiles*	useless

Adjectives ending in *-í* often make their plural in *-ís* in spontaneous speech, e.g. *iranís* 'Iranian'; but *iraníes* is the standard written form. Some words, e.g. *maorí/maoríes* or *maorís* 'Maori' are uncertain, but at the present stage of the language, *-íes* is still felt to be the correct plural in formal styles of most adjectives ending in *-í*.

If a diminutive or augmentative suffix is added to a type 2 adjective it then becomes type 1: *mayor* 'large'/ 'older'-*mayorcito/mayorcita* 'grown-up'; *grande* 'big'-*grandote/grandota* 'extremely large'; *vulgar* 'vulgar'-*vulgarzote/vulgarzota* 'pretty vulgar'.

Dominante forms a popular feminine *dominanta* 'bossy'/'domineering'. A few other popular or slang forms in *-nta* occur, e.g. *atorrante/atorranta* (Lat. Am.) 'lazy'/'loafer'; but other adjectives ending in *-nte* are not marked for gender whereas some nouns ending in *-nte* are. See 1.2.5 and 19.4 for further discussion.

4.2.3 Type 3 adjectives (marked for neither number nor gender)

These have only one form and are not numerous: *una rata macho* 'male rat', *unas ratas macho* 'male rats'. (See also 2.1.7b for discussion of the plural of compound nouns like *perros policía* 'police dogs', *hombres rana* 'frogmen'). Other examples are: *alerta** 'alert' (*estamos alerta* 'we're alert'), *los puntos clave* 'the key issue(s)', *encinta* 'pregnant' (literary: Seco recommends plural *encintas*), *estándar* 'standard', *extra** 'extra', *hembra* 'female' (see 1.3), *esnob* 'snobbish' or, in Spain, 'trendy'; *modelo* 'model', *monstruo* 'monster', *sport* (*los coches sport* 'sports cars'), *tabú** 'taboo', *ultra** 'extreme right-wing'.

This group is unstable, and the words asterisked often agree in the plural: *los problemas claves, los pagos extras, los temas tabúes, nuestra obligación es vivir constantemente alertas* (M. Vargas Llosa, Pe.) 'our obligation is to live constantly alert'.

Although they look like nouns, *maestro, virgen, perro* and *gigante* agree like normal adjectives: *llaves maestras* 'master keys', *tierras vírgenes* 'virgin territories', *¡qué vida más perra!* 'what a rotten life!', *berenjenas gigantes* 'giant aubergines'/(US 'eggplants'). *Gigante* has a feminine form *giganta* used only when it is applied to people.

NB: Type 3 (invariable) adjectives also occur in French, cf. *des chemises marron* 'brown shirts', but French words like *violète, extra, tabou, modèle, rose* have separate plural forms.

4.2.4 Invariable adjectives of colo(u)r

The more usual adjectives—*negro* 'black', *rojo* 'red', *azul* 'blue'—are ordinary type 1 or type 2 adjectives. However, any suitable noun, preceded by *color, de color* or *color de*, can be used: *ojos color (de) humo* 'smoke-colo(u)red eyes', *color barquillo* 'wafer-colo(u)red'. The phrase with *color* is sometimes dropped and the noun is then used like a type 3 adjective, i.e. it does not agree in number and gender: *tres botones naranja/rosa/malva/violeta/esmeralda* 'three orange/pink/mauve/violet/emerald buttons', *corbatas salmón* 'salmon ties', *cintas fresa* 'strawberry-colo(u)red ribbons'. Similar nouns are:

añil indigo	*cereza* cherry	*granate* dark red	*turquesa* turquoise
azafrán saffron	*chocolate* choco-	*lila* lilac	*violeta* violet
beige beige	late brown	*oro* gold	
azur azure	*escarlata* scarlet	*paja* straw	
café coffee brown	*grana* dark red	*sepia* sepia	

(i) Colloquially, and in some writers, especially Latin-American, *naranja, rosa, malva, violeta* and a few others may be pluralized: *flores malvas* 'mauve flowers', *los jacarandaes se pusieron violetas* (E. Sábato, Arg.) 'the jacarandas turned violet', *las uñas violetas* 'violet fingernails' (C. Barral, Sp.), ...*los ojos violetas eran de Mary* (C. Fuentes, Mex.) 'the violet eyes were Mary's', *rayos ultravioletas* (*Granma*, Cu.) 'ultraviolet rays'. But this generally seems to be avoided, especially in Spain: *sus ojos violeta parpadean* (J. Marsé, Sp.) 'her violet eyes are blinking', *pliegos de papel azules, malva, rosa, verdes* (F. Umbral, Sp.) 'blue, mauve, pink, green folds of paper', *rayos ultravioleta* (*El País*, Sp.), *la muchacha de ojos violeta* (C. Fuentes, Mex.) 'the girl with violet eyes'. *Carmesí* 'crimson' is usually pluralized like a regular type 2 adjective (*carmesíes*), but cf. *grandes rosas carmesí* (A. Gala, Sp.)

(ii) It is very unusual to find these adjectives before a noun. *Como sonreía la rosa mañana. . .* (A. Machado, Sp., poetry written before 1910) 'as pink dawn was smiling...' is a rare exception.

(iii) *Color* or *de color* is usually inserted before the more exotic hues: *eran ambas prendas de color salmón* (J. Marías, Sp.) 'both articles were salmon colo(u)r', *la pantalla de moaré color geranio* (I. Aldecoa, Sp.) 'the geranium-colo(u)red moiré lampshade', *esto se está poniendo color de hormiga* (M. Vargas Llosa, Pe.) 'this is getting ant-colo(u)red' (i.e. this is starting to look ugly/bad).

NB: *Beige* is pronounced *beis* in Spain. Seco and *El País* recommend the latter spelling.

4.3 Compound colo(u)r adjectives

All compound colo(u)r adjectives of the type 'dark blue', 'light green', 'signal red' are invariable in form (in this respect Spanish resembles French, e.g. *des yeux bleu clair*):

hojas verde oscuro	dark green leaves
calcetines rojo claro	pale/light red socks
una masa gris castaño	a grey/US gray-brown mass
[*Mis ojos*] *son azul pálido* (E. Poniatowska, Mex.)	My eyes are pale blue

Well-established compound adjectives of this kind may be used on their own, but new or unusual formations may require the addition of *de color*, e.g. *una mancha de color rojo apagado* 'a dull red stain/patch', not ?*una mancha rojo apagado*.

There are special words for some common mixed colo(u)rs: *verdirrojo* 'red-green', *verdiblanco* 'greenish-white', *verdinegro* 'very dark green', *blanquiazul* 'bluish-white', *blanquinegro* 'black-and-white', *blanquirrojo* 'red-and-white'. These agree like normal adjectives: *verdinegros/verdinegras*, etc..

NB: There is no single word for 'brown' in Peninsular Spanish. *Marrón* (type 2) is chiefly used for artificial things like shoes, and also for eyes. *Castaño* is used for hair and eyes: *pelo castaño, ojos castaños*. 'Brown skin' is *piel morena*. 'Brown earth' is *tierra parda* or *tierra rojiza*. *Café* (no agreement) is used for 'brown' in many parts of Latin America.

4.4 *Hirviendo* and *ardiendo*

Gerunds (see glossary) cannot be used as adjectives in Spanish: one cannot say **un objeto volando* for 'a flying object' (*un objeto volante/volador* or *un objeto que vuela/volaba*); see 20.3 for details. But there are two apparent exceptions, *hirviendo* 'boiling' and *ardiendo* 'burning' which look like gerunds but can be used as adjectives:

Tráeme agua hirviendo	Bring me some boiling water
Tienes la frente ardiendo	Your forehead is burning
Yo más bien soy un carbón ardiendo (i.e. sexually excited; M. Vargas Llosa, Pe., dialogue)	I'm more like a burning coal

Hirviendo, ardiendo are invariable in form, take no suffixes and cannot appear before a noun.

Chorreando 'dripping wet' may be another exception in *llevo la ropa chorreando* 'my clothes are dripping wet'.

4.5 Adjectives formed from two words

Some compound adjectives are made into single words and behave like any adjective: *muchachas pelirrojas* 'red-haired girls' (from *pelo* 'hair' and *rojo* 'red'), *cuernos puntiagudos* 'sharp-pointed horns' (from *punta* 'point' and *agudo* 'sharp').

In compound adjectives joined by a hyphen, only the second word agrees with the noun: *movimientos político-militares* 'political-military movements', *teorías histórico-críticas* 'historical-critical theories'. Such examples excepted, use of hyphens to join words is very rare in Spanish; cf. *contrarrevolucionario* 'counter-revolutionary', *latinoamericano* 'Latin-American'. See 39.4.6 for details about the use of the hyphen.

4.6 Short forms of some adjectives

A number of common adjectives lose their final syllable in certain circumstances.

(a) *Grande* is shortened to *gran* before any noun: *un gran momento* 'a great moment', *una gran comida* 'a great meal'. The *-de* is occasionally retained in formal literary styles before words beginning with a vowel. This archaism is rare nowadays, but cf. *¿busca un nuevo grande amor?* (J. César Chaves, Sp.) 'is he seeking a new great love?', *...y con un grande alboroto de pitos y timbales* (G. García Márquez, Col.) '...and with a great din of whistles and kettledrums'.

Grande is not shortened if *más* or *menos* precede: *el más grande artista de su especialidad en América* (E. Poniatowska, Mex.) 'the greatest artist in his field in America' (or *el mayor artista*), *la más grande ofensiva de terrorismo dinamitero* (G. García Márquez, Col.) 'the biggest terrorist bombing campaign'.

(b) The following lose their final vowel when placed before a singular **masculine** noun or combination of adjective and masculine noun:

alguno: algún remoto día some remote day	*postrero: tu postrer día* (archaic) your last day
bueno: un buen cocinero a good cook	
malo: un mal ingeniero a bad engineer	*primero: mi primer amor* my first love
ninguno: en ningún momento at no moment	*tercero: el tercer hombre* the third man

In all cases, the full form is used if a conjunction or adverb separates the adjective from the noun or noun phrase: *esta grande pero costosa victoria* 'this great but costly victory', *un bueno aunque agrio vino* 'a good though sour wine'.

(i) Popular speech, especially Latin American, sometimes uses short forms of adjectives before feminine nouns. This is also occasionally seen in several good Spanish writers of the first half of the twentieth century, but it is nowadays avoided: *la primera mujer* 'the first woman', not **la primer mujer*, *buena parte de* 'a good part of', not **buen parte de.*

(ii) *Santo* 'saint' is shortened to *San* before the names of all male saints except those beginning with *Do-* or *To-*: *san Juan, san Blas, santo Tomás, Santo Domingo.* It is not shortened when it means 'holy': *el santo Padre* 'the Holy Father', *todo el santo día* 'the whole day through', *el Santo Oficio* 'the Holy Office' (i.e. the Inquisition).

(iii) For *alguna* and *ninguna* before feminine nouns beginning with a stressed *a-* or *ha-* see 3.1.2, 9.4 and 23.5.5. For *cualquiera* see 9.8. For the short forms of *tanto* and *cuánto* (*tan* and *cuán*) see 9.16 and 24.6.

4.7 Agreement of adjectives

Some questions of number agreement of adjectives are also discussed under 2.3, particularly agreement with collective nouns (2.3.1). For the agreement of adjectives with titles like *Alteza* 'Highness', *Excelencia* 'Excellency' see 1.2.11.

4.7.1 Agreement of adjectives that follow the noun

(a) One or more masculine nouns require a masculine adjective: *un elefante asiático* 'an Asian elephant', *platos combinados* (Sp.) 'single-dish courses' (usually mystifyingly translated in Spain as 'combined plates': it means meat and vegetables served together, foreign-style, on one plate); *cien mil pesos mexicanos*, '100,000 Mexican pesos'.

(b) One or more feminine nouns require a feminine adjective: *la Grecia antigua* 'ancient Greece', *mil libras británicas* '1000 British pounds', *mi madre es inglesa* 'my mother's English'.

(c) Two or more nouns of different gender require a masculine plural adjective: *profesores y profesoras ingleses* 'English men and women teachers', *puentes y casas decrépitos* 'derelict bridges and houses'.
   'White irises and roses' should therefore be *lirios y rosas blancos*, but a plural adjective is sometimes given the gender of the last noun even though it qualifies all the nouns. *Adornado con lirios y rosas blancas* (M. Vargas Llosa, Pe.) may mean 'adorned with irises and white roses' or '...with white irises and roses', the *blancas* being explained by the awkwardness of following a feminine noun by a masculine adjective.
   French rejects a masculine adjective following a feminine noun: **des hommes et des femmes gros* is incorrect, but *hombres y mujeres gordos* 'fat men and women' is correct.

(i) Seco (1998), 124, notes the possibility of singular agreement with two or more nouns denoting a single complex idea, e.g. *talento y habilidad extremada* 'extreme talent and skill' for *talento y habilidad extremados.*

(ii) If several adjectives follow a plural noun and each adjective refers to only one individual item, the adjective will be singular: *los presidentes venezolano y peruano* 'the Peruvian president and the Venezuelan president'. *Los presidentes venezolanos y peruanos* means 'the presidents of Venezuela and (the presidents of) Peru'.

NB: Adverbs that have the form of adjectives are invariably masculine singular in form: *María habla muy claro* 'Maria speaks very clearly'. See 31.3.3 for further discussion.

4.7.2 Agreement with nouns joined by *o* or *ni*

(a) With the conjunction *o* agreement is optional. Plural agreement emphasizes the fact that the *o* is not exclusive (i.e. either one or the other or possibly both) and it indicates that the adjective refers to both nouns:

Buscaban una tienda o un restaurante abiertos (*abiertos* clearly refers to both)	They were looking for an open shop or (an open) restaurant
Buscaban la mujer o el hombre capaces de asumir el cargo (for the absence of personal *a* see 22.2)	They were looking for the woman or man capable of taking on the job

Singular agreement with a verb placed before its subject emphasizes exclusivity: *puede venir Mario o su hermano, pero no los dos* 'Mario or his brother can come, but not both'.

(b) With *ni* 'nor' a plural verb is usual: *ni Mario ni Juan eran tontos* 'neither Mario nor Juan was stupid'.

4.7.3 Agreement with collective nouns

An adjective that modifies a collective noun is usually singular: *la organización de profesores se dio por vencida* 'the teachers' association gave up/admitted defeat', but there are exceptions, discussed at 2.3.1.

4.7.4 Agreement of pre-posed adjectives

When an adjective precedes two or more nouns and qualifies them all, it usually agrees only with the first. This avoids the awkward combination of a plural adjective with a singular noun or a masculine adjective with a feminine noun (e.g. to avoid the peculiar ?*frescos rosas*...below):

su habitual sabiduría y tolerancia (E. Sábato, Arg.)	his usual wisdom and tolerance
esas frescas rosas y claveles (J. L. Borges, Arg.)	those fresh roses and carnations

The plural may occasionally appear to avoid ambiguities: *sus amados hijo y nieto* 'his beloved son and grandson' (both beloved), *pobres Mario y Jean Pierre* (A. Bryce Echenique, Pe., dialogue) 'poor Mario and Jean Pierre' (both poor).

NB: French does not allow this construction. Compare *una profunda inspiración y reflexión* and *une inspiration et une réflexion profondes* 'deep inspiration and reflection'.

4.7.5 'Neuter' agreement

An adjective that refers to no noun in particular is neuter in gender and masculine singular in form:

Es absurdo hacerlo sin ayuda	It's absurd to do it without help
Es peligroso, pero lo haré	It's dangerous, but I'll do it
Fantástico. . . la cantidad de dinero que gasta en tabaco	Fantastic … the amount of money he spends on tobacco
La miseria no tiene nada de sano y placentero (M. Vargas Llosa, Pe.)	Extreme poverty has nothing healthy or agreeable about it

Neuter agreement is sometimes found even where a noun is present: *tampoco es bueno demasiada natación* (L. Goytisolo, Sp., dialogue) 'too much swimming isn't good either'. Here the adjective does not qualify the noun *natación* but the general idea of *demasiada natación*; *buena* would also be correct. This phenomenon is quite common in everyday speech when the noun is not accompanied by a determiner (see Glossary), e.g. *mucha comida así no es bueno* (or *buena*) 'a lot of that sort of food isn't good', but always *esa comida no es buena* 'that food's not good'.

(i) In Asturian dialects mass nouns have neuter gender to distinguish them from nouns referring to individual items: compare *una cebolla fresca* 'a (single) fresh onion' and *cebolla fresco* 'fresh onion' (i.e. a quantity of onions), …*fresca* in standard Spanish. This occasionally invades the Castilian spoken in those parts. The *GDLE*, 1.2.4, gives details.

(ii) For adjectives with the article *lo* (*lo bueno*, *lo grande*, etc.) see 7.2.

4.8 Formation of adjectives of place

4.8.1 Adjectives referring to countries and regions

These are formed unpredictably. The following are noteworthy (for the use of the definite article with the names of countries, see 3.2.17):

Alemania: alemán Germany, German
Argelia: argelino Algeria, Algerian
(la) Argentina: argentino
Austria: austriaco or *austríaco*
Bélgica: belga Belgium, Belgian
Bolivia: boliviano
(el) Brasil: brasileño
(el) Canadá: canadiense
Canarias: canario
Castilla: castellano Castile/ Castilian. See (ii)
Cataluña: catalán
Chile: chileno
(la) China: chino
Colombia: colombiano
Costa Rica: costarriqueño, costarricense
Dinamarca: danés Denmark, Danish
Ecuador: ecuatoriano
Egipto: egipcio (not **egipciano*)

Escocia: escocés Scotland, Scottish
Estados Unidos: estadounidense. See (i)
Europa: europeo
Francia: francés
Gales: galés Wales, Welsh
Galicia: gallego
Gibraltar: gibraltareño
Gran Bretaña: británico
Grecia: griego
Guatemala: guatemalteco
Holanda: holandés
Honduras: hondureño
Hungría: húngaro
Inglaterra: inglés, often used for 'British'
Irlanda: irlandés
(el) Japón: japonés
la India: indio see (iii) for *hindú*
Marruecos: marroquí Moroccan (*moro* is pejorative)

Méjico/México: mejicano/mexicano
   see (iv)
Nicaragua: nicaragüense
Panamá: panameño
(el) Paraguay: paraguayo
(el) Perú: peruano
Polonia: polaco Polish
Portugal: portugués

Puerto Rico: puertorriqueño
El Salvador: salvadoreño
Rusia: ruso
Suecia: sueco Sweden, Swedish
Suiza: suizo Switzerland, Swiss
(el) Uruguay: uruguayo
Vascongadas, el País Vasco: vasco: see (v)
Venezuela: venezolano

(i) The adjective from *América Latina* or *Latinoamérica* is *latinoamericano*. *Hispanoamericano* or 'Spanish-American' is a linguistically accurate but ethnically imprecise term for the Spanish-speaking zones and peoples. *Latinoamérica* is a politically favoured but linguistically unscientific description of the region since other Latin-based languages are spoken there—e.g. in Brazil, Haiti, Martinique, French Guyana, etc.

In Latin America *norteamericano* means our 'American': *estadounidense* (in Mexico and in some nearby republics *estadunidense*) is used in newspapers but is rare in speech. *Americano* is assumed to mean *latinoamericano*. In Spain it usually means our 'American', but it can mean 'Latin-American' in appropriate contexts. For agreement with *Estados Unidos*, see 3.2.17 note (i).

The adjective from *América del sur* or *Sudamérica* (or *Suramérica*) 'South America'—which does not include Central America, Mexico or the Caribbean—is *sudamericano*. Seco (1998), 421, is non-committal about the forms *Suramérica*, *suramericano*, which he says are generally thought 'less acceptable' in Spain than the forms with *sud-*, but *El País* (*Libro de estilo*, 2002) prefers the prefix *sur-*, e.g. *Suráfrica*, *suroeste* 'South-West', *sureste* 'South-East', etc.

(ii) *El castellano* is the Castilian language, i.e. what is described in this book, strictly speaking the dialect of Old Castile which became the majority language of Spain, so that *el castellano* now means the same as *el español*. Now that Spain has several official languages, Catalans, Basques and Galicians sometimes object to *el castellano* being called *el español*. The same objection is also heard from some Latin Americans.

(iii) In Latin America the word *indio* is always assumed to mean Amerindian (Native American), so *hindú* is used there—but less often in Spain—for Asian Indian, although it properly means Hindu: *los empleados hindús del raj británico* (C. Fuentes, Mex., dialogue), 'the Indian employees under the British Raj' (*hindús* is colloquial for *hindúes:* see 2.1.3c). In Spain *indios americanos* or, less commonly, *amerindios*, are used for Native Americans. *Indiano* denotes a 'colonial' who has made a fortune in Latin America and returned home.

(iv) Mexicans always write *México/mexicano*, even though they are pronounced *Méjico, mejicano*: the *x* conmemorates the *Mexica* or Aztec tribe. *El País* (Sp.) uses *México, mexicano*, but Manuel Seco objects because it tempts Spanish newsreaders to say [méksiko], [meksikáno]. The spellings *Méjico, mejicano* are common outside Mexico. A few other Mexican place names are similarly affected, e.g. Oaxaca, Xalapa (or Jalapa). See 39.1.3g for further remarks on the pronunciation of *x*.

(v) The Basque words *Euskadi* or *Euzkadi* 'Basque Country', *euskalduna* 'Basque' /

'Basque-speaker', *euskera* 'the Basque language', are commonly seen in Spanish newspapers.

4.8.2 Adjectives referring to towns

There is no general rule for forming adjectives referring to towns, and some places pride themselves on obscure forms, e.g. *Huelva–onubense*. Some of the more common are:

Álava: alavés	*Lima: limeño*	*Río de Janeiro: carioca*
Alcalá: complutense. See (i)	*Londres: londinense*	after a local Indian tribe
Ávila: abulense	(note spelling)	*Roma: romano*
Badajoz: pacense	*Lugo: lucense*	*Salamanca: salmantino/*
Barcelona: barcelonés	*Madrid: madrileño*	*salamanqués*
Bilbao: bilbaíno	*Málaga: malagueño*	*San Sebastián: donos-*
Bogotá: bogotano	*Moscú: moscovita*	*tiarra* a Basque word
Buenos Aires: porteño/	*Murcia: murciano*	*Santander: santanderino*
bonaerense. See (ii)	*Nápoles: napolitano*	*Santiago: santiaguino*
Burgos: burgalés	*Nueva York: neo-*	(Ch.), *santiagués*
Cádiz: gaditano	*yorquino/ neoyorkino*	(Sp.)
Caracas: caraqueño	*Oviedo: ovetense*	*Segovia: segoviano*
Córdoba: cordobés	*Pamplona: pamplonés/*	*Sevilla: sevillano*
La Coruña: coruñés	*pamplonica* invariable	*Toledo: toledano*
Florencia: florentino	*París: parisiense.* See (iii)	*Valencia: valenciano*
Granada: granadino	*La Paz: paceño/pacense*	*Valladolid: vallisoletano*
La Habana: habanero	*Quito: quiteño*	*Zaragoza: zaragozano*

(i) *La complutense* is the old university of Alcalá, now located in Madrid.

(ii) *Bonaerense* refers to the Province of Buenos Aires.

(iii) *El País* objects to the use of *parisién* and *parisino*, but they are heard colloquially.

4.9 Intensive forms of the adjective

4.9.1 The suffix *-ísimo*: meaning and formation

The suffix *-ísimo* can be added to many adjectives. It intensifies the original meaning—*Ana es riquísima* 'Ana is extremely rich' (from *rico*)—and it should be used sparingly. It cannot be added to all adjectives, and there are irregularities. This suffix is sometimes misnamed a 'superlative' suffix, but it cannot be used in comparisons and is best thought of simply as an intensifier. *-ísimo* is added after removing any final vowel: *grande-grandísimo*, *guapa-guapísima*. The following spelling changes occur:

(**a**) adjectives ending in *-co/-ca* and *-go/-ga* require a silent *u* to keep the hard sound of the *c* or *g*: *rico-riquísimo* 'rich', *vago-vaguísimo* 'vague'/'lazy'.

(**b**) Adjectives ending in *-z* change the *z* to *c*: *feliz-felicísimo* 'happy', *feroz-ferocísimo* 'ferocious'.

(**c**) For adjectives ending in two vowels, see 4.9.2.

(**d**) Adjectives ending in *-ble* change this ending to *-bil*: *amable-amabilísimo* 'friendly', *posible-posibilísimo*. *Endeble-endeblísimo* 'feeble' is a rare exception.

4.9.2 Adjectives which do not take *-ísimo*

The following adjectives do not take the suffix *-ísimo*:

(**a**) those ending in *-í, -uo, -io,* or *-eo* if not stressed on the *e*: e.g. *baladí* 'trivial', *arduo* 'arduous', *espontáneo* 'spontaneous', *rubio* 'blond', *tardío* 'late'. Exceptions: *agrio-agrísimo* 'sour', *amplio-amplísimo* 'wide' / 'extensive', *frío-friísimo* 'cold', *limpio-limpísimo* 'clean', *ordinario-ordinarísimo* 'ordinary' / 'vulgar', *pío-piísimo* 'pious', *sucio-sucísimo* 'dirty', *vacío-vaciísimo* 'empty'.

(**b**) Words stressed on the last syllable but two (*palabras esdrújulas*) ending in *-ico, -fero, -eno, -voro, político* 'political', *mamífero* 'mammal(ian)', *homogéneo* 'homogeneous', *carnívoro* 'carnivorous'.

(**c**) Diminutives and comparatives: *grandote* 'enormous', *menor* 'smaller' / 'younger'. But *mayorcísimo* 'very old' is often heard, e.g. *es mayorcísimo* 'he's very old'.

(**d**) Compound adjectives, e.g. *patizambo* 'knock-kneed', *ojituerto* 'one-eyed'.

(**e**) Many adjectives of more than three syllables ending in *-ble*: *inexplicable, incontestable* 'unquestionable', *desmontable* 'collapsible'. There are exceptions, though some are uncommon: *agradable-agradabilísimo* 'agreeable', *apacible-apacibilísimo*, 'mild', *miserable-miserabilísimo* 'wretched', *venerable-venerabilísimo* 'venerable'.

(**f**) Those whose meaning cannot be further intensified: *fantástico, ideal, infinito, inmortal* 'immortal', *total*, etc. Exceptions: *mismo-mismísimo* 'very' (*la mismísima persona* 'the very same person'), *singular-singularísimo* 'singular'.

(**g**) Time and number adjectives: *anual* 'annual', *diario* 'daily', *nocturno* 'night-time', *semanal* 'weekly', *quinto* 'fifth', *último* 'last', *vigésimo* 'twentieth', etc. Exception: *primero-primerísimo* 'first' / 'very first of all'.

(**h**) *Hirviendo* 'boiling' and *ardiendo* 'burning'.

(**i**) Technical and scientific adjectives and most adjectives ending in *-ista*, e.g. *decimal, termonuclear* 'thermo-nuclear', *transformacional* 'transformational', *separatista* 'separatist', *nacionalista* 'nationalist', etc.

4.9.3 Irregular intensive forms

(**a**) The following are best learned as separate words:

antiguo: *antiquísimo* ancient
cursi: *cursilísimo* affected / pseudo-refined
inferior: *ínfimo* (literary) inferior / least / lowest
joven: *jovencísimo* young
lejos: *lejísimos* distant / far

mayor: *máximo* supreme / greatest
menor: *mínimo* slightest / least
mejor: *óptimo* superb (literary)
peor: *pésimo* bad / dreadful
superior: *supremo* superior / supreme

Augmentative forms ending in *-ón* insert a *c*: *guapetón* 'handsome'/'good-looking'-*guapetoncísimo*, *juguetón* 'playful'-*juguetoncísimo*, but they are rarely used.

(b) Some of the following forms are occasionally found in older texts and or in flowery written styles:

		Literary form	Current form
amigo	friendly/keen	*amícisimo*	*amiguísimo*
áspero	harsh	*aspérrimo*	*asperísimo*
benévolo	charitable	*benevolentísimo*	none
célebre	famous	*celebérrimo*	none
cruel	cruel	*crudelísimo*	*cruelísimo*
difícil	difficult	*dificílimo*	*dificilísimo*
fácil	easy	*facílimo*	*facilísimo*
fértil	fertile	*ubérrimo*	*fertilísimo*
fiel	faithful	*fidelísimo*	*fidelísimo*
frío	cold	*frigidísimo*	*friísimo*
íntegro	whole/entire	*integérrimo*	*integrísimo*
libre	free	*libérrimo*	*librísimo*
magnífico	magnificent	*magnificentísimo*	none
munífico	munificent	*munificentísimo*	none
pobre	poor	*paupérrimo*	*pobrísimo*
sabio	wise	*sapientísimo*	none
sagrado	sacred	*sacratísimo*	none

(c) The old rule whereby the diphthongs *ue* and *ie* are simplified to *o* or *e* when *-ísimo* is added is nowadays usually ignored, although *novísimo* 'very recent' must be distinguished from *nuevísimo* 'very new'. Bracketed forms are literary:

bueno	*buenísimo*	*(bonísimo)*	good
cierto	*ciertísimo*	*(certísimo)*	certain
diestro	*diestrísimo*	*(destrísimo)*	skilled
fuerte	*fuertísimo*	*(fortísimo)*	strong
reciente	*recientísimo*	*(recentísimo)*	recent
tierno	*tiernísimo*	*(ternísimo)*	tender

In some words the diphthong is never modified, e.g. *viejo-viejísimo* 'old', *cuerdo-cuerdísimo* 'sane'.

4.10 Use of nouns as adjectives and adjectives as nouns

(a) Nouns may occasionally be used as adjectives:

Tienes que ser más persona decente	You've got to be more of a decent person
Este libro es menos novela que el otro	This book is less of a novel than the other
Es más bailarina que actriz	She's more a dancer than an actress
Su reacción es puro teatro	His/her reaction is pure theatre

Such nouns are invariable in form, and when they are modified by words like *más*, *menos*, *tan* they are not accompanied by a definite or indefinite article. See 24.4.4 for nouns and adjectives modified by *qué*: *¡qué bandido eres!*, what a villain you are!; *¡qué guapa estás!* 'you look great!'

(b) Spanish adjectives can very often be made into nouns by using a determiner (see Glossary): *valiente/un valiente* 'brave'/'a brave man', *viejo/tres viejas* 'old'/'three old ladies', *extranjero/los extranjeros* 'foreign'/'the foreigners'. Unfortunately this process is subject to constraints too numerous for full discussion here. The noun may acquire a special meaning, as in *impreso/un impreso* 'printed'/'a printed form', *helado/un helado* 'frozen'/'an ice-cream', *rojo/un rojo* 'red'/'a Communist'. Some noun forms are simply not used: *¿*sale con un feliz* is not said for '(s)he's going out with a happy man' = *sale con un hombre feliz*; *llegó con una chica guapa* '(s)he arrived with an attractive girl', not *con una guapa*, etc.

An adjective may remain an adjective after a determiner, it which case *uno* and not *un* is used, cf. English 'the greens' (noun = 'environmentalists' or 'green-leaved vegetables') and 'the green ones' (adjective). Thus *un parecido* = 'similarity', but *uno parecido* = 'a similar one', as in *le voy a encargar a alguna modista que haga uno parecido* (A. Buero Vallejo, Sp., dialogue) 'I'm going to get a dressmaker to make a similar one'.

See also 3.3.11 on the use of the indefinite article to distinguish nouns from adjectives, as in *es generoso* and *es un generoso*.

4.11 Position of adjectives in relation to nouns

4.11.1 General

For the position of *alguno, ninguno, cualquiera, mismo*, possessive adjectives, etc., consult these words in the index. For the position of ordinal number-adjectives, e.g. *primero* 'first', *sexto* 'sixth', see 10.12.3.

The rules governing the position of Spanish adjectives are much more flexible than in English and a good deal more flexible than in French, but the underlying rules that determine whether one says *un lejano ruido* or *un ruido lejano* 'a distant noise' are difficult to explain. The basic rule for all adjectives other than ordinal numbers seems to be:

(a) **Restrictive adjectives follow the noun.**

(b) **Non-restrictive adjectives may precede or follow the noun. Some always precede the noun.**

Restrictive adjectives narrow the scope of the noun that precedes them: *vino espumoso* 'sparkling wine' denotes a restricted type of wine; *odio las novelas históricas* 'I hate historical novels' refers only to novels that are historical. Non-restrictive adjectives typically refer to the whole of the thing denoted by the noun: *las aburridas conferencias del decano* 'the dean's boring lectures', *la poco apetitosa cocina británica* 'unappetizing British cooking' both attribute a quality to every member or aspect of the class of thing or things referred to by the noun. Unfortunately the distinction between restrictive and non-restrictive adjectives is not always clear, and the decision about where to put the adjective often relies on a feel for the language rare among non-natives.

As a useful, though not absolutely foolproof guide to whether an adjective is restrictive, native speakers of English can apply the following test: if an English adjective sounds correct when spoken with a heavy stress (or, more accurately, with falling intonation)—'I don't like **sour** apples, but I do like **sweet** apples'—then it is almost certainly restrictive and its Spanish equivalent must follow the noun: *no me gustan las manzanas agrias, pero sí me gustan las manzanas dulces*. If an English adjective sounds wrong when stressed it is probably non-restrictive and its Spanish counterpart may well precede the noun. If one stresses 'beautiful' in 'the beautiful sun of Spain', it suggests that there is another less beautiful Spanish sun. This is absurd, so the Spanish adjective will probably precede the noun: *el hermoso sol de España*. Ordinal number adjectives do not follow this rule, cf. *está en el quinto capítulo, no en el cuarto* 'it's in the fifth chapter, not in the fourth'. See 10.12.3.

4.11.2 Examples of restrictive adjectives

The following adjectives are restrictive and therefore always follow the noun:

(a) those that create a new type or sub-set of the thing described by the noun:

el pan integral wholemeal bread   *la teoría cuántica* quantum theory
el papel secante blotting paper   *la tracción delantera* front-wheel drive
los cazas computerizados computerized
   fighter aircraft

All the other examples in this section are in fact instances of this type of adjective, which can be thought of as a transformed clause: *la poesía romántica = aquella poesía que es romántica, las manzanas verdes = aquellas manzanas que están/son verdes.*

(b) Those used for purposes of contrast, whether explicit or implied:

Tráigame una cuchara limpia, no una sucia   Bring me a clean spoon, not a dirty one
Tengo un boli verde y otro azul   I have a green ballpoint pen and a blue
                                               one
Adoro los ojos azules   I adore blue eyes
No queremos agua salada   We don't want salty water

(c) Scientific or technical adjectives:

la gramática transformativa   *el laboratorio lingüístico* language
   transformational grammar   laboratory
la crítica estructuralista structuralist *el correo electrónico* e-mail
   criticism

NB: *El emilio* was an ingenious colloquialism for 'e-mail' in Spain, but it has lost ground to *el correo* or *el email*. In formal Spanish one should use *el mensaje electrónico*.

Only the most far-fetched styles would use such adjectives poetically or as epithets, though some, e.g. *unilateral, microscópico, (p)sicoanalítico, materialista*, might conceivably be used as value judgements (see 4.11.4a).

(d) Relational adjectives. These express the origin, substance, contents or purpose of a noun. Their use is discussed at 4.12:

la nave espacial spaceship   *el material bélico* war matériel
el túnel ferroviario railway tunnel   (= *material de guerra*)
la guerra nuclear nuclear war

(e) Adjectives of nationality, which are almost always restrictive:

el clima argentino   the Argentine climate
la paella valenciana   paella Valencia-style
los monumentos mayas   the Mayan monuments

Adjectives of nationality can occasionally be used as epithets (because they express allegedly typical qualities. See 4.11.4 for a discussion of epithets): *mi española impul-*

sividad me hace escribir estas líneas (reader's letter in *Cambio16*, Sp.) 'my Spanish impulsiveness makes me write these lines'; *su británica reserva* 'her/his British reserve'.

4.11.3 Adjectives put before a noun to indicate impression, reaction or subjective assessment

The most common reason for putting an adjective before the noun is to emphasize its emotional content, e.g. *una tremenda tragedia* 'a tremendous tragedy', *un gran poeta* 'a great poet', *el inquietante problema del efecto invernadero* 'the worrying problem of the greenhouse effect'. These adjectives are non-restrictive in context because the speaker wants to eliminate any allusion to another tragedy, poet or problem: in the previous quotation, there is obviously no suggestion that there is also a non-worrying greenhouse effect.

Native speakers often report that such adjectives are in some way 'emphatic', but this is misleading since in the English translation the adjective is definitely not stressed, as explained at 4.11.1.

These pre-posed adjectives can describe the speaker's impression, assessment or evaluation of a thing, or its appearance. They include a vast range of adjectives indicating shape, distance, size, colo(u)r, texture, passage of time, praise, blame or subjective appraisal of any kind. The more emotional the language, therefore, the more pre-posed adjectives are likely to occur, as in poetry, poetic prose, journalism and advertising. Examples:

las magníficas ruinas de Machu Picchu	the magnificent ruins at/of Macchu Picchu
¡No voy a permitir que a tu hija la envenenes con las ideas de tu enferma cabeza! (L. Esquivel, Mex., dialogue)	I'm not going to let you poison your daughter with the ideas in your sick brain!
un profesor, dueño de una amplísima cultura (S. Pitol, Mex., dialogue)	a teacher, a highly educated man
¡Sensacional promoción de verano!	Sensational Summer Special Offer!

Sometimes the difference of meaning between post-posed and pre-posed adjectives can be significant, as in *el poético lenguaje de Lorca* 'the poetic language of Lorca' (aesthetic opinion) and *el lenguaje poético de Lorca* 'the language of Lorca's poetry' (factual), or *las decimonónicas actitudes del ministro* 'the nineteenth-century attitudes of the minister' (an opinion) and *la novela decimonónica* 'the nineteenth-century novel' (factual). But very often a pre-posed adjective is merely more poetic or dramatic, a post-posed one more matter-of-fact. The following examples will help to train the ear. In every case the adjective or adjectival phrase in bold letters could have followed the noun or noun-phrase:

el casi olvidado nombre de James MacPherson (J. L. Borges, Arg.)	the almost forgotten name of James MacPherson
Hay barcos anclados en permanente contacto con los aviones nocturnos (G. García Márquez, Col., dialogue)	There are boats anchored at sea in permanent contact with the night aircraft
La revolución significó para mí una justa redistribución de la riqueza (M. Vargas Llosa, Pe.)	The revolution meant for me a just redistribution of wealth

una guirnalda de blancas flores (L. Goytisolo, Sp.)	a wreath of white flowers
La pera es de fácil digestión (cookery book, Spain)	Pears are easily digested
el creciente costo de la tierra urbana	The rising cost of land in the cities

(i) Adjective position is arbitrarily fixed in many set phrases: *Alto Egipto* 'Upper Egypt', *el Sumo Pontífice* 'the Pope', *Baja California* 'Lower California' (cf. *América Central*, *los Estados Unidos*, *la China Popular*, 'People's China', etc.), *altos hornos* 'blast-furnaces', *en alta mar* 'on the high seas', *Dios Todopoderoso* 'Almighty God', *sentido común* 'common sense', etc.

(ii) If an adjective is qualified by an adverb it usually follows the noun in ordinary styles: *esta noticia altamente reveladora* 'this highly revealing news item', *una chica frígidamente agresiva*, 'a frigidly aggressive girl', *con tres amigos igualmente roñosos* 'with three equally stingy friends'. Compare *anuncian una útil linterna* (not *linterna útil*) 'they are advertising a useful torch/US flashlight' and *anuncian una linterna* **muy** *útil* 'they are advertising a very useful torch/flashlight'. With *más* and *menos* either position is possible: *el más popular presentador de la TV italiana* (*Cambio16*, Spain) 'the most popular presenter on Italian TV', or *el presentador más popular de la TV italiana*.

Constructions like *la altamente reveladora noticia* 'the highly revealing news item', *esa siempre sorprendente inteligencia de los perros* (S. Galindo, Mex.) 'that ever-surprising intelligence of dogs', *la sorprendente y para Julián desconocida noticia…* (I. Aldecoa, Spain) 'the surprising and—for Julian—unknown news …' are, however, found in literary styles.

(iii) For nouns with two or more adjectives see 4.11.5.

4.11.4 Other uses of adjectives placed before the noun

The following types of adjectives are also placed before the noun:

(a) Epithets, i.e. adjectives used to describe qualities typically associated with the noun. These are not common in everyday or matter-of-fact language, except in set phrases, but they are very common in literary, poetic or other types of emotive language:

mi distinguido colega	my distinguished colleague
el peligroso tigre asiático	the dangerous Asian tiger
un valiente torero	a brave bullfighter
los volubles dioses romanos	the fickle Roman gods

Epithets describe predictable or typical qualities: one can say *un enorme elefante* 'an enormous elephant' but only *un elefante cojo* 'a lame elephant' since lameness is not typical of elephants, unlike bigness; *mi leal amigo* 'my loyal friend' but only *mi amigo vegetariano* 'my vegetarian friend'; *un difícil problema* or *un problema difícil* 'a difficult problem', but only *un problema (p)sicológico*, since problems are not *typically* psychological.

(b) Adjectives that clearly refer to every one of the items denoted by a plural noun: *tuvo que parar en boxes para cambiar sus deterioradas ruedas* (*El País*, Sp.) 'he had to stop in the pits to change his worn tyres/US tires' (*ruedas deterioradas* could imply that only some of his tyres were worn), *muchas gracias por las magníficas rosas* (*rosas magníficas* suggests that some of the roses were less magnificent) 'many thanks for the magnificent roses', *sus evasivas respuestas empezaban a irritarme* 'his/her evasive replies were starting to irritate me', *las simpáticas peticiones de nuestros oyentes* 'our listeners' kind requests'.

For this reason, adjectives applied to unique entities are likely to be pre-posed, unless they apply only to an aspect or part of the thing:

Se veía el imponente Everest	One could see imposing Mount Everest
el izquierdista Frente Farabundo Martí	the left-wing Farabundo Martí Front
tu alarmante edad... (you have only one age)	your alarming age...

But

Existe un Unamuno político y comprometido, y otro contemplativo	There is a political, committed Unamuno, and another contemplative one
También visitamos la ciudad moderna	We also visited the modern (part of the) city

(c) Intensifiers, hyperboles and swear words—which are extreme examples of adjectives used emotively and often stripped of all real meaning:

mi increíble suerte	my incredible luck
¡este maldito ordenador! (Lat. Am. *computadora* or *computador*)	this damned computer!
Valiente soldado eres tú	A great soldier you are (I don't think...)
tu dichosa familia	your blessed family
estas condenadas hormigas	these damned ants
cinco cochinos/piojosos euros	five lousy euros

4.11.5 Position of adjectives with nouns connected by *de*

Choice of position here depends on whether the noun phrase is a compound word, i.e. a new concept, or merely a loose cluster of words. Thus *las flores de España* 'the flowers of Spain' is not a compound, so one says *las flores silvestres de España* 'the wild flowers of Spain' not **las flores de España silvestres*. But *una casa de muñecas* 'a dolls' house' is a compound and is inseparable: *una casa de muñecas barata* 'a cheap dolls' house', not **una casa barata de muñecas*. Only long familiarity with Spanish provides a guide as to what is or is not a compound noun. Some noun phrases are uncertain: one can say *una bicicleta amarilla de hombre* or *una bicicleta de hombre amarilla* 'a yellow man's bicycle' (the Spanish is unambiguous!). Further examples:

un cochecito de niño verde	a green pram/baby carriage
un buque de asalto anfibio	an amphibious assault craft
un médico de cabecera simpático	a nice family doctor
un libro lleno de curiosas referencias de índole personal (J. L. Borges, Arg.)	a book full of curious references of a personal nature

NB: Relational adjectives cannot be separated from their nouns: one cannot say **un virus peligroso informático* for *un peligroso virus informático* or *un virus informático peligroso* 'a dangerous computer virus': see 4.12.

4.11.6 Position of *bueno, malo, grande, pequeño*

The general rule applies: when they are clearly restrictive, they follow the noun. When used restrictively, they usually indicate objective qualities. When they precede the noun they usually express a subjective evaluation (which is usually the case, but see note iv for the special case of *pequeño*).

According to the *GDLE*, 3.4.2.2, in the case of *bueno* and *malo*, the preposed adjective may unambiguously refer to competence rather than moral qualities. So *un buen poeta* may be a scoundrel but a competent poet, whereas *un poeta bueno* may be a good poet and a good person. Likewise *un mal músico* and *un músico malo* 'a bad musician', *un buen amigo* = 'good as a friend' and *un amigo bueno* = 'a good friend and a good person'. The distinctions do not seem so clear-cut to us.

(a) Objective qualities

Tengo un abrigo bueno para los fines de semana, y uno regular para los laborables	I've got a good coat for weekends, and a so-so one for weekdays
Oscar Wilde dijo que no hay libros buenos o malos sino libros bien o mal escritos (J. L. Borges, Arg., contrast)	Oscar Wilde said there are no good or bad books, only well or badly written books
Ponlo debajo del árbol grande	Put it under the big tree
Trae la llave grande	Bring the big key/spanner
Era un hombre grande	He was a big man
mi hermana mayor/menor	my elder/younger sister

(b) Subjective qualities

un buen carpintero	a good carpenter
un gran éxito	a great success
un gran ruido/poeta/ embustero	a great noise/poet/fraud
los grandes narcotraficantes	the major drug dealers
un pequeño problema (see note iv)	a slight problem
el mayor poeta mexicano	the greatest Mexican poet
ni la menor impresión de insinceridad	not even the slightest impression of insincerity

(i) With *hombre* and *mujer*, *bueno* tends to mean 'good' after the noun and 'harmless' before: *un buen hombre* means 'a harmless/simple man'. *Malo* is weaker before the noun, e.g. *pasamos un mal rato* 'we had a bad time'. *Mala mujer* may be a euphemism for prostitute.

(ii) There are many set expressions: *lo hizo de buena gana* '(s)he did it willingly', *oro de buena ley* 'pure gold', *en buen lío te has metido* 'you're in a fine mess', *a mí siempre me pone buena cara* '(s)he always makes an effort with me', *¡qué mala pata!* 'what bad luck', etc.

(iii) *Grande* is pre-posed when it means 'great', but it may mean 'big' in either position.

(iv) *Un pequeño problema* is normal since *problema* is an abstract noun. However *una pequeña casa* is less usual than *una casita*. For discussion of this phenomenon see 38.2.

4.11.7 Position of *nuevo* and *viejo*

The usual explanation is that these are pre-posed when they mean 'another' and 'previous'/'long-standing' respectively, but in practice it is doubtful whether the distinction is always clear-cut: *tenemos un nuevo presidente/un presidente nuevo* 'we've got a new president', *nuevos progresos técnicos* 'new (i.e. more) technological developments', *un viejo amigo* 'an old friend' (i.e. long-standing, not necessarily old in years).

Nuevo is usually post-posed when it means 'brand-new' as is *viejo* when it means 'not new': *un coche nuevo* 'a brand-new car', *un coche viejo* 'an old car'. But *viejo* may be pre-posed when it means 'not young': *un viejo americano* 'an old American'. This distinction is overridden for purposes of contrast: *prefiero el coche nuevo al viejo* 'I prefer our new (i.e. latest) car to the old (i.e. previous) one'.

4.11.8 Adjectives whose meaning varies according to position

The following are some common cases of changes of meaning determined by adjective position, but in many cases the distinction is not rigid and a good dictionary should be consulted for further information:

	After noun	Before noun
antiguo	ancient	former or ancient
medio	average	half
pobre	poor (= not rich)	miserable/wretched
puro	pure/clean	sheer
raro	strange/rare	rare
rico	rich	delicious
simple	simple-minded	simple (= mere)
triste	sad	wretched
valiente	courageous	'great' (ironic)
varios	assorted/various	several

For *mismo* see 9.11, *propio* 9.14, *sólo/solo* 9.15.

4.11.9 Adjectives that occur only in front of the noun

The following phrases contain adjectives that normally occur only in front of a noun:

Lo haré en ambos casos	I'll do it in both cases
las llamadas democracias	the so-called 'democracies'
la mera mención del asunto	the mere mention of the topic
Llevaba mucho dinero	(S)he was carrying a lot of money
Busquemos otro médico	Let's look for another doctor
Me dejó en pleno centro	(S)he left me right in the town centre/US center
el presunto culpable	the allegedly guilty person
pocas veces	rarely
poca paciencia	little patience
el pretendido autor	the alleged/supposed author
un sedicente budista	a self-styled Buddhist
Trajeron sendos paquetes (literary)	They brought a parcel each
el supuesto ladrón	the alleged thief
ante tamaña tontería	in the face of such a great act of stupidity
No puedo comer tanta cantidad	I can't eat such a quantity

4.12 Relational adjectives

'Relational' adjectives are usually equivalent to *de* plus a noun: *la vida familiar = la vida de familia* 'family life'. Spanish has numerous relational adjectives formed from nouns cf. *mañana* 'morning' - *matinal* (*la televisión matinal* 'breakfast TV'), *impuesto* 'tax' - *impositivo* (*política impositiva* 'taxation policy'), *agua* 'water' - *hidráulico* (*avión hidráulico* 'firefighting aircraft'), or *acuático*: *planta acuática* 'water-plant'.

Relational adjectives cannot normally precede a noun (**matinal televisión* is not Spanish); they usually cannot be made comparative by using *más* or *menos*, and many of them cannot be predicates of verbs like *ser*: one can say *tasas universitarias* 'university fees', but not **estas tasas son universitarias*. There are exceptions like *constitucional, acuático*.

New relational adjectives constantly appear, probably because the combination noun + adjective more effectively translates English compound nouns of the type 'computer virus' (*virus informático*), 'film text' (*texto fílmico*). Some of these formations are short-lived or are rejected as journalese by educated speakers.

There is no fixed rule for forming relational adjectives from nouns, and Latin-American coinages occasionally differ from Peninsular ones, cf. Sp. *presupuestario*, Lat. Am. *presupuestal*; Sp. *programa de radio*, Lat. Am. *programa radial* 'radio program(me)'. In a few cases, e.g. *viento-eólico* 'wind' as in *la energía eólica* 'wind energy' (from *Eolo* 'Aeolus', the Roman god of the winds), *caza-cinegético* 'hunting', the adjective is derived from a completely different root. The following are taken from various printed sources:

de + noun	Relational adjective
carestía del petróleo	*carestía petrolera* high oil prices
crisis de la banca	*crisis bancaria* bank crisis
defectos del oído	*defectos auditivos* hearing defects
estancia en la cárcel	*estancia carcelaria* prison term
industria de automóviles	*industria automovilística* car industry
industria de hoteles	*industria hotelera* hotel industry
peces de río	*peces fluviales* river-fish
política de energía	*política energética* energy policy
programa de informaciones	*programa informativo* information program(me)
programa de televisión	*programa televisivo* television program(me)
sindicato de pilotos	*sindicato piloteril* pilots' union

In both languages an adjective may be descriptive or relational according to context: compare 'theatrical equipment' (relational) and 'theatrical reaction' (descriptive). Such pairs seem to be more common in Spanish, and this may confuse English-speakers, who tend to misinterpret a phrase like *calidad constructiva* as meaning 'constructive quality' when it in fact means 'quality of construction'. Further examples:

lenguaje shakespeariano	Shakespearean language/the language of Shakespeare
una cantidad masiva	a massive quantity
los medios masivos	the mass media
un gesto hospitalario	a hospitable gesture
un centro hospitalario	a hospital centre/US center
política defensiva	defence/US defense policy
actitud defensiva	defensive attitude
poesía amorosa	love poetry
una sonrisa amorosa	a loving smile
educación infantil	infants' education
actitud infantil	childish attitude

(i) The *GDLE*, 3.3.1.1, points out that other adjectives cannot separate a noun + a relational adjective: one says *los medios masivos americanos* not **los medios americanos masivos* for 'the American mass media'.

4.13 Translating the English prefix 'un-'

The Spanish prefix *in-* is much less common than the English 'un-' and English speakers should resist the temptation to invent imaginary words like **ineconómico* from 'uneconomical' (*poco económico*). The two languages often coincide: *inimaginable* 'unimaginable', *insobornable* 'unbribable', *intocable* 'untouchable', *irreal* 'unreal'. But often a solution with *poco, no* or *sin* must be found:

no autorizado/sin autorizar unauthorized	*poco inteligente* unintelligent
no usado/sin usar unused	*poco práctico* impractical (not **impráctico*)
poco amistoso unfriendly	*poco profesional* unprofessional
poco apetitoso unappetizing	*sin comprender* uncomprehending
poco atractivo unattractive	*sin convencer* unconvinced
poco caritativo uncharitable	*sin principios* unprincipled
poco elegante inelegant	*sin probar* untried
poco favorable unfavo(u)rable	

The above list shows that *poco*, like the French *peu*, negates an adjective: *poco deseable* means 'undesirable', not 'a bit desirable'. A preceding indefinite article restores the meaning 'little': *un poco cansado* 'a bit tired'/'slightly tired'.

5

Comparison of adjectives
and adverbs

The main points discussed in this chapter are:

- Comparison of adjectives and adverbs (how to say 'more/less beautiful', etc.) (Sections 5.1–2)
- The superlative of adjectives ('most/least beautiful', etc.) (Section 5.3)
- The superlative of adverbs ('most fluently'/'least convincingly', etc.) (Section 5.4)
- The difference between *más que* and *más de* (Section 5.5)
- When to use *más del/de la/de los/de las–que* and *más de lo que* (Section 5.6)
- *Mayor* and *menor* (Sections 5.8–9)
- Comparisons of equality: 'as...as...', 'the same as...', etc.) (Section 5.15)

Comparison in Spanish is not complicated, but English-speaking students are often affected by interference from French, which encourages misuse of the article in the superlative and failure to use *tanto como* 'as...as' in comparisons of equality (cf. French *aussi...que*). French-speakers must remember to use *yo* and *tú* after comparisons: *es más rubia que yo/tú* = *elle est plus blonde que moi/toi* 'she's blonder than me/you', never *...que mí/ti.

5.1 Regular comparison of adjectives and adverbs

With the exception of the six adjectives and adverbs listed at 5.2, all adjectives and adverbs form the comparative with *más...que* 'more...than' or *menos...que* 'less... than':

Los limones son más agrios que las cerezas	Lemons are more bitter than cherries
Tú andas más despacio que yo	You walk more slowly than me
Tiene un traje menos/más de moda	(S)he's got a less/more fashionable suit
Más vale solos que mal acompañados (M. Vargas Llosa, Pe., dialogue)	better alone than in bad company

(i) For the difference between *más que/menos que* and *más de/menos de* see 5.5.

(ii) Before clauses, verb phrases and neuter adjectives and participles, *más/menos de lo que* or the appropriate gender and number of *más/menos del que* are required, as in *es más joven de lo que parece* '(s)he's younger than (s)he looks'. See 5.6 for discussion.

(iii) The comparative of adverbs and, in some circumstances, of adjectives, has the same form as the superlative. See 5.3.2 for discussion.

(iv) *Más* and *menos* need not be repeated provided some point of comparison follows: *él es más/menos inteligente y emprendedor que su hermano* 'he's more/less intelligent and enterprising than his brother', *me pareció el lugar más refinado y elegante del mundo* (M. Vargas Llosa, Pe., dialogue) 'it seemed to me the most refined and elegant place in the world'. But if nothing follows, *más/menos* should not be omitted: *María es más guapa y más inteligente* 'María is more attractive and intelligent' (not *más guapa e inteligente*).

(v) '...than ever...' is translated ...*que nunca* (but not **que jamás*): *¡estás más joven que nunca!* 'you're younger than ever!' This use of *nunca* and of other negative words used with a positive meaning is discussed at 23.4.

(vi) The verb *llevar*, which has numerous meanings (see Index), is used in personal comparisons involving age or height: *me lleva dos años/dos centímetros* '(s)he's two years older/two centimetres taller than me'.

5.2 Irregular comparative forms

There are five adjectives and adverbs that have irregular comparative forms:

Adjective	Adverb		Comparative singular	Comparative plural (adjective only)	
bueno	*bien*	good/well	*mejor*	*mejores*	better
malo	*mal*	bad/badly	*peor*	*peores*	worse
pequeño		small/little	*menor/ más pequeño*	*menores/más· pequeños*	smaller
grande		big	*mayor/más grande*	*mayores/más grandes*	greater/bigger
poco	*poco*	little/few	*menos*	*menos* (invariable)	less/fewer

NB: The comparative forms have no separate feminine forms. *Más* is invariable.

Examples:

Estas manzanas son mejores que ésas/esas	These apples are better than those
El mundo es peor que yo (E. Mendoza, Sp.)	The world is worse than me/than I

When these words are used as adverbs only the singular form is used:

Sus hermanas hablan mejor que ella (adverb)	Her/His sisters speak better than she does
Aquí estamos mejor (adverb)	It's better for us here/We're better off here

Menos and *más* can be adjectives or adverbs: *hablas más/menos que antes* 'you talk more/less than before' (adverbs), but *somos más/menos* 'there are more/fewer of us' (lit. 'we are more/fewer').

NB: Use of *más* or *menos* with these comparative forms, e.g. **más mejor*, is sub-standard and comparable to English forms like **'more better'*, **'less worse'*. One says *mucho mejor/peor* 'much better/worse'.

(i) The uses of *mayor* and *menor* are discussed at 5.8 and 5.9.

(ii) *Más bueno, más malo* are used of moral qualities though *mejor/peor* are more usual: *a mí no me gusta pegar a los niños...pero es que éste es el más malo de todos* (E. Arenas, Sp., dialogue) 'I don't like hitting children, but this one's the worst of all', *tu papá es el más bueno de todos, más bueno que el mío* (M. Puig, Arg., dialogue) 'your father's the nicest of all, nicer than mine', *es más bueno que el pan* (set phrase) 'he has a heart of gold' (lit. 'he is more good than bread').

5.3 Superlative of adjectives

See 5.4 for the superlative of adverbs. See 16.14.5 for the use of the subjunctive after superlative expressions.

5.3.1 Superlative of adjectives formed with the definite article

In statements of the type 'the nearest station', 'the smallest tree', the superlative of adjectives (but not of adverbs) is formed with *el/la/los/las/lo* and the comparative form, or *el/la/los/las/lo menos* 'the least': *ella es la más inteligente/la mejor/la menos tímida* 'she's the most intelligent/the best/the least shy':

una infernal espiral de sangre y muertes	an infernal spiral of blood and deaths
que nos ha convertido en el país más	that has turned us into the unsafest
inseguro y violento del mundo, con la más	and most violent country in the
alta tasa de homicidios (El Tiempo, Col.)	world, with the highest murder rate
lo mejor/peor que te puede suceder... (See	the best/worst thing that can happen
Ch. 7 for the uses of *lo*)	to you...

However, in certain cases, listed at 5.3.2, the definite article is not used.

(i) Students of French must avoid repeating the article: *l'exemple le plus intéressant* = *el ejemplo más interesante* or *el más interesante ejemplo.* *El ejemplo el más interesante is not Spanish.

(ii) Translation of sentences like 'the best restaurant in Madrid' usually require *de* not *en*, i.e. *el mejor restaurante **de** Madrid.* See 34.7.1c (i) for discussion.

5.3.2 Superlative of adjectives formed without the definite article

The definite article is not used in superlative constructions in the following cases:

(**a**) When a possessive adjective precedes *más* or *menos* (contrast French *mon ami le plus loyal*):

mi más leal amigo/mi amigo más leal	my most loyal friend
Pero mi capa más profunda se entristeció	But the deepest layer in me (lit. 'my
(E. Sábato, Arg.)	deepest layer') was saddened

(**b**) After *ponerse* and other verbs of becoming, and *quedar(se)*:

María se pone más nerviosa	Maria gets most nervous
Queda mejor así	It's best/better like that

Such sentences could also be understood as comparatives. The superlative meaning can be made clear by using *ser* + *el que* or *quien*: *María es la que/quien se pone más nerviosa, éste/este es el que queda mejor.*

(**c**) In relative clauses and after nominalizers, i.e. after *el/la/los/las que, quien, aquel que*, etc. when they mean 'the one(s) who/which':

el curso que es menos interesante es...	the course that's least interesting is...
la que es más abordable...	the girl/woman who's most approachable ...
los que son más laboriosos...	the ones who are most hard-working
quienes tienen mejores notas son...	the ones with the best marks are...

(**d**) When the superlative does not involve comparison with another noun (this includes cases in which something is compared with itself):

El idealismo siempre es más fácil cuando uno es joven	Idealism is always easiest (or 'easier') when one's young
Los domingos es cuando la lluvia es más deprimente	It's on Sundays that the rain is most depressing
Aquí es donde el Rin es más romántico (the Rhine compared with itself)	The Rhine is at its most romantic here

Compare the following where true comparison with another noun is involved: *el amor sin celos es el más noble* (compared with other loves) 'love without jealousy is the noblest', *las pizzas con anchoas son las mejores* 'pizzas with anchovies are (the) best'.

(**e**) In the construction *qué...más* 'what a...!':

Qué hombre más cabeza dura... (M. Puig, Arg., dialogue)	What an obstinate man ...
¡Qué respuesta más cínica!	What a cynical answer!

5.4 Superlative of adverbs (including *más* and *menos*)

The definite article cannot be used to form the superlative of an adverb (including *más* and *menos* used as adverbs). Students of French must remember not to use the article: compare *c'est Richard qui danse le mieux* and *Ricardo es el que mejor baila.* Examples:

Cuando más llueve es en verano	It's in summer that it rains most (or 'more')
Era el cuento que mejor nos permitía pelear (A. Bryce Echenique, Pe.)	It was the short story that allowed us to quarrel most (lit. 'best'; i.e. 'short stories provoked our greatest quarrels')
...el ser que más lo amaba y al que más amaba (García Márquez, Col.)	...the person who loved him most and whom he loved most
El patrón fue uno de los que más peces capturó (*Granma*, Cu.)	The skipper was one of those who caught most fish

NB: The difference between *el que más me gusta* and *el que me gusta más* 'the one I like more/most' is one of emphasis, the former being stronger and therefore more likely to carry a superlative meaning. Note that with the verb *gustar*, *más* must be used, not *mejor*; contrast English 'I like this one best/most'.

5.5 *Más/menos que* or *más/menos de?*

The difference is crucial: *más de* is used before numbers or quantities:

Mi abuelo tiene más de cien años	My grandfather is more than a hundred years old
Son más de las tres y media	It's past three thirty
Estaba seguro de que no aguantarías quieta durante más de 6 meses (A. Mastretta, Mex., dialogue)	I was sure you wouldn't stay still for more than six months

Compare the following examples in which the expression following *más* or *menos* is not a quantity:

Este restaurante es más caro que antes	This restaurant is dearer than before
Cansa más el viaje que el empleo	The travel(l)ing is more tiring than the job
Le escriben de Italia más que a nosotros (M Puig, Arg., dialogue)	They write to him from Italy more than they do to us

(i) *No más de* 'not more than' must not be confused with *no. . .más que. . .* meaning 'only': the *GDLE*, 17.1.3.4, contrasts *Juan no compró más de veinte libros* 'Juan bought twenty books' or 'fewer/not more than twenty' and *Juan no compró más que veinte libros* 'Juan bought only twenty books'. Cf also *no he pasado en Marbella más que unos días* (S. Puértolas, Sp., dialogue) 'I only spent a couple of days in Marbella', *las clases de pintura no eran más que una manera más entretenida de pasar el tiempo* (G. García Márquez, Col.) 'the art classes were only a more entertaining way of killing time'.

(ii) In the following examples *que* must be used, even though a number follows: *tiene más fuerzas que tres hombres juntos* '(s)he's stronger than three men together', *habla más que siete* '(s)he never stops talking' (lit. '(s)he talks more than seven people'). The reason is that the comparison is not with the numbers but with the *strength of* three men, *the talking* done by seven people. Spanish thus avoids an ambiguity that affects English: compare *comió más que tres personas* '(s)he ate more than three people (would eat)' and *comió (a) más de tres personas* '(s)he ate more than three people' (cannibalism).

5.6 Comparison with clauses, verb phrases and neuter adjectives/participles

Más. . .que cannot be used before clauses, verb phrases or past participles, e.g. in sentences like 'she's more intelligent than you think'. *Más/menos de* must be used, but this phrase can be used only in front of noun phrases: **es más inteligente de crees* is clearly not Spanish for '(s)he's more intelligent than you think'. The appropriate form of *del que* must therefore be used to convert the verb phrase into a noun phrase: *es más inteligente de lo que crees*.

(a) If a comparison is made with a clause containing a noun or pronoun, *del que* must be used and must agree in number and gender with the noun or pronoun:

Has traído menos aceite del que necesitamos	You've brought less oil than we need
La conozco desde hace aún más años de los que lleva fuera de España (J. Marías, Sp., dialogue)	I've know her for even more years than she has been out of Spain
más novedades de las que Diego hubiera podido imaginar (A. Mastretta, Mex.)	more novelties than Diego could have imagined
Tienen mejores posibilidades de las que yo podría tener jamás (E. Poniatowska, Mex., dialogue)	They have better opportunities than I could ever have

(b) If the comparison is made with a verb phrase, a participle or an adjective, *de lo que* must be used (this is the neuter form, required when no gendered noun or pronoun is referred to):

El viento me vuelve mucho más loca de lo que mi marido y ex maridos dicen que estoy (Carmen Rico-Godoy, Sp.; comparison with adjective *loca*)	The wind drives me much crazier than my husband and ex-husbands say I am
No se haga el estúpido más de lo que es (M. Vargas Llosa, Pe., dialogue; Sp. *no se haga más estúpido de lo que es*)	Don't try to be more stupid than you are
más impresionante de lo esperado (= *de lo que se esperaba*)	more impressive than was hoped
...o si la noche era cálida y menos húmeda de lo habitual (E. Mendoza, Sp.)	...or if the night was warm and less humid than usual

NB: Popular English—especially British—also converts verb phrases into noun phrases in comparisons: ?'she's more intelligent than *what* you think', for the standard '...than you think'.

(i) This construction seems an unnecessary complication to English-speakers, but it is needed in Spanish because *más/menos de* can only precede noun phrases, and because *más que* before a verb or adjective usually means 'rather than' or 'instead of': *gasta más que gana* '(s)he spends more (i.e. 'rather') than earns'.

(ii) *Que* was sometimes used in these sentences in good writers in the past, cf. Unamuno (Sp., writing before 1920), *porque España ha tenido un proceso mucho más homogéneo que se cree* 'because Spain has had a much more homogeneous process than is believed'. A few informants thought this might occur in spontaneous speech, but most condemned the construction.

(iii) French is free of the problems raised by *del/de lo que*, but, unlike Spanish, it uses a redundant negative (*ne*) in comparisons with a clause: *il en sait plus qu'il n'avoue* = *él sabe más de lo que admite* 'he knows more than he admits'.

5.7 *Más* as a colloquial intensifier

Más is often used as an intensifier in familiar speech on both continents, without any comparative meaning:

Es que eres más tonto...	Heavens, you're stupid...
Está más borracho...	Is he *drunk*!

For the standard construction *qué vida más triste* 'what a sad life!', *¡qué hombre más guapo!* 'what an attractive man!', see 5.3.2 (e).

5.8 Uses of *mayor*

Mayor, which means both 'greater' and 'bigger', is used as follows:

(a) In the same way as *más grande* 'bigger' in comparisons involving physical objects, although it is not normally used of small things like pins and insects, etc., and its use for physical comparisons is more characteristic of written language:

Esta aula es más grande/mayor que la otra	This lecture room is bigger than the other
Mallorca es la más grande/la mayor de las Baleares	Majorca is the biggest of the Balearic Islands

NB: One can never say **lo mayor*: *lo más grande lo ponemos abajo* 'let's put the biggest things underneath'.

(**b**) To translate 'older' or 'oldest' when applied to people:

Mi hermano es mayor que el tuyo	My brother is older than yours
mi hermano mayor	My elder brother
Tienes dieciséis años pero pareces mayor	You're sixteen but you look older
Es ya mayor que su hermana mayor...en realidad mayor de lo que fue nunca Teresa (J. Marías, Sp., dialogue)	She's already older than her elder sister... actually older than Teresa ever was

Mayor is also a euphemism for *viejo*: *una señora mayor* 'an elderly lady'.

(**c**) *Mayor* is used to mean 'greater' or 'greatest': *su mayor éxito* 'his greatest success', *el mayor criminal del mundo* 'the greatest criminal in the world', *el mayor peligro* 'the greatest danger', *su mayor preocupación/alegría* 'his/her greatest worry/joy'.

(**d**) Before nouns denoting sizes, intensity, frequency, power or quantity, *mayor* or *más* can be used, with *mayor* considered more elegant: *mayor/más anchura* 'greater width', *mayor/más intensidad*, *mayor/más fuerza* 'greater strength', *mayor/más potencia* 'more power', *mayor/más frecuencia* 'greater frequency', *mayor/más peso* 'more weight'. Further examples:

Más acentuado será el sabor del ajo, cuanta mayor cantidad lleve (cookery book, Sp.)	The greater the quantity it contains, the more pronounced the garlic flavour will be
A mayor servicio prestado, mayor dignidad (*El Diario de Hoy*, El Salvador)	The greater the service done, the greater the dignity
Deseo recibir mayor información	I would like to receive more information

In all the examples under (d) *más* is possible and much more usual in relaxed styles.

(**e**) Before *número* or words and phrases indicating number, *mayor* is obligatory: *en mayor número de casos* 'in a greater number of cases', *mayor índice de mortalidad infantil* 'a higher rate of infantile mortality', *mayor incidencia de accidentes de tráfico* 'a higher rate of traffic accidents', *la mayor parte de las víctimas* 'the majority of the victims'.

(**f**) Set phrases: *mayor de edad* 'of age', *hacerse mayor* 'to get old', *ganado mayor* 'livestock' (horses, cows, mules only), *calle mayor* 'high street'.

(**g**) *Más grande* can be used as a superlative: *el más grande/mayor pensador moderno* 'the greatest modern thinker', but not in pejorative statements: *el mayor granuja del país* 'the biggest rogue in the country' (not *más grande*).

5.9 Uses of *menor*

Menor differs from *mayor* in that it is not used for physical size: *esta habitación es más pequeña que ésa/esa*, not **menor que ésa/esa*; *ella es más pequeña de tamaño/más baja* 'she's smaller in size', not **menor de tamaño*. However, it can be used for dimensions where English would allow 'less': *el área es menor de lo que parece* 'the area is less/smaller than it looks'. Note also *mi hermano menor/pequeño* 'my younger brother', but *mi hermano es más joven/pequeño que yo* 'my brother is younger than me'. Also *el más pequeño de la familia* 'the youngest in the family', not **el menor de la familia*.

*Lo menor is also impossible: *lo más pequeño* 'what's smallest'/'the smallest things'.

Menor is used in the same contexts as *mayor* in (b), (c), (d) and (e) in the previous section. Examples:

Diego es tres años menor que Martita y cuatro que Sergio (C. Rico-Godoy, Sp.)	Diego is three years younger than Martita and four younger than Sergio
Virginia era unos meses menor que yo (A. Mastretta, Mex., dialogue)	Virginia was a few months younger than me
Usted no tendrá la menor dificultad (or *mínima* or *más pequeña*)	You won't have the slightest difficulty
El riesgo de un enfrentamiento es cada vez menor	The risk of a confrontation is declining

(i) Common set phrases: *menor de edad* 'under age', *apto para menores* 'suitable for minors/young people'.

(ii) Colloquially the phrase *ser de tamaño menor* 'to be smaller in size' is possible.

5.10 *Mucho más, mucho menos, poco más*, etc.

Before *más, menos, mayor* and *menor*, when these four words qualify a noun, *mucho* and *poco* are adjectives and must agree in number and gender with the following noun—a point that English-speakers are prone to forget: *tienen muchos menos hijos que tú* 'they have far fewer children than you'. See 9.12b (i) for a discussion.

5.11 'The more...the more...'/'the less...the less...'

Cuanto más. . .más. . ., cuanto menos. . .menos. . . are the standard formulas (no accent on *cuanto*):

Cuantas más fotos, mejor	The more photos the better
Cuanto mayor sea la distancia de una galaxia a la Tierra, más deprisa se aleja (*Abc*, Sp. For *deprisa/de prisa* see 31.3.1, ii)	The more distant a galaxy is from the Earth, the faster it recedes
Cuanto más pensaba más me afligía (J. Cortázar, Arg., dialogue)	The more I thought, the more upset I got...

The use of *mientras* in this construction sounds popular or sub-standard in Spain but is normal in Latin America. Use of *contra* or *entre* for *cuanto* is typical of every-day speech in many parts of Latin America, but they are generally avoided in writing. (*Contra* is also heard in Spain, but it is stigmatized):

Mientras más pienses en ella, más tuya la harás (C. Fuentes, Mex., dialogue)	The more you think of her, the more you will make her yours
...la cabeza gacha, entre menos me vea, mejor (E. Poniatowska, Mex., dialogue)	...with my head bowed, the less he sees of me the better
Aquí, contra menos somos, peor avenidos estamos (M. Delibes, Sp., illiterate, rural dialogue)	Here, the less of us there are the worse we get on

'Not so much. . .but that. . .' may be translated by *tanto. . .cuanto*: *no es tanto que entre dos personas. . .no haya secretos porque así lo deciden. . .cuanto que no es posible dejar de contar. . .* (J. Marías, Sp.) 'it's not so much that there are no secrets between two people because they decide that it should be that way, but that it's not possible to avoid telling'.

5.12 'More and more...', 'less and less...'

Cada vez más/menos are the usual Spanish equivalents:

Está cada vez más delgado	He's getting thinner and thinner
Hace cada vez menos calor	The weather's getting less and less hot

5.13 Superlative time expressions

A neuter construction may be required:

Lo más tarde que cenamos es a las ocho	We have dinner/supper at eight at the latest
Lo antes/Lo más temprano que puedo salir de casa es a la una...	The earliest I can leave house is at one...
Levántense lo más temprano posible	Get up as early as you can

5.14 Miscellaneous translations of English comparatives and superlatives

Todos le interesaban, el párroco no el que menos	All the men interested her/him, not least the parish priest
Ninguno trabaja mucho, y tú menos que todos	None of them works much, and you least of all
lo menos que podrías hacer...	the least you could do...
Estoy agradecidísimo/muy agradecido	I'm most/extremely grateful
De los dos, este libro es el que más se lee	Of the two, this book is read more/the most
En esas circunstancias la gastronomía es lo de menos (M. Vázquez Montalbán, Sp.)	In those circumstances gastronomy is the least important part of it
Dale cuanto dinero puedas/Dale todo el dinero que puedas	Give him/her as much money as you can
la mejor solución posible	the best possible solution
el segundo mejor/peor	the second best/worst
Sabe sacar el mejor partido de todo	(S)he knows how to make the most of everything
Tan duquesa es como mi padre	She's as much a duchess as I am...(ironic; lit. 'she's as much a duchess as my father is')

5.15 Comparisons of equality

5.15.1 *Tan como, tanto como*

The formula is *tan...como* or *tanto...como* 'as...as', not *tanto...que* which means 'so much that', as in *se rió tanto que por poco revienta* '(s)he laughed so much (s)he nearly burst'. *Tan* is used before adjectives, adverbs and nouns; *tanto* is used before *como* itself or when nothing follows:

No soy tan joven como tú	I'm not as young as you
Usted lo sabe tan bien como yo (M. Vargas Llosa, Pe., dialogue)	You know as well as I do
No eres tan hombre como él	You're not as much of a man as he is
No hablo tanto como tú	I don't talk as much as you

5.15.2 *Igual que, lo mismo que, tal como*

These are used to express equality. *Igual que* is used after verbs, not *igual a* (for which see 5.15.3):

Escribe igual que/lo mismo que tú (not **igual* *como*, **lo mismo como*)	(S)he writes the same way as you
Me trató igual que siempre (G. García Márquez, Col.)	She treated me the same as always

(i) Comparison of equality with verb phrases can also be expressed by the formula *del mismo modo que/de la misma manera que/de igual modo que/de igual manera que*: *argüía de la misma manera que muchos filósofos de la época* '(s)he argued in the same way as many philosophers of the day'.

(ii) *Diferente, distintos*: *es diferente del que tú tienes* 'it's different to/from the one you have', *esta silla es diferente de la otra* 'this chair's different to/from the other', *es diferente/distinto a ti* 'he's different to/from you'. The construction *diferente a* is found in Latin America and is heard in Spain, although Seco (1998), 164, says it is uncommon in educated Peninsular usage.

(iii) Note the following translations of 'exactly/just as...' *lo hice tal como me lo dijiste/lo hice exactamente como me lo dijiste* 'I did it just as you told me to/exactly as you told me'.

5.15.3 *Igual or igualmente?*

Igualmente means 'equally', but *igual* (as well as being an adjective meaning 'equal') is an invariable adverb in its own right meaning 'the same'. Compare *otros problemas igualmente difíciles* 'other equally difficult problems' and *una bata que le caía igual que hecha a medida* (L. Goytisolo, Sp.) 'a housecoat that fitted her exactly as if made to measure'. Further examples:

Cuando te conozcan sabrán apreciarte igual que yo (L. Otero, Cu., dialogue)	When they get to know you they'll value you the same way as I do
En eso ustedes son igual a las mujeres (M. Puig, Arg., dialogue. Also *igual que...*)	You're the same as women in that respect
Es igual que tú (also *igual a ti*)/*Es lo mismo que tú*	(S)he's the same as you
Tú eres igualmente delgado/Tú eres igual de delgado	You're just as slim
Lo hace igual de bien que tú	(S)he does it as well as you

In Spain, *igual* very often functions colloquially as an adverb meaning 'maybe' (i.e. the same as *quizá*, *tal vez* or *a lo mejor*). See 16.3.2(c).

5.15.4 *Como para...*

Como para (or simply *para*) is used after *bastante* and *lo suficiente*, as in *bastantes problemas de violencia tiene el país como para que ahora la Fiscalía se dedique a actividades proselitistas* (*El Tiempo*, Col.) 'the country has enough problems with violence without the Public Prosecution Office now getting involved in proselytizing activities'.

6

Demonstrative adjectives and pronouns

The main points discussed in this chapter are:

- Forms of the demonstratives (Section 6.1)
- The difference between *esta mujer* and *la mujer esta* (Section 6.2)
- The difference between *este/ese/aquel* and *éste/ése/aquél* (Section 6.3)
- The different meanings of *este, ese* and *aquel* (Section 6.4)
- Translating 'the former and the latter' (Section 6.4.2)
- Some translation problems involving demonstratives (Section 6.5)

Spanish differs from French, German and English in having two words for 'that', *ese* and *aquel*, depending on the distance in time or space between the speaker and the object referred to. The demonstratives have neuter forms, *esto, eso* and *aquello*, which are discussed separately in Chapter 7.

6.1 Forms of demonstrative adjectives and pronouns

	this	that (near)	that (far)
masculine	este	ese	aquel
feminine	esta	esa	aquella
neuter (see Chapter 7)	esto	eso	aquello
	these	those (near)	those (far)
masculine	estos	esos	aquellos
feminine	estas	esas	aquellas

(i) See 6.3 for when to write these with an accent.

(ii) The masculine singular forms do **not** end in *-o*!

(iii) *Esta, esa* and *aquella* should be used before feminine nouns beginning with stressed *a-* or *ha-*: *esta agua* 'this water', *esa aula* 'that lecture hall', *aquella haya* 'that beech tree over there' (see 3.1.2 for a list of these nouns). This is the opinion of Seco (1998, articles on *aquel, ese* and *este*) and of the Academy's *Esbozo...,* 2.6.2d, and the practice of well-edited texts everywhere. But forms like *este arma* 'this weapon', *este área* 'this area' are very common in spontaneous speech and quite often appear in informal writing.

(iv) In Latin America *este*, and in Spain *esto*, are used and abused like the English 'er...' to fill pauses while the speaker is thinking.

(v) When two or more nouns are involved the demonstratives are repeated unless the nouns refer to the same thing: *este hombre y esta mujer* 'this man and (this) woman' but *este poeta y filósofo* 'this poet and philosopher' (same man).

6.2 Position of demonstrative adjectives

Normally before the noun: *esta miel* 'this honey', *ese árbol* 'that tree', *aquellas regiones* 'those regions'. In spoken language they may appear after the noun, in which case they strongly imply that the thing referred to has been mentioned before or is very familiar. In most cases this implies exasperation or sarcasm, and the construction should be used cautiously. Compare *esa mujer* 'that woman' (neutral tone) and *la mujer esa* 'that woman...' (often with a sarcastic or insinuating tone). But the construction may simply indicate a reference to a well-known topic, as in *¿quiere la bata esta? Se va a enfriar* (C. Martín Gaite, Sp., dialogue) 'do you want this dressing gown/US bathrobe? You'll get cold' (refers to an article familiar to both). Further examples:

Pero con la agencia esa que ha montado, se está forrando el riñón (A. Buero Vallejo, Sp., dialogue)	But with that agency he's set up, he's simply raking it in
En seguida dejé de tener importancia para la gente aquella (F. Umbral, Sp., dialogue)	I immediately ceased to have any importance for those people
Me voy de aquí, no resisto el frío este (interview, *Granma*, Cu.)	I'm leaving. I can't stand this cold (i.e. New York's)
...desde la tarde aquella en que me ayudaron a llenar los formularios de ingreso a la seguridad social (A Bryce Echenique, Pe.; Sp. *rellenar un formulario*)	...after that afternoon when they helped me fill in my Social Security application forms

The definite article is obligatory if a demonstrative adjective follows the noun: *la gente aquella*. The demonstrative in this case remains an adjective even though it follows the noun, so it is not written with an accent.

6.3 When does one write *éste, ése, aquél*?

There is still no clear answer to this vexing question.

Before 1959, the accent was always written on demonstrative pronouns (i.e. when *este/ese/aquel* mean 'this one', 'that one'): *ésta es mía* 'this one is mine', *un libro como ése* 'a book like that one', but *esta casa, ese libro* (demonstrative adjectives).

In 1959 the Academy decreed that the accent was needed only to avoid ambiguities of the sort found in *esta protesta* 'this protest' and *ésta protesta* 'this woman is protesting'; *esa compra* 'that purchase', *ésa compra* 'that woman is buying', *aquella baja* 'that decrease' and *aquélla baja* 'that woman is going down'. Such ambiguities are rare in practice, and the Academy, Seco (1998), 55, 200, 206, J. Martínez de Sousa (2001) and the Spanish daily *Abc* now consider the following to be correct: *Juan compró más libros que esos* 'Juan bought more books than those', *esta es mía* 'this one's mine', *un libro como ese* 'a book like that one'. The neuter pronouns *esto, eso* and *aquello* were and are *never* written with an accent.

However, many publishers, newspaper editors, the more cautious grammarians and ordinary citizens everywhere stick to the old rule: the Spanish dailies *El Mundo* and *El País* order their journalists always to write the accent on the pronouns and the Latin-American press generally does the same. Foreign students must therefore choose between obeying the Academy and upsetting many educated Spanish-speakers, or ignoring the Academy and systematically distinguishing demonstrative adjectives from pronouns, which is not always easy.

In this book we show both possibilities, e.g. *un libro como ése/ese* 'a book like that one', although we omit the accent in a few cases where we cannot decide whether the demonstrative is an adjective or a pronoun.

There is one important inconsistency in the traditional system. It has always been the practice in modern times even before 1959 and even among the most conservative writers to omit the accent from demonstrative pronouns that are the antecedent of a relative clause or act as nominalizers (*aquel que, este de,* etc.; see Glossary for terminology); the reason for this is not entirely clear. As a result we write *esta novela es mejor que* **aquella** *en que...* 'this novel is better than that in which...', **este/ese** *que...* 'this/that one that...', **aquel** *de ayer...* 'the one from yesterday...' etc. This practice is encouraged by Seco (1998, articles on *aquel, ese, este*).

Examples of demonstrative pronouns:

Dame otro cuchillo—éste/este no corta	Give me another knife—this one doesn't cut
Ése/Ese sí que es inteligente	Now that one—he really is intelligent
Antonio salía cada vez más de casa, circunstancia ésta/esta que a su madre no le pasaba inadvertida (Note position of demonstrative pronoun in apposition)	Antonio left the house more and more, this being a circumstance which did not pass unnoticed by his mother
... su proximidad o lejanía respecto de la persona que habla o de **aquella** *a quien se habla* (Academy Grammar, 1928, 39; accent omitted from *aquella* followed by relative pronoun)	...one's closeness or distance in relation to the person speaking or to whom one is speaking

NB: Use of demonstratives to refer to someone present is humorous or insulting: *pregúntaselo a éste/este* 'ask this one here' (e.g. pointing to her husband), *¡éstos/estos fuera!* 'get this lot out!'

6.4 Uses of *este*, *ese* and *aquel*

(a) *Este/esta/estos/estas* refers to things near to or associated with the speaker and is equivalent to 'this': *este libro* 'this book', *estos arbustos* 'these bushes', *esta catástrofe* 'this catastrophe (that has just happened)', *estas circunstancias* 'these circumstances (that have just arisen/that we are talking about here)'.

(b) As far as physical distance is concerned, *ese/esa/esos/esas* means 'that': *ese libro* 'that book', *esos árboles* 'those trees'. It can refer to objects at any distance from the speaker and can therefore in practice always replace *aquel* when space rather than time is involved. But *aquel* cannot always replace *ese* since it is not used for things close to the hearer or speaker.

(c) *Aquel/aquella/aquellos/aquellas* resembles the old English 'yonder' or the modern 'that/those **over there**'. Spatially, it suggests distance, and it is rarely obligatory. As far as time is concerned, it refers to the more remote past: *en aquella época* 'at that (distant) time' and may be obligatory. It is discussed in detail at 6.4.1.

éste/este de aquí	this one here
ése/ese de ahí	that one just there
aquél/aquel de allí	that one over there
(see 31.5.1 for the difference between *ahí* and *allí*).	
no ése/ese sino aquel/aquél	Not that one, but that one over there
Alcánzame ese/aquel libro rojo	Pass me that red book
Prefiero ese que tú tienes	I prefer that one (masc.) that you've got
¿Cómo se llama aquella/esa estrella?	What's that star (up there) called?
¿Quién se acuerda ya de aquellas tardes sin televisión? (not *esas* for remote time)	Who can still remember those evenings without television?

6.4.1 *Aquel* or *ese*?

Aquel seems to be dying out. Some grammarians complain about a tendency to use *ese* where *aquel* is more elegant, so learners will probably do well, when in doubt, to translate 'that' as *ese*: it is almost always correct, although *aquel* is obligatory in certain phrases referring to the distant past. However, *aquel* is still instinctively used by the majority of Spaniards and Latin Americans.

(**a**) When distances in space are compared, *aquel* implies the more distant item, and it is usual:

—*¿Quién plantó ese árbol?*	'Who planted that tree?'
—*¿Ése/Ese? —No, aquél/aquel*	'That one?' 'No, the one behind'
No esa torre sino aquélla/aquella	Not that tower but the one further away

Even in these cases *ese*, perhaps reinforced by some phrase like *ese de detrás* or *ese de más allá*, could have been used.

(**b**) When only one item is involved, it is optionally but usually used to indicate something at some distance from the speaker. The difference between *ese libro* and *aquel libro* is about the same as between 'that book' and 'that book over there':

Tráeme aquella/esa taza	Bring me that cup (from over there)
¿Ves aquella/esa montaña?	Can you see that mountain (over there)?

(**c**) As far as time is concerned, *aquel* indicates the distant past. Once an event in the past has been mentioned, *ese* can be used in subsequent references to it. In phrases indicating time there is sometimes a difference of meaning between *ese* and *aquel*:

Debe de haber andado ya por los sesenta años cuando se embarcó con aquel horror de mujer (S. Pitol, Mex., dialogue; *ese* would imply that he is still with her)	He must have been getting on for sixty when he fell in with (lit. 'set sail with') that frightful woman
¿Te acuerdas de aquel escritorio que el abuelo quemó cuando tenías cinco años? (*aquel* for something no longer in existence)	Do you remember that desk that grandfather burnt when you were five?
. . . la luna ya como de invierno, con su halo violeta de medusa y aquellas estrellas como un hielo hecho añicos (L. Goytisolo, Sp.) (*aquellas* appropriate for a childhood memory)	...the moon like a winter moon now, with its violet halo like a jellyfish's, and those stars like shattered ice

In some set phrases *aquel* is obligatory: *¡qué noche aquélla/aquella!* 'what a night that was!', *¡qué tiempos aquéllos/aquellos!* 'what times they were!'

(i) *Aquel que* (no written accent) is used and not *el que* when a preposition plus a relative pronoun follows (as in 'the one in which...*aquel/aquella en el que/la que*). See 6.5(c) and 35.13 for discussion.

(ii) *Aquel* should not be used with a historic present since it is absurd to stress both the remoteness and the closeness of an action: not **en aquel año Cervantes escribe el Quijote* 'in that year Cervantes wrote *Don Quixote*' but either *en este año Cervantes escribe el Quijote*, or *en aquel año Cervantes escribió el Quijote*.

6.4.2 'The former, the latter'

Since *aquél/aquel* denotes something remote and *éste/este* something close, they conveniently translate 'former' and 'latter':

Existían dos partidos, el conservador y el liberal, éste/este anticlerical y aquél/aquel partidario de la Iglesia	There were two parties, the conservatives and the liberals, the latter anticlerical and the former a supporter of the Church

Éste/este is much used on its own for 'the latter': *uno de los guardaespaldas se inclinó hacia el inválido, y éste/este dirigía el brillo de sus gafas oscuras hacia Ornella* (L. Sepúlveda, Ch.) 'one of the bodyguards leaned over to the invalid, and the latter directed the glint of his sunglasses towards Ornella'.

6.5 Translation problems involving demonstratives

(a) 'The... which/who', 'those... who', etc.

El que or *quien* are the usual equivalents. *Aquel que* (no accent) is used in formal language: *que se ponga de pie la que* (or *aquella que*) *ha dicho eso* 'stand up the girl who said that', etc. See Chapter 36 (Nominalizers) for discussion.

(b) 'Those of them', 'those of you', etc. *Aquellos de* is frowned on, except perhaps before *ustedes* or *vosotros*:

Los que aplaudieron ayer	Those of them who applauded yesterday
Los nicaragüenses que sabemos la verdad	Those of us Nicaraguans who know the truth
Aquellos de (entre) ustedes que afirmen eso	Those of you who claim that
Los que no hayan firmado el formulario (**los de ellos* or **aquellos de ellos* in this context are not Spanish)	Those (of them/you) who haven't signed the form

(c) 'The one in which', 'those where', etc.

Aquel que, written without an accent, is a literary alternative for *el que* when a preposition governs a relative pronoun. One writes *la habitación era más cómoda que aquella en que había dormido antes* 'the room was more comfortable than the one he had slept in before'. Spoken language usually repeats the noun: *la habitación era más cómoda que la habitación en la que/donde había dormido antes;* *en la en que is not possible. See also 35.13.

(**d**) 'This/that is why...', 'this/that is where', 'this/that's who', 'this/that was when' etc. Translating these phrases may involve the problem of 'cleft' sentences, e.g. *fue por eso por lo que pagó demasiado* (Lat. Am. *fue por eso que pagó...*) 'that was why he paid too much'. See 36.2 for a detailed discussion.

7

Neuter article and neuter pronouns

This chapter discusses:

- *lo bueno, lo más rápido posible* (Section 7.2.1)
- *lo inteligentes que son…* (Section 7.2.2)
- *ello* (Section 7.3)
- Neuter *lo* as in *no lo sé* (Section 7.4)
- *vérselas, arreglárselas*, etc. (Section 7.4.2)
- *esto, eso, aquello* (Section 7.5)

7.1 Neuter gender: general

Spanish nouns are either masculine or feminine, but a few neuter pronouns and an article have neuter as well as masculine and feminine gender and they are important in the modern language.

Neuter gender is considered necessary in Spanish to refer to concepts, ideas or statements (e.g. a preceding remark or a sentence) which are neither grammatically masculine nor feminine. Masculine and feminine articles and pronouns can refer only to nouns, present or implied, and nouns can be only masculine or feminine. Examples should make this clear:

No quiero hablar de aquél/aquel/aquélla/ aquella (for the optional accent on these pronouns see 6.3)	I don't want to talk about that one (i.e. some masculine or feminine noun. French *celui- là/ celle-là*)
No quiero hablar de aquello	I don't want to talk about **that** (Fr. *cela*)
No me gusta ése/ese/ésa/esa	I don't like that one (Fr. *celui-là/celle-là*)
No me gusta eso	I don't like that (Fr. *cela*)
los nuevos/las nuevas	the new ones (masc.)/the new ones (fem.)
lo nuevo	what is new

For *lo que, lo cual* as relative pronouns (meaning 'which…'), see 35.6. For *lo que* and *lo de* as nominalizers (i.e. 'the thing that/of…'), see 36.1.5 and 36.1.3. For the humorous *la que…* for *lo que…* see 36.1.4 (iii). For the colloquial *la de* meaning 'the quantity of…' see 3.2.30. For the neuter pronouns *todo* 'everything', *algo* 'something', *mucho* 'a lot' and *poco* 'a little' see Chapter 9.

7.2 The 'neuter article' *lo*

7.2.1 *Lo* with masculine singular adjectives and participles, and with adverbs

(a) With adjectives and participles:

Lo followed by a masculine singular adjective, or *lo de...* + a noun or adverb, may become a sort of abstract noun. This is often an equivalent of an English adjective + 'thing', but the translation may require some thought:

Lo importante es que digan la verdad	The important thing is for them to tell the truth
Lo bueno de tu casa es que tiene mucha luz	What's good about your house is that it's full of light
Lo monótono es la felicidad (C. Solórzano, Mex., dialogue)	Monotony is happiness (or 'happiness is things not changing')
Papá se ha enterado de lo nuestro	Father has found out about us
Felicitas había estudiado lo justo (S. Puértolas, Sp.)	Felicitas had studied just as much as was necessary
Lo mío ha sido igual de duro que lo de ustedes (G. García Márquez, Col., dialogue)	What happened to me was as tough as what happened to you
a pesar de lo antes dicho	despite what was said earlier
en lo alto de la colina	on the top of the hill
Baja lo de allí arriba	Take down everything from up there
lo ya dicho en el capítulo anterior	what was said in the previous chapter
lo nunca visto en Estados Unidos	what has never been seen before in the USA

NB: *En/a lo de Antonio* may mean 'in/to Antonio's house' in Southern Cone countries.

In sentences with *ser* the verb agrees with the predicate: *lo mejor de la película **son** los actores* 'the best thing in the film is (lit. 'are') the actors': see 2.3.3.

(i) Other Romance languages lack this device: the French *le plus tragique* can mean both 'the most tragic thing' and 'the most tragic one (masc.)'; the Italian *il bello e il brutto* can mean 'beauty and ugliness' (*lo bello y lo feo*) or 'the beautiful one (masc.) and the ugly one' (*el bello y el feo*).

(ii) For the choice between the indicative and the subjunctive in constructions with *lo* + adjective + *es que*, e.g. *lo increíble/curioso es que...*, see 16.6.3.

(iii) *Lo* is sometimes found with a noun used adjectivally: *pues sí, Diego, ya sabes lo desastre que soy* (C. Martin-Godoy, Sp., dialogue) 'well yes, Diego, you know what a disaster I am', *ya te salió lo mujer* (A. Mastretta, Mex., dialogue) 'here goes the woman in you' (lit. 'the woman in you came out').

(**b**) With adverbs or adverbial phrases:

Combinations of *lo* + *más/menos* + an adverb + some phrase meaning 'as possible' are particularly common and useful:

Hazlo lo más rápidamente que puedas	Do it as quickly as you can
Cuélgalo lo más arriba que puedas	Hang it as high/as far up as you can
lo más atrás posible	as far back as possible
Lo antes que puedo salir de casa es a las seis	The earliest I can leave home is at six

When *bastante* and *suficiente* occur in phrases like 'clever enough to...', 'she did it well enough to...' they are preceded by *lo* and followed by *para*: *el cuello de su gabardina estaba lo bastante abierto para permitirme contemplar el collar de perlas* (J. Marías, Sp.) 'the collar of her raincoat was open enough to let me see her pearl necklace', *ya tenía lo suficiente para aquellos paseos* (S. Galindo, Mex.) 'he already had enough (money) for those excursions'. *Como* may optionally precede the *para*: *era lo suficientemente ingenua como para tragarse cualquier cuento* (L. Sepúlveda, Ch.) 'she was naive enough to swallow any story'.

7.2.2 *Lo* plus adjectives or adverbs translating 'how', etc.

Lo with an adjective or adverb often translates the English 'how' or some similar word + an adjective or adverb. When used thus an adjective must agree with the noun. The construction often occurs after verbs of perception ('see', 'realize', 'understand', 'know') and after verbs of liking or disliking:

(**a**) with adjectives and nouns used adjectivally:

No se ha fijado en lo delgada que se ha quedado? (A. Buero Vallejo, Sp., dialogue)	Haven't you noticed how thin she's become?
Lo que resulta increíble es lo modernos y antiguos que son al mismo tiempo (A. Bryce Echenique, Pe.)	What's incredible is how modern and ancient they are at the same time
Tal vez no haya salido todo lo buena que yo creía (M. Puig, Arg., dialogue)	Perhaps she hasn't turned out to be as good as I thought

(**b**) with adverbs and adverbial phrases

Yo llegué confiando en lo bien que lo iba a pasar	I arrived sure of what a good time I was going to have
Haga que hablen de usted por lo bien que habla inglés (advertisement, Sp.)	Get them talking about you because you speak English so well
Si vieras lo mal que patina	If you could see how badly (s)he skates
Hay que ver lo tarde que es	I can't believe how late it is (lit. 'you have to see how late it is')

(i) A common colloquial construction is *con lo* + adjective. Translation varies with context: *pobre Ana, con lo enferma que está...* 'Poor Anna, and her being so ill...', *tú, con lo inteligente que eres, a ver si lo puedes abrir* 'you're so intelligent, let's see if you can open it', *...con lo metomentodo que es* '...since (s)he's such a nosy-parker'.

(ii) *De lo más* + an adjective is found in familiar speech as an intensifying phrase: *viene de lo más arregladita* 'she's coming all dressed-up', *tomaban su cerveza de lo más tranquilos* (M. Vargas Llosa, Pe., dialogue) 'they were drinking their beer really quietly', *hice un pudín de pan. Mi marido me dijo que estaba de lo más bueno* (A. Arrufat, Cu., dialogue) 'I made a bread pudding. My husband said it was really delicious'.

(iii) In expressions of cause *por* or *de* can be used before *lo* + adjective: *no pudieron pasar por lo gordos que estaban/...de (lo) gordos que estaban* 'they couldn't get through because they were so fat'.

7.3 *Ello*

This is a neuter third-person pronoun. It is invariable in form and can be used to translate 'it' when this pronoun does not refer to a specific noun. Compare *en cuanto al régimen militar, prefiero no hablar de él* 'as for the military regime, I prefer not to talk about it' (*régimen* is masculine singular) and *todo fue tremendamente violento, y prefiero no hablar de ello* 'it was all tremendously embarrassing, and I prefer not to talk about it' (neuter).

Ello can be used as a subject pronoun or it can be combined with a preposition, but *lo* is its direct object form and *le* its indirect object form: *yo lo sabía* = 'I knew it', never **yo sabía ello*:

No te preocupes por ello, que no se me olvida (see 33.4.4b for this use of *que*)	Don't worry about it—I haven't forgotten it (or 'I won't forget')
Por ello ya no se fía de nadie	Because of that (s)he doesn't trust anybody any more
Las cosas que no importan no se entienden porque no se pone uno a ello (C. Martin Gaite, Sp. *Ello* is not an indirect object here)	Things that don't matter aren't understood because we don't apply our minds to it

When it is the subject of a verb it is usually translated 'this' and it clearly refers to the whole of the preceding utterance (*esto* could often be used instead).

Habitó un siglo en la Ciudad de los Inmortales. Cuando la derribaron, aconsejó la fundación de otra. Ello no debe sorprendernos... (J. L. Borges, Arg.)	He dwelt for a century in the City of the Immortals. When they demolished it, he recommended the foundation of another. This (fact) should not surprise us...

If *ello* is omitted in such sentences, the following verb will take a nearby gendered noun or pronoun as it subject and the meaning may change: *el director dijo que no vamos excedidos con el presupuesto, pero ello no permite que podamos ser extravagantes* 'the director said that we're not over-budget, but *this fact* does not allow us to be extravagant'. ... *pero no permite que seamos extravagantes* would mean '...but he doesn't allow us to be extravagant'.

7.4 Lo as a neuter pronoun

7.4.1 General uses

Lo is the direct object pronoun corresponding to *ello* (but *lo* can also mean 'him' or 'it' referring to masculine nouns; see Chapter 12). *Lo* as a neuter pronoun does not refer to any specific noun, but to an idea, action, situation, clause or sentence that has no gender:

¿Lo hacemos o no?	Shall we do it or not?
—¿No sabíais que estaba prohibido?	'Didn't you know it was forbidden?'
—No, no lo sabíamos	'No, we didn't know (it)'
Soy incapaz de hacer eso porque mi orgullo de trabajadora femenina me lo impide (C. Martin Gaite, Sp.)	I'm incapable of doing that because my pride as a woman worker prevents me
El ministro lo tiene difícil (*Cambio16*, Sp.)	The minister is in a difficult situation

(i) *Lo* is used to echo or resume the predicate of *ser*, *estar* and *parecer*, the object of transitive verbs and of *haber* 'there is/are'. Spanish does not like to leave these verbs isolated, as English does in a sentence like *puedo aguantar el estar cansado, pero preferiría no estarlo* 'I can stand being tired, but I'd rather not be'. Compare also *lo hacían sentirse estúpido. Pensó: "lo soy". Lo era, demostró serlo* (M. Vargas Llosa, Pe., dialogue) 'they made him feel stupid. He thought "I am." He was. He'd shown he was'; *¿tolera estar solo, o tolera la necesidad que tenga su cónyuge de estarlo?* (quiz on marriage in *Abc*, Sp.) 'can you stand being alone, or can you stand your partner's need to be?'; *ya nadie la llamaba Clarita, como lo habían hecho siempre sus difuntos padres y marido* (M. Puig, Arg., dialogue) 'by now nobody called her Clarita, as her late parents and husband had done'.

Resumptive *lo* is not used when a gerund is dropped after *estar*: —*¿estás escribiendo otra novela?* —*Sí, estoy/Sí, lo estoy haciendo* (not *lo estoy*) '"are you writing another novel?' "Yes, I am."'

Resumptive *lo* is often omitted in Latin-American speech and sometimes in Latin-American writing. See 30.2.2 for more details about the resumptive pronoun with *haber* 'there is/are'.

(ii) *Lo* is sometimes used before *todo* to make the latter more specific. Compare *Miguel lo sabe todo* 'Miguel knows it all/all about it' and *Miguel sabe todo* 'Miguel knows everything'.

(iii) For Latin-American *?se los dije* 'I said it to them', standard Spanish *se lo dije*, see 11.13.2.

(iv) *La* is used in a few colloquial set phrases where we would expect *lo*. This seems to be more frequent in Latin America than in Spain: *la vamos a pasar muy rico* (S. Galindo, Mex., dialogue; Sp. *lo vamos a pasar*) 'we're going to have a great time', *si los matan la pagarán también ustedes, la pagarán sus familias* (G. García Márquez, Col., dialogue; Sp. *lo pagarán*), 'if they kill them you'll pay for it too, your families will pay', *te la estás jugando* 'you're taking a big risk', *se la está pegando con su primo* '(s)he's cheating on him with her/his/your cousin', *te la vas a ganar* 'you're asking for trouble'.

(v) *Le* is the indirect object form of *lo*: *¿qué le vamos a hacer?* 'ah well, what can be done about it?', *no le hace* (S. Cone) 'it's got nothing to do with it' (Sp. *no tiene que ver*).

7.4.2 *Vérselas, arreglárselas, habérselas*, etc.

The feminine plural *las* is used idiomatically with a few *se* verbs where we would expect *lo*. Some of these verbs have unexpected meanings. The most common are:

agenciárselas to wangle something/to get something by 'fiddling'
apañárselas* to manage/to cope
arreglárselas to find a way to do something
cantárselas to tell someone a few home truths
dárselas de to fancy oneself as
echárselas de to fancy oneself as
entendérselas con to have it out with someone
habérselas con to be faced with/to have it out with

ingeniárselas para to manage to fix things so that...
prometérselas muy felices* to have high hopes
traérselas* to be difficult/treacherous
vérselas y deseárselas* to find something difficult to do
vérselas con to have it out with/to have a showdown with

All are in use on both continents except those marked with an asterisk, which seem to be confined to Spain. Examples:

Si haces eso te las vas a tener que haber conmigo or *te las vas a tener que ver conmigo*

If you do that you're going to have to have it out/face up to me

Él se las echa/se las da de ligón (colloquial, Spain)	He fancies himself as a great womanizer/as a great hit with the ladies
Eso me pasó por dármelas de genio (G. García Márquez, Col., dialogue)	That happened to me because I figured I was a genius
—Arréglatelas como puedas —me dijo, llorando (A. Bryce Echenique, Pe., dialogue)	'You manage as best you can', she said, weeping (i.e. 'I don't care what you do')
Tenía que ingeniárselas para mantener ocupados a sus guardianes (G. García Márquez, Col.)	She had to do her best to keep her guards occupied
Por eso te digo que ella también se las trae (C. Rico-Godoy, Sp., dialogue)	That's why I'm telling you that she's also not to be trusted
La Policía se las ve y se las desea para controlarlos (Cambio16, Sp.)	The police have a hard time controlling them

NB: The second-person present plural of *habérselas* is *nos las habemos*, not the expected *nos las hemos*: *en don Luis nos las habemos nuevamente con el Hombre y la Mujer* (J. Montesinos, quoted Seco 1998, 237) 'in Don Luis we are dealing once again with Man and Woman'.

7.5 Neuter demonstrative pronouns

These take the invariable forms *esto, eso* and *aquello*. Since they cannot be confused with demonstrative adjectives they *never* have a written accent—something that both learners and native speakers constantly forget. They refer to no noun in particular (cf. Fr. *ceci, cela*).

The difference between *esto* 'this', *eso* 'that' and *aquello* 'that' (distant) reflects the difference between *este, ese* and *aquel*, discussed at 6.4:

¿Quién ha hecho esto?	Who did this?
—Quisiera llamar a cobro revertido. *—De eso nada*	'I'd like to make a reverse-charge/US collect call.' 'No way/out of the question'
Había comprendido cómo todo aquello jamás tuvo nada que ver con el humor ni con el buen humor (A. Bryce Echenique, Pe.)	I had understood how all that never had anything to do with humo(u)r or good temper
¿Qué hay de aquello/eso de los billetes falsos?	What's happening about that business of the forged notes?
¿Cómo podía yo pensar que aquello que parecía tan mentira era verdadero? (J. Cortázar, Arg., dialogue)	How could I think that that thing which seemed such a lie was true?

(i) *Aquello de (que)* or *eso de (que)* often corresponds to 'the saying that': *Spengler dijo aquello de que "la civilización en última instancia siempre es salvada por un puñado de soldados"* (Cambio16, Sp.) 'Spengler made that remark that "in the final instance civilization is always saved by a handful of soldiers"', *pensé que lo más parecido que existe a eso de ir por lana y volver trasquilado era…*(A. Bryce Echenique, Pe.) 'I thought that the nearest thing to that saying "to go for wool and come back fleeced" was…'.

(ii) The difference between a neuter or non-neuter demonstrative may be crucial. Compare *esto es un desastre* 'this (situation) is a disaster' and *éste/este es un desastre*—'this (man, boy, book or some other masc. noun) is a disaster'. If the speaker is thinking of a specific noun, the masculine or feminine pronoun must be used as appropriate unless the speaker is referring to a *type* of thing. Pointing to a coat in a shop window one could say *eso es lo que quiero* 'that's the (type/sort of) thing I want' or *ése/ese es el que quiero* 'that's the *one* I want'.

In some sentences the pronoun can refer either to a situation or to a specific noun, in which case the neuter and gendered forms are interchangeable: *no tengo ni talento, ni fuerza. Ésa/Esa es la verdad* (E. Sábato, Arg., dialogue; *eso* also possible) 'I have neither talent nor strength. That's the truth'; *esto es una operación militar* (G. García Márquez, Col., dialogue. *Ésta/Esta es. . .*also possible) 'this is a military operation'; *ésa/esa es otra de las invenciones de ustedes* (M. Vargas Llosa, Pe., dialogue) 'that's another of your inventions'. Note also: *¿qué es esto?* 'what's this?', *¿quién es éste/este?* 'who's this (man or boy)?', *éste/este es el problema* 'this is the problem', *esto es un problema* 'this is **a** problem'.

When the subject of the verb is a noun, the pronoun agrees with it: *la verdad es ésta/esta* 'the truth is this', *los problemas son éstos/estos* 'the problems are these'.

8

Possessive adjectives and pronouns

The main points discussed in this chapter are:

- Forms of possessive adjectives and pronoun (Section 8.2)
- Uses of *mi, tu, su, nuestro, vuestro, su* (Section 8.3)
- Replacement of possessive adjectives by *el/la/los/las* (Section 8.3.4)
- Uses of *mío, tuyo, suyo* (Section 8.4)
- *Detrás mío, delante suyo* for *detrás de mí, delante de él/ella/usted* (Section 8.7)

8.1 General

Spanish possessives have two forms. The short forms, *mi, tu, su*, etc., appear in front of a noun or noun phrase and correspond to the English 'my', 'your', 'his', 'her', etc. The full forms, *mío, tuyo, suyo*, etc. roughly correspond to 'mine', 'yours', 'hers', etc., and can only follow a noun or stand alone.

In all cases number and gender agreement is determined by the number and gender of the noun possessed, not of the possessor, so *su libro* can mean 'his book', 'her book', 'your book' (*de usted* or *de ustedes*) or 'their book'. All forms agree in number—*mi libro* but *mis libros*—, but only those whose masculine singular ends in -*o* agree in gender.

The most important difference between English and Spanish is that the latter constantly uses definite articles and not possessives when the identity of the possessor is obvious: *me he roto el brazo* 'I've broken my arm', *dame la mano* 'give me your hand' (see 8.3.4). This occurs more frequently than in French and it sometimes confuses English-speakers.

8.2 Forms of the possessives

8.2.1 Short forms of possessives

Personal pronoun	Singular possessive	Plural possessive	Translation
yo	*mi*	*mis*	my
tú (and *vos*, where it is used)	*tu* (no accent!)	*tus*	your (familiar)
él/ella	*su*	*sus*	his/her/its
usted	*su*	*sus*	your (formal)
nosotros/nosotras	*nuestro* (masc.) *nuestra* (fem.)	*nuestros* (masc.) *nuestras* (fem.)	our
vosotros/vosotras	*vuestro* (masc.) *vuestra* (fem.)	*vuestros* (masc.) *vuestras* (fem.)	your (familiar)
ellos/ellas	*su*	*sus*	their
ustedes	*su*	*sus*	your (formal)

NB: In Latin America *su/sus* is the only second-person plural possessive, and *vuestro* is not used; see 8.6 for discussion. For the forms corresponding to *vos* (archaic in Spain, common for *tú* in some parts of Latin America) see 11.3 and 8.6a.

8.2.2 Long forms of possessives

All are marked for number and gender (*vuestro* is not used in Lat. Am.). For *vos* see 11.3 and 8.6a.

Personal pronoun	Masc. singular & plural	Fem. singular & plural	Translation
yo	*mío – míos*	*mía – mías*	mine
tú/vos	*tuyo – tuyos*	*tuya – tuyas*	yours (familiar)
él/ella	*suyo – suyos*	*suya – suyas*	his/hers/its
usted	*suyo – suyos*	*suya – suyas*	yours (formal)
nosotros/nosotras	*nuestro – nuestros*	*nuestra – nuestras*	ours
vosotros/vosotras	*vuestro – vuestros*	*vuestra – vuestras*	yours (familiar)
ellos/ellas	*suyo – suyos*	*suya – suyas*	theirs
ustedes	*suyo – suyos*	*suya – suyas*	yours (formal)

8.3 Uses of the short form of possessives

8.3.1 Basic uses

These words agree in number with the thing possessed. *Nuestro* and *vuestro* agree in gender as well:

mi padre/mis padres	my father/my parents
mi madre/mis flores	my mother/my flowers
¿Dónde está tu coche?	Where's your car?
¿Dónde están tus zapatos?	Where are your shoes?
Me fío de su amigo	I trust his/her/your/their friend
Me fío de sus amigos	I trust his/her/your/their friends
nuestro dinero/nuestra dignidad	our money/our dignity
vuestra casa/vuestras casas (Sp.)	your house/your houses
Usted dejó sus cosas aquí	You (sing.) left your/his/her/their things here.
Ustedes dejaron sus cosas aquí	You (plur.) left your things here.
Si ellos no quieren dejarnos su cortacésped. . .	If they don't want to lend us their/your/his/ her lawnmower...

As can be seen, *su* and *sus* mean several things. 8.5a shows how to remove the ambiguity.

8.3.2 Possessives with more than one noun

If more than one noun is involved, Spanish differs from English in that it uses one possessive only when the nouns refer to the same, or to aspects of the same thing. One says *mi padre y mi madre* 'my father and mother' (different persons), *mi chaqueta y mi corbata* 'my jacket and tie' (different things), but *mi amigo y colega* 'my friend and colleague' (same person), *su paciencia y valor* 'his patience and courage' (aspects of a single virtue).

8.3.3 Possessive in military usage

In military circles, possessives are used to address officers: *sí, mi general* 'yes, General', *no, mi coronel* 'no, Colonel'.

8.3.4 Definite article instead of possessives

Spanish very frequently prefers the definite article where English uses possessive adjectives. *Sacó su pañuelo de su bolsillo* '(s)he took his/her handkerchief out of his/her pocket', although not incorrect, sounds unnatural: *se sacó el pañuelo del bolsillo* (provided it is from his/her own pocket) is much more idiomatic. The Academy's *Esbozo. . .*, 3.10.9a, remarks that sentences like *pase sus vacaciones en la playa de X,* 'spend your holidays/vacation on the beach at X' for *pase las vacaciones. . .* sound foreign.

The definite article is used when a verb, pronoun, or context make it clear who the possessor is. The article is especially common with parts of the body, and is normal with clothing and other close possessions, e.g. wristwatches, purses, wallets, pens, glasses, etc.

This may confuse English-speakers. 'Have you got the passport' normally implies that we do not know who owns it, otherwise we say 'his', 'her', 'your'. In *¿tienes el pasaporte?* the second-person ending of the verb shows that the sentence probably means 'have you got your passport', unless context suggests that someone else is involved. Spanish therefore often relies on context to identify the possessor. In the following sentence only the fact that purses are associated with women makes us translate *el monedero* as 'my purse' (the speaker is female): *metí en una bolsa de playa el bronceador, las toallas, la radio portátil, el libro que estoy leyendo, dos camisetas, el monedero. . .* (C. Rico-Godoy, Sp.) 'I put the suntan lotion, the towels, the portable radio, the book I'm reading, two T-shirts, my purse. . .in a beach-bag'. Further examples:

Cierre la boca	Shut your mouth
Llegó con los zapatos cubiertos de lodo	S(h)e arrived with his/her shoes covered in mud
Llegaba a pensar que Alicia había perdido la razón (S. Puértolas, Sp.)	I was starting to think that Alicia had lost her reason
Introduje la mano izquierda en el bolsillo derecho del pantalón (A. Bryce Echenique, Pe.)	I inserted my left hand in the right pocket of my trousers (*sic*)
Se sacó de la manga una camándula de oro (G. García Márquez, Col. Sp. *camándula = rosario*)	She took from her sleeve a gold rosary
Bébete el café/Arréglate el pelo	Drink your coffee/Tidy your hair
Juan le quitó la novia a Miguel	Juan stole Miguel's girlfriend
La rabia le puso las orejas coloradas y los ojos húmedos (A. Mastretta, Mex.)	Rage made his ears red and his eyes damp

But when there is no word that makes clear who is the possessor, a possessive must be used: *mis ojos son azules* 'my eyes are blue' (cf. *tengo los ojos azules*), *tus medias tienen una carrera* 'your stockings are laddered', *he corregido tu redacción* (cf. *te he corregido la redacción*) 'I've marked/graded your essay'. With clothes, use of the possessive may suggest that the thing is not being worn: *he visto tu nueva falda en el Corte Inglés* 'I saw your new skirt (on sale) in Corte Inglés'.

When the thing possessed is emphasized or particularized by context, or by an adjective or some other words, or whenever ambiguity must be avoided, the possessive adjective usually reappears:

Usted póngase su camisa, no la mía	You put on your shirt, not mine
Vi sus ojos grandes, fatigados, sonrientes y como lacrimosos (F. Umbral, Sp.)	I saw her eyes, big, tired, smiling and seemingly tearful
Acerqué mi cabeza a la suya (C. Fuentes, Mex., dialogue; contrast)	I moved my head closer to his
X deja sus/tus manos suaves y perfumadas (or *le/te deja las manos...*)	X leaves your hands soft and perfumed
Toco tus labios... (popular song)	I touch your lips...

(i) Use of the definite article downplays the thing possessed. *Te toco los labios* can sound accidental or matter-of-fact. A mother says *dame la mano, que vamos a cruzar la calle* 'hold my hand, we're going to cross the road', but an old-fashioned lover might say *dame tu mano y te haré feliz* 'give me your hand (i.e. in marriage) and I will make you happy'.

In polite speech one therefore avoids the definite article when the possession is a human being: *¡cuánto echo de menos a mis hijas!* 'I miss my daughters so much!', *siempre voy de vacaciones con mi mujer/mi novia* (?*con la mujer/la novia* is humorous or popular, cf. popular British 'with "the" wife') 'I always go on holiday/vacation with my wife/girlfriend', *ha despedido a su secretaria* '(s)he's fired his/her secretary'.

(ii) In spoken Latin-American Spanish, especially Mexican, possessive adjectives are sometimes combined with indirect object pronouns: *les pintamos su casa* (street sign, Oaxaca, Mex.) 'we'll paint your house for you'; *me duele mi cabeza* (colloquial Mexican) 'my head aches', standard Spanish *me duele la cabeza*; *¿te quitas tu ropa?* (E. Poniatowska, Mex., dialogue) 'why don't you take your clothes off?', standard Spanish *¿te quitas la ropa?*

(iii) Unlike English, Spanish normally uses the singular when each person possesses one each of a thing: *les confiscaron el pasaporte* 'they confiscated their passports'. See 2.2.4.

(iv) One say *me quité la camisa* 'I took my shirt off', not *quité la camisa* (= 'I removed the shirt'), because shirts do not come off by themselves. For this reason one says *abrí los ojos* 'I opened my eyes': *me abrí los ojos* suggests that your eyelids were stuck together and had to be separated by hand.

8.4 Long or pronominal forms of the possessives

8.4.1 Use of the long or pronominal forms of the possessive

(a) To translate English '...of mine/yours/his/ours', etc.:

un amigo mío	a friend of mine
un conocido tuyo	an acquaintance of yours
un poema muy malo mío (Granma, Cu.; Sp. *un poema mío muy malo*)	a very bad poem of mine
Antonio ha vuelto a hacer una de las suyas	Antonio's up to his usual tricks again (lit. 'a thing of his')
una actitud muy suya	a very typical attitude of his/hers/yours/theirs
algo mío/nada nuestro	something of mine/nothing of ours

(**b**) As a literary, rather stilted variation on the usual possessive:

en mi novela/en la novela mía	in my novel/in this novel of mine
nuestro pan/el pan nuestro de cada día	our daily bread

(**c**) In Spain, in formulas of address:

Bueno, hijo mío/hija mía, me voy	Well, dear, I'm off
Te aconsejo que no, amigo mío	I advise you not to, my friend

Latin-American Spanish typically says *mi hijo, mi hija*, etc.: *no, mi amiga. Me quedaré en casa. Iré otro día* (A. Arrafut, Cu., dialogue) 'no my friend. I'll stay at home. I'll go another day'. This gives rise to terms of endearment like *mijita* (= *mi hijita*), *mi amor*, etc. In Spain a number of loving expressions also optionally use the normal order, e.g. *mi vida/vida mía, mi cielo/cielo mío, mi amor, mi cielín*, etc. 'darling'/US 'honey', etc.

(**d**) To translate the pronouns 'mine', 'yours' (see the following section for the use of the definite article in this construction):

—*¿De quién es este bloc?* —*Mío*	'Whose notepad is this?' 'Mine'
Este garabato es tuyo	This scrawl is yours
Éste/Este es el vuestro, ¿verdad?	This one is yours, isn't it?

The long forms are used in a number of set phrases:

de nuestra parte/de parte nuestra for our part	*a costa mía* at my cost	*muy señor mío* (S. Cone *de mi consideración*) Dear
a pesar mío/suyo despite me/despite him/her/you	*en torno suyo* around him/ her/them/you	Sir (in letters)
	a propuesta suya at his/ her/your/their suggestion	

8.4.2 Definite article with the long forms

The definite article is obligatory in the following cases:

(**a**) After prepositions. Compare —*¿De quién es el coche?* —*Mío* 'Whose car is it?' 'Mine' and —*¿En qué coche vamos?* —*En el mío* '"Which car are we going in?"' "In mine"'. Further examples:

No hablo del tuyo sino del nuestro	I'm not talking about yours but ours
A tu primo sí lo/le conozco, pero no al suyo	I know your cousin, but not his/hers

(**b**) When the pronoun is the subject or object of a verb (even though the verb may not be present):

Toma el mío	Take mine
Tu padre te deja salir, el mío no	Your father lets you go out, mine doesn't
Qué vida tan triste la suya	What a sad life his/hers/yours/theirs is
Los dos vídeos son buenos, pero el nuestro es mejor	The two videos are good but ours is better

(**c**) After *ser* 'to be', omission of the article emphasizes actual possession. One would say *esta casa es mía* 'this house is mine' (it is my property or I live in it), but in an office where there are several telephones one would say *ese teléfono que suena* *es el tuyo* 'that phone that's ringing is yours' (i.e. you use it but don't own it). Compare

la casa de Jeremiah Saint-Amour, que desde ahora era suya (G. García Márquez, Col.)	Jeremiah Saint-Amour's house, which from now on was hers
Pero estas cualidades eran mucho más suyas que mías (A. Bryce Echenique, Pe.)	But these qualities were much more hers than mine

and

¿Ves estas tres camas? Ésta/Esta es la mía, ésa/esa es la tuya y aquélla/aquella es la de Rafael (temporary use, not possession)	Do you see these three beds? This is mine, that's yours and that one's Rafael's

8.4.3 The neuter article with *lo mío*, *lo suyo*, etc.

The neuter form of the possessive has various meanings (discussed in detail at 7.2.1):

Mi marido sabe lo nuestro	My husband knows about us
Ahora estás en lo tuyo	Now you're in your element
Lo vuestro es alucinante	What happened to you is mind-boggling

8.5 Clarification or replacement of possessive by *de* + pronoun

In some cases *de* + a pronoun may be used instead of a possessive. Moreover, when *su/sus* refer to *usted* or *ustedes*, *de usted* or *de ustedes* are often added. This happens:

(a) When it is necessary to clarify the meaning of *su/suyo*, which can mean 'his', 'her', 'its', 'your' (*usted*), 'their', 'your' (*ustedes*). Context nearly always makes ownership clear, but it can be emphasized or clarified by using *de él/ella, de usted, de ellos/ellas, de ustedes*: *los paraguas de ustedes* 'your (plural) umbrellas', *la camisa de él* 'his shirt'.

The possibility of ambiguity is illustrated by the question 'is this handkerchief yours or hers?', where one would probably say *¿este pañuelo es de usted o de ella?* whereas *¿este pañuelo es suyo?* 'is this handkerchief yours?' is clear if no one else is present.

In Spain, *su* is assumed out of context to be third-person, so that *de usted/ustedes* may be needed to show that the meaning is 'your'. (For Latin-American usage, see 8.6.)

(b) When *de* means 'from' and not 'of', as in *hace tiempo que no tengo noticias de vosotros* (or *noticias vuestras*) 'it's been some time since I've had news from you'.

8.6 Possessives: Latin-American usage

Latin-American usage differs from Peninsular Spanish in a number of ways:

(a) Where *vos* is used instead of *tú* (especially Argentina and much of Central America), *tu/tuyo* are the possessive forms: *vos tenés tu birome* (Arg.) 'you've got your ballpoint pen', in Spain *tú tienes tu bolígrafo*.

NB: 'Ballpoint pen' has numerous translations in Latin America, e.g. *la birome* (Arg.), *el lápiz (de pasta)* (Ch.), *el esfero(gráfico), esferógrafo* (Col.), *la pluma (atómica)* (Mex.), *el lapicero* (Pe., C. America).

(b) Since *vosotros* is not used in everyday Latin-American Spanish (see 11.3.3 for details), *su/sus* is the only second-person plural possessive in all styles.

(c) In Latin America *su/suyo* is assumed, out of context, to mean *de usted / de ustedes* 'of you'. Third-person possession may be represented in everyday speech by *de él* 'his' / 'its' (masc.), *de ella* 'her' / 'its' (fem.), *de ellos* 'their' (masc.), *de ellas* 'their' (fem.):

¿Quieres que vayamos al cuarto de él a ver si está? (Costa Rican dialogue, quoted Kany, 69; Sp. *a su cuarto*)	Do you want to go to his room to see if he's there?
En la oficina de ella no hay la mitad de trabajo que en la mía (M. Puig, Arg., dialogue; Sp. *en su oficina*)	There isn't half the work in her office that there is in mine

(d) *De nosotros* for *nuestro* is also common in Latin-American speech: *la casa de nosotros está en la esquina* (Colombian informant, standard Spanish *nuestra casa*) 'our house is on the corner', —*¿A quién se lo entregó?* —*Al jefe de nosotros* (*Vindicación de Cuba*, Cu., dialogue) '"Whom did you hand it over to?" "To our boss"', standard Spanish *a nuestro jefe*.

(e) In spoken Spanish in Mexico and the Andes there is a tendency to use *su/sus* in phrases of the type noun + *de* + noun, e.g. *su libro de Juan* 'Juan's book', *su casa de mi amigo* 'my friend's house', standard Spanish *el libro de Juan, la casa de mi amigo*.

8.7 Possessives after prepositions and adverbs

A common construction in spoken Latin-American Spanish, also heard in popular speech in Spain, is the use of the long possessive forms after prepositions that usually require *de* + a pronoun, and after some adverbs: *?detrás mío* = *detrás de mí* 'behind me', and even, in sub-standard speech, *?entró antes mío* '(s)he went in before me', for *entró antes que yo*. Examples:

Adentro mío yo soy igual que todos los reaccionarios (M. Puig, Arg. dialogue; Sp. *dentro de mí* or *por dentro*)	Inside (me) I'm the same as all the reactionaries
Quiero estar cerca tuyo (ibid., Sp. *cerca de ti*)	I want to be near you
No lo consiguió por lo intimidado que estaba en mi delante (M. Vargas Llosa, Pe., dialogue; Sp. *delante de mí*)	He was so intimidated in my presence that he didn't manage it
Pero un segundo autobús que iba por detrás suyo lo embistió con gran violencia (*El País*, Sp.; better *detrás de él*)	But a second bus trave(l)ling behind collided violently with it

and also (the bracketed forms are used in standard Spanish):

?alrededor mío	(*a mi alrededor / alrededor de mí*)	around me
?encima mía	(*encima de mí*)	above/over me
?enfrente suyo	(*enfrente de él/ella/usted ustedes/ellos/ellas*)	opposite him/her/you/them
?aparte suyo	(*aparte de él/ella*, etc.)	apart from him/her, etc.
?fuera suyo	(*fuera de él/ella*, etc.)	apart from him/her, etc.

This construction is found in the best writers in Argentina, but it is considered colloquial in other Latin-American countries and incorrect in Spain and Mexico;

foreign students should avoid it. However, *en torno nuestro* (literary) 'around us' is considered correct. Both *contra mí/ti* and *en contra mía/tuya*, 'against me/you', etc. are correct, but there is a tendency to make the possessive precede in Latin America, and this seems to be spreading in Spain: *está en mi contra* (*Peanuts*, Arg.) '(s)he/it's against me', *el hecho de que el teléfono se hubiera puesto en mi contra...* (S. Puértolas, Sp.) 'the fact that the phone had turned against me...'.

9

Miscellaneous adjectives
and pronouns

This chapter discusses a series of important words that may cause problems for English-speaking learners:

ajeno 9.1	*cada* 9.6	*mismo* 9.11	*tanto* 9.16
algo 9.2	*cierto* 9.7	*mucho* & *poco* 9.12	*todo* 9.17
alguien 9.3	*cualquier(a)* 9.8	*otro* 9.13	*varios* 9.18
alguno 9.4	*demasiado* 9.9	*propio* 9.14	
ambos 9.5	*medio* 9.10	*solo* 9.15	

9.1 *Ajeno*: adjective, marked for number and gender

A rather literary word meaning 'someone else's': *el dolor ajeno* (= *el dolor de otros*) 'other people's sorrow', *en casa ajena* (= *en casa de otra persona*) 'in someone else's house':

> *Te preocupas demasiado por lo ajeno*   You concern yourself too much with other people's business

(i) It is not used in this meaning after *ser*: *esta agenda es de otro* 'this is someone else's diary'.

(ii) *Ajeno* often translates 'a stranger to', 'remote from': *éstos/estos son problemas ajenos a mi responsabilidad* 'these are problems outside my responsibility', *. . .una mujer adulta pero atractiva que tomaba el sol tumbada y ajena, aparentemente, a todo* (C. Rico-Godoy, Sp.) '. . .an adult but attractive woman who was lying there sunbathing and apparently oblivious to everything'.

9.2 *Algo*: invariable pronoun or adverb

Used as a pronoun, it usually means 'something' or, in questions and after *poco* and a few other words discussed at 23.4, 'anything':

> *Detrás se veía algo grande, negro*   Behind one could see something big, black
> *Aquella frase era el preámbulo de algo*   That phrase was the prelude to something
>   *muy grave* (G. García Márquez, Col.)   very serious
> *¿Ves algo?*   Can you see anything?
> *Serán pocos los que hayan traído algo*   There probably won't be many who have brought anything

NB: The English question-opener 'do you know something...?' is *¿sabes una cosa? ¿Sabes algo?* means 'do you know anything?'

Used as an adverb it means 'rather', 'somewhat', though *un poco*, *un tanto* or *más bien* are more common in speech:

Estamos algo/un poco/más bien inquietos	We're rather/a bit worried
...achinada y de hermosas piernas, aunque algo cargada de caderas (L. Otero, Cu.)	[She had an] oriental face and lovely legs, although she was rather heavy in the hips

(i) *Algo así, algo así como*, are translations of 'something like...': *pesa algo así como siete kilos* 'it weighs around 7 kilos', *se llama Nicanora, o algo así* 'she's called Nicanora, or something like that'.

(ii) In negative sentences *nada* translates 'anything': *no sabe nada* '(s)he doesn't know anything', *yo no sé dónde está nada en esta casa* 'I don't know where anything is in this house'.

(iii) *Algo* is neuter in gender, so one says *algo en* **lo** *que podían creer* 'something they could believe in'.

9.3 *Alguien*: invariable pronoun

It means 'someone', 'somebody', as in *vi a alguien* 'I saw someone'. It also translates 'anyone', 'anybody' in questions and certain other types of sentence. It is not marked for gender:

Le pidió a Andrés que se quedara en casa por si alguien llamara (G. García Márquez, Col.)	He asked Andrés to stay at home in case someone phoned
¿Conoces a alguien que pueda darme un presupuesto para reparar el coche?	Do you know anyone/someone who could give me an estimate for fixing my car?

(i) **Alguien de los estudiantes*, **alguien de ellos* are rejected by grammarians in favour of *alguno de los estudiantes, alguno de (entre) ellos*, although *alguien de entre ustedes* is accepted by some authorities: *si alguien de entre ustedes/alguno de ustedes lo sabe, que lo diga* 'if someone among you/any of you knows, say so'. Occasionally *alguien de* is necessary since, unlike *alguno*, it does not indicate gender: *yo creo que alude a alguien de esta casa* 'I think (s)he's alluding to someone in this house'.

(ii) María Moliner notes that *?darle una cosa a alguien que él no desea* is awkward since *alguien* is too vague to be specifically masculine: *darle una cosa a alguien que no lo desea* 'to give something to someone who doesn't want it' avoids the problem.

(iii) 'Give it to someone else' is *dáselo a algún otro/alguna otra/alguna otra persona*. **Alguien otro* is not Spanish.

(iv) *Uno* is sometimes colloquially used for 'someone' when gender is an important part of the message (for other uses of *uno* as a pronoun see 28.7.1): *se ha peleado con uno en la calle* '(s)he's had a fight with some man in the street', *se casó con una de Valencia* 'he married some girl from Valencia'.

9.4 *Algún*, *alguno*, *algunos*; *alguna*, *algunas*: adjective or pronoun marked for number and gender

9.4.1 General uses of *alguno*

(**a**) As an adjective:

The usual translation is 'some', French *quelque(s)*. It is shortened to *algún* before a singular masculine noun or noun phrase: *algún día* 'some day', *¡o si te gusta algún otro!* (A. Buero Vallejo, Sp., dialogue) 'or if you like some other man!', but *alguna región* 'some region'.

Alguna is normally pronounced 'algún' immediately before feminine nouns beginning with a stressed *a-* or *ha-*, i.e. *algún alma perdida* 'some lost soul', *algún arma defensiva* 'some defensive weapon'; but Seco (1998), 36, says that this is avoided in careful language and *alguna* should be used in writing. When followed by *que* and a masculine noun phrase, either *algún* or *alguno* may be used: *algún que otro libro* or *alguno que otro libro* 'some book or other', the short form being commoner. Only *alguna que otra* is allowed with feminine nouns.

In the singular, *alguno* often means a vague 'one or another', 'some or other'. (For the difference between *unos* and *algunos*, see 9.4.2):

en algún momento de la historia de Perú	at one time or another in the history of Peru
Alguna vez la echaba de menos (S. Puértolas, Sp.)	From time to time he used to miss her
Deben cuidar bien esos platos. Alguna vez, en el futuro, podrían donarlos a un museo (L. Otero, Cu., dialogue)	You should look after those plates well. Some time in the future you could donate them to a museum
Mira a ver si queda alguna botella de vino	Look and see whether there is some bottle of wine or other left

In formal styles *alguno* may follow a noun, in which case it is an emphatic equivalent of *ninguno*, 'none', 'no...at all': *no cultivaba forma alguna de contacto con el pueblo* (J. Marsé, Sp.) 'he cultivated absolutely no kind of contact with the common people', *ninguna autoridad militar quiere dar explicación alguna* (*La Prensa*, Bol.) 'no military authority wishes to give any explanation whatsoever', *no puede tolerar pregunta alguna* (E. Poniatowska, Mex.) 'she can't stand any questions at all'.

(**b**) *Alguno* as a pronoun (the short form *algún* is not used as a pronoun):

Again, the meaning may be a vague 'one' or 'one or two':

Alguno lo sabrá	One or other of them will know
—*¿Has recibido cartas de tu familia?* —*Bueno, alguna, sí*	'Have you had any letters from your family?' 'Well, one or two, yes'
Una noche la policía entró y nos palpó. Alguno tuvo que ir a la comisaría (J. L. Borges, Arg., dialogue; Sp 'to frisk' = *cachear*)	One night the police came in and frisked us. At least one had to go to police station

In the plural 'some' or 'a few' are the usual translations:

Con algunos de tercero vas a tener que hacer ejercicios de verbos irregulares	You're going to have to do irregular verb exercises with some of the third year
Algunos ya están deseando marcharse	Some already want to go

(i) When the singular *alguno/alguna* is combined with a second-person pronoun, the verb is optionally either second- or third-person, the latter being more usual: *si alguno de vosotros lo sabéis/lo sabe* 'if any of you know(s) it'. In the plural, agreement is always with the pronoun: *algunas de vosotras lo sabéis* 'some of you women know', *algunas de nosotras generalmente caminamos despacito* (*La Jornada*, Mex.) 'some of us women generally walk slowly'.

(ii) The English 'some' (and 'any') have no visible equivalent in Spanish when they precede a partitive noun, i.e. a noun that refers to only a part or specific quantity of something, as in 'give me some water' *dame agua/un poco de agua*, 'you haven't bought any pins' *no has comprado alfileres*, *¿tiene usted pan integral?* 'have you got any wholemeal bread?'

In some cases *un poco* or *ninguno* may be good translations of 'some': *yo también quiero un poco* 'I want some (a little) too', *chuletas de ternera? No tenemos* 'veal chops? We haven't got any', *no tenemos ninguna* 'we haven't got a single one'; *no queda apenas ninguna* 'there are hardly any left'. 'Any' in the sense of 'it doesn't matter which' is *cualquiera* (see 9.8): *comidas a cualquier hora* 'meals at any time'.

(iii) When *alguno* is the direct or indirect object of a verb and it comes before the verb for purposes of focus, agreement is governed by the number of an accompanying noun or pronoun: *a alguno de vosotros **os** quisiera ver yo en un lío como éste/este* 'I'd like to see one of you in a mess like this', *a alguno de ellos **les** quiere dar el premio* 'it's one of them that (s)he wants to give the prize to'.

9.4.2 *Unos* and *algunos* contrasted

These two plural words are not always easily distinguished (*unos* has other uses discussed at 3.4).

(a) The two words are interchangeable in the phrase *algunos/unos...otros*:

Algunos/unos vinieron, otros no	Some came, others didn't
...las explicaciones teológicas que hacían plausible la venta de unos terrenos y la compra de otros (A. Mastretta, Mex.; or *algunos terrenos*)	...the theological (i.e. obscure) explanations that made plausible/acceptable the sale of some plots of land and the purchase of others
Algunos/Unos días estoy de mal humor, otros no	Some days I'm in a bad mood, others I'm not

(b) Only *algunos* is possible in the phrase *algunos de*: *salí a cenar con algunos de los alumnos* 'I went out to dinner with some of the students'.

(c) Only *unos/unas* can be used to make non-generic nouns and adjectives: compare *son payasos* 'they are clowns (by profession)', *son unos payasos* 'they act like clowns'. See 3.4.1(c) for details.

(d) Only *unos* can be used in the reciprocal construction: *se admiran los unos a los otros* 'they admire one another'.

(e) *Algunos* is used when no implication of 'a few' is intended: *algunos mexicanos hablan tres idiomas* 'some Mexicans speak three languages' (since *unos* here would mean 'a certain small group of'). When 'a few' is intended, the two are interchangeable and *unos* is usually followed by *cuantos*: *me dio unas (cuantas)/algunas monedas de un euro* '(s)he gave me a couple of one-euro coins', ...*o cuando arriesgábamos algunos dólares en el casino* (A. Bryce Echenique, Pe.; or *unos cuantos*) '...or when we gambled a few dollars in the casino'.

9.5 *Ambos*: adjective marked for number and gender

'Both', though it is rather literary and *los/las dos* is more usual in speech.

en ambos/los dos casos	in both cases
La idea de una pelea de novios le pareció tan ridícula a la edad y en la situación de ambos (G. García Márquez, Col.)	The idea of a lovers' quarrel seemed so ridiculous to her, given the age and situation of both of them
—*¿Cuál de los dos es correcto?*	'Which of the two is correct?' 'Both'
—*Ambos/Los dos*	

9.6 *Cada*: invariable

'Each', 'every'. *Cada* always precedes the noun:

Cada loco con su tema	'Each to his/her own' (lit. 'every madman with his obsession')
un libro por cada tres alumnos	one book for every three students
Me llama a cada momento	(S)he's constantly on the phone to me
Cada día me preocupa más esto de la taquicardia (A. Bryce Echenique, Pe.)	Every day I'm more worried by this tachycardia business (increased heart-rate)

(i) *Cada vez más/menos* usually translate 'more and more' and 'less and less': *es cada vez más complicado* 'it gets more and more complicated', *era cada vez menos generosa* 'she was less and less generous'.

(ii) In colloquial speech in Spain and Latin America *cada* means 'all sorts of...': *dice cada tontería* 'the nonsense (s)he talks...', *hay cada ladrón por ahí* 'there are all sorts of thieves there...', *¡me hace usted cada pregunta!* (S. Pitol, Mex., dialogue), 'the things you ask me!'.

(iii) 'Each one', 'each person': *que cada uno* (or *cada cual/cada quien*) *haga la lectura que le parezca conveniente* 'let each person read it as it suits him/her'.

(iv) *?Me baño cada día* or *?voy cada mañana* for ...*todos los días*, ...*todas las mañanas* are widespread, but are rejected by some speakers as Catalanisms. They are, however, correct in certain contexts. See 9.17.

9.7 *Cierto*: adjective, marked for number and gender

'Certain', i.e. 'specific'. Used thus it precedes the noun:

en ciertos casos	in certain cases
cierto alemán	a certain German
en cierta novela suya	in a certain novel of his/hers/yours/theirs
Y esto, claro, flotaba de cierta manera en el ambiente (A. Bryce Echenique, Pe.)	And this, of course, was to some extent floating in the atmosphere

Determinado is a more formal synonym: *en determinados trenes existe un servicio de camareros* 'on certain trains waiter service is provided'.

(i) *Un cierto/una cierta* for 'a certain' are sometimes condemned as borrowings from French or English, but are common in all styles. *Un cierto* is found before partitive nouns—*yo era consciente de (una) cierta tendencia suya a exagerar* 'I was aware of a certain tendency of his to exaggerate'—and as a colloquial alternative to *un tal*: *se casó con un cierto/un tal Dionisio de México* 'she married a certain Dionisio from Mexico'.

(ii) Placed after a noun or verb *cierto* means 'fixed', 'accurate', 'true': *hemos tenido noticias ciertas de otro enfrentamiento* 'we have received accurate reports of another clash', *¿Está enfermo? ¿Es cierto o no?* (M. Puig, Arg., dialogue) 'Is he ill/sick? Is it true or not?'

9.8 *Cualquier, cualquiera, cualesquiera*: adjective or pronoun, marked for number

As an adjective 'any'; as a pronoun 'anybody'/'any one' (Fr. *n'importe quel*).

(a) As an adjective

Before any noun or noun phrase, the *a* of *cualquiera* (but not, usually, of *cualesquiera*) is dropped: *en cualquier momento* 'at any moment', *cualquier mujer* 'any woman', *yo puedo andar con cualquier complejo* (L. Otero, Cu., dialogue. *Andar* can mean 'to work properly' in Lat. Am. In Spain the verb is *funcionar*) 'I can function with any complex' (i.e. whatever complexes I may have); *en cualesquiera circunstancias* 'in any circumstances'.

However, the plural adjective *cualesquiera* is nowadays frequently expressed by the singular since the meaning is virtually the same: *cualquier mujer que no simpatice con el feminismo...* 'any woman who doesn't/any women who don't sympathize with feminism...'.

Cualquier(a) normally precedes the noun: *duerme a cualquier hora del día* '(s)he sleeps at any hour of the day', *se puede pagar con cualquier moneda* 'one can pay in any currency'. The idea of random choice is strengthened if it follows the noun, cf. English 'any at all'. When used thus of people the effect is often pejorative, as is the English 'any old':

...no una muerte cualquiera, sino la muerte propia (M. Benedetti, Ur.)	...not any old death, but one's own death
Un martes cualquiera...él dijo de un modo que apareciera casual (G. García Márquez, Col.)	One Tuesday (i.e. 'one Tuesday out of the blue') he said, in a way designed to seem casual
Vamos a pasear por una calle cualquiera	Let's just walk down any street
Su esposa no es una mujer cualquiera	His wife isn't just any woman (i.e. she is something special)

(i) One occasionally hears *cualquiera* used before a feminine noun, but foreigners should avoid this: *?de cualquiera manera* (C. Fuentes, Mex. dialogue *?y más malvados que cualquiera otra tribu* (M. Vargas Llosa, Pe., dialogue) 'and more wicked than any other tribe'. This use is seen in Ortega y Gasset, Valera and a few other pre-mid-20th-century stylists.

(**b**) As a pronoun (the final -*a* is always retained):

cualquiera de estos tres modelos	any one of these three models
Cualquiera que sea el resultado	Whatever the result is
Cualquiera diría que eres un millonario	Anybody would think you're a millionaire
...la necesidad en que se ven de desahogarse con cualquiera (A. Bryce Echenique, Pe.)	...the need they find themselves in to let off steam in front of anybody
No cualquiera tiene un auto como el de nosotros (S. Vodanovic, Ch., dialogue; Sp. *...como el nuestro*)	Not everyone (lit. 'not anyone') has a car like ours
Cualesquiera que sean los desafíos en el camino de la construcción del comunismo (Fidel Castro, speech)	Whatever the challenges along the path to the building of Communism...

There is a tendency in spontaneous speech and even in informal written styles to use the singular where the plural is needed. This applies to both the pronoun and the adjective: *se les garantiza plaza escolar a sus hijos cualquiera que sean sus estudios* (*El País*, Sp.; better *cualesquiera*) 'their children are guaranteed school places, whatever their studies' (i.e. whatever they have studied). Careful speakers usually reject this.

9.9 *Demasiado*: adjective marked for number and gender, or invariable adverb

As an adjective 'too many'/'too much'; as an adverb 'too'/'too well'.

(**a**) Used as an adjective, it must agree in number and gender:

Has comido demasiadas uvas	You've eaten too many grapes
...pero el calor era demasiado hasta para una danza tan calma (M. Puig, Arg., dialogue)	...but the heat was too much even for such a placid dance
Has traído demasiados pocos tornillos (*demasiado* is treated as an adjective before *poco*)	You've brought too few screws

Nowadays *demasiado* is always placed before the noun.

(**b**) As an adverb (invariable in form)

Tú hablas demasiado	You talk too much
A ése/ese me lo conozco demasiado	I know him only too well
No cuentes demasiado conmigo	Don't count on me too much

9.10 *Medio*

In standard European Spanish this word functions as an adverb (invariable in form) or as an adjective (inflected for number and gender), both meaning 'half':

Están medio borrachos	They're half-drunk
La recogieron medio muerta	They picked her up half-dead
media pinta/media luna	half a pint/half-moon
media hora	half an hour

It is also often used colloquially in Latin America to mean 'rather', 'pretty' (Sp. *bastante, más bien*) as in *es medio linda* (Sp. *guapa*) 'she's pretty good-looking', *son medio tontos* 'they're pretty stupid', *yo también estoy medio enredado estos días* (L. Otero, Cu., dialogue) 'I'm pretty tied up too these days'.

In Galicia and Latin America there is a popular tendency to make the adverb agree in gender: *ella es media loca* 'she's half crazy', for *medio loca*; *llegó media desilusionada* (popular Mexican, quoted Kany, 55) 'she arrived pretty disillusioned', *la tenía media atragantada* (M. Puig, Arg., popular dialogue) '...she had it half-stuck down her throat'.

9.11 *Mismo* (and Latin-American variants): adjective, marked for gender and number

(a) 'The same'

When it means 'the same', which is its usual meaning on both continents, it is always placed before the noun or noun phrase that it qualifies:

Lleváis la misma blusa	You're wearing the same blouse
...con los mismos mozos pero un día griegos, otro andaluces, otro franceses, aunque vinieran de donde vinieran (A. Bryce Echenique, Pe. In Spain *mozos* = *camareros*)	...with the same waiters, but (dressed as) Greeks one day, Andalusians another, French on yet another, regardless of where they came from
Estos dos casos son el mismo	These two cases are the same (i.e. identical)
Estos dos son los mismos	These two are the same (i.e. as before)
—¿Es usted don Francisco? —El mismo	'Are you Don Francisco?' 'I am indeed' (lit. 'the same')

(i) *Lo mismo* may mean *la misma cosa*, or it may be adverbial: *como me vuelvan a decir lo mismo/la misma cosa...* 'if they say the same thing to me again...', *lo mismo hace imitaciones de políticos que juegos de manos* '(s)he just as easily does imitations of politicians as conjuring tricks', *no nos divertimos lo mismo que si hubieras estado tú* 'we didn't have such a good time as we would have if you'd been there'. **Lo mismo como* is sub-standard for *lo mismo que* 'the same as'. For *lo mismo* as a rather slangy Peninsular word for 'perhaps' see 16.3.2c.

(ii) The following should be noted: *esa casa es lo mismo que (igual que) aquélla/aquella* 'that house is the same as that other one' (i.e. the same thing is true of it, not the same house), *esa casa es la misma que compró Agustín* 'that house is the same one that Agustín bought'.

(b) Placed either before or after a noun, but always after a pronoun, *mismo* means 'selfsame'/'very'/'right':

Vivo en Madrid mismo/en el mismo Madrid	I live in Madrid itself
Aparca el helicóptero en su mismo jardín/su jardín mismo	(S)he parks the helicopter right in his/her garden

If there is danger of ambiguity, *mismo* must be placed after the noun if it means 'very', 'selfsame': *el mismo Papa* 'the Pope himself' or 'the same Pope', *el Papa mismo* = only 'the Pope himself'. *Propio* placed before the word can mean the same thing: see 9.14b.

(c) Placed after a pronoun it emphasizes the pronoun e.g. *yo mismo* 'I myself', *ella misma* 'she herself':

—*¿Quién construyó el chalet?* —*Yo mismo/misma (el chalet =* 'detached house' in Spain)	'Who built the house?' 'I did myself'
Parece que convencí a Graciela, pero yo mismo ¿estoy convencido? (M. Benedetti, Ur.)	It seems I convinced Graciela, but am I convinced myself?

(d) Placed after an adverb or adverbial phrase, *mismo* is itself an adverb and is therefore invariable:

por eso mismo	for that very reason
ahora mismo/ya mismo	right now/right away
aquí mismo	right here
Mañana mismo empiezo a escribir (A. Bryce Echenique, Pe. *Mañana* is an adverb here)	I'll start writing *tomorrow* without fail

But if the adverbial phrase contains a noun not accompanied by the definite article, *mismo* may or may not agree with it (Seco, 1998, 298, recommends agreement):

esta noche mismo/misma	this very night
Vino esta mañana mismo/misma	(S)he/it came this very morning
En España mismo/misma no se pudo evitar la llegada del bikini	In Spain itself it was impossible to prevent the arrival of the bikini

When the definite article is used, *mismo* is an adjective and must agree in number and gender: *lo descubrieron en la chimenea misma* 'they found it in the chimney itself'.

(i) *Mismísimo* is a colloquial emphatic form of *mismo* in sense (b): *el mismísimo presidente le/lo felicitó* 'the President himself congratulated him'.

(ii) Mexican and Central-American everyday speech often uses *mero* in contexts under (b): *en la mera (misma) esquina* 'right on the corner', *lo hizo él mero (él mismo)* 'he did it himself', *ya mero (ahora mismo)* 'right now'. In various parts of Latin America, from Chile to Mexico, *puro* may be used: *en la pura cabeza (en la misma cabeza)* 'right on the head', etc. (from Kany, 57ff), *a puro Villa* (bus-driver in Tabasco, Mex.) '(I'm going) only to Villahermosa' (Sp. *sólo/solo a*). . . ; *había puras mujeres* (colloquial Chilean) 'there were only women there' (Sp. *no había más que mujeres*).

(iii) *Mismamente* (= *igual*) is rustic or jocular.

9.12 *Mucho* and *poco*: adjectives, marked for number and gender, or invariable adverbs

'Much' or 'many', and 'little' or 'few'. Used as adjectives they agree in number and gender. Used as adverbs they are invariable.

(a) As adjectives:

Mis hijos no me hacen mucho caso	My children don't pay much attention to me
En el patio hay muchos limoneros	There are a lot of lemon trees on the patio
Pon poca pimienta	Don't put much pepper on/in it
Somos muchos/pocos	There are a lot/not many of us
su poca paciencia	her/his scant patience

—¿Cuánta harina has comprado?	'How much flour have you bought?'
— Poca	'Not much'
Lo poco gusta, lo mucho cansa	Brevity is the soul of wit (lit. 'little pleases, much tires')
Muchas se quejan de las nuevas horas de apertura	Many women are complaining about the new opening hours

(i) In the following sentences *mucho* and *poco* do not agree with the preceding noun, but refer to the general idea underlying the sentence: *¿trescientos mil dólares? Es mucho* '300,000 dollars? That's a lot', *¿tres cajas de ciruelas? Es poco* 'three boxes of plums? That's not much'. Compare *mil cajas para cien días son pocas* '1000 boxes for 100 days isn't/aren't a lot', *setenta libros por estante son muchos* 'seventy books to a shelf is/are a lot', *y será mucha la cerveza que consumirán, para provecho del dueño* (M. Puig, Arg., dialogue) 'and great will be the quantities of beer that they'll consume, to the owner's profit'.

(**b**) Adverbial uses:

Estoy añorando mucho a mi patria	I'm missing my home country a lot
Poco antes de las siete llegó su hijo Andrés (G. García Márquez, Col.)	Shortly before seven his son Andrés arrived
Sale poco últimamente	(S)he hasn't been out much lately
Por mucho que te quejes. . .	However much you complain…
Por poco que lo quieras	However little you want it
No sabes lo poco que me gusta ese hombre	You don't know how little I like that man

(i) Before *más, menos, mayor* and *menor*, when these are followed by a noun (present or implied), *mucho* or *poco* agree in number and gender—a fact that English-speakers are prone to forget: *tienen muchos más hijos que tú*/*tienen muchos más que tú* 'they have many more children than you'/'they have many more than you', *no en balde han transcurrido 27 años, hay mucha más experiencia, mucha más madurez* (Fidel Castro, Cu.) 'twenty-seven years have not passed in vain, there is much more experience, much more maturity'. This construction is apparently not obligatory in Latin America: *cuando me jubile, me pasarán sin duda mucho menos cosas* (M. Benedetti, Ur., Sp. *muchas menos cosas*) 'when I retire, no doubt a lot fewer things will happen to me'. Informants from Peru and Mexico found this acceptable, but it is rejected by Spaniards.

Before adjectives and adverbs, *mucho* and *poco* are adverbs and invariable in form: *los problemas eran mucho mayores* 'the problems were much greater'.

(ii) *Muy* 'very' can be thought of as a shortened form of *mucho*, used before adjectives and adverbs. The full form therefore reappears when it is used alone: *—¿Es laborioso? —Mucho.* '"Is he hard-working?" "Very"'.

(iii) *Poco* (but not *un poco*) negates a following adverb or adjective: *poco frecuente* = 'not frequent'. See 4.13.

(iv) 'Very much' = *muchísimo*. *Muy mucho* is archaic or jocular.

(v) *Un poco de* is invariable, but phrases like *?una poca de sal* 'a bit of salt' are heard in popular or jocular speech.

9.13 *Otro*: adjective/pronoun, marked for number and gender

Adjectivally 'other'/'another'; pronominally 'another one'/'others':

Otra persona no te creería	Another person wouldn't believe you
Ponle otro sello (Lat. Am. *estampilla*)	Put another stamp on it
en circunstancias otras que aquellas en que...	in circumstances other than those in which...
El que lo hizo fue otro	The one who did it was someone else
Hay quienes ven la vida lógica y ordenada, otros la sabemos absurda y confusa (G. Cabrera Infante, Cu., dialogue)	There are some who see life as logical and ordered, others of us know it's absurd and confused
Se lanzaban la pelota unos a otros	They were throwing the ball to one another

(i) **Un otro* for 'another' (Fr. *un autre*, Catalan *un altre*) is not Spanish: *dame otro* 'give me another'. *El otro/la otra*, etc., means 'the other one'.

(ii) The possessives *mi, tu, su, nuestro, vuestro* precede *otro*, but other adjectives follow it, although *mucho* may appear in either position: *tu otro pantalón* 'your other trousers', *sé que estoy manipulada como otra mucha gente* (interview in *Cambio16*, Sp., also *mucha otra...*) 'I know I'm being manipulated like a lot of other people', *...cosa que sólo celebraron Carmen Serdán y otras cuatro maestras* (A. Mastretta, Mex., dialogue) '...something that only Carmen Serdán and four other women teachers greeted enthusiastically', *en otros pocos casos* (cf. *en pocos otros casos* 'in not many other cases') 'in a few other cases', *otros varios millones de campesinos* (M. Vargas Llosa, Pe.) 'several million other peasants'.

(iii) *Los/las demás* may be a synonym of *los otros/las otras* if the latter means 'the rest'/'the remainder': *todos los demás países europeos* 'all the other European countries', *si de mí dependiera ya le habría regalado todos los demás muebles* (A. Bryce Echenique, Pe., dialogue) 'if it had depended on me, I'd have made you a present of all the other furniture'.

(iv) The phrase *alguno...que otro* is noteworthy: *...y todo porque un día les habrá colocado alguna amonestación que otra* (M. Puig, Arg., dialogue) '...and all because one day he gave them some kind of dressing-down'. For the choice between *algún que otro* and *alguno que otro* before masculine nouns, see 9.4.1a.

9.14 *Propio*: adjective, marked for number and gender

(a) Usually it means 'own', as in:

mi propio taxi/ tus propias convicciones	my own taxi/your own convictions
Manuel tiene chófer propio (Lat. Am. *chofer*)	Manuel has his own driver
Intentar comprender su realidad es comprender mejor la tuya propia (Queen Sofía of Spain, quoted in *El País*)	Trying to understand their [i.e. artists'] reality is to understand your own better

(b) Placed before a noun (but not a pronoun), 'selfsame', 'very', etc. (same as *mismo* at 9.11b.):

Las tachaduras son del propio autor	The crossings-out are by the author himself
Nos dio audiencia el propio obispo	The Bishop himself granted us an audience

(c) 'Appropriate', 'right', 'peculiar', 'characteristic':

Ese olor es propio del butano	That smell is characteristic of butane
Ese lenguaje no es propio de un diplomático	That language is not suitable for a diplomat
Es propio de ella llegar tres horas tarde	It's like her/typical of her to arrive three hours late

9.15 *Solo*: adjective, marked for number and gender; *sólo* or *solo*: invariable adverb

The adjective means 'alone', the adverb 'only' (i.e. *solamente*). The adverb was always marked with a written accent, but the Academy's *Nuevas normas* of 1959 decreed that the accent is needed only for clarity, so one may now write *solo tres* or *sólo tres* for 'only three'. Seco (1998), 417, agrees, but more than forty years later most editors and publishers follow the old rule, and the Academy seems to have backtracked, since the *GDLE* of 1999 always uses *sólo* for 'only'. Confusion is possible only with the masculine singular adjective, e.g. *un hombre solo/un hombre sólo* 'a man alone'/'only one man', *solo en casa/sólo en casa* 'alone in the house'/'only at home'.

(a) Adjectival uses:

Yo me quedé solo	I was left alone
Octavia me dijo que tenía que regresar sola (A. Bryce Echenique, Pe.)	Octavia told me she had to go back alone
Por el solo tono de la voz comprendió que era una llamada alarmante (G. García Márquez, Col.)	By the tone of the voice alone he understood that it was an alarming phone-call
dos cafés solos	two black coffees
(cf. *dos cafés sólo/solo*	only two coffees)

(b) Adverbial examples (in every case *solamente* could be used instead):

Sólo/Solo así se solucionarán estos problemas	Only in this way will these problems be solved
Millones de personas disfrutan de la luz eléctrica con sólo/solo accionar un simple conmutador	Millions of people enjoy electric light merely at the press of a switch
Tan sólo se me ocurrió en ese instante lo que podría haber pedido Graciela (M. Puig, Arg., dialogue)	It only occurred to me at that moment what Graciela might have asked for

(i) A negative + *más. . .que* means 'only' (cf. French *ne. . .que. . .*): *no hizo más que reírse* 'all he did was laugh', *no piensa más que en sí misma* 'she only thinks of herself'. It must not be confused with *más de*, used with numbers to mean 'more than'. See 5.5.

(ii) *A solas* strictly means 'alone' (i.e. unaccompanied), and is occasionally required for the sake of clarity to avoid confusion between *sólo* and *solo*, as in *necesito estar a solas/solo contigo* 'I want to be alone with you' (*solo* might be heard as *sólo* 'only with you'), or *lo solucionó a solas* '(s)he solved it alone (no one else present)' and *lo solucionó solo* 'he solved it alone' (without help). Cf. also *pero nunca había fumado a solas* (G. García Márquez, Col.) 'but she had never smoked on her own'.

A solas cannot be used of inanimate things. In sentences like *estuve a solas con mis pensamientos* 'I was alone with my thoughts' it is an elegant, rather poetic alternative to *solo*.

(iii) 'Not only... but also' is *no sólo/solo... **sino***. See 33.1a.

(iv) 'The only...', 'the only one...', 'his only', etc. *Único* is required if no noun follows: *él es el único que sabe conducir* 'he's the only one who can drive', *es lo único concreto que tenemos* (L. Otero, Cu.) 'it's the only real thing we have', *lo único es que no sé nadar* 'the only thing is I can't swim', *es hijo único* 'he's an only child'. Compare *el único/solo ser por quien deseo vivir* 'the only person I want to live for', *son el único/solo sustento del gobierno* 'they're the government's only support'.

(v) In some Latin-American countries, e.g. Cuba, *único* may be used as an adverb meaning 'only', where other regions use *únicamente*, cf. *único* (for *únicamente/solamente/sólo*) *en esta región* 'only in this region'.

9.16 *Tanto*: adjective, marked for number and gender; or invariable adverb

For the use of *tanto* and *tan* in comparisons see 5.15.1. *Tanto* basically means 'so much', 'so many' (French *tant **de***).

(**a**) As an adjective it must agree in number and gender:

tanta nieve/tantas hormigas/tantos problemas	so much snow/so many ants/so many problems
...uno de tantos consuelos del pobre (M. Puig, Arg., dialogue)	...one of so many consolations that the poor have

It can also function as a noun or pronoun (invariable in form as *tanto*):

No creí que se atreviera/atreviese a tanto	I didn't think (s)he/you would be that daring
Es un tanto místico	He's a bit of a mystic (or 'he lives in the clouds')
Cobran un tanto por ciento de comisión	They take a certain percentage as commission

(**b**) As an adverb it is invariable in form:

—Hay más de tres kilos. —¡No tanto!	'There are more than three kilos.' 'Not that much!'
Corrió tanto que no podía hablar	(S)he ran so much that (s)he couldn't speak
tanto era así que...(see ii for ?*tan era así...*)	so much was it so that...
tanto mejor/tanto peor para ellos	all the better/so much the worse for them
—Es nada menos que de cincuenta pesos. —¡Tanto mejor! (J. J. Arreola, Mex., dialogue)	'It's only fifty pesos.' 'So much the better!'
Es tanto un problema para la oposición como para el Gobierno	It's as much a problem for the opposition as for the government

(i) Before adjectives or adverbs, *tan* is required: *usted ha sido tan acogedor* 'you've been so welcoming', *se levanta tan de mañana que nadie le/lo ve salir* 'he gets up so early in the morning that no one sees him leave', *tan a propósito* 'so much on purpose'/'so relevantly', *te lo enviaré tan pronto como pueda* 'I'll send it to you as soon as I can'.

Mejor, peor, mayor and *menor* are exceptions: *tanto mejor/peor para usted* 'so much the better/worse for you', *el peligro era tanto mayor debido a la radiactividad* 'the danger was all the greater due to radioactivity'.

(ii) *Tan* before verbs is considered sub-standard in Spain but is found in Latin-American speech and writing: *tan es así = tanto es así* 'it was so true', *tan no la conocen que la dejan morir de hambre* (E. Poniatowska, Mex.; Sp. *tanto...*, *tan poco la conocen*) 'they know so little of her that they let her starve to death'.

(iii) *Tanto* plus a singular noun is colloquial for 'lots of', 'so many': *hay tanto ricacho por aquí* 'there are loads of stinking-rich people round here'.

(iv) *Tanto...que* for 'as much as' is not Spanish: *no viaja tanto **como** tú* '(s)he doesn't travel as much as you'. *Tanto...que* can only mean 'so much...that'. See 5.15.1.

9.17 *Todo*: adjective/pronoun, marked for number and gender

'All', 'every', 'the whole of', 'any'.

(**a**) When not followed by a definite or indefinite article it usually means 'every' or 'any':

todo producto alimenticio que contenga colorantes artificiales...	any food product containing artificial colouring...
todo español sabe que...	every Spaniard knows that...
en todo caso	in any case

In all these cases *cualquier* could be used instead of *todo*.

(**b**) With the definite article, possessives or demonstratives, or before proper names, its usual meaning is 'the whole of'/'all':

toda la noche	all night
todos los cinco	all five of them
Varadero. Es una playa increíble. Todos los extranjeros nos envidian (L. Otero, Cu., dialogue)	Varadero. It's an incredible beach. All the foreigners envy us
Incluso Ricardo, con toda su paciencia, se salió del seminario	Even Ricardo, with all his patience, walked out of the seminar
Todo Barcelona habla de ello (see 1.4.7 for the gender of *todo* here)	All Barcelona's talking about it

(**c**) With the definite article and periods of time it means 'every':

El fontanero (Lat. Am. *plomero*) *viene todos los meses*	The plumber comes every/once a month
todos los viernes/años	every Friday/year

(i) *Cada* is used if the actions are new ones rather than repetitions, or when the period of time is preceded by a number: *cada día sale con una chica nueva* 'every day he goes out with a new girl', *cada diez minutos sale con alguna nueva burrada* 'every ten minutes (s)he comes out with some new nonsense', *tres gotas cada cuatro horas* 'three drops every four hours'.

(ii) Moliner, **II**, 1330, notes that *al...* is more elegant than *todos los...* to indicate rate or quantity per period of time: *se fuma cuatro paquetes al día* '(s)he smokes four packets/US packs a day', *lee un par de novelas a la semana* '(s)he reads a couple of novels a week', etc.

(iii) *Cuanto* may be used to translate 'absolutely every': *no es cosa de obligar a leer cuanto libro se ha escrito* (E. Sábato, Arg., interview) 'it's not a question of obliging people to read every book that was ever written'. *Cuanto* is not used in phrases like *todos los días* 'every day'.

 Cuanto or *todo cuanto* may also mean 'absolutely everything': *heredó de él una tremenda bronca a (todo) cuanto sonara a autoridad* (L. Sepúlveda, Ch.; in Spain *bronca* means 'row'/'argument' and *rabia* would be used here) 'he inherited from him a tremendous rage against everything that sounded like authority'.

(**d**) Pronominally, the singular means 'everything', the plural 'everyone'/'everybody'/'all of them': *se enfada por todo* '(s)he gets cross about everything', *es todo propaganda* 'it's all propaganda:

—*¿Dónde están las fresas?* —*Me las he comido todas*	'Where are the strawberries?' 'I've eaten them all'
Pago por todos	I'm paying for everyone

After a neuter *todo*—as after all singular nouns and pronouns—Spanish usually makes the verb *ser* (and one or two others) agree with a following plural noun: *con nuestro nuevo plan de ahorros, todo **son** ventajas* 'with our new savings plan it's all advantages'. See 2.3.3.

(**e**) Agreement of *todo* should be noted in the following cases:

When an adjectival phrase follows *todo*, the latter agrees with the subject: *la verja está toda oxidada* 'the railings are all rusty', *estaba toda cubierta de harina* 'she was completely covered in flour'. But when a noun follows there is some uncertainty: *su cara era toda pecas* 'his/her face was all freckles', *el cielo era todo nubes* 'the sky was all clouds', *esa niña es toda ojos* (from Moliner, II, 1930), 'that girl's all eyes'; but *su madre es todo corazón* 'his/her mother is all heart' (*GDLE* 16.6.5), *los soldados eran todo ímpetu y coraje* 'the soldiers were all fighting spirit and courage' (ibid.). Women usually say *soy toda oídos* 'I'm all ears' but one hears *todo…*; also *es toda/todo sonrisas esta mañana* 'she's all smiles this morning'.

 The invariable *todo* may avoid ambiguity: *esos hombres son todo músculo* means 'those men are all muscle', whereas …*todos músculos* sounds like 'all muscles', i.e. 'all from the Muscle family'. So *estas chuletas son todo hueso* is more likely for 'these chops/cutlets are all bone'.

(**f**) Relative clauses involving *todo*

The following sentences illustrate some translation problems:

todos los que dicen eso	all who say that
todo el que diga eso/todo aquel que diga eso (the latter is literary)	anyone who says that
Todo lo que escribe es bueno	Everything (s)he writes is good
Cuanto/Todo cuanto escribe es bueno (literary)	Everything (s)he writes is good
este poeta, cuyas palabras todas quedarán grabadas en nuestro corazón	this poet, whose every word will remain engraved on our hearts
el césped, por toda cuya superficie crecían malas hierbas	the lawn, over all of whose surface weeds were growing

esta ciudad, de la que conozco todas las iglesias	this city, all of whose churches I know
estas novelas, todas las cuales he leído	these novels, all of which I have read
estos niños, los padres de todos los cuales yo conozco	these children, all of whose parents I know
estas páginas, escritas todas ellas en japonés	these pages, all of which are written in Japanese
el palacio, del que no hay habitación que yo no haya visitado	the palace, all of whose rooms I have visited

(i) *Todo* occasionally follows the noun in flowery styles: *el cielo todo estaba sembrado de estrellas* 'the whole sky was strewn with stars', *el mundo todo le parecía un jardín encantado* 'the whole world seemed to him an enchanted garden'.

(ii) *Todo el mundo* (singular agreement) is a set phrase meaning 'everybody': *todo el mundo los conoce* 'everyone knows them'.

(iii) *Todo* followed by the indefinite article usually translates 'a whole…': *se comió toda una tarta de melocotones* '(s)he ate a whole peach tart', *hubo toda una serie de malentendidos* 'there was a whole series of misunderstandings'.

9.18 *Varios*: adjective, marked for number and gender

(a) 'Several', in which case it normally—but not always—precedes the noun: *en varias partes del país* 'in several parts of the country', *mis motivos son varios* 'my motives are several', *los aspectos varios de la cuestión* (literary: from Moliner, II, 1442) 'the several aspects of the question'.

(b) 'Various', 'varied', in which case it can also follow or precede the noun. When used with *hay* or *ser* it precedes the noun:

flores de varios colores/de colores varios (the second option is more literary)	flowers of various colours
La fauna de esta zona es muy varia/variada	The fauna of this zone is very varied
tapas varias	selection of tapas (snacks)

Translating 'various': *en diversas ocasiones* 'on various occasions', *en diferentes puntos de los Andes* 'in various places in the Andes'.

10

Numerals

The main points discussed in this chapter are:

- Numbers 1 to a billion (Section 10.1)
- Gender of numbers (Section 10.2)
- Agreement of *uno* and *cientos* (Section 10.3)
- Millions and billions (Section 10.4)
- *Un* or *uno?* (Section 10.5)
- *Cien* or *ciento?* (Section 10.6)
- Percentages (Section 10.7)
- 'score', 'dozen', etc. (Section 10.8)
- Fractions (Section 10.10)
- First, second, third, etc. (Section 10.12)
- Rules for writing numbers (Section 10.16)
- Phone numbers (10.17)

Spanish numerals are simple and regular, although this makes the three unexpected forms *quinientos* 500 (not **cinco cientos*), *setecientos* 700 (not **sietecientos*) and *novecientos* 900 (not **nuevecientos*) easy to forget. Remember also that 16–29 are written as one word (*dieciséis*, *veintidós*, etc.) whereas other tens plus units, i.e. 31–99, are joined by *y*: *treinta y uno*, *ochenta y seis*, etc.

10.1 Cardinal numbers: forms

Spanish cardinal numerals (the numbers used for counting) do not change their form, except for *uno* 'one' and *cientos* 'hundreds', which agree in gender with the thing counted:

0 *cero*	12 *doce*	23 *veintitrés*	41 *cuarenta y*
1 *uno/una*	13 *trece*	24 *veinticuatro*	*uno/una/un*
2 *dos*	14 *catorce*	25 *veinticinco*	50 *cincuenta*
3 *tres*	15 *quince*	26 *veintiséis*	60 *sesenta*
4 *cuatro*	16 *dieciséis*	27 *veintisiete*	70 *setenta*
5 *cinco*	17 *diecisiete*	28 *veintiocho*	80 *ochenta*
6 *seis*	18 *dieciocho*	29 *veintinueve*	90 *noventa*
7 *siete*	19 *diecinueve*	30 *treinta*	100 *cien/ciento*
8 *ocho*	20 *veinte*	31 *treinta y*	101 *ciento uno/*
9 *nueve*	21 *veintiuno/a*	*uno/una/un*	*una/un*
10 *diez*	*veintiún*	32 *treinta y dos*	102 *ciento dos*
11 *once*	22 *veintidós*	40 *cuarenta*	

185 *ciento ochenta y cinco*	400 *cuatrocientos/*	1001 see note (iv)
200 *doscientos/ doscientas*	*cuatrocientas*	1006 *mil seis*
205 *doscientos cinco/*	500 **quinientos/quinientas**	1107 *mil ciento siete*
doscientas cinco	600 *seiscientos/seiscientas*	1998 *mil novecientos/as*
300 *trescientos/trescientas*	700 **setecientos/setecientas**	*noventa y ocho*
357 *trescientos/as*	800 *ochocientos/ ochocientas*	2022 *dos mil veintidós*
cincuenta y siete	900 **novecientos/novecientas**	5000 *cinco mil*
	1000 *mil*	10.000 *diez mil*

500.014 *quinientos/as mil catorce*   936.257 *novecientos/as treinta y seis mil*
                                          doscientos/as cincuenta y siete
1.000.000 *un millón*   100.000.000 *cien millones*
$1.000.000 *un millón de dólares* (for the use of *de* see 10.4a)
7.678.456 *libras: siete millones seiscientas setenta y ocho mil cuatrocientas cincuenta y seis*
    libras
1.000.000.000 *mil millones*   1.000.000.000.000 *un billón* (see 10.4b)

(i) 16–19 and 21–29 are written as one word, as are 200, 300, 400, 500, 600, 700, 800 and 900. Forms like *diez y seis* for *dieciséis* are old-fashioned.

(ii) *Uno* is not used before *ciento* or *mil*: *una pareja de ratas es capaz de procrear más de ciento veinte crías por año* 'a pair of rats is capable of producing more than 120 offspring per year', *más de mil colegios equipados con televisores en color* 'more than one thousand schools equipped with colo(u)r television'. But *un* is used to avoid ambiguity: compare *trescientos/as **un** mil ochenta y cuatro* 301.084 and *trescientos/as mil ochenta y cuatro* 300.084.

(iii) A point (US 'period') is used to separate thousands: *19.000 dólares* = $19,000. Typists sometimes write years with a point, e.g. 1.998, but the grammarians disapprove. A comma is used to separate decimals: *3,45* (pronounced *tres coma cuarenta y cinco*, not '*tres coma cuatro cinco*') = British and American 'three point four five'. However, Mexico, Puerto Rico, the Dominican Republic and the Central-American countries (but not Cuba or the other republics) use the system of the English-speaking world, i.e. 20,550 = *veinte mil quinientos/as cincuenta* and 1.25, pronounced *uno punto veinticinco*.

(iv) 1001 is theoretically *mil uno* and this form is used when counting and no noun follows. Seco (1998), 446, notes that *mil y uno* comes from the famous book *Las mil y una noches* 'One Thousand and One Nights' and is correct only in the vague sense of 'a lot': *tengo mil y una cosas que hacer* 'I've got a thousand and one things to do', *las mil y una aplicaciones domóticas permiten descansar al propietario* (*El País*, Sp.) 'the innumerable applications available in a computerized household allow the owner to take it easy'. However, *mil y uno/a* is usual before nouns: *mil y un euros* '1001 euros', *tres mil y un dólares* '3001 dollars'. Forms like *mil un euros* are confined to formal writing.

(v) Certain forms ending in *-ón* are used pejoratively to refer to people of a specific age: *un cuarentón* 'a forty-year-old man', *un cincuentón* 'a fifty-year-old', *una sesentona* 'a sixty-year-old woman'. Forms ending in *–añero* are merely descriptive, e.g. *un quinceañero* 'a fifteen-year-old', *una veinteañera* (C. Martín Gaite, Sp.) 'a twenty-year-old woman'.

El País's *Libro de estilo* (2002), 34, says that *el/la joven* or *el/la adolescente* is a person aged between 13 and 18, so they are close equivalents of our 'teenager'.

10.2 Gender of numbers

Numbers are masculine (unlike letters of the alphabet, which are all feminine):

Yo puse un siete, no un nueve	I put a 7, not a 9
Los dos ochos del anuncio giraban	The two 8s on the advertisement were
velozmente en sentido contrario	spinning rapidly in opposite directions
(C. Martín Gaite, Sp.)	
un cinco de bastos	a five of clubs
Tú eres el cinco	You're number five

This is also true of *cientos* and *miles* when used as nouns (i.e. when followed by *de*):

los miles de víctimas de los tifones	the thousands of victims of the typhoons
los escasos cientos de personas que asistían	the few hundred persons present at the
a la manifestación	demonstration

In informal styles *miles de* is often made feminine before feminine nouns: *la acumulación de los plaguicidas es un continuo peligro de envenenamiento para las miles de aves* (*La Vanguardia*, Sp.) 'the build-up of pesticides represents (lit. 'is') a continual threat of poisoning for the thousands of birds'. Seco (1998), 297, says *las miles* is 'abnormal'.

10.3 Agreement of *uno* and the hundreds

Uno and *cientos* (but not *ciento/cien*) agree in gender with the noun counted. Foreign students constantly forget to make *cientos* agree:

un peso/una libra	one peso/one pound
veintiuna casas	twenty-one houses
quinientos dólares	five hundred dollars
setecientas mujeres	seven hundred women
en la página quinientas catorce	on page 514
Yo duermo en la cuatrocientas (*habitación*	I'm sleeping in (room) 400
omitted)	

Combinations of tens plus one and thousands (21,000, 31,000, 41,000, etc.) are problematic. Logically one should say *veintiuna mil mujeres* '21,000 women' since the nouns are feminine and *mil* is an adjective, and this is often seen: *se han visto afectadas treinta y una mil personas* 'thirty-one thousand people have been affected' (TVE broadcast). However, forms like *veintiún mil pesetas*, *treinta y un mil mujeres* '31,000 women', etc., are in common use, and many speakers do not accept *veintiuna/treinta y una mil*. Seco (1998), 445, notes that the masculine is in fact the traditional form.

When thousands are multiplied by hundreds the expected gender agreement must be used: *doscientas mil mujeres* '200,000 women', never **doscientos mil mujeres*.

10.4 Millions and billions

(**a**) *Millón* is a masculine noun and is connected by *de* to the following noun or noun phrase:

una inversión global de más de 6.000	an overall investment of more than
*millones **de** pesetas, de **los** que mil*	6 billion pesetas, of which 1 billion
millones se invertirán el próximo	will be invested next year
año (*El País*, Sp. The *peseta* was	
abolished in 2002)	

The phrase *un millón* is singular, so a following verb or noun must agree accordingly: *el millón y medio restante **fue** invertido...* 'the remaining million and a half were/was invested...'. 'A million and one' is *un millón y uno/una*, and *y* is used whenever a single number-word follows: *un millón y cien, tres millones y mil*, but *un millón doscientos mil* = 'one million two hundred thousand'.

(b) Our billion is a thousand million (*mil millones*), French *un milliard*, Italian *un miliardo* (*un millardo* was approved by the Academy in 1995, but is apparently used only in Venezuela). The Hispanic *billón* is a million million, a value confirmed by the International Conference on Weights and Measures of 1948, and applied in the press of all Spanish-speaking countries. An alarming number of people, especially foreigners, seem to be unaware of the difference. The construction is also with *de*: *un billón de liras turcas*= a **thousand billion** Turkish lira.

10.5 *Un* or *uno*?

Uno loses its final vowel before a masculine noun or noun phrase, as does *una* before nouns beginning with stressed *a-* or *ha-*. *Veintiuno* is shortened to *veintiún* in the same contexts:

un tigre, dos tigres, tres tigres	one tiger, two tigers, three tigers (a tongue-twister)
veintiún mil hombres	21,000 men
veintiún mil mujeres (see note to 10.3)	21,000 women
un águila, veintiún armas, treinta y un hachas	one eagle, 21 weapons, 31 axes

But in the following examples the final vowel is retained since the numeral does not precede a noun: *no hay más que veintiuno* 'there are only twenty-one', *párrafo ciento uno* 'paragraph 101', *Inglaterra, país tradicional de los fantasmas, ve uno nuevo por sus calles* (*Cambio16*, Sp.) 'England, the traditional land of ghosts, is witnessing a new one in its streets'.

10.6 *Cien* or *ciento*?

Ciento is shortened to *cien* before another numeral which it multiplies, or before a noun or noun phrase:

cien mil bolívares	100,000 bolivares
cien millones	100 million
cien buenas razones	100 good reasons
but	
ciento once	one hundred and eleven
en la página ciento dieciocho	on page one hundred and eighteen

The old rule was that *ciento* should be used when the number stands alone: — *¿Cuántos son?* —*Ciento* '"How many are there?" '"A hundred"'. But this rule is obsolete in Latin America and virtually extinct in Spain, so the answer is now *cien*. Further examples: *yo vivo en el cien* 'I live in number 100', *pues faltan cien o sobran cincuenta* (A. Mastretta, Mex., dialogue) 'well, there are either a hundred missing or fifty too many'. However, *ciento* is still used in percentages: see next section.

10.7 Expression of percentages

Por ciento is used for 'per cent', although the phrase *cien por cien* 'one hundred per cent' is accepted in the meaning 'absolutely'/'totally': *es cien por cien honrada* 'she's one hundred per cent honest'. Forms like *cincuenta por cien, diez por cien* are heard in Latin America and occasionally in Spain, but . . .*por ciento* is used in writing on both continents:

el cuarenta y tres por ciento	forty-three per cent
tanto por ciento	so much per cent
El PCE sólo obtuvo el 8 y pico por ciento de los votos (*El País*, Sp.)	The Spanish Communist Party only obtained just over 8% of the votes
. . .*el costo de la construcción creció el 0,7 por ciento* (*La Nación*, Arg.)	Building costs rose 0.7 per cent
. . .*la seguridad, cien por cien, de que los vertidos son inocuos* (*El País*, Sp.)	. . .a hundred-per-cent guarantee that the waste is harmless

10.8 Collective numerals

There is a series of collective numerals, cf. our 'score', sometimes used to express approximate quantities:

un par de veces a couple of times	*una cuarentena* about forty/quarantine
una decena about ten	*una cincuentena* about fifty
una docena a dozen (often approximate, used less than in English)	*un centenar* about a hundred
	un millar about a thousand
una veintena a score/about twenty	

(i) *Cuatro* is much used colloquially in Spain and Mexico, and no doubt elsewhere, to mean 'a couple'/'a handful': *no hay más que cuatro gatos* 'there's not a soul about' (lit. '. . .only four cats about'), *no son más que cuatro desgraciados los que ponen las pegatinas fascistas* 'it's only a handful of wretches who put up fascist stickers'.

(ii) *Centenar* and *millar* are used for expressing rate: *mil dólares el centenar/millar* '1000 dollars the hundred/the thousand' (or, more colloquially, . . .*cada cien/por cada cien, cada mil*).

(iii) Like all collective nouns, collective numerals are often treated as singular: *una veintena de casas se ordenaba formando una calle frente al río* (L. Sepúlveda, Ch.) 'a score of houses were laid out to form a street in front of the river'. See 2.3.1 for further remarks on collective nouns.

(iv) An informal way of expressing 'slightly above' is by using *y pico*, as in *el piso veintipico* (M. Vázquez Montalbán, Sp.) 'flat/apartment twenty-something', *treinta y pico* 'thirty and a bit'. Note also *son las cinco y poco* 'it's just after/gone five o'clock'.

10.9 Mathematical expressions

Dos y tres son cinco	Two plus three equals five
Dos por tres son seis	Two times three equals six
Ocho dividido por dos son cuatro (or *ocho entre dos. . .*)	Eight divided by two is four
Once menos nueve son dos	Eleven minus nine equals two

Tres es la raíz cuadrada de nueve	Three is the square root of nine
Nueve es el cuadrado de tres	Nine is three squared
Forma un cuadrado de diez metros	It's 10 metres square
dos metros cuadrados	two square metres
menos veinte	minus twenty

The division sign is a colon, e.g. 3:6 = 0,5 (*tres dividido por seis son cero coma cinco*) '3 ÷ 6 = 0.5'.

10.10 Fractions

There are nouns to express some lower fractions, e.g. *la/una mitad* 'the/a half', *el/un tercio* 'the/a third', *dos tercios* 'two thirds', *el/un cuarto* 'the/a quarter'.

From 'fifth' to 'tenth' the masculine ordinal numeral can be used: *un quinto/ sexto/séptimo/octavo/noveno/décimo* 'a fifth/sixth/seventh/eighth/ninth/tenth'; but this is more typical of mathematical, technical or sporting language, although not unknown in educated speech: *ganó por tres quintos de segundo* '(s)he won by three-fifths of a second'.

Everyday language uses the forms *quinta parte, sexta parte, séptima parte*, etc., although usage is fickle in a few cases and the *parte* may be dropped. Note *tengo unas décimas de fiebre* 'I've got a couple of tenths of a degree of fever', *unas décimas de segundo después* 'a few tenths of a second later': *un décimo* is a tenth share in a Spanish national lottery ticket. *La tercera parte* is usual in non-mathematical speech for *el tercio*. Examples:

La mitad se salvó	Half were saved
un cuarto (de) kilo	a quarter (of a) kilo
Un tercio/La tercera parte de los	A third of Spaniards think that…
españoles piensa(n) que…	
Alaska y Venezuela sólo nos aseguran las	Alaska and Venezuela only guarantee
dos terceras partes de ese suministro	us two-thirds of that supply
(C. Fuentes, Mex., dialogue)	

In both languages complex fractions like 'four twenty-sevenths' are usually nowadays expressed as percentages or decimals. If fractions must be used, the usual practice in Spain is to use the ordinary cardinal numbers: '1/20th' = *la veinte parte*, '1/90th' = *la noventa parte*, '1/53rd' = *la cincuenta y tres parte*. Forms like *la vigésima parte* '1/20th', *la nonagésima parte* '1/90th', *la quincuagésima tercera parte* '1/53rd', are avoided in all but very formal language.

Ordinal forms with *parte* are however used in everyday language for hundredths, thousandths, millionths and billionths: *la centésima/milésima/ millonésima parte*, *tres doscentésimas* '3/200ths'; the word *parte* is often dropped:

A partir de la primera cienmilésima de	After the first one hundred-thousandth of
segundo, el Universo empieza a cobrar	a second the Universe begins to take on
un aspecto conocido (Abc, Sp.)	a familiar appearance
Greene corrió el fin de semana pasado en	Greene clocked (lit 'ran') 6.4 seconds last
Atlanta en 6,40, una centésima de	weekend in Atlanta, a hundredth of a
segundo menos que…(ibid.)	second less than…

The tinier fractions can alternatively be expressed, and generally are in mathematical language and in Latin America, by adding the suffix *–avo* to the ordinal number: *la veinticincava parte* '1/25th', *tres ochenta y seisavas partes* '3/86ths'. Mathematical language may use the masculine noun form, e.g. *tres ochenta y seisavos*. If two *a*'s come together when –*avo* is added, one can optionally be dropped and usually is in non-mathematical language: *treinta(a)vo* '30th'.

Medio/a/os/as is the adjectival form for 'half': *una media docena/pinta* 'a half-dozen/half-pint'; *la mitad* is the noun 'the half'. *Cuarto* may function as an adjective or noun: *un cuarto kilo* or *un cuarto de kilo* '1/4 kilo', but always *un cuarto de hora* 'a quarter of an hour'.

10.11 Articles with numbers

Certain common numerical expressions, especially percentages, appear with *el* or *un*. This is particularly true when the numerical value is preceded by a preposition, and after *cumplir, al llegar a...* meaning 'to reach the age of':

Vivo en el cinco	I live in number five
Cuando George Burns cumplió los noventa años... (La Jornada, Mex.)	When George Burns reached the age of ninety
Lo dijo al llegar a los ochenta años	(S)he said it when (s)he reached eighty
... una reducción del 55% en el total de sentencias dictadas y un incremento del 102% en la suma de causas archivadas (La Nación, Arg.)	... a 55% drop in the number of sentences handed out and a 102% rise in the total number of shelved prosecutions
El 20 por ciento de los mexicanos dice(n) que...	20 per cent of Mexicans say that...

But

Ha costado entre tres mil y cinco mil euros	It cost between 3,000 and 5,000 euros
Tengo cuarenta y tres años	I'm forty-three

The article is not used everywhere with percentages: *el año pasado el gasto programable representó 18.2 por ciento del PIB (La Jornada.* Mexico uses points and commas as in English) 'last year the predicted cost represented 18.2% of GDP'; *acaba de obtener 46,4% del total de votos (El Nacional,* Ven.) 'he has just obtained 46.4% of the votes'.

10.12 Ordinal numbers

10.12.1 Ordinal numerals first to tenth

These translate 'first', 'second', 'third', etc. They agree in number and gender: *el quinto libro, la quinta casa* 'the fifth book', 'the fifth house'. The special ordinal forms 1st–10th are in everyday use, but the cardinal numbers encroach even on them in phrases like *el siglo nueve/noveno* 'the ninth century', *Alfonso diez/décimo* 'Alfonso the tenth', the ordinal being considered more correct:

primer(o) first	*quinto* fifth	*octavo* eighth
segundo second	*sexto* sixth	*noveno* ninth
tercer(o) third	*séptimo/sétimo* seventh	*décimo* tenth
cuarto fourth		

el tercer hombre the third man	*la tercera vez* the third time
Carlos III (tercero) Charles III	*el siglo décimo/diez* the tenth century
Fernando VII (séptimo) Ferdinand VII	

(i) *Primero* and *tercero* lose their final vowel before a masculine singular noun or noun phrase: *el primer récord mundial* 'the first world record', *el tercer gran éxito* 'the third great success'. For more details see 4.6b.

(ii) *Séptimo* is often pronounced *sétimo* and the Academy approves of this spelling. Many Spanish-speakers find it unacceptable.

(iii) *Nono* is used for *noveno* when referring to Popes: *Pío nono* 'Pope Pius IX'.

(iv) In the titles of royalty and Popes, the usual rule is that the ordinal number is used below eleven, the cardinal for numbers above ten: *Enrique V (Enrique Quinto)* 'Henry the Fifth', but *Juan XXIII (Juan Veintitrés)* 'John 23rd'.

(v) See 32.9.1 for how to say and write dates.

10.12.2 Ordinal numbers above tenth

The use of special ordinal forms for these numbers is declining, and they are now mainly found only in official or very formal language. Forms in bold type are used for fractions in technical language: *tres doceavos* 'three-twelfths'. They are used as ordinal numbers in Latin America: *la doceava parte de un sexenio* (Carlos Fuentes, Mex., dialogue) 'one twelfth of six years', and occasionally in Spain, although this is condemned by Seco (1998), 70, and by the *Libro de estilo* of *El País*.

undécimo eleventh ***onceavo***
duodécimo twelfth ***doceavo***
decimotercero thirteenth ***treceavo***
decimocuarto fourteenth ***catorceavo***
decimoquinto fifteenth ***quinceavo***
decimosexto sixteenth ***dieciseisavo***
decimoséptimo seventeenth ***diecisieteavo***
decimoctavo eighteenth ***dieciochavo***
decimonoveno/decimonono nineteenth ***diecinueveavo***
vigésimo twentieth ***veinteavo***
vigésimo/a primero/a twenty-first
vigésimo/a quinto/a etc. twenty-fifth ***veinticincavo***
trigésimo thirtieth ***treinta(a)vo***
trigésimo/a sexto/a thirty-sixth ***treintiseisavo***
cuadragésimo fortieth ***cuarenta(a)vo***
quincuagésimo fiftieth ***cincuenta(a)vo***

sexagésimo sixtieth ***sesenta(a)vo***
septuagésimo seventieth ***setenta(a)vo***
octogésimo eightieth ***ochenta(a)vo***
nonagésimo ninetieth ***noventa(a)vo***
centésimo (in common use) hundredth ***centavo***
ducentésimo two-hundredth
tricentésimo three-hundredth
cuadringentésimo four-hundredth
quingentésimo five-hundredth
sexcentésimo six-hundredth
septingentésimo seven-hundredth
octingentésimo eight-hundredth
noningentésimo nine-hundredth
milésimo (in common use) thousandth
dosmilésimo two-thousandth
cuatrocientosmilésimo four-hundred thousandth
millonésimo millionth

(i) In informal styles, written and spoken, ordinal forms over tenth are avoided and the ordinary cardinal number is used, e.g. *el veinticinco aniversario* 'the twenty-fifth anniversary', *la trescientas cincuenta reunión del comité* 'the 350th meeting of the committee', *faltaban quince días para mi cincuenta cumpleaños* (C. Martín Gaite, Sp., dialogue) 'there were fifteen days to go to my fiftieth birthday', *el tren de alta velocidad español está a punto de contabilizar su pasajero medio millón* (El País, Sp., instead of *quinientosmilésimo pasajero*) 'the Spanish High Speed Train is about to get (lit. 'enter in its accounts') its 500,000th passenger'.

(ii) **Decimoprimero, *decimosegundo*, for *undécimo, duodécimo*, are common mistakes in spoken Spanish.

(iii) Forms like *décimo tercero, décimo cuarto*, in which both words agree in number and gender, are nowadays old-fashioned. Joined forms like *vigesimoquinto/a, vigesimoséptimo/a*, etc. are also common for '21st' to '29th'.

(iv) When addition of *–avo* creates a double *a*, as in *treinta(a)vo*, the *a*s may be written single or double, the latter being usual among mathematicians, the former among non-specialists.

10.12.3 Position of ordinals

They usually precede, but used contrastively, or with titles, they may follow the noun, sometimes with a change of meaning:

en el tercer capítulo/en el capítulo tercero (latter order unusual)	in the third chapter
los tres párrafos primeros	the first three paragraphs (i.e. paras 1, 2 & 3)
los tres primeros párrafos	the three first paragraphs (i.e. para. 1 of three different chapters)
Isabel segunda (Isabel II)	Elizabeth the Second
por la enésima vez	for the umpteenth time

10.13 Distribution

cada cinco meses	every five months
Cada uno paga lo suyo	Each will pay his share
Di cien mil pesos a cada uno	I gave 100,000 pesos to each of them
Traían sendos ramilletes de flores (literary style, informally *cada uno traía un ramillete*)	Each bore a bouquet of flowers/Each one was carrying a bouquet

Use of *sendos* to mean 'several' (i.e. *varios*) is a common mistake on both continents.

10.14 Single, double, treble, etc.

un billete de ida	a one-way ticket
una habitación individual	a single room
todos y cada uno de los problemas	every single problem
con una sola excepción/con una excepción única	with a single exception
ni uno solo	not a single one
El aire contiene el doble de óxido de nitrógeno que en Washington (*Granma*, Cu.)	The air contains twice more nitrous oxide than in Washington
Mi sueldo es el doble del suyo	My salary is double his
el doble acristalamiento	double glazing
una cama de matrimonio	double bed
Duplicaron la suma	They doubled the sum
Esta cantidad es el triple de ésa/esa	This quantity is triple that

10.15 Dimensions and other numerical expressions

Este cuarto mide 2,5 (dos coma cinco) por *3,75 (tres coma setenta y cinco)*	This room measures 2.5 by 3.75
El área es de tres metros cuadrados	The area is three square metres
Forma un cuadrado de dos metros	It's two metres square
mil centímetros cúbicos	1000 cc
El cable tiene cien metros de largo/de *longitud*	The cable's 100m long
Tiene cinco metros de hondo/ancho	It's five metres/US meters deep/wide
un motor de ocho caballos	an 8-horsepower engine
un motor de dos tiempos	a two-stroke engine
un ángulo de treinta grados	a 30-degree angle
Forma un ángulo recto	It makes a right-angle
Debe haber cinco bajo cero	It must be five degrees below zero
números pares/impares/ primos	even/odd/prime numbers
dos nueveavos dividido por tres sieteavos (see 10.12.2 for discussion of *-avo*)	two-ninths divided by three-sevenths
diez elevado al cubo/sexto/noveno	ten to the third/sixth/ninth

10.16 Numerals: rules for writing

There is no universal agreement about the rules for writing numbers, but the following recommendations are based on *El País*'s *Libro de estilo*, 2002, Chapter 10:

Digits are used:

(**a**) for all numbers over nine: *siete, ocho,* 21, 5532;

(**b**) for all numbers when some are over nine: *3 ministros, 45 senadores y 100 diputados* 'three ministers, 45 senators and 100 members of Congress'. But approximate numbers are spelled out. See (**b**) below;

(**c**) in timetables: *salida a las 20.30* 'departure at 2030', *llegada a las 09.15* 'arrival at 0915'; note the use of the point in Spanish;

(**d**) for dates: *el 23 de marzo de 2006*; see 32.9.1 for more on the format of dates. Numbers are used for years (*1998, 2005*) but not for decades: *los años noventa* 'the nineties';

(**e**) for exact figures (e.g. ones that include decimals) and addresses: *2,38 kilómetros* '2.38 km', *58 por ciento* '58%', *419 páginas* '419 pages', *63 grados bajo cero* '63 degrees below zero', *Avenida de la Libertad 7, 2º izquierdo* '7 Liberty Avenue, left-hand flat/apartment on second floor', *N-342* 'National Highway 342'.

Words are used:

(**a**) for zero to nine inclusive: *cero, seis, ocho,* etc.;

(**b**) for time elapsed: *veinticinco años* 'twenty-five years', *han pasado quince segundos* 'fifteen seconds have gone by';

(**c**) for approximate figures: *hubo más de quinientos heridos* 'there were more than five hundred injured', *tengo mil y una cosas que hacer* 'I've got a thousand and one things to do';

(**d**) for numbers that are quoted as spoken by someone: *me dijo que quería comprar quince* '(s)he told me wanted to buy fifteen';

(**e**) for telling the time other than in timetables: *llegó a las diez y media/a las cuatro cuarenta y cinco* '(s)he arrived a 10.30'/'at 4.45'.

El País (Sp.) says in its *Libro de estilo* that one should not begin a sentence with a number except in headlines and abbreviated messages. It forbids its journalists to open with *Diez personas resultaron heridas. . .'* 'Ten persons were injured. . .'; better *Un total de diez personas resultaron heridas* (*Libro de estilo*, 10.10). This is not always observed in Latin America: *Tres personas murieron y 22 quedaron heridas...* (*El Comercio*, Pe.).

10.17 Telephone numbers

The *Libro de estilo* of *El País* recommends that telephone numbers should be expressed by pairs: 54 06 72, spoken as *cincuenta y cuatro–cero seis–setenta y dos*; and this is the usual way that phone numbers are said in Spanish. If the number of figures is uneven, the first group is written, and may be said, as a combination of hundreds: *542 67 22*, spoken as *quinientos–cuarenta y dos–sesenta y siete–veintidós*, or, usually, *cinco–cuarenta y dos–sesenta y siete–veintidós*. Extensions are sometimes written in brackets: 033 527 76 89 (19) = 033 527 7689 (ext. 19). Phone numbers are often written with hyphens separating the figures that are spoken as single numbers.

11

Personal pronouns

The main points discussed in this chapter are:

- Forms of personal pronouns (Section 11.1)
- Use of subject pronouns (Section 11.2)
- Formal and informal modes of address (*tú, vos* and *usted(es)*) (Section 11.3)
- *Nosotros* (Section 11.4)
- Forms of pronouns after prepositions (Section 11.5)
- The pronoun *sí* (Section 11.5.3)
- Pronouns and agreement (Section 11.6)
- First- and second-person object pronouns (*me, te, nos, os*) (Section 11.7)
- Object pronouns and verbs of motion (Section 11.8)
- Pronouns with *ser* and *resultar* (Section 11.9)
- 'Resumptive' *lo* with *ser* and *estar* (Section 11.10)
- Object pronouns used to show personal involvement (Section 11.11)
- Order of object pronouns (Section 11.12)
- Replacement of *le* by *se* (the 'rule of two l's') (Section 11.13)
- Position of object pronouns in sentences (Section 11.14)
- *Quiero verlo* or *lo quiero ver*? (Section 11.14.4)
- Emphasis of object pronouns (Section 11.15)
- 'Redundant' object pronouns (Section 11.16)

The use of the third-person object pronouns *le* and *lo* is discussed separately in Chapter 12. For possessive adjectives and pronouns, see Chapter 8. For the pronoun *se* and pronominal (i.e. 'reflexive') verbs in general, see Chapters 26 and 28.

11.1 Classification and forms

'Subject' pronouns are used to emphasize the subject of a verb: *yo hablo*, 'I am talking', *él duerme* 'he is sleeping'. See 11.2.1 for details about their use.

'Object' pronouns (other than third-person) are used for both direct and indirect objects: *te quiero* 'I love you', *te hablo* 'I'm talking **to** you'; *nos vio* '(s)he saw us', *nos dio* '(s)he gave (to) us'. This dual function means that there is no need to distinguish between 'direct' and 'indirect' object pronouns in Spanish except in the case of the third person, where the difference between the 'direct' object forms (*lo/la/los/las*) and the 'indirect' forms (*le/les*) does not exactly reflect the usual distinction between direct and indirect objects. This problem is discussed separately in Chapter 12.

'Prepositional' pronouns are used after most prepositions. See 11.5 for details.

Spanish Personal Pronouns

This table contains the personal pronoun forms currently in use:

SINGULAR

Person	Subject	Object	Prepositional		Remarks
1st	*yo*	*me*	*mí*	I, me	
2nd	*tú*	*te*	*ti* (no accent!)	you	informal: see 11.3.2
	vos	*te*	*vos*	you	informal: see 11.3.1
	usted	masc. *lo* or *le* fem. *la* or *le*	*usted*	you	formal: see 11.3.2
3rd masc.	*él*	*lo* or *le*	*él*	he, him	see 11.2.1–2
3rd fem.	*ella*	*la* or *le*	*ella*	she, her	see 11.2.1–2
3rd neuter	*ello*	*lo, le*	*ello*	it	see 7.3
'reflexive'		*se*	*sí*: see 11.5.3		chapters 26 & 28

PLURAL

Person	Subject	Object	Prepositional		Remarks
1st masc.	*nosotros*	*nos*	*nosotros*	we, us	see 11.4
1st fem.	*nosotras*	*nos*	*nosotras*	we, us	see 11.4
2nd masc.	*vosotros*	*os*	*vosotros*	you	informal: see 11.3.3
2nd fem.	*vosotras*	*os*	*vosotras*	you	informal: see 11.3.3
2nd formal	*ustedes*	masc. *los* or *les* fem. *las* or *les*	*ustedes*	you	formal: see 11.3.3
3rd masc.	*ellos*	*los*	*ellos*	they	see 11.2.1–2
3rd fem.	*ellas*	*las*	*ellas*	they	see 11.2.1–2
'reflexive'		*se*	*sí*: see 11.5.3		chapters 26 & 28

11.2 Use of subject pronouns

11.2.1 Emphasis and contrast

The identity of the subject of a Spanish verb is usually made clear by the verb ending: *hablo* 'I speak', *habló* 'he/she/you/it spoke', *vendimos* 'we sold', *salieron* 'they/you (*ustedes*) went out', etc. The forms *yo/tú/él/ella/usted(es)/ellos/ellas* are therefore usually only required for emphasis or contrast. It is a bad error, common among English-speakers, to use Spanish subject pronouns unnecessarily. As the *GDLE* 19.3.1 points out, **yo me vestí, y después yo fui a recoger a mi hijo, pero yo llegué tarde* is completely unacceptable for 'I got dressed, then I went to pick up my son, but I arrived late'. All the *yos* must be deleted except, perhaps, the first, and only if it is needed for one of the reasons given in this section.

The subject pronouns are used only:

(a) when the pronoun stands alone:

—*¿Quién ha venido?* —*Ellos*	'Who's come?' 'They have'
—*¿Quién lo ha hecho?* —*Nosotros*	'Who did it?' 'We did'
—*¿Quién es?* —*Yo*	'Who is it?' 'Me'

(b) When there is a change of subject (not necessarily within the same sentence) and the subjects are contrasted with one another:

Tú eres listo, pero ella es genial	You're clever but she's a genius
Mi mujer trabaja y yo me quedo en casa con los niños	My wife works and I stay at home with the children
¿Mami le cuenta a Dios que Mita no va a misa y que yo me porto mal? (M. Puig, Arg., dialogue)	Does Mummy tell God that Mita doesn't go to Mass and that I'm naughty?
—A París no llegamos nunca —le dio la razón Tita. —Perfecto —celebré yo (A. Bryce Echenique, Pe., dialogue)	'We'll never get to Paris,' Tita agreed. 'Great,' I said enthusiastically

Great confusion is caused by English-speakers who ignore this rule. *Mi hermana es médica y ella nunca está en casa* means 'my sister's a doctor and *she* (i.e. someone else) is never at home', whereas '*...y nunca está en casa* refers to my sister.

(c) To emphasize the subject pronoun (this is really only a case of **(b)** in which the other subject has been omitted):

Pues yo no quiero salir	Well **I** don't want to go out (even if you do)
Tú haz lo que te dé la gana	**You** do whatever you like (implies 'what do I care?')

(d) To clarify ambiguous verb endings: *yo tenía/él tenía* 'I had'/'he had', *que yo fuese/que él fuese* 'that I should go/be'/'that he should go/be', *yo estaba trabajando* 'I was working'. However, in such cases context often makes the meaning clear.

(i) English can focus on or emphasize almost any word simply by pronouncing it louder, e.g. 'you want to talk to **her** not to her **brother**'; but this use of loudness or stress usually produces an unfortunate effect in Spanish. The latter uses other devices, e.g. cleft sentences (*es con ella con la que deberías hablar, no con su hermano*; see 36.2) or changes of word order: *con ella deberías hablar, no con su hermano*.

Further examples (bold type in English shows stress and loudness): 'where are **you** going?' *¿tú adónde vas?/¿adónde vas tú?*', 'I'm talking to **you**' *contigo es con quien estoy hablando/te estoy hablando a ti*, 'what's **he** doing?' *¿y él qué está haciendo?/¿qué está haciendo él?*, '**you're** not coming with **us**' *con nosotros no vienes tú/tú con nosotros no vienes*'. See 11.15 and 37.5 for more remarks on this subject.

(ii) *Usted/ustedes* 'you' are used more frequently, either to avoid ambiguity or to emphasize the polite tone of an utterance: *¿adónde van ustedes?* 'where are you going?, *si (usted) quiere, iré con usted* 'if you like, I'll go with you'. See 11.3.4.

11.2.2 Subject pronouns for inanimate nouns

Él/ella/ellos/ellas may translate 'it' or 'them' when applied to non-living things, especially after prepositions: *no fuera de la casa sino dentro de ella* 'not outside the house but in it'. But they are taken to stand for human beings when they are used as the subject of a verb. One does not express *el viento sopla* 'the wind's blowing' as **él sopla*, which means 'he's blowing' (*sopla* = 'it's blowing'), and one cannot say **compré una mesa y un sillón. Él tiene tapizado de cuero y ella es de diseño italiano* for '*el sillón tiene... y la mesa es de...* 'I bought a table and an armchair. The chair is leather-covered and the table is of Italian design' (example from *GDLE* 19.2.2). Subject pronouns are, however, sometimes used in Latin America for a non-living subject where Peninsular speakers would use either no pronoun at all or an appropriate form of *éste* 'this'/'the latter' or *ése/aquél* 'the former':

> La *"oposición" ha desaparecido de la radio, de la televisión y de la prensa diaria en el Perú. **Ella** subsiste, mínima, hostigada, desde las columnas de todos los periódicos* (M. Vargas Llosa, Pe.)
>
> The 'opposition' has vanished from radio, television and the daily press in Peru. It continues to operate, minimal, harassed, from the opinion columns of all the newspapers

11.3 Formal and informal modes of address

11.3.1 *Voseo*

In Spain *vos* for 'you' is archaic, but it is used instead of *tú* in many parts of Latin America. *Vos* for *tú* is nowadays universal in Argentina, and students of this variety should use it (but see 16.2.8 for a note on the subjunctive forms used with *vos*). It is common in most social circles in Uruguay, Paraguay and most of Central America (in Costa Rica, for example, *tú* is considered unnatural), and it is also heard in the extreme south of Mexico. In Colombia, Ecuador and Venezuela it is often heard, and is possibly spreading, but may be considered 'lower-class' or provincial, although usage and attitudes vary locally: in Chile, for example, it is shunned by the middle and upper classes (see 11.3.2 note iii for further remarks on Chile). It is not usual in Bolivia, Peru, Panama, Cuba, central and northern Mexico, and Puerto Rico, but there are pockets of *voseo* in some of these countries.

The possessive adjective for *vos* is *tu/tus*, the object pronoun is *te*, and the prepositional form is *vos*: *¿te das cuenta de que estoy hablando de vos y de tu amiga?* 'do you realize I'm talking about you and your friend?' The verb forms used with *vos* fluctuate according to region and are best learned locally. For the verb forms used in Buenos Aires see 13.1.and 16.2.8.

Vos was once used as a polite second-person singular pronoun in Spain, and it survived there until the 1830s, to judge by Larra's *Artículos de costumbres*. It is still used in Spain in ritual language in official documents, in some prayers, when addressing the King on very formal occasions, and in pseudo-archaic styles, e.g. in Buero Vallejo's play *Las meninas*. In Spain this archaic *vos* takes the normal verb endings for *vosotros*, and the possessive adjective/pronoun is *vuestro/a/os/as*.

11.3.2 *Tú (vos) or usted?*

In Spain *tú* is nowadays used for persons with whom one is on first-name terms (but see note i), i.e. between friends, fellow workers, family members, to children and animals, and in prayers. It is also much used between strangers under the age of about forty. *Tú* is therefore used far more than the French *tu* or German *Du*, and it is more common than fifty years ago. However *tú* (or *vos* in Latin America) should not be used anywhere to persons in authority or to elderly persons unless they invite its use. Use of *tú* where *usted* is expected may express over-familiarity, contempt or threat: muggers call their victims *tú*, not *usted*.

In most of Latin America *tú* (or *vos*) is used less readily than in Spain and learners should probably err on the side of caution by sticking to *usted(es)* with strangers, except children. One finds varieties, e.g. Antioquía in Colombia, and Uruguay, where all three pronouns, *usted*, *tú* and *vos*, may be used in the course of a single conversation, depending on the degree of intimacy reached at any moment. Chilean Spanish is unusual in that *usted* can be used as well as *tú* for familiar address. In the following extract from a Chilean play an upper-class mother sitting on the beach calls to her little son: *Alvarito, **métase** un poco al agua. **Mójese** las patitas siquiera. . . ¿**Ves** que es rica el agüita?* (S. Vodanovic) 'Alvarito, go into the water a bit. At least get your feet wet. Do you see how lovely the water is?' See also note (iii) for *tú* in Chile.

(i) *Usted* and a first name can be combined when one wishes to mark a distance from someone well-known, e.g. an employee: *bueno, Pura, pues hasta mañana. Y cierre al salir* (C. Martín Gaite, Sp., spoken to the maid) 'Right, Pura, well, see you tomorrow. And shut the door on the way out'. *Usted* is also used to elderly persons when they are addressed respectfully as *don* + their first name: *¿cómo está usted, don Roberto?*

(ii) In some families, especially in rural areas, *usted(es)* is used to address grandparents, but the custom is dying.

(iii) Students of Chilean Spanish will hear special endings used with *tú* (*voseo* is not usual in Chile). These resemble the standard *vosotros* forms minus the final *–s*: *tú estay* (*estás*), *tú soy* (*tú eres*), *tú hablay* (*hablas*), *tú viví* (*vives*). *–Er* verbs take *–í*: *tú comí* (*comes*), *tení* (*tienes*). These forms are confined to very familiar language.

11.3.3 *Vosotros/as or ustedes?*

Vosotros (*vosotras* to females) is the plural of *tú* and is used in Spain for two or more persons in the same circumstances as *tú* is used for one person. It is universal in standard Peninsular Spanish, but in Latin America only *ustedes* is used in all but archaic styles, a phenomenon also found in the Canary Islands and locally in popular speech in Southern Spain. A Latin-American mother addresses her child as *tú* or, in some places, *vos*, and her children as *ustedes*. Even animals are called *ustedes* in Latin America.

Vosotros and its possessive *vuestro* is found in business correspondence, flowery speeches and similar solemn texts in Latin America, cf. *. . .dada la recomposición de relaciones entre la Argentina y vuestro país* '. . .given the re-establishment of relations between Argentina and your country' (from a business letter sent to England). The reason is apparently that since *vosotros* is archaic in Latin America it sounds appropriate in very elevated styles. But in Spain it is in fact familiar in tone.

11.3.4 Use of *usted, ustedes*

Usted is a formal or polite pronoun meaning 'you' and is similar to the French *vous*, German *Sie*—but French and German usage is a poor guide, so see 11.3.2 and 11.3.3 for details of their relationship with *tú/vos*. In Spain *ustedes* is the plural of *usted* and is reserved for formal situations, but in Latin America it is both familiar and formal, and is the only second-person plural subject pronoun in daily use.

Since they descend from the archaic formula *Vuestra Merced* 'Your Grace', they require third-person verb forms: *usted habla* 'you speak', *ustedes hablan* 'you (plural) speak'. *Usted/ustedes* may optionally be abbreviated to *V./Vs.*, *Vd./Vds.*, or *Ud./Uds* in official documents or business letters, but the full, lower-case forms *usted/ustedes* are now most common. Object forms of *usted/ustedes* are discussed under third-person pronouns (11.7.3 and Chapter 12).

(i) As subject pronouns *usted/ustedes* need only appear once at the beginning of a text or utterance and then occasionally thereafter to recall the polite tone. Whereas total omission of *usted/ustedes* may sound too informal, constant repetition may sound obsequious.

(ii) When one subject is *tú* or *vosotros/as* and the other *usted* or *ustedes*, agreement is as for *ustedes*: *tú y usted, quédense aquí* 'you and you stay here'.

(iii) Use of *vosotros* endings with *ustedes*, e.g. *ustedes habláis* for *ustedes hablan*, is common in popular speech in parts of Andalusia for the normal *vosotros habláis*, etc.

11.4 *Nosotros/as, nos*

Females referring to themselves and to other females should use *nosotras*.

The first-person plural is constantly used in books and articles when the author is modestly referring to her/himself. It is less pompous than the English 'royal We': *en este trabajo hemos procurado enfocar el problema de la inflación desde...* 'in this work I ('we') have tried to approach the problem of inflation from...'.

Nos for *nosotros* is obsolete, but is used by popes, bishops and monarchs in official documents or ritual language.

(i) The following construction is peculiar to Latin America, especially the Southern Cone, Peru and Colombia: *fuimos con* mi hermano... (Sp. *fui con mi hermano/mi hermano y yo fuimos*) 'I went with my brother' (lit. 'we went with my brother'), *y así nos fuimos a la Patagonia, con Matilde* (E. Sábato, Arg., interview; Sp. *fui con Matilde/Matilde y yo fuimos*) 'so Matilde and I went to Patagonia'.

11.5 Forms of pronouns after prepositions

11.5.1 Use after prepositions

Only *yo*, *tú* and *se* have separate prepositional forms: *mí*, *ti* and *sí* (the latter discussed at 11.5.3). In the other cases the normal subject forms, *él, ella, ello, nosotros/as, vosotros/as, usted/ustedes, ellos/ellas*, are used after prepositions. *Mí* and *sí* have an accent to distinguish them from *mi* 'my' and *si* 'if'. *Ti* has no accent, a fact constantly forgotten by foreigners and natives alike:

No sabe nada de mí	(S)he knows nothing about me
No tengo nada contra ti	I've nothing against you
Creo en vos (Argentina, etc.)	I believe in you
no delante de usted	not in front of you
Me refiero a él/ella	I'm referring to him/her
Confiamos en ustedes/vosotros/vosotras	We trust in you
Corrió tras ellos	(S)he ran after them
aparte de ellas	except for them (fem.)

Seven prepositions or preposition-like words require the ordinary form of all the subject pronouns (but the pronoun *se* obeys slightly different rules: see 11.5.3 note i). These are: *entre* 'between'/'among' (but see note iv), *excepto* 'except', *hasta* when it means 'even' rather than 'as far as', *incluso* 'including'/'even', *menos* 'except', *salvo* 'except'/'save', *según* 'according to':

Todos lo hicieron menos/excepto/salvo tú	They all did it except/save you
Que se quede entre tú y yo	Let's keep it between you and me
Hasta tú puedes hacer eso	Even you can do that
según tú y él	according to you and him

(i) It is necessary to repeat the preposition after conjunctions (*y, o*): *para ti y para mí* 'for you and me', not **para ti y mí*; *para Mamá y para ti* 'for Mother and you', not **para Mamá y ti*.

(ii) Note the set phrases *de tú a tú* 'on equal terms', *hablar de tú* (i.e. *tutear*) 'to address someone as *tú*'.

(iii) For constructions like *?detrás tuyo* for *detrás de ti* 'behind you', or *?delante mío* for *delante de mí* 'in front of me', see 8.7.

(iv) *Mí* is used after *entre* in the set phrase *entre mí* as in *esto va a acabar mal, decía entre mí* 'this is going to end badly, I said to myself'.

There is a popular tendency in some regions to use the prepositional forms with *entre* when this refers to actual spatial location: *esta noche a la Inés la voy a poner a dormir en mi cama, entre mí y la Pelusa* (M. Puig, Arg., dialogue; Sp. *entre la Pelusa y yo*) 'tonight I'm going to put Inés to sleep in my bed between me and Pelusa' (*la Inés* for *Inés* is popular style; see 3.2.21).

11.5.2 *Conmigo, contigo*

These special forms are used instead of *con + yo, con + tú*: *¿vienes conmigo?* 'are you coming with me?', *no quiero discutir contigo* 'I don't want to argue with you'. In areas of *voseo, contigo* is rarely heard: *no quiero discutir con vos* 'I don't want to argue with you'.

11.5.3 *Sí, consigo*

These are special prepositional forms of the pronoun *se*. *Sí* is used after prepositions other than *con*: the accent distinguishes it from *si* meaning 'if'. *Consigo* is used for *con + se* and means 'with him/herself'. *Sí* is combined with *mismo* when it is used reflexively: *se lavan a sí mismos* 'they wash themselves'. In other cases use of *mismo* with *sí* is variable, with no clear agreement among native speakers.

No se refiere a sí misma	She's not referring to herself
Este fenómeno ya es muy interesante de por sí	This phenomenon is in itself very interesting
Un brillante que para sí lo quisieran muchos (advert., Sp.)	a diamond many would like for themselves
Volvió en sí	(S)he came round (regained consciousness)
Colocó el vaso junto a sí (Luis Ortega, Cu.)	He put the glass next to himself
...tan perezosa que difícilmente era capaz de leer por sí sola	...so lazy that she was hardly able to read by herself
No puede dar más de sí	(S)he's doing the best (s)he can
Está disgustada consigo misma	She's cross with herself

NB: Some speakers insist on adding *mismo* to *sí* and do not accept phrases like *junto a sí* without it.

(i) *Se* is unique in being the only pronoun requiring a prepositional form after *entre*: *entre tú y yo* 'between you and me', but *entre sí* 'among themselves': *hablan castellano entre sí* (or *entre ellos*) 'they speak Spanish among themselves'. *Decía Juan entre sí* means 'John was saying to himself'; see 11.5.1 (iv).

(ii) *Sí* can sometimes mean 'one another', as in *el acento sirve para que los ingleses se distingan entre sí* 'accent enables Englishmen to distinguish themselves from one another'.

(iii) There is a colloquial tendency, frowned on by the Academy, to retain *sí* in the first and second persons of *volver en sí* 'to regain consciousness' and *dar de sí* 'to give of oneself'. One hears *recobré el conocimiento* (correct) or even *volví en sí*, but the expected *volví en mí* is often avoided, even by educated speakers (although it is heard: the last of the following examples reflects the hesitation of some people): *volví en sí ya estando en la clínica* (interview, *El Nacional*, Mex.) 'I came round when I was (lit. 'already being') in the clinic', *—Perdona, ¿no te importa ponerte de pie para que te veamos? —Estoy de pie, es que no doy más de sí* (E. Arenas, Sp., dialogue) 'Excuse me, would you mind standing up so we can see you?' 'I *am* standing up. This is all there is of me', *cuando volví en sí, o en mí, escuché un rumor* (S. Puértolas, Sp., dialogue) 'when I came round I heard a noise'.

(iv) There is a good deal of disagreement about *sí* in the modern language. *Sí* is required when it does not refer to identified persons: *hay personas que hablan mucho de sí (mismas)* 'there are people who talk about themselves a lot'. It is also required in reflexive sentences where it is the reinforced direct object of the verb: *se lava a sí mismo* 'he's washing himself', *se criticó a sí misma* 'she criticized herself'; never *...a él mismo, a ella misma....*

But in other cases when *sí* refers to a specific person, the modern tendency is to prefer a non-reflexive prepositional pronoun. In answer to a questionnaire, the great majority of informants (professional people and students, Spanish) rejected *sí* in the following sentences: *hablan francés entre ellos (?entre sí)* 'they speak French among themselves', *lo mantuvo contra ella con uno de sus brazos* (E. Sábato, Arg.) 'she held him against herself with one arm', *tenía las manos apoyadas en la barra, delante de él (ante sí)* 'his hands were resting on the bar, in front of him(self)'. In the previous example, *ante sí* is tolerable, since *ante* is itself literary; but *delante de él* is normal in speech, although some speakers respect the difference between 'in front of him(self)' and 'in front of him' (someone else). *Sí* is obligatory in set phrases like *de por sí* 'in itself', *por sí, en sí (mismo)* 'in itself'.

(v) *Sí* seems to be avoided with *usted*, probably because the latter is unconsciously felt to be second-person while *sí* is third-person: *usted tiene ante usted a un hombre que...* (interview, *El Nacional*, Mex.) 'you have before you a man who...', *guárdeselo para usted* 'keep it for yourself', *yo sé que usted toca para usted misma* (J. Cortázar, Arg., dialogue) 'I know you play (music) for yourself'.

(vi) The French pronoun *soi* has suffered a similar decline over the years, and has been replaced in many contexts by *lui-même, elle-même* (*él mismo, ella misma*).

11.6 Pronoun agreement in English and Spanish

Verbs sometimes agree with personal pronouns in ways strange to English-speakers:

Soy yo/Somos nosotros/Fuisteis	It's me/It's us/It was you/It was them
vosotros/Fueron ellos	(lit. 'I am me', 'we are we', 'you were
	you', 'they were they')

El feo de la foto **eres** *tú* — The ugly one in the photo is you
Debería volver a escribir, pero no tiene — She ought to start writing again, but
estímulos ya. Y luego que tampoco la — there's nothing to stimulate her any
ayudamos nadie (C. Martín Gaite, — more. And after all, none of us helps
Sp., dialogue) — her either
—*¿Quién ha dicho eso?* —**He** *sido yo* — 'Who said that?' 'It was me'
[any second- or third-person] *y yo* or — You/(S)he and I are going
nosotros **vamos**
Tú or *vosotros y* [*usted(es)* or third — You and (s)he/you are going
person] **van**
Él y usted(es) [or any third-person — He and you/they are going
pronoun] **van**

When answering the phone one says *soy Ana* 'it's Ana', literally 'I'm Ana', *soy Antonio* 'it's Antonio speaking'. *Es Ana* 'it's Ana' is only possible when said by someone else about her.

11.7 Object pronouns

The term 'object pronouns' is used in this book to refer to *me, te, lo, la, le, nos, os, los, las, les* and *se*.

Traditional grammars often divide these pronouns into two lists, 'direct object' pronouns, and 'indirect object' pronouns; but only the third-person set has two forms, *lo/la/los/las* as opposed to *le/les*, and the difference between them is not always the traditional distinction between 'direct' and 'indirect' objects; this problem is discussed separately in Chapter 12. For 'pronominal' verbs (sometimes inaccurately called 'reflexive' verbs), see Chapter 26.

11.7.1 Forms of first- and second-person object pronouns

Subject pronoun	Singular	Plural
yo, nosotros/nosotras	*me* 'me'	*nos* 'us'
tú, vosotros/vosotras	*te* 'you' (familiar)	*os* 'you' (familiar)

(i) *Usted/Ustedes* take third-person object pronouns: *los* (in Spain also *les*) *vi a ustedes ayer* 'I saw you (plural) yesterday'. See 11.7.3.

(ii) *Te* is the object form of *tú* and also of *vos* where *vos* is used: see 11.3.1.

(iii) *Os* corresponds to *vosotros* and is therefore not heard in Latin America, where *ustedes* is used for both polite and familiar address: see 11.3.3.

11.7.2 Uses of first- and second-person object pronouns

The main problem that these and the third-person object pronouns pose for English-speakers is the wide range of meanings they seem to have. Spanish object pronouns merely indicate the person or thing 'affected' by a verb phrase: they do not clearly indicate *how* the object is affected. This must be worked out from the meaning of the verb, from context or by common sense. English makes the meaning clear by using prepositions, as can be seen from the following thirteen different translations of *me*:

Me han visto	They've seen **me**
Me dejó una finca	(S)he left an estate **to me**
Me ha aparcado el coche	(S)he's parked the car **for me**
Me compró una agenda	(S)he bought a diary **off/from me/for me**
Me sacaron tres balas	They took three bullets **out of me**
Me han quitado a mis hijos	They've taken my children **from me** (or 'they have taken me away from my children')
Me tiene envidia	(S)he's envious **of me**
Me tiró una bola de nieve	(S)he threw a snowball **at me**
Me encontraron mil pesetas	They found 1000 pesetas **on me**
Me echaron una manta	They threw a blanket **over me**
Voy a comprarme un helado	I'm going to buy **myself** an ice-cream
Siempre me pone pegas	(S)he always finds fault **with me**
Me rompió el brazo	(S)he broke **my** arm

For more examples, see Lists A and B (at 12.3 and 12.4), where *me/te/os/nos* can be substituted for *le/les* or *lo/la/los* if the meaning permits it.

A special case arises when the object pronoun and the subject pronoun (usually indicated by the verb ending) refer to the same person or thing, e.g. *me lavo* 'I'm washing (myself)', *te equivocaste* 'you were mistaken', *Miguel se va* 'Miguel's leaving', *nos caímos* 'we fell over'. We call such verbs 'pronominal verbs' and discuss them in Chapter 26.

11.7.3 Use of 3rd-person object pronouns

The distinction between *le/les* and *lo/las/los/las* is discussed in Chapter 12. These overworked pronouns also have a second-person meaning since they are used for *usted/ustedes* 'you':

Doctora Smith, le aseguro que la llamé ayer	Dr Smith (fem.), I assure you I rang you/her yesterday
Le vi ayer (Spain only; see 12.5.1 & 2)	I saw you/him yesterday
Lo vi ayer (Latin America and, optionally, Spain too)	I saw it/him/you yesterday
Los vi ayer	I saw you/them yesterday

11.7.4 Constraints on the number of object pronouns

Spanish allows the following combinations of object pronouns before a verb:

(a) One direct object pronoun: *la vi* 'I saw her/it', *nos conocen* 'they know us';

(b) One indirect object pronoun *me dijiste* 'you said to me', *les hablé* 'I spoke to them/you';

(c) An indirect object pronoun followed by a direct object pronoun *me lo diste* 'you gave it to me', *se lo dieron* 'they gave it to him/her/you/them', *te lo pusiste* 'you put it on (yourself)'.

(d) Occasionally, two indirect object pronouns: *me le has estropeado la camisa* 'you've spoilt his shirt for me!' This is not very common: see 11.11 and 11.12 for a discussion;

(e) Infrequently, a direct object followed by an indirect object, as in *¡qué guapa te me has puesto!* 'how attractive you have made yourself for me!': see 11.12 (iii).

The combination of two *direct* object pronouns is not possible in Spanish and very peculiar in English, cf. ?'he was declared president, and after they declared **him it**, he went on to...', which would have to be recast in Spanish: *después de que le/lo nombraran presidente, pasó a... .* This constraint on the use of direct object pronouns in Spanish clarifies the difference between passive and impersonal *se*. See 28.5.2;

(i) For the impossibility of **lo y la vi for 'I saw him and her', see 11.12 (iv).

11.8 Pronouns with verbs of motion

Object pronouns cannot replace the preposition *a* plus a noun if mere physical arrival or approach is involved: *voy a la reunión—voy allí* (not *le voy) 'I'm going to the meeting'—'I'm going to it'; *acude a ella* '(s)he goes to her', not *le acude:

Cuando él tiene problemas siempre va a ella	When he has problems he always goes to her
Me dirijo a ustedes	I'm turning to you/addressing you/ writing to you
todo el occidente que vino a nosotros... (M. Vargas Llosa, Pe.)	the whole of the west (i.e. western world) which came to us...
Suele recurrir a él cuando no le queda más remedio	(S)he usually turns to him when (s)he has no alternative

However, object pronouns are often used colloquially with the following verbs, particularly if the verb is third-person:

Él se le acercó por la espalda (J. Marsé, Sp.)	He approached her from behind
Ella se le reunió al doblar la esquina (L. Goytisolo, Sp.)	She caught up with him as she turned the corner
Hoy, el que se te acerca es a menudo un drogadicto (A. Bryce Echenique, Pe., dialogue)	Nowadays, the person coming up to you is often a drug-addict
No sólo los sollozos de los niños se alzaron entonces, sino que se les unieron los de los sirvientes (J. Donoso, Ch.)	Not only did the children's sobs ring out, but the servants' sobbing was added to it

(i) This construction is rare in the first and second persons: *se le opuso* '(s)he opposed him/her', but *te opusiste a él* 'you opposed him' rather than ?*te le opusiste*. First- and second-person forms are more common in Latin America, especially Mexico (J. Lope Blanch, 1991, 20), so one finds sentences like *te ruego que te nos incorpores* (for ...*que te incorpores a nosotros*) 'I'm asking you to join us', *me le acerqué y le dije...* (J. L. Borges, Arg.) 'I went up to him and said to him...'.

(ii) *Se le puso delante, se me puso delante* '(s)he stood in front of him/her', '(s)he/you stood in front of me' occur colloquially for *se puso delante de él/se puso delante de mí*, and are more dramatic in tone.

(iii) The example from José Donoso unusually breaks the rule that object pronouns are not used with such verbs when the sentence refers to non-human things: the normal construction would be *se unieron a ellos*. One says for *se acercaron al puente* 'they approached the bridge', *se acercaron a él* 'they approached it', not **se le acercaron*.

(iv) Object pronouns are used with *llegar*, *venirse* and *venir con* when their object is human: *cuando me llegó la noticia de su triunfo...* 'when news of his/her/your triumph reached me...', *el armario se le vino encima* 'the cupboard/US closet collapsed on him/her/you', *a mí no me venga usted con cuentos porque yo todo lo sé* (A. Bryce Echenique, Pe., dialogue) 'don't come to me with stories because I know all about it'.

(v) In *le viene a decir que...* '(s)he's coming to tell him/her that...' the *le* belongs to the *decir*: *viene a decirle que...* In *le viene bien* 'it suits him/her' and *¿qué tal te va?* 'how are things going'/'how're you doing?', advantage, not motion, is involved.

11.9 Pronouns with *ser* and *resultar*

(a) With adjectives:

The choice is between *me es necesario* and *es necesario para mí* 'it's necessary for me'. The former is possible with *ser* only if the adjective expresses a meaning included in List A in section 12.3. *Resultar* allows the construction with a wider range of adjectives, and may be thought of as the 'involving' counterpart of *ser*:

Les es/resulta necesario	It's necessary for them
Me es/resulta importante	It's important to me
Nos era imprescindible contactar a sus padres	We absolutely had to contact her/his parents
Le era más fácil soportar los dolores ajenos que los propios (G. García Márquez, Col.)	It was easier for him to put up with other people's suffering than his own
Voy a serle muy franca (A. Bryce Echenique, Pe., dialogue)	I'm going to be very frank with you

But

La casa era demasiado blanca para mí/me resultaba demasiado blanca (not **me era demasiado blanca*)	The house was too white for me
Era muy feo para ella/ Le resultaba muy feo	It/He was very ugly for her

The following list shows the kind of adjective that can take object pronouns with *ser*:

aconsejable advisable	*indiferente* indifferent
agradable/desagradable agreeable/ disagreeable	*leal* loyal
ajeno strange	*molesto* bothersome
conocido/desconocido known/unknown	*necesario/innecesario* necessary/ unnecessary
conveniente/inconveniente suitable/ unsuitable	*permitido/prohibido* allowed/prohibited
doloroso painful	*posible/imposible* possible/impossible
fácil/difícil easy/difficult	*simpático/antipático* nice/nasty (persons)
familiar familiar	*sincero, franco* sincere, frank
fiel/infiel faithful/unfaithful	*suficiente/insuficiente* sufficient/insufficient
grato/ingrato pleasing/displeasing	*urgente* urgent
	útil/inútil useful/useless

(i) Many of these adjectives could also be constructed with *para* or *con*: *¿tan difícil te es vivir conmigo?* (A. Buero Vallejo, Sp., dialogue) or *¿tan difícil es para ti vivir conmigo?* 'is it so hard for you to live with me?', *es conveniente para ellos/les es conveniente* 'it's suitable for/to them', *voy a ser franco con usted/le voy a ser franco* 'I'll be frank with you'. The object pronouns convey a higher level of personal involvement.

(ii) *Grande, pequeño* take *le/les* if they mean 'too big', 'too small' (note use of *estar*): *ese puesto le está grande* 'that job's too big for him'. Otherwise *resultar* or *ser para* must be used: *es/resulta grande para él* 'it's big to/for him', etc.

(iii) The nuance conveyed by *resultar* is often almost untranslatable. Compare *es feo* = 'it/he's ugly' and *resulta feo* 'the effect is ugly'/'he/it is ugly as a result'.

(**b**) *Ser* plus personal pronouns with nouns:

This occurs only with a few nouns, most derived from or close in meaning to the adjectives listed above.

Si le es molestia, dígamelo	If it's a nuisance for you, tell me
Nos es de interés. . .	It's of interest to us…
Me/Le era un gran placer/Era un gran	It was a great pleasure for/to me/him, etc.
placer para mí/él	

(i) Spanish does not allow a pronominal construction in translations of sentences like 'I was always a good mother to him': *siempre fui una buena madre para él* (not **siempre le fui. . .*).

(ii) *Resultar* has limited use with nouns: *pues atrévase a contarla…. Resultaría una gran novela* (C. Martín Gaite, Sp., dialogue) 'well have the courage to tell it [*la historia*]…. It would make a great novel', *mi temporada aquí me está resultando un verdadero viaje de estudios* (J. L. Borges, Arg.) 'my stay here is turning out to be a real study trip for me', *la señorita María ha resultado una excelente secretaria* (J. J. Arreola, Mex.) 'Señorita María has turned out to be an excellent secretary', *si le resulta un problema. . .* 'if it turns out to be a problem for you…'.

11.10 'Resumptive' *lo* with *ser*, *estar*, *parecer* and *hay*

The predicate of *ser, estar* and *parecer* is echoed or resumed by *lo*: —*Parece buena la tierra desde aquí.* —*Lo es.* '"The land looks good from here." "It is."' This construction is discussed at 7.4.1. For *lo hay, los hay/las hay*, etc., see 30.2.2.

11.11 Object pronouns used to denote personal involvement

Object pronouns may simply show that a person is intensely affected, as in the indignant Frenchman's *regardez-moi ça!* 'just look at that for me!', 'just look at that, will you!' Usually the effect is untranslatable in standard English, but popular English sometimes uses 'on me', 'on you', etc., to include the person affected: *se me han ido de casa* 'they've left home "on me"', *se le ha averiado el coche* 'his/her car's broken down "on him/her"'. In Spanish this device is most common when there is a strong emotional involvement on the speaker's part, e.g. when parents are speaking about their children:

Me le has estropeado tres camisas	You've spoilt three of his shirts for me
—*Pues, yo eché a una porque me fumaba y ahora tengo otra que, además de fumar, me bebe* (E. Arenas, Sp., dialogue, very colloquial)	Well, I fired one [maid] because she smoked ('on me') and now I've got another who not only smokes but drinks ('on me')
Los alumnos se me habían largado a una manifestación (A. Bryce Echenique, Pe., dialogue)	The students (better 'my students') had gone off to a demonstration
No estará pensando embalsamarnos al Presidente. . . (I. Allende, Ch., dialogue)	You aren't thinking of having the President embalmed for us?
Mi suegra compró un reloj y al mes no le caminaba (A. Arrafut, Cu., dialogue; Sp. *No le funcionaba*)	My mother-in-law bought a watch and a month later it didn't work ('on her')
Sírvamele un café a la señorita (Arg., quoted García, 1975; possible, but rare in Spain)	Serve a coffee to the young lady for me
Cuídamele (or *cuídamelo*) *bien*	Look after him well for me
Péiname al niño	Do the child's hair for me

This device of including an emotionally involved person is used more in parts of Latin America than in Spain. *Me le pintaste la mesa* 'you painted the table for him/her for me' is acceptable for some Latin American speakers, but, with some exceptions, European Spanish tends to avoid clusters of two indirect object pronouns, as is explained in note (i) of the next section.

11.12 Order of object pronouns

The invariable order of object pronouns when two or more appear together is:

1	2	3	4
se	*te/os*	*me/nos*	*le/lo/la/les/los/las*

i.e. *se*, if it occurs, comes first-, second-person precedes first-person, and third-person pronouns come last:

María te lo dijo	Maria told it to you
Me lo habré dejado en casa	I must have left it at home
No querían comunicárnoslo	They didn't want to tell it to us
¿Por qué no se lo prueba?	Why don't you try it on?
Se te ha caído la tinta	You've dropped the ink
Nos los vamos a comprar	We're going to buy them for ourselves
Se nos ha vuelto listísimo	He's turned into a genius 'on us'
Yo me le fui encima, pero ella chilló (J. Cortázar, Arg.; Sp. *yo me le eché encima*)	I lunged at her, but she screamed
¿Se te ha comido la lengua el gato?	Has the cat eaten your tongue?

(i) As mentioned at 11.7.4, the combinations of two indirect object pronouns is quite rare in Peninsular Spanish, but not unknown: *te le dieron una paliza terrible* 'they gave him/her a terrific blow "on you"/"for you"', *échamele un vistazo a esta carta* 'have a look at this letter for me'; *hágasemeles un buen recibimiento* 'make sure for me that they get a good reception' (from *GDLE* 30.7.1.2). But in practice it is usually avoided when the first pronoun is not *me*, so the following are not found: **te le dieron malas notas* 'they gave him/her bad grades "on you"', **nos te dieron una multa* 'they gave you a fine "on us"'.

In Spain *le* is constantly used as a direct object pronoun referring to human males, so the following is possible: *al abuelo nos le llevamos de vacaciones todos los años* 'we take grandfather with us on holiday every year'. But even this is usually avoided by replacing the *le* by *lo*: *al abuelo nos lo llevamos.* . . .

(ii) Reversal of the correct order with *se*, e.g. *?me se ha caído* for *se me ha caído* 'I've dropped it' (lit. 'it's fallen down "on me"'), *?¿me se oye?* for *¿se me oye?* 'can anyone hear me?'/'is anyone listening?', is a well-known mistake of uneducated speech.

(iii) In all the examples given, the pronouns are in the order indirect object—direct object (*te lo doy* 'I give it to you', *se lo tragaron* 'they swallowed it', etc.).

However, if *te me criticaron* means 'they criticized you to me' (IO-DO), how does one say 'they criticized me to you' (DO-IO)? Apparently the same order is used for both meanings, so **te me** *recomendaron/alabaron/criticaron/ presentaron* 'they recommended/praised/criticized/introduced you to me' could also be understood as '...me to you': the *GDLE* 19.5.7 can find no explanation for this breakdown in the normal rules of pronoun order. In practice the problem is avoided, e.g. by dropping the *te* and simply saying *me recomendaron*, etc. There is no problem if the verb-form makes the meaning clear: *¡qué guapa te me* **has** *puesto!* displays the unusual order direct object-indirect object, but can only mean 'how attractive you have become for/to me!'

In the case of pronominal verbs of motion, the 'reflexive' pronoun (here *te*) is certainly not a direct object (it is not clear what it is), so *no te me escaparás* 'you won't escape from me', *te me fuiste de casa* 'you left home "on me"' are normal.

(iv) One can never join these unstressed pronouns with 'and', 'but' or any other word: 'I saw him and her' is **never** **lo y la vi*. The only possibility is to use the contrastive forms (11.15a): *lo/le vi a él y la vi a ella* or *los vi a él y a ella*. 'I saw him but not her' is *lo/le vi a él pero no a ella*.

(v) Identical pronouns cannot appear side by side, so combinations like *me me, se se* cannot occur (see 26.11 for how to avoid the latter). This also applies to combinations *lo/la/los/las* with *le* or *les*. See next section.

11.13 Replacement of *le* by *se*

11.13.1 *Se* for *le* when the latter is followed by a pronoun beginning with *l*

If *le* or *les* are immediately followed by an object pronoun beginning with *l*, i.e. by *lo, la, los* or *las*, the *le* or *les* must be replaced by *se*: *le doy* 'I give to him/her/you' + *lo* 'it' > *se lo doy* 'I give **it** to him/her/you'—**never** **le lo doy*:

Quiero dárselo	I want to give it to him/her/you/them
Se lo dije a ella	I told her
Se lo dije a ellos	I told them (masc.)
¿Quiere usted que se lo envuelva?	Do you want me to wrap it for you?
El guiso está a punto, pero no se lo voy a servir todavía	The stew's ready but I'm not going to serve it to you (*usted* or *ustedes*) yet

This phenomenon, which has no counterpart in French, Italian or Portuguese, is traditionally explained by the 'ugliness' of too many *l*'s. This explanation is implausible, but it helps to remind students that in Spanish two object pronouns beginning with *l* can *never* stand side by side. This is a strong rule: combinations of pronouns like **le lo*, **le la*, **le los*, **les lo*, **les los* are not heard anywhere in the Spanish-speaking world.

11.13.2 Latin American *se los* for *se lo*

The combination *se* + neuter *lo* is very ambiguous. *Se lo dije* may mean 'I told it to him, her, you (*usted*)', 'them' (*ellos* or *ellas*) or 'you' (*ustedes*)'. *A él/ella/usted/ellos/ ellas/ustedes* may be added if context does not make the issue clear: *se lo dije a ustedes* 'I told you', etc.

There is a widespread tendency in spontaneous Latin-American speech to show that *se* stands for *les* by pluralizing the direct object pronoun, i.e. *?se los dije*, for *se lo dije a ellos/ellas* 'I told it to them':

*A un policía le había gustado más bien poco la gracia y se **los** había dicho* (J. Cortázar, Arg., dialogue, for *se lo había dicho*)	One policeman really didn't like the joke and told them so
*sin que nadie se **los** hubiera dicho* (M. Vargas Llosa, Pe. = *se lo hubiera dicho*)	without anyone telling them

DeMello (1992), 1, reports that in Mexico City this construction is of about equal frequency in educated and uneducated speech, and it is apparently on the way to tacit acceptance throughout Latin America, although less common in Lima, La Paz and a few other places. It is vehemently rejected in Spain.

11.14 Position of object pronouns

The position of object pronouns in relation to a verb depends on the form of the verb.

11.14.1 Pronouns with finite verbs (see Glossary)

Pronouns appear in the order given at 11.12 immediately before finite verbs, i.e. all verb forms save the infinitive, gerund, participle and imperative. In compound tenses the pronouns are placed before the auxiliary verb, as *la he visto* 'I've seen her':

Se los entregamos	We gave them (masc.) to him/her/ it/them/you
Te los enviaré luego	I'll send you them (masc.) later
Os las guardaré (Sp.; Lat. Am. *se las...*)	I'll keep them (fem.) for you
Se me ha roto el cinturón	My belt's broken

(i) No word may come between the object pronouns and a verb. In pronunciation these pronouns are always unstressed.

(ii) In pre-twentieth-century literary style, object pronouns were often joined to finite verbs: *contestóles así* '(s)he answered them thus' = *les contestó así*, *encontrábase exiliado* 'he found himself exiled' = *se encontraba exiliado*, *ocurriósele* 'it occurred to him/her' = *se le ocurrió*. Rules for this construction are not given here since it is now extinct except in a few set phrases, e.g. *habráse visto...* 'well, did you ever...', *diríase* (literary) 'one might say', *dícese* (literary) 'it is said': the latter survives in various forms in spoken Latin-American Spanish, e.g. *dizque*; see 28.4. The construction is also still found in very flowery styles, and in headlines in some Latin-American countries: *Enrédanse gobiernos de Washington y Londres en mentiras sobre Iraq* (*Granma*, Cu.) 'Governments in Washington and London bogged down in lies over Iraq'.

11.14.2 Position with imperatives: see 17.4

11.14.3 Position with infinitives

(**a**) If the infinitive is used as a noun or follows an adjective or a participle plus a preposition, pronouns are suffixed to it in the usual order:

Sería una locura decírselo	It would be madness to tell it to him
Mejor enviárselo ahora	Best send it to him/her/them now
Rechazaron el proyecto por considerarlo demasiado caro	They rejected the project on the grounds it was too expensive
Estamos hartos de oírtelo	We're fed up with hearing it from you
Usted no puede quitármela. Eso sí sería de mal agüero (G. García Márquez, Col., dialogue)	You can't take it (a gold chain) off me. That *would* be a bad omen

As the examples show, when two pronouns are attached to an infinitive a written accent is needed to show that the position of the stress has not changed, as in *quitármela*.

(**b**) If the infinitive depends on a previous verb, there are two possibilities:

(1) Join the pronouns to the infinitive, as in the previous examples:

Quiero hacerlo	I want to do it
Pudieron salvarla	They managed to save her
Intentaron robárnoslo	They tried to steal it from us
Propusieron alquilárnoslos	They suggested renting them to us
Acabo de dártelo	I've just given it to you

This is the safest, and in the view of some strict grammarians, e.g. Francisco Marsá (1986), 6.1.2, the only correct option. But *Don Quijote*, the purists' Bible, contains many examples of the shifted pronouns described in 11.14.4, e.g. *tu simplicidad, que por ahora no le quiero dar otro nombre* (I, Ch. 33) 'your simplicity—I would rather not call it anything else for now'.

(2) Place the pronouns before the finite verb: *lo quiero hacer*, etc. See the following section for discussion.

11.14.4 *Quiero verlo or lo quiero ver?*

Suffixed object pronouns are very often put before the finite verb when the infinitive depends on a preceding verb: *quiero verlo* > *lo quiero ver* 'I want to see it/him', etc. This construction is possible with a large number of common verbs, but it is not allowed with all verbs. When shifting is possible, both the suffixed and the shifted forms are equally acceptable in spoken Spanish. In Spain the two constructions seem to be about equally frequent in ordinary speech, but to judge by the dialogue of modern novels, Latin-American speech strongly prefers the shifted forms. The suffixed forms are everywhere preferred in formal written styles. The following verbs are especially affected:

querer

Te la quiero enviar/Quiero enviártela	I want to send it (fem.) to you
Por mucho que yo se lo quiera dar/quiera dárselo, no puedo	However much I want to give it (masc.) to you/him/her/them, I can't

poder

No puedo atenderle/No le puedo atender en este momento	I can't attend to you/her/him at this moment
Usted no me lo puede quitar/. . .no puede quitármelo	You can't take it off/away from me

deber

Deberías explicárnoslo/Nos lo deberías explicar	You ought to explain it to us

tener que

Tiene que devolvértelo/Te lo tiene que devolver/	(S)he has to give it back to you

acabar de

Pero acabo de verlo/lo acabo de ver	But I've just seen him!

llegar a

Incluso llegué a caerme/me llegué a caer por unas escaleras	I even managed to fall down a flight of stairs

haber de

He de consultarlo/Lo he de consultar con la almohada	I'd better sleep on it (lit. 'consult my pillow')

dejar de

No dejes de llamarla/No la dejes de llamar	Don't forget to phone her

ir a

Me temía que Roberto fuera a contárselo/ se lo fuera a contar a mamá	I was worried that Roberto would go and tell it to mother

volver a

Como vuelvas a decírmelo/Como me lo vuelvas a decir, me voy	If you say it to me again, I'm going

hacer

Me hizo abrirlo/Me lo hizo abrir	(S)he made me open it

The list at 18.2.3 shows most of the numerous other verbs that allow this shifting of suffixed pronouns, although some of them, e.g. *fingir*, are controversial. Note that the following common verb phrases do not allow shifting (an asterisk marks an incorrect or popular/sub-standard form): *hay que hacerlo -?lo hay que hacer* 'it has to be done', *parece saberlo -*lo parece saber* '(s)he seems to know it', *conviene hacerlo - *lo conviene hacer* 'it ought to be done'. (NB: Previous editions of 'B&B' failed to mark *lo hay que...* as popular or sub-standard. The form is frequently heard but is rejected by careful speakers.)

If two pronouns are joined as suffixes they must stay together if they are shifted leftwards. So, starting from *tienes que decírselo a Enrique*, the only permitted shift is *se lo tienes que decir a Enrique* 'you'll have to tell Enrique', never **le tienes que decirlo a Enrique*. Further examples: *¿quieres bebértelo ahora/te lo quieres beber ahora?* 'do you want to drink it now?', *¿vas a entregárselo ahora/se lo vas a entregar ahora?* 'are you going to hand it over to him/her now?', *¿vino a decírtelo ayer/te lo vino a decir ayer?* 'did (s)he come and tell it to you yesterday?'.

The shifted construction (i.e. *te lo voy a decir*) is not allowed in the following circumstances:

(a) When the finite verb already has a pronoun. In *te interesa hacerlo* 'it's in your interest to do it' the *te* goes with *interesar*, so **te lo interesa hacer* is not possible; and *?me lo permitieron hacer* is substandard for *me permitieron hacerlo* 'they allowed me to do it'.

This particularly affects pronominal ('reflexive') verbs (see Chapter 26). *Volverse* 'to turn round' is a pronominal verb (it has other meanings, discussed at 26.6.13 and 27.3.2), so one says *se volvió a mirarla* '(s)he turned to look at her' but not *se la volvió a mirar*. The latter is only possible when *volver* is not a pronominal verb, in which case we would take the *se* to stand for *le*, as in *el médico volvió a mirarle la lengua* 'the doctor looked at his/her tongue again' > *se la volvió a mirar* 'he looked at it again'.

Other common pronominal verbs that appear with an infinitive are: *ponerse a* 'to begin', *echarse a* 'to begin' (*echar a* means the same and also does not allow pronoun shifting), *meterse a* 'to begin', *atreverse a* 'to dare'. Examples: *se puso a hacerlo* (not **se lo puso a hacer*) '(s)he started to do it', *se metió a venderlos* (not **se los metió a vender*) '(s)he started to sell them', *se atrevió a hacerlo* (not **se lo atrevió a hacer*) '(s)he tried to do it'.

The verbs *ver* seems to be an exception to the general rule: *nos ha visto hacerlo/nos lo ha visto hacer* '(s)he saw us do it', *quiero verte hacerlo/quiero vértelo hacer* 'I want to see you do it'.

?Os la dejaron llamar is heard, but the unshifted forms should be used, e.g. *os dejaron llamarla* 'they let you call her', *me dejaron hacerlo*, etc.

(b) When another word intervenes between the finite verb and the infinitive: *preferiría no hacerlo* 'I'd prefer not to do it' but not **lo preferiría **no** hacer*; *quiero mucho verla*, not **la quiero mucho ver* 'I really want to see her', etc. An exception is made of a few common verb phrases that include a preposition, usually *a* or *de*, or the conjunction *que*: *lo trató **de** hacer/trató de hacerlo* '(s)he tried to do it', *le tengo **que** hablar/tengo que hablarle* 'I've got to talk to him/her', *lo empezó **a** hacer/empezó a hacerlo* '(s)he began to do it'. The rule is also sometimes broken in familiar speech, cf. *no le tengo **nada** que envidiar*, familiar for *no tengo nada que envidiarle* 'I've got nothing to envy him/her/you for', *el que no se tiene que andar metiendo eres tú* (A. Mastretta, Mex., dialogue) 'the one who shouldn't go round getting involved is you'.

(c) When the main verb is a positive imperative: *procura hacerlo* 'try to do it', *vamos a comprarlos* 'let's go and buy them' (or 'we're going to buy them'), *venga a verla* 'come and see her'. But with a negative imperative shifting may occur in familiar speech: *no intentes hacerlo/no lo intentes hacer* 'don't try to do it', *cuidado, no vayas a mancharlo/no lo vayas a manchar* 'be careful not to make it dirty', *no te empieces a incluir tú en las culpas* (C. Martín Gaite, Sp., dialogue) 'don't start including yourself among the guilty ones'/'don't start blaming yourself as well', for *no empieces a incluirte tú en las culpas.*

NB: *Dejar* does allow shifting in positive imperatives in familiar language: *déjamelo hacer a mi estilo* (A. Buero Vallejo, Sp., dialogue, for *déjame hacerlo…*), 'let me do it my way'.

(**d**) When the infinitive follows a verb of saying, believing, claiming, etc. *Creen saberlo todo* but not **lo creen saber todo*, 'they think they know everything', *negabas haberlo hecho* but not **lo negabas haber hecho* 'you denied having done it' (*GDLE* 19.5.5).

(i) In *voy a verla* 'I'm going to see her' either motion or futurity is meant. Usually *la voy a ver* is interpreted as a future form of the verb: 'I'll see her'/'I intend to see her', although familiar speech may allow shifting with both meanings: *ellos me fueron a comprar el billete* (Interview in *Triunfo*, Sp.) 'they went and bought my ticket for me'.

(ii) If more than one infinitive is involved in a construction that allows pronoun shifting, several solutions are possible, the first being safest for foreigners:

No quiero volver a decírtelo/No quiero volvértelo a decir/ No te lo quiero volver a decir	I don't want to tell you it again
Puedes empezar a hacerlo/Puedes empezarlo a hacer/Lo puedes empezar a hacer	You can start to do it
Debes tratar de hacerlo/Debes tratarlo de hacer/Lo debes tratar de hacer	You must try to do it

(iii) It is difficult to explain why some verbal phrases allow pronoun shifting whereas others do not. The difference between a phrase like *tratar de* 'to try', which allows pronoun shifting, and *tardar en* 'to be late in'/'to take time over…', which does not, is presumably that the preposition *de* has become so intimately fused to *tratar* that the two words are processed by the speaker as a single word. A list of verbs that allow shifting appears at 18.2.3.

11.14.5 Position of pronouns with the gerund

(**a**) In combination with *estar* (continuous verb forms) and a few other verbs, e.g. *andar, ir, venir, quedarse*, the pronouns may be either attached or shifted:

Te lo estoy contando/Estoy contándotelo	I'm telling you it
Se estaba dejando ganar por la autocompasión (M. Vargas Llosa, Pe.; or *estaba dejándose ganar*)	He was giving in to self-pity
Os lo estoy diciendo/Estoy diciéndooslo (note the double *o*. Lat. Am. *se lo estoy diciendo*)	I'm telling you
Se lo va contando a todos/Va contándoselo a todos	(S)he goes around telling it to everyone
Se me quedó mirando/Se quedó mirándome (the *se* belongs to *quedarse*)	(S)he remained gazing at me

The second construction is slightly more formal and probably safer for foreign students.

(**b**) In other cases the pronouns are always attached to the gerund: *disfruta mirándolos* '(s)he enjoys himself/herself by looking at them', *se divierte quemándolos* '(s)he amuses himself/herself by burning them', *contesta insultándolos* '(s)he replies by insulting them', *llevo horas esperándote* 'I've been waiting for you for hours', etc.

(i) *Seguir* allows both constructions, but some native speakers did not accept pronoun shifting with *continuar*: *se seguían viendo/seguían viéndose* 'they went on seeing one another', *me sigue dando la lata/sigue dándome la lata* '(s)he's still pestering me', *ella lo siguió encontrando todo muy natural* (A. Bryce Echenique, Pe.) 'she continued to find it all very natural'; but *continuaban viéndose, continúa dándome la lata* rather than *se continuaban viendo*, etc.

(ii) In case (**a**), if the auxiliary verb is an infinitive preceded by one of the verbs that allow pronoun shifting (see 11.14.4), several solutions are possible: *debe estar recordándolo/debe estarlo recordando/lo debe estar recordando* '(s)he must be remembering it/him'; *tenía que quedarse mirándola/tenía que quedársela mirando/se la tenía que quedar mirando* '(s)he had to remain looking at her'.

11.14.6 Position with past participles

Pronouns come before the auxiliary verb:

Se ha equivocado	(S)he's made a mistake
Se lo ha traído de China	(S)he's brought it from China
Te lo hemos mandado ya	We've already sent it to you

(i) In phrases in which pronoun shifting is possible (discussed at 11.14.4), there are two options: *se lo hemos tenido que vender/hemos tenido que vendérselo* 'we had to sell it to him', *la he vuelto a ver/he vuelto a verla* 'I've seen her again', *no he podido abrirlo/no lo he podido abrir* 'I couldn't open it', *ha debido hablarle/le ha debido hablar* '(s)he must have spoken to him/her'.

(ii) Literary language used to join personal pronouns to past participles, especially when the auxiliary verb was omitted; but this construction is obsolete except in flowery styles in some Latin-American republics: Kany, 156, cites *un accidente ocurrídole en el corral de yeguas* 'an accident that happened to him in the yard where the mares are kept' from Uruguay. Manuel Seco (1998), 334, says the construction is 'inelegant'. A sentence like *era un propietario rico de Cáceres, donde había nacido y criádose* 'he was a rich landowner from Cáceres, where he had been born and brought up' would nowadays be expressed ... *donde había nacido y se había criado*.

11.15 Emphasis of object pronouns

(**a**) Object pronouns may be emphasized by adding *a* and the prepositional form of the pronoun:

La vi a ella, pero no a él	I saw **her** but not **him**
Te lo darán a ti, pero no a él	They'll give it **to you**, but not **to him**
¡A mí me lo dices!	You're telling **me**!?
Si me retirara, pues, tampoco lo vería a usted (S. Galindo, Mex., dialogue)	If I retired, well, I wouldn't see **you** either

(b) Reflexive phrases may be emphasized by the appropriate number and gender of *mismo* added to a prepositional pronoun. Reciprocal sentences can be emphasized by the appropriate form of *el uno* and *el otro*:

Se lavaron	They washed (themselves)/They were washed
*Se lavaron **a sí mismos***	They washed **themselves**
Es difícil vivir con quien no se estima a sí mismo (Abc, Sp.)	It is difficult to live with someone who does not value himself/herself
Se quieren el uno al otro	They love one another
Se quieren la una a la otra (two females)	They love one another
Se envidian los unos a los otros	They envy one another (three or more people)

If a male and a female are involved in a reciprocal sentence one might expect *el uno a la otra*, but both pronouns are left in the masculine in order to preserve the idea of reciprocity: *Antonio y María se quieren **el uno al otro*** 'Antonio and Maria love one another'.

(i) The unstressed pronouns must not be omitted in these constructions. **Vi a ella* is not Spanish for *la vi a ella* 'I saw *her*', nor is **lavaron a sí mismos* for *se lavaron a sí mismos*. However, *usted* occasionally appears alone: *¿en qué puedo servir a ustedes?* (example from *GDLE* 19.4.1) 'how can I help you', more often ...*servirles a ustedes*.

11.16 Redundant object pronouns

Spanish constantly uses object pronouns even when the thing they refer to is already named by a noun: in this it is very different from French and English. Some of these redundant pronouns are virtually obligatory; others are more typical of informal styles.

11.16.1 Redundancy when object precedes verb

If, for purposes of emphasis or focus, a direct or indirect object precedes a verb, a redundant pronoun is obligatory (but see note iii). Compare *compré esta casa hace cinco años* and *esta casa **la** compré hace cinco años* 'I bought this house five years ago'. Examples:

Eso no me lo negarás	You won't deny me that
Aviones los tenemos a patadas (quantitystated: see note iii	We've got tons/heaps of aircraft
A alguno de vosotros os quisiera ver yo en un buen fregado (D. Sueiro, familiar dialogue, Sp.)	I'd like to see one of you in a real mess
Al profesor Berlin no le parece tan importante que Maquiavelo propusiera esa disyuntiva (M. Vargas Llosa, Pe.)	It does not seem so important to Professor Berlin that Machiavelli suggested this dilemma

(i) The pronoun is not used after *eso* in such phrases as *eso creo yo* 'that's what I think', *eso digo yo* 'that's what I think' (but compare *eso lo digo yo* 'that's what I **say**').

(ii) For a discussion of the effect of putting the object before the verb see 28.2.3.

(iii) Redundant pronouns are not used with indefinite *direct* objects, i.e. ones that refer to an unspecified or unidentified quantity or number, as in *mucha prisa ha debido tener* '(s)he *must* have been in a hurry', *carne no como* 'meat I *don't* eat!', *aviones tenemos aquí que han costado más de cincuenta millones* 'we've got planes here that cost more than 50 million', *¡cuántas tonterías dices!* 'what a lot of nonsense you talk!' For this reason use of *las* in this example is incorrect: —*¿compraste flores? — Sí, compré* (GDLE 24.2.1; not *las compré*) 'Did you buy flowers?' 'Yes, I did' (but *las compré* must be used in answer to *¿compraste las flores?*). The *GDLE* 5.3.2.4 and 5.5 notes that use of pronouns in sentences like *?fiebre no la tiene* is typical of some northern dialects in Spain.

11.16.2 Redundant pronouns and indirect objects

When an indirect object follows a verb, a redundant pronoun is very frequently used to show that a noun is 'involved' by the verb in one of the ways listed in List A at 12.3 (i.e. 'receiving', 'losing', 'advantage', 'involvement', etc.). In other words, an indirect object is often reinforced by a redundant indirect object pronoun:

Bueno, si no le dicen a uno cómo hay que hacerlo...	Well, if they don't tell one how to do it...
Esta solución le pareció a doña Matilde la más acertada (J. María Guelbenzu, Sp.)	This solution seemed to be the best one to Doña Matilde
Se le notan cada vez más los años a Martínez	You can tell Martínez's age more and more
Les tenía mucho miedo a los truenos	(S)he was very frightened of thunder
Se la tienen jurada a María	They've got it in for María
Le puso un nuevo conmutador a la radio	(S)he put a new knob on the radio
Tráigale un jugo de naranja a la niña (A. Mastretta, Mex., dialogue. *Jugo* = juice of meat in Spain; *zumo* = fruit juice)	Bring the girl an orange juice

Absence of the redundant pronoun in such cases depersonalizes the indirect object and would be natural in official documents or business letters when a formal tone is required: *escriba una carta al Ministerio de Hacienda* 'write a letter to the Ministry of Finance', *comunique los detalles al señor Presidente* 'inform the President of the details', *esto no corresponde a Odradek* (J. L. Borges; Arg. Odradek is a non-human creature) 'this is not a trait of Odradek's'; *es necesario dar cera a este tipo de suelo todas las semanas* (instruction leaflet, Sp.) 'this type of floor must be waxed every week'.

In most other cases the redundant pronoun is used, more so than fifty years ago and always with proper names: *dáselo a Mario* 'Give it to Mario', *se lo robaron a Mariluz* 'they stole it from Mariluz' (*robar a...* 'to steal from...'). However, the redundant pronoun is sometimes not used with other nouns, cf. *una forma estudiada de acentuar la ironía que gusta a todas las mujeres* (J. Marías, Sp.) 'a studied way of emphasizing the irony that all women like', where *les gusta a las mujeres* is less literary; or *todo lo que sobra de esta mañana lo podés dar a las gallinas* (M. Puig, Arg., dialogue; or *se lo podés dar a las gallinas*. Spain *puedes* for the *vos* form *podés*) 'you can give the chickens everything left over from this morning'. The *GDLE*, 19.4.1, says that omission is very rare, although slightly more frequent with *decir* and *dar*.

(i) This rule does not apply to *direct* objects that follow the verb, for which see 11.16.4.

11.16.3 *Le* for redundant *les*

There is a strong tendency in spontaneous language everywhere to use the singular *le* in this construction for the plural *les*, especially, but not exclusively, when the pronoun refers to a human being. DeMello (1992), 2, reports that in Latin America it is equally common with non-human and humans, but Peninsular informants generally reported it as less acceptable with humans. *Le* for *les* is widespread even in quite formal speech:

Cualquiera le da vuelta a las razones por las que te viniste conmigo (J. María Guelbenzu, Sp., dialogue)	Anyone might ponder on the reasons why you came to me
no darle importancia a los detalles	not to ascribe importance to details
¿Quieres devolverle la isla de Manhattan a los Algonquins? (Carlos Fuentes, Mex., dialogue)	Do you want to give Manhattan Island back to the Algonquins?
?Le viene natural a los niños (educated Spaniard, overheard; not universally accepted in Spain)	It comes naturally to children
Bayardo San Román le puso término a tantas conjeturas (G. García Márquez, Col.)	Bayardo San Román put an end to so much conjecture

Sentences like *él les* (for *le*) *da mucha importancia a las apariencias* '(s)he ascribes a lot of importance to appearances' may sound odd to some speakers. But use of the singular *le* for *les* is technically 'wrong', and should be avoided in formal writing—e.g. in this case by omitting the redundant pronoun altogether.

11.16.4 Redundant direct object pronouns

As was said at 11.16.1, a redundant pronoun is usually obligatory when an object precedes the verb, as in *las flores las compré ayer* 'I bought the flowers yesterday'. When the direct object *follows* the verb, use of a redundant object pronoun is common with *todo*: *ahora me lo tienes que contar todo* 'now you have to tell me everything'. It is also required when it is necessary to reinforce an object pronoun, e.g. *la vi a ella pero no a él* 'I saw *her* but not *him*' (not *vi a ella*). In other cases use of a redundant pronoun with direct objects is generally avoided in Spain, but it is common in Latin America in spontaneous speech, and in Argentina it appears even in literary styles, especially with proper names:

Le quiere mucho a ese hijo (Spain, familiar)	(S)he loves that son a lot
Morgan también lo mandó llamar a Abdulmalik (J. L. Borges, Arg., dialogue; Sp. ...*mandó llamar a Abdulmalik*)	Morgan also had Abdulmalik sent for
No lo conocen a Perón en Córdoba, lo confunden con un cantante de tangos (J. Asís, Arg., dialogue; Sp. *no conocen...*)	They've never heard of Perón in Córdoba. They think he's a tango singer
Convénzalo a su amigo de que acepte la beca (M. Vargas Llosa, Pe., dialogue; Sp. *convenza a su amigo...*)	Persuade your friend to accept the grant

This is less usual, but not unknown, with non-human direct objects.

11.16.5 Redundant pronouns in relative clauses

Redundant pronouns occur in spoken Spanish in relative clauses to 'resume' or echo a direct or indirect object relative pronoun, especially in non-restrictive clauses, and they may appear in writing, particularly if several words separate the *que* and the verb that depends on it:

*Los gramáticos aconsejan muchas cosas que nadie **las** dice* (Sp., informant)	Grammarians recommend lots of things that no one says
Te voy a hacer una confesión que nunca me animé a hacerla a nadie (Lat. Am., from Kany, 150)	I'm going to make you a confession I never had the courage to make to anybody
Sólo por ti dejaría a don Memo a quien tanto le debo (Carlos Fuentes, Mex., dialogue)	Only for you would I leave Don Memo, whom I owe so much

DeMello (1992), 4, shows that the construction is very widespread, even in quite formal speech in Spain and Latin America, but it may sound uneducated to some, especially in restrictive clauses (the first two examples), and it is best left to native speakers.

12

Le/les *and* lo/la/los/las

The main points discussed in this chapter are:

- Basic rules for choice between *lo/la/los/las* and *le/les* (Section 12.2)
- The uses of *le/les* as an indirect object pronoun (Section 12.3)
- The uses of *lo/la/los/las* as direct object pronouns (Section 12.4)
- Regional variations in the rules (Section 12.5)
- Use of *le/les* as direct object pronouns in standard Spanish everywhere (Section 12.6)

This chapter is devoted exclusively to the problem of the relationship between the third-person object pronouns *le/les* and *lo/la/los/las*. For first- and second-person pronouns (including *usted* and *ustedes*) and for third-person subject pronouns (*él, ella, ellos, ellos*), see Chapter 11.

12.1 The *le/lo* controversy: summary of the arguments contained in this chapter

The rules governing the correct choice of third-person object pronouns vary a great deal in everyday spoken language throughout the Hispanic world: the eighty pages that the *GDLE* devotes to the subject reveal that usage sometimes even differs between places less than fifty kilometres apart.

However, the situation in the written language is fairly stable, and can be summarized (and over-simplified) thus: the pronoun used for third-person direct objects, human and non-human, in more than 90% of the Spanish-speaking world is *lo/la* for the singular and *los/las* for the plural. *Le* and *les* are used for indirect objects as defined at 11.7.2 and 12.3. This scheme is recommended for beginners learning Latin-American Spanish, and it usually produces acceptable sentences in Peninsular Spanish. However, *le* and *les* are also used for direct objects in the following cases:

(a) In the standard language of Spain when the direct object is singular, human and male: compare *yo le vi* 'I saw him' and *yo lo vi* 'I saw it (masc.)'. See 12.5.1.

(b) Sometimes as the object pronoun for *ustedes* in order to denote respect. See 12.6.1.

(c) Frequently when the subject of the verb is inanimate and the direct object is human and is reacting emotionally to the action described. See 12.6.2.

(d) Frequently, when the subject is impersonal *se* and the direct object is human. See 12.6.3.

(e) In all countries, *le/les* is used with certain verbs, listed at 12.6.4.

12.2 Third-person object pronouns: basic rules

Beginners can apply the following scheme, valid for all of Latin America and acceptable to most Spaniards. These rules will produce correct sentences in over 90% of cases.

Third-person object pronouns (from the Academy's *Esbozo de una nueva gramática de la lengua española*, 3.10.5c)

	Direct object	Indirect object
	SINGULAR	
Masculine	*lo*	*le*
Feminine	*la*	*le*
	PLURAL	
Masculine	*los*	*les*
Feminine	*las*	*les*

Ángela vio a Antonio Angela saw Antonio	***Lo*** *vio* She saw him
Antonio vio a Ángela Antonio saw Angela	***La*** *vio* He saw her
Vio el libro (S)he saw the book	***Lo*** *vio* (S)he saw it
Vio la casa (S)he saw the house	***La*** *vio* (S)he saw it
María dijo hola a Juan Maria said hello to Juan	***Le*** *dijo hola* She said hello to him
Juan dijo hola a María Juan said hello to Maria	***Le*** *dijo hola* He said hello to her
Vio a los hombres (S)he saw the men	***Los*** *vio* (S)he saw them
Vio a las mujeres (S)he saw the women	***Las*** *vio* (S)he saw them
Vio los libros (S)he saw the books	***Los*** *vio* (S)he saw them
Vio las casas (S)he saw the houses	***Las*** *vio* (S)he saw them
Dijo hola a María y a José (S)he said hello to María and José	***Les*** *dijo hola* (S)he said hello to them
Dijo hola a María y a Ángela (S)he said hello to Maria and Angela	***Les*** *dijo hola* (S)he said hello to them

(i) Standard European Spanish prefers the form *le* for a **human** male direct object—*le vi* 'I saw him': see 12.5.1 for details. In the plural *los* is more common than *les* for male human direct objects and is generally preferred; see 12.5.2 for details.

(ii) *Usted/ustedes* 'you' (polite) takes third-person object pronouns: *lo vi ayer* 'I saw him/it/you yesterday', *le vi ayer* (Spain only) 'I saw you (masc.)/him yesterday', *los vi ayer* 'I saw them/you yesterday', *las vi ayer* 'I saw them/you (fem.) yesterday'. This possibility that a third-person object pronoun may also refer to *ustede(es)* must be borne in mind since it is not systematically shown in the translations in this book.

12.3 Use of *le/les* as 'indirect object' pronouns: detailed rules

(*Le/les* are also used in Spain as direct object pronouns: see 12.5–12.6.)

Le/les are often described as third-person 'indirect object' pronouns (*pronombres de complemento indirecto*). However, 'indirect object' is a term that covers many different meanings, and the more general principle underlying the use of *le/les* seems to be the following: *le/les* **can replace any person or thing gaining from or losing by the action described in the verb phrase** (in English an indirect object can only gain or receive: we cannot say *'they stole him fifty dollars' = *le robaron cincuenta dólares*). The nature of these gains or losses must be inferred from the meaning of the verb phrase or from clues provided by context. Whatever departures from these examples they may hear, foreign students are advised to use *le/les* in the following contexts:

List A Typical uses of *le/les*

In the translations, 'you' appears as a reminder that *lo/los/la/las* and *le/les* can refer to *usted* or *ustedes* as well as to 'him', 'her', 'it' or them'.

(**a**) Receiving or acquiring any thing, impression or sensation

Le di/mandé la carta	I gave/sent her/him/you the letter
No les dije la verdad	I didn't tell you/them the truth
Le tirábamos bolas de nieve	We were throwing snowballs at him/her/you
Le pusieron una inyección	They gave you/him/her an injection
Le echaron una sábana	They threw a sheet over him/her/you
Se le pegó una brizna de hierba	A blade of grass stuck to him/her/you
Les enseñé el camino	I showed them/you the way
Esa chaqueta no le va	That jacket doesn't suit him/her/you
No le parece mucho	It doesn't seem much to them/you
Le suena mal	It sounds wrong to him/her/you
La secretaria le cayó bien	(S)he took a liking to the secretary
Les gusta la miel	They/You like honey
Cuánto les pesaba haber hablado	How sorry they/you were for having talked

and also words meaning 'to happen to', e.g. *suceder, acontecer, sobrevenir, pasar*: *les sobrevino una tragedia* ' they/you suffered a tragedy', *no le pasó nada* 'nothing happened to him/her/you'.

(**b**) Loss or removal from

Les han robado un millón de pesos	They've stolen a million pesos from them/you
Mario le ha quitado a Ana	Mario's taken Ana away from him/her/you (NB: personal *a*)
Le he comprado un cuadro	I've bought a picture from him/her/you
Le están sacando una muela	They're taking one of her/his teeth out
Le costó un dineral	It cost him/her a fortune
Se le cae el pelo	His/Her hair's falling out
Se le ha muerto un hijo	A son of his/hers/yours has died
Se le pasa pronto	(S)he gets over it quickly/You get over…
No te acepto ese tipo de comentarios	I'm not taking that kind of remark from you

Also, in Latin America, *recibir*: *desolado porque ésta no aceptó recibirle el presente de amor* (popular press, Ch.) 'distraught because she refused accept the love gift from him', Sp. *…ésta se negó a aceptarle el regalo de amor.*

(**c**) Sufficiency, insufficiency, lack, excess

Les basta decir que sí	All they/you have to do is say 'yes'
Le faltan mil pesos	(S)he's/You're 1000 pesos short
Le faltaba un dedo meñique	One of his/her little fingers was missing
Veinte euros al día le alcanzaban para vivir	(S)he/You could manage on 20 euros a day
Le sobraba (la) razón	(S)he was/You were only too right
El traje le está grande	His/Her/Your suit is too big for her

(**d**) Requesting, requiring, ordering

Le hicieron varias preguntas	They asked him/her/you several questions
Les pidieron nuestras señas	They asked them/you for our names and addresses
Les rogaron que se sentasen/sentaran	They/You requested them/you to sit down
Les ordenamos rendirse	We ordered them/you to surrender
Les exigía un esfuerzo continuo	It required continuous effort from them/you
Les llamaste la atención	You attracted their attention (or 'you told them off')

Compare *le mandó que comprara/comprase pan* '(s)he ordered her/him to buy bread' and *la mandó a comprar pan* '(s)he sent her to buy bread'.

(**e**) Numerous phrases involving *tener* plus an emotion (although the equivalent verbs, *respetar*, *temer*, etc., may take *lo/la/las/los*)

Mario le tiene miedo	Mario fears him/her/you
Su madre le tenía poco cariño	His/Her/Your/Their mother felt little fondness for him/her/you
Ana le tiene ojeriza	Ana has it in for him/her/you
Le tenías una envidia tremenda	You were enormously envious of her/him

(**f**) Numerous set phrases consisting of *hacer* plus a noun

El frío les hacía mucho daño	The cold did them/you a lot of harm
El chico le hizo una mueca	The boy pulled a face at him/her/you
Mi nieto nunca les hacía caso	My grandson never heeded them/you
Tienes que hacerle frente a la realidad	You have to face up to reality
Le hacía falta reflexionar	(S)he/You needed to reflect

(**g**) To indicate persons or things affected by something done to a part of their body or to some intimate possession (for further details about this construction and for the omission of the possessive adjective with parts of the body and intimate possessions, see 8.3.4)

¡Le estás pisando los pies!	You're treading on his/her feet!
A esa edad se les ablanda el cerebro	Their brains go soft at that age
Los nervios le jugaban malas partidas	His/Her nerves were playing tricks on him/her
Se le ha hundido la moral	Her/His morale has collapsed
No le veo la gracia	I don't see what's funny about it/him/her
Le dejaron las gafas hechas añicos (*las gafas* = Lat. Am. *los anteojos* or *los lentes*)	They shattered her/his/your glasses

(**h**) In a number of less easily classified cases which may all be seen to convey ideas of 'giving', 'removing', 'benefiting', 'involving', 'affecting intimately'

¿Qué le vamos a hacer?	What can be done about it?
No le hace (Southern Cone; Sp. *no tiene que ver*)	That's irrelevant
¡Dale!	Hit him!/Go on!/Get moving!
Le agradezco	I thank you
El cura les (also *los*) *aconsejaba que no lo hicieran/hiciesen*	The priest advised them/you not to do it
Le encontraron mil pesos	They found 1000 pesos on her/him/you
La respuesta del abogado le afectó mucho (*lo* or *le* possible in Latin America)	The lawyer's reply affected him/her/you a lot

This multiplicity of meanings can give rise to ambiguities: *le compré un vestido* 'I bought a dress off her/for her', *cómprame algo* 'buy something for/off me', *Ángel me robó una manzana* 'Ángel stole an apple from me/for me/on my behalf'. Context nearly always makes the sense plain, or the sentence can be recast: *compró una calculadora para mí* '(s)he bought a calculator for me', etc.

12.4 Uses of *lo/la/los/las*

Lo/la/los/las are the third-person 'direct object' pronouns, 'direct' object understood here as the person or thing directly affected by a verb phrase but not 'losing' or 'gaining' in the ways described in List A above. In the following examples it will be seen that even when dramatically affected by the verb phrase (as in 'they killed her') the person or thing denoted by the pronoun is not actively involved as a participant in the action or as an interested party. In fact the condition of the pronoun is very often literally that of an object which merely has the action of the verb done to it.

List B: Contexts normally requiring *lo/la/los/las* (direct object)

The use of *lo* for human males in this list reflects standard Latin-American usage. The second of the alternative forms reflects widespread, preferred, but not obligatory usage in Spain. See 12.2 and 12.5.1 for discussion. 'You' in the translation reflects the possibility of *usted/ustedes*.

(**a**) Direct physical actions (although there are exceptions, like *le pega* '(s)he beats him/her'; see 12.6.4):

Lo/Le interrogaron	They interrogated him/you
La operaron	They operated on her/you
Coge estos papeles y quémalos	Take these papers and burn them
A usted lo durmieron con algún mejunje en la sidra (J. L. Borges, Arg., dialogue; Sp. *le*)	They put you to sleep with some potion in the cider
Saca el carburador y límpialo	Take out the carburettor and clean it
—¿Y tu cámara? —La he perdido	'What about your camera?' 'I've lost it'

(**b**) Verbs of perception, e.g. 'seeing', 'hearing', 'knowing', etc.

Al director no lo/le conozco	I don't know the director
La vi ayer en el mercado	I saw her/you yesterday in the market
Sabía que el ladrón estaba en la habitación porque lo/le oí	I knew the thief was in the room because I heard him
El padre lo miraba con orgullo (I. Aldecoa, Sp., or *le*)	His father gazed at him with pride
A uno de ellos lo identifiqué enseguida (J. Marías, Sp.; or *le*)	One of them I identified immediately

(**c**) Praise, blame, admiration, love, hatred and other actions denoting attitudes towards a person or thing:

Sus profesores lo/le alaban	His/her/your teachers praise him/you
A las monjas las envidio mucho	I envy nuns a lot
Lo/le admiro profundamente	I admire him/you deeply
Su marido la adora	Her/Your husband adores her
Yo la quiero mucho	I love her/you a lot

(For some speakers *lo quieren* = 'they want him/you', *le quieren* = 'they love him/her/you'.)

(**d**) 'Naming', 'nominating', 'describing' (but see 12.6.4 for the verb *llamar*):

Los denominaron "los decadentes"	They named them/you 'the decadents'
Lo/Le nombraron alcalde	They nominated him/you mayor
Las describió en términos despectivos	(S)he described them/you (fem.) in pejorative terms
Lo calificó de tragedia	(S)he described it as a tragedy

(**e**) Many other actions done to things or persons but not 'involving' them in the ways described at 12.3 List A:

La crisis energética no la podrá solucionar ningún gobierno elegido	The energy crisis can't be solved by any elected government
El Canciller los recibirá a las siete y cuarto	The Chancellor will receive you/them at 7.15
Este país no hay quien sepa gobernarlo	There's no one who can govern this country
Habrá que defenderlos	We'll have to defend them/you
No pude convencerla	I couldn't convince her/you
Yo intentaba evitarlos	I was trying to avoid them/you

(i) *Lo/la/los/las* agree in gender with the noun they stand for. If they do not replace a specific noun, *lo* is used: *dijo que llegaría a las siete, pero no lo creo* '(s)he said he'd arrive at seven, but I don't believe it', *esto no lo aguanta nadie* 'no one can stand this'. This neuter use of *lo* is discussed at 7.4.

(ii) The first- and second-person pronouns *me/te/nos/os* could be used in any of the above sentences in place of the third-person pronoun, provided the result makes sense.

12.5 The *le/lo* controversy: general remarks

The use of *le/les* as *direct* object pronouns has always been a source of controversy. Beginners may follow the scheme given in 12.2, but they will soon come across at least some of the variants described hereafter. Some of these are dialectal and not to be imitated by foreigners. But some are basic features of certain varieties Spanish and fluent foreigners will need to use them. Section 12.5 describes regional variations. Section 12.6 describes certain subtleties in the use of *le* and *lo* found in the best written and spoken Spanish.

12.5.1 *Le* for *lo* in Spain (*leísmo*): further details

The most prestigious styles in Spain, i.e. the variety used in publishing, the media, and by most educated speakers in central and northern Spain, favours *le vi* for *lo vi* when the sentence means 'I saw him' as opposed to 'I saw it':

—*¿Has visto a Miguel? —No, no le he visto*	'Have you seen Miguel?' 'No, I haven't seen him'
—*¿Has visto mi lápizi? —No, no lo he visto*	'Have you seen my pencil pen?' 'No, I haven't seen it'

The Academy has itself changed its mind about this phenomenon several times in the last 150 years. Its most recent preference (*Esbozo. . .*, 3.10.5) was to advocate the

Latin-American use of *lo* for both human males and masculine non-human direct objects, but in the face of massive resistance in Spain it officially 'tolerates' forms like *le vi* for 'I saw **him**'. The new *GDLE* simply notes differences of dialect and declares no preferences, but it considers that *leísmo* is spreading in Spain because it is considered prestigious (*GDLE* 21.6.2).

Students may still encounter anti-*loísta* prejudice in *leísta* regions: some Spaniards claim that *lo vi* applied to a male human being sounds vaguely sub-standard or regional. However, they will also note much inconsistency in the use of *le* or *lo* with reference to human males in Spain, *lo* being more frequent in the South and not uncommon elsewhere, cf. *lo tiene por vecino de calle y desde la ventana lo ve pasar todos los días* (Carlos Casares, *El País*, Sp.) 'he assumes that he's a neighbour from the same street and from the window he sees him go by every day'. The *leísmo* of Spain usually sounds incorrect to Latin Americans, but section 12.6 will show that, although less common, the use of *le* in Latin America for human direct objects, male and female, is in fact more widespread in certain countries and circumstances than is usually claimed.

Much of the controversy arose from traditional grammarians' over-rigid distinction between 'direct' and 'indirect' object pronouns in Spanish, which they based on the example of Classical Latin rather than of modern Castilian. The following pages attempt to provide a succinct account. For a full discussion see E. García (1975) or the *GDLE*, chapter 21.

Feminists will note that in the *leísta* system of standard Peninsular Spanish, only males are exalted above non-living objects by the use of *le*: *la vi* means both 'I saw her' and 'I saw *it*'.

12.5.2 *Les* for *los* in Spain

Use of *les* for *los*, e.g. *les vi* 'I saw them' (masc.) is also frequent in colloquial language in Spain, especially in Castile, when the pronoun refers to human males; but this construction is less common than *los vi* and is not, in fact, 'tolerated' by the Academy or favoured in writing. Seco (1998), 180, says of *no les he visto* applied to human males for *no los he visto* that 'literary language does not generally admit it', but examples are so common in good Spanish writers that foreign students need not worry unduly about using it:

Les llevaron a una casa donde estuvieron mucho rato esperando (Juan Benet, Sp.; for *los llevaron...*)	They took them to a house where they waited for a long time
La colonización les explotó (P. Laín Entralgo, Sp.)	Colonization exploited them

12.5.3 *Le* for *la* in Spain: regional usage

Speakers from north and north-western Spain, especially Navarre and the Basque provinces, often use *le* for female human direct objects as well as for males: *le vi* = both 'I saw him' and 'I saw her', *lo vi* (masc.) and *la vi* (fem.) = 'I saw it'. This usage sometimes appears in literature and is generally accepted as a regional variant. The same phenomenon is sporadically heard elsewhere, e.g. in Valencia and in Paraguay.

12.5.4 *La* for *le* (*a ella*) in Spain (*laísmo*)

People from Madrid and the provinces of central Spain often use *la* for the indirect object pronoun to refer to a female or feminine noun:

?*Yo la dije la verdad* (for *yo le dije la*   I told her the truth
    verdad)

?*Yo la alabo el gusto* (M. Delibes,   I praise her taste
    Sp., dialogue; for *yo le alabo*
    el gusto)

¿*Desde entonces yo la he escrito*   Since then I've written to her several times
    varias veces (A. Martín, Sp.,
    dialogue; for *le he escrito*)

Schoolteachers have battled relentlessly against this type of *laísmo* and it may now be in decline in the speech of Madrid. It is common in pre-twentieth-century literature, but foreign students should not imitate it.

12.5.5 *Lo* for *le* in Latin America

Extreme *loísmo*, i.e. use of *lo* for the indirect object, is reported in popular speech in many parts of Latin America: Kany, 137, cites from Guatemala *ya no tarda en llegar. ¿Quiere hablarlo?* 'he won't be long now. Do you want to speak to him?' (for *hablarle*). The same phenomenon is occasionally heard in dialects in Spain, but it should not be imitated.

12.5.6 *Le* for *lo/la* applied to inanimate objects in Spain

In familiar speech in Madrid, in Quito, Ecuador, and in pre-twentieth-century texts, one finds *le* used as the direct object pronoun even for inanimate nouns: ?*no le he leído todavía* 'I haven't read it [*el libro*] yet', ?*unos niegan el hecho, otros le afirman* 'some deny the fact, others assert it' (B. Feijoo, Sp., mid-18th century). This extreme *leísmo*, endorsed by the Academy until the 1850s, is nowadays considered sub-standard unless it is a rare instance of genuine personification. Foreign students should avoid it, although it occasionally appears in written language, cf. *en esta historia mal concertada hacen que San Prudencio y otros obispos maldigan al pueblo y le destruyan* (J. Caro Baroja, Sp.) 'in this disjointed story they make Saint Prudentius and other bishops curse the village and destroy it'.

12.6 *Le* used for human direct objects throughout the Spanish-speaking world

Even when all the regional and dialectal factors are taken into account, *le* is still used as a direct object pronoun in the best styles in Spain where *la/las* would be expected, and in Latin America where either *lo/los* or *la/las* would be predicted. This problem arises because the difference between *lo/la/los/las* and *le/les* is not a simple distinction between 'direct' and 'indirect' objects. This can been seen from the translation of the following sentences, in both of which 'her' is the direct object of 'flattered': (a) 'he flattered her', (b) 'the joke flattered her'.

We expect the Spanish translations to be (a) *él la halagó*, (b) *la broma la halagó*, and this is what many native speakers accept. However, many speakers, Spanish and

Latin-American, translate (b) as *la broma le halagó*, this being the more common form in educated speech. In an attempt to replicate García's (1975) experiments on natives of Buenos Aires, we issued a questionnaire to 28 educated speakers (mostly university students or professionals, 80% from Madrid) asking them to insert *la* or *le* in the following sentences: (i) *A María todo el mundo. . . halaga* 'everyone flatters Maria', (ii) *María comprendió que fue una broma, pero. . .halagó que esa broma fuera posible* 'Maria understood it was a joke, but . . . it flattered her that the joke was possible'. In (i) 87% put *la*, in (ii) 90% put *le*. When the sample was increased by adding 20 Latin Americans from 5 different countries the picture did not change. As a result, although the rules for the use of *le/les* already given at 12.3 and the rules for *lo/la/los/las* given at 12.4 will enable foreign learners to form sentences that are acceptable to the majority of native speakers, they do not always explain the actual use of these pronouns.

12.6.1 *Le* to denote respect

In certain areas some speakers use *le* for human direct objects as a mark of respect. Spaniards who say *lo vi* for 'I saw him' may prefer *le vi* for the *usted* form 'I saw you'. Argentine informants were convinced that they would say *no quería molestarle* 'I didn't mean to bother you' when speaking to their boss, but *molestarlo* when speaking about him; the *GDLE* 24.5 reports the phenomenon in Chile, Venezuela and Ecuador. Colombian informants said *molestarlo* in both cases. Similarly one might hear in Spain *si le molesta el humo, señora, lo apago* 'if the smoke's bothering you, Señora, I'll put it out', but *lo apagué porque la molestaba el humo* 'I put it out because the smoke was bothering her'.

It is possible that, for some speakers of European Spanish, use of *lo* can, on the other hand, express the idea that the male person referred to is helpless or held in low esteem, although this distinction is not made in central Spain, where there is no detectable difference of meaning between *lo* and *le* when they refer to male direct objects. The following examples may show *lo* used with the nuance described, but the choice seems arbitrary and *le* is clearly preferred in the singular for human males:

Lo agarramos por los sobacos y por las piernas y lo subimos. . .dejándole tendido en la puerta de aquel pisito (J. Marsé, Sp., dialogue, about a drunkard; inconsistent use of *le/lo*)	We grabbed hold of him under the arms and by the legs, and carried him up and left him lying in the doorway to that little flat/apartment
Después lo hemos traído aquí (A. Buero Vallejo, Sp.; *lo* refers to a corpse)	Then we brought him here

García (1975) reports that some speakers in Buenos Aires detect a difference between *le llevaron al hospital* and *lo llevaron al hospital* 'they took him to the hospital', the former implying that the patient was walking or co-operative, the latter that he was carried; and it seems that some Spaniards also accept the distinction. For Colombian informants only *lo llevaron* was possible.

12.6.2 *Le/les* preferred when the subject is inanimate

Le or *les* are often the preferred direct object pronouns in Spain and Latin America when they denote a human being and the subject of the verb is non-living. Compare the following sentences: *la espera su marido* 'her husband's waiting for her' and *le espera una catástrofe* 'a catastrophe awaits her/him'. *Le* is most often used when the human direct object is reacting emotionally, as in sentences like 'it surprised him', 'it shocked her'. The phenomenon is vividly illustrated in this Peruvian sentence where *le* reflects an inanimate subject (a tooth) with a human direct object, but the *lo* reflects both a human subject (the dentist who is speaking) and a human direct object: *si [la muela] le molesta mucho, lo puedo atender hoy mismo* (from *Variedades*, 238) 'if it [the tooth] is troubling you a lot, I can attend to you today'. Further examples:

Le amargaba la idea de haber estrangulado las palabras que estaba a punto de dirigirle (C. Carmen Gaite, Sp.)	She was embittered by the idea of having choked back (lit. 'strangled') the words she was about to say to him
Él se miraba la sangre que le había salpicado (M. Vargas Llosa, Pe.)	He looked at the blood that had spattered him
Sin embargo, le molestaba encararse con Parodi (J. L. Borges, Arg.)	Yet it troubled him to come face to face with Parodi
Durante mucho tiempo le angustió esa novedad (E. Sábato, Arg.)	For a long while that new turn of events (lit. 'novelty') filled him with anguish
...lo que más le preocupaba de la muerte al doctor Urbino... (G. García Márquez, Col.)	...what worried doctor Urbino most about the death...

The following pairs further illustrate the rule:

La angustia le acompañaba siempre	Anguish went with her/him always
Yo la acompañaba siempre	I always went with her
A Consuelo le admiró que no contestase	It surprised Consuelo that he did not reply
A Consuelo la admiro mucho	I admire Consuelo a great deal
Le alcanzan mil euros para vivir	1000 euros are enough for him/her to live on
No pude alcanzarla	I couldn't catch up with her
El gas les hace reír	The gas makes them laugh
Yo los haré reír	I'll make them laugh

The following verbs are also especially likely to be affected: *acometer* 'to assail' (doubts, etc.), *afligir* 'to afflict' (pain, etc.), *asustar* 'to frighten', *ayudar* 'to help', *calmar* 'to calm', *coger* 'to catch', *complacer* 'to please', *convencer* 'to convince', *distraer* 'to amuse'/'distract', *encantar* 'to enchant'/'charm', *estorbar* 'to impede'/'get in the way of', *exasperar* 'to exasperate', *fascinar* 'to fascinate', *fatigar* 'to fatigue', *indignar* 'to outrage', *inquietar* 'to worry', *molestar* 'to trouble', *preocupar* 'to worry', *seducir* 'to charm', *tranquilizar* 'to calm', etc.

The rules given in this section reflect the best usage in Spain, the Southern Cone and Mexico, but many native speakers do not exploit all the potential of these subtleties so they may disagree about the correct pronoun to use. Moreover, strongly *loísta* speakers, e.g. Colombians, may use *lo/la* where others prefer *le*.

12.6.3 Preference for *le/les* after impersonal or reflexive *se*

If impersonal (or, occasionally, reflexive *se*) precedes a third-person pronoun there is a widespread tendency to prefer *le/les* when the object is human.

Se le notaba tímida y cortada (L. Goytisolo, Sp.)	One could see she was timid and embarrassed
Se le notaba alegre (M. Vargas Llosa, Pe.; *lo* expected)	One could see he was cheerful
Entonces se le leerá como se le debió leer siempre... (M. Vargas Llosa, Pe., essay on Camus; *lo* expected)	Then he will be read as he always should have been read...
Hola doctor, ¡qué bien se le ve! (Peruvian speaker, *Variedades* 238; *lo* expected)	Hallo, doctor, you're looking well!
Licha se le prendió de la solapa (C. Fuentes, Mex.)	Licha pulled him to her by his lapels

(i) Use of *le/les* for the direct object removes the ambiguities caused in Spanish by the lack of object pronoun forms. Use of *lo/la* after *se* invites us to read *se* as a substitute for *le* by the rule that two object pronouns beginning with *l* cannot occur side by side (11.13.1). Thus *le cortaron la cabeza* 'they cut his/her head off' is pronominalized *se la cortaron* 'they cut it off (him/her)' (*not *le la cortaron!*). For this reason *se la notaba pálida* may suggest '(s)he noticed that his/her/their hand, face, head, cheek, chin (or some other feminine noun) was pale'; *se le notaba...* shows that the whole person is referred to. In the following examples *se* replaces *le* but the object is not human: *se lo cobró* '(s)he took it (money) off him/her/you', *se lo leyó a su padre* '(s)he read it to his/her father'.

(ii) In Spain *le* is occasionally seen even for non-human direct objects after impersonal *se*, although in this example *los* would have been more usual: *a los esperpentos de Valle-Inclán siempre se les ha considerado ejemplos de expresionismo español* (A. Buero Vallejo, Sp.) 'Valle-Inclán's *esperpentos* have always been considered examples of Spanish expressionism'. Cf. *paralización súbita...Se la conoce también como muerte súbita* (L. Sepúlveda, Ch., dialogue) 'sudden paralysis...It is also known as sudden death' (for *se la* ... here see 28.2.5 note i).

(iii) Use of *la* after impersonal *se* to refer to a female and of *lo* to refer to a male is not, however, impossible: *la luz se apagó y apenas se lo veía* (M. Vargas Llosa, Pe.) 'the light went out and one could scarcely see him', *se lo veía pálido en las fotos* (J. Marías, Sp.) 'he looked pale in the photographs', *al término de la temporada se le dio de baja, se lo traspasó al fútbol francés* (J. Marías, Sp.) 'at the end of the season he was released and transferred to French soccer', *—No se **le** acusa de ningún hecho. —Y entonces ¿de qué se **lo** acusa?* (interview *La Nación*, Arg.) '"He's not being accused of any action." "What is he being accused of then?"'(both forms used).

(iv) The verb *llevarse* encourages use of *lo* for human and non-human direct objects. Most informants from the strongly *leísta* regions of Madrid, Segovia and Valladolid preferred *lo* to *le* in *se rompió una pierna y se lo/le llevaron al hospital en ambulancia* 'he broke a leg and they took him to hospital in an ambulance' (*lo* 75%, *le* 25%); *a mi padre me lo/le voy a llevar a pasar las vacaciones con nosotros* 'I'm going to take my father on vacation with us' (*lo* 62%, *le* 38%). This is apparently a peculiarity of the verb *llevar*: *le* is reserved for the meaning 'carry *to* him/her', and *lo* for the meaning 'to take' or 'to wear'.

12.6.4 *Le/les* preferred with certain verbs

Some verbs usually take *le* for what English-speakers take to be their direct object pronoun. However, many native speakers of Spanish would analyse the *le* or *les* in the following sentences as an 'indirect object':

> *Creer* 'to believe', when its object is human: *yo no le creo, señora,* 'Señora, I don't believe you', but *sí que lo creo* 'I *do* believe it'.
>
> *Discutir* 'to argue'/'to discuss', when it means 'to answer back': *¿desde cuándo le discutía?* 'since when had she been answering him back?' (M. Vargas Llosa, Per., dialogue).
>
> *Enseñar* 'to teach'/'to show', when its object is human: *les enseñaba* '(s)he taught/showed them' but *lo enseñaba* '(s)he showed it'.
>
> *Entender* 'to understand', when its object is human: *no le entiendo* 'I don't understand him/her/you' but *lo entiendo* 'I understand it'.
>
> *Gustar/agradar/complacer/placer* 'to please', and all verbs of similar or opposite meaning: *le gusta la miel* '(s)he/it likes/you like honey', *le disgustaba encontrarse sola* 'she disliked finding herself alone'.
>
> *Importar* 'to matter', *concernir* 'to concern' and verbs of similar meaning: *no les importa que no tengan dinero* 'they don't care that they have no money'; *eso no le concierne a usted* 'that doesn't concern you'.
>
> *Interesar* '**to interest**': *reiteró que solo/solo un hombre le interesaba en el mundo* 'she repeated that only one man in the world interested her'.
>
> *Llamar* 'to call': many speakers prefer *le/les* when the verb means 'to give a name', although *lo/la* are also common: *por eso le llaman mami* (A. Buero Vallejo, Sp., dialogue) 'that's why they call her "mummy"', *se nos informó en un "briefing", que le llaman* (TV interview, Cu.) 'we were told in a "briefing", as they call it'; but this usage is not universal: *al más alegre lo llamaban el Trompo* (G. García Márquez, Col.) 'they called the most cheerful one "Spinning Top"'. (For christening, educated usage says *le pusieron María de nombre* 'they called her "Maria"'). *La/lo/(le)/ los/las* are the usual object pronouns used when the verb means 'phone' or 'call': *yo la llamaré apenas haya alguna novedad* 'I'll call you/her as soon as there's news'. However, *telefonear* takes *le/les*.
>
> *Obedecer* 'to obey': *¿le han obedecido a Mademoiselle Durand?* 'did you obey Mlle Durand?' (E. Poniatowska, Mex., dialogue), although the verb is also found with *la/lo*.
>
> *Pegar* 'to beat': [*Lalita*] *te contó que le pegué* (M. Vargas Llosa, Pe., dialogue) 'Lalita told you I hit her', *dicen que le pega mucho* 'they say he hits him/her/you a lot'. *Pegarlo/ pegarla*, etc., is assumed to mean 'to stick (i.e. glue) it'. *La pegaba* for '(s)he beat her' is, however, heard in familiar language, cf. *luego él cambió y le daba achares y la pegaba* (R. Montero, Sp.) 'then he changed and made her jealous and hit her', *la insultaba y la pegaba* (S. Puértolas, Sp.) 'he insulted her and hit her'.
>
> *Preocupar, inquietar* 'to worry': *le preocupa* 'it worries him/her/you'.
>
> *Recordar*: when it means 'to remind': *la recuerdo* 'I remember her', but *recuérdale que viene esta noche* 'remind her/him that (s)he's coming tonight'.
>
> *Tirar* when it means 'to pull' rather than to 'throw' or 'throw away': *la amiga le tiraba de la mano* (J. Marías, Sp.) 'his/her friend was pulling her/him/you by the hand'. Compare *lo/la tiró* '(s)he threw it/(s)he threw it away'.
>
> *Tocar* when it means 'to be the turn of' rather than 'to touch': compare *le toca a usted, señora* 'it's your turn, Señora' and *la tocó a usted, señora* '(s)he touched you, Señora'.

12.6.5 *Le/les* in double accusative constructions

In *Juan la oyó* 'John heard her' *la* is normal since 'she' is not 'actively participating' in any of the ways described at 12.3, List A. In 'John heard her sing an aria' there are two objects, one, 'aria', less active than the other, 'her'. Spanish-speakers normally use *le* to denote the more active object *Juan le oyó cantar un aria* (*la* occurs, particularly in Spain, but may be rejected by educated speakers). Questionnaires, based on examples from García (1975), elicited the following replies from twenty educated *madrileños*, which confirmed García's finding with Latin-American-speakers: *María no quería venir, pero. . .obligamos a venir* (*la* 70%, *le* 30%) 'Maria didn't want to come, but we obliged her to come' (single accusative); *pobre María, su padre siempre. . .obliga a decir la verdad* (*la* 35%, *le* 65%) 'poor Maria, her father always obliges her to tell the truth' (two objects, 'her' and *la verdad*).

(i) *Ver* normally takes *lo* (in Spain *le*)/*la*/*los*/*las*: *yo me quedé con ella porque quería verla firmar el contrato* 'I stayed with her because I wanted to see her sign the contract'.

(ii) *Dejar* 'to let' may take *la* (and in Latin America *lo*): *la dejaron hacerlo* 'they let her do it'. *Permitir* takes *le*: *le permitieron hacerlo*.

12.7 Pronouns with verbs of motion

For *acude a ella* '(s)he goes to her', *se les acercó* '(s)he approached them', see 11.8.

12.8 'Resumptive' or 'echoing' *lo* with *ser*, *estar* and *haber*

The predicate of *ser, estar, parecer* and *haber* is resumed or 'echoed' by *lo*: *parecía alemana y lo era* 'she looked German and she was'. See 7.4 note (i) and 30.2.2 for details.

12.9 *Se* for *le*/*les* when they are followed by *lo*/*la*/*los*/*las*

For the obligatory replacement of *le* by *se* when it precedes *lo*/*la*/*los*/*las*, as in *se lo di* 'I gave it to him' (*never *le lo di*), see 11.13.1.

12.10 Latin America *se los* for *se lo*

For the very frequent colloquial Latin-American form *?se los dije* 'I told them/you (plural)', for the standard *se lo dije a ellos/ellas/ustedes*, see 11.13.2.

12.11 *Le* for *les*

For the universal colloquial tendency to use *le* for *les* when the latter is a 'redundant' pronoun, as in *siempre le digo la verdad a mis padres* 'I always tell my parents the truth', for *les digo la verdad*, see 11.16.3.

13

Forms of verbs

The main points discussed in this chapter are:

- The three conjugations (Section 13.1.1)
- Irregular and radical-changing verbs (Section 13.1.3–4)
- The different tense forms (Section 13.1.5–17)
- Spelling rules affecting all verbs (Section 13.2. & 13.5.3)
- Forms and list of irregular verbs (Section 13.3–4)
- Forms of regular verbs (Section 13.5)

Argentine *vos* forms are mentioned since they are standard in that country. See 11.3.1 for details.

13.1 General remarks about the Spanish verb system

13.1.1 The three conjugations

All Spanish verbs belong to one of three conjugations distinguished by the vowel of the infinitive: (1) *-ar* (2) *-er* (3) *-ir*, or *-ír* in the case of the verbs listed at 13.1.4f.

The full conjugation of three typical regular verbs in *-ar*, *-er* and *-ir* is shown at 13.5.2. As this list shows, the endings of verbs of the *-ir* conjugation are the same as those of the *-er* conjugations except for the forms shown in bold.

13.1.2 Regular spelling changes

There are important, predictable spelling changes that affect all verbs. They are discussed at 13.2.2 and the main ones are shown at 13.5.3.

13.1.3 Irregular verbs: general remarks

Only about two dozen Spanish verbs (not counting compound verbs formed from them) are traditionally defined as truly 'irregular'. These are:

andar to walk 13.3.5	compounds) 13.3.16	*poder* to be able 13.3.34
asir to seize (rarely used) 13.3.6	*estar* to be 13.3.21	*poner* to put (and several compounds) 13.3.35
caber to fit into 13.3.8	*haber* auxiliary verb or 'there is/are' 13.3.22	*producir* to produce (and all verbs ending in
caer to fall (and some compounds) 13.3.9	*hacer* 'to do'/'to make' 13.3.23	– *ducir*) 13.3.37
dar to give 13.3.15	*ir* to go 13.3.24	*querer* to want 13.3.38
decir to say (and a few	*oír* to hear 13.3.29	*saber* to know 13.3.42

salir to go out 13.3.43
ser to be 13.3.45
tener to have (and several compounds) 13.3.46

traer to bring (and a few compounds) 13.3.47
valer to be worth (and compounds) 13.3.48

venir to come (and compounds) 13.3.49
ver to see 13.3.50

13.1.4 Radical-changing verbs

'Radical-changing' verbs are numerous: several hundred are in everyday use, although many of them are derived from more familiar verbs, e.g. *descontar* 'to discount' is conjugated like *contar* 'to count'/'to tell a story'. Radical-changing verbs have regular endings, but a vowel in the stem is modified in some forms, cf. *contar* 'to tell a story' > *cuenta* '(s)he tells', *perder* 'to lose' > *pierdo* 'I lose', *sentir* 'to feel' > *siente* '(s)he feels' > *sintió* '(s)he felt', etc.

Grammarians have traditionally been reluctant to call these verbs 'irregular', but they must be learned separately since their infinitive is no guide to whether they are radical-changing or not. Compare *renovar* 'to renovate', which is a radical-changing verb, and *innovar* 'to innovate', which is not.

A few verbs are uncertain or have become regular. These include: *cimentar* 'to cement' like *cerrar* or, more usually, regular; *derrocar* 'to overthrow', nowadays regular; *mentar* 'to mention', though educated usage still prefers to conjugate it like *cerrar*; *derrengarse* 'to be exhausted', nowadays regular; *plegar* 'to fold' like *cerrar* or optionally regular.

Note also the following variant meanings: *apostar* reg. 'to post a sentry', conj. like *contar* ' to bet'; *aterrar* reg. 'to terrorize', conj. like *cerrar* 'to level/raze to the ground'; *asolar* reg. 'to parch', conj. like *contar* ' to level/raze to ground' (nowadays often always regular).

The following list shows the common types of radical-changing verbs and a selection of verbs that occur constantly and should be learned first.

(a) Conjugated like *contar* 'to tell'/'to count', 13.3.14:

acordarse de 'to remember', *acostarse* 'to go to bed', *apostar* 'to bet', *aprobar* 'to approve/'to pass an exam', *avergonzarse* 'to be ashamed', *colarse* 'to slip through/ gatecrash', *colgar* 'to hang', *comprobar* 'to check', *consolar* 'to console', *costar* 'to cost', *demostrar* 'to demonstrate' (a fact or technique), *desaprobar* 'to disapprove', *encontrar* 'to find'/'to meet', *esforzarse* 'to make an effort', *mostrar* 'to show', *probar* 'to prove'/'to try' (i.e. 'to sample'/'to test'), *recordar* 'to remember'/'to remind', *renovar* 'to renew', *rodar* 'to roll', *soltar* 'to release'/ 'let out', *sonar* 'to sound', *soñar* 'to dream', *tronar* 'to thunder', *volar* 'to fly'.

(b) Conjugated like *cerrar* 'to close', 13.3.11:

acertar 'to get right'/'to hit the mark', *apretar* 'to squeeze/tighten', *atravesar* 'to cross', *calentar* 'to heat', *comenzar* 'to begin', *confesar* 'to confess', *despertar(se)* 'to wake up', *empezar* 'to begin', *encerrar* 'to lock/shut in', *enterrar* 'to bury', *gobernar* 'to govern', *helar* 'to freeze' (liquids), *manifestarse* 'to demonstrate' (i.e. protest), *negar* 'to deny', *nevar* 'to snow', *pensar* 'to think', *recomendar* 'to recommend', *sentarse* 'to sit down', *temblar* 'to tremble', *tropezar* 'to stumble'.

(c) Conjugated like *mover* 'to move', 13.3.28:

desenvolverse 'to develop', *devolver* 'to give back', *disolver* 'to dissolve', *doler* 'to hurt', *envolver* 'to wrap up', *llover* 'to rain', *morder* 'to bite', *oler* 'to smell' (see 13.3.30), *remover* 'to stir up' (Lat. Am. 'to remove'), *resolver* 'to resolve', *soler* 'to be accustomed to' (+ infinitive), *volver(se)* 'to return'/'to become', etc.

(**d**) Conjugated like *perder* 'to lose', 13.3.32:

atender 'to attend' (i.e. pay attention), *defender* 'to defend', *encender* 'to light/set fire to', *entender* 'to understand', *extenderse* 'to extend/stretch' (over a distance), *tender a* 'to tend to'.

(**e**) Conjugated like *pedir* 'to ask for', 13.3.31:

competir 'to compete', *concebir* 'to conceive', *conseguir* 'to achieve'/'to manage', *corregir* 'to correct', *derretirse* 'to melt', *despedir* 'to fire' (i.e. dismiss from job), *despedirse* 'to say goodbye', *elegir* 'to elect'/'to choose', *gemir* 'to groan', *impedir* 'to hinder'/'to impede', *medir* 'to measure', *perseguir* 'to persecute'/'to chase', *proseguir* 'to pursue' (a course of action), *rendirse* 'to surrender', *repetir* 'to repeat', *reñir* 'to scold' (see 13.3.40), *seguir* 'to follow', *servir* 'to serve'/'to be useful', *vestir(se)* 'to wear'/'to dress'.

(**f**) Conjugated like *reír* 'to laugh', 13.3.39:

desleír(se) 'to dissolve/melt', *engreírse* 'to grow conceited', *(re)freír* 'to fry', *sonreír* 'to smile'.

(**g**) Conjugated like *sentir* 'to feel', 13.3.44:

advertir 'to warn', *arrepentirse* 'to repent', *consentir* 'to consent', *convertir* 'to convert', *convertirse en* 'to turn into', *desmentir* 'to deny', *disentir* 'to dissent', *divertir(se)* 'to amuse oneself', *herir* 'to wound', *interferir* 'to interfere', *invertir* 'to invest', *mentir* 'to tell lies', *preferir* 'to prefer', *referirse a* 'to refer to', *sugerir* 'to suggest'.

(**h**) *dormir* 'to sleep' and *morir* 'to die', 13.3.18.

(**i**) *jugar* 'to play', 13.3.25.

(**j**) *adquirir* 'to acquire', 13.3.3.

(**k**) Conjugated like *discernir* 'to discern', 13.3.17:

cernirse 'to hover'/'to loom'; *concernir* 'to concern' (third-person only).

13.1.5 Forms of the present indicative

The endings of the present indicative of regular verbs and of all but a few irregular verbs are shown at 13.5.2. However, there are numerous verbs in the *-er* and *-ir* conjugations in which the first-person singular ending is attached to an irregular stem, e.g. *producir* 'to produce' > *produzco* 'I produce', *poner* 'to put' > *pongo* 'I put', etc. These must be learned separately.

Four irregular verbs have a first-person singular ending in *-y*: *dar* 'to give' > *doy*, *estar* 'to be' > *estoy*, *ir* 'to go' > *voy*, *ser* 'to be' > *soy*.

Learners can discover the Argentine *vos* forms of the present tense by dropping any unaccented *i* from the ending of the Peninsular *vosotros* form: *vosotros habláis* > *vos hablás* 'you speak', *vosotros teméis* > *vos temés* 'you fear', *vosotros sois* > *vos sos* 'you are'; but *vosotros vivís > vos vivís* 'you live', *vosotros decís > vos decís* 'you say'. The verb forms used with *vos* in other areas of *voseo*, e.g. much of Central America, should be learned locally.

13.1.6 Forms of the imperfect indicative

The endings of the imperfect indicative (*tú* and *vos*) are shown at 13.5.2. The endings are added to the stem left after removing the infinitive ending. There are only three exceptions:

>*ser*: to be: *era, eras, era, éramos, erais, eran*   *ver*: to see: *veía, veías, veía, veíamos, veíais,*
>*ir*: to go: *iba, ibas, iba, íbamos, ibais, iban*   *veían* (not the expected* *vía*, **vías*, etc.)

13.1.7 Forms of the preterite (US 'preterit': the British spelling is used in this book)

The endings of the preterite (*tú* and *vos*) are shown at 13.5.2. The third-person plural ending is *-eron* (not *-ieron*) in the case of the preterite of:

>*conducir* 'to drive', and all verbs whose infinitive ends in *–ducir*: *condujeron,*
>   *redujeron*
>*decir* 'to say': *dijeron*
>*ser* & *ir* 'to be' & 'to go': *fueron*
>*traer* 'to bring': *trajeron*

Verbs whose infinitive ends in *-ñer*, *-ñir* or *-llir* also lose the *i* in the third-person singular and third-person plural endings. See 13.5.3, 6.

Most of the irregular verbs listed at 13.1.3 have an irregular preterite stem, and many of them have unexpected first-person and third-person singular endings, and no accent on the final vowels. *Hacer* 'to do' and *caber* 'to fit into' are typical: *hacer: hice, hiciste, hizo, hicimos, hicisteis, hicieron; caber: cupe, cupiste, cupo, cupimos, cupisteis, cupieron.*

Verbs conjugated like *sentir* 'to feel', *pedir* 'to ask', and *dormir* 'to sleep' have irregularities in the third person of the preterite:

>*sintió > sintieron*   *pidió > pidieron*   *durmió > durmieron*

13.1.8 The future and the conditional

The future and the conditional tenses (*tú* and *vos*) are formed in the same way for all verbs, regular and irregular: they are shown at 13.5.2. These endings are always added to the infinitive except in the cases of the following twelve verbs which have a special future/conditional stem, shown in bold:

>*caber* to fit in: ***cabr–***   *poder* to be able: ***podr–***   *salir* to go out: ***saldr–***
>*decir* to say: ***dir–***   *poner* to put: ***pondr–***   *tener* to have: ***tendr–***
>*haber* (aux. verb): ***habr–***   *querer* to want: ***querr–***   *valer* to be worth: ***valdr–***
>*hacer* to do/make: ***har–***   *saber* to know: ***sabr–***   *venir* to come: ***vendr–***

13.1.9 Forms of the present subjunctive

The endings of the present subjunctive are easily memorized: ***-ar*** verbs take the endings of the present indicative of regular *-er* verbs except that the first-person ending is *-e*; *-er* and *-ir* verbs take the endings of the present indicative of regular *-ar* verbs, except that first-person ending is *–a*. See 13.5.2 for examples.

As far as regular verbs and most irregular verbs are concerned, these endings are added to the stem left after removing the *-o* of the first-person present indicative: e.g. *vengo* 'I come' > *venga*, *conduzco* 'I drive' > *conduzca*, *quepo* 'there's room for me' > *quepa* (from *caber*, 13.3.8), etc. The six exceptions among the irregular verbs are :

dar to give	*dé, des, dé*, etc. (the accent distinguishes the word from *de* = 'of').
estar to be	*esté, estés, esté, estemos, estéis, estén*
haber	*haya, hayas, haya, hayamos, hayáis, hayan*
ir to go	*vaya, vayas, vaya, vayamos, vayáis, vayan*
saber to know	*sepa, sepas, sepa, sepamos, sepáis, sepan*
ser to be	*sea, seas, sea, seamos, seáis, sean*

In the case of radical-changing verbs, the usual vowel changes occur, e.g. *cuente, cuentes, cuente, contemos, contéis, cuenten* (from *contar*; see 13.3.14). Verbs like *sentir* 'to feel' have another irregularity in the present subjunctive: *sienta, sientas, sienta, sintamos, sintáis, sientan*.

Morir 'to die' and *dormir* 'to sleep' also show extra irregularities in the present subjunctive. See 13.3.18 for details.

In Argentina the *vos* forms of the present subjunctive used by careful speakers are the same as the standard *tú* forms. See 16.2.8 for discussion of this point.

13.1.10 Forms of the past (imperfect) and future subjunctives

There are two sets of imperfect subjunctive endings: the imperfect subjunctive in *–ra* and the imperfect subjunctive in *–se*. They are shown at 13.5.2 (Argentine *vos* forms are the same as the standard *tú* forms). When used as subjunctive forms, these two sets of forms are interchangeable, although the *–ra* forms are more frequent. For the slight differences between their uses see 16.2.3.

The future subjunctive is virtually obsolete, so foreign learners can ignore it: its limited uses in modern Spanish are discussed at 16.17. Its endings are identical to those of the *-ra* past subjunctive, except that the last vowel is *e*: *-ar* verbs: *-are, -ares, -are, -áremos, -areis, -aren*; *-er* & *-ir* verbs: *-iere, -ieres, -iere, -iéremos, -iereis, -ieren*.

The past (imperfect) and the future subjunctive endings are added to the stem of the third-person singular of the preterite indicative. In the case of regular verbs this stem is found by removing the infinitive ending, e.g. *habl(ar)* > *habl-*: *yo hablara/hablase, tú hablaras/hablases, él hablara/hablase*, etc. But in the case of irregular verbs the preterite stem is often irregular, e.g.

Infinitive	third-person preterite stem	Past & future subjunctives
sentir 'to feel' & verbs like it	*sint(ió)*	*sintiera/sintiese/sintiere*, etc.
pedir 'to request' & verbs like it	*pid(ió)*	*pidiera/pidiese/pidiere*, etc.
ser 'be'	*fu(e)*	*fuera/fuese/fuere*, etc.
producir 'to produce', & all verbs ending in *-ducir*	*produj(o)*	*produjera/produjese/produjere*, etc.
tener 'to have'	*tuv(o)*	*tuviera/tuviese/tuviere*, etc.

Morir and *dormir* have the third-person preterite stems *mur(ió)* and *durm(ió)*, so the past subjunctives are *muriera/muriese, durmiera/durmiese*, etc.

The forms *-ese, -era, -ere*, etc. (i.e. not *-iese, -iera, -iere*) are used with the following verbs:

decir 'to say'	*dijera/dijese/dijere*, etc.
ser 'to be'	*fuera/fuese/fuere*, etc.
traer 'to bring'	*trajera/trajese/trajere*, etc.
all verbs whose infinitive ends in *-ducir*	*condujera, produjese*, etc.
all verbs whose infinitive ends in *-ñer*, *-ñir* or *-llir*	*bullera, tañese*, etc.

13.1.11 The imperative

See 13.5.2 for the regular forms, and Chapter 17 for its uses. Argentine *vos* imperatives can be found by removing the *–d* of the standard *vosotros* imperative: *contad > contá, decid > decí*, etc.

13.1.12 Forms of the past participle: see 19.2.1

13.1.13 The compound tenses

The compound tenses, e.g. *he hablado* 'I have spoken', *has visto* 'you've seen', *habían tenido* 'they'd had', *habrán hecho* 'they'll have made', etc., are always predictable if one can conjugate *haber* (see 13.3.22) and knows the past participle of the verb. For this reason individual compound tenses are not listed, but the full compound tense forms of *ver* 'to see' is shown in 13.5.4. The use of the compound tenses is discussed at 14.8.–10.

13.1.14 Forms of the gerund: see 20.2

13.1.15 Forms of the adjectival participle

This refers to forms like *preocupante* 'worrying', *convincente* 'convincing', discussed at 19.4.

13.1.16 Continuous forms of verbs

Spanish has a full range of continuous forms, e.g. *estoy hablando* 'I'm talking', *estuve esperando* 'I was waiting' / 'I waited for a time', etc. They are all formed from the appropriate tense of *estar* (see 13.3.21) and the invariable gerund. Their use is discussed in Chapter 15.

13.1.17 Forms of the passive: see 13.5.1

13.2 Variants and spelling rules

13.2.1 Colloquial variants

The Spanish verb system is remarkably stable throughout the Hispanic world, despite the large number of forms and exceptions. Popular regularizations of irregular forms, e.g. **cabo* for *quepo* (from *caber* 'to fit into'), **produció* for *produjo* (from *producir* 'to produce'), **andé* for *anduve* (from *andar* 'to walk') are stigmatized.

Four other popular spoken forms are heard:

(**a**) use of the infinitive for the *vosotros* form of the imperative (used in Spain only): *dar* for *dad* 'give', *callaros* for *callaos* 'shut up!' / 'be quiet', *iros* for *idos* 'go away', etc. For discussion see 17.2.4;

(**b**) addition of *-s* to the second-person preterite singular, e.g. *?distes* for *diste* 'you gave', *?hablastes* for *hablaste* 'you spoke'. This is common on both continents, but it is stigmatized and is not seen in printed texts;

(**c**) pluralization of forms *haber* (other than *hay*) when it means 'there is' / 'there are', e.g. *?habían muchos* for *había muchos* 'there were many'. See 30.2.1. note (i);

(**d**) a tendency in some popular Latin-American dialects to regularize radical-changing verbs, e.g. **cuentamos* for *contamos* 'we tell', **detiénete* for *detente* 'stop'. Such forms sometimes appear in the dialogue of novels, but they are strongly stigmatized.

13.2.2 General spelling rules

Certain spelling changes are applied systematically throughout the verb system, e.g. *pago > pagué, saco > saqué, rezo > recé*. The most common are shown at 13.5.3.

13.2.3 Spelling and pronunciation of *aislar, reunir, prohibir* and similar verbs whose stem contains a diphthong

When the last syllable but one of an infinitive contains a falling diphthong (one whose second letter is *i* or *u* pronounced *y* or *w*), this diphthong may or may not be broken into two syllables when it is stressed, e.g.

prohibir to prohibit	[proyβír] (two syllables)
prohíbe (s)he prohibits	[proíβe] (three syllables)
reunir to join together	[rrewnír] (two syllables)
reúnen they join	[rreúnes] (three syllables)

Compare the following verb in which the diphthong is not broken:

causar to cause	[kawsár] (two syllables)
causa it causes	[káwsas] (two syllables)

Since 1959 the stressed vowel in such broken diphthongs has been written with an accent; in the Academy's view the fact that *-h-* appears between the two vowels makes no difference. *Aislar* 'to isolate', *reunir* 'to bring together', and *prohibir* 'to prohibit' are common examples. The ruling affects the following forms of the verb (bracketed forms are unaffected):

Tú imperative:	*aísla*	*reúne*	*prohíbe*
Usted(es) imperative:	*aísle/aíslen*	*reúna/reúnan*	*prohíba/prohíban*

Present Indicative	*aíslo, aíslas, aísla (aislamos), (aisláis), aíslan*
	reúne, reúnes, reúne (reunimos), (reunís), reúnen
	prohíbe, prohíbes, prohíbe (prohibimos), (prohibís), prohíben

Present Subjunctive:	*aislar: aísle, aísles, aísle, (aislemos), (aisléis), aíslen*
	reunir: reúna, reúnas, reúna, (reunamos), (reunáis), reúnen
	prohibir: prohíba, prohíbas, prohíba, (prohibamos), (prohibáis), prohíban

The following verbs are similarly affected, but bracketed verbs are now archaic or rare:

ahijar to adopt (child)	*(amohinar* to vex)	*(desahitarse* to digest)	*prohijar* to adopt
(ahilar to line up)	*arcaizar* to archaize	*enraizar* to take root	*rehilar* to quiver
(ahincar to urge)	*aullar* to howl	*europeizar* to Europeanize	*rehusar* to refuse
(ahitar to cloy)	*aunar* to unite	*hebraizar* to Hebraicize	*sahumar* to incense
ahumar to smoke (food)	*aupar* to help up	*judaizar* to Judaize	*sobrehilar* to over-
(airar to anger)	*cohibir* to restrain	*maullar* to meow	cast (in sewing)

NB: The meaning of *desahitarse* is, more accurately, 'to get rid of a sensation of excessive fullness'. It is rarely used, but the adjective *ahíto* is found, at least in Spain: *estoy ahíto/a* 'I'm full'.

The new spelling is in general use in printed texts in Spain, but most people still omit the accent in handwriting and many Latin-American publishers use the old, unaccented forms.

In other verbs the diphthong is not broken: when the diphthong is stressed the accent falls on its first vowel and no written accent appears, e.g. *arraigarse* 'to take root' > *arraigo, encausar* 'to sue' > *encausa*, etc. Similar are *amainar* 'to shorten'/'to calm', *causar* 'to cause', *desahuciar* 'to evict'/'to give up hope for' (variable, usually the diphthong is retained), *desenvainar* 'to unsheathe', *embaucar* 'to swindle', *embaular* 'to pack' (a trunk/suitcase: variable—the verb is hardly ever used), *envainar* 'to sheathe', *peinar* 'to comb'/'to do someone's hair', *reinar* to reign', etc.

13.2.4 Verbs whose infinitive ends in *-iar*

These are of two types. The majority conjugate like *cambiar* 'to change': the *-ia* survives as a diphthong throughout and is always pronounced [ya], so the verb is conjugated as a regular *–ar* verb and no accent is written on the *i*.

But about fifty verbs conjugate like *liar* 'to tie in a bundle'. These verbs are conjugated like *cambiar* (i.e. regularly) except that the *i* of the diphthong is stressed and written with an accent in the following cases (bracketed forms are regular):

Imperative: *(tú) lía, (usted) líe, (ustedes) líen*
Present Indicative: *lío, lías, lía, (liamos), (liáis), lían*
Present Subjunctive: *líe, líes, líe, (liemos), (liéis), líen*

The following list shows common verbs which conjugate like *liar*:

agriar to sour (usu. like *cambiar*)	*autografiar* to autograph	*desafiar* to challenge
aliar to ally	*auxiliar* to aid (disputed, usually like *cambiar*)	*descarriar* to misdirect
amnistiar to grant an amnesty to	*averiar* to damage	*desliar* to untie
ampliar to expand/enlarge	*aviar* to fit out	*desvariar* to rave
ansiar to yearn for	*biografiar* to write the biography of	*desviar* to divert
arriar to flood/to haul down	*conciliar* to reconcile (usually like *cambiar*)	*enfriar* to chill
ataviar to array (with clothes)	*contrariar* to counter	*enviar* to send
	criar to breed/raise	*escalofriar* to feel shivery
		espiar to spy
		expatriarse to emigrate (also like *cambiar*)

expiar to expiate
extasiar to make ecstatic
  (usually like *liar*)
extraviar to mislead
fiar to confide
fotografiar to photograph
gloriar(se) to glory
guiar to guide
hastiar to weary
historiar to chronicle
  (usually like *cambiar*)

inventariar to inventory
litografiar to lithograph
malcriar to pamper
mecanografiar to type
paliar to palliate
  (usually like *cambiar*)
piar to cheep
porfiar to argue
  stubbornly
radiografiar to X-ray
resfriar to cool

rociar to sprinkle
telegrafiar to telegraph
vaciar to empty
vanagloriarse to be
  boastful (almost always
  like *cambiar*)
variar to vary
vidriar to glaze (also
  like *cambiar*)

13.2.5 Verbs whose infinitive ends in *-uar*

Nearly all conjugate like *actuar* 'to act', i.e. the *u* may be stressed and written with an accent. The only forms affected are (bracketed forms are as a regular *–ar* verb, as are all the unlisted forms):

> Imperative: (*tú*) *actúa*, (*usted*) *actúe*, (*ustedes*) *actúen*
> Present Indicative: *actúo*, *actúas*, *actúa*, (*actuamos*) (*actuáis*) *actúan*
> Present Subjunctive: *actúe*, *actúes*, *actúe*, (*actuemos*), (*actuéis*), *actúen*

Verbs that conjugate like *actuar*:

acentuar to emphasize
atenuar to attenuate
conceptuar to deem
continuar to continue
desvirtuar to spoil
efectuar to carry out
evaluar to assess
exceptuar to except

extenuar to emaciate
fluctuar to fluctuate
graduar to grade
habituar to habituate
individuar to
  individualize
infatuar to infatuate
insinuar to hint

perpetuar to perpetuate
preceptuar to establish as a
  norm/precept
puntuar to punctuate/to
  assess
redituar yield (profit, etc.)
situar to situate
valuar to value

Averiguar ('to find out') is conjugated as a regular *–ar* verb and the *u* is never stressed (i.e. it is always pronounced [w]). *Aguar* 'to spoil' (a party, fun) is similar. A dieresis is written over the *u* before a following *e* in order to preserve the pronunciation [gw]. The only forms with a dieresis are (bracketed forms are unaffected):

> Imperative: (*usted*) *averigüe*, (*ustedes*) *averigüen*
> Preterite: *averigüé*, (*averiguaste*), (*averiguó*), (*averiguamos*), (*averiguasteis*), (*averiguaron*)
> Present Subjunctive: *averigüe*, *averigües*, *averigüe*, *averigüemos*, *averigüéis*, *averigüen*

(i) Verbs ending in *-cuar*, e.g. *evacuar* and *adecuar*, should be conjugated like *averiguar* (without the dieresis). *El País, Libro de estilo*, 2002, 155, insists on this, but conjugation like *actuar* is a common error in Spain and is accepted in some Latin-American countries.

13.2.6 Verbs ending in *-ear*

All regular. The combination *ee* is never written with an accent, cf. *pasear* 'to go for a walk':

> Present Indicative: *paseo*, *paseas*, *pasea*, *paseamos*, *paseáis*, *pasean*
> Present Subjunctive: *pasee*, *pasees*, *pasee*, *paseemos*, *paseéis*, *paseen*

13.2.7 Verbs ending in *-cer*

If the infinitive ends in *-cer* the spelling changes shown at 13.5.3 are applied in the case of a few verbs (*c* > *z* before *a, o*). However, the only verbs ending in *-cer* that are conjugated in this way are:

(**a**) those in which the *c/z* occurs after a consonant:

coercer to coerce	*ejercer* to practise/US	*(re)torcer* to twist (radical-
convencer to convince	practice	changing; see 13.3.12)
destorcer to untwist		*vencer* to defeat

(**b**) the following exceptional verbs:

(re)cocer to boil (food) (radical-changing; see 13.3.12)
escocerse to sting/smart (conj. like *cocer*; *picar* 'to sting' is more usual)
mecer to rock/swing; *mecerse* 'to sway'

The rest are like *parecer*, i.e. *-zc-* appears before *-o* or *-a*. See 13.3.10. For *hacer, placer, yacer* see 13.4.

13.2.8 Verbs ending in *–eer*: see 13.3.36

13.2.9 Verbs ending in *-cir*

The spelling change shown at 13.5.3 must be applied if the infinitive ends in *-cir*: *c* > *z* before *a, o*. But the only totally regular verbs ending in *-cir* are *esparcir* 'to scatter/strew', *fruncir* 'to pucker/wrinkle' (the eyebrows), *resarcir* 'to repay (effort)', *uncir* 'to yoke' and *zurcir* 'to darn'/'to sew together'. Any others, e.g. *producir*, *lucir*, should be viewed with suspicion, and checked in the list at 13.4.

13.2.10 Verbs whose infinitive ends in *–uir*: see *construir* 'to build', 13.3.13

13.3 Irregular verbs

13.3.1 General

Irregular verbs and model radical-changing verbs are listed in alphabetical order. The list omits oddities like the archaic *abarse*, found only in the form *ábate* 'get thee hence!', or *usucapir* 'to acquire property rights through customary use', used in legal jargon and only in the infinitive. In general only the irregular forms are shown, except in the cases of some very common verbs.

13.3.2 *Abolir* 'to abolish'

Defective verb. Only those forms are used in which the verb ending begins with *-i*:

Infinitive: *abolir*   Gerund: *aboliendo*   Past Participle: *abolido*
Imperative: *abolid* (**abole* is not used)
Present Indicative: only *abolimos* and *abolís* are used
Present Subjunctive: not used

All other tenses are regular. Other verbs or constructions are used to avoid unused forms, e.g. **sin que se abola* by *sin que sea abolido*. A few other verbs are defective, but only *abolir* and *agredir* are common nowadays:

aguerrir 'to inure'/'to harden' (only past participle in current use)
agredir see 13.3.4
arrecirse (Lat. Am.) 'to be frozen stiff'
aterirse 'to be numb with cold' (only infinitive and participle in current use)
blandir 'to brandish'

despavorir 'to be terrified' (only past participle in current use)
empedernir 'to harden'/'to petrify' (only participle in current use)
garantir 'guarantee' (*garantizar* in Spain but still used in Peru and the Southern Cone, where it is often conjugated regularly)

13.3.3 *Adquirir* 'to acquire' (also *inquirir* 'to enquire')

The infinitive was once *adquerir*, hence the *-ie-* when the stem vowel is stressed. Bracketed forms are regular, as are all forms not shown, e.g. *adquirí, adquiría, adquiriré, adquiriera*, etc.

Imperative: *(tú) adquiere, (usted) adquiera, (ustedes) adquieran*
Present Indicative: *adquiero, adquieres, adquiere, (adquirimos), (adquirís), adquieren*
Present Subjunctive: *adquiera, adquieras, adquiera, (adquiramos), (adquiráis), adquieran*

13.3.4 *Agredir* 'to assault'/'to attack'

Classified by some as defective (like *abolir*; see 13.3.2), by others as a regular *-ir* verb, the former usage being the more conservative. The new Academy dictionary declares it to be a normal *–ir* verb.

13.3.5 *Andar* 'to walk'/'to go about'

A regular *-ar* verb except for the preterite and the past subjunctives:

Preterite: *anduve, anduviste, anduvo, anduvimos, anduvisteis, anduvieron*
Imperfect Subjunctive (*-ra*): *anduviera, anduvieras, anduviera, anduviéramos, anduvierais, anduvieran*
Imperfect Subjunctive (*-se*): *anduviese, anduvieses, anduviese, anduviésemos, anduvieseis, anduviesen*

Preterite forms like **andé, *andaste* are heard, but they are strongly stigmatized.

13.3.6 *Asir* 'to grasp/'to seize'

Agarrarse is now much more common. Forms that contain a *g* are avoided, but other forms are heard, e.g. *me así a una rama para no caerme* 'I clutched hold of a branch so as not to fall'. It is conjugated like a regular *–ir* verb except for (bracketed forms are regular):

Imperative: *(usted) asga, (ustedes) asgan*
Present Indicative: *asgo, (ases, ase, asimos, asís, asen)*
Present Subjunctive: *asga, asgas, asga, asgamos, asgáis, asgan*

13.3.7 *Balbucir* 'to stammer'

Nowadays found only in those forms whose ending begins with *i*, e.g. *balbucía, balbució*. For other forms the regular *balbucear* is used and is the usual verb in spontaneous speech.

13.3.8 *Caber* 'to fit in'

Numerous irregularities:

> Gerund: *cabiendo*   Past Participle: *cabido*
> Imperative: (*tú*) *cabe,* (*vosotros*) *cabed,* (*usted*) *quepa,* (*ustedes*) *quepan*
> Present Indicative: *quepo, cabes, cabe, cabemos, cabéis, caben*
> Imperfect (regular): *cabía, cabías, cabía, cabíamos, cabíais, cabían*
> Preterite: *cupe, cupiste, cupo, cupimos, cupisteis, cupieron*
> Future: *cabré, cabrás, cabrá, cabremos, cabréis, cabrán*   Conditional: *cabría,* etc.
> Present Subjunctive: *quepa, quepas, quepa, quepamos, quepáis, quepan*
> Imperfect Subjunctive (*-ra*): *cupiera, cupieras, cupiera, cupiéramos, cupierais, cupieran*
> Imperfect Subjunctive (*-se*): *cupiese, cupieses, cupiese, cupiésemos, cupieseis, cupiesen*

Usage: *¿quepo yo?* 'is there room for me?', *no cabe* 'it won't fit', *no cabíamos* 'there wasn't room for us', *no cabe la menor duda de que...* 'there isn't the slightest doubt that...'.

13.3.9 *Caer* 'to fall'

> Gerund: *cayendo*   Past Participle: *caído*
> Imperative: (*tú*) *cae,* (*vosotros*) *caed,* (*usted*) *caiga,* (*ustedes*) *caigan*
> Present Indicative: *caigo, caes, cae, caímos, caéis, caen*
> Imperfect (regular): *caía, caías, caía, caíamos, caíais, caían*
> Preterite: *caí, caíste, cayó, caímos, caísteis, cayeron*
> Future (regular): *caeré,* etc.   Conditional (regular): *caería,* etc.
> Present Subjunctive: *caiga, caigas, caiga, caigamos, caigáis, caigan*
> Imperfect Subjunctive (*-ra*): *cayera, cayeras, cayera, cayéramos, cayerais, cayeran*
> Imperfect Subjunctive (*-se*): *cayese, cayeses, cayese, cayésemos, cayeseis, cayesen*

13.3.10 Verbs ending in *-cer*

All verbs ending in *-cer* conjugate like *nacer*, shown below, except the regular verbs *coercer, ejercer,* (*con*)*vencer* and *mecer,* for which see 13.5.3 item (1), and the radical-changing verbs *escocer,* (*re*)*cocer* and (*re*)*torcer,* for which see 13.3.12 and 13.2.7. In all other verbs ending in *–cer, c > zc* before *a* or *o*. All forms are as for a regular *–er* verb except for (bracketed forms are regular):

> Imperative: (*usted*) *nazca,* (*ustedes*) *nazcan*
> Present Indicative: *nazco,* (*naces, nace, nacemos, nacéis, nacen*)
> Present Subjunctive: *nazca, nazcas, nazca, nazcamos, nazcáis, nazcan*

13.3.11 *Cerrar* 'to shut/'to close'

A common type of radical-changing verb. The endings are those of regular *-ar* verbs, but the *e* of the stem changes to *ie* when stressed. All forms are as for a regular *–ar* verb, save (bracketed forms are regular):

Imperative: (*tú*) *cierra*, (*usted*) *cierre*, (*ustedes*) *cierren*
Present Indicative: *cierro, cierras, cierra*, (*cerramos*), (*cerráis*), *cierran*
Present Subjunctive: *cierre, cierres, cierre*, (*cerremos*), (*cerréis*), *cierren*

13.3.12 *Cocer* 'to boil' (food)

This, and three verbs like it, *torcer* 'to twist', *destorcer* 'to untwist' and *retorcer* 'to wring'/'to twist', conjugate exactly like *mover* save for the predictable spelling change *c* > *z* before *a, o* (bracketed forms are regular):

Imperative: (*tú*) *cuece*, (*usted*) *cueza*, (*ustedes*) *cuezan*
Present Indicative: *cuezo, cueces, cuece*, (*cocemos*), (*cocéis*), *cuecen*
Present Subjunctive: *cueza, cuezas, cueza*, (*cozamos*), (*cozáis*), *cuezan*

13.3.13 *Construir* 'to build'

Verbs ending in *-uir* are quite common. An unstressed *i* between vowels is spelt *y*, e.g. *construyó* for the expected **construió* and an unexpected *y* is inserted in a number of forms, e.g. *construyes* for the predicted **construes*.

Gerund: *construyendo*   Past Participle: *construido* (no accent! See 39.2.3b for explanation)
Imperative: (*tú*) *construye*, (*vosotros*) *construid*, (*usted*) *construya*, (*ustedes*) *construyan*
Present Indicative: *construyo, construyes, construye, construimos* (no accent!), *construís, construyen*
Imperfect (regular): *construía, construías, construía, construíamos, construíais, construían*
Preterite: *construí, construiste, construyó, construimos, construisteis, construyeron*
Future (regular): *construiré*, etc.   Conditional (regular): *construiría*, etc.
Present Subjunctive: *construya, construyas, construya, construyamos, construyáis, construyan*
Imperfect Subjunctive (*-ra*): *construyera, construyeras, construyera, construyéramos, construyerais, construyeran*
Imperfect Subjunctive (*-se*): *construyese, construyeses, construyese, construyésemos, construyeseis, construyesen*

Argüir 'to argue (a point)' is spelt with a dieresis whenever the *u* is followed by *i*. This preserves the pronunciation [gwi]: *arguyo, argüimos, argüí, arguya*, etc.

13.3.14 *Contar* 'to count'/'to tell a story'

A common type of radical-changing verb: the *o* of the stem changes to *ue* when it is stressed. All forms are as for a regular *–ar* verb except (bracketed forms are regular):

Imperative: (*tú*) *cuenta*, (*usted*) *cuente*, (*ustedes*), *cuenten*
Present Indicative: *cuento, cuentas, cuenta*, (*contamos*), (*contáis*), *cuentan*
Present Subjunctive: *cuente, cuentes, cuente*, (*contemos*), (*contéis*), *cuenten*

13.3.15 *Dar* 'to give'

Gerund: *dando*   Past Participle: *dado*
Imperative: (*tú*) *da*, (*vosotros*) *dad*, (*usted*) *dé*, (*ustedes*) *den*
Present Indicative: *doy, das, da, damos, dais, dan*

Imperfect (regular): *daba, dabas, daba, dábamos, dabais, daban*
Preterite: *di, diste, dio* (no accent!), *dimos, disteis, dieron*
Future (regular): *daré*, etc.   Conditional (regular): *daría*, etc.
Present Subjunctive: *dé, des, dé, demos, deis, den*
Imperfect Subjunctive (*-ra*): *diera, dieras, diera, diéramos, dierais, dieran*
Imperfect Subjunctive (*-se*): *diese, dieses, diese, diésemos, dieseis, diesen*

The accent on the present subjunctive forms distinguishes them from the preposition *de* 'of'. This accent becomes unnecessary (although it is constantly printed) when a pronoun is suffixed: *dele, deles*.

13.3.16 *Decir* 'to say'

Gerund: *diciendo*   Past Participle: *dicho*
Imperative: (*tú*) *di*, (*vosotros*) *decid*, (*usted*) *diga*, (*ustedes*) *digan*
Present Indicative: *digo, dices, dice, decimos, decís, dicen*
Imperfect (regular): *decía, decías, decía, decíamos, decíais, decían*
Preterite: *dije, dijiste, dijo, dijimos, dijisteis, dijeron*
Future: *diré, dirás, dirá, diremos, diréis, dirán*   Conditional: *diría*, etc.
Present Subjunctive: *diga, digas, diga, digamos, digáis, digan*
Imperfect Subjunctive (*-ra*): *dijera, dijeras, dijera, dijéramos, dijerais, dijeran*
Imperfect Subjunctive (*-se*): *dijese, dijeses, dijese, dijésemos, dijeseis, dijesen*

(i) *Predecir* 'to foretell' is conjugated regularly in the future, conditional and imperative forms: *prediciré*, etc., *prediciría*, etc., imp. *predice, prediga*, etc. Forms like *prediré, prediría* are said by Seco (1998), 351, to be 'rare'.

(ii) *Desdecir* (e.g. *desdecirse de* 'to go back on') has the *tú* imperative *desdice*, but is otherwise regular, although rarer forms like *desdeciré, desdeciría* are not considered incorrect. The same is true of *contradecir* 'to contradict': *contradice, contradiré, contradiría*, rarely *contradeciré, contradeciría*.

13.3.17 *Discernir*, 'to discern'

This shows the common radical-changing modification *e > ie*, but verbs like *discernir* are very unusual in the *-ir* conjugation: only *cernir* 'to hover'/'to loom', *concernir* (third-person only) 'to concern' and *hendir* (in Spain also *hender*, like *entender*) 'to cleave' conjugate like it (bracketed forms are regular):

Imperative: (*tú*) *discierne*, (*usted*) *discierna*, (*ustedes*) *disciernan*
Present Indicative: *discierno, disciernes, discierne*, (*discernimos*), (*discernís*), *disciernen*
Preterite (regular): *discerní, discerniste, discernió**, *discernimos, discernisteis, discernieron**
Present Subjunctive: *discierna, disciernas, discierna*, (*discernamos*), (*discernáis*), *disciernan*
Imperfect Subjunctive (*-ra*) (regular): *discerniera*, etc.
Imperfect Subjunctive (*-se*) (regular): *discerniese*, etc.

*Not the expected *discirnió, *discirnieron

All other forms are as for a regular *-ir* verb.

13.3.18 *Dormir* 'to sleep', *morir* 'to die'

Dormir and *morir* are the only verbs of this kind. Apart from the common change *o > ue*, the third-person preterite stem vowel is *u*. The *u* also appears in the first and second-person plural of the present subjunctive and in the gerund. Forms in brackets are regular:

> Gerund: *durmiendo*   Past Participle: *dormido* (reg.), but *muerto* is the p.p. of *morir*
> Imperative: (*tú*) *duerme*, (*vosotros dormid*), (*usted*) *duerma*, (*ustedes*) *duerman*
> Present Indicative: *duermo, duermes, duerme, (dormimos), (dormís), duermen*
> Imperfect (regular): *dormía, dormías, dormía, dormíamos, dormíais, dormían*
> Preterite: (*dormí*), (*dormiste*), *durmió*, (*dormimos*), (*dormisteis*), *durmieron*
> Future (regular): *dormiré*, etc.   Conditional (regular): *dormiría*, etc.
> Present Subjunctive: *duerma, duermas, duerma, durmamos, durmáis, duerman*
> Imperfect Subjunctive (-*ra*): *durmiera, durmieras, durmiera, durmiéramos, durmierais, durmieran*
> Imperfect Subjunctive (-*se*): *durmiese, durmieses, durmiese durmiésemos, durmieseis, durmiesen*

13.3.19 *Erguir(se)* 'to rear up'/'to sit up straight'

This verb has alternative forms in some of its tenses, the forms with *y-* being more common. Forms in brackets are regular:

> Gerund: *irguiendo*   Past Participle: *erguido*
> Imperative: (*tú*) *yergue / irgue*, (*vosotros erguid*), (*usted*) *yerga/irga*, (*ustedes*) *yergan/irgan*
> Present Indicative: *yergo/irgo, yergues/irgues, yergue/irgue*, (*erguimos*), (*erguís*), *yerguen/irguen*
> Preterite: (*erguí*), (*erguiste*), *irguió*, (*erguimos*), (*erguisteis*), *irguieron*
> Present Subjunctive: *yerga/irga, yergas/irgas, yerga/irga, yergamos/irgamos, yergáis/irgáis, yergan/irgan*
> Imperfect Subjunctive (-*ra*): *irguiera, irguieras, irguiera, irguiéramos, irguierais, irguieran*
> Imperfect Subjunctive (-*se*): *irguiese, irguiese, irguiese, irguiésemos, irguieseis, irguiesen*

All other forms are regular. Usage: *no te agaches—ponte erguido* 'stop slouching—sit up straight', *se irguió como una serpiente* 'it rose up like a snake', *el perro irguió las orejas* 'the dog pricked up its ears'.

13.3.20 *Errar* 'to wander'/'err'

This verb conjugates like *cerrar*, i.e. *e* > *ie* when stressed, but the *ie* is written *ye*. In the Southern Cone and Colombia, and in some other parts of Latin America, it is regular, i.e. *erro, erras, erra*, etc. Conjugated like a regular –*ar* verb except for (bracketed forms are regular):

> Imperative: (*tú*) *yerra*, (*usted*) *yerre*, (*ustedes*) *yerren*
> Present Indicative: *yerro, yerras, yerra*, (*erramos*), (*erráis*), *yerran*
> Present Subjunctive: *yerre, yerres, yerre*, (*erremos*), (*erréis*), *yerren*

13.3.21 *Estar* 'to be'

This constantly occurring irregular verb is conjugated like a regular –*ar* verb except for the final accented vowel in several forms of the present indicative and subjunctive, and except also for the preterite, which is unexpected. The difference between *estar* and *ser* is discussed in Chapter 29.

Gerund (reg.): *estando* Past   Participle (reg.): *estado*
Imperative: (*tú*) *está*, (*vosotros estad*, reg.), (*usted*) *esté*, (*ustedes*) *estén*
Present Indicative: ***estoy***, *estás, está, estamos, estáis, están*
Imperfect (regular): *estaba, estabas, estaba, estábamos, estabais, estaban*
Preterite: *estuve, estuviste, estuvo, estuvimos, estuvisteis, estuvieron*
Future (regular): *estaré*, etc.   Conditional (regular): *estaría*, etc.
Present Subjunctive: *esté, estés, esté, estemos, estéis, estén*
Imperfect Subjunctive (*-ra*): *estuviera, estuvieras, estuviera, estuviéramos, estuvierais, estuvieran*
Imperfect Subjunctive (*-se*): *estuviese, estuvieses, estuviese, estuviésemos, estuvieseis, estuviesen*

(i) The imperative is often formed from the pronominal ('reflexive') form, i.e. *estate, estaos, estese, estense*. These are frequently spelled with an accent, e.g. *estáte*. See 17.2.6.

(ii) *Estar* is never used in the continuous form: **está estando* is not Spanish.

13.3.22 *Haber*, auxiliary verb, and also 'there is', 'there are', 'there were', etc.

This common verb is used to form the compound tenses of all regular and irregular verbs (for discussion of compound tenses see 14.8). It is also used in the third person only as the main 'existential' verb, cf. *había muchos* 'there were a lot', *habrá menos de cinco* 'there will be less than five'. When used thus its present indicative form is *hay*: see Chapter 30 for discussion.

Gerund: *habiendo*   Past Participle: *habido*
Imperative: (not used)
Present Indicative: *he, has, ha* (*hay*), *hemos, habéis, han*
Imperfect (regular): *había, habías, había, habíamos, habíais, habían*
Preterite: *hube, hubiste, hubo, hubimos, hubisteis, hubieron*
Future: *habré, habrás, habrá, habremos, habréis, habrán*
Conditional: *habría, habrías, habría, habríamos, habríais, habrían*
Present Subjunctive: *haya, hayas, haya, hayamos, hayáis, hayan*
Imperfect Subjunctive (*-ra*): *hubiera, hubieras, hubiera, hubiéramos, hubierais, hubieran*
Imperfect Subjunctive (*-se*): *hubiese, hubieses, hubiese, hubiésemos, hubieseis, hubiesen*

(i) The *-ra* subjunctive form is also commonly used to form the conditional perfect, i.e. *te hubiera llamado* for *te habría llamado* 'I would have phoned you'. See 14.7.5 for discussion.

(ii) When it means 'there is/was/will be', etc., this verb is always singular: *había cinco* 'there were five'. Forms like ?*habían cinco* are unacceptable in Castilian-speaking Spain and in careful writing everywhere, but they are usual in spoken Spanish in Catalonia and Latin America.

(iii) *Habemos* is used in the phrase *nos las habemos* 'we're dealing with'. See 7.4.2 for an example.

(iv) The form ?*haiga* is sometimes heard for the subjunctive *haya* but it is stigmatized as rustic or illiterate.

13.3.23 *Hacer* 'to do'/'to make'

There are several compounds, e.g. *deshacer* 'to undo', *contrahacer* 'to counterfeit'

Gerund: *haciendo*   Past Participle: *hecho*
Imperative: (*tú*) *haz*, (*vosotros*) *haced*, (*usted*) *haga*, (*ustedes*) *hagan*
Present Indicative: *hago, haces, hace, hacemos, hacéis, hacen*
Imperfect (regular): *hacía, hacías, hacía, hacíamos, hacíais, hacían*
Preterite: *hice, hiciste, hizo, hicimos, hicisteis, hicieron*
Future: *haré, harás, hará, haremos, haréis, harán*   Conditional: *haría*, etc.
Present Subjunctive: *haga, hagas, haga, hagamos, hagáis, hagan*
Imperfect Subjunctive (-*ra*): *hiciera, hicieras, hiciera, hiciéramos, hicierais, hicieran*
Imperfect Subjunctive (-*se*): *hiciese, hicieses, hiciese, hiciésemos, hicieseis, hiciesen*

13.3.24 *Ir* 'to go'

Gerund: *yendo*   Past Participle: *ido*
Imperative: (*tú*) *ve*, (*vosotros*) *id* (see note), (*usted*) *vaya*, (*ustedes*) *vayan*
Present Indicative: *voy, vas, va, vamos, vais, van*
Imperfect: *iba, ibas, iba, íbamos, ibais, iban*
Preterite: ***fui*** (no accent!), *fuiste*, ***fue*** (no accent!), *fuimos, fuisteis, fueron*
Future (regular): *iré, irás, irá, iremos, iréis, irán*   Conditional (regular): *iría*, etc.
Present Subjunctive: *vaya, vayas, vaya, vayamos, vayáis, vayan*
Imperfect Subjunctive (-*ra*): *fuera, fueras, fuera, fuéramos, fuerais, fueran*
Imperfect Subjunctive (-*se*): *fuese, fueses, fuese, fuésemos, fueseis, fuesen*

The *vosotros* imperative of *irse* is irregularly *idos* (for the predicted *íos). See 17.2.4 for further discussion of this form.

13.3.25 *Jugar* 'to play' (a game. *Tocar* = 'to play an instrument')

This verb is unique in that *u>ue* when stressed. Note also *g>gu* before *e*. All forms are as for a regular –*ar* verb except (bracketed forms are regular):

Imperative: (*tú*) *juega*, (*usted*) *juegue*, (*ustedes*) *jueguen*
Present Indicative: *juego, juegas, juega, (jugamos), (jugáis), juegan*
Preterite (regular): *jugué, jugaste, jugó, jugamos, jugasteis, jugaron*
Present Subjunctive: *juegue, juegues, juegue, (juguemos), (juguéis), jueguen*

13.3.26 *Lucir* 'to show off' (transitive)

C > zc before *a* or *o*. All other forms are as for a regular –*ir* verb (bracketed forms are also regular):

Imperative: (*usted*) *luzca*, (*ustedes*) *luzcan*
Present Indicative: *luzco, (luces, luce, lucimos, lucís, lucen)*
Present Subjunctive: *luzca, luzcas, luzca, luzcamos, luzcáis, luzcan*

Verbs ending in -*ducir* are conjugated like *producir*, shown at 13.3.37.

13.3.27 *Maldecir* 'to curse', *bendecir* 'to bless'

Conjugated like *decir* in some tenses, and regularly in others. Forms that differ from *decir* are shown in bold type:

Gerund: *maldiciendo*   Past Participle: ***maldecido***
Imperative: (*tú*) ***maldice***, (*vosotros*) *maldecid*, (*usted*) *maldiga*, (*ustedes*) *maldigan*
Present Indicative: *maldigo, maldices, maldice, maldecimos, maldecís, maldicen*
Imperfect (regular): *maldecía*, etc.

Preterite: *maldije, maldijiste, maldijo, maldijimos, maldijisteis, maldijeron*
Future (regular): **maldeciré, maldecirás, maldecirá, maldeciremos, maldeciréis, maldecirán**
Conditional (regular): **maldeciría, maldecirías, maldeciría, maldeciríamos, maldeciríais, maldecirían**
Present Subjunctive: *maldiga, maldigas, maldiga, maldigamos, maldigáis, maldigan*
Imperfect Subjunctive (-*ra*): *maldijera, maldijeras, maldijera, maldijéramos, maldijerais, maldijeran*
Imperfect Subjunctive (-*se*): *maldijese, maldijeses, maldijese, maldijésemos, maldijeseis, maldijesen*

13.3.28 *Mover* 'to move'

A common type of radical-changing verb. The *o* of the stem changes to *ue* when stressed. All other forms (including bracketed ones) as for regular –*er* verbs:

Imperative: (*tú*) *mueve*, (*usted*) *mueva*, (*ustedes*) *muevan*
Present Indicative: *muevo, mueves, mueve, (movemos), (movéis), mueven*
Present Subjunctive: *mueva, muevas, mueva, (movamos), (mováis), muevan*

13.3.29 *Oír* 'to hear' (also *desoír* 'to disregard', 'to turn a deaf ear to a request')

Gerund: *oyendo* Past Participle: *oído*
Imperative: (*tú*) *oye*, (*vosotros*) *oíd*, (*usted*) *oiga*, (*ustedes*) *oigan*
Present Indicative: *oigo, oyes, oye, oímos, oís, oyen*
Imperfect (regular): *oía, oías, oía, oíamos, oíais, oían*
Preterite: *oí, oíste, oyó, oímos, oísteis, oyeron*
Future (regular): *oiré*, etc. Conditional (regular): *oiría*, etc.
Present Subjunctive: *oiga, oigas, oiga, oigamos, oigáis, oigan*
Imperfect Subjunctive (-*ra*): *oyera, oyeras, oyera, oyéramos, oyerais, oyeran*
Imperfect Subjunctive (-*se*): *oyese, oyeses, oyese, oyésemos, oyeseis, oyesen*

There is a confusing tendency among the younger generation to replace *oír* by *escuchar*, which means 'to listen'. One occasionally hears answerphone messages like ?*deja un mensaje cuando escuches la señal* for *cuando oigas la señal*.

13.3.30 *Oler* 'to smell'

Oler is conjugated like *mover* but shows the predictable spelling *hue* for *ue* when this diphthong is at the beginning of a word. All forms, including bracketed ones, as for a regular –*er* verb except:

Imperative: (*tú*) **huele**, (*usted*) **huela**, (*ustedes*) **huelan**
Present Indicative: **huelo, hueles, huele**, (*olemos*), (*oléis*), **huelen**
Present Subjunctive: **huela, huelas, huela**, (*olamos*), (*oláis*), **huelan**

13.3.31 *Pedir* 'to ask for'

The endings are regular, but the *e* of the stem changes to *i* when stressed, and also in the gerund, third-person preterite and imperfect subjunctive:

Gerund: *pidiendo* Past Participle: *pedido*
Imperative: (*tú*) *pide*, (*vosotros*) *pedid*, (*usted*) *pida*, (*ustedes*) *pidan*

Present Indicative: *pido, pides, pide, pedimos, pedís, piden*
Imperfect (regular): *pedía, pedías, pedía, pedíamos, pedíais, pedían*
Preterite: *pedí, pediste, pidió, pedimos, pedisteis, pidieron*
Future (regular): *pediré*, etc.   Conditional (regular): *pediría*, etc.
Present Subjunctive: *pida, pidas, pida, pidamos, pidáis, pidan*
Imperfect Subjunctive (-*ra*): *pidiera, pidieras, pidiera, pidiéramos, pidierais, pidieran*
Imperfect Subjunctive: (-*se*): *pidiese, pidieses, pidiese, pidiésemos, pidieseis, pidiesen*

13.3.32 *Perder* 'to lose'

A common type of radical-changing verb. The endings are regular, but the *e* of the stem changes to *ie* when stressed. All forms, included bracketed ones, are as for a regular –*er* verb except:

Imperative: (*tú*) *pierde*, (*usted*) *pierda*, (*ustedes*) *pierdan*
Present Indicative: *pierdo, pierdes, pierde, (perdemos), (perdéis), pierden*
Present Subjunctive: *pierda, pierdas, pierda, (perdamos), (perdáis), pierdan*

13.3.33 *Placer* 'to please'

Found only in the third person and nowadays very rare: *gustar* (regular) is the usual word for 'to please'. It is conjugated like *nacer* (see 13.3.10) except that irregular alternatives (none nowadays used) exist for the following third-person forms:

Preterite	Present Subjunctive	Imperfect Subjunctive
sing. *plugo*, plural *pluguieron*	*plega*	*pluguiera/pluguiese*

13.3.34 *Poder* 'to be able'

Gerund: *pudiendo*   Past Participle: *podido*
Imperative: not used
Present Indicative: *puedo, puedes, puede, podemos, podéis, pueden*
Imperfect (regular): *podía, podías, podía, podíamos, podíais, podían*
Preterite: *pude, pudiste, pudo, pudimos, pudisteis, pudieron*
Future: *podré, podrás, podrá, podremos, podréis, podrán*   Conditional: *podría*, etc.
Present Subjunctive: *pueda, puedas, pueda, podamos, podáis, puedan*
Imperfect Subjunctive (-*ra*): *pudiera, pudieras, pudiera, pudiéramos, pudierais, pudieran*
Imperfect Subjunctive (-*se*): *pudiese, pudieses, pudiese, pudiésemos, pudieseis, pudiesen*

13.3.35 *Poner* 'to put'

Gerund: *poniendo*   Past Participle: *puesto*
Imperative: (*tú*) *pon*, (*vosotros*) *poned*, (*usted*) *ponga*, (*ustedes*) *pongan*
Present Indicative: *pongo, pones, pone, ponemos, ponéis, ponen*
Imperfect (regular): *ponía, ponías, ponía, poníamos, poníais, ponían*
Preterite: *puse, pusiste, puso, pusimos, pusisteis, pusieron*
Future: *pondré, pondrás, pondrá, pondremos, pondréis, pondrán* Conditional: *pondría*, etc.
Present Subjunctive: *ponga, pongas, ponga, pongamos, pongáis, pongan*
Imperfect Subjunctive (-*ra*): *pusiera, pusieras, pusiera, pusiéramos, pusierais, pusieran*
Imperfect Subjunctive (-*se*): *pusiese, pusieses, pusiese, pusiésemos, pusieseis, pusiesen*

Also compounds like *componer* 'to compose', *imponer* 'to impose', *proponer* 'to propose', *descomponer* 'to split something up', *suponer* 'to suppose', etc. An accent is written on the *tú* imperative of these compounds, e.g. *componer* 'to compose' > *compón*, *posponer* 'to postpone' > *pospón*.

13.3.36 *Poseer* 'to possess'

This verb and others like it, e.g. *leer* 'to read', *creer* 'to believe', requires that a *y* sound between vowels should be written *y* and not *i*. This is a spelling rule, not an irregularity:

> Gerund: *poseyendo*   Past Participle: *poseído*
> Imperative: (*tú*) *posee*, (*vosotros*) *poseed*, (*usted*) *posea*, (*ustedes*) *posean*
> Present Indicative: *poseo, posees, posee, poseemos, poseéis, poseen*
> Imperfect (regular): *poseía, poseías, poseía, poseíamos, poseíais, poseían*
> Preterite: *poseí, poseíste, poseyó, poseímos, poseísteis, poseyeron*
> Future (regular): *poseeré*, etc.   Conditional (regular): *poseería*, etc.
> Present Subjunctive: *posea, poseas, posea, poseamos, poseáis, posean*
> Imperfect Subjunctive (*-ra*): *poseyera, poseyeras, poseyera, poseyéramos, poseyerais, poseyeran*
> Imperfect Subjunctive (*-se*): *poseyese, poseyeses, poseyese, poseyésemos, poseyeseis, poseyesen*

13.3.37 *Producir* 'to produce'

Conjugated like *lucir* except for the preterite and for forms (imperfect and future subjunctive) based on the preterite stem. The preterite endings, and therefore the past and future subjunctive endings, are *-eron, -era, -ese*, etc., not *-ieron, -iera, -iese*.

> Imperative: (*tú*) *produce*, (*vosotros*) *producid*, *usted produzca*, *ustedes produzcan*
> Present Indicative: *produzco, produces, produce, producimos, producís, producen*
> Imperfect (regular): *producía*, etc.
> Preterite: *produje, produjiste, produjo, produjimos, produjisteis, produjeron*
> Future (regular): *produciré*, etc   Conditional (regular): *produciría*, etc.
> Present Subjunctive: *produzca, produzcas, produzca, produzcamos, produzcáis, produzcan*
> Imperfect Subjunctive (*-ra*): *produjera, produjeras, produjera, produjéramos, produjerais, produjeran*
> Imperfect Subjunctive (*-se*): *produjese, produjeses, produjese, produjésemos, produjeseis, produjesen*

Preterite forms like *produció, *conducí are common mistakes, but they are stigmatized.

13.3.38 *Querer* 'to want'/'to love'

> Gerund: *queriendo*   Past Participle: *querido*
> Imperative (rarely used): (*tú*) *quiere*, (*vosotros*) *quered*, (*usted*) *quiera*, (*ustedes*) *quieran*
> Present Indicative: *quiero, quieres, quiere, queremos, queréis, quieren*
> Imperfect (regular): *quería, querías, quería, queríamos, queríais, querían*
> Preterite: *quise, quisiste, quiso, quisimos, quisisteis, quisieron*
> Future: *querré, querrás, querrá, querremos, querréis, querrán* Conditional: *querría*, etc.
> Present Subjunctive: *quiera, quieras, quiera, queramos, queráis, quieran*
> Imperfect Subjunctive (*-ra*): *quisiera, quisieras, quisiera, quisiéramos, quisierais, quisieran*
> Imperfect Subjunctive (*-se*): *quisiese, quisieses, quisiese, quisiésemos, quisieseis, quisiesen*

13.3.39 *Reír* 'to laugh'

This verb is in fact conjugated in almost the same way as *pedir*, although the absence of a consonant between the vowels obscures the similarity:

Gerund: *riendo*   Past Participle: *reído*
Imperative: (*tú*) *ríe*, (*vosotros*) *reíd*, (*usted*) *ría*, (*ustedes*) *rían*
Present Indicative: *río*, *ríes*, *ríe*, *reímos*, *reís*, *ríen*
Imperfect (regular): *reía*, *reías*, *reía*, *reíamos*, *reíais*, *reían*
Preterite: *reí*, *reíste*, *rió*,* *reímos*, *reísteis*, *rieron*
Future (regular): *reiré*, *reirás*, *reirá*, *reiremos*, *reiréis*, *reirán*   Conditional (regular): *reiría*, etc.
Present Subjunctive: *ría*, *rías*, *ría*, *riamos*, *riáis*, *rían*
Imperfect Subjunctive (-*ra*): *riera*, *rieras*, *riera*, *riéramos*, *rierais*, *rieran*
Imperfect Subjunctive (-*se*): *riese*, *rieses*, *riese*, *riésemos*, *rieseis*, *riesen*

*Note the written accent. The only third-person singular preterites ending in *-io* that have no written accent are *dio* (from *dar*) and *vio* (from *ver*); see 39.2.3 note (ii) for further remarks.

13.3.40 *Reñir* 'to scold'

This and other verbs in -*eñir* are conjugated like *pedir*, except that, as usual, *ie > e* and *ió > ó* after *ñ*; see 13.5.3, item 6. Only the forms that differ from *pedir* are shown, and bracketed forms are also regular:

Gerund: *riñendo*
Preterite: (*reñí*), (*reñiste*), *riñó*, (*reñimos*), (*reñisteis*), *riñeron*
Imperfect Subjunctive (-*ra*): *riñera*, *riñeras*, *riñera*, *riñéramos*, *riñerais*, *riñeran*
Imperfect Subjunctive (-*se*): *riñese*, *riñeses*, *riñese*, *riñésemos*, *riñeseis*, *riñesen*

13.3.41 *Roer* 'to gnaw'

The bracketed forms are little-used alternatives. In practice the first-person singular indicative is avoided and may be expressed by *estoy royendo* 'I'm gnawing'.

Gerund: *royendo*   Past Participle: *roído*
Imperative: (*tú*) *roe*, (*vosotros*) *roed*, (*usted*) *roa* (*roiga/roya*), (*ustedes*) *roan* (*roigan/royan*)
Present Indicative: *roo* (*roigo/royo*), *roes*, *roe*, *roemos*, *roéis*, *roen*
Imperfect (regular): *roía*, *roías*, *roía*, *roíamos*, *roíais*, *roían*
Preterite: *roí*, *roíste*, *royó*, *roímos*, *roísteis*, *royeron*
Future (regular): *roeré*, etc.   Conditional (regular): *roería*, etc.
Present Subjunctive: *roa* (*roiga/roya*), *roas* (*roigas/royas*), *roa* (*roiga/roya*), *roamos* (*roigamos/royamos*), *roáis* (*roigáis/royáis*), *roan* (*roigan/royan*)
Imperfect Subjunctive (-*ra*): *royera*, *royeras*, *royera*, *royéramos*, *royerais*, *royeran*
Imperfect Subjunctive (-*se*): *royese*, *royeses*, *royese*, *royésemos*, *royeseis*, *royesen*

13.3.42 *Saber* 'to know'

Gerund: *sabiendo*   Past Participle: *sabido*
Imperative (rarely used): (*tú*) *sabe*, (*vosotros*) *sabed*, (*usted*) *sepa*, (*ustedes*) *sepan*
Present Indicative: *sé*, *sabes*, *sabe*, *sabemos*, *sabéis*, *saben*
Imperfect (regular): *sabía*, *sabías*, *sabía*, *sabíamos*, *sabíais*, *sabían*
Preterite: *supe*, *supiste*, *supo*, *supimos*, *supisteis*, *supieron*
Future: *sabré*, *sabrás*, *sabrá*, *sabremos*, *sabréis*, *sabrán*   Conditional: *sabría*, etc.

Present Subjunctive: *sepa, sepas, sepa, sepamos, sepáis, sepan*
Imperfect Subjunctive (-*ra*): *supiera, supieras, supiera, supiéramos, supierais, supieran*
Imperfect Subjunctive (-*se*): *supiese, supieses, supiese, supiésemos, supieseis, supiesen*

13.3.43 *Salir* 'to go out'/'to leave'

Gerund: *saliendo*   Past Participle: *salido*
Imperative: (*tú*) *sal*, (*vosotros*) *salid*, (*usted*) *salga*, (*ustedes*) *salgan*
Present Indicative: *salgo, sales, sale, salimos, salís, salen*
Imperfect & Preterite: regular
Future: *saldré, saldrás, saldrá, saldremos, saldréis, saldrán*   Conditional: *saldría*, etc.
Present Subjunctive: *salga, salgas, salga, salgamos, salgáis, salgan*
Imperfect Subjunctive (-*ra*): *saliera*, etc.
Imperfect Subjunctive (-*se*): *saliese*, etc.

13.3.44 *Sentir* 'to feel'

A common type of -*ir* verb. The endings are regular, but the stem vowel changes to *ie* or to *i* in certain forms. All forms as for a regular –*ir* (including bracketed ones), except:

Gerund: *sintiendo*
Imperative: (*tú*) *siente*, (*usted*) *sienta*, (*ustedes*) *sientan*
Present Indicative: *siento, sientes, siente, (sentimos), (sentís), sienten*
Preterite: (*sentí*), (*sentiste*), *sintió*, (*sentimos*), (*sentisteis*), *sintieron*
Present Subjunctive: *sienta, sientas, sienta, sintamos, sintáis, sientan*
Imperfect Subjunctive (-*ra*): *sintiera, sintieras, sintiera, sintiéramos, sintierais, sintieran*
Imperfect Subjunctive (-*se*): *sintiese, sintieses, sintiese, sintiésemos, sintieseis, sintiesen*

13.3.45 *Ser* 'to be'

A very common verb. For its relationship with *estar* see Chapter 29. Its preterite and past subjunctive forms are the same as those of *ir* 'to go':

Gerund: *siendo*   Past Participle: *sido*
Imperative: (*tú*) *sé* (see note), (*vosotros*) *sed*, (*usted*) *sea*, (*ustedes*) *sean*
Present Indicative: *soy, eres, es, somos, sois, son*
Imperfect: *era, eras, era, éramos, erais, eran*
Preterite: *fui* (no accent!), *fuiste, fue* (no accent!), *fuimos, fuisteis, fueron*
Future (regular): *seré, serás, será, seremos, seréis, serán*   Conditional (regular): *sería*, etc.
Present Subjunctive: *sea, seas, sea, seamos, seáis, sean*
Imperfect Subjunctive (-*ra*): *fuera, fueras, fuera, fuéramos, fuerais, fueran*
Imperfect Subjunctive (-*se*): *fuese, fueses, fuese, fuésemos, fueseis, fuesen*

The accent on the imperative *sé* distinguishes it from the pronoun *se*.

13.3.46 *Tener* 'to have'

Note the irregular preterite and future:

Gerund: *teniendo*   Past Participle: *tenido*
Imperative: (*tú*) *ten*, (*vosotros*) *tened*, (*usted*) *tenga*, (*ustedes*) *tengan*
Present Indicative: *tengo, tienes, tiene, tenemos, tenéis, tienen*
Imperfect (regular): *tenía, tenías, tenía, teníamos, teníais, tenían*
Preterite: *tuve, tuviste, tuvo, tuvimos, tuvisteis, tuvieron*

Future: *tendré, tendrás, tendrá, tendremos, tendréis, tendrán* Conditional: *tendría*, etc.
Present Subjunctive: *tenga, tengas, tenga, tengamos, tengáis, tengan*
Imperfect Subjunctive (-ra): *tuviera, tuvieras, tuviera, tuviéramos, tuvierais, tuvieran*
Imperfect Subjunctive (-se): *tuviese, tuvieses, tuviese, tuviésemos, tuvieseis, tuviesen*

The *tú* imperative of compounds like *retener* 'to retain', *detener* 'to stop', has an accent: *retén, detén*.

13.3.47 *Traer* 'to bring'

Gerund *trayendo*   Past Participle *traído*
Imperative (*tú*) *trae*, (*vosotros*) *traed*, (*usted*) *traiga*, (*ustedes*) *traigan*
Present Indicative: *traigo, traes, trae, traemos, traéis, traen*
Imperfect (regular): *traía, traías, traía, traíamos, traíais, traían*
Preterite: *traje, trajiste, trajo, trajimos, trajisteis, trajeron* (**not** **trajieron*)
Future (regular): *traeré*, etc.   Conditional (regular): *traería*, etc.
Present Subjunctive: *traiga, traigas, traiga, traigamos, traigáis, traigan*
Imperfect Subjunctive (-ra): *trajera, trajeras, trajera, trajéramos, trajerais, trajeran*
Imperfect Subjunctive (-se): *trajese, trajeses, trajese, trajésemos, trajeseis, trajesen*

The preterite *truje, trujiste*, etc., is found in Golden-Age texts and occasionally in dialects.

13.3.48 *Valer* 'to be worth'

Gerund: *valiendo*   Past Participle: *valido*
Imperative: (*tú*) *vale*, (*vosotros*) *valed*, (*usted*) *valga*, (*ustedes*) *valgan*
Present Indicative: *valgo, vales, vale, valemos, valéis, valen*
Imperfect (regular): *valía, valías, valía, valíamos, valíais, valían*
Preterite (regular): *valí, valiste, valió, valimos, valisteis, valieron*
Future: *valdré, valdrás, valdrá, valdremos, valdréis, valdrán* Conditional: *valdría*, etc.
Present Subjunctive: *valga, valgas, valga, valgamos, valgáis, valgan*
Imperfect Subjunctive (-ra): *valiera, valieras, valiera, valiéramos, valierais, valieran*
Imperfect Subjunctive (-ra): *valiese, valieses, valiese, valiésemos, valieseis, valiesen*

13.3.49 *Venir* 'to come'

Gerund: *viniendo*   Past Participle: *venido*
Imperative (*tú*) *ven*, (*vosotros*) *venid*, (*usted*) *venga*, (*ustedes*) *vengan*
Present Indicative: *vengo, vienes, viene, venimos, venís, vienen*
Imperfect (regular): *venía, venías, venía, veníamos, veníais, venían*
Preterite: *vine, viniste, vino, vinimos, vinisteis, vinieron*
Future: *vendré, vendrás, vendrá, vendremos, vendréis, vendrán* Conditional: *vendría*, etc.
Present Subjunctive: *venga, vengas, venga, vengamos, vengáis, vengan*
Imperfect Subjunctive (-ra): *viniera, vinieras, viniera, viniéramos, vinierais, vinieran*
Imperfect Subjunctive (-se): *viniese, vinieses, viniese, viniésemos, vinieseis, viniesen*

The *tú* imperative of compounds like *prevenir* 'to forewarn' has an accent: *prevén*.

13.3.50 *Ver* 'to see'

Gerund: *viendo*   Past Participle: *visto*
Imperative: (*tú*) *ve*, (*vosotros*) *ved*, (*usted*) *vea*, (*ustedes*) *vean*
Present Indicative: *veo, ves, ve, vemos, veis, ven*
Imperfect: *veía, veías, veía, veíamos, veíais, veían*

Preterite: *vi* (no accent!), *viste, vio* (no accent!), *vimos, visteis, vieron*
Future (regular): *veré,* etc.   Conditional (regular): *vería,* etc.
Present Subjunctive: *vea, veas, veas, veamos, veáis, vean*
Imperfect Subjunctive (*-ra*): *viera, vieras, viera, viéramos, vierais, vieran*
Imperfect Subjunctive (*-se*): *viese, vieses, viese, viésemos, vieseis, viesen*

The root verb is stressed in compound form in the first-person and third-person singular of the preterite and the third-person singular present indicative, e.g. *entreví* 'I glimpsed', *entrevió* '(s)he glimpsed', *prevé* '(s)he foresees', *previó* '(s)he foresaw'.

13.3.51 *Yacer* 'to lie' (as in 'he lay there') (US 'to lay')

Almost never used nowadays, except on gravestones: *estar tumbado, estar acostado* are the usual translations. It is conjugated like *nacer,* except for the alternative forms shown in brackets:

Imperative: (*usted*) *yazca* (*yaga/ yazga*), (*ustedes*) *yazcan* (*yagan/ yazgan*)
Present Indicative: *yazco* (*yago, yazgo*), other persons regular
Present Subjunctive: *yazca* (*yaga/ yazga*), etc.

13.4 List of irregular verbs

A number of very rare verbs have been omitted, but this is no guarantee that all of the verbs listed are in common use today. Bracketed forms indicate verbs which are found in the infinitive or past participle forms, which are often the only surviving remains of the verbs that are otherwise obsolete (cf. *aterirse*). For verbs beginning with the prefix in *re-* that are not listed here see the root verb.

abastecer: -cer 13.3.10
abolir: 13.3.2
aborrecer: -cer 13.3.10
abrir: past participle *abierto*
absolver: mover 13.3.28
    past participle *absuelto*
abstenerse: tener 13.3.46
abstraer: traer 13.3.47
acaecer: -cer 13.3.10
acertar: cerrar 13.3.11
acontecer: -cer 13.3.10
acordar: contar 13.3.14
acostar(se): contar 13.3.14
acrecentar: cerrar 13.3.11
adherir: sentir 13.3.44
adolecer: -cer 13.3.10
adormecer: -cer 13.3.10
adquirir: 13.3.3
aducir: producir 13.3.37
advertir: sentir 13.3.44
aferrar(se): cerrar 13.3.11
    but usually regular
agradecer: -cer 13.3.10
agredir: 13.3.4
(*aguerrir: abolir* 13.3.2)

alentar: cerrar 13.3.11
almorzar: contar 13.3.14
    z > c before *e*
amanecer: -cer 13.3.10
andar: see 13.3.5
anochecer: -cer 13.3.10
anteponer: poner 13.3.35
apacentar: cerrar 13.3.11
aparecer: -cer 13.3.10
apetecer: -cer 13.3.10
apostar: contar 13.3.14
    reg. in meaning 'to station'
apretar: cerrar 13.3.11
aprobar: contar 13.3.14
argüir: construir 13.3.13
(*arrecirse: abolir* 13.3.2)
arrendar: cerrar 13.3.11
arrepentirse: sentir 13.3.44
ascender: perder 13.3.32
asentar: cerrar 13.3.11
asentir: sentir 13.3.44
asir: 13.3.6
asolar: contar 13.3.14 if it means 'to parch', but usually reg. nowadays

atañer: see 13.5.3, item 6
    third-person sing. only
atender: perder 13.3.32
atenerse: tener 13.3.46
(*aterirse: abolir* 13.3.2)
atraer: traer 13.3.47
atravesar: cerrar 13.3.11
atribuir: construir 13.3.13
avenir: venir 13.3.49
aventar: cerrar 13.3.11
avergonzar: contar 13.3.14
    z > c before *e.*
    Diphthong spelt *üe,* e.g. subjunctive *avergüence,* etc.
balbucir: 13.3.7
bendecir: maldecir 13.3.27
(*blandir: abolir* 13.3.2)
bruñir: gruñir see 13.5.3, item 6
bullir: zambullir see 13.5.3, item 6
caber: 13.3.8
caer: 13.3.9
calentar: cerrar 13.3.11
carecer: -cer 13.3.10

cegar: cerrar 13.3.11
  g > gu before *e*
ceñir: reñir 13.3.40
cerner: perder 13.3.32
cernir: discernir 13.3.17
cerrar: 13.3.11
circunscribir: irreg. past
  participle *circunscrito*
cocer: 13.3.12
colar: contar 13.3.14
colegir: pedir 13.3.31
  -g > j before *a, o*
colgar: contar 13.3.14
  g > gu before *e*
comenzar: cerrar 13.3.11
  z > c before *e*
compadecer: -cer 13.3.10
comparecer: -cer 13.3.10
competir: pedir 13.3.31
complacer: -cer 13.3.10
componer: poner 13.3.35
comprobar: contar 13.3.14
concebir: pedir 13.3.31
concernir: discernir 13.3.17
concertar: cerrar 13.3.11
concluir: construir 13.3.13
concordar: contar 13.3.14
condescender: perder
  13.3.32
condolerse: mover 13.3.28
conducir: producir 13.3.37
conferir: sentir 13.3.44
confesar: cerrar 13.3.11
confluir: construir 13.3.13
conmover: mover 13.3.28
conocer: -cer 13.3.10
conseguir: pedir 13.3.31
  gu > g before *a, o*
consentir: sentir 13.3.44
consolar: contar 13.3.14
consonar: contar 13.3.14
constituir: construir 13.3.13
constreñir: reñir 13.3.40
construir: 13.3.13
contar: 13.3.14
contender: perder 13.3.32
contener: tener 13.3.46
contradecir: 13.3.16
contraer: traer 13.3.47
contrahacer: hacer 13.3.23
contraponer: poner 13.3.35
contravenir: venir 13.3.49
contribuir: construir
  13.3.13
controvertir: sentir 13.3.44
convalecer: -cer 13.3.10
convenir: venir 13.3.49

convertir: sentir 13.3.44
corregir: pedir 13.3.31
  g > j before *a, o*
costar: contar 13.3.14
crecer: -cer 13.3.10
creer: poseer 13.3.36
cubrir: irreg. past part.
  cubierto
dar: 13.3.15
decaer: caer 13.3.9
decir: 13.3.16
decrecer: -cer 13.3.10
deducir: producir 13.3.37
defender: perder 13.3.32
deferir: sentir 13.3.44
degollar: contar 13.3.14
  diphthong spelt *üe*
demoler: mover 13.3.28
demostrar: contar 13.3.14
denegar: cerrar 13.3.11
  g > gu before *e*
denostar: contar 13.3.14
dentar: cerrar 13.3.11
  often *dientar* (reg.)
  nowadays
deponer: poner 13.3.35
derrengar: cerrar 13.3.11
  often regular
  nowadays; *g > gu*
  before *e*
derretir: pedir 13.3.31
derrocar: nowadays
  regular; *c > qu* before *e*
desacertar: cerrar 13.3.11
desacordar: contar 13.3.14
desagradecer: -cer 13.3.10
desalentar: cerrar 13.3.11
desandar: andar 13.3.5
desaparecer: -cer 13.3.10_
desapretar: cerrar 13.3.11
desaprobar: contar 13.3.14
desasosegar: cerrar 13.3.11
  g > gu before *e*
desatender: perder 13.3.32
desavenir: venir 13.3.49
descender: perder 13.3.32
desceñir: reñir 13.3.40
descolgar: contar 13.3.14
  g > gu before *e*
descollar: contar 13.3.14
descomedirse: pedir 13.3.31
descomponer: poner 13.3.35
desconcertar: cerrar 13.3.11
desconocer: -cer 13.3.10
desconsolar: contar 13.3.14
descontar: contar 13.3.14
desconvenir: venir 13.3.49

describir: past participle
  descrito
descubrir: past participle
  descubierto
desdecir: 13.3.16
desempedrar: cerrar 13.3.11
desengrosar: contar 13.3.14
desentenderse: perder
  13.3.32
desenterrar: cerrar 13.3.11
desenvolver: mover 13.3.28
  past part. *desenvuelto*
desfallecer: -cer 13.3.10
  past participle *disuelto*
desgobernar: cerrar 13.3.11
deshacer: hacer 13.3.23
deshelar: cerrar 13.3.11
desherrar: cerrar 13.3.11
desleír: reír 13.3.39
deslucir: lucir 13.3.26
desmembrar: cerrar 13.3.11
desmentir: sentir 13.3.44
desmerecer: -cer 13.3.10
desobedecer: -cer 13.3.10
desoír: oír 13.3.29
desollar: contar 13.3.14
despedir: pedir 13.3.31
despedrar: cerrar 13.3.11
despertar: cerrar 13.3.11
despezar: cerrar 13.3.11
  usually *despiezar,*
  reg.; *z > c* before *e*
desplacer: -cer 13.3.10
desplegar: cerrar 13.3.11
  g > gu before *e*; now
  often regular
despoblar: contar 13.3.14
desproveer: poseer 13.3.36
  past participle *despro-*
  visto/desproveído
desteñir: reñir 13.3.40
desterrar: cerrar 13.3.11
destituir: construir 13.3.13
destruir: construir 13.3.13
desvanecer: -cer 13.3.10
desvergonzarse: contar
  13.3.14 *z > c* before *e*;
  diphthong spelt *üe*
detener: tener 13.3.46
detraer: traer 13.3.47
devolver: mover 13.3.28
  past participle *devuelto*
diferir: sentir 13.3.44
digerir: sentir 13.3.44
diluir: construir 13.3.13
discernir: 13.3.17
disentir: sentir 13.3.44

disminuir: *construir* 13.3.13
disolver: *mover* 13.3.28
disponer: *poner* 13.3.35
distender: *perder* 13.3.32
distraer: *traer* 13.3.47
distribuir: *construir* 13.3.13
divertir: *sentir* 13.3.44
doler: *mover* 13.3.28
dormir: 13.3.18
elegir: *pedir* 13.3.31
  g > j before *a, o*
embebecer: *-cer* 13.3.10
embellecer: *-cer* 13.3.10
embestir: *pedir* 13.3.31
embravecer: *-cer* 13.3.10
embrutecer: *-cer* 13.3.10
empedrar: *cerrar* 13.3.11
empequeñecer: *-cer* 13.3.10
empezar: *cerrar* 13.3.11
  z > c before *e*
empobrecer: *-cer* 13.3.10
enaltecer: *-cer* 13.3.10
enardecer: *-cer* 13.3.10
encanecer: *-cer* 13.3.10
encarecer: *-cer* 13.3.10
encender: *perder* 13.3.32
encerrar: *cerrar* 13.3.11
encomendar: *cerrar* 13.3.11
encontrar: *contar* 13.3.14
encubrir: past participle
  encubierto
endurecer: *-cer* 13.3.10
enflaquecer: *-cer* 13.3.10
enfurecer: *-cer* 13.3.10
engrandecer: *-cer* 13.3.10
engreírse: *reír* 13.3.39
engrosar: *contar* 13.3.14
  now usually reg.
engullir: *zambullir* see
  13.5.3, item 6
enloquecer: *-cer* 13.3.10
enmendar: *cerrar* 13.3.11
enmohecer: *-cer* 13.3.10
enmudecer: *-cer* 13.3.10
ennegrecer: *-cer* 13.3.10
ennoblecer: *-cer* 13.3.10
enorgullecer: *-cer* 13.3.10
enriquecer: *-cer* 13.3.10
enronquecer: *-cer* 13.3.10
ensangrentar: *cerrar* 13.3.11
ensoberbecer(se)-cer 13.3.10
ensordecer: *-cer* 13.3.10
entender: *perder* 13.3.32
enternecer: *-cer* 13.3.10
enterrar: *cerrar* 13.3.11
entreabrir: past participle
  entreabierto

entredecir: *decir* 13.3.16
entreoír: *oír* 13.3.29
entretener: *tener* 13.3.46
entrever: *ver* 13.3.50
entristecer: *-cer* 13.3.10
entumecer(se)-cer 13.3.10
envanecer: *-cer* 13.3.10
envejecer: *-cer* 13.3.10
envilecer: *-cer* 13.3.10
envolver: *mover* 13.3.28
  past participle *envuelto*
equivaler: *valer* 13.3.48
erguir: 13.3.19
errar: 13.3.20
escabullirse: *zambullir* see
  13.5.3, item 6
escarmentar: *cerrar* 13.3.11
escarnecer: *-cer* 13.3.10
escocer: *cocer* 13.3.12
escribir: past participle
  escrito
esforzar: *contar* 13.3.14
  z > c before *e*
establecer: *-cer* 13.3.10
estar: 13.3.21
estremecer: *-cer* 13.3.10
estreñir: *reñir* 13.3.40
excluir: *construir* 13.3.13
expedir: *pedir* 13.3.31
exponer: *poner* 13.3.35
extender: *perder* 13.3.32
extraer: *traer* 13.3.47
fallecer: *-cer* 13.3.10
favorecer: *-cer* 13.3.10
florecer: *-cer* 13.3.10
fluir: *construir* 13.3.13
fortalecer: *-cer* 13.3.10
forzar: *contar* 13.3.14
  z > c before *e*
fregar: *cerrar* 13.3.11
  g > gu before *e*
freír: *reír* 13.3.39
  past participle *frito*
gemir: *pedir* 13.3.31
gobernar: *cerrar* 13.3.11
gruñir: see 13.5.3, item 6
guarecer: *-cer* 13.3.10
guarnecer: *-cer* 13.3.10
haber: 13.3.22
hacer: see 13.3.23
heder: *perder* 13.3.32
helar: *cerrar* 13.3.11
henchir: *pedir* 13.3.31
hender: *perder* 13.3.32
hendir: *discernir* 13.3.17
herir: *sentir* 13.3.44
herrar: *cerrar* 13.3.11

hervir: *sentir* 13.3.44
holgar: *contar* 13.3.14
  g > gu before *e*
hollar: *contar* 13.3.14
huir: *construir* 13.3.13
humedecer: *-cer* 13.3.10
impedir: *pedir* 13.3.31
imponer: *poner* 13.3.35
  imp. sing. *impón*
incensar: *cerrar* 13.3.11
incluir: *construir* 13.3.13
indisponer: *poner* 13.3.35
inducir: *producir* 13.3.37
inferir: *sentir* 13.3.44
influir: *construir* 13.3.13
ingerir: *sentir* 13.3.44
injerir: *sentir* 13.3.44
inquirir: *adquirir* 13.3.3
instituir: *construir* 13.3.13
instruir: *construir* 13.3.13
interferir: *sentir* 13.3.44
interponer: *poner* 13.3.35
intervenir: *venir* 13.3.49
introducir: *producir*
  13.3.37
intuir: *construir* 13.3.13
invernar: *cerrar* 13.3.11
  now usually reg.
invertir: *sentir* 13.3.44
investir: *pedir* 13.3.31
ir: 13.3.24
jugar: 13.3.25
languidecer: *-cer* 13.3.10
leer: *poseer* 13.3.36
llover: *mover* 13.3.28
lucir: 13.3.26
maldecir: 13.3.27
manifestar: *cerrar* 13.3.11
mantener: *tener* 13.3.46
medir: *pedir* 13.3.31
mentar: *cerrar* 13.3.11
mentir: *sentir* 13.3.44
merecer: *-cer* 13.3.10
merendar: *cerrar* 13.3.11
moler: *mover* 13.3.28
morder: *mover* 13.3.28
morir: 13.3.18
mostrar: *contar* 13.3.14
mover: 13.3.28
mullir: *zambullir* see
  13.5.3, item 6
nacer: *-cer* 13.3.10
negar: *cerrar* 13.3.11
  g > gu before *e*
nevar: *cerrar* 13.3.11
obedecer: *-cer* 13.3.10
obscurecer: *-cer* 13.3.10

obstruir: construir 13.3.13
obtener: tener 13.3.46
ofrecer: -cer 13.3.10
oír: 13.3.29
oler: 13.3.30
oponer: poner 13.3.35
oscurecer: -cer 13.3.10
   (*obscurecer* is an older
   spelling)
pacer: -cer 13.3.10
padecer: -cer 13.3.10
palidecer: -cer 13.3.10
parecer: -cer 13.3.10
pedir: 13.3.31
pensar: cerrar 13.3.11
perecer: -cer 13.3.10
permanecer: -cer 13.3.10
perseguir: pedir 13.3.31
   gu > g before *a, o*
pertenecer: -cer 13.3.10
pervertir: sentir 13.3.44
placer: 13.3.33
plegar: cerrar 13.3.11
   g > gu before *e*
poblar: contar 13.3.14
poder: 13.3.34
podrir: variant of *pudrir*,
   common in Lat. Am.,
   rare in Spain: *-u-* used
   for all other forms
   save past part. *podrido*
poner: 13.3.35
poseer: 13.3.36
posponer: poner 13.3.35
   tú imperative *pospón*
predecir: 13.3.16
predisponer: poner 13.3.35
preferir: sentir 13.3.44
prescribir: past participle
   prescrito
presuponer: poner 13.3.35
prevalecer: -cer 13.3.10
prevaler: valer 13.3.48
prevenir: venir 13.3.49
prever: ver 13.3.50
probar: contar 13.3.14
producir: 13.3.37
proferir: sentir 13.3.44
promover: mover 13.3.28
proponer: poner 13.3.35
proseguir: pedir 13.3.31
   gu > g before *a*
prostituir: construir 13.3.13
proveer: poseer 13.3.36
   past participle *provisto/*
   proveído
provenir: venir 13.3.49

pudrir: regular; see also
   podrir
quebrar: cerrar 13.3.11
querer: 13.3.38
raer: caer 13.3.9 (*rayo* is an
   alternative to *raigo*)
reaparecer: -cer 13.3.10
reblandecer: -cer 13.3.10
recaer: caer 13.3.9
recluir: construir 13.3.13
recocer: cocer 13.3.12
recomendar: cerrar 13.3.11
reconocer: -cer 13.3.10
reconvenir: venir 13.3.49
recordar: contar 13.3.14
recostar(se)contar 13.3.14
reducir: producir 13.3.37
reelegir: pedir 13.3.31
   g > j before *a, o*
referir: sentir 13.3.44
reforzar: contar 13.3.14
   z > c before *e*
refregar: cerrar 13.3.11
   g > gu before *e*
regar: cerrar 13.3.11
   g > gu before *e*
regir: pedir 13.3.31
   g > j before *a, o*
rehacer: hacer 13.3.23
reír: 13.3.39
rejuvenecer: -cer 13.3.10
remendar: cerrar 13.3.11
remorder: mover 13.3.28
remover: mover 13.3.28
rendir: pedir 13.3.31
renegar: cerrar 13.3.11
   g > gu before *e*
renovar: contar 13.3.14
reñir: 13.3.39
repetir: pedir 13.3.31
replegar: cerrar 13.3.11
   g > gu before *e*
repoblar: contar 13.3.14
reponer: poner 13.3.35
reprobar: contar 13.3.14
reproducir: producir 13.3.37
requebrar: cerrar 13.3.11
requerir: sentir 13.3.44
resentirse: sentir 13.3.44
resollar: contar 13.3.14
resolver: mover 13.3.28
   past participle *resuelto*
resonar: contar 13.3.14
resplandecer: -cer 13.3.10
restablecer: -cer 13.3.10
restituir: construir 13.3.13
restregar: cerrar 13.3.11

   g > gu before *e*
retemblar: cerrar 13.3.11
retener: tener 13.3.46
reteñir: reñir 13.3.40
retorcer: cocer 13.3.12
   c > z before *a, o*
retraer: traer 13.3.47
retribuir: construir 13.3.13
retrotraer: traer 13.3.47
reventar: cerrar 13.3.11
reverdecer: -cer 13.3.10
reverter: perder 13.3.32
revestir: pedir 13.3.31
revolar: contar 13.3.14
revolcar(se)contar 13.3.14
   c > qu before *e*
revolver: mover 13.3.28
   past participle *revuelto*
robustecer: -cer 13.3.10
rodar: contar 13.3.14
roer: 13.3.41
rogar: contar 13.3.14
   g > gu before *e*
romper: past participle
   roto
saber: 13.3.42
salir: 13.3.43
satisfacer: hacer 13.3.23
seducir: producir 13.3.37
segar: cerrar 13.3.11
   g > gu before *e*
seguir: pedir 13.3.31
   gu > g before *a* or *o*
sembrar: cerrar 13.3.11
sentar: cerrar 13.3.11
sentir: 13.3.44
ser: 13.3.45
serrar: cerrar 13.3.11
servir: pedir 13.3.31
sobre(e)ntender: perder
   13.3.32
sobreponer: poner 13.3.35
sobresalir: salir 13.3.43
sobrevenir: venir 13.3.49
sofreír: reír 13.3.39, past
   participle *sofrito*
soldar: contar 13.3.14
soler: mover 13.3.28
   future, conditional and
   past and future
   subjunctives not used
soltar: contar 13.3.14
sonar: contar 13.3.14
sonreír: reír 13.3.39
soñar: contar 13.3.14
sosegar: cerrar 13.3.11
   g > gu before *e*

sostener: *tener* 13.3.46
soterrar: *cerrar* 13.3.11
subarrendar: *cerrar* 13.3.11
subscribir: see *suscribir*
subvenir: *venir* 13.3.49
subvertir: *sentir* 13.3.44
sugerir: *sentir* 13.3.44
suponer: *poner* 13.3.35
suscribir past participle
   suscrito
sustituir: *construir* 13.3.13
sustraer: *traer* 13.3.47
tañer: see 13.5.3, item 6
temblar: *cerrar* 13.3.11
tender: *perder* 13.3.32
tener: 13.3.46
tentar: *cerrar* 13.3.11
teñir: *reñir* 13.3.40
torcer: *cocer* 13.3.12
   c > z before *a, o*

tostar: *contar* 13.3.14
traducir: *producir* 13.3.37
traer: 13.3.47
transcribir: past participle
   transcrito
transferir: *sentir* 13.3.44
transgredir: *abolir* 13.3.2
   sometimes reg.
transponer: *poner* 13.3.35
trascender: *perder* 13.3.32
trasegar: *cerrar* 13.3.11
   g > gu before *e*
traslucir: *lucir* 13.3.26
trasponer: *poner* 13.3.35
trastrocar: *contar* 13.3.14
   c > qu before *e*
trocar: *contar* 13.3.14
   c > qu before *e*
tronar: *contar* 13.3.14
tropezar: *cerrar* 13.3.11

   z > c before *e*
tullir: see 13.5.3, item 6
valer: 13.3.48
venir: 13.3.49
ver: 13.3.50
verter: *perder* 13.3.32
vestir: *pedir* 13.3.31
volar: *contar* 13.3.14
volcar: *contar* 13.3.14
   c > qu before *e*
volver: *mover* 13.3.28
   past participle *vuelto*
yacer: 13.3.51
zaherir: *sentir* 13.3.44
zambullir: see 13.5.3,
   item 6

13.5 Regular verb forms

The following remarks apply throughout these verb tables:

(i) *Vosotros* forms are not used in everyday Latin-American language.

(ii) The *-ra* form of *haber* (*hubiera*, etc.) is an optional alternative for the conditional *habría* in the conditional tenses of the perfect.

(iii) The future subjunctive is almost obsolete. See 16.17.

(iv) All compound tenses are formed with the auxiliary *haber* (see 13.3.22) and the past participle, which is invariable in form in these tenses.

13.5.1 Overview of the Spanish verb

Spanish verbs may appear in the following forms:

Infinitive   *hablar* discussed in Chapter 18
Gerund   *hablando* discussed in Chapter 20
Past participle   *hablado* discussed in Chapter 19
Imperative   *habla* (*tú*), *hablá* (*vos*) (see 11.3.1), *hablad* (*vosotros/vosotras*)
                          hable (*usted*), *hablen* (*ustedes*) discussed in Chapter 17

ACTIVE VOICE

INDICATIVE MOOD

The uses of the indicative tense forms are discussed in Chapter 14.

Present   *yo hablo*, etc. I speak
Imperfect   *yo hablaba*, etc. I was speaking
Preterite   *yo hablé*, etc. I spoke
Future   *yo hablaré*, etc. I shall/will speak
Conditional   *yo hablaría*, etc. I would speak
Perfect   *yo he hablado*, etc. I have spoken

Pluperfect	*yo había hablado*, etc. I had spoken
Future Perfect	*yo habré hablado*, etc. I will have spoken
Conditional Perfect	*yo habría hablado*, etc., or *yo hubiera hablado* I would have spoken
Pretérito anterior:	*yo hube hablado* I had spoken, etc. (see 14.10.4)

Continuous (discussed in Chapter 15)

Present	*yo estoy hablando*, etc. I am speaking
Imperfect	*yo estaba hablando*, etc. I was speaking
Preterite	*yo estuve hablando*, etc. I spoke/had a talk
Future	*yo estaré hablando*, etc. I will be speaking
Conditional	*yo estaría hablando*, etc. I would be speaking
Perfect	*yo he estado hablando*, etc. I have been speaking
Pluperfect	*yo había estado hablando*, etc. I had been speaking
Future Perfect	*yo habré estado hablando*, etc. I shall/will have been speaking
Conditional Perfect	*yo habría estado hablando*, etc. I would have been speaking

SUBJUNCTIVE MOOD (no English translation)

Present	(*que*) *yo hable*, etc.
Imperfect	(*que*) *yo hablara*/(*que*) *yo hablase*, etc.
Future	(*que*) *yo hablare*, etc. (obsolete, except in third person in very formal styles)
Perfect	(*que*) *yo haya hablado*, etc.
Pluperfect	(*que*) *yo hubiera*/*hubiese hablado*, etc.
Future Perfect	(*que*) *yo hubiere hablado*, etc.(obsolete)

Continuous

Present	(*que*) *yo esté hablando*, etc.
Imperfect	(*que*) *yo estuviera*/*estuviese hablando*, etc.
Future	(*que*) *yo estuviere hablando*, etc. (obsolete)
Perfect	(*que*) *yo haya estado hablando*, etc.
Pluperfect	(*que*) *yo hubiera*/*hubiese estado hablando*, etc.
Future Perfect	(*que*) *yo hubiere estado hablando* (obsolete)

PASSIVE VOICE

There are a number of ways of translating the English passive, the most common being the passive with *ser*, e.g. *esta novela fue publicada en México*, or (in the case of the third person) passive *se*, e.g. *esta novela se publicó en México*. These forms, not always interchangeable, are discussed in Chapter 28, but a selection of the chief tenses is shown here by way of illustration. The participle in the *ser* form must agree in number and gender with the subject of *ser*.

INDICATIVE (third person only shown)

Present	*es publicado*/*se publica* it is published
Imperfect	*era publicado*/*se publicaba* it used to be published
Preterite	*fue publicado*/*se publicó* it was published
Future	*será publicado*/*se publicará* it will be published
Conditional	*sería publicado*/*se publicaría* it would be published
Perfect	*ha sido publicado*/*se ha publicado* it has been published
Pluperfect	*había sido publicado*/*se había publicado* it had been published
Future Perfect	*habrá sido publicado*/*se habrá publicado* it will have been published
Conditional Perfect	*habría sido publicado*/*se habría publicado* it would have been published

Continuous

The passive continuous with *ser* is not very common.

Se may optionally be shifted in the continuous forms, i.e. *se está publicando*, etc.

Present	*está siendo publicado/está publicándose* it is being published
Imperfect	*estaba siendo publicado/estaba publicándose* it was being published
Future	*estará siendo publicado/estará publicándose* it will be being published
Conditional	*estaría siendo publicado/estaría publicándose* it would be being published
Perfect	*ha estado siendo publicado/ha estado publicándose* it has been being published
Pluperfect	*había estado siendo publicado/había estado publicándose* it had been being published
Future Perfect	*habrá estado siendo publicado/habrá estado publicándose* it will have been being published
Conditional Perfect	*habría estado siendo publicado/habría estado publicándose* it would have been being published

SUBJUNCTIVE

Present	*(que) sea publicado/(que) se publique*
Imperfect	*(que) fuera publicado/(que) se publicara/(que) fuese publicado/(que) se publicase*
Future	*(que) fuere publicado/(que) se publicare* (obsolete)
Perfect	*(que) haya sido publicado/que se haya publicado*
Pluperfect	*(que) hubiese/hubiera sido publicado/que se hubiera/hubiese publicado*

Continuous

The subjunctive continuous passive is also rare in practice.

Present	*(que) esté siendo publicado/(que) esté publicándose*
Imperfect	*(que) estuviera/estuviese siendo publicado/(que) estuviera/estuviese publicándose*
Perfect	*(que) haya estado siendo publicado/que haya estado publicándose*
Pluperfect	*(que) hubiera/hubiese estado siendo publicado/que hubiera/hubiese estado publicándose*

13.5.2 Conjugation of regular verbs

The three verbs *hablar* 'to speak', *comer* 'to eat' and *vivir* 'to live' conjugate regularly throughout and are unaffected by spelling changes. The *–ir* conjugation differs from the *–er* only in the forms shown in bold:

(Stem	*habl-*	*com-*	*viv-*)
Infinitive	*hablar*	*comer*	*vivir*
Gerund	*hablando*	*comiendo*	*viviendo*
Past Participle	*hablado*	*comido*	*vivido*
Imperative			
(*tú*)	*habla*	*come*	*vive*
vos	*hablá*	*comé*	*viví* (Argentine forms: see 11.3.1)
(*vosotros/as*)	*hablad*	*comed*	*vivid* (Spain only)
(*usted*)	*hable*	*coma*	*viva*
(*ustedes*)	*hablen*	*coman*	*vivan*

INDICATIVE

Present (the bracketed forms are Argentine *vos* forms: see 11.3.1)

hablo	*hablamos*	*como*	*comemos*	*vivo*	*vivimos*
hablas (hablás)	*habláis*	*comes (comés)*	*coméis*	*vives (vivís)*	*vivís*
habla	*hablan*	*come*	*comen*	*vive*	*viven*

Perfect

he hablado, etc.   *he comido*, etc.   *he vivido*, etc.

Imperfect

hablaba	*hablábamos*	*comía*	*comíamos*	*vivía*	*vivíamos*
hablabas	*hablabais*	*comías*	*comíais*	*vivías*	*vivíais*
hablaba	*hablaban*	*comía*	*comían*	*vivía*	*vivían*

Preterite

hablé	*hablamos*	*comí*	*comimos*	*viví*	*vivimos*
hablaste	*hablasteis*	*comiste*	*comisteis*	*viviste*	*vivisteis*
habló	*hablaron*	*comió*	*comieron*	*vivió*	*vivieron*

Pluperfect   *Pretérito anterior*

había hablado, etc.   *hube hablado*, etc.
había comido, etc.   *hube comido*, etc.
había vivido, etc.   *hube vivido*, etc.

Future

hablaré	*hablaremos*	*comeré*	*comeremos*	*viviré*	*viviremos*
hablarás	*hablaréis*	*comerás*	*comeréis*	*vivirás*	*viviréis*
hablará	*hablarán*	*comerá*	*comerán*	*vivirá*	*vivirán*

Future perfect

habré hablado, etc.   *habré comido*, etc.   *habré vivido*, etc.

Conditional

hablaría	*hablaríamos*	*comería*	*comeríamos*	*viviría*	*viviríamos*
hablarías	*hablaríais*	*comerías*	*comeríais*	*vivirías*	*viviríais*
hablaría	*hablarían*	*comería*	*comerían*	*viviría*	*vivirían*

Perfect conditional

habría hablado, etc. *habría comido*, etc. *habría vivido*, etc., or—
hubiera hablado, etc. *hubiera comido*, etc. *hubiera vivido*, etc.

SUBJUNCTIVE

Present

hable	*hablemos*	*coma*	*comamos*	*viva*	*vivamos*
hables	*habléis*	*comas*	*comáis*	*vivas*	*viváis*
hable	*hablen*	*coma*	*coman*	*viva*	*vivan*

NB: See 16.2.8 for a note on the forms preferred in Argentina, where the pronoun *vos* is used.

Perfect

haya hablado, etc.   *haya comido*, etc.   *haya vivido*, etc.

Imperfect

(a) -*ra* form

hablara	*habláramos*	*comiera*	*comiéramos*	*viviera*	*viviéramos*
hablaras	*hablarais*	*comieras*	*comierais*	*vivieras*	*vivierais*
hablara	*hablaran*	*comiera*	*comieran*	*viviera*	*vivieran*

(b) -*se* form

hablase	*hablásemos*	*comiese*	*comiésemos*	*viviese*	*viviésemos*
hablases	*hablaseis*	*comieses*	*comieseis*	*vivieses*	*vivieseis*
hablase	*hablasen*	*comiese*	*comiesen*	*viviese*	*viviesen*

Pluperfect

hubiera hablado, etc.   *hubiera comido*, etc.   *hubiera vivido*, etc.
hubiese hablado, etc.   *hubiese comido*, etc.   *hubiese vivido*, etc.

Future (more or less obsolete)

hablare	*habláremos*	*comiere*	*comiéremos*	*viviere*	*viviéremos*
hablares	*hablareis*	*comieres*	*comiereis*	*vivieres*	*viviereis*
hablare	*hablaren*	*comiere*	*comieren*	*viviere*	*vivieren*

13.5.3 Spelling changes in the verb system

The following spelling rules apply to the endings of all Spanish verbs, regular and irregular (see Chapter 39 for the phonetic symbols used):

(1) Infinitives ending in -*zar*, -*cer* and -*cir*:

The sound /θ/ (or /s/ in Latin America and often in southern Spain) is written *c* before *i* and *e*, and *z* before *a*, *o*, *u*. However, in the majority of verbs ending in –*cer*, *c* becomes *zc* before *a*, and *o*):

rezar 'to pray'   *vencer* 'to defeat'   *esparcir* 'to scatter'

Gerund

rezando   *venciendo*   *esparciendo*

Past Participle

rezado   *vencido*   *esparcido*

Present indicative

rezo	*rezamos*	*venzo*	*vencemos*	*esparzo*	*esparcimos*
rezas	*rezáis*	*vences*	*vencéis*	*esparces*	*esparcís*
reza	*rezan*	*vence*	*vencen*	*esparce*	*esparcen*

Preterite

recé	*rezamos*	*vencí*	*vencimos*	*esparcí*	*esparcimos*
rezaste	*rezasteis*	*venciste*	*vencisteis*	*esparciste*	*esparcisteis*
rezó	*rezaron*	*venció*	*vencieron*	*esparció*	*esparcieron*

Present subjunctive

rece	*recemos*	*venza*	*venzamos*	*esparza*	*esparzamos*
reces	*recéis*	*venzas*	*venzáis*	*esparzas*	*esparzáis*
rece	*recen*	*venza*	*venzan*	*esparza*	*esparzan*

No other forms affected.

Verbs ending in *-cer* or *-cir* are usually irregular and should be checked against the list at 13.4.

(2) Infinitives ending in *-car*, *-quir*:

The sound /k/ is written *qu* before *e* and *u*, but *c* before *a*, *o*:

| *sacar* 'to take out' | | *delinquir* 'to commit a crime' | |

Present indicative

saco	*sacamos*	*delinco*	*delinquimos*
sacas	*sacáis*	*delinques*	*delinquís*
saca	*sacan*	*delinque*	*delinquen*

Preterite

saqué	*sacamos*	*delinquí*	*delinquimos*
sacaste	*sacasteis*	*delinquiste*	*delinquisteis*
sacó	*sacaron*	*delinquió*	*delinquieron*

Present subjunctive

saque	*saquemos*	*delinca*	*delincamos*
saques	*saquéis*	*delincas*	*delincáis*
saque	*saquen*	*delinca*	*delincan*

No other forms affected.

Delinquir seems to be the only living example of a verb ending in *-quir* and it is very rarely used.

(3) Infinitives ending in *-gar* *-guir*.

The sound γ (as in *hago*) is written *gu* before *i* and *e*, and *g* before *a*, *o*:

| *llegar* 'to arrive' | | *seguir* 'to follow' (radical-changing, like *pedir*; see 13.3.31) | |

Gerund

| *llegando* | | *siguiendo* | |

Past Participle

| *llegado* | | *seguido* | |

Present indicative

llego	*llegamos*	*sigo*	*seguimos*
llegas	*llegáis*	*sigues*	*seguís*
llega	*llegan*	*sigue*	*siguen*

Preterite

llegué	*llegamos*	*seguí*	*seguimos*
llegaste	*llegasteis*	*seguiste*	*seguisteis*
llegó	*llegaron*	*siguió*	*siguieron*

Present subjunctive

llegue	*lleguemos*	*siga*	*sigamos*
llegues	*lleguéis*	*sigas*	*sigáis*
llegue	*lleguen*	*siga*	*sigan*

No other forms affected.

(4) Infinitives ending in -*guar*:

The *u* is written *ü* before *e* and pronounced /w/. See 13.2.5 for examples.

(5) Infinitives ending in -*ger*, -*gir*:

The sound /χ/ (like ch of 'loch') is written *g* before *e* and *i*, and *j* before *a*, *o*:

proteger 'to protect'   *fingir* 'to pretend'

Present indicative

protejo	*protegemos*	*finjo*	*fingimos*
proteges	*protegéis*	*finges*	*fingís*
protege	*protegen*	*finge*	*fingen*

Present subjunctive

proteja	*protejamos*	*finja*	*finjamos*
protejas	*protejáis*	*finjas*	*finjáis*
proteja	*protejan*	*finja*	*finjan*

No other forms affected.

Verbs ending in -*jar*, e.g. *amortajar*, and -*jer*, e.g. *tejer*, retain the *j* throughout.

(6) Infinitive in -*ñer*, *ñir*, -*llir*:

ie becomes *e*.
ió becomes *ó*.

tañer 'to chime'   *gruñir* 'to grunt'   *zambullir* 'to dive'

Gerund

tañendo   *gruñendo*   *zambullendo*

Preterite

tañí	*tañimos*	*gruñí*	*gruñimos*	*zambullí*	*zambullimos*
tañiste	*tañisteis*	*gruñiste*	*gruñisteis*	*zambulliste*	*zambullisteis*
tañó	*tañeron*	*gruñó*	*gruñeron*	*zambulló*	*zambulleron*

Imperfect subjunctive

tañera	*tañéramos*	*gruñera*	*gruñéramos*	*zambullera*	*zambulléramos*
tañeras	*tañerais*	*gruñeras*	*gruñerais*	*zambulleras*	*zambullerais*
tañera	*tañeran*	*gruñera*	*gruñeran*	*zambullera*	*zambulleran*
tañese	*tañésemos*	*gruñese*	*gruñésemos*	*zambullese*	*zambullésemos*
tañeses	*tañeseis*	*gruñeses*	*gruñeseis*	*zambullese*	*zambulleseis*
tañese	*tañesen*	*gruñese*	*gruñesen*	*zambullese*	*zambullesen*

Future subjunctive (almost obsolete): *tañere*, etc., *gruñere*, etc., *zambullere*, etc.

(7) Verbs in -*eer*: all conjugate like *poseer* at 13.3.36.

(8) Verbs in -*uir*: all conjugate like *construir* at 13.3.13.

13.5.4 Full conjugation of the compound tenses of *ver*

The forms of the compound tenses are completely predictable provided one knows the full conjugation of *haber* (13.3.22) and the past participle of the verb.

The conjugation of the compound tenses of *ver* 'to see' is shown here as an example. Note the irregular past participle, *visto*.

INDICATIVE

Perfect 'I have seen' Pluperfect 'I had seen', etc.

he visto	*hemos visto*	*había visto*	*habíamos visto*
has visto	*habéis visto*	*habías visto*	*habíais visto*
ha visto	*han visto*	*había visto*	*habían visto*

Future perfect 'I shall have seen' Conditional 'I would have seen', etc.

habré visto	*habremos visto*	*habría visto*	*habríamos visto*
habrás visto	*habréis visto*	*habrías visto*	*habríais visto*
habrá visto	*habrán visto*	*habría visto*	*habrían visto*

Pretérito anterior 'I had seen'

hube visto	*hubimos visto*
hubiste visto	*hubisteis visto*
hubo visto	*hubieron visto*

SUBJUNCTIVE

Perfect

haya visto	*hayamos visto*
hayas visto	*hayáis visto*
haya visto	*hayan visto*

Imperfect

hubiera visto hubiéramos visto		or	*hubiese visto hubiésemos visto*
hubieras visto hubierais visto			*hubieses visto hubieseis visto*
hubiera visto hubieran visto			*hubiese visto hubiesen visto*

14

Use of indicative (non-continuous) verb forms

The main points discussed in this chapter are:

- Uses of the present tense (*hablo, vamos*, etc.) (Section 14.3)
- Uses of the preterite tense (*hablé, fuimos*, etc.) (Section 14.4)
- Uses of the imperfect tense (*hablaba, íbamos*, etc.) (Section 14.5)
- Uses of the future tense (*hablaré, iré*, etc.) (Section 14.6)
- Uses of the conditional tense (*hablaría, iría*, etc.) (Section 14.7)
- General remarks on the compound tenses (Section 14.8)
- Uses of the perfect tense (*he hablado, hemos ido*, etc.) (Section 14.9)
- Uses of the pluperfect tense (*había hablado, habían ido*, etc.) (Section 14.10)
- The *–ra* pluperfect (Section 14.10.2)

Continuous verb forms (*estoy hablando, estamos trabajando*, etc.) are discussed in Chapter 15; the subjunctive is discussed in Chapter 16. The possible forms of a typical regular verb are shown at 13.5.1.

14.1 Names of the tenses

There is little agreement among Hispanic linguists about the names of the tenses. Another source of confusion for English-speakers is the fact that *pretérito* simply means 'past' (*las glorias pretéritas* = 'bygone glories'), whereas 'preterite' (US 'preterit': the British spelling is used in this book) refers to a specific Spanish past tense. The main variants are listed below:

Name used in this book	Example	Common alternative names
Imperfect indicative	*hablaba, tenías*	*pretérito imperfecto, copretérito*
Preterite	*hablé, tuviste*	*pretérito perfecto simple, pretérito indefinido, pretérito perfecto absoluto*, past definite
Perfect	*he hablado, has tenido*	*pretérito perfecto (compuesto), pretérito perfecto actual, antepresente*, present perfect
Pluperfect	*había hablado, habías tenido*	*pretérito pluscuamperfecto, antecopretérito*
Future	*hablaré, tendrás*	*futuro imperfecto*
Conditional	*hablaría, tendrías*	*potencial, futuro hipotético*

14.2 Tense in Spanish: general remarks

The following points need emphasis:

(**a**) The name 'present tense' for forms like *hablo, voy*, is misleading since this form can also express the future, the past, and timeless statements. See 14.3.

(**b**) The name 'future tense' for forms like *hablaré, irá*, is misleading since it can also be used for suppositions, and there is also more than one way of expressing the future. See 14.6.

(**c**) The difference between the imperfect and the preterite tenses, e.g. between *hablaba* and *hablé*, can be subtle for English-speakers since both can be translated 'I spoke', even though they mean different things: see 14.4. This difference is especially troublesome for English-speakers when the verb *ser* 'to be' is involved: see 14.4.3–4.

(**d**) Spanish resembles English and differs from French and German in having a full range of continuous forms: *está lloviendo* 'it's raining', *estabas pensando* 'you were thinking', *he estado comiendo* 'I have been eating'. However, the similarity to the English progressive forms ('I'm going', 'you're waiting', etc.) is misleading; see 15.1–2 for details.

(**e**) The difference in meaning between the preterite *hablé* 'I spoke' and the perfect *he hablado* 'I *have* spoken' is respected in Spanish and English, but blurred or lost in spoken French, Italian and German. But the relationship between the Spanish tenses is not exactly the same as between 'I spoke' and 'I have spoken'; see particularly 14.9.3. Use of the perfect tense is also much affected by regional variations.

14.3 Uses of the present tense

For the use of the present in conditional sentences, e.g. *si sales, compra pan* 'if you go out, buy some bread', see 25.2. For the use of the present as a future tense see 14.6.3.

14.3.1 Present tense to indicate timeless or habitual events that still occur

The simple present tense is used to express eternal or timeless truths, or habitual states or events. This is probably the commonest use of this verb form:

Llueve mucho en Irlanda	It rains a lot in Ireland
Fumo más de sesenta al día	I smoke more than sixty a day
María es venezolana	Maria's Venezuelan
No tengo tarjeta de crédito	I don't have a credit card
Me deprime comer sola (C. Martín Gaite, Sp.)	Eating on my own depresses me
Los que son creyentes tienen ese consuelo (M. Puig, Arg.)	Those who are believers have that consolation

As in English, use of the present continuous for a habitual event makes it in some way unusual, surprising or temporary, i.e. not necessarily a habit: *últimamente estoy fumando más de sesenta al día* 'lately I'm smoking more than sixty a day'.

14.3.2 The present tense for events occurring in the present

The simple present in Spanish can also show that an action is happening in the present: *duermen* = 'they are sleeping' as well as 'they sleep'. English-speakers find this overlap confusing: to say 'he comes' for 'he is coming' nowadays sounds Shakespearean. The difference between the Spanish simple present and the present continuous is therefore not clear-cut, and the following remarks should be read together with the discussion of continuous forms in Chapter 15.

(a) With some verbs and in some contexts there is often only a slight difference between the simple present and the continuous:

Escribe una novela/Está escribiendo una novela	(S)he's writing a novel
¿Qué haces?/¿Qué estás haciendo? (they mean the same when they express surprise)	What are you doing?
¡Mira cómo llueve!/¡Mira cómo está lloviendo!	Look at the way it's raining!

(b) The simple present, not the continuous, is used for states rather than actions, e.g. *parece cansada* 'she seems tired', *brilla la luna* 'the moon is shining'. See 15.3b for discussion.

(c) The simple present is much used for events that happen in the present but are not necessarily actually in progress *now*, e.g. for imminent or very recent events:

Acusamos recibo de su carta del 3 de enero	We acknowledge receipt of your letter of 3 January
A mí me suena poco natural	It sounds unnatural to me
La oposición considera una maniobra el aperturismo anunciado por el régimen	The opposition considers the liberalization policy announced by the regime to be a manoeuvre
¿Por qué te metes en ese asunto?	Why are you getting involved in that business?
¿Qué dices? (= *¿qué estás diciendo?* when indignation or surprise are intended)	What did you say (just then)?' or 'What do you say?' or 'What are you saying?'
¿No oyes los perros?	Can't you hear the dogs?
¡Que me ahogo!	I'm drowning!
¡Ya voy!/Disiento	I'm coming!/I disagree
Merino pasa la pelota a Andreas	Merino passes the ball to Andreas
¿Vienes?/¿Interrumpo?	Are you coming?/Am I interrupting?

None of the sentences under **(c)** refers to an event which is strictly speaking actually in progress, but to events that have either just happened or are just about to happen (*¿qué dices?*, *pasa la pelota*, *¿interrumpo?*, *¡que me ahogo!*), or which are present but not necessarily happening at this moment, e.g. *la oposición considera...*, *¿por qué te metes?...*, *yo disiento*. English-speakers constantly misuse the Spanish continuous, as in ?*mi hermano se está casando* 'my brother's getting married' when they mean *se casa* or *se va a casar*. See 15.1.2–3 for further discussion.

14.3.3 The *presente histórico* or historic present

The present tense is used much more than in English to refer to the past as a way of dramatizing a story. This device is usually restricted to popular English ('Annie walks in and says to me...') and it may sound unfortunate in serious English styles; but it is very common both in literary and spoken Spanish:

Por fin, distingue a unos pasos, acuclillado, a un hombre con sandalias y sombrero de cuero (M. Vargas Llosa, Pe.)	Eventually he spotted (spots), a few paces away, a man in leather sandals and hat, crouching
Bueno, pues me llama y me dice que por qué no nos vemos. ¿Vernos? ¿Dónde?, le digo yo. En cualquier sitio, me dice. Pero, ¿qué es lo que les pasa a tus amiguitas?, le digo. Es que no son tan guapas como tú, me dice. A buenas horas lo has descubierto, le digo (S. Puértolas, Sp., dialogue; very colloquial)	Anyway, he rings me and asks me why we don't meet. 'Meet!? Where?', I say to him. 'Anywhere,' he says. 'But what's happened to your lady friends?' I say to him. 'Actually they're not as attractive as you.' 'A fine time to discover that,' I say to him

This historic present is almost always used after *por poco* 'all but', and often after *casi* 'nearly': *me caí por unas escaleras y por poco/casi me rompo/me rompí el tobillo* 'I fell down a flight of stairs and nearly broke my ankle', *casi me mata, lo cual no era nada difícil por aquel entonces* (A. Bryce Echenique, Pe.) 'she nearly killed me, which wasn't at all difficult at that time', *casi enloquezco al abrir el telegrama* (ibid.) 'I nearly went crazy on opening the telegram'. Exceptions can be found on both continents: *por poco me hizo llorar de lo cariñosa que es* (M. Vargas Llosa, Pe., dialogue) 'she's so affectionate she nearly made me cry'.

14.3.4 Present tense used as an imperative

This is frequently used in everyday speech to make strong orders: *tú te callas* 'you just keep quiet'. All matters connected with the imperative are discussed in Chapter 17.

14.3.5 Use of the present to ask permission

The present is much used when asking for someone's consent:

¿Te lo mando yo?	Shall I send it to you?
¿Escribo a los abuelos para decírselo?	Should I write to our grandparents to tell them?
¿Vamos al cine esta noche?	Shall we go to the movies tonight?

14.3.6 Use of the present as a future tense

Spanish makes constant use of the simple present to refer to the future: *mañana vamos a California* 'we're going to California tomorrow', *te veo luego* 'I'll see you later'. See 14.6.3.

14.3.7 Present in sentences like 'it's the first time I've seen you' and other expressions of time

English uses the perfect in sentences of the type 'this is the first time that...' and 'I've been... for *n* days/weeks', etc. Spanish uses the present:

Es la primera vez que la veo	It's the first time I have seen her
No es la primera vez que los noruegos	It isn't the first time that the
entran en Nueva York (J. L. Borges, Arg.)	Norwegians have entered New York
Hace tres años que no vengo	I haven't been here for three years
Desde hace dos días estoy tratando de	I've been trying to contact Mr Morales
comunicarme con el señor Morales	for two days
(*Prensalibre*, Guatemala, dialogue)	

The past tense used in such constructions is the imperfect. See 14.5.3.

14.4 The preterite: general

The Spanish preterite describes events that were completed in the past or are *viewed* as completed in the past (see 14.4.1 for the reason for this distinction). Occasionally it highlights the fact that an event is beginning in the past: see 14.4.8.

English constantly fails to distinguish the preterite from the imperfect: 'I looked' may be *miré* (*en aquel momento miré por la ventana* 'just then I looked out of the window') or *miraba*: *estuve pensando mientras miraba por la ventana* 'I was thinking as I looked out of the window'. This ambiguity of English is a recurrent problem for learners of Spanish.

It is easy to explain that the preterite is used for 'one-off' past events like *Marco se rompió la pierna* 'Marco broke his leg'. ?*Marco se rompía una pierna* 'Marco was breaking his leg' or '...used to break his leg' is unlikely (but see 14.5.8 for a rare exception). It is also possible to say confidently that the preterite is used for events that continue for the whole of a specified period or throughout a number of specified periods in the past: *fue rey durante ocho años* 'he was king for eight years', *habló tres veces durante dos horas* '(s)he spoke three times for two hours (each time)'. But a difficulty arises when the past event is habitual or prolonged, since one can then sometimes optionally use either the imperfect or the preterite, as in *mi padre fumó mucho cuando era joven* or *fumaba mucho cuando era joven* 'my father smoked a lot when he was young' or *la Guerra Civil era un desastre/la Guerra Civil fue un desastre* 'the Civil War was a disaster'; see 14.4.3 and 14.4.4 for a discussion.

The preterite is often used in Latin-American Spanish where the perfect tense is used in Spain. See 14.9.8 for discussion.

14.4.1 Preterite for events occurring throughout a finite period

The preterite tense must be used for an event that continued throughout the whole of a finite period of time, regardless of whether the action then ended. By 'finite' is meant a period of time of a specific length, i.e. one whose beginning and end are stated or clearly implied:

Estuve destinado en Bilbao dos años	I was stationed in Bilbao for two years
Por un instante pensé que me caía	For a moment I thought that I was falling
Los dinosaurios reinaron sobre la tierra durante millones de años	The dinosaurs reigned on earth for millions of years
La ETA tuvo menos actividad durante el régimen de Franco que al instalarse la democracia (M. Vargas Llosa, Pe.)	ETA (Basque terrorists) was less active during the Franco regime than when democracy was introduced
Durante años no pudimos hablar de otra cosa (G. García Márquez, Col.)	For years we could talk of nothing else

En toda mi vida supe de dos casos (D. Navarro Gómez, Sp.)	In all my life I've known of two cases
La fiesta fue un éxito	The party was a success (from start to finish)
Fue un día magnífico	It was a magnificent day (from start to finish)

The question is whether the period ended, not the action: *habló durante dos horas, y luego continuó hablando durante tres horas más* '(s)he talked for two hours and then went on talking for three more hours' is possible. For the optional alternative *estuvo hablando durante dos horas* see 15.2.3.

(i) Compare the last two examples in the columns with *cuando llegué vi que la fiesta era/estaba siendo un éxito* 'when I arrived I saw that the party was a success' (it wasn't over yet), and *como era un día magnífico, fuimos al zoo* 'as it was a lovely day, we went to the zoo' (but it may have rained later).

(ii) Words like *siempre* and *nunca* often indicate actions continuing throughout the whole of a period of time: *siempre procuré pasarlo bien* 'I always tried to have a good time', *nunca me hizo gracia ese hombre* 'I never really liked that man', *nunca Fermín Eguren me pudo ver* (J. L. Borges, Arg.) 'Fermín Eguren never was able to stand me' (i.e. throughout the time I'm referring to). But they may refer to habitual actions that occur over no specified period and therefore require the imperfect, as in *antes siempre ibas a misa* 'you always used to go to Mass', *nunca hacía tanto calor como ahora* 'it never used to be as hot as now'.

(iii) In sentences involving phrases like *todos los días*, *todos los años*, either tense may be possible, depending on whether we look at the action as complete or as going on at the time: *todos los veranos veraneaban en San Sebastián/veranearon en San Sebastián* 'every summer they spent their holidays/vacation in San Sebastian', *aquella semana regaba/regó el jardín todas las mañanas* 'that week he watered the garden every morning', but *cuando yo era pequeño yo lo/le veía pasar casi todos los días* (not *lo/le vi* since the period is too vague), 'when I was little I saw him pass nearly every day'.

(iv) Actions performed throughout a period of time can be habitual, in which case the imperfect is used, as in *hablaba durante tres horas* (or *solía hablar durante tres horas*) '(s)he used to speak for three hours', i.e. on an unspecified number of different occasions.

14.4.2 Preterite used to indicate single events or sets of events completed in the past

A single completed past event, or a single set of completed past events, is expressed by the preterite:

La Segunda Guerra Mundial empezó en 1939	World War Two began in 1939
Hubo una explosión	There was an explosion (i.e. at that moment)
Momentos después Pepe tosió	A few moments later Pepe coughed
Lo primero que escribí fue un cuento (A. Grandes, Sp.)	The first thing I wrote was a short story
Martín la abrazó cuatro veces	Martín embraced her four times
Lo escribió ochenta veces	(S)he wrote it eighty times

(i) The preterite is used to describe a series of completed events that occurred separately (in whichever order), as in *di un paseo, fui a casa, sentí miedo, y aquí estoy* (L. Sepúlveda, Ch., dialogue) 'I went for a walk, went home, felt scared, and here I am'. In such lists of events, the imperfect tense suggests that they occurred simultaneously or habitually. Compare *lloraba, gritaba, se reía...* '(s)he was weeping, shouting, laughing' (simultaneously) or '(s)he used to weep', etc.

(ii) The imperfect is occasionally also used in journalistic styles for single completed events. See 14.5.8.

(iii) Compare *lo hicimos tres veces* 'we did it three times' and *lo hacíamos tres veces/ solíamos hacerlo tres veces* 'we used to do it three times'. The latter does not refer to a specific number of events: we cannot count the total number of events.

14.4.3 Preterite used to distinguish narrative events from descriptive background

The preterite is sometimes used to show that an event is a part of a story, while the imperfect shows that it is descriptive background. This is clear for English-speakers in a sentence like *tuvieron tres niños* 'they had (i.e. 'produced'/'gave birth to') three children', which is usually three separate events, and *tenían tres niños*, which is a state of affairs, not an event. Less obvious is the difference between *querían hacerlo* 'they wanted to do it', which is a state of mind, and *quisieron hacerlo*, which is an event with an outcome, i.e. they wanted to do it *and tried to*, successfully or not (it usually implies failure).

English-speakers find this distinction most confusing with the verb *ser*. María Luz Gutiérrez Araus (1995), 32, cites an interesting example from García Márquez: *un perro... mordió a cuatro personas que se le atravesaron en el camino. Tres **eran** esclavos negros. La otra **fue** Sierva María* 'a dog bit four people who got in its way. Three were black slaves. The other was Sierva María'. Luz Gutiérrez explains the difference between *eran* and *fue* here as a difference between the 'non-active', i.e. 'descriptive', imperfect and the 'active' (i.e. 'narrative') preterite *fue*. The preterite brings Sierva María into the foreground—she is a major character in the novel. The imperfect pushes the other three characters into the descriptive background. But such clear-cut examples are rare and literary: ordinary language would say *era*.

In the following example, the preterite presents the publication of the statistics as events while the imperfect paints the background:

*En noviembre se registraron 851.320 contratos, de los cuales 83.419 **fueron** indefinidos. Es decir, las colocaciones han caído significativamente respecto a la cifra récord del pasado octubre, que **fue** de más de un millón. El paro ha caído en 157.444 personas desde noviembre de 1996, cuando la tasa de paro **era** del 14,04%* (El País, Sp.)

851,320 job contracts were registered in November, of which 83,419 were long-term. In other words, the number of persons hired has fallen significantly compared with last October's record figure, which was more than a million. Unemployment has fallen by 157,444 persons since November 1996, when unemployment stood at 14.04%

14.4.4 Use of the preterite to denote habitual events

Habitual events in the past are usually expressed by the imperfect, as explained at 14.5.2. But the preterite can sometimes describe habitual or prolonged events in the past. The preterite views the event as having gone on for a finite period whereas the imperfect merely describes it as going on at the time or as part of the background: compare English 'what were you doing in the garden yesterday?' (at the time: imperfect) and 'what did you do in the garden yesterday?' (looking back on it as completed: preterite).

In *mi padre fumaba/fumó mucho cuando era joven* 'my father smoked a lot when he was young', either tense is possible, whether or not he carried on smoking afterwards and whether or not he is still alive (it is this possibility that makes the linguistic terms 'perfective' or 'completed aspect' and 'imperfective' or 'non-complete aspect' unhelpful for learners of Spanish). The imperfect tense views the habit as in progress at the time; the preterite looks back on it as an event viewed as a whole, i.e. something that continued throughout whichever period of time the speaker has in mind, e.g. his youth, those years, that period I'm talking about, etc.

Since we cannot always know what is in the speaker's or writer's mind, it often happens that either the preterite or the imperfect can be used in Spanish with a difference of nuance that is virtually untranslatable in English:

Mi niñez fue/era feliz	My childhood was happy
Recuerdo que llovió/llovía mucho cuando vivíamos en Irlanda (it still rains in Ireland!)	I remember it rained a lot when we lived in Ireland
Alonso se levantó/se levantaba todos los días a las ocho para ir al trabajo	Alonso got up every day at eight to go to work
Cuando vivíamos juntos no tuvimos/teníamos problemas	When we lived together we had no problems
Siempre dormía como durmió su padre, con el arma escondida dentro de la funda de la almohada (G. García Márquez, Col.; ...*durmió como dormía su padre* would have meant roughly the same thing)	He always used to sleep as his father (had) slept, with his gun hidden in his pillowcase

Intrinsic characteristics are likely to be expressed by the imperfect since they tend to be part of a general background. Thus *la casa era muy grande* 'the house was very big', *mi padre era indio/blanco* 'my father was Indian/white'. Use of *fue* in these cases is very unlikely since such descriptions are obviously not 'events', but cf. *su padre fue un hombre muy alto, muy guapo, muy inteligente* (A. Gala, Sp.).

Non-intrinsic characteristics can take either tense, but are more likely to appear with the imperfect if they refer to some more or less permanent attribute. However, choice of tense depends whether we consider an event viewed as a whole (preterite) or whether we are focusing on what was true at the time (imperfect), as in *yo, de pequeño, fui tímido* or *era tímido* 'as a child I was/used to be timid'. Students are advised to use the imperfect in such cases, since use of the preterite for a more or less inherent characteristic can sound strange or very literary, as in *Sir Thomas Browne (1605–82)* **supo** *el griego, el latín, el francés, el italiano y el español, y fue uno de los primeros hombres de letras que estudiaron anglosajón* (J. L. Borges, Arg., more usually *sabía griego*) 'Sir Thomas Browne (1605–82) knew Greek, Latin, French, Italian and Spanish, and was one of the first men of letters to study Anglo-Saxon'.

14.4.5 Use of the preterite to denote an event that has reached completion

The preterite may indicate that a process has finally reached completion, as in:

Una vez el dinero estuvo en mis manos, compré la casa	As soon as the money came into my hands, I bought the house
Estuvo lista a las once (G. García Márquez, Col.)	She was ready by eleven
Cuando el café estuvo listo le alcanzó una tacita (E. Sábato, Arg.)	When the coffee was ready she handed him a small cup
La conversación se fue espaciando (*ir* + gerund indicates a longish process, *fue* shows it ended)	The conversation gradually petered out

14.4.6 Use of the preterite to indicate an event that actually happened

Sometimes the preterite clearly indicates that the event referred to happened, while the imperfect does not give us this information. Compare: *tuvimos que atravesar dos desiertos para llegar al oasis* 'we had to cross two deserts to get to the oasis' (and we did), and *teníamos que atravesar dos desiertos para llegar al oasis* 'we had (still) to cross two deserts to get to the oasis'. The second does not tell us whether we crossed it or turned back. Further examples:

Fue un error decírselo	It was a mistake to tell him (we committed it)
Era un error decírselo	It was a mistake to tell him (we may or may not have committed it)
Fue una presa fácil	(S)he/It was an easy prey (and was caught)
Era una presa fácil	(same translation, but the victim may have escaped)
Costó trabajo conseguirlo	It was hard work getting it (but we did)
Costaba trabajo conseguirlo	It was hard work to get it (we may or may not have done)

*Fue un error devolverle el dinero, por eso no lo hice has the absurd meaning *'I committed the mistake of giving him back the money, so I didn't': *era un error…* must be used.

14.4.7 Preterite to denote a rapid or short-lived event

The preterite can sometimes show that an event lasted only a moment. The imperfect would, in these cases, indicate an event that had not yet ended at the time referred to:

Hubo una nota de alarma en su voz	There was a (brief) note of alarm in his/her voice
Cuando abrí el horno, se sintió calor	When I opened the oven it felt hot (i.e. there was a gust of heat)
Estuvo a punto de pensar que esas manos no eran suyas (C. Fuentes, Mex., dialogue)	(For a second) he was on the verge of thinking that those hands weren't his own

14.4.8 Preterite used to indicate the beginning of a state or action

The preterite may indicate the beginning of an action. Compare *mi hija habló a los once meses* (i.e. *empezó a hablar*) 'my daughter started talking *at* eleven months', and *mi hija hablaba a los once meses* 'my daughter was talking *by* eleven months'. Also:

Me cayó bien (cf. *me caía bien* 'I was getting on well with him/her')	I took a liking to her/him
Ana me gustó desde el primer momento	I liked ('took a liking to') Ana right from the start
Fue niña y le pusimos Rita (M. Rodoreda, Castilian translation, Sp.)	It was a girl and we called her Rita
Todo lo que había dentro me pareció lejano y ajeno (L. Sepúlveda, Ch.)	Everything inside (suddenly) seemed to me distant and alien
desde 1957, cuando por primera vez estuve consciente de la Revolución Cubana (interview, *Granma*, Cu.; Sp. *fui consciente*)	since 1957, when I first became aware of the Cuban Revolution...

14.4.9 Preterite used to indicate certainties in the future

The preterite is occasionally used to indicate an absolute certainty in the future:

Cuando llegue, llegó	(S)he'll be here when (s)he's here (and that's that!)
Cuando se acabe, se acabó	When it's finished, it's finished

This construction is more common in Latin America than in Spain. The following three examples are not heard in Spain:

Para las dos ya lo acabé (Mex., from Lope Blanch, 1991; Sp. *ya lo tengo/tendré acabado*)	I'll have it finished by two o'clock
Mañana ya llegó el día (L. Rafael Sánchez, Puerto Rico, dialogue; Sp. *mañana es el día*)	Tomorrow's the day!
Nos fuimos (colloquial La. Am.; Sp. *nos vamos*)	We're going/We're leaving right now (lit. 'we left')

14.4.10 Special meanings of the preterite of some verbs

Some verbs require special translations when they appear in the preterite. This is especially true of the modal verbs *deber, poder, querer, saber*, discussed in Chapter 21. Two other verbs affected are:

(a) *Tener*: the preterite may mean 'to receive'/'to get', the imperfect means 'had' in the sense of 'was in my possession':

tuve la impresión de que...	I got the impression that...
tenía la impresión de que...	I had the impression that...
Tuve una carta/Tenía una carta	I got a letter/I had a letter
Cuando tuvo ocasión de estudiar consiguió con la universidad a distancia el título de ingeniero (*Cambio16*, Sp.)	When he got the chance to study, he graduated as an engineer from the Open University

This does not override the rule given at 14.4.1 that the preterite must be used for actions continuing throughout a specified period: *tuvo fiebre durante tres días* '(s)he had a fever for three days'.

(**b**) *Conocer*: contrast *conocí a Antonia* 'I met Antonia' (for the first time), *conocía a Antonia* 'I knew Antonia'.

14.5 The imperfect: general

The Spanish imperfect form indicates an event viewed as not yet complete at the past time referred to. It is therefore much used as a background tense to describe something that was already in progress when another event occurred (14.5.1), and to express habitual events in the past (14.5.2), although the preterite can also sometimes describe habitual events, as explained at 14.4.4.

In colloquial language the Spanish imperfect may be a substitute for the conditional. See 14.5.4 and 25.5 for discussion.

14.5.1 Imperfect tense to denote past events in progress when something else happened

The imperfect is much used to indicate any state or event that was in progress when something else happened. It is thus the correct tense for background descriptions; the preterite is used for the events set against the background (imperfects in bold type):

Yo **volvía** del cine cuando vi a Niso	I was coming back from the cinema when I saw Niso
Miró por encima del hombro para estar segura de que nadie la **acechaba** (G. García Márquez, Col.)	She looked over her shoulder to be sure that no one was lying in wait for her
Cuando entré en el cuarto noté que **olía** a quemado	When I entered the room I noticed there was a smell of burning
Los monumentos y estatuas que **adornaban** los paseos y las plazas fueron triturados (E. Mendoza, Sp.)	The monuments and statues that adorned the avenues and squares were pulverized
Volví a la sala, pero él ya no **estaba** (A. Mastretta, Mex., dialogue: i.e. his absence was still continuing when I arrived)	I went back to the living room, but he was no longer there

For the possible use of the continuous imperfect in some of these sentences, e.g. *estaba acechando*, instead of the non-continuous imperfect, see 14.5.5.

14.5.2 Imperfect used to denote events that continued in the past for an unspecified period

The imperfect can indicate that an event continued in the past for an unspecified period (and may or may not have continued). It is thus much used for characteristics, situations, habitual actions and other events that have no clear beginning and end:

Las catapultas romanas lanzaban piedras	Roman catapults threw stones
Cada vez que os veíais lo decía (I. Aldecoa, Sp., dialogue)	He used to say it every time you met
Le exasperaban estas comidas mexicanas de cuatro o cinco horas de duración (C. Fuentes, Mex.)	These four- or five-hour Mexican meals exasperated him

A veces le dolían el aire y la tierra que pisaba, el sol del amanecer, las cuencas de los ojos (A. Mastretta, Mex.)	Sometimes the air and the ground she trod on hurt her; and the rising sun, and her eye-sockets

The preterite must be used if a period of time is specified, as in 'she was (*fue*) president for eight years'; see 14.4.1.

14.5.3 Imperfect in phrases of time of the kind 'I hadn't seen her for years', 'it was the first time that...'

English-speakers should note the use of the imperfect in the following type of sentence where English uses the pluperfect tense (for the use of the present tense in sentences of this type see note to 14.3.7):

Hacía años que no la veía	I hadn't seen her for years
Era la primera vez que la veía	It was the first time I had seen her

14.5.4 Imperfect for the conditional

The imperfect is often used in familiar speech instead of the conditional. This most commonly occurs in four cases (the examples under **b** and **c** reflect European Spanish: we are not sure about the distribution of these constructions in Latin America):

(a) When the conditional would refer to an immediate future. In this case Spanish resembles English: one can say 'he said he would come' or 'he said he was coming':

Prometieron que venían/vendrían	They promised they were coming/would come
Juró que lo hacía/haría	(S)he swore (s)he'd do it
Pensaba que ya no venías/vendrías	I thought you weren't coming/ wouldn't come any more
Sabíamos que los refuerzos llegaban/ llegarían de un momento para otro	We knew the reinforcements were arriving/would arrive at any moment

This is not possible if the future is not immediate: *juró que me amaría siempre* (not *amaba...*) '(s)he swore (s)he would love me for ever'.

NB: *Querer* means to love a person in all senses, as a friend, relative or lover. *Amar* is used between people who are passionately in love, and also for religious love: *amar a Dios* 'to love God', *ama al pecador* 'love the sinner'.

(b) With *deber* and *poder*, in which case the imperfect is slightly more colloquial:

Podía ser una solución, mira... (C. Martín Gaite, Sp., dialogue)	It could be a solution, you know...
Debías/Deberías hacerlo ahora	You should do it now

This usage is especially frequent with *poder* and *deber* to show that someone should or could have acted differently in the past, e.g. *podías/podrías haberlo hecho, ¿no?* 'you could have done it, couldn't you?'; see 21.2.3d and 21.3.3 for details.

(c) In 'remote' and 'unfulfilled' conditions in familiar Spanish (see 25.5 for details):

Aunque no me gustara, me casaba/casaría con ella	I'd marry her even if I didn't like her

Usted no tenía más que decírmelo y le cambiaba el plato (very colloquial for *le habría cambiado*)	You only had to tell me and I'd have changed your plate
Un paso más y te rompías el pescuezo (colloquial for *te habrías roto/te hubieras roto*)	One more step and you'd have broken your neck

The imperfect cannot replace the conditional when the latter indicates a guess or estimate (as explained at 14.7.2).

(**d**) In familiar Spanish, to express a wish:

Ya le decía yo cuatro verdades	I wouldn't mind giving him/her a piece of my mind! (lit. 'telling him/her four truths')
Tenían que hacer un monumento al tío que inventó el café (M. Delibes, Sp., dialogue)	They ought to build a monument for the guy who invented coffee
Yo ahora me tomaba un helado y me quedaba tan bien	I'd (like to have) have an ice-cream now and I'd feel great

14.5.5 *Hablaba* or *estaba hablando?*

If the action is not habitual and is truly past (e.g. 'I was leaving the next day' is in fact a future in the past), the difference between the continuous and non-continuous imperfect is often blurred, although modern Spanish prefers the continuous form in such cases if it is possible with the verb (see Chapter 15): *yo hablaba/estaba hablando con los vecinos cuando llegaron los bomberos* (*estaba hablando* preferred) 'I was talking to the neighbo(u)rs when the firemen arrived'.

However, the verbs *ir* and *venir* and a few others are not generally used in the continuous form: see 15.3c.

14.5.6 Imperfect in children's language

An interesting use of the imperfect is found in children's language (called the *imperfecto lúdico* or 'imperfect of play'): *vamos a jugar a que yo era un vaquero y tú eras un indio* 'let's pretend I'm a cowboy and you're an Indian'.

14.5.7 Imperfect to make courteous requests

The imperfect can be used to show courtesy in requests and enquiries:

¿Qué deseaba?	What would you like?
Perdone, quería hablar con el director	Excuse me, I'd like a word with the manager

14.5.8 Imperfect used for preterite in literary styles

In literary styles the imperfect is sometimes used as an alternative to the preterite for dramatic effect. Normally the sentence includes an adverb of time that shows that the action is a single completed event:

Poco después, la policía francesa arrestaba a DM, de 56 años (*El País*, Sp.)	Shortly after, the French police arrested 56-year-old DM
Un día antes, en Santiago de Cuba, era asesinado Frank País (*Granma*, Cu.)	The day before, in Santiago de Cuba, Frank País was murdered

This construction is uncommon outside sensational journalism, but it is frequent in literary French (the *imparfait dramatique*).

14.5.9 Imperfect used in reported speech and in stream of consciousness (*monólogo interior*)

In reported speech the present tense becomes an imperfect and the perfect tense becomes a pluperfect. The following is an extract from a letter in a novel written by Josefina Aldecoa (Spain). Annick writes to David: *Lo que ocurre es que tu carta me ha dejado inquieta. No hablo de tus planteamientos generales; sabes que los comparto. Pero estoy libre de emociones viscerales…. Y me preocupo por ti. No se trata de tu seguridad sino de tu pérdida de rumbo. Temo que estás buscándote salidas nobles pero falsas, porque tú, no te engañes, eres un diletante, un señorito que juega a derribar tiranías.* 'The thing is that your letter has left me worried. I'm not referring to your views in general; you know I share them. But I'm not prone to gut reactions … And I worry about you. Not about your safety but about your loss of direction. I'm afraid you're looking for a noble but false way out, because, don't fool yourself, you're a dilettante, an upper-class boy playing at overthrowing tyrants'.

In reported speech, this would read: *Annick le decía en su carta que lo que **ocurría era** que su carta la **había dejado** inquieta. **No hablaba** de sus planteamientos generales; ya **sabía** él que ella los **compartía**. Pero ella **estaba** libre de emociones viscerales… Y se **preocupaba** por él. **No se trataba** de su seguridad, sino de su pérdida de rumbo. **Temía** que se estaba buscando salidas nobles pero falsas porque, no se **debía** engañar, él **era** un diletante, un señorito que **jugaba** a derribar tiranías.*

The following paragraph is an example of 'stream of consciousness' (*monólogo interior*): *sola en la tienda, Felicitas se quedó reflexionando. Vaya, al chico le **parecía** mejor que esperase la visita del director (….) Ella **quería** trabajar en el hotel y el director **decía** que **quería** una chica como ella (…) Ya no **parecía** fácil el acceso a la recepción del hotel, que **hacía** unos días se **había** abierto ante sus ojos como una visión prometedora, pero **debía** trazarse un plan de acción* (S. Puértolas, Sp.) 'alone in the shop, Felicitas was thinking. So the boy thought it was better for her to wait for the manager to come and see her. She wanted to work in the hotel and the manager said he wanted a girl like her. It didn't seem easy any more to get a job in the hotel reception, which a few days ago had seemed to her a promising possibility, but a plan of action had to be drawn up'.

14.6 Future tense: general

Spanish has several ways of expressing the future, and the so-called 'future tense' (*hablaré, vendrás*) is not the most common in everyday speech (from which it is said to be disappearing except in its 'suppositional' role described at 14.6.5):

(a) *Esta noche vamos al cine*	Tonight we're going to the cinema
(b) *Esta noche vamos a ir al cine*	Tonight we're going to go to the cinema
(c) *Esta noche iremos al cine*	Tonight we'll go to the cinema
(d) *Esta noche hemos de ir al cine*	Tonight we're to go/we're due to go to the cinema

(a) describes an event which is prearranged or scheduled.

(**b**) is a foreseen or 'intentional' future and it is also often an informal substitute for the future tense proper *iremos, seré*, etc.

(**c**) often excludes the idea of pre-arrangement or a scheduled event. Consequently it may sound rather uncertain or, depending on tone and context, may sound like an order or promise.

(**d**) is discussed at 21.4.1. It is sometimes heard in Latin America with a future meaning, but in Castilian-speaking areas of Spain it usually implies obligation and is now old-fashioned, rather like the English 'tonight we are to go to the cinema'. But it has other, still current, uses, discussed at 21.4.1. It is common in Mexico as an alternative to *deber de*. The latter is discussed at 21.3.2, the Mexican construction at 21.4.1b.

As was mentioned earlier, the future tense is gradually disappearing from spoken (but not written) Spanish, this decline being more advanced in Latin America than in Spain and more deep-rooted in familiar or popular styles. It is usually replaced by the simple present—*te llamo mañana* 'I'll call you tomorrow' (see 14.6.3)—or by *ir a* + infinitive: *la voy a ver mañana* 'I'm going to see her tomorrow' (see 14.6.4).

14.6.1 Uses of the future tense form to denote future time

Often, particularly in informal speech, the present and future forms are interchangeable. However, the future is used:

(**a**) For provisional or less certain statements about the future, e.g. for forecasts, or for statements about the future when no other word makes it clear that the future is meant:

Si llueve se aplazará el partido	If it rains the match will be postponed
En el remoto futuro el sol se apagará	In the remote future the sun will go out
Para entonces todos estaremos calvos	We'll all be bald by then (said of something that will take a long time)
Me ha dado cien euros. Con esto tiraré hasta la semana próxima, y luego veremos (*luego vemos* is impossible here)	(S)he gave me 100 euros. I'll manage with that until next week, and then we'll see
En cuanto pasemos el túnel ya verás cómo cambia el tiempo. Hará más frío (I. Aldecoa, Sp., dialogue)	When we get through the tunnel you'll see how the weather changes. It'll be colder
Nos veremos mañana en Palacio, ¿no es cierto? (C. Fuentes, Mex., dialogue. *Nos vemos...* would imply more certainty)	We'll see one another tomorrow at the Palace won't we?'

(i) The difference between sentences like *te veo mañana* and *te veré mañana* 'I'll see you tomorrow' may be merely one of tone. Some informants claimed they would use the present tense in *te veo mañana* (informal) and the future in *le/lo veré (a usted) mañana* (formal).

(ii) *Acaso, tal vez, quizá(s)*, which mean 'perhaps', *posiblemente* 'possibly' and *probablemente* 'probably' may, when they refer to a future event, appear either with the future tense or the conditional, but much more usually with the present subjunctive. See 16.3.2 for details. **Tal vez/quizá/acaso **viene** mañana* is not Spanish.

(b) The future is much used for promises, especially long-term ones, since these by nature are not pre-arrangements:

Ten confianza en mí. No te decepcionaré	Have confidence in me. I won't disappoint you
¡No pasarán!	They shall not pass!
Hoy eres la Cenicienta, pero mañana serás una princesa	Today you're Cinderella, but tomorrow you'll be a princess
Pero cuídalo como si fuera ya mío, porque en ese caso algún día será de mis hijas (A. Bryce Echenique, Pe., dialogue)	But look after it as though it already belonged to me, because in that case one day it will belong to my daughters
Una verdadera revolución no admitirá jamás la impunidad (*Vindicación de Cuba*, Cu.)	A true revolution will never allow crimes to go unpunished

However, the present can be used colloquially (but not with *ser* 'to be') for short-term promises presented as pre-arrangements, e.g. *no te preocupes, te lo devuelvo mañana* 'don't worry, I'll give it back to you tomorrow'.

14.6.2 Future tense used for stern commands

The future is occasionally used for very for solemn or stern commands, as in English:

No matarás	Thou shalt not kill
No saldrás de esta casa hasta que yo no te lo permita (see 23.2.4d for the second *no*)	You will not leave this house until I allow you to

14.6.3 Present tense with future meaning

The present is much used in informal language to refer to the future. If the subject is human this conveys an idea of pre-arrangement and is therefore especially used for fixtures or scheduled events, cf. English 'I'm going to Spain next year', 'we attack tomorrow'. If the subject is non-living, the action is foreseen as a certainty or a fixture, e.g. *el tren sale mañana a las 7* 'the train's leaving tomorrow at 7' (scheduled departure). Compare *el tren saldrá mañana a las siete* 'the train will leave tomorrow at seven', which implies an unscheduled departure in both languages.

The fact that the verb refers to the future is normally shown by some time phrase like *mañana, esta noche, el año que viene*. The following examples are informal in tone:

Vamos a España el año que viene	We're going to Spain next year
Te llamo/Nos vemos	I'll call you/See you again/later
Si viene por aquí, ¿qué digo?	If (s)he comes round here, what shall I say?
Esta noche hay tormenta, verás	Tonight there'll be a storm, you'll see
Espera, lo hago en un momento	Wait, I'll do it in a moment
El día menos pensado le tiran a tu madre la casa (C. Martín Gaite, Sp., dialogue; expresses certainty)	One fine day (lit. 'the day least expected') they're going to knock your mother's house down
¡Repite eso y te mato! (A. Bryce Echenique, Pe., dialogue)	Say that again and I'll kill you!

(i) This use of the present tense is particularly common with verbs of motion (*ir*, *venir*, *salir*, *llegar*).

(ii) Events predicted in an unspecified future are by nature less certain, so the present tense should not be used: *si las cosas continúan así, ya no habrá árboles* 'if things go on like this there will be no more trees left'.

(iii) If there is nothing in the sentence or context that clearly shows that the statement refers to the future, the present tense is assumed to be a true present and the future must be shown by some unambiguous form, e.g. *ir a* + infinitive or the future tense proper. Compare *me parece que no hay sitio* 'I think there's no room' and *me parece que no habrá/va a haber sitio* 'I think there won't be room'.

(iv) The present tense of *ser* is usually used for the future only in calendar statements: *mañana es jueves* 'tomorrow is Thursday', but *mañana el discurso será pronunciado por el presidente* 'tomorrow the speech will be delivered by the president'.

14.6.4 *Ir a...* + infinitive

The future is very often expressed by *ir a* + the infinitive. This may express firm intention or it may simply be a colloquial variant for the future tense (but not for the suppositional future mentioned at 14.6.5). In this second use it is so frequent that it virtually replaces the ordinary future-tense form in the speech of many people. Kany, 192, gives several Latin-American examples like *ya va usted a querer pelear con nosotros por semejante porquería* (Pe., popular; Spain *se va usted a pelear con nosotros por...*) 'sure, you'll want to fight us over a bit of rubbish like this', *¿cuánto va a querer, señor?* (Mex., popular; Sp. *¿cuánto va a ser?/¿cuánto quiere?*) 'how much will you want, Sir?'. But the future tense is by no means extinct in spoken Spanish in Spain or in Latin America, as can be seen in this passage of colloquial Cuban:

—¿Y qué harás entre estas cuatro paredes? —Limpiaré el cuarto, me lavaré la cabeza, plancharé una blusita para ir al trabajo el lunes, me sentaré en la butaca, sacaré un crucigrama, me asomaré al balcón, cocinaré, me comeré las uñas. ¡No tengo ni un solo minuto libre! (A. Arrufat, Cu., dialogue; Spain *haré un crucigrama*)	'And what'll you do (shut up) between these four walls?' 'I'll clean my room, wash my hair, iron a blouse for work on Monday, sit in the armchair, do a crossword, look out of the window, cook, bite my nails... I don't have a single minute free!'

The imperfect *iba a*, etc. may also be used as a future in the past. See 14.7.3.

14.6.5 Suppositional future

An important use of the future tense, especially in Spain, is to express suppositions or approximations. Use of the future in approximations often produces much more idiomatic Spanish than clumsy sentences involving *aproximadamente* or *alrededor de*. In questions, the future expresses wonder, incredulity or conjecture:

Serán las nueve y media, por ahí (C. Martín Gaite, Sp., dialogue)	It must be around 9.30
Un par de años hará...Gannon me escribió de Gualeguaychu (J. L. Borges, Arg.)	It must be a couple of years ago that Gannon wrote to me from Gualeguaychu
Pase usted, por favor. Siéntese. Estará cansado (J. de J. Martínez, Panama, dialogue)	Please come in. Sit down. You must be tired

—¿Dónde está tu monedero? —Me lo habré dejado en casa	'Where's your purse?' 'I must have left it at home'
¡Habráse visto semejante tontería!	Did anyone ever see such nonsense!
¿Qué hora será? (Lat. Am.¿Qué horas serán?)	I wonder what the time is?
¿Qué estará tramando ella?	I wonder what she's up to?
Eh, no querrás que mi jefe vea eso (J. Marías, Sp., dialogue)	Hey, you don't want my boss to see that, do you?

(i) Kany, 190, notes that this use of the future is more common in Spain than in Latin America, where *deber (de)...* is more usual: *deben (de) ser las cinco = serán las cinco* or *deben (de) ser las cinco*. See 21.3.2 for *deber de*, which is also used in Spain.

(ii) In Mexico *haber de* is commonly used instead of *deber de* in this construction. See 21.4.1b.

(iii) For additional remarks on the use of the future perfect tense for conjectures, see 14.11a.

14.7 The conditional: general

(For the forms of the conditional see 13.1.8.) The name 'conditional' is accurate insofar as it often shows that an event is conditional on some other factor, as in *podríamos ir mañana* 'we could go tomorrow' (if the weather's nice, if we're free, etc.). But it has other functions that have nothing to do with the idea of conditionality, especially the expression of suppositions or approximations in the past (14.7.2) and the expression of the future in the past (14.7.3).

For the purpose of agreement, the conditional counts as a past tense, so the subjunctive in a subordinate clause governed by the conditional must also be in the past. Compare *es absurdo que vengas mañana* 'it's absurd for you to come tomorrow' and *sería absurdo que vinieras/vinieses mañana* 'it would be absurd for you to come tomorrow' (see 16.16 for detailed discussion).

Colloquial language may use the imperfect instead of the conditional by the imperfect, especially in conditional sentences (see 14.5.4 and 25.5 for discussion).

Replacement of the imperfect subjunctive by the conditional, e.g. *?si yo tendría dinero* for *si yo tuviera dinero* 'if I had some money' is very common in popular speech in Navarre and neighbouring regions, in Argentina and perhaps locally elsewhere, but foreigners should avoid it.

14.7.1 Uses of the conditional to express conditions

(For the conditional in conditional sentences, see Chapter 25.) The conditional is also used for implied conditions, i.e. conditional statements which contain no if-clause:

Sería una locura ponerlo en marcha sin aceite	It would be crazy to start it up with no oil
¿Quieres ir a la manifestación? Sería interesante	Do you want to go to the demonstration? It would be interesting
De nada serviría un nuevo golpe porque sólo perjudicaría al país (headline, Bolivian press)	Another coup d'état would be pointless because it would only damage the country

14.7.2 Conditional for suppositions about the past

The conditional is used for suppositions and approximations about the past in the same way as the future is for the present (see 14.6.5 and 14.11):

Aquel día andaríamos más de cincuenta kilómetros	That day we must have walked more than fifty kilometres
Tendría (or tenía/debía de tener) unos treinta años	(S)he must have been about thirty
Los guardé algún tiempo...; luego supongo quo los quemaria (C. Martín Gaite, Sp., dialogue)	I kept them (*los diarios* –'the diaries') for a while...; then I guess I must have burnt them
Llevaba un saco sport que en algún tiempo habría sido azul marino (E. Sábato, Arg. *Saco = chaqueta* in Spain)	He was wearing a sports jacket which must once have been navy blue

In some styles, especially journalism and more so in Latin America, the conditional is used for rumours, inferences or unsubstantiated reports. This construction is condemned by grammarians, and by the editors of *El País*, as an imitation from French:

Gregorius habría nacido en Glasgow... (J. Cortázar, Arg.)	Gregorius was reportedly born in Glasgow
La desaparición de los etarras estaría motivada por cuestiones de seguridad (*Abc*, Sp.)	Security reasons are said to be the motive for the disappearance of the ETA members (*ETA* is a Basque separatist movement)

(i) For the use of *deber de* for suppositions see 21.3.2.

(ii) In questions, the conditional perfect may express amazement or anxiety. See 14.11.

14.7.3 Conditional for the future in the past

The conditional is used to express the future in the past (i.e. as a close equivalent of *iba a* + an infinitive):

Yo sabía que papá bajaría/bajaba/iba a bajar a las once	I knew father would come down at 11 o'clock
Cerró la puerta con cuidado; su mujer dormía profundamente. Dormiría hasta que el sol hiciera su primera presencia en la ventana (I. Aldecoa, Sp.)	He shut the door carefully; his wife was fast asleep. She would sleep until the sun first showed at the window
En un rato todo el mundo se iría a dormir la siesta (A. Mastretta, Mex., dialogue; Sp., *dentro de un rato*)	Soon everyone would go and take a siesta

14.7.4 Conditional in rhetorical questions

As in English, the conditional is much used for questions to which the speaker already knows the answer:

¿Alguien se atrevería a decir que la "socialización" ha hecho más libres a los diarios? (M. Vargas Llosa, Pe.)	Would anyone dare to say that 'socialization' has made newspapers more free?

14.7.5 Replacement of the conditional by the *-ra* form of the subjunctive

With a few verbs the *-ra* subjunctive form is a stylistic variant for the conditional when this is used as a true conditional (and not, for example, as a suppositional tense or future in the past). This is common with the auxiliary *haber: habría/hubiera sido mejor* 'it would have been better'. Use of the *-ra* form for the conditional is slightly more formal in tone:

Hubiera podido ser una buena novela de misterio…(C. Martín Gaite, Sp., dialogue)	It could have been a good mystery novel…
El mal lo mismo se hubiera colado por alguna grieta de las piedras del castillo (M. Puig, Arg., dialogue)	The disease would have crept in just the same through some crack in the walls of the castle
A lo mejor me hubiera hecho mucho bien seguir con la terapia (A. Mastretta, Mex., interview)	Perhaps it would have done me a lot of good to continue with therapy

Habría could have been used in all these examples.

(i) The *–ra* form is also common with *querer* and *deber*, although it is more formal than the plain conditional: *yo querría/quisiera hacerlo* 'I'd like to do it', *deberías/debieras haberlo hecho* 'you should have done it'. With *poder* it is literary: *podría haber sido/pudiera haber sido* 'it could have been'. See Chapter 21 for discussion of these modal verbs. With other verbs it is nowadays uncommon and archaic: *Abril, sin tu asistencia clara,* **fuera** *invierno de caídos esplendores…* (Juan Ramón Jiménez, poetry; i.e. *sería…*) 'April, without thy bright presence, would be a winter of fallen splendours', *un libro* **fuera** *poco…para dar cauce a un país como La Mancha* (C. J. Cela, Sp.) 'a book would be little (lit. 'were little…') to do justice to (lit. 'to give channel to') a land like La Mancha'.

It is common in the Latin-American literary formula *pareciera que…* (for *parecería que…*) 'it would seem that…': *pareciera que al señor Doens se le detuvo la historia nacional en 1992* (*La Prensa*, Panama) 'it would seem that for Mr Doens the country's history stopped in 1992'.

(ii) Use of the *-se* subjunctive in place of the *-ra* form for the conditional is rejected by the grammarians: *El País's Libro de estilo* bans it. But it is common in spontaneous speech: *y* **hubiese** *(for hubiera/habría) sido muy sospechoso que yo me negase* (M. Puig, Arg., dialogue) 'and it would have been very suspicious if I'd refused'.

(iii) In pre-18th-century Spanish the use of the *-ra* form for the conditional with all verbs was very common: *y si estas calamidades no me acontecieran, no me* **tuviera** *yo por caballero andante* (Cervantes, *Don Quijote*) 'and had these calamities not befallen me, I would not consider myself a knight errant'. This recalls the archaic English equivalent '…I had not considered myself a knight errant'.

14.8 Compound tenses: general remarks

'Compound tenses' are tenses formed from *haber* plus the past participle. The compound tenses are as follows:

Perfect (14.9)	*he hablado,* etc.	I have spoken
Pluperfect (14.10)	*había hablado,* etc.	I had spoken
Pretérito anterior (14.10.4)	*hube hablado,* etc.	I had spoken
Future Perfect (14.11)	*habré hablado,* etc.	I will have spoken
Conditional Perfect (14.11)	*habría hablado,* etc.	I would have spoken
Perfect Subjunctive (14.9.9)	*haya hablado,* etc.	(no exact translation)
Pluperfect Subjunctive (14.10.5)	*hubiera* or *hubiese hablado,* etc.	(no exact translation)

All of these, except the *pretérito anterior*, can also appear in the Continuous Form (see Chapter 15):

Perfect	*he estado hablando,* etc.	I've been speaking
Pluperfect	*había estado hablando,* etc.	I had been speaking
Future Perfect	*habré estado hablando,* etc.	I will have been speaking
Conditional Perfect	*habría estado hablando,* etc.	I would have been speaking
Perfect Subjunctive	*haya estado hablando,* etc.	(no exact translation)
Pluperfect Subjunctive	*hubiera* or *hubiese estado hablando,* etc.	(no exact translation)

Compound tenses all use the auxiliary *haber* or, much less commonly and the *pretérito anterior* excepted, *tener* (see 14.8.3). No verbs in modern Spanish form the perfect with *ser* 'to be' as an auxiliary (*llegar, ir, venir* are very rare archaic or journalistic exceptions, cf. *el verano es ido* 'Summer is gone', *Cambio16*, Sp.).

Unlike French and Italian, the past participle does not agree in number and gender with the object of the verb (unless *tener* is used instead of *haber*: see 14.8.3). For an example of a verb conjugated in the compound tenses, see 13.5.4.

14.8.1 Compound tenses: word order

Learners should not insert words between *haber* and the past participle: French *j'ai toujours dit* = *siempre he dicho*. *He siempre dicho* is not heard in normal Spanish, but the rule is occasionally broken in literary style with such words as *ni siquiera, incluso, todavía, aún, ya, nunca, jamás, más que, quizá(s), tal vez*:

Se habrá tal vez olvidado	You may have forgotten
Se ha más que duplicado la cifra (*Hoja del lunes,* Sp.)	The figure has more than doubled
. . .en buena parte por no habérselo aún propuesto con entera seriedad (S. Pitol, Mex.)	. . .to a great extent because he had not yet suggested it to him in all seriousness

(i) When *haber* is in the infinitive or the gerund form, personal pronouns are always attached to it: *. . .habérselo propuesto* '. . .to have suggested it to him/her/you', *habiéndonoslos enviado* 'having sent them to us'.

14.8.2 Omission of *haber* and of the past participle in compound tenses

The auxiliary verb *haber* may optionally be omitted before a second or subsequent past participle to avoid repetition:

Yo también he pasado por baches y conocido la duda (L. Goytisolo, Sp., dialogue)	I've been through rough patches as well and known doubt
No sólo había tocado la mano y mirado los ojos de la mujer que más le gustaba tocar y mirar del mundo… (C. Fuentes, Mex.)	Not only had he touched the hand and looked at the eyes of the woman he most liked to touch and look at in the world…

(i) The past participle may be deleted in English, but not in Spanish: 'Have you tried the sausages?' 'Yes, I have.' —*¿Has probado las salchichas? —Sí* or —*Sí, las he probado*. However, deletion occasionally occurs with the pluperfect tense, to judge by *¿Se había reído? Sí, se había. Pero esta vez sin sarcasmo* (M. Vargas Llosa, Pe., dialogue) 'Had he laughed? Yes, he had. But without sarcasm this time'. Spanish informants considered this more typical of Latin-American Spanish.

14.8.3 *Tengo hecho, tengo comprado*, etc.

Tener is occasionally used as an auxiliary, like the English 'to have got', to denote the successful acquisition of some object or the fulfilment of some task. Compare 'I've done my homework' and 'I've got my homework done'. The participle must agree in number and gender with the object of the verb, and the verb must be transitive and have a direct object (**tengo sido*, cf. Portuguese *tenho sido* 'I have been' is not Spanish):

*Ya tengo comprad**as** las entradas*	I've already bought the tickets
Para el viernes tendré hechos todos mis deberes	By Friday I'll have all my homework done
Yo tenía concertada hora con el jefe	I had arranged an appointment with the boss
Que persigan a los pillos que tienen tomadas las calles (El Tiempo, Col.)	Let them chase after the hoodlums that have taken over the streets
Tenía pensado cruzar a la orilla derecha (J. Cortázar, Arg., dialogue)	I had planned to cross to the right bank

(i) *Llevar* is also occasionally used in the same way for accumulative actions: *llevo tomadas tres aspirinas, pero todavía me duele la cabeza* 'I've taken three aspirins, but my head's still aching', . . .*y le llevan encontradas ya creo que hasta tres calaveras en la catedral de Lima* (A. Bryce Echenique, Pe., dialogue; Sp. *y llevan encontradas...*) 'I think they've already found three of his skulls in Lima Cathedral'(referring to a famous saint), *yo llevo vendidos cuatrocientos* (Mexico City, overheard) 'I've sold four hundred'.

(ii) In Galicia one sometimes hears sentences like **no la tengo visto*. This is not Castilian but a borrowing from the Galician *non a teño visto*. It should be *no la he visto*.

14.9 The perfect tense

European Spanish and literary Latin-American Spanish differ sharply from French, German and Italian, and broadly resemble English in respecting the different meanings of the preterite, *hablé* 'I spoke', and the perfect, *he hablado* 'I've spoken'. Students of languages in which the difference is blurred must not imitate sentences like *je l'ai vu hier, ich habe ihn gestern gesehen, l'ho visto ieri* 'I saw him yesterday' to produce bad Spanish like **lo/le he visto ayer* (correctly *lo/le vi ayer*). Such misuse of the perfect is heard in popular Madrid speech.

European Spanish usually uses the perfect wherever English does, but the converse is not true: the European Spanish perfect often requires translation by the English simple past. Moreover, in most of the Spanish-speaking world (Galicia, Asturias and most of Latin America) the preterite is in fact more common than the perfect, cf. *ya llegó* (Latin America) '(s)he has already arrived' (some varieties of North-American English are like Latin-American Spanish in preferring the simple past to the compound perfect: '(s)he already arrived'). In Spain one says *ya ha llegado*. See 14.9.8 for further remarks on the perfect tense in Latin America.

14.9.1 Perfect to denote events occurring in a period that includes the present

The perfect is used for events that have happened in a period of time that is still current, e.g. today, this afternoon, this week, this month, this year, this century, always, already, never, still, yet. In this respect, English—especially British English—and European Spanish coincide, and the construction is common in written Latin-American Spanish:

No he visto a tu madre esta semana	I haven't seen your mother this week
Hemos ido dos veces este mes	We've been twice this month
En sólo dos generaciones se ha desertizado un 43% de la superficie terrestre (*Abc*, Sp.)	In only two generations 43% of the earth's surface has been reduced to desert
A sus 42 años, este funcionario jamás ha visto la luz del sol, pero se ha convertido en un colombiano ejemplar (*El Tiempo*, Col.)	At the age of 42, this (blind) government employee has never seen the light of day but he has become an exemplary Colombian
Ya han llegado	They've already arrived
Siempre he pensado que. . .	I have always thought that...
Aún/Todavía no han llegado	They haven't arrived yet

(i) The preterite may be used with the effect of severing the link between the event and the present moment. Compare *vi a tu suegra esta mañana* and *he visto a tu suegra esta mañana* 'I saw/have seen your mother-in-law this morning'. Use of the preterite suggests either that the statement was made after midday (the most likely explanation), or that the speaker feels that the event is by now further in the past.

(ii) Words like *siempre*, *nunca* may or may not include the present: compare *yo siempre he sido un problema para mis padres* 'I've always been a problem for my parents' (and still am) and *yo siempre fui un problema para mis* padres 'I always was a problem for my parents' (e.g. when I was young). But some speakers do not systematically respect the difference of meaning in either language.

(iii) For the common Latin-American (and Canary Islands) use of the preterite in the above contexts see 14.9.8

14.9.2 Perfect for events whose effects are still relevant in the present

As in English, the perfect is used for recent past events that are relevant to or explain the present, or whose effects persist in the present. This is also common in written Latin-American Spanish:

Alguien ha fumado un cigarrillo aquí. Huelo el humo	Someone has smoked a cigarette here. I can smell the smoke
¿Quién ha roto esta ventana?	Who's broken this window?
Todo el mundo habla de Fulano porque ha publicado otra novela	Everyone's talking about so-and-so because he's published a new novel

Es evidente que Simone de Beauvoir ha leído con detenimiento a estos autores y aprovechado sus técnicas (M. Vargas Llosa, Pe.)	It is obvious that Simone de Beauvoir has read these authors closely and (has) made use of their techniques

(i) Latin-American speech generally uses the preterite in such sentences. See 14.9.8 for discussion.

(ii) The perfect is sometimes used in European Spanish in conjunction with some word or phrase that refers to a past not continuing into the present, e.g. 'yesterday', 'two months ago'. This may express the idea that an event is relevant to or explains something in the present, as in *está en muy mala edad para cambiar. Ha cumplido cincuenta años en junio* (C. Martín Gaite, dialogue) 'he's really not the best age for changing. He was fifty last June', *mi padre ha muerto hace un par de meses* 'my father died a couple of months ago' (which explains why I'm still sad). Seco (1998), 357, says that this shows that the action took place in what for the speaker is the 'psychological present', but many Spaniards from the north and many Latin Americans insist on the preterite in such cases and in sentences like the following:

Pero el padre murió, y la madre ha muerto hace unos años (A. Buero Vallejo, Sp., dialogue; makes her death more immediate)	But the father died, and the mother died a few years ago
?*Bueno, he ido a hacerme el análisis hace quince días* (*Cambio16*, Sp., Madrid interviewee)	Anyway, I went and had the test two weeks ago
A mí todo lo que me ha sucedido me ha sucedido ayer, anoche a más tardar (J. Cortázar, Arg., dialogue)	Everything that has happened to me happened yesterday, last night at the latest

DeMello (1994), 1, reports the same phenomenon in the speech of Lima and La Paz, but he finds virtually no other Latin-American examples.

14.9.3 Perfect of recency

In Spain, but rarely in Latin America, the perfect may optionally be used for any very recent event, in practice any event that has happened since midnight. Very recent events (e.g. seconds ago) are almost always expressed by the perfect tenses in Peninsular Spanish:

Esta mañana me he levantado/me levanté a las seis	I got up at six this morning
Han sonado hace poco dos tiros. ¿Los has oído? (A. Buero Vallejo, Sp., dialogue)	There were two shots a moment ago. Did you hear them?
—¿Quién ha dicho eso? —No he sido yo. Ha sido él	'Who said that (just now)?' 'It wasn't me. It was him'
La he visto hace un momento	I saw her a moment ago
No he podido hacerlo	I couldn't do it
Perdone, no he entendido bien lo que ha dicho (C. Martín Gaite, Sp., dialogue)	Sorry, I didn't fully understand what you said (just now)
Ha muerto Franco (headline)	Franco is dead

(i) The uses of the perfect described in 14.9.1 and 14.9.2 have a long history in Spanish, but the perfect of recency described here seems to be a more recent innovation of European Spanish, although Kany, 200, notes its colloquial use in Bolivia and Peru, cf. *te he hecho daño porque no has entendido nada* (A. Bryce Echenique, Pe., dialogue) 'I hurt you because you didn't understand a thing'. Other Latin-American regions favour the preterite in these examples.

Many persons from northern Spain use the preterite in examples like *me he levantado a las ocho* or *la he visto hace un momento* on the grounds that—as in English—the perfect cannot be used when the time of the event is specified. Use of the perfect of recency is most developed in Madrid. A. Moreira Rodríguez, private communication, recalls a friend's eight-year-old daughter, a native of Galicia, rebuking her little cousin from Madrid: *¡Siempre estás con "he corrido", "he visto", "he ido". Hablas mal. Hay que decir "corrí", "vi", "fui"!*

(ii) The above examples are chosen to show how European Spanish freely uses the perfect of recency with verbs like *querer, ser*, where English allows only the simple past: *no he querido hacerlo* 'I didn't want to do it', *¿quién ha sido el gracioso que se ha llevado las llaves?* 'who was the clown that took the keys away?'

(iii) European Spanish thus differs from English in that the perfect is used of any very recent event, completed or not. English allows 'have you heard the news?' since the news can still be heard, but not *'have you heard that explosion?' Cf. *¿habéis visto el relámpago?* 'did you see the flash?'

(iv) In view of the frequent occurrence of the perfect of recency in Spain, it is not clear why Peninsular radio announcers often end programmes with remarks like **oyeron** *la novena sinfonía de Beethoven* 'you have been listening to Beethoven's Ninth Symphony' (more usually *acaban de oír...*).

14.9.4 Perfect in time phrases

The perfect is often used in Spain in negative time phrases of the sort *hace años que no te he visto* (or *no te veo*; Latin Americans and Spaniards from the north-west may not accept the perfect) 'I haven't seen you for years'. Positive sentences of this type usually require the present tense: *hace años que lo/le veo todos los días* 'I've been seeing him every day for years'. See Chapter 32 (Time expressions).

14.9.5 Use of the perfect for quotations

The perfect is sometimes used for famous quotations, e.g. *Aristóteles ha dicho que...* 'Aristotle said...', though this sounds affected. The present, preterite or imperfect are safer.

14.9.6 Perfect used for future certainties

The perfect is occasionally used in familiar European Spanish, at least in Central Spain, for future actions that are described as certainties: *cuando vuelvas ya he acabado*; formal usage requires the future perfect *...ya lo habré acabado* 'I'll have finished by the time you get back'. See 14.4.9 for the Latin-American tendency to use the preterite (*ya acabé)* in similar sentences.

14.9.7 Perfect with future reference in conditional sentences

As in English, the perfect may refer to the future in the if-clause of a conditional sentence: *si la situación no ha cambiado para el viernes, avísame* 'if the situation hasn't changed by Friday, let me know'.

14.9.8 The perfect tense in Latin America: further remarks

In most of Latin America, all completed actions tend to be expressed in informal language by the preterite tense, more so in some regions than others. This solution is so favoured in informal styles in some regions that the perfect tense is rarely heard:

Ya nos llegó la moderna solución (El Tiempo, Col.; Sp. *ha llegado*)	Now we've got the modern answer!
En el curso de los últimos años se lograron (Sp. *se han logrado...*) *notables progresos en el conocimiento de la función de los riñones* (Chilean press, quoted *Variedades*)	In recent years notable progress has been made in (our) knowledge of the function of the kidneys
—¿Ya organizaste? —le pregunté. *—Sí, ya organicé* (A. Mastretta, Mex., dialogue; Sp. *has, he organizado*)	'Have you organized it?', I asked him. 'Yes, I've organized it'
¿Nunca te fijaste en eso? (ibid.; Sp. *nunca te has fijado*)	Haven't you ever noticed/Didn't you ever notice that?

The perfect tense seems to be least popular in everyday speech in Buenos Aires city and is said to sound 'bookish' there. In the spoken language of Bolivia and Peru the perfect is more frequent and its use seems to correspond quite closely to the usage of central Spain in that the perfect of recency is also heard there: see 14.9.3 note (i).

In Mexico, according to J. M. Lope Blanch ('Sobre el uso del pretérito en el español de México', in Lope Blanch, 1991, 131–43), the preterite is used in speech for all completed actions, however recent, including actions that happened in a period including the present or ones that are still relevant to the present: *estudié mucho este mes* 'I've done a lot of studying this month' (and now I've stopped), — *¿ya viste la película? —Sí, la vi* '"have you seen the film?" "Yes, I have"', *la vi dos veces esta semana* 'I've seen her twice this week', *nos podemos ir. El maestro no vino* 'we can go. The teacher hasn't come' (and he won't be coming now). The perfect is reserved for actions that are still continuing or being repeated in the present and for events that may still occur: *he estudiado mucho este mes* 'I've been doing a lot of studying this month (and I still am)', *les he escrito* = 'I have been writing to them and still am', *el maestro no ha venido* 'the teacher hasn't come yet' (but he may still come). With words like *aún, todavía* the event still can happen, so the perfect is used, as in Spain: *aún/todavía no ha llamado* '(s)he hasn't phoned yet' (but may still phone). For Spaniards, on the other hand, *les he escrito* is a completed action: 'I wrote/have written to them'. This difference may affect the meaning of sentences like *¿cuánto tiempo has estado en México.* See 32.2 note (i).

14.9.9 The perfect and imperfect subjunctive

In general, the perfect subjunctive, *haya dicho, hayamos contestado*, etc., is used where Spanish grammar requires that a perfect indicative verb must be put in the subjunctive mood (*creo que lo he visto* – *no creo que lo haya visto*), and the imperfect subjunctive is used when the original sentence would have had the preterite or imperfect indicative: see 14.10.5. But it often seems that the perfect and imperfect subjunctives can be used interchangeably:

Es imposible que lo haya hecho/que lo hiciera/hiciese	It's impossible that (s)he did it
Niega que su mujer le abriera/abriese/le haya abierto la puerta	He denies that his wife opened the door for him/her
Algunos no aceptan que Colón descubriera/descubriese/haya descubierto América	Some people don't accept that Columbus discovered America

14.10 The pluperfect: general

The pluperfect is formed with the imperfect of *haber* plus a past participle: *habías comido* 'you had eaten', *habían llegado* 'they/you had arrived'. The *-ra* form of the verb can also sometimes have an indicative pluperfect meaning in literary Spanish. See 14.10.2.

14.10.1 Uses of the pluperfect

The use of the Spanish pluperfect corresponds quite closely to the English pluperfect. It is used for events or states that preceded some past event and are felt to be relevant to it.

Ya se habían dado cuenta de que no estabas	They had already realized you weren't there
Sabíamos que ya había vendido el coche	We knew that he had already sold the car
Yo me había levantado, duchado y desayunado...cuando sonó el teléfono (A. Bryce Echenique, Pe.)	I had got up, showered and breakfasted ... when the phone rang

(i) Colloquially, especially in Latin-American Spanish, the pluperfect may be expressed by the preterite or, when it refers to habitual actions, by the imperfect: *lo encontré donde lo dejé* (for ... *donde lo había dejado*) (J. M. Lope Blanch, 1991, 152) 'I found it where I'd left it/where I left it', *cuando terminábamos* (for *habíamos terminado*) *volvíamos a casa* (habitual) 'when we had finished, we used to return home', *le faltaban dos dientes y nunca se puso* (Sp. *se había puesto/se ponía*) *a dieta ni fue* (Sp. *había ido/iba*) *al gimnasio* (A. Mastretta, Mex., dialogue) 'he had two teeth missing and he had never been on a diet or gone to the gym'.

(ii) In some cases the English pluperfect will require translation by the preterite: '...nights alone in the double bed after a divorce which left me stranded' (Mary Ingram, *Now we are Thirty*) ... *noches sola en la cama matrimonial después de un divorcio que me había dejado abandonada sin saber qué hacer.*

(iii) The pluperfect is occasionally used to make polite enquiries: *¿usted me había pedido otro té?* 'did you ask for another tea?'

14.10.2 Pluperfect in *-ra*

The *-ra* form of Spanish verbs—*hablara, dijéramos*, etc.—descends from the Latin indicative pluperfect: Latin *fueram* 'I had been' > Spanish *fuera*. The Spanish form gradually acquired a subjunctive meaning and for most purposes it is now identical in use to the *-se* imperfect subjunctive (see 16.2.3 for further details). But the old indicative pluperfect use of the *-ra* forms survives in literature and journalism as a supposedly elegant alternative for the ordinary pluperfect with *había*. This is a very common construction in Latin America, but it is also found in Spain in writers who fancy they are stylists. Lorenzo (1980), 135, warns against it: *evidentemente, la sentimos como afectada, pero hay muchas gentes que lo son. . . .*

When used thus, the *-ra* form has no subjunctive meaning at all. However, this construction seems to have been contaminated by a feature of the subjunctive: it only occurs in subordinate, chiefly relative clauses: *el libro que había leído* 'the book he had read' can be recast in supposedly 'elegant' style as *el libro que leyera*, but the sentence *había leído el libro* '(s)he had read the book' cannot be rewritten **leyera el libro.* Examples:

Fue el único rastro que dejó en el que fuera su hogar de casada por cinco horas (G. García Márquez, Col.; for *había sido*)	It was the only trace she left in what had been her marital home for five hours
Parece ser además que en el solar donde se construyera el hotel se alzaba antes el palacio (A. Grosso, Sp.)	It seems, moreover, that the palace once stood on the land where the hotel had been built

Había sido, se había construido would have been equally correct, and preferable for many people.

(i) One even finds examples of the imperfect subjunctive in *-se* used as an indicative pluperfect in the same contexts as the *-ra* form described above: *así había dado con el hombre capaz, muy versado en asuntos económicos, que conociese en la Logia* (A. Carpentier, Cu.; for *había conocido* or *conociera*) 'he had thus come across the able man, well-versed in economic matters, whom he had met in the (Masonic) Lodge'. But this is very rare on both continents and rather forced.

(ii) Use of the *–ra* pluperfect in spoken Spanish is typical of Galicians since the *–ra* form still has an indicative pluperfect meaning in Galician (and in Portuguese).

14.10.3 *-ra* and *-se* verb forms after *después de que, desde que, luego (de) que,* etc.

The rule for the choice of verb form after *después (de) que* and *luego de que* 'after', and *a los pocos/dos/cinco días de que* 'a few/two/five days after' is: subjunctive for as yet unfulfilled events: *comeremos después de que lleguen los demás* 'we'll eat after the rest arrive', and indicative for fulfilled events: *comimos después de que **llegaron** los demás* 'we ate after the rest arrived'. If the subject of both verbs is the same *después (de) que* is replaced by *después de* + infinitive: *nos fuimos después de haber hecho todo* 'we left after we had done everything'. Further examples:

...después de que las hijas mayores la ayudaron a poner un poco de orden en los estragos de la boda (G. García Márquez, Col.)	...after the elder daughters (had) helped her to put a bit of order in the devastation left by the wedding
...después de que Victoriano Huerta mató a Madero (A. Mastretta, Mex., dialogue)	...after Victoriano Huerta killed Madero
Desde que se casó, Octavia nunca volvió a besarme (A. Bryce Echenique, Pe.)	From the moment she got married, Octavia never kissed me again

Él le entregó…los planos, las copias. Luego que ella los hubo recogido de sus manos…dijo (J. Aldecoa, Sp.; *pretérito anterior*, discussed at 14.10.4)	He gave her … the maps, the copies. After she had taken them from his hands…he said

However, the media everywhere frequently use the *–ra* or (rarely) the *-se* verb forms even for fulfilled events in the past and even with subordinators like *desde que* 'from the moment that…', which obviously introduces fulfilled events. This is clearly a use of the *–ra* pluperfect discussed at 14.10.2:

…después de que Nigeria hiciese pública su decisión de firmar el acta (*El País*, Sp.)	…after Nigeria made public its decision to sign the communiqué/ minutes
Vargas Llosa, que conserva muchos amigos en Barcelona desde que residiera en España (*Abc*, Sp.)	Vargas Llosa, who has kept many friends in Barcelona from when he lived in Spain
… luego de que por problemas de tipo legal les fuera impedido el paso ayer en la mañana (*La Época*, Ch.)	…after their entry had been prevented for legal reasons yesterday morning

14.10.4 *Pretérito anterior: hube hablado, hube acabado, etc.*

This tense, formed with the preterite of *haber* plus the past participle, is used to indicate an event completed just before another past event. It is normally confined to literature and is now extremely rare in speech:

Cuando hubieron terminado de reírse, examinaron mi situación personal (A. Cancela, quoted *Esbozo*, 3.14.7)	When they had finished laughing, they examined my personal situation
Le escribió el mismo día, no bien se hubo marchado (L. Goytisolo, Sp.)	He wrote to her the same day, when she had only just left
…así que, una vez que me hube quitado la blusa… (E. Sábato, Arg., dialogue)	…so, as soon as I had taken my blouse off…
…porque no bien hube entrado a Octavia Carrión (A. Bryce Echenique, Pe.)	…because I'd scarcely carried Octavia Carrión in

(i) This tense is only used after *después (de) que* 'after', *luego que, así que, no bien, enseguida que, en cuanto, tan pronto como* and *apenas*, all translatable as 'as soon as', and after *cuando* and other phrases of similar meaning, to emphasize that the event was completed just before the main event in the sentence. In ordinary language it is expressed by the preterite: *tan pronto como llegamos, pasamos al comedor* 'as soon as we (had) arrived, we went through to the dining room', *pero apenas entró cambió de opinión* (J. Ibargüengoitia, Mex., dialogue) 'but he'd hardly entered when he changed his mind', *apenas terminamos el almuerzo llegó Casals* (M. Puig, Arg., dialogue) 'we'd scarcely finished lunch when Casals arrived'; or, less commonly, by the pluperfect: *apenas había ordenado el señor juez el levantamiento del cadáver para llevarlo al depósito judicial, rompieron el silencio unos gritos de mujer* (F. García Pavón, Sp.) 'the judge had scarcely ordered the removal of the body to the official morgue when the silence was broken by women shouting'.

(ii) The *pretérito anterior* refers to a single completed event. After the same time phrases, repeated or habitual events are expressed by the ordinary pluperfect—*en cuanto habíamos terminado el trabajo, volvíamos a casa* 'as soon as we had finished work, we used to return home'—or, colloquially, by the imperfect: *en cuanto ter-minábamos el trabajo, volvíamos a casa*.

(iii) The French equivalent of *hube terminado* is *j'eus fini*, or in popular French *j'ai eu fini*. This tense survives in French, but the *pretérito anterior* is obsolete in spoken Spanish and rare in written styles.

14.10.5 The pluperfect subjunctive

Normally this form, e.g. *hubiera hablado, hubiese hablado*, is used when Spanish grammar requires that a pluperfect indicative form be put in the subjunctive form. Compare *yo estaba convencido de que Manuel lo había hecho* 'I was convinced Manuel had done it' and *yo no estaba convencido de que Manuel lo hubiera/hubiese hecho* 'I wasn't convinced that Manuel had done it'. These rules are explained in Chapter 16.

Students must beware of confusing the pluperfect subjunctive with the conditional perfect. The latter can be formed either with the conditional or with the *-ra* form of *haber*: *habría sido mejor* and *hubiera sido mejor* both mean 'it would have been better'. The pluperfect subjunctive can only be formed with the *-ra* or *-se* forms.

14.11 The future perfect and conditional perfect

The future perfect, *habré hecho* 'I will have done' and the conditional perfect *habría hecho* or *hubiera hecho* 'I would have done' are used in more or less the same ways as their English equivalents. But the following points are worthy of note:

(a) The future perfect is very often used to express conjecture or, in questions, mystification or perplexity: *se lo habrá dicho Miguel* 'Miguel must have told him/her/you', *¿dónde lo habrá puesto?* 'where *can* (s)he have put it?' The negative expresses a conjecture or may make a statement rhetorical, i.e. it expects or hopes for the answer 'of course not': *no lo habrán hecho* 'I guess they haven't done it' or 'they *can't* have done it'. In questions, the negative may make a tentative suggestion: *¿no se lo habrán llevado a casa?* 'do you think that possibly they've taken it home' / 'could it possibly be that they've taken it home?', *¿no será que ya han tomado la decisión?* 'couldn't it be that they've already taken the decision?' It may also make a question rhetorical (i.e. it expects or hopes for the answer 'no'): *¿no la habrás vuelto a llamar?* 'you haven't called her again, have you?!'

(b) The conditional perfect frequently occurs in conditional sentences of the type 'if I had had enough money I would have bought it' *si hubiera tenido suficiente dinero, lo habría/hubiera comprado*'. Use of the *-ra* form of *haber* in this tense is a common alternative, as explained at 14.7.5.

It may also express a conjecture or supposition about the past: *se lo habría dicho Miguel* 'Miguel must have told him/her'. In questions it adds a note of perplexity or anxiety: *¿no se lo habría dicho Miguel?* 'it couldn't be that Miguel told her, could it?', *¿la habría oído?* (C. Martín Gaite, Sp., dialogue) 'could he possibly have heard her?'

(i) As far as we know, use of the perfect for the future perfect (i.e. to mean 'will have done something') is confined to colloquial language in Spain: *para mañana ya lo he acabado* = ...*ya lo habré acabado* 'I'll have finished it by tomorrow'. See 14.4.9 for Latin-American alternatives.

14.12 Tense agreement

Tense agreement with the subjunctive is discussed in full at 16.16.

As far as the indicative tenses are concerned, Spanish is stricter than English about the agreement of past with past. In sentences like 'John said he is/was coming' English seems optionally to use either tense in the subordinate clause. Spanish requires *Juan dijo que* **venía**. Sentences like ?*Juan dijo que viene* usually sound careless or sub-standard. The present is, however, possible with the perfect tense when John's arrival is still awaited: *Juan ha dicho que viene*.

15

Continuous forms of the verb

The main points discussed in this chapter are:

- *Estoy hablando, están cenando*, etc., compared with English 'I'm talking', 'they're having supper' (Section 15.1.2)
- Uses of the Spanish continuous forms (Section 15.2)
- Restrictions on the use of the Spanish continuous (Section 15.3)
- The continuous form of *ser* (Section 15.4)
- Continuous forms in Latin-American Spanish (Section 15.5)

15.1 General

15.1.1 Forms and equivalents of the continuous

The continuous forms of Spanish verbs are based on the appropriate tense of *estar* 'to be' and the gerund: *estoy hablando* 'I'm talking', *estuve cenando* 'I was having dinner/supper', *estaremos escribiendo* 'we'll be writing', etc.; the forms of the gerund are discussed at 20.2.

French has an equivalent of the Spanish continuous: *je suis en train de parler* 'I'm (in the process of) speaking' emphasizes an ongoing action in much the same way as *estoy hablando*, but the Spanish continuous is used much more frequently. Students who know French well should note that if *en train de...* is impossible in French, the continuous will usually be impossible in Spanish. *Je pars demain = salgo mañana.* **Je suis en train de partir demain*/**Estoy saliendo mañana* are both impossible for 'I'm leaving tomorrow' (but see 15.5b).

The Italian continuous, *sto lavorando* (= *estoy trabajando* 'I'm working') is much more restricted in use than its Spanish counterpart. The Spanish continuous can appear in any tense except the *pretérito anterior*, whereas in the past only the imperfect continuous *stavo lavorando* is used in Italian.

The Spanish continuous form is apparently more common than fifty years ago and some of its current uses seem to reflect the influence of English. The Academy's *Esbozo...*, 3.12.5, complains bitterly about the modern over-use of the continuous.

15.1.2 The Spanish continuous and the English progressive compared

Spanish continuous forms, e.g. *estoy leyendo, estaban hablando*, etc., misleadingly resemble the much-used English progressive verb form, e.g. 'I'm reading', 'they were talking'. The Spanish continuous differs from its English counterpart in several important respects:

(a) The present and imperfect tenses of the Spanish continuous can only refer to actions that are or were actually in progress or are or were being repeated, whereas the English progressive is constantly also used as a future tense and also, sometimes, to express habit:

Estoy comiendo	I'm (actually) eating (right now)
Estabas hablando	You were (in the middle of) talking

But

Llegamos mañana	**We're arriving** tomorrow (future)
Si te pones así, me voy	If you get like that, **I'm going** (future)
Mi hijo va a un colegio mixto	My son **is going** to a mixed (i.e. co-educational) school (habitual)
Te envío ésta para decirte que. . .	**I'm sending** you this to tell you that... (really means 'I shall send': you haven't sent it yet)
Solicito un puesto en la Administración (*estoy solicitando* suggests you are actually filling out the form)	**I'm applying** for a Government job (really means 'I've applied for' or 'I'm going to apply'))
Se casan (*se están casando* suggests they are in mid-ceremony)	**They're getting** married (i.e. they are going to get married)
Yo salía a la mañana siguiente para París	**I was leaving** the following morning for Paris (future in the past)
Hoy el Barça juega en casa	Today Barcelona **is/are playing** at home (*está jugando* possible only if the game is in progress)

See 15.5.b for exceptions to this rule in the Spanish of some Latin-American regions.

(b) The Spanish continuous is very rarely used with the common verbs *ir*, *venir*, *volver* (but see 15.5a for exceptions in parts of Latin America):

¿Adónde vas?	Where are you going?
Viene la policía	The police are coming
Yo volvía cuando te vi	I was coming back when I saw you
Ya voy	I'm coming

NB: One says *voy* for 'I'm coming' because one is leaving the place one is at, not coming towards it. English uses 'go' and 'come' vaguely.

(c) The Spanish continuous adds a nuance to, but does not always radically alter the meaning of the non-continuous verb form, so the two forms are sometimes virtually interchangeable. This tends to confuse English-speakers, who see a sharp difference between 'she smokes' and 'she's smoking':

¡Que se queman/se están quemando las salchichas!	The sausages are burning!
Yo hablaba con Mario	I was talking to Mario/I used to talk to Mario
Yo estaba hablando con Mario	I was talking to Mario (but not 'I used to...')
—¿Qué haces? —Leo esta revista (S. Vodanovic, Ch., dialogue; or *¿Qué estás haciendo? —Estoy leyendo...*)	'What are you doing?' 'I'm reading this magazine.'
No te conocía, ¿qué te pasa? Hablas raro (C. Martín Gaite, Sp., dialogue)	I didn't recognise you. What's the matter with you. You're talking strangely
Dígame en qué piensa, por favor (ibid.)	Tell me what you're thinking about, please

El otro hombre está sentado en un sillón.	The other man is sitting in an
Fuma (El País, Sp.)	armchair. He is smoking

(**d**) A number of common Spanish verbs do not appear in the continuous form, whereas their English counterparts do. See 15.3 for discussion.

15.1.3 Further remarks on the relationship between the simple present tense and the present continuous

The simple present tense, *escribo, hago*, etc., is imprecise: it may indicate present, future, habitual events, eternal truths or even past events (see 14.3 and 14.6.3). Continuous forms are much more specifically present: compare *fuma* '(s)he smokes' or '(s)he's smoking' and *está fumando* '(s)he's (actually) smoking (*now*)'.

An action must be perceived to be actually in progress for the continuous to be possible. Peninsular informants said *está lloviendo* on seeing rain through a window, and thought that *llueve*, in this case, sounded vaguely poetic or archaic. But most avoided the continuous in the sentences *asómate a ver si llueve* 'look out and see if it's raining' and *¿llueve o no llueve?* 'is it raining or not?', the reason being that the speaker has obviously not actually seen or heard rain falling (in this and several other cases, Latin-American informants tended to use the continuous more readily). Similarly, when someone up a tree shouts 'I'm falling!', (s)he literally means 'I'm going to fall', not 'I'm already in mid-air', so a Spanish speaker shouts *¡que me caigo!*, not **¡que me estoy cayendo!*

With some verbs that refer to actions that are self-evidently more or less prolonged events, e.g. *leer* 'to read', *charlar* 'to chat', or where the duration of an action is emphasized, the continuous makes better Spanish than the simple form. Most informants thought that *está leyendo* 'he's reading' was better than *lee* in reply to the question **¿qué hace Miguel?* 'what's Miguel doing?

When an action is by nature more or less instantaneous, i.e. it cannot be extended, as is the case with verbs like *toser* 'to cough', *romper* 'to break', *firmar* 'to sign', etc., the continuous can normally only indicate a series of repeated actions, as in English: *estaba tosiendo* '(s)he was coughing'.

15.2 Uses of the continuous forms

15.2.1 Continuous used to emphasize events in progress

It follows that the main use of the continuous forms of the present and imperfect tenses is to emphasize that an event is or was actually in progress at the time. In cases in which the action is emphatically in progress at the time, the continuous is obligatory:

Ahora no se puede poner—está haciendo sus cuentas (not *...hace sus cuentas*)	(S)he can't come to the phone now— (s)he's doing his/her accounts
Estaba dándole una propina al mozo que me había subido la maleta cuando sonó el teléfono (L. Sepúlveda, Ch.)	I was (just) giving a tip to the boy who'd carried my bags up when the phone rang
Octavia estaba abriendo la puerta cuando regresé (A. Bryce Echenique, Pe.)	Octavia was (just) opening the door when I returned
Pero ¡si te estoy escuchando!/¡si te escucho!	But I *am* listening to you!

(i) In the case of the imperfect tense, the continuous and non-continuous are more or less interchangeable if they really refer to the past and the action is not habitual; i.e. *pensaba* and *estaba pensando* both mean 'I/(s)he was thinking'/'you were thinking'. See 14.5.5 for discussion.

(ii) As far as the present and imperfect are concerned, English-speakers will often find that if the phrase 'in the middle of' makes at least possible sense in the translation, the Spanish continuous is possible: 'Octavia was in the middle of opening the door' makes sense, so *estaba abriendo* is correct.

(iii) The preterite, perfect and pluperfect continuous, e.g. *estuve hablando*, *he estado hablando*, differ in meaning from the non-continuous equivalents of these tenses. See 15.2.3.

15.2.2 Continuous used to denote temporary or surprising events

The continuous may optionally be used to show that an action is temporary or in some way unusual or surprising:

Vive en París, pero últimamente está viviendo/vive en Madrid	(S)he lives in Paris, but at the moment (s)he's living in Madrid
Me estoy sintiendo mal/Me siento mal	I'm (suddenly) feeling ill
¡Qué sueño me está entrando! (C. Martín Gaite, Sp., dialogue)	I suddenly feel so sleepy!
¿Qué me estás contando?/¿Qué me cuentas?	What *are* you telling me!?
—¿En qué estábamos pensando tú y yo cuando engendramos a estos seres, me quieres explicar? —le pregunta la madre al padre (Carmen Rico-Godoy, Sp. dialogue; or ...*en qué pensábamos*)	'Do you mind explaining to me what you and I were thinking of when we conceived these creatures?', the mother asks the father

15.2.3 Preterite, perfect, pluperfect and periphrastic future continuous used to denote prolonged events

The continuous forms of the preterite, perfect, pluperfect and the periphrastic future (i.e. *ir a* + infinitive) show that an action is, was or will be prolonged over a period of time:

Estuve hablando dos horas con tu hermano	I was talking with your brother for two hours
Pero, ¿vas a estar esperándola todo el día?	But are you going to keep on waiting for her all day?
Estuve andando hasta el amanecer (S. Puértolas, Sp.)	I was walking/walked until dawn
Acuérdense, el señor ese con el que estuvimos tomando nieves en el zócalo de Atlixco (A. Mastretta, Mex., dialogue; *nieves* = *helados* in Spain)	Remember, that gentleman we had an ice-cream with in the main square in Atlixco...
He estado pensando que tú no siempre dices la verdad	I've been thinking that you don't always tell the truth
El rostro de María sonreía. Es decir, ya no sonreía, pero había estado sonriendo un décimo de segundo antes (E. Sábato, Arg.)	Maria's face was smiling. I mean, it wasn't smiling now, but it had been smiling a tenth of a second before

The preterite continuous, *estuve hablando/comiendo* 'I was speaking/eating for a time' indicates an action that was prolonged in the past but is viewed as finished, unlike the imperfect forms *hablaba/estaba hablando*, which merely indicate that an action was going on at the time. It has no clear counterpart in English or French: *ahí está el libro que me hizo perder pie…lo estuve buscando antes no sé cuánto rato…* (C. Martín Gaite, Sp., dialogue) 'there's the book I tripped over…I don't know how long I spent looking for it earlier', *abandonó la sala y corrió en busca del teléfono…Estuvo hablando horas* (A. Bryce Echenique, Pe.) 'she left the room and ran in search of the phone. She spent hours talking/She talked for hours'. When a period is 'viewed as finished' the action itself does not literally have to have finished with it: *estuve leyendo durante tres horas, y continué leyendo hasta el amanecer* 'I read for three hours then went on reading until morning' is possible.

The preterite continuous is really only possible with verbs that refer to naturally drawn-out actions, e.g. 'think', 'talk', 'read', 'wait', 'eat', etc. Verbs that refer to instantaneous actions cannot be extended: **estuvo rompiendo una ventana* '(s)he was breaking a window (for a certain time)' is not possible, and *estaba rompiendo una ventana* is only possible with the unlikely meaning '(s)he was (in the middle of) breaking a window'. Instantaneous actions can, however, be repeated over a period of time: *estuvo disparando al aire durante tres minutos* '(s)he spent three minutes firing into the air'.

15.2.4 Continuous to express repeated events:

The continuous may express the idea that an event is or has been constantly recurring:

Está yendo mucho al cine estos días	(S)he's going to the cinema a lot these days
En sus diarios siempre está hablando de la familia (J. Cercas, Sp.)	in his diaries he's always talking about the family
Lleva años que se está yendo pero nunca acaba de irse	(S)he's been leaving for years but never gets round to going
Está haciendo frío	It's been cold lately/The weather's cold at the moment
Pero está usted tomando muy seguido esas hierbas y seguido hacen daño (A. Mastretta, Mex., dialogue)	But you're taking those herbs over long periods, and they cause harm when taken continuously

Venir and *ir* may appear in the continuous form in this sense, but not usually in other contexts, at least in Spain and in written Spanish elsewhere. *Tener* is also found in the continuous to refer to repeated events: *estoy teniendo problemas con los vecinos* 'I'm having problems with the neighbo(u)rs'. But the continuous is not used for single events: *tiene un problema con el vecino*, not **está teniendo un problema con el vecino*.

15.2.5 Future and conditional continuous

The future continuous is used either (**a**) to describe events which will be in progress at a certain time, or (**b**) to conjecture about what may actually be happening now:

Mañana a estas horas estaremos volando sobre el Pacífico	Tomorrow at this time we'll be flying over the Pacific
¿Qué sabes tú lo que es vivir para ponerle las zapatillas a un hombre? Pruébalo dos meses y al tercero ya estarás maldiciendo tu destino (T. Moix, Sp., dialogue)	What do you know about living in order to put a man's slippers on? Try it for two months and by the third you'll be cursing your fate!
Estarán comiendo a estas horas	They'll probably be eating at this time of day
¿Me estarán viendo/Me ven desde esa ventana?	I wonder if they can see me from that window?

The future perfect continuous can also be used to express conjectures: *no me habrás estado esperando, ya te dije que no te preocuparas* (C. Martín Gaite, Sp., dialogue) 'I hope you haven't been waiting for me, I told you not to worry'.

The conditional continuous is used like its English counterpart 'would be ...-ing': *yo sabía que a esa hora estarían comiendo* 'I knew that at that time they would be eating'. It can also express conjectures or suppositions about events that may have been going on: —*¿Por qué no contestaba al teléfono? —Estaría durmiendo* '"Why wasn't (s)he answering the phone?" "(S)he must have been sleeping."'

15.3 Restrictions on the use of the continuous

(a) Continuous forms are not normally used with certain verbs that refer to inner mental activities, e.g. *aborrecer* 'to loathe', *amar* 'to love', *odiar* 'to hate', *saber* 'to know': *odio tener que quedarme en casa* 'I hate having to stay at home'. In this respect Spanish and English coincide, but some verbs which denote inner states or 'invisible' actions may appear in the continuous in Spanish but not in English, e.g.

No estaba creyendo nada de lo que ella decía (A. Gala, Sp., dialogue)	She 'wasn't believing' a word she said
Estoy viendo que vamos a acabar mal	I can see we're going to end badly
Asegura que está deseando conocerte (A. Buero Vallejo, Sp. dialogue)	He insists that he wants to meet you
Te estás mereciendo una bofetada	You deserve (i.e. 'are asking for') a slap
Estoy temiendo que va a llegar tarde	I'm afraid (s)he's going to arrive late

(i) Use of the continuous with the 'mental' verbs is very rare, but not impossible, if the action is presented as changing or increasing, as in *te estoy queriendo cada vez más* 'I'm getting to love you more and more', *estoy sabiendo cada vez más cosas sobre ese amigo tuyo tan misterioso* 'I'm finding more and more out about that mysterious friend of yours' (from *GDLE* 46.3.2.1).

(ii) *Doler* 'to hurt' may appear in either form, much as in English: *me duele/me está doliendo la barriga* 'my belly aches/is aching'.

NB: *La barriga* = 'belly' or 'intestines'. Embarrassed English-speakers who call their intestines their 'stomach' (*estómago*) cause great anatomical confusion. *Los intestinos, las tripas* or *la barriga* are not indelicate words.

(b) The continuous is not used to describe states rather than actions (English often allows the progressive form for states):

Normalmente lleva corbata azul, pero hoy lleva una corbata roja	Normally he wears a blue tie, but today he's wearing a red tie
Tres arañas de luces colgaban del techo	Three chandeliers were hanging from the roof

Lo que falta es...	What's lacking is...
La luna brillaba sobre las olas	The moon was shining on the waves
Parece cansada	She's looking tired
¡Qué bien huele la madreselva hoy!	Isn't the honeysuckle smelling good today!

(**c**) The continuous is not used with *estar* (*estar estando is not Spanish), *poder, haber* or, usually, at least in European and standard literary Spanish, with *ir, venir, regresar, volver, andar,* except in the frequentative sense discussed at 15.2.4:

¿Adónde vas?	Where are you going?
Viene ahora	(S)he's coming now
Cuando volvíamos del cine (me) subí un momento a ver a la abuela	When we were coming back from the cinema I went up to see grandmother for a moment
Estás estúpido hoy	You're being stupid today

(**d**) Finite forms of verbs that describe physical posture or position can refer only to an action, not to a state. English-speakers are often misled by forms like 'he was sitting down', which almost always means *estaba sentado* 'he was seated'. *Estaba sentándose* means '(s)he was in the process of sitting down' and *se sentaba* means '(s)he used to sit down'. Further examples:

Estaban tumbados	They were lying down
Estaba agachada	She was bending down
(compare *Estaba agachándose*	(S)he was in the process of bending down)

(i) For the continuous of *tener* 'to have' see 15.2.4.

(ii) *Llevar* is used in the continuous only with the sense of 'to take from one place to another': *lleva camisa* '(s)he's wearing a shirt', *llevabas una maleta en la mano* 'you were carrying (= 'holding') a suitcase in your hand', but *estoy llevando/llevo una camisa a mi madre* 'I'm taking a shirt to my mother'.

(iii) *Parecer* 'to seem' occasionally appears in the continuous: *la situación me está pareciendo/me parece cada vez más fea* 'the situation's looking uglier and uglier to me'.

(iv) The continuous of *ir, venir* and, regionally, of some other of these verbs of motion, is found in colloquial speech in parts of Latin America. See 15.5 for Latin-American usage.

15.4 Continuous forms of *ser*

Some grammarians claim that forms like *está siendo* are borrowed from English, but they are not uncommon, especially in Latin America, and they occur in speech as well as in writing, to judge by the dialogue of some novels. It seems unreasonable to deny to Spanish the nuance that distinguishes our 'he was good' from 'he was being good':

Por un instante pensó que de algún modo él, Martín, estaba de verdad siendo necesario a aquel ser atormentado (E. Sábato, Arg.)	For an instant he thought that he, Martín, was really being necessary to that tormented creature
La convocatoria a las distintas manifestaciones está siendo variada (*La Vanguardia*, Sp.)	The people attending the demonstrations come from various sources (lit. 'the calling to the various demonstrations is varied')

Yo no estoy siendo juzgado (C. Fuentes, Mex., dialogue)	I'm not being judged
Estás siendo muy bueno hoy	You're being very good today

15.5 Latin-American uses of the continuous

Written—or at least printed—Latin-American Spanish seems to obey the same rules as European Spanish as far as the use of the continuous is concerned. However, there are numerous regional colloquial variants, and it seems, in general, that the continuous is used more extensively in Latin-American speech than in Spain.

(a) In many places the continuous of *ir*, *venir* and other verbs of motion is regularly heard:

—*Estamos yendo a Pato Huachana* —*dijo Lalita* (M. Vargas Llosa, Pe., dialogue)	'We're going to Pato Huachana,' Lalita said
Estaba yendo a tomar un café con leche en Brosa (ibid.)	I was on my way to Brosa to have a white coffee
¿Cómo le va yendo? (Chile, quoted Kany, 282; Sp. *¿Cómo le va?*)	How are things with you?

In Spain one would use *vamos*, *iba* in these sentences.

(b) In colloquial language in a number of places including Chile, Bolivia, Peru, Ecuador and Colombia, the present continuous is used, as in English, to express a pre-scheduled future: *mañana estoy yendo a París* 'tomorrow I'm going to Paris' (= *mañana voy a París*). This is not possible in Peninsular or literary Latin-American Spanish.

(c) Kany, 282ff, reports that in the Andean region, including Chile, verbs like *poder*, *tener*, *haber* also appear in the continuous form, especially in popular styles: *estás pudiendo* = *puedes* 'you can', *¿está habiendo?* 'is there any?' (Spain *¿hay?*). This usage is not heard in standard Spanish. The Peninsular colloquial form *irse yendo* is worth noting: *me voy a ir yendo ¿sabes?* (C. Martín Gaite, Sp., dialogue), 'I'm on my way/I'm off/I'm out of here'.

(d) In colloquial, but not written, Mexican, *andar* is much used instead of *estar* to form the continuous: *ando trabajando* 'I'm working', *¿qué andas haciendo?* 'what are you doing?' Similar forms with *andar* are sometimes heard in popular speech in Spain, e.g. *¿qué andas haciendo?* for *¿qué estás haciendo?*, but *andar* + gerund normally means 'to go around doing something'; see 20.8.1 for discussion and examples.

16

The subjunctive

The subjunctive is an important feature of Spanish in all styles and countries, and it will not die out in the foreseeable future. It occurs most often in clauses preceded by *que, cuando, en cuanto* and after other subordinating conjunctions (see Glossary), and also in imperatives of the type *diga, no digas*.

16.1 Index to chapter

The use of the subjunctive in conditional sentences is discussed in Chapter 25. All matters involving the imperative are discussed in Chapter 17.

16.2 General remarks on the subjunctive

16.2.1 The importance of the Spanish subjunctive

English-speakers sometimes wonder why Spanish needs the subjunctive, but it expresses nuances that English ignores—see 16.14.1 for a vivid example. It also removes some ambiguities that affect English—especially the British variety—now that our language has more or less lost the subjunctive. Compare the modern British habit of saying 'we insist that the children are looked after properly' both to state a fact (indicative) and to express a wish, i.e. '...*be* looked after properly' (subjunctive). Spanish-speakers may also find sentences like 'we decided to eat when they arrived' unclear: does it mean 'when they arrived, we decided to eat' (...*cuando llegaron*) or 'we decided not to eat until they arrived' (...*cuando llegaran/llegasen*)?

16.2.2 Forms of the subjunctive

There are three simple (i.e. non-compound) tenses of the Spanish subjunctive: present, imperfect and future. Only the first two are in everyday use: the present, formed as explained at 13.1.9, and the imperfect, of which there are two forms, one in *-ra* and one in *-se*. The latter forms are explained at 13.1.10 and all the forms are shown at 13.5.2. The relationship between the *–ra* and *–se* forms is discussed in the next section. The future subjunctive, discussed at 16.17, is virtually obsolete.

Compound tenses of the subjunctive, e.g. *haya hablado, hubiera/hubiese hablado* (also mentioned at 14.9.9 and 14.10.5), and continuous forms of the subjunctive, e.g. *esté hablando, estuviera/estuviese hablando*, are also common.

16.2.3 The *-ra* and *-se* forms compared

When the *-ra* and *-se* forms are used as subjunctives they are interchangeable and the two forms are shown side by side in the following examples. The *–ra* form is more frequent everywhere, is gaining ground, and in some parts of Latin America has all but replaced the *-se* form. The *-ra* form also has a few uses as an indicative form which it does not share with the *-se* form, at least in normal styles:

(**a**) It may be a supposedly elegant literary variant for the indicative pluperfect, especially in Latin-American texts: *el hombre que ella **conociera** años antes* 'the man she had met years ago', for *que había conocido....* See 14.10.2 for discussion.

(**b**) It frequently replaces the conditional of *haber*—*habría sido mejor/**hubiera** sido mejor* 'it would have been better'—and less commonly of a few other verbs. See 14.7.5 for discussion.

(**c**) It is used in a few set phrases: e.g. *acabáramos* 'now I see what you're getting at...', *otro gallo nos cantara* 'that would be another story...'.

16.2.4 Tense agreement and the subjunctive

This is discussed in detail at 16.16. The idea that there is a 'Rule of Agreement' that dictates which tense of the subjunctive must be used in Spanish is one of the myths of traditional grammar, but in the majority of cases the following scheme applies:

Tense of verb in main clause	Tense of subjunctive verb
Present, Perfect, Future, Imperative	Present
Conditional, Imperfect, Preterite, Pluperfect	Imperfect

Examples: *le digo/he dicho/diré que se **vaya*** 'I tell/have told/will tell him to go away'; *le diría/decía/dije/había dicho que se **fuera/fuese*** 'I would tell/was telling/told/had told him to go away'.

16.2.5 When the subjunctive is *not* used in clauses introduced by *que*

It is easier to state categorically when the subjunctive is **not** used in clauses introduced by *que* than to list all the cases in which it **is** used. The subjunctive is not used:

(a) After affirmative statements that declare that an event happened, is happening or will happen: *es cierto que hubo una conspiración* 'it's true that there was a conspiracy', *era obvio que lo había hecho* 'it was obvious that (s)he'd done it', *se prevé que habrá déficit* 'a deficit is forecasted', *se queja de que está cansada* 'she complains that she's tired' (*quejarse de* is usually treated as a verb of statement: see 16.6.2.)

(b) After affirmative statements that declare the subject's belief or opinion: *creo/me parece que habla inglés* 'I think (s)he speaks English', *yo pensaba que él era más honrado* 'I thought he was more honest', *dicen que vienen* 'they say they're coming', *parece que su mujer está enferma* 'it seems that his wife is ill/sick'. There are occasional exceptions to (b) discussed at 16.11.1.

NB: As far as (b) is concerned, Spanish differs from Italian and resembles French. Compare *creo que es verdad / je crois que c'est vrai* (both verbs indicative) and Italian *credo che sia certo* (second verb subjunctive).

However, negative statements + *que* usually require the subjunctive, e.g. *no creo/no me parece que **hable** inglés* 'I don't think (s)he speaks English'. See 16.2.9.

(c) After subordinators (words like *cuando, después de que, mientras que*, etc.), when the verb refers to an action that either habitually happens or had already happened at the time of the main verb. Compare *les pagaré cuando lleguen* 'I'll pay them when they arrive' and *les pago cuando llegan / les pagué cuando llegaron* 'I pay them when they arrive' (habitual)/'I paid them when they arrived' (past). See 16.12.1 for further discussion.

16.2.6 Subjunctive or infinitive?

In many cases a subjunctive can, or must be, avoided by using an infinitive. As far as phrases and clauses + *que* are concerned, a subjunctive subordinate verb is usually only required when the subject of the verb in the main clause and the subject of the subordinate verb are different. When they are the same, the infinitive is used. Thus *yo quiero* 'I want' + *yo voy* 'I go' must be expressed as *yo quiero ir* 'I want to go' (same subject), but *yo quiero* + *él va* 'he goes' = *yo quiero que él vaya*, 'I want him to go' (different subjects, subjunctive obligatory). However, verbs of prohibiting, permitting, requesting, suggesting and advising—i.e. most verbs that can be constructed with an indirect object pronoun—may allow either construction: see 16.5.2.

The infinitive may also be used after certain subordinators when the subjects are identical, e.g. *la llamé después de llegar a casa* 'I rang her after I got home'. See 16.12.2.

16.2.7 The subjunctive does *not* always indicate doubt or uncertainty

One widespread misconception about the Spanish subjunctive is that it expresses doubt or uncertainty. This is sometimes true, but the subjunctive is not in fact always obligatory after some common words that express uncertainty, e.g. 'perhaps', 'probably' (see 16.3.2) and 'to doubt' (see 16.8). Moreover, the sentence *me acostaré cuando se ponga el sol* 'I'll go to bed when the sun sets' does not imply that the sun may not set: the subjunctive is required after *cuando* simply because the sunset is still in the future.

In this respect students of French or Italian must remember that Spanish uses the present subjunctive to indicate the future in subordinate clauses after words like 'when', 'after', 'as soon as', etc., where the other two languages often use the future indicative. Compare *on y ira quand il **fera** beau temps* and *ci andremo quando **farà** bel tempo* (all verbs future indicative) with *iremos allí cuando **haga** buen tiempo* (second verb present subjunctive). Portuguese differs from all three in using a future subjunctive in this context: *iremos lá quando **fizer** bom tempo*.

The subjunctive also expresses certainties in other types of sentence. In *el hecho de que España no tenga petróleo explica en parte las dificultades económicas del país* 'the fact that Spain has no oil explains in part the country's economic difficulties', there is no doubt about Spain's having no oil. It is simply a rule of Spanish grammar that phrases meaning 'the fact that' usually require the subjunctive, possibly because an idea of cause is involved. See 16.10.1 for further discussion.

16.2.8 Regional variations in the use of the subjunctive

There is very little variation in the use of the subjunctive in educated usage throughout the Spanish-speaking world. In some regions, especially Navarre, the Basque Provinces and Argentina, there is a strong tendency in familiar speech to use the condtional instead of the imperfect subjunctive, e.g. *?si tendría dinero, lo compraría* for *si tuviera/tuviese dinero lo compraría* 'If I had some money, I'd buy it'. This should not be imitated by foreign learners, although it is acknowledged (at least in Spain and not in writing) as a well-known regionalism.

Nor should foreign students imitate the tendency, heard in popular speech in parts of Latin America, to use the indicative after subordinators of time that point to the future, e.g. *?se lo diré cuando viene* for *se lo diré cuando venga* 'I'll tell him when he comes'. Another tendency to be avoided by foreigners is the popular Latin-American use of the future indicative after phrases like *es posible que* 'it is possible that', which require the subjunctive in standard Spanish; see 16.3.1.

In Argentina, where *voseo* is normal in the spoken language (see 11.3.1) and should be imitated by foreigners learning that variety, careful speakers may nevertheless use standard Spanish subjunctive forms with *vos*: the expected *vos* forms with a stressed final vowel are considered a shade too popular for many tastes. In the following examples the speakers address one another as *vos*: *tengo miedo que no vengas... que aflojes* (J. Asís, Arg.; Spain *...miedo **de** que*) 'I'm scared you won't come...that you'll go off the idea', *no digas nada pero papá fue a matar un pollo...* (M. Puig, Arg., dialogue) 'don't say anything, but father went to kill a chicken...'. Compare this example of very familiar language: *yo no tengo inconveniente en hablar de perros todo lo que **querás*** (Mafalda cartoon, Arg.; 'correct' style *todo lo que quieras*) 'I don't mind talking about dogs as much as you like'.

16.2.9 Subjunctive required after negative statement + *que*

Sentences of the type negative statement + *que* are almost always followed by the subjunctive. Compare the following pairs

Es cierto que su mujer está enferma	It's true that his wife is ill
No es cierto que su mujer esté enferma	It isn't true that his wife is ill

Parece que es verdad	It seems that it's true
No parece que sea verdad	It doesn't seem that it's true
Es que quiero verla	It's that/The fact is that I want to see her/it
No es que quiera verla	It isn't that I want to see her/it
...porque habla ruso	...because (s)he speaks Russian
...no porque hable ruso	...not because (s)he speaks Russian
Esto no significa que ya sepan todo el uno del otro (*Reforma*, Mex.)	This doesn't mean that they already know everything about one another

Exceptions occur, especially after *no saber que* 'not to know that', *no decir que* 'not to say (i.e. 'state') that' and *no ser que* 'not to be that'. See section 16.7.

16.3 Subjunctive after statements of possibility and probability (including words meaning 'perhaps')

16.3.1 *Es posible/probable que...* and similar statements

In sentences of the pattern statement of possibility/probability/plausibility + *que* + subordinate verb, the latter is in the subjunctive. 'Possibility' also includes meanings like 'the risk that', 'the danger that', 'it is inevitable that...', etc.:

Es posible que haya tormenta	There may be a storm
Era probable/previsible que sucediera/sucediese así	It was probable/foreseeable that it would happen that way
La sola posibilidad de que aquella muchacha no lo viese más lo desesperaba (E. Sábato, Arg.)	The mere possibility that that girl wouldn't see him again filled him with despair
Corrías el riesgo de que te vieran/viesen	You were running the risk of them seeing you
Es inevitable que los autores... pierdan su capacidad creadora (J. Marías, Sp.)	It is inevitable that authors will lose their creative ability
También puede ocurrir que Santiago prefiera tener a Graciela en una relación deteriorada... (M. Benedetti, Ur., dialogue)	It may also be the case that Santiago prefers being with (lit. 'having') Graciela in a shaky relationship...

(i) *Pueda que* is a common Latin-American alternative for *puede que/puede ser que* 'maybe'/'it may be that': *pueda que algo te den y te mejores* (M. Puig, Arg., dialogue) 'maybe they'll give you something and you'll get better'.

(ii) The future indicative, or, when the verb in the main clause is in the past, the conditional, are quite often found in informal Latin-American Spanish after such statements, e.g. *... la posibilidad de que no podrán* (Spain *puedan*) *moler fábricas que no cuenten con caña suficiente* (*Granma*, Cu.) '...the possibility that mills that do not have enough sugar-cane will not be able to do any crushing'. This is banned from careful styles.

(iii) Use of *capaz que* for 'possibly', usually, but apparently not always, with the subjunctive, is typical of familiar Latin-American speech: *capaz que a la semana siguiente se lo ofrecen* [sic] *a Jane Fonda y para que acepte convierten el personaje en mujer* (*La Jornada*, Mex.) 'it's possible that the following week they'll offer it (the part) to Jane Fonda and make the character a woman so that she'll accept'. This construction is banned from formal styles and unheard in the standard language of Spain, but it is found in regional dialects in Spain.

16.3.2 Subjunctive after words meaning 'perhaps', 'possibly', 'probably'

Spanish has several words meaning 'perhaps': *acaso, tal vez, quizá* or *quizás, a lo mejor, igual* (Sp.), *lo mismo* (Sp.), *posiblemente, de repente* (Lat. Am.). These words may appear in main or subordinate clauses, but they are discussed here in order to group them with statements of possibility.

(a) *Tal vez, quizá(s), acaso, posiblemente, probablemente*

Tal vez (written *talvez* in Latin America) and *quizá(s)* are equally common on both continents. Both *quizá* and *quizás* are acceptable, but the former is more common in writing in Spain according to Seco. *Acaso* is rather literary in the meaning of 'perhaps' (it has another use described at 16.3.3). *Posiblemente* and *probablemente* mean 'possibly' and 'probably'.

With all these words, when the event referred to is happening in the present or happened in the past, use of the subjunctive is optional. The subjunctive makes the possibility rather weaker:

Tal vez fuese una discusión auténtica. Tal vez representaban una comedia en mi honor (interview, Madrid press; both moods used)	Maybe it was a real argument. Maybe they were putting on an act for my benefit
Tal vez debió irse (El País, Sp., or *debiera/debiese haberse ido*)	Perhaps he should have gone (i.e. 'resigned')
Tal vez tengamos algo de culpa nosotros mismos (S. Vodanovic, Ch., dialogue; or *tenemos*)	Perhaps we're partly to blame ourselves
Quizá ni siquiera entabláramos conversación (J. Marías, Sp.; or *entablamos*)	Perhaps we didn't even start up a conversation
Quizá era pena lo que se traslucía en la sonrisa de. . .mi padre (ibid.; *fuera/fuese* possible)	Perhaps it was sorrow that came through in my father's smile
Posiblemente quedara algo de alcohol etílico en nuestras venas humorísticas (G. García Márquez, Col.; *quedaba* or *quedase* possible)	Perhaps there was still some ethyl alcohol left in the veins of our humo(u)r
Posiblemente lo más criollo de nuestra cocina radica en las sopas y los guisos (Cuba Internacional, Cu.; *radique* possible, Spain *consiste en.* Guiso more or less interchangeable with *guisado* in Spain)	Possibly the most authentic (lit. 'creole') aspect of our cuisine lies in the soups and stews
Posiblemente lleguen/llegarán mañana (not *llegan*)	Possibly they'll arrive tomorrow
Probablemente en ningún momento te fuiste del cuarto. . . (J. Cortázar, Arg.)	Probably you never left the room for a moment
Probablemente el mérito sea de Ada (C. Rico-Godoy, Sp., dialogue)	You can probably thank Ada for that

If the event is still in the future, the present subjunctive or, much less commonly, the future indicative, is used, but not the present indicative:

Quizá/tal vez/acaso venga/vendrá mañana (not **viene mañana*)	Perhaps (s)he'll come tomorrow
Quizá tengamos una nueva generación afectada por un envejecimiento cerebral temprano a causa de los teléfonos móviles (Granma, Cu.)	Perhaps we are going to have a new generation affected by premature cerebral ageing because of mobile phones
Tal vez me lo expliques cuando te llegue la hora (L. Sepúlveda, Ch., dialogue)	Perhaps you'll explain it to me when the time's right for you
Quizá España podrá desempeñar un papel particularmente activo en el restablecimiento de la paz en Europa Central (El País, Spain; *pueda* possible)	Perhaps Spain will be able to play a particularly active part in re-establishing peace in Central Europe
Posiblemente sea mañana	Possibly it'll be tomorrow

NB: *Posiblemente* is less common than the English 'possibly': *ser posible que...* (always followed by subjunctive), *quizá(s)* or *tal vez* are more common.

The conditional of *haber* and *poder* is also common after these words to make the statement more tentative: *quizá habría que revisar asimismo estos conceptos* (A. Gala, Sp.) 'it may also possibly be necessary to modify these ideas'.

If the event *was* still in the future, only the imperfect subjunctive or the conditional can be used: *quizá/tal vez vinieran/viniesen/vendrían al día siguiente* (not **venían*) 'perhaps they would come the following day', *...una generación que acaso no volviera a ser feliz fuera de sus retratos* (G. García Márquez, Col.) '...a generation that would perhaps never again be happy outside its portraits'.

NB: The subjunctive can only be used if the word meaning 'perhaps' precedes the verb it modifies: one can only say *era, tal vez, un efecto de esta política...* 'it was, perhaps, an effect of this policy...'.

(b) *A lo mejor* also means 'perhaps', but it does not take the subjunctive. It is heard everywhere on both continents, but it is confined to spoken language or informal writing:

A lo mejor se ha quedado en casa	Perhaps/Maybe (s)he's stayed at home
Ni siquiera la nombró. A lo mejor se ha olvidado de ella (M. Vargas Llosa, Pe., dialogue)	He didn't even mention her. Maybe he's forgotten her

(c) In Spain *igual* and *lo mismo* are also used in familiar speech in the meaning 'perhaps': *yo no sé lo que me espera hoy. Igual llego tarde* (C. Rico-Godoy, Sp., dialogue) 'I don't know what's in store for me today. Maybe I'll get back late', *llama a la puerta. Lo mismo te da una propina* 'knock on the door. Maybe he'll give you a tip'. These two constructions are considered sub-standard by some speakers and they are not heard in Latin America. Latin Americans may interpret *igual* as 'anyway'/'all the same', e.g. *también mi estómago se mueve pero igual estoy contento* (M. Benedetti, Ur., dialogue) 'my stomach's churning too, but I'm happy all the same'.

(d) In parts of Latin America, especially Peru, *de repente* is used colloquially to mean 'perhaps'; the word means 'suddenly' in Spain and in standard language. It does not take the subjunctive: *de repente viene mañana = a lo mejor viene mañana* 'perhaps (s)he's coming tomorrow'. In colloquial Argentine Spanish *por ahí* + indicative is also used for 'perhaps'.

16.3.3 Further remarks on *acaso*

We said earlier that *acaso* is rather literary in the meaning 'perhaps', but it is found in all styles with the indicative in rhetorical, often sarcastic, questions, i.e. ones to which the speaker already knows the answer:

¿Acaso has visto alguna vez que no *llueva en verano?* (implies 'of course you haven't...')	Have you ever known it not to rain in summer? (lit. 'have you ever seen that it didn't rain in summer?')
¿Acaso todos los paganos no odian *a los huambisas?* (M. Vargas Llosa, Pe., dialogue)	Don't all the Indians (lit. 'pagans') hate the Huambisa tribe?

16.4 'Depending'

Statements + *que* that mean 'to depend on...' require the subjunctive:

Yo dependo de que me devuelvan *el dinero a tiempo*	I'm depending on them giving me the money back in time
De las mujeres depende que se coma *en el mundo* (A. Mastretta, Mex., dialogue)	It's women who ensure that people eat in this world (lit. 'that one eats in this world depends on women')
Miguel contaba con que lo/le *llamaran/llamasen aquella noche*	Miguel was counting on them calling him that night

16.5 Statements of 'influence' + *que*

16.5.1 General

In a statement of 'influence' the subject of the verb in the main clause tries to influence the outcome of the action in the subordinate clause by wanting, ordering, needing, causing, allowing, prohibiting, advising, persuading or encouraging it to happen, or by avoiding it.

When the subject of the main verb is not the same as the subject of the subordinate verb, the subjunctive must be used for the subordinate verb: *yo quiero que Mario lo haga* 'I want Mario to do it'. When the subjects are the same, the infinitive is used: *yo quiero hacerlo* 'I want to do it'; see 16.5.2a. However, some verbs of 'influence', especially verbs of permitting and prohibiting, can optionally be used with an infinitive even when the subjects are different. This possibility is discussed in 16.5.2b–c.

The following verbs always require the subjunctive when the subject of the subordinate verb is different from the subject of the main verb (although asterisked forms can be used impersonally with the infinitive. See 16.5.2b):

causar que to cause...
conseguir/lograr que to succeed in...
contribuir a que to contribute to...
cuidar de que to take care that...
decir que to tell someone to...
dificultar que to hinder...
esforzarse porque to make an effort to...
evitar*/impedir que to avoid...
exigir* que to require that...
hacer falta* que to be necessary that...
insistir/empeñarse en que to insist on...

necesitar que to need to...
oponerse a que to be against...
pedir que (but see 16.5.3) to ask/request that...
preferir que to prefer that...
pretender que... to aim for/to aspire to
querer/desear que to want...
salvar de que to rescue/save from...
ser necesario que to be necessary that...
suplicar que to implore to...
tratar de que... to try to ensure that...
vigilar que/asegurarse de que to make sure that...

NB: *Decir de* + infinitive is not standard Spanish: cf. French *dire à quelqu'un **de** faire quelque chose* = *decirle a alguien que* ***haga** algo* 'to tell someone to do something'. But *decir de* occurs in popular speech in Latin America.

There are many alternative ways of expressing the ideas associated with these verbs, e.g. by using adjectives, as in *es necesario/deseable que...* 'it's necessary/ desirable that...', or nouns, as in *la petición/obligación de que...* 'the request/ obligation that...'. These also require the subjunctive when they are followed by *que*, e.g. *su insistencia en que contestaran/contestasen en seguida* 'his/her insistence on them replying immediately'. Examples:

Quiero que estudies más	I want you to study more
Se esforzaba porque los demás vivieran/viviesen en mejores condiciones (*esforzarse **por** * 'to make an effort to')	(S)he strove to ensure that the others lived in better conditions
Organicé que todas nos vistiéramos como ellas (A. Mastretta, Mex., dialogue)	I arranged it so that all of us women should dress like them
Soy partidario de que lo publiquen	I support their publishing it
Esto dio como resultado que no le hicieran/hiciesen caso	The upshot of this was that they ignored him/her
Me salvé de puro milagro de que los ladrones me mataran/matasen	By a sheer miracle I avoided being killed by the thieves
Cierta impaciencia generosa no ha consentido que yo aprendiera a leer (J. L. Borges, Arg.)	A certain generous impatience did not allow me to learn to read
No puedes pretender que cambien las cosas (J. Aldecoa, Sp., dialogue)	You can't expect things to change
El primer paso, le dijo, era lograr que ella se diera cuenta de su interés (G. García Márquez, Col.)	The first thing to do, she said to him, was to get her to notice his interest
Nadie impidió que Hemingway escribiera y publicase sus libros (G. Cabrera Infante, Cu.)	Nobody stopped Hemingway writing and publishing his books
Hay que evitar que ellos se enteren	We have to avoid them finding out
Es necesario/imprescindible que lo reciban para mañana	It is necessary/essential that they receive it by tomorrow

(i) As was mentioned earlier, a noun phrase like *la decisión de que* 'the decision that', *la orden de que* 'the order that', *el deseo de que* 'the wish that', can be used instead of a main clause: *la orden de que se apagaran/apagasen las luces* 'the order for the lights to be turned off', *el anhelo de que Dios exista* 'the longing for God to exist', *la idea era que las chicas ayudasen/ayudaran a los chicos* 'the idea was that the girls should help the boys', *la petición de que se la indultara/indultase no llegó a tiempo* 'the petition for her reprieve didn't arrive in time'. When such a noun phrase immediately precedes *que*, *de* is inserted: *la necesidad de que nos mantengan informados* 'the need for them to keep us informed'. See 33.4.2 for details and exceptions.

(ii) Some verbs may or may not imply 'influence', according to their meaning. They take the subjunctive only when an order or wish is implied: *decidió que lo firmaran/firmasen* '(s)he decided that they should sign it', *decidió que lo habían firmado* '(s)he decided (i.e. 'came to the conclusion') that they had signed it'; *dijo que se terminara/terminase* '(s)he said (ordered) that it should be finished', *dijo que se había terminado* '(s)he said (i.e. 'announced') that it was finished'; and likewise *decir que* 'to tell someone to...' (subjunctive)/'to say that' (indicative), *establecer que* 'to stipulate that' (subjunctive)/'to establish the truth that' (indicative), *pretender que* 'to try to'/'to aim at'/'wish that' (subjunctive)/'to claim that' (indicative); *escribir* 'to write that' (indicative)/'to write instructing that' (subjunctive).

(iii) Statements of 'hope' are discussed at 16.11.3.

16.5.2 Use of the infinitive with verbs of influence

Some of the verbs listed under 16.5.1, and certain other verbs of influence not mentioned so far, may appear with the infinitive in the following circumstances (for *pedir* and similar verbs of requesting, see 16.5.3):

(**a**) if the subject of the main clause and the subject of the subordinate clause refer to the same person or thing:

Quiero hacerlo but *Quiero que **tú** lo hagas*	I want to do it/I want you to do it
No se deja pensar en ella	(S)he doesn't let himself/herself think of her
No pude evitar caerme (but) *No pude evitar que se cayera/cayese*	I couldn't help falling (but) I couldn't stop him/her falling
Ya has logrado enfadarme/Ya has logrado que me enfade	Now you've managed to make me angry
Pidió ir/Pidió que fueran/fuesen (but see 16.5.3)	(S)he asked to go/(S)he asked them to go

(**b**) In impersonal constructions (i.e. when there is no identifiable subject):

Hacía falta conseguir más gasolina	It was necessary to get more petrol/US gas
Se evitaba hablar de ellos	People avoided talking about them
Se exigía presentar los documentos	The documents were required to be presented
Esto obliga a pensar que...	This obliges one to think that...

(**c**) With certain verbs, even when they are not impersonal and have different subjects. These are verbs that can be constructed with an indirect object, as in *te ayudaré a conseguir/a que consigas lo que quieres* 'I'll help you to get what you want'.

Many of these are always followed by the preposition *a*, and the infinitive is almost always then used in preference to the subjunctive (as a general rule Spanish-speakers avoid the subjunctive when the rules of grammar allow it). The most common of these verbs are:

acostumbrar a to get used to	*desafiar a* to challenge to	*invitar a* to invite to
ayudar a to help to	*enseñar a* to teach to	*mandar a* to send to do
autorizar a to authorize to	*forzar a* to force to	something
animar a to encourage to	*impulsar a* to impel to	*obligar a* to oblige to
condenar a to condemn to	*incitar a* to encourage to	*persuadir a* to persuade to
contribuir a to contribute to	*inducir a* to persuade to	*retar a* to challenge to
convidar a to invite to	*instar a* to urge	*tentar a* to tempt to

Thus we can say

Le acostumbré/animé/autoricé/ayudé a hacerlo/a que lo hiciera/hiciese	I accustomed/encouraged/allowed/helped him/her to do it
Le condené/desafié/enseñé/forcé/impulsé/incité a hacerlo/a que lohiciese/hiciera	I condemned/challenged/taught/forced/impelled/incited him/her to do it
Le induje/invité/mandé/obligué/persuadí/reté/tenté a hacerlo/a que lo hiciera/hiciese	I induced/invited/sent/obliged/persuaded/challenged/tempted her to do it

Verbs not followed by *a* can be divided into two categories. The following are usually followed by the infinitive, although the subjunctive is also found:

dejar to let
hacer to make (i.e. cause to)
impedir to prevent

mandar to order
ordenar to order
permitir to allow/to permit

prohibir to forbid

Le dejó/hizo hacerlo/que lo hiciera/hiciese — (S)he let/made him/her do it
Le impidió hacerlo/que lo hiciese/hiciera it — (S)he prevented him/her from doing it
Le mandó/permitió/prohibió hacerlo/que lo hiciera — (S)he ordered/allowed/prohibited him/her from doing it
Si te prohíbo que faltes tú, ¿me obedecerás? (A. Buero Vallejo, Sp., dialogue) — If I forbid you not to be there, will you obey me?
Déjanos a los hombres conversar en paz (M. Vargas Llosa, Pe., dialogue) — Leave us men to talk in peace
La dosis de vanidad que todos tenemos dentro hizo que me sintiera el hombre más orgulloso de la Tierra (Che Guevara, quoted in *Granma*, Cu.) — The dose of vanity that we all have within us made me feel the proudest man on Earth
Estos actos sólo hacen perder la confianza en la democracia (*La Época*, Ch.) — These actions only make people lose confidence in democracy
Irala me convidó a acompañarla (J. L. Borges, Arg., dialogue; *a que la acompañara* also possible) — Irala invited me to accompany her
Había ordenado retirarse a todas sus sirvientas (A. Gala, Sp.; or *...a todas sus sirvientas que se retirasen/retiraran*) — She had ordered all her ladies-in-waiting to withdraw

But, some verbs are in a transitional state. The older construction is with the subjunctive and is safer for foreigners, but the infinitive construction is often heard and is creeping into the written language:

aconsejar to advise
obstaculizar to hinder

pedir to ask (but see 16.5.3)
proponer to propose

recomendar to recommend
sugerir to suggest

Te propuse hacerlo/que lo hiciéramos/hiciésemos — I suggested to you that we should do it
Te confieso que te propuse fugarnos (A. Bryce Echenique, Pe., dialogue) — I admit that I suggested to you that we should elope
Además, aprende de Octavia, a quien una vez le sugerí pasar a la otra parte (ibid.) — Moreover, learn from Octavia, to whom I once suggested that she should go over to the other side
Incluso las radioemisoras aconsejaron con insistencia a los capitalinos abstenerse de salir (*La Jornada*, Mex.) — Even the radio stations strongly advised residents of the capital to avoid going out

(i) Some of the verbs listed in this section can appear without an object in their main clause where English requires a dummy object like 'one' or 'people': *un delgado vestido que impedía llevar nada bajo él/...que se llevara/llevase nada debajo de él* 'a thin dress that prevented one from wearing anything underneath it', *que hagan respetar los derechos humanos* (*El Tiempo*, Col.) 'let them get people to respect human rights', *esto permite pensar que...* 'this allows one to think that'.

(ii) When the object is non-living and the subject is human the subjunctive should be used. One can say *la hiciste llorar* 'you made her cry', but not **se puede hacer un texto significar cualquier cosa* for *...hacer que un texto signifique cualquier cosa* 'one can make a text mean anything' (impersonal *se* counts as a human subject); *el experto técnico puede hacer que el acompañamiento se oiga menos* 'the technical expert can make the backing sound less loud' but not *...*puede hacer al acompañamiento oírse menos*.

When both subject and object are non-living it seems that either construction is possible, although the safe option is the subjunctive: *el embalse permite que las aguas del río alcancen unos niveles adecuados* (possibly *permite a las aguas alcanzar...*) 'the dam allows the water of the river to reach suitable levels', *...vientos flojos que harán bajar las temperaturas* (*Radio Nacional de España*) '...light winds that will cause temperatures to fall'.

16.5.3 Use of the infinitive with *pedir* and verbs of similar meaning

Pedir and other verbs of similar meaning, e.g. *rogar* 'to request', seem to be in a complex transitional state with respect to the use of the infinitive. They may appear in requests with the infinitive when the subjects are identical—*pidió hablar con el director* '(s)he asked to speak to the director', *pidió verme a las seis* '(s)he asked to see me at six o'clock'. They normally require *que* and the subjunctive when the subjects are different, as do other verbs of requesting: *pidió/suplicó/rogó que contestaran/contestasen cuanto antes* '(s)he asked/implored/requested them to answer as soon as possible'. Nevertheless, when the subject of the main verb is impersonal *se*, the infinitive is found in public notices of the type *se ruega a los residentes no llevar las toallas a la piscina* 'residents are asked not to take the towels to the swimming pool'.

In other cases, use of the infinitive when the subjects differ is not normally accepted as correct in standard language, but it is heard in familiar Latin-American speech and sometimes appears in Latin-American writing: *piden restituir a empleados de Correos que fueron despedidos* (*La Prensa*, Panama) '(unions) ask for reinstatement of dismissed Post Office workers', normally *...piden que se restituya a los empleados...*; *le pidió dejarlo solo con los varones* (G. García Márquez, Col.) 'he asked her to leave him alone with the men', normally *le pidió que lo dejara/dejase solo*; *te pido exigir que te den lo que nos ofrecieron* (idem, dialogue) 'I ask you to insist on them giving us what they offered us', usually *te pido que exijas que...*; *hoy nos hemos reunido por lo del wáter y les ruego permanecer sentados hasta que se solucione el problema* (A. Bryce Echenique, Pe., dialogue) 'we've met today over the question of the lavatory and I ask you to remain seated until the problem is solved', usually *...que permanezcan sentados*.

This infinitive construction is rejected in Spain, but it is increasingly common in journalistic styles, especially headlines, e.g. ?*Amnistía Internacional pide al gobierno español presionar* (better *que presione*) *a Chile* (*El País*, Sp.) 'Amnesty International asks Spanish Government to pressure Chile'. Moreover, sentences like ?*me pidió salir con él* 'he asked me to go out with him' are heard in the informal speech of young Spaniards. This seems to be limited to this third-person singular dating formula: informants who thought that this form was natural would not accept **nos pidieron ir con ellos al cine* for *nos pidieron que fuéramos/fuésemos con ellos*, or **les pedimos salir con nosotros* for *les pedimos que salieran/saliesen con nosotros*.

16.6 Emotional reactions and value judgements

16.6.1 Emotional reaction or value judgement + *que* + subjunctive

See also 26.4.2 for further remarks on the use and non-use of *de que* with such expressions.

In standard Spanish, the subjunctive is used in sentences of the pattern emotional reaction + *que* + subordinate verb. 'Emotional reaction' covers a vast range of possibilities including regret, pleasure, blame, displeasure, surprise, understanding, toleration, excusing, rejection, statements of sufficiency and insufficiency, importance, etc. It also includes value judgements like 'it's logical that..'., 'it's natural that...', 'it's enough that...'. Examples:

Es natural/comprensible que esté alterada	It's natural/understandable for her to be upset
Que estuviera todo tal cual, era hasta cierto punto lógico (E. Lynch, Arg.; subordinate clause precedes main clause)	It was logical to some extent that everything was as it was
Que te protejan no está mal (A. Buero Vallejo, Sp., dialogue)	It's not a bad thing that they protect you
No aguanto/perdono que me hablen de esa manera	I can't stand them/anyone talking to me like that
Basta que te ofrezcan mucho dinero para que de repente no sepas ni para qué sirve (S. Puértolas, Sp., dialogue)	You only need to be offered a lot of money to suddenly realize that you don't even know what use it is
Estoy hasta el moño de que tengamos que ser siempre nosotras las que debamos recoger la mesa (C. Rico-Godoy, Sp.)	I'm sick to death with the fact that it's always us women who have to clear the table
Andrés era el culpable de que me pasaran todas esas cosas (A. Mastretta, Mex., dialogue)	It was Andrés's fault that all these things were happening to me

A number of impersonal verbs denoting value judgements require the infinitive when their *indirect* object and the subject of the following verb are the same, as in *¿te importa hacer menos ruido?* 'do you mind making less noise' or *nos gusta comer mejillones* 'we like eating mussels'. Similar verbs are: *afligir* 'to afflict', *agobiar* 'to oppress/overwhelm', *agradecer* 'to thank for', *alarmar* 'to alarm', *alegrar* 'to cheer up', *apetecer* as in *me apetece hacerlo* 'I feel like doing it', *bastar* as in *te basta con decir gracias* 'all you have to do is say thanks', *conmover* 'to move' (emotionally), *convenir* as in *me conviene hacerlo mañana* 'it suits me to do it tomorrow', *costar* 'to be hard work', *disgustar* 'to displease', *doler* 'to hurt', *fastidiar* 'to annoy', *interesar* 'to be of interest'/'to be advantageous', *preocupar* 'to worry', *sorprender* 'to surprise', etc.

Some verbs take the infinitive when there is a shared subject, as in *odio hablar en público* 'I hate speaking in public'. Similar are: *aceptar* 'to accept', *avenirse a* 'to agree to', *conformarse con* 'to agree to', *consentir en* 'to consent to', *contentarse con* 'to be content to', *deplorar* 'to deplore, *lamentar* 'to lament', *resignarse a* 'to be resigned to', *soportar/aguantar* 'to put up with', etc. (based on *GDLE* 36.3.2.3).

A fuller list of infinitive constructions appears at 18.2.3.

(i) One must differentiate between value judgements and statements of fact like *es verdad que* 'it's true that', *es obvio/evidente que* 'it's obvious that', *es indiscutible que* 'it is beyond dispute that', *afirma/pretende que...* '(s)he claims that...'. The latter require the indicative, even though the distinction may sometimes appear arbitrary to English-speakers, particularly when they notice that *ser natural que* 'to be natural that' takes the subjunctive whereas *quejarse de que* 'to complain that' usually takes the indicative; see note to 16.6.2. For statements like 'it is *not* true that', see 16.7.

(ii) *Menos mal que* 'thank heavens that' takes the indicative: *menos mal que no se ha roto* 'thank heavens it's not broken'. *Qué bien que* takes the subjunctive in Spain: *qué bien que haya venido Tito* 'it's great/good news that Tito's come'. In Latin America it may appear with the indicative.

(iii) The form *mejor...* 'it would be best that...' is also followed by the indicative. This abbreviation of *sería mejor que* is very common in Latin America, but it is also heard in colloquial language in Spain: *mejor lo dejamos para más tarde* 'we'd better leave it until later'. Compare *sería mejor que lo dejáramos/dejásemos para más tarde* 'it would be better if we left it until later'.

(iv) In spontaneous language in Latin America, and to a lesser extent in some parts of Spain, an emotional reaction to a past, present or habitual event may be expressed by the indicative; this tendency is rather stronger with verbs followed by *de que*: see 16.6.2.

The indicative is sometimes seen in writing in Latin America, especially in Argentina. Examples:

El innegable genio de Joyce era puramente verbal; lástima que lo gastó en la novela (J. L Borges, Arg.)	Joyce's undeniable genius was purely verbal; a pity that he wasted it on the novel
Es curioso que uno no puede estar sin encariñarse con algo (M. Puig, Arg., dialogue)	It's strange that one can't manage (lit. 'can't be') without getting fond of something
Me da lástima que terminó (ibid., dialogue)	I'm sorry it's ended
Me parece raro que este hombre baja y dice "Mire..." (Ven., quoted DeMello, 1996, (2), 367)	It seems strange to me that this man gets out and says 'Look...'

DeMello's (1996), 2, study of recordings from Hispanic capital cities suggests that colloquial Spanish distinguishes between value judgements accompanied by emotional reactions (subjunctive) and value judgements that simply inform the speaker of a fact (s)he didn't know (indicative). But he notes that whereas the indicative was found in 57% of Latin-American sentences involving value judgements, it occurred in only 36% in Spain. Literary language strongly prefers the subjunctive after value judgements + *que*.

(v) English-speakers should beware of over-using *si* 'if' in sentences involving a value judgement: *sería maravilloso que/si no hubiera/hubiese hambre en el mundo* 'it would be wonderful if there were no hunger in the world'.

(vi) The subjunctive is still required when the main clause is deleted: *...pero que él diga eso...* (some phrase like *es increíble que...* having been deleted from the sentence) '...that he should say that...'/'...that he should have the nerve to say that...'.

16.6.2 Further remarks on emotional reactions followed by *de que*

For further remarks on *de que* after such expressions, see 26.4.2.

It was stated in 16.6.1 that the subjunctive is used with expressions of emotion and value judgements, and foreigners should respect this rule. But when the verb is followed by *de que* the indicative mood is sometimes heard in relaxed speech when the verb is in the present or past. This tendency should not be imitated by foreign students:

Me alegré de que (pensaban)/pensaran/ pensasen hacerlo	I was glad that they intended to do it
Se indignaba de que sus suegros (creían)/creyeran/creyesen en la pena de muerte	(S)he was outraged that his/her in-laws believed in the death penalty
Se asombra de que todo el mundo tiene un ticket (quoted DeMello, 1996 (2), 367; Madrid speech)	(S)he's surprised everyone's got a ticket

Quejarse de que 'to complain that...' seems to foreign learners to be an emotional reaction, but it is usually followed by the indicative (although the subjunctive is possible): *se queja de que Berta la hace quedarse a dormir la siesta* (M. Puig, Arg., dialogue) 'she complains about Berta making her stay in to sleep in the afternoon'. *Lamentar que* 'to regret the fact that' takes the subjunctive. *Lamentarse de que* 'to lament the fact that...' takes the subjunctive when it expresses an emotional reaction and the indicative when it merely makes a statement. *Protestar de que* 'to protest that' takes the indicative: *protestaba de que/se lamentaba de que el gobierno había subido los impuestos* '(s)he was protesting at/lamenting the fact that the Government had raised taxes', *lamento que ustedes no me hayan comprendido* 'I regret that you did not understand me'.

16.6.3 *Lo* + emotional reactions

If a value judgement is expressed by a phrase involving the 'neuter article' *lo*, the rule for the use of the subjunctive is as follows:

(**a**) *Lo lógico es que.../lo normal es que.../lo habitual/corriente es que...* are followed by a subjunctive:

Lo lógico/lo normal/lo habitual es que no venga	The logical thing/the normal thing/the usual thing is that he doesn't come
En nuestro país, lo habitual es que en todo asunto en que una persona pobre reclama de algún abuso...termine con problemas mayores que aquellos por los cuales reclama (La Época, Ch.)	In our country, it's usual that, in any matter in which poor people complain about some abuse, they end up with worse problems than the ones they are complaining about

(**b**) *Lo peor es que/lo mejor es que.../lo malo es que.../lo terrible es que.../lo molesto es que...*, etc., are followed by a subjunctive when the verb in the main clause points to an event still in the future:

Lo peor será/es que no venga nadie	The worst thing will be if no one comes
Lo malo sería que no terminaran/ terminasen el trabajo a tiempo	The problem would be if they didn't finish the work on time
Lo más provocante de la ley es que provoque una reacción violenta del gobierno cubano (La Jornada, Mex.)	The most provocative thing about the law is that it may produce a violent reaction from the Cuban government

But if the main verb is timeless, habitual or in the past, the verb is usually in the indicative, although the subjunctive is also possible, in which case the event seems more doubtful:

Lo peor fue que no vino nadie	The worst thing was that no one came
Lo que me indigna es que la sociedad todavía condena los amores o amoríos entre una señora madura y un jovencito (C. Rico-Godoy, Sp.)	What makes me mad is that society still condemns romances or love affairs between a mature woman and a young man
Lo malo es que soñé nuevamente con Emilio (M. Benedetti, Ur., dialogue)	The worst is that I dreamt of Emilio again
Lo que más me sorprendió...fue que...se habían detenido y vuelto (J. Marías, Sp.)	What surprised me most was that they had stopped and turned round

The subjunctive could have been used in these examples with the effect of making them more hesitant.

In some cases use of the subjunctive depends on the meaning: *lo increíble era que Pedro no lo sabía* or *supiera/supiese* 'the incredible thing was that Pedro didn't know about it'. Here the indicative assumes that Pedro did not know whereas the subjunctive leaves open the question whether he knew or not. The choice depends on whether the action denoted by the subordinate verb is a reality to the speaker. Compare: *lo peor es que mi padre nunca dice nada* 'the worst thing is that my father never says anything', and a possible reply to this: *sí, lo peor es que no diga nada* 'yes, the worst thing is that he doesn't say anything' (i.e. *if* that is the case). In the second example the speaker does not claim knowledge of the facts described by the first speaker. This subtle distinction will be found to operate in many examples of subjunctive use.

16.7 Subjunctive after denials

In sentences of the pattern denial + *que* + subordinate clause, the subordinate verb is usually in the subjunctive:

Mayta negó que hubiera intervenido en el rapto (M. Vargas Llosa, Pe., dialogue; or *hubiese*)	Mayta denied he was involved in the kidnapping
Yo no he dicho que seas una histérica (C. Rico-Godoy, Sp., dialogue)	I never said you were a hysteric
Esto no significa que haya que esperar un cambio radical de actitud (J. Cortázar, Arg.)	This doesn't mean that one must expect a radical change of attitude
No ocurre/sucede que haya eclipse todos los días	It doesn't happen that there's an eclipse every day
No se trata de que tengas que quedarte todos los días hasta las nueve de la noche	It's not a question of your having to stay till nine p.m. every day
Pero nunca creí que Marta se acostumbrara a vivir en un pueblo (M. Puig, Arg., dialogue)	But I never thought Marta would get used to living in a small town
Nunca pensé que fueras así (A. Arrafut, Cu., dialogue)	I never imagined you were like this

However the subjunctive is sometimes optional after verbs of knowing or believing, depending on the degree of uncertainty involved. Choice of the subjunctive in such cases depends on the speaker's background knowledge. If one knows for a fact that X is a thief, one says *no confesaba que había robado el dinero* '(s)he didn't confess to stealing the money'. If X may be innocent one says *no confesaba que hubiese/hubiera robado el dinero.* For this reason, negated statements of demonstrable fact, e.g. *yo no sabía que la puerta estaba abierta* 'I didn't know the door was open' (it was) are more likely to take the indicative (although *estuviera/estuviese* is also correct), and negated opinions, e.g. *no creo que sea muy útil* 'I don't think it's very useful', are almost certain to take the subjunctive.

(i) The indicative is occasionally found after *negar que* and verbs of similar meaning, although this construction is unusual, especially in Spain: *niego que hubo bronca* (*Proceso*, Mex.; usually *hubiera, hubiese* or *haya habido bronca*) 'I deny there was a row'; *¿también va Vd. a negar que los ingleses se lavan?* (J. Camba, Sp.; indicative used because a denial would be unreasonable) 'are you also going to deny that the English wash?', *pero negaban tozudamente que transportaban marihuana en esta ocasión* (*Granma*, Cu.) 'but they stubbornly denied that they were carrying marijuana on this occasion', *rechaza que Dios existe* (from Navas Ruiz (1986), 69, usually *exista*) '(s)he denies that God exists'.

(ii) Negative questions and negative orders take the indicative. See note (v).

(iii) *No ser que* and *no que…* are denials and are normally followed by the subjunctive: *no es que yo diga que es mentira* 'it's not that I'm saying that it's a lie', *no es que se dijeran grandes cosas* (J. Marías, Sp.) 'it isn't that important (lit. 'great') things were said', *no era que no hubiese pobres por toda la ciudad* (A. Mastretta, Mex.) 'it wasn't that there were no poor people all over the city'. But *no ser que* takes the indicative in questions: see note (v).

Exceptionally *no ser que* is followed by the indicative, in which case the denial is more confident and assertive: *no era que tomaba posesión del mundo* (M. de Unamuno, Sp.) 'it wasn't that he was taking possession of the world'.

For the formula *no sea que* 'lest'/'so that not…', see 16.12.3b.

(iv) Compare the different translations of *decir* in the following examples: *ha dicho que venía* '(s)he said (s)he was coming', *no he dicho que venía* 'I didn't say I was coming', *no he dicho que viniera/viniese* 'I didn't tell him/her to come'.

(v) Negative questions and negative orders are not denials, so the indicative is used: *¿no es verdad que ha dicho eso?* 'isn't it true that he said that?', *¿no sientes que el corazón se te ensancha al ver esto?* (J. Ibargüengoitia, Mex., dialogue) 'don't you feel your heart getting bigger when you see this?', *no digas que es verdad* 'don't say it's true', *no creas que esto es lo único que hacemos* (A. Mastretta, Mex., dialogue) 'don't think that this is the only thing we do', *pero no crean ustedes que me vio* (C. Rico-Godoy, Sp., dialogue) 'but don't get the idea that he saw me', *no será que no quiere hacerlo?* 'isn't it the case that he doesn't want to do it?', *¿no sería que no quedaban más?* 'wouldn't it be the case that there were none left?'.

16.8 Statements of doubt

Dudar que takes the subjunctive, but after statements meaning 'not to doubt that…' the indicative is used when the meaning is 'to be sure that…':

Dudo que sea verdad	I doubt whether it's true
No dudo que sea verdad lo que dices	I don't doubt whether what you say is true (tentative remark)

But:

No dudo que es verdad lo que dices	I don't doubt (i.e. 'I'm convinced') that what you say is true
No dudo que vendrá/venga	I don't doubt he'll come
Dudo que yo pueda venir mañana/Dudo poder venir mañana (infinitive possible since the verbs are in the same person)	I doubt I can come tomorrow
No hay duda que ella puede ser discutida (M. Vargas Llosa, Pe.; Sp. *no hay duda de que...*)	There is no doubt that it can be debated

(i) For the possibility *dudar de que* see 33.4.3 note (ii).

16.9 Statements of fear

Temer/Tener miedo de que 'to fear' and other statements of similar meaning may take the subjunctive or a future indicative tense (including future time expressed by *ir a* 'to be going to...'), or, if they refer to the past, a past subjunctive or an indicative future in the past. For *temerse que* see note (ii):

Temo que le moleste/Temo que le va a molestar/molestará/le vaya a molestar	I'm afraid it may upset him/her
Temíamos que le molestara/molestase/ molestaría/Temíamos que le iba/fuera a molestar	We were afraid it would upset him/her
Yo tenía miedo de que te hubieras ido (G. Cabrera Infante, Cu., dialogue)	I was scared that you'd gone
...para no ver el mar por la escotilla porque nos da miedo de que entre (E. Poniatowska, Mex.)	...so as not to see the sea through the hatchway, because we're afraid it'll come in

The subjunctive is always used if the main verb is negated: *no temía que me fuera/fuese a atacar* 'I wasn't afraid he/she/it was going to attack me'.

(i) Use of redundant *no* (see 23.2.4) instead of *que* after *temer(se)* changes the meaning: the subjunctive is then obligatory. Compare *temo que no te va a gustar* 'I'm afraid you're not going to like it' and redundant *no* in *temo no te vaya a gustar demasiado* 'I'm afraid in case/lest you're going to like it too much', *temo no te vayas a enfadar* 'I'm afraid in case/lest you get cross'.

(ii) *Temerse que* usually means little more than 'I'm sorry to say that...' and it therefore takes the indicative: *me temo que no he sido muy delicado* 'I fear I haven't been very discreet', *de eso me temo que no puedo hablarte* (L. Sepúlveda, Ch., dialogue) 'I'm afraid I can't talk to you about that'. But the subjunctive is possible: *mucho nos tememos que se trate de los primeros* (*Terra*, Ur.) 'we are very much afraid that the former are involved.

(iii) *Temer que* may also be found with the indicative when it refers to timeless or habitual actions: *temo que la verdadera frontera la trae cada uno dentro* (C. Fuentes, Mex., dialogue) 'I fear that each one of us carries the real frontier inside ourselves', *empezaba a temer que las imágenes de los dos mundos...pertenecían a dos caras de la misma moneda* (J. Aldecoa, Sp.) 'I was beginning to fear that the images of the two worlds...belonged to the two sides of the same coin'.

16.10 Subjunctive after 'the fact that...' and after other noun phrases

16.10.1 'The fact that...'

There are three common ways of translating 'the fact that': *el hecho de que, el que,* and *que;* the latter two items have various other meanings, for which see the Index.

(a) With all of these the subjunctive is used whenever any kind of value judgement or emotional reaction is involved, or whenever any idea of cause or influence is involved:

(El) que no digan nada no debería afectar tu decisión	The fact that they say nothing shouldn't affect your decision
No hay duda de que el hecho de que me hayan dado el Nobel va a dar mayor resonancia a todo lo que diga y haga (G. García Márquez, Col.)	There is no doubt that the fact that they've given me the Nobel prize will give more weight to everything I say and do
El que yo escriba un diario se debe también a Virginia (J. J. Arreola, Mex., dialogue.)	The fact that I keep a diary is also thanks to Virginia
Que tres aviones se destrocen, se desplome un tren,... arda una discoteca, y todo en menos de un mes, quizá sea simplemente casualidad (Cambio16, Sp.)	The fact that three planes are destroyed, a train plunges into a ravine, ...a discotheque catches fire, and all in less than a month, is perhaps pure chance

(b) The indicative is required when the main verb is a verb of knowing or perceiving (e.g. *enterarse de* 'to find out', *darse cuenta de* 'to realize'). When *el hecho de que* is preceded by a preposition it almost always takes the indicative:

Se ha dado cuenta del hecho de que tiene que trabajar para vivir	(S)he has realized (s)he has to work in order to live
...parten del hecho de que muchos mayores tienen dificultades para usar correctamente los aparatos (El Mundo, Sp.)	...are based on the fact that many elderly persons find it difficult to use the equipment
Que el poder tiende al abuso...no debe escandalizar a nadie (El País, Sp.)	That power tends to abuse ... is a fact that should scandalize no one

(c) In some cases the subjunctive and indicative appear to be interchangeable. After years of reconsidering these examples we can still detect no difference of meaning between them, but foreigners will not go wrong if they apply the rules set out in (a) and (b):

Le molesta el hecho de que no venga/viene a verlo/le	The fact that (s)he doesn't come to see him annoys him
No le daba importancia al hecho de que él no le hacía/hiciera/hiciese caso	(S)he didn't mind the fact that he paid her/him no attention
No quiero que el hecho de que te conozco/conozca sea un obstáculo	I don't want the fact that I know you to be an obstacle
El hecho de que no me veía/viera/viese me hacía sentirme seguro	The fact that (s)he couldn't see me made me feel safe

El que 'the fact that' must be distinguished from *el que* 'the person that' (discussed at 36.1.4). Sometimes only context makes the sense clear: *el que haya dicho eso no sabe lo que dice* 'the person who/whoever said that doesn't know what (s)he's talking about', *el que haya dicho eso no tiene importancia* 'the fact that (s)he said that has no importance'.

(i) English-speakers tend to overdo *el hecho de que* for 'the fact that'. *El que...* or *que...* alone are in fact as common if not more so.

16.10.2 Subjunctive after other noun phrases used as subordinators

When a noun phrase replaces a verb phrase it is normally connected to a following subordinate clause by *de que*: compare *esperamos que llueva* 'we hope it will rain' and *la esperanza de que llueva* 'the hope that it will rain': see 33.4.2 for more detailed discussion of the use of *de que* after nouns.

In general the mood of the subordinate verb after such noun phrases is governed by the same rule that would affect verb phrases of the same meaning, i.e. *la posibilidad de que...* 'the possibility that...' takes the subjunctive because *es posible que...* 'it's possible that...' does. However, there is a series of miscellaneous noun phrases after which choice between the subjunctive and indicative is determined by meaning. Two factors may combine or operate independently to invoke the subjunctive: (a) the type of verb in the main clause, (b) the reality or non-reality of the event expressed by the subordinate clause.

(a) In the following examples the verb in the main clause is of a type (emotional reaction, possibility, etc.) which would itself require the subjunctive:

Le contrarió la casualidad de que encontrase/encontrara ahí a su primo	(S)he was annoyed by happening to find his/her cousin there
No podía soportar la idea de que no le dieran/diesen el puesto	(S)he couldn't stand the idea of them not giving her the job

(b) In the following sentences the indicative is used because the subordinate verb indicates an established fact or reality, even though in some cases the person affected may not yet know the truth of the situation:

Siempre daba la casualidad de que no llegaban a tiempo	It always happened that they never arrived on time (habitual fact)
Se tenían que enfrentar con el problema de que no tenían dinero	They had to face up to the problem of not having any money (fact)
Consiguió que aceptara la idea de que no le darían el puesto	(S)he managed to get him to accept the idea that they wouldn't give him/her the job (i.e. accepting a fact)
Tengo la convicción de que no hace nada	I'm convinced (s)he doesn't do anything (knowledge)
Se encontró con la sorpresa de que estaba de mal humor	(S)he was surprised to find that (s)he was in a bad mood (factual)
Le atormentaba la obsesión de que su mujer le engañaba	He was tormented by the obsession that his wife was being unfaithful to him (factual, as far as he knows)

(c) In some sentences, the difference between the subjunctive and the indicative reflects a very subtle distinction between statements of fact (indicative) and value judgements (subjunctive):

Tuve la suerte de que no me viera/vio	I was lucky in that he didn't see me (on that occasion; factual, but subjunctive more usual)

But:

Tenía la suerte de que no me veía	I was lucky in that he didn't see me (on one or several occasions. Indicative only)
Tenía siempre la preocupación de que le iba/fuera a pasar algo	(S)he always worried that something might happen to her/him
Vivían con la pesadilla de que perderían su dinero	They lived with the nightmare of losing their money (indicative only)
Le animaba la ilusión de que lo conseguiría	She was encouraged by the dream of getting it (same subject for both verbs)
Le animaba la ilusión de que ella lo conseguiría/consiguiera/consiguiese	(S)he was encouraged by the dream that (s)he would get it (different subjects)

16.11 Subjunctive after special verbs

16.11.1 Subjunctive after *creer, parecer, suponer* and *sospechar*

We said at 16.2.5b and 16.7 that expressions of belief + *que* take the indicative—*creo que Dios existe* 'I believe that God exists'—unless they are negated: *no creo que Dios exista* 'I don't believe God exists'. However, the subjunctive occasionally appears after some of these verbs even when they are affirmative. The meaning is then more hesitant, but the difference can barely be translated into English:

Sospecho que es/sea mentira	I suspect it's a lie
Como si la Historia fuera una especie de saltamontes; y parece que lo sea pero en otro sentido (A. Sastre, Sp., dialogue)	As if History were a sort of grasshopper; and it seems that it is, but in a different sense
¿Por qué estás así? Parece que te estuvieras ahogando (E. Bryce Echenique, Pe., dialogue)	Why are you like that? It looks as though you were drowning

Use of the subjunctive to make a question ironic (i.e. the speaker already knows the answer) seems to be confined to Latin-American Spanish:

¿Usted cree que esto ayude? (M. Puig, Arg., dialogue; incredulous tone)	Do you really think that this helps?
¿Usted cree que yo quiera lastimar a esta niña preciosa? (A. Mastretta, Mex., dialogue)	Do you really think I want to hurt this lovely girl?

In Spain the indicative (*ayuda, quiero*) would have been used.

16.11.2 Subjunctive after *comprender/entender que, explicar que*

All of these verbs take the subjunctive when they are negated, e.g. *no entiendo que ahora me pregunten sobre la ponencia* (interview in *El País*, Sp.) 'I don't understand why people are asking me now about the written statement/paper'.

Comprender and *entender* take the subjunctive when they mean 'to sympathize with':

Yo comprendo que los concejales defendieran sus posiciones dentro del partido (Interview in *Cambio16*, Sp.; or *defendiesen*)	I understand the councillors/US councilors defending their positions inside the party

Explicar usually takes the indicative when it really means 'to state' or 'to say': *Manuel explicó que había estado enfermo* 'Manuel explained that he had been ill'. But the subjunctive is used when the verb means 'gives the reason why': *esto explica que las mutaciones de la literatura estén estrechamente ligadas a las innovaciones técnicas* 'this explains how changes in literature are intimately linked to technical innovations'.

16.11.3 Subjunctive after *esperar que*

Esperar 'to hope' may be followed by the subjunctive, by the future indicative, by the indicative of *ir a*, or by the conditional. The subjunctive is by far the commoner form when the verb means 'to hope'. Use of the indicative of these tenses suggests the meaning 'to expect':

Espero que le convenzas/convencerás ...*con la esperanza de que ella haría lo mismo* (C. Fuentes, Mex.)	I hope/expect you'll convince him ...in the hope that she'd do the same
Por un momento la invadió la esperanza de que su marido no habitara ya el reino de los vivos (S. Pitol, Mex., or *habitase*)	For a moment she was overcome by (lit. 'invaded by') the hope that her husband no longer dwelt in the realm of the living
Espero que me vas a pagar	I hope you're going to pay me

(i) *Esperar a que* and *aguardar a que* 'to wait for...' take the subjunctive: *yo estaba esperando/aguardando a que fuera/fuese otro el que lo hiciera/hiciese* 'I was waiting for someone else to do it'.

(ii) *No esperar que* always takes the subjunctive: *yo no esperaba que me fuera a escribir* 'I didn't expect (s)he was going to write to me'.

16.12 The subjunctive after subordinators

16.12.1 Introductory

Subordinators are words like 'before', 'after', 'provided that', 'because', 'when', 'unless', which introduce subordinate clauses. The general rule governing the use of the subjunctive after subordinators is: if the event referred to has or had occurred, the verb is in the indicative; if the event has or had not yet occurred, the verb is in the subjunctive. Example:

Te lo di cuando llegaste	I gave it to you when you arrived
Te lo daré cuando llegues	I'll give it to you when you arrive
Yo iba a dártelo cuando llegaras/llegases	I was going to give it to you when you arrived

It follows from this that a few subordinators, e.g. *antes de que* 'before', *para que/a que* 'in order that', always take the subjunctive because they must refer to something that has or had not yet happened. In some cases, e.g. *puesto que* 'since' (i.e. 'because'), *debido a que* 'due to the fact that', the event referred to has obviously already happened, so the indicative is obligatory (these subordinators are also discussed in Chapter 33). But in most cases use of the subjunctive depends on the rule given above.

As in English, the subordinate clause may precede or follow the main clause: *después de que llegaron, empezamos a hablar/empezamos a hablar después de que llegaron* 'after they arrived we started talking'/'we started talking after they arrived'.

_{NB:} The rules given in this section do not refer to question-words like *cuándo, dónde, cómo*, which are not subordinating conjunctions. In direct and indirect questions they are followed by the indicative: *¿sabes cuándo llega?* 'do you know when (s)he's coming?', *¿te acordarás de dónde lo has/habrás dejado?* 'will you remember where you've left it?', *dudo que sepa cómo se dice* 'I doubt (s)he knows how to say it'. Note that *depender* and *según* are followed by non-interrogative forms: *depende de cuando lleguen* 'it depends when they arrive', *según quien sea* 'according to who it is'.

16.12.2 Use of the infinitive after subordinators (see also 18.3)

The infinitive is used after certain subordinators when both verbs have the same subject. Compare *entré sin verla* 'I came in without seeing her' (same subject 'I') and *entré sin que ella me viera/viese* 'I came in without her seeing me' (different subjects). This is possible with the following subordinators:

(a) All those that include the word *de*, e.g. *con tal de que* 'provided that', *antes de que*, 'before', *después de que* 'after', *bajo la condición de que* 'on condition that', *con el objeto de que/a fin de que* 'with the intention of', *a cambio de que* 'in return for', *a pesar de que* 'despite', *en caso de que* 'in the event of', *el hecho de que* 'the fact that', etc. The *que* is dropped before the infinitive:

Lo haré antes de salir	I'll do it before I going out
Lo escribió con el objeto de criticar a sus colegas	(S)he wrote it with the intention of criticizing his/her colleagues
El hecho de saber cuatro lenguas me ayuda	The fact of knowing four languages helps me

_{NB:} Exception: *en vista de que* 'in view of the fact that', always takes an indicative finite verb, never an infinitive.

(b) *Sin que* 'without', *para que/porque/a que* 'in order to', *nada más* 'as soon as', *hasta que* 'until'. The *que* is dropped before an infinitive. Compare: *entré sin hacer ruido* 'I came in without making any noise', *entré sin que me viera/viese* 'I came in without him/her seeing me', *fue al dentista a que le sacara/sacase una muela* 'she went to the dentist for him to take one of her teeth out' and *fui al supermercado a comprar pan* 'I went to the supermarket to buy bread'. Compare also *cerré los ojos por no llorar* 'I shut my eyes so as not to cry', *estábamos cruzando la Plaza de San Martín para tomar el colectivo* (M. Vargas Llosa, Pe., dialogue) 'we were crossing San Martin square in order to get the bus'.

In the case of the other subordinators, e.g. *cuando, mientras que* 'while', *en cuanto/una vez que* 'as soon as', a subordinate finite verb cannot be replaced by an infinitive: *te lo diré cuando te vea* 'I'll tell you when I see you', never **te lo diré cuando verte*, which is not Spanish.

(i) Some of these subordinators that allow the infinitive construction are sometimes found with an infinitive in very informal speech even when the subjects are not the same, as in *?cómprame unas postales para mandárselas yo a mi madre* for *cómprame unas postales para que yo se las mande a mi madre* 'buy me some postcards for me to send to my mother'. But this is banned from careful language and should be avoided by foreigners.

16.12.3 Subjunctive with subordinators of purpose

(**a**) Phrases meaning 'in order to' such as *a fin de que, para que/porque, con el objeto de que, con el propósito de que, con la intención de que* and *a que* (which also has other meanings, e.g. *a que sí* 'I bet it's true'), are always followed by a subjunctive because they must point to an event that has or had not yet happened. (When the subjects of the verbs are identical the infinitive is used, e.g. *lo hice para fastidiarte* 'I did it to annoy you'; see 16.12.2b):

Afuera, para que la solidaridad se sienta, hay que reunir un millar de personas (M. Benedetti, Ur., dialogue)	Outside, so that people should sense the (level of) solidarity, one ought to assemble about a thousand people
Me callé porque/para que no me acusaran/acusasen de metomentodo	I kept silent so that they wouldn't accuse me of interfering
He escrito una circular a fin de que se enteren todos	I've written a circular so that everybody knows about it

For the difference between *por* and *para* when both mean 'in order to', see 34.14.7.

(**b**) A number of phrases express negative intention or avoidance, i.e. 'so that not', and always take the subjunctive. They are awkward to translate now that our word 'lest' has become obsolete. These phrases do not allow replacement of the subjunctive by an infinitive:

Trabaja más, no sea que te despidan	Work harder so that they don't (lit. 'lest they') fire you
Me subí al coche en tres minutos no se me fuera a arrepentir de la invitación (A. Mastretta, Mex., dialogue)	I got into the car within three minutes lest he regretted/so that he wouldn't regret the invitation
No corras tanto, no vaya a darte un infarto	Don't hurry (lit. 'run') so much—you don't want to give yourself a heart attack
Devuélvele el dinero, no ocurra que nos demande	Give her/him back the money. We don't want her/him to sue us

16.12.4 Subjunctive with subordinators of cause and consequence

These do not allow replacement of the finite verb by an infinitive.

(**a**) The following are always followed by the indicative:

pues because (see 33.5.3)   *ya que* since/seeing that   *debido a que* due to the fact that
puesto que since   *en vista de que* seeing that

   Como, when it means 'since'/'because', is also usually followed by the indicative and is discussed in detail at 33.5.2. When followed by the subjunctive *como* means 'if' and is discussed at 25.8.2. For the use of *como* in sentences like *hazlo como quieras* 'do it as/how you like', see 16.12.5b. *Cómo* means 'how' in direct and indirect questions, and is best thought of as a different word: see 24.7.

Invítame ya que/puesto que tienes tanto dinero/Como tienes tanto dinero me puedes invitar (in this meaning *como* must appear at the head of the clause; see 33.5.2)	Since you have so much money you can pay for me

(**b**) *Porque* is usually followed by an indicative but requires the subjunctive when it means 'just because'/'only because' or 'not because' and the main verb is negated. Sometimes it can be preceded by *sólo/solo*:

No lo hago porque tú lo digas	I'm not doing it just because *you* say so
Que nadie venga a nosotros porque piense que va a obtener enchufes (Cambio16, Sp.)	Let no one come to us (just) because they think that they'll get special favo(u)rs

NB: *El enchufe*, literally 'plug', is used in Spain to mean 'connections': *está muy enchufado* 'he's well-connected', *el enchufismo* 'the old-boy network', 'the inside-favours system'; also *el amiguismo*.

But:

No lo hago porque tú lo dices	I won't do it because you say so/said I should
No lo hago sólo/solo porque tú lo dices	I'm doing it, but not simply because you're telling me to
No salgo contigo sólo/solo porque tienes un Ferrari	The fact that you have a Ferrari isn't the only reason I go out with you

Compare also: *sólo/solo porque tengas un Ferrari no voy a salir contigo* 'the fact that you have a Ferrari isn't a good enough reason for me to go out with you'.

The subjunctive is used after *bien porque. . . o/ya porque. . . o, fuera porque...fuera porque* meaning 'whether. . . or':

Bien/ya porque tuviera algo que hacer o porque estuviera cansado, el caso es que no estuvo muy amable con nosotros	Whether he had something to do or whether he was tired, the fact is that he wasn't very kind to us
...ya fuese para apuntalar al Gobierno, ya para atacarlo (Abc Color, Par.)	...whether in order to support the government, or to attack it
Fuera porque no sea costumbre de los arrabales estadounidenses, fuera porque a nadie le interesara demasiado su vida. . . (S. Puértolas, Sp.; bien porque...o porque could have been used)	Whether because it wasn't usual in the suburbs in the USA, or because her life didn't interest people too much...

(i) If *porque* means *para que* (as it does after verbs like *esforzarse porque* 'to make an effort in order that...'), the verb is always subjunctive: *nos esforzamos porque/para que todos tengan agua limpia* 'we're making an effort to ensure that everyone has clean water', *estoy un tanto apurado y como impaciente porque pase el trago* 'I'm a bit worried and rather impatient for this unpleasantness to pass'.

(ii) *No porque...* 'not because' always take the subjunctive: *me perdí y llegué tarde. No porque yo me oriente mal, sino porque iba un poco sonada* (C. Martin Gaite, Sp.) 'I lost my way and was late. Not because I have no sense of direction but because I was a bit high/stoned'.

(c) *De ahí que* 'hence the fact that' is almost always followed by a subjunctive:

De ahí que el Papa haya incluso presionado al nuevo Gobierno (El País, Sp.)	This is why the Pope has even put pressure on the new Government
De ahí que visitar nuestra casa se convirtiese de vez en cuando en motivo de excursión (L. Goytisolo, Sp.)	This is why visiting our house occasionally became the pretext for an excursion

(d) *Dado que* takes the indicative if it means 'given that', the subjunctive if it means 'if it is the case that':

dado que él quiera hacerlo	if it's the case that he wants to do it...
dado que es así. . .	given that this is the case...

16.12.5 Subjunctive with subordinators of result, aim and manner

The basic rule is that these take the indicative when they imply result and the subjunctive when they refer to an aim or intention. They do not allow replacement of the finite verb by an infinitive.

(**a**) When they indicate the result of an action the following take the indicative:

así que so (= 'as a result')	*de manera que* in such a way that/so
conque so (esp. in questions, e.g.	*de suerte que* in such a way that/so
¿conque lo has hecho tú? 'so it was *you*	*de forma que* in such a way that/so
that did it?')	
de modo que in such a way that/so	

Tú tienes la culpa, de modo que/así que/	You're to blame, so you can't complain
conque no te puedes quejar	
Lo hicieron en silencio de modo/forma/	They did it in silence so (as a result)
manera que no se enteró el portero	the doorman didn't find out
Se han dispuesto helicópteros que sobrevuelen	Helicopters have been ordered to
la zona, de manera que podría ser factible	overfly the area, so it could be
hacerlo por esa vía (*La Época*, Ch.)	feasible to do it (i.e. 'enter the area')
	using that route

De modo que/de manera que/de forma que may also indicate aim or purpose, in which case they take the subjunctive. Unfortunately some varieties of English, especially British, no longer always mark the difference between result and aim in this kind of sentence, so *lo hizo de modo que nadie se enteró* and *lo hizo de modo que nadie se enterase/enterara* may both be translated '(s)he did it so no one realized', despite the fact that in Spanish the indicative implies that no one realized and the subjunctive that (s)he *hoped* that no one would. It seems that North Americans usually differentiate 'he did it so no one realized' (indicative) and 'he did it so no one would realize' (subjunctive), so they should know when to use the subjunctive:

Compórtate de modo/manera que no sospeche	Behave so as to avoid him/her
	suspecting
Entró silenciosamente de modo/manera que	She came in quietly so that I wouldn't
yo no la oyera/oyese	hear her
Entró silenciosamente de modo/manera que	(S)he came in quietly so (i.e. 'and') I
no la oí	didn't hear her
—Está sobreactuando —me dijo a mí en el	'She's overacting,' he said to me in
pasillo, de forma que nuestra madre no le	the corridor so that our mother
pudiera oír (S. Puértolas, Sp.)	wouldn't hear him

(**b**) *Como* requires the subjunctive when it refers to an action which is or was still in the future:

Hazlo como quieras	Do it however you like
Lo hizo como quiso	(S)he did it the way (s)he wanted
Te dije que podías venir como quisieras/	I told you could come any way you
quisieses	liked

In literary styles, *como* is occasionally found with the *-se* or *-ra* forms when it refers to a past action: *como se diese/diera cuenta de que...* 'as/when he realized that...'.

For *como* + subjunctive meaning 'if' see 25.8.2; for *como* meaning 'as' (i.e. 'seeing that') see 33.5.2.

(c) *Cual si* (literary: see 24.3.1), *como si* 'as if', and *sin que* 'without' always take the subjunctive (but for *como si* = 'just as if'/'it's just the same as when', see note (ii)):

Me miró como si no me viera/viese	(S)he looked at me as if (s)he couldn't see me
Las trató con gran familiaridad, como si las viera todos los días (C. Fuentes, Mex.)	He treated them very familiarly, just as if he saw them every day
Debes hacerlo sin que yo tenga que decírtelo	You must do it without my having to tell you

(i) *Comme si* takes the indicative in French: *comme si elle avait quinze ans* = *como si **tuviera** quince años* 'as if she was fifteen years old'.

(ii) *Hacer como si* 'to act as if' and *ser como si* 'to be as if...' take the indicative when *como si* means the same as *como cuando...* '...the same as when...': *hicieron como si no se enteraban* (S. Puértolas, Sp.) 'they acted as if they didn't understand', *es como si/como cuando no puedes respirar y te asustas* 'it's the same as when you can't breathe and you get scared', *el niño pasa de todo, como si le llevo a una manifestación en favor del divorcio o contra los bocadillos de calamares* (M. Vázquez Montalbán, Sp., dialogue) 'my little boy doesn't worry about a thing: it's the same whether I take him on a demonstration in support of divorce or against squid sandwiches'.

Como si... is also found colloquially in Spain with the indicative to mean 'even if': —*No iré hasta las ocho.* —*Como si no vienes, a mí me da igual* (Spain, colloquial) '"I won't come until eight o'clock." "Even if you don't come it's the same to me"'.

(iii) *Tan...como que...* 'such...as that...' takes the subjunctive: *dos héroes como nosotros no pueden retroceder por cosas tan sin importancia como que le coma a uno un gigante* (children's story book, Sp.) 'two heroes like us can't turn back because of such unimportant things as being eaten by a giant' (lit. 'as that a giant eats one').

(iv) *Como que*, which can also means 'as if', takes the indicative: *últimamente lo he venido notando preocupado, como que desea comunicarme algo* (J. J. Arreola, Mex., dialogue) 'lately I've been noticing that he's preoccupied, as if he wanted to tell me something'.

16.12.6 Subjunctive with subordinators of possibility (words meaning 'perhaps' are discussed at 16.3.2.)

En caso de que and *en el caso de que* call for the subjunctive:

En caso de que no esté, llámame	If (s)he's not in call me
Esperaremos dos minutos para darle tiempo de ponerse cómodo, en el caso de que se esté usted duchando (A. Bryce Echenique, Pe.)	We'll wait two minutes for you to make yourself comfortable if it should happen that you're having a shower
Las puse en la maleta en caso de que las necesitaras/necesitases	I put them in the suitcase in case you needed them

But *por si* usually (but not invariably) takes the indicative, although *por si **acaso*** may take either mood, the subjunctive making the possibility less likely:

Llévate el paraguas por si (acaso) lluveve/lloviera/lloviese	Take the umbrella in case it rains
Siempre estaba haciendo favores a la gente por si acaso a alguien se le ocurría devolvérselos (S. Puértolas, Sp.)	She was always doing people favo(u)rs in case someone thought of repaying them
Está apuntando hacia la otra acera, por si hay un ataque por retaguardia (J. Ibargüengoitia, Mex., dialogue)	He's aiming at the other pavement/ sidewalk in case there's an attack from the rear
Por si fuera poco... (set phrase)	As if that wasn't enough...
Conviene que vayas enterado por si alguien te pidiera una aclaración (E. Mendoza, Sp., or *pidiese*)	It would be best if you were informed (lit 'went informed') in case anyone asks you for an explanation

Suponiendo que 'supposing that' requires the subjunctive: *suponiendo que **venga**, ¿le/lo vas a dejar entrar?* 'supposing he comes, are you going to let him in?'

16.12.7 Subjunctive with subordinators of time

These include such words and phrases as the following:

a medida que/según/ conforme as	*después (de) que* after	*mientras que* as long as
antes (de) que before	*en cuanto/nada más/apenas/ tan pronto como/una vez que/nomás que* (Lat. Am.) as soon as	*siempre que* every time
cuando when		
desde que since	*hasta que* until	

After subordinators of time the subordinate verb is in the subjunctive when its action is or was still in the future. Students of French and Italian must not use the future tense after these subordinators: compare *je lui donnerai son livre quand il **arrivera**, gli darò il suo livro quando **arriverà** and le daré su libro cuando **llegue** 'I'll give him his book when he arrives':

Llegamos antes de que empezara/empezase a nevar (for *antes de que* see note ii)	We arrived before it started snowing
No sea muy dura con su empleada, después que se haya tranquilizado (S. Vodanovic, Ch., dialogue. Spain *después de que...*)	Don't be very hard on your maid after she's calmed down (or 'after you've calmed down')
Me saludará cuando llegue	(S)he'll greet me when I arrive/(s)he arrives
Me saluda cuando llega	(S)he greets me when (s)he arrives (habitual)
Tú conoces a mi prima. Cuando venga le diré que te lo cuente (A. Arrafut, Cu., dialogue)	You know my cousin. When she comes I'll tell her to tell you about it
Iban a cenar cuando llegaran/llegasen los demás	They were going to have supper when the rest arrived (i.e. they had not yet arrived)
Las ideas se irán haciendo más y más claras en la medida en que nos aventuremos más y más por la senda que iremos construyendo (El País, sp.)	The ideas will get progressively clearer as we venture further along the path we will be building
Me doy cuenta, a medida que Rosita pasa mis notas a máquina, de que he reunido cerca de doscientas páginas (C. Fuentes, Mex.)	I realize, as Rosita types out my notes, that I've assembled more than 200 sheets of paper
tan pronto como acabe la huelga...	as soon as the strike is over...
tan pronto como acabó la huelga...	as soon as the strike was over...

En cuanto pueda me compraré un reloj (M. Benedetti, Ur., dialogue)	As soon as I can, I'll buy a watch
Nomás que oscurezca te vas por la carretera (J. Ibargüengoitia, Mex., dialogue; Sp. *en cuanto oscurezca*....For *nomás* see 23.2.5)	As soon as it gets dark you go down the road
Apenas pueda, te llamo (J. Asís, Arg. *Apenas* is discussed more fully at 23.5.7. See also note i)	As soon as I can, I'll ring you
Hasta que no llegue a ser ministro no se quedará contento	He won't be satisfied until he becomes a Minister
Hasta que no llegó a ser ministro no se quedó contento	He wasn't satisfied until he became a Minister
Siempre que la vea se lo diré	I'll tell her every time I see her

(i) Of these subordinators of time, only *antes de, después de, hasta* and *nada más* (and in Latin America *nomás*) can take an infinitive construction when the subjects of both verbs are identical: *me fui después de comer* 'I went after I had eaten', *hazlo antes de acostarte* 'do it before you go to bed', *trabajó hasta no poder más* '(s)he worked until (s)he could work no longer', *la llamaré nada más llegar a casa* 'I'll call her as soon as I get home'. In the case of *nada más*, the subjects do not need to be identical: *salí nada más entrar ella* 'I left as soon as she came in'. *Apenas* is heard with the infinitive in very informal speech when the subjects are identical, although this is stigmatized: ?*lo hice apenas llegar a casa* (good Spanish *lo hice apenas llegué a casa*) 'I did it as soon as I got home'. The rest allow only a finite verb, indicative or subjunctive according to the rule given.

(ii) *Antes de que* is always followed by the subjunctive because it must refer to a future event. Both *antes de que* and *antes que* are correct, the former being more common in Spain. *Antes que* also means 'rather than' and must not be confused with *antes (de) que* 'before': *cualquier cosa antes que casarse* 'anything rather than get married'.

(iii) *Después (de) que* 'after' and similar phrases, e.g. *a los pocos días de que*, 'a few days after', *desde que* 'since', *luego de que* 'after', always take the subjunctive when they refer to an action still in the future. If they refer to a past action they should logically take the indicative, but in written Spanish the *-ra* and *-se* forms are quite common: see 14.10.3. *Después que* for *después de que* is quite common in Latin America.

(iv) *Mientras* 'as long as'/'while' is variable with respect to the subjunctive. When it means 'on condition that'/'provided that', the subjunctive is obligatory: *no irá a la cárcel mientras no robe* '(s)he won't go to prison provided/as long as (s)he doesn't steal anything'. When it refers to simultaneous events in the past or the present, or to habitual events, the indicative is used: *ayer me arreglé el abrigo mientras oía la radio* 'yesterday I mended my coat while I listened to the radio', *siempre pongo la televisión mientras como* 'I always switch the television on while I eat'. When it refers to simultaneous actions in the future the subjunctive or indicative can be used: *mañana puedes hacer la comida mientras yo arreglo/arregle la casa* 'tomorrow you can do the cooking while I tidy the house'.

In all the above contexts *mientras que* may be heard instead of *mientras*, but students are advised to use *mientras* alone (see Seco, 1998, 296). However, when contrast is implied (i.e. when it means 'on the other hand'), the *que* is usual: *él es inaguantable mientras que ella es muy simpática* 'he's unbearable while she's very nice'.

(v) *Nada más* is followed by an indicative when it means *sólo*: *sólo/nada más voy un momento a comprar el periódico* 'I'm just going out for a moment to buy a newspaper'.

16.12.8 Subjunctive with subordinators of condition and exception

They all take the subjunctive. (For *si* 'if' and *como* when it means 'if' see 25.8.1 and 25.8.2.) Those that include the word *de*, e.g. *con tal de…*, are used with the infinitive when the subject of both verbs is identical, as explained at 16.12.2, e.g. *me lo llevaré a condición de no tener que leerlo* 'I'll take it on condition that I don't have to read it'.

(**a**) Condition: the following mean 'provided that', 'on condition that':

con tal (de) que	*a condición de que*	*a cambio de que*
siempre que (also	*con la condición de que*	(also 'in return for')
'whenever'. See 16.13.6 ii)	*bajo (la) condición de que*	
siempre y cuando (emphatic)		

El Gobierno está dispuesto a negociar siempre que/siempre y cuando/con tal (de) que/a condición de que sean razonables	The Government is ready to negotiate provided they are reasonable
…sin la condición previa de que se anule el contrato… (*El País*, Sp.)	…without the precondition that the contract should be cancelled…
…siempre que su muerte se debiera a causas naturales (L. Sepúlveda, Ch., dialogue)	…provided his death was due to natural causes
Añadió cincuenta mil pesetas a la minuta a cambio de que yo hiciera esta llamada telefónica (M. Vázquez Montalbán, Sp.)	He added fifty thousand pesetas to my professional fees in return for my making this telephone call

(**b**) Exception (occasionally followed by the indicative in the cases discussed in note i). The infinitive cannot be used with these subordinators:

a no ser que unless	*a menos que* unless	*como no (sea que)* unless
salvo que unless/save that	*fuera de que* (less common)	(in suggestions)
excepto que unless/except	unless	*como no fuera que*
that		unless

Me casaré contigo a no ser que/salvo que/como no sea que/a menos que hayas cambiado de idea	I'll marry you unless you've changed your mind
Íbamos de vacaciones en agosto salvo/a no ser que/como no fuera que yo estuviera/estuviese muy ocupado	We took our holidays/vacation in August unless I was very busy
No sé qué sugerir. Como no (sea que) vayamos al teatro…	I don't know what to suggest, unless we go to the theatre

Excepto/salvo que and *con la salvedad de que* are followed by the indicative when they mean 'except for the fact that' : *ella hablaba mejor, excepto que/salvo que/con la salvedad de que pronunciaba mal las eñes* 'she spoke better/best, except (for the fact) that she pronounced the *eñes* badly'.

16.12.9 Subjunctive with subordinators of concession

There are several ways of saying 'although', of which *aunque* is the most common:

aunque	siquiera	si bien
así	aun cuando	y eso que

Words meaning 'despite the fact that' have a similar meaning:

| a pesar de que | pese a que (literary) | a despecho de que (literary) |

With the exception of *si bien que* and *y eso que*, which are always used with the indicative (see 33.6), these require the subjunctive if they point to an event which is or was still in the future. *Así* always requires the subjunctive when it means 'although'. Those that contain the word *de* may be constructed with an infinitive in the circumstances described at 16.12.2:

Es un valiente, no lo confesará así/aunque le maten	He's a brave man, he won't admit it even if they kill him
No lo confesó aunque le ofrecieron dinero	(S)he didn't confess although they offered him/her money
No lo confesaría aunque le/lo mataran/matasen	(S)he wouldn't confess it even if they killed him
A estas alturas de la campaña nadie aguanta un rollo de estos así le den veinte duros (M. Delibes, Sp., dialogue)	At this stage in the [election] campaign no one's going to put up with a lot of old nonsense like that even if they give them 100 pesetas
. . .tienen que cumplir, así caminen bajo la lluvia (La Jornada, Mex.)	They have to fulfil/US fulfill their mission, even if they walk in the rain
Vendieron la finca, a pesar de que el abuelo se oponía	They sold the estate, despite the fact that grandfather opposed it
¿A pesar de que tus padres se opongan? (A. Buero Vallejo, Sp., dialogue)	Even though your parents will/may be against it?
...pese a que muchos de quienes iniciaron la tarea ya no están ahora (Abc Color, Par.)	...despite the fact that many who began the task are no longer here now

(i) The subjunctive may be used with *aunque* to refer to past or habitual events. In this case it strengthens the concession, making it an equivalent to 'even though': *jamás culparé a Octavia, aunque lo haya intentado alguna vez* (A. Bryce Echenique, Pe., dialogue) 'I'll never blame Octavia, even though I may have tried to sometimes', *aunque no te gusten las películas ésta/esta te va a gustar* 'even though you don't like films you'll like this one', *aunque sea español no me gustan los toros* 'even though I'm Spanish I don't like bullfights'.

(ii) When *siquiera* is used to mean 'although' (literary style) it requires the subjunctive: *...dos fuentes independientes... a las que se aludirá, siquiera sea vagamente* (Libro de estilo de El País, Sp.) '...two independent sources, which will be mentioned, even if in vague terms'.

16.13 Translating 'whether... or', 'however', 'whatever', 'whoever', 'whichever' and 'the more... the more...'

The phrases discussed in this section are often translated by the *forma reduplicativa*, i.e. constructions in which a subjunctive verb is repeated, as in *pase lo que pase* 'whatever happens', *no hay salida para ti, hagas lo que hagas, vayas a donde vayas* (C. Fuentes, Mex., dialogue) 'there's no way out for you, whatever you do, wherever you go'. After a negative the second verb is sometimes omitted: *quieras o no (quieras)* 'whether you want to or not'.

16.13.1 'Whether... or'

The *forma reduplicativa* is used:

Lo único que tengo que hacer es informar sobre unos hechos escuetos, que son los que son, guste o disguste a unos u otros (El Mundo, Sp.)	The only thing I have to do is to inform about certain simple facts, which are what they are whether certain people like it or not
Escuchaba las conversaciones con sus amigas, repararan o no repararan en mí (S. Puértolas, Sp.)	I listened to her (lit. 'the') conversations with her women friends, whether they noticed me or not

The second verb is sometimes replaced by *hacer* or, in negative phrases, omitted altogether:

trabaje en una red, o lo haga desde un PC en casa. . . (Spanish computer manual)	whether you work on a network or from a PC at home. . .
Estuviese o no enfermo, lo cierto es que no vino al trabajo	Whether he was ill/US sick or not, the fact is he didn't come to work
Estaré de tu parte, tengas razón o no (la tengas)	I'll be on your side, whether you're right or wrong

16.13.2 'However much/little...', etc.

Por mucho que/por más que + verb, *por mucho* + noun + verb, *por (muy)* + adjective + verb. Use of the subjunctive follows the usual rule: if the event referred to is or was a reality, the indicative is used: *por mucho que/más que se lo dijo, no lo hizo* '(s)he didn't do it however much she asked him/her', but *por mucho que se lo digas, no lo hará* '(s)he won't do it however much you ask him/her'. Further examples:

Por mucho calor que haga, no abrirán la ventana (the heat is still in the future)	However hot it gets, they won't open the window
Por más que las esperanzas de Eulalia y su padre crecían, no lograban contagiar a Andrés (A. Mastretta, Mex., dialogue; real event)	However much Eulalia's and her father's hopes grew, they didn't manage to inspire (lit. 'infect') Andrés
Por más que llueva no se le van a resucitar los novillos muertos (M. Puig, Arg.)	However much it rains, his dead steers won't come back to life

(i) The subjunctive may be used even for actions that are realities; the force of the concession is then stronger: *por mucho que/más que se lo dijera, no lo hacía* 'however often (s)he told him/her, (s)he didn't do it', *en Mendoza a esa hora cae el frío, por más sol que haya habido durante el día* (M. Puig, Arg., dialogue; subjunctive, because it happens whether there was sun or not) 'the cold sets in at that time in Mendoza, however sunny it may have been during the day'.

(ii) To translate 'however it is', 'however it was', etc., either the *forma reduplicativa* is used or *como quiera que* + subjunctive, e.g. *. . .pero como quiera que sea, yo he comprado. . .una media docena por lo menos* (J. J. Arreola, Mex.) 'but however it is/but all the same, I've bought at least a half a dozen', or *. . .sea como sea. . . .*

16.13.3 'The more... the more', 'the less... the less'

Cuanto/a/os/as más. . . más and *cuanto/a/os/as menos. . . menos* are the standard formulas. The general rule is applied: if the event is a reality (i.e. has occurred or is occurring) the indicative is used:

Cuanto más comas más querrás	The more you eat the more you'll want
Cuanto más comías, más querías	The more you ate the more you wanted
Yo sabía que cuanto más bebiera/bebiese	I knew that the more I drank, the
más me emborracharía	drunker I would get
Cuanto menos digas, menos se inquietarán	The less you say, the less they'll worry

For the use of *mientras* instead of *cuanto* in this construction, and, in parts of Latin America (e.g. Mexico), of *entre*, instead of *cuanto*, see 5.11.

16.13.4 'Whatever'

The *forma reduplicativa* is normally used:

digan lo que digan	whatever they say
hagas lo que hagas	whatever you do
Den lo que den, siempre vamos al	Whatever's on (lit. 'whatever they
Metropolitan (E. Poniatowska,	give'), we always go to the
Mex., dialogue)	Metropolitan cinema
Cómpralo sea como sea	'Buy it whatever it looks like' or 'buy it
	whatever the cost'
Dijo que lo compraría fuera como	(S)he said she'd buy it whatever it was
fuera/fuese como fuese	like

Comoquiera que sea and *comoquiera que fuera* could be used in the last two examples, but they are less usual. *Como quiera* is a less frequently seen alternative spelling.

Lo que + the subjunctive may also be used in some contexts:

Aquella novela o lo que quiera que fuese era	That novel, or whatever it was, was
muy difícilmente publicable (J. Marías, Sp.)	very unlikely to be publishable
...por temor, por pereza o por lo que sea...	...because of fear, laziness, or
(S. Puértolas, Sp.)	whatever...

(i) The English 'whatever' may mean 'whichever', in which case it is best translated by an appropriate tense of *sea cual sea*.... This construction is preferred in written and spoken language to the rather stilted *cualquiera que* and *comoquiera que*: *las camelias, cualquiera que/sea cual sea su color, son bonitas* 'camellias are pretty whatever their colo(u)r'. (For a general discussion of *cualquiera* see 9.8.)

(ii) When 'whatever' means 'everything' it will usually be translated by *todo lo que* or *cuanto*: *trae todo lo que puedas* 'bring whatever/everything you can', *aprenderé todo lo que/cuanto pueda* 'I'll learn whatever/everything I can'.

16.13.5 'Whichever'

When this word means 'which', 'whichever one' or 'the one that' it is usually translated by *que* or *el que* + subjunctive (for more details on the subjunctive in relative clauses, see 16.14):

Escoge la maceta que más te guste	Choose whichever flowerpot you like most
—¿Cuál me llevo? —El que usted quiera	'Which should I take?' 'Whichever (one) you like'

16.13.6 'Whenever'

Cuando with the subjunctive when the event referred to is or was still in the future, and the indicative in all other cases:

Vienen cuando quieren	They come whenever they like
Vendrán cuando quieran	They'll come whenever they like
Dijeron que vendrían cuando quisieran/quisiesen	They said they'd come when they wanted to

(i) *Cuando quiera que* is old-fashioned for *cuando*, but it is used as an occasional literary alternative for *siempre que*: *...cuando quiera que en la vida española se ponen tensos los ánimos...* (R. Pérez de Ayala, Sp., quoted Seco, 1998, 139) '...whenever passions are stirred in Spanish life...'.

(ii) *Siempre que*, as well as meaning 'provided that' (see 16.12.8) may also mean 'whenever'; *cada vez que* can also mean the same thing: *yo la saludaba siempre que/cada vez que la veía* 'I said hello to her whenever I saw her'. However, when used with the subjunctive *siempre que* is assumed to mean 'provided that', so an alternative should be used for 'whenever': *no se te olvide saludarla cada vez que la veas* (future reference) 'don't forget to say hello to her whenever you see her'.

16.13.7 'Anyone who...', 'whoever...'

Cualquiera que 'anyone who...' cannot be replaced by the *forma reduplicativa*:

Cualquiera que te vea pensará que vas a una fiesta	Anyone who sees you will think you're going to a party

If 'anyone who...' means 'those who...', 'people who...', a nominalizer (*el/la/los/las que* or *quien/quienes*) with the subjunctive is used: *el que/quien se crea eso está loco* 'anyone who believes that is mad'. *Quienquiera...* is also found. Seco (1998), 378, says that it is exclusively literary in Spain, but the following example suggests that it survives colloquially elsewhere: *quienquiera se crea eso está loco* (G. Cabrera Infante, Cu., dialogue; Spain *el que crea...* or *quien crea...*).

However, *quienquiera que sea* 'whoever it is' seems to alternate freely with the *forma reduplicativa*: *no abras la puerta, sea quien sea/quienquiera que sea* 'don't open the door whoever it is', *íntimo amigo del Jefe del Gobierno, fuera el que fuese* (M. Vázquez Montalbán, Sp., or *quienquiera que fuera/fuese*) 'a close friend of the Prime Minister, whoever he happened to be'.

16.13.8 'Wherever'

Dondequiera or *forma reduplicativa*:

Dondequiera que voy/Vaya donde vaya me lo encuentro	Wherever I go I meet him
Dondequiera que vaya/Vaya donde vaya me lo encontraré	Wherever I go I'll meet him
Dondequiera que fuese/Fuese donde fuese, me lo encontraba (or *fuera...*)	Wherever I went I met him
Estés donde estés, busca un teléfono público (L. Sepúlveda, Ch., dialogue)	Wherever you are, look for a public phone

(i) The *que* is sometimes omitted, e.g. *dondequiera se encuentren* 'wherever they're found', but Seco (1998), 170, disapproves.

(ii) *Adondequiera* should be used when the meaning is 'wherever…to': *adondequiera que vayan* 'wherever they go (to)' or *vayan a donde vayan*. But *dondequiera que vayan* is common.

16.14 Subjunctive in relative clauses

In this section nominalizers like *el que* 'the one that', *quien* 'the one who', *aquellos que* 'those who' etc., are treated as relative pronouns. They are also discussed under Nominalizers at 36.1. See 16.13. for *cualquiera que, quienquiera que, cuandoquiera que, dondequiera*.

16.14.1 Subjunctive in relative clauses that refer to something not yet identified

Spanish uses the subjunctive in these cases to express a nuance that English usually ignores. Compare *los que digan eso* 'those who say that' (if anyone does) and *los que dicen eso* 'those who say that' (some do). The difference in Spanish is clear: contrast *me voy a casar con una mujer que tiene mucho dinero* 'I'm getting married to a woman who has a lot of money' (you've already met her) and *…que tenga mucho dinero* (you're still looking for her); *busco un médico que sepa acupuntura* (n.b. no personal *a*) 'I'm looking for a doctor (i.e. 'any doctor') who knows acupuncture', *conozco a un médico que sabe acupuntura* 'I know a doctor who knows acupuncture'. Further examples:

Haz lo que quieras	Do whatever you like
Necesitamos a alguien que esté en el local	We need somebody who'll be on the spot
Cualquier reacción que uno pueda tener suena a sobreactuado (C. Rico-Godoy, Sp.)	Any reaction one might have sounds like overacting/sounds overdone
Me pregunto si hay alguien en el mundo a quien no le haya ocurrido lo mismo (J. Marías, Sp.)	I wonder if there is anyone in the world to whom the same thing hasn't occurred (i.e. 'hasn't had the same thought')
¿Sabes de alguien que tenga apellido en este país? (E. Sábato, Arg., dialogue)	Do you know anyone in this country who has a surname (i.e. a famous name)?
Dígame qué tienen que esté muy sabroso (J. Ibargüengoitia, Mex., dialogue)	Tell me what you've got that tastes really good

NB: French uses the subjunctive in similar circumstances: *quiere comprar una casa que tenga piscina* = *il/elle veut acheter une maison qui **ait** une piscine*.

In literary styles, the subjunctive is common in relative clauses when the main clause is introduced by *como* 'like' or *como si fuera/fuese* 'as if it were…': *…como un ángel que perdiera/perdiese las alas* '…like an angel that had lost its wings', *el sol se pone súbitamente—como si fuera un interruptor que lo apagara* (J. Marías, Sp.) 'the sun sets suddenly—as if a switch had turned it off'.

16.14.2 Subjunctive in relative clauses that refer to non-existent things

If the relative clause refers to something that does not exist, the subjunctive must be used:

No hay nadie que sepa tocar más de un violín
 a la vez

There is no one who can play more
 than one violin at the same time

Jamás la oí hablar de algo que mereciera la
 pena (S. Puértolas, Sp., dialogue)

I never heard her talk about anything
 worthwhile

No hay quien le entienda

There's no one who can understand
 him/her

En realidad no existen culturas
 "dependientes" y emancipadas ni nada
 que se les parezca (M. Vargas Llosa, Pe.)

In reality there are no 'dependent' and
 emancipated cultures or anything
 like them

¿A quiénes conoces que se vean feas
 esperando un hijo? (A. Mastretta, Mex.,
 dialogue; *se vean = estén* in Spain)

What women do you know who look
 ugly when they're expecting a baby?

NB: The rule is similar in French: *il n'y a personne qui puisse = no hay nadie que pueda.*

16.14.3 Subjunctive in relative clauses when the main verb is in the future tense

The subjunctive is used in relative clauses when the main clause refers to the future:

Seré yo el que tenga que solucionar mis
 propios problemas (cf. *soy yo el que
 tengo/tiene que solucionar…*)

I'll be the one who has to solve my
 own problems

No será hasta el primer Consejo de Ministros
 cuando el Gobierno apruebe el proyecto de
 ley (*La Vanguardia*, Sp.; for the use of
 cuando here see 36.2.3b)

It won't be until the first Council of
 Ministers (Brit. 'Cabinet meeting')
 that the Government will approve
 the draft law

Pero serán las investigaciones las que
 determinen qué fue lo que sucedió
 (*El Diario de Hoy*, El Salvador)

But the police investigation will
 discover what happened

16.14.4 Subjunctive after the relatives *donde* and *cuanto* (for *dondequiera que* see 16.13.8)

The subjunctive is used if the reference is to a yet unknown or to a non-existent entity:

Comeré en el pueblo donde me pare

I'll eat in whichever village I stop in

Comí en el pueblo donde me paré

I ate in the village where I stopped

Buscó una zona donde el mar llegara
 debilitado (M. Vázquez Montalbán, Sp.)

(S)he looked for an area where the sea
 was coming in with less force

Te daré cuanto/todo lo que me pidas

I'll give you anything you ask

Le di (todo) cuanto/todo lo que me pidió

I gave her/him everything (s)he asked

16.14.5 Subjunctive in relative clauses after superlative expressions

The subjunctive may appear in literary styles in relative clauses following superlative statements, but it is unusual in everyday written or spoken language:

El mayor incendio que jamás se ha/haya visto

The greatest fire ever seen

La mayor transacción con divisas fuertes que
 se haya hecho en el Río de la Plata
 (E. Sábato, Arg.)

The largest hard-currency transaction
 ever made in the River Plate region

…y el aburrimiento general más importante
 que haya presenciado en mi vida
 (A. Bryce Echenique, Pe.)

…and the greatest general boredom
 I've ever witnessed in my life

Compare these less literary examples:

*Eres la chica más simpática que **he** conocido*	You're the most likeable girl I've ever met
Yo debía ser el extranjero más inteligente que madame Forestier había visto en su vida (A. Bryce Echenique, Pe.)	I must have been the most intelligent foreigner Madame Forestier had seen in her life
Dijo que era la mayor barbaridad que a nadie se le había ocurrido (or *hubiera/hubiese*)	(S)he said it was the greatest stupidity anybody had ever thought of

The indicative is normal in affirmative sentences after words like 'first', 'only': *es la primera vez que se habla de esto* 'it's the first time people have talked about this', *es la única película que ha hecho* 'it's the only film (s)he's made'. French uses the subjunctive in these cases and after superlative statements in general.

16.15 Subjunctive in main clauses

The subjunctive is primarily a feature of subordinate clauses, but it may appear in a main clause in certain circumstances.

16.15.1 Subjunctive with the imperative

(a) The subjunctive is used to form all negative imperatives: *no me hables* 'don't talk to me', *no se vayan ustedes* 'don't go away'.

(b) The subjunctive is used for affirmative imperatives with the pronouns *usted* and *ustedes*: *guarden silencio* 'keep quiet', *váyase* 'go away'.

(c) The subjunctive is used to form first- and third-person imperatives, e.g. *sentémonos* 'let's sit down', *que entre* 'let him/her come in'.

The imperative is discussed in detail in Chapter 17.

16.15.2 Subjunctive to express wishes

The verb is usually preceded by *ojalá*, *quién* or simply by *que*—the latter is omitted in some set phrases. *Así*, used jokingly, parodies a typical gypsy curse and is frequently heard in colloquial language, at least in Spain:

¡Ojalá nos toque la lotería!	Let's hope we win the lottery!
Ojalá se le queme el arroz (A. Arrafut, Cu., dialogue)	I hope her rice burns
...y pensé quién fuera escritor... (A. Bryce Echenique, Pe.)	...and I thought: if only I were a writer...

NB: *Quién* in this construction should not be confused with the word meaning 'who'.

¡Que no se vaya! —pensaba —¡que no eche a volar! (A. Mastretta, Mex., dialogue)	'Please don't let him leave!' I thought, 'don't let him fly away!'
Bendita seas, cuñada... (A. Mastretta, Mex., dialogue)	God bless you, sister-in-law...
¡Dios se lo pague!	May God repay you!
¡Así se te pegue mi catarro!	I hope you get my cold!

There is a less common expression with the same meaning as *ojalá*: *fueran* (or *así/ya fueran) como tú todas las mujeres...* 'if only all women were like you...'.

16.15.3 Subjunctive in some common set phrases

(**a**) *O sea que* 'in other words':

Ha dicho que tiene que trabajar, o sea que no quiere venir	(S)he said (s)he had to work, in other words (s)he doesn't want to come

(**b**) In the phrases *que... sepa/que. . .recuerde*:

Que yo recuerde es la primera vez que le/lo veo	As far as I remember it's the first time I've seen him
Nada que yo sepa (J. Madrid, Sp.)	Nothing, as far as I know
Que se sepa nadie lo ha hecho antes	As far as anybody knows, it hasn't been done before

(**c**) In a few other set phrases:

¡Acabáramos!	Now I see what you're getting at!
Otro gallo nos cantara si le hubiéramos/hubiésemos hecho caso	It would have been another story if we had listened to him/her
¡Cómo tiras el dinero! Ni que fueras millonario. . .	The way you throw money around anyone would think you're a millionaire...
¡Vaya tontería!	What nonsense!

16.16 Tense agreement: subjunctive

Despite the claims of many traditional grammars, there are no rigid rules of tense agreement between main and subordinate clauses, but the following patterns are the most usual combinations:

(a) Main clause in Present Indicative Tense
(1) Present subjunctive: *me gusta que hable* 'I like her/him to talk', *quiero que dejes de fumar* 'I want you to stop smoking'.
(2) Perfect subjunctive: *me encanta que hayas venido* 'I'm really glad you've come'.
(3) Imperfect subjunctive (see note i): *es imposible que lo dijera/dijese* 'it's impossible that he said it'.

(b) Main clause in Future Tense
Present subjunctive: *nos contentaremos con que terminen para finales del mes* 'we'll be content with them finishing by the end of the month', *¡jamás soportaré que mi sobrina se case con un tipo que va por el mundo vestido de profesor en vacaciones!* (A. Bryce Echenique, Pe., dialogue) 'I'll never tolerate my niece marrying a guy who goes around dressed like a teacher on vacation!'

(c) Main clause in Conditional or Conditional Perfect Tense
Imperfect subjunctive: *nos contentaríamos con que terminaran/terminasen para finales del mes* 'we'd be content with them finishing by the end of the month', *yo habría preferido que se pintara/pintase de negro* 'I'd have preferred it to be painted black'.

(d) Main clause in Perfect Tense (see note ii)
(1) Present subjunctive: *le he dicho que se siente* (A. Gala, Sp., dialogue; perfect of recency) 'I told you to sit down'.

(2) Perfect subjunctive: *ha sido un milagro que no te hayan reconocido* 'it was a miracle they didn't see you'.

(3) Imperfect subjunctive: *ha sido un milagro que no te reconocieran/reconociesen* 'it was a miracle that they didn't recognize you'.

(e) Main clause in Imperfect, Preterite or Pluperfect Tense (see notes iii and iv)

(1) Imperfect subjunctive: *La idea era que cobrarais/cobraseis los viernes* 'The idea was that you'd get paid on Fridays', *me sorprendió que fuera/fuese tan alto* 'it surprised me that he was so tall', *yo te había pedido que me prestaras/prestases cien dólares* 'I'd asked you to lend me 100 dollars'.

(2) Pluperfect subjunctive: *me sorprendía que hubiera/hubiese protestado* 'I was surprised that (s)he had protested'.

(3) Present subjunctive. This is common, especially in newspapers, when the main clause refers to the past and mentions an action that has still not taken place in the reader's or hearer's present: *el secretario de Naciones Unidas pidió ayer a Estados Unidos que no actúe unilateralmente contra Irak* (*El País*, Sp.) 'The UN secretary asked the US yesterday not to act unilaterally against Iraq'. It is also common in popular Latin-American speech where standard language requires the past subjunctive. See note (iv).

(f) Main clause in Imperative Mood

Present subjunctive: *díganles que se den prisa* 'tell them to hurry'.

(i) The combination present + imperfect or perfect subjunctive occurs when a comment is being made about a past event. There seems to be little difference between the perfect and imperfect subjunctive in this case, and occasionally the present subjunctive can also be used: *algunos niegan que Cristóbal Colón fuera/fuese/haya sido/sea el primer descubridor de América* some deny that Christopher Columbus was the first discoverer of America'.

(ii) The perfect (*ha dicho, ha ordenado*, etc.) is strictly speaking classified as a present tense for the purposes of agreement, but the imperfect subjunctive is occasionally used with it when the event in the subordinate clause is also in the past. Compare *ha dado órdenes de que nos rindamos* '(s)he's given orders for us to surrender' and *el clima que se está creando ha llevado a que se hablara de intervención del Ejército* (*Cambio16*, Sp.; also *hable*) 'the climate that is being created has led to talk of Army intervention'.

(iii) The combination past indicative + present subjunctive is optionally possible when the subordinate clause refers to a timeless or perpetual event: *Dios decretó que las serpientes no tengan/tuvieran/tuviesen patas* 'God decreed that snakes should have no legs' (*las piernas* is used only for human legs).

(iv) Use of the present when both verbs refer to the past is common in popular Latin-American speech but is unacceptable to Peninsular speakers: *el inspector aduanero le pidió a la muchacha que le muestre su casaca* (*La Prensa*, Pe.; Spain *mostrara/mostrase*. In Spain *la casaca* = 'dress coat') 'the Customs inspector asked the girl to show him her coat', *Eva abogó por Perón, pidió, clamó, imploró, para que entiendan lo que quería decirles* (A. Posse, Arg.; normally *entendieran* or *entendiesen*) 'Eva pleaded for Perón, asked, clamo(u)red, implored them [i.e. the Communists] to understand what he was trying to say to them', *logró impedir que frases como ésta destruyan mi vida* (A. Bryce Echenique, Pe.; for *destruyeran/destruyesen*) 'she managed to prevent phrases like this from destroying my life'. This construction seems to be spreading to the media in Spain and it is not unknown there in spontaneous speech, a tendency that may indicate that the imperfect subjunctive will one day become obsolete, as it has in French.

(v) After *como si* 'as if', *igual que si/lo mismo que si* 'the same as if', the verb is always in the imperfect subjunctive: *le hablaré como si yo no supiese/supiera hablar bien el castellano* 'I'll talk to him as if I didn't know how to speak Spanish well'. See also 16.12.5c for *como si*.

16.17 The future subjunctive

The future subjunctive (see 13.1.10 for its forms) is nowadays obsolete in everyday Spanish, except in a few literary variants of set phrases such as *sea lo que fuere* (more usually *sea lo que sea*) 'whatever it may be', *venga lo que viniere* (usually *venga lo que venga*) 'come what may': the present or imperfect subjunctive is used instead. But it is still used in legal jargon and official documents:

> *APUESTA: Contrato bilateral en el que se acuerda que el que **acertare** un pronóstico o **tuviere** razón en una disputa recibirá del perdedor lo pactado* (legal dictionary)

> 'BET': A bilateral contract whereby it is agreed that a person who makes an accurate forecast or wins an argument shall receive an agreed sum from the loser

It occasionally appears in flowery language to indicate a very remote possibility:

> *...lo cual ofrece amplísimas ventajas en la extracción del motor o en reparaciones, caso de que las hubiere* (advert., Sp., *hubiera/hubiese* more normal).

> ...which offers very wide advantages when removing the engine or in repair work—should such a thing ever arise

It is also quite common in Latin-American newspapers in some regions:

> *Sólo la aplicación de un plan de estrictas medidas, aun cuando éstas resultaren antipopulares, permitirá salir de la actual situación* (La Nación, Arg.)

> Only the application of a plan of strict measures, even if these were unpopular, would allow us to get out of the present situation

Kany, 225, notes examples in written usage from nine republics.

17

The imperative

The main points discussed in this chapter are:

- The *tú, vos, vosotros/as* and *usted(es)* imperative (Sections 17.2.2–5)
- The imperative of *estar* (Section 17.2.6)
- How to form negative imperatives (*no lo hagas*, etc.) (Section 17.3)
- The position of pronouns with the imperative (Section 17.4)
- First-person plural imperative ('let's go', 'let's sit down', etc.) (Section 17.5)
- Third-person imperatives ('let her come in', 'let them go', etc.) (Section 17.6)
- Impersonal imperatives (*véase, escríbase*, etc.) (Section 17.8)
- Use of the infinitive as an imperative (*empujar, tirar*, etc.) (Section 17.9)
- Present tense used as an imperative (Section 17.10)
- Making imperatives more mellow (Section 17.11)

17.1 General remarks

The imperative is used to give orders or to make requests. As in English, a simple imperative, e.g. *hazlo* 'do it', can sound rude or abrupt, so intonation and attitude are important. In Spanish a friendly manner counts for much more than the constant repetition of *por favor* or *haga el favor* 'please', which, like *gracias*, English-speakers constantly over-use. In Spain, *por favor* is strictly speaking used when asking a favo(u)r, and since barmen, waiters or salespersons are simply doing their job, *por favor* is not really necessary. However, *por favor* seems nowadays to be heard more often than before, especially in Mexico, where everyday language is very polite.

Other points to watch are: **(a)** all negative imperatives (e.g. 'don't do', 'don't say') are formed with the subjunctive: *vete* 'go away', *no te vayas* 'don't go away'; **(b)** for Latin Americans there is no *vosotros* imperative: *ustedes* + the subjunctive is used for both strangers and friends, and even for children and animals.

17.2 Affirmative forms of the imperative

For negative imperatives ('don't do', 'don't say', etc.) see 17.3.

17.2.1 General

As in English, addition of a subject pronoun to an imperative can make an order emphatic and brusque:

¡***Tú** bájate de ahí!*/*Usted bájese*   You get down from there!
¡***Vosotros** callaos!* (familiar *callaros*;   You shut up!
    Lat. Am. *ustedes cállense*)

However, *usted* may be added after an imperative to reinforce the politeness: *venga usted a las ocho* 'come at eight o'clock'.

(i) Spoken Mexican often adds *le* to certain common imperatives, e.g. *aváncenle* 'move on', *pásenle* 'come in', *ándale* 'wow!'

17.2.2 The *tú* imperative

The familiar singular imperative (*tú* form) is, with eight exceptions, formed by removing the *-s* of the second-person singular of the present indicative: *llamas* > *llama, lees* > *lee*. The exceptions are:

decir to say: *di*	*poner* to put: *pon*	*venir* to come: *ven*
hacer to do/make: *haz*	*salir* to leave/go out: *sal*	
ir to go: *ve* (*vete* = 'go away')	*ser* to be: *sé*	
	tener to have: *ten*	

Anda, sé bueno y márchate (J. Madrid, Sp.)	Come on, be good and go away
Ven a tomar el café cuando quieras	Come and have coffee whenever you want
—Vete —le dijo—. Vete, antes de que te cobre el dinero que me debes (A. Mastretta, Mex., dialogue)	'Go away,' she told him. 'Go away before I take back the money you owe me'

(i) The *tú* imperative of *haber* is theoretically *he*, but it is never used. As Seco (1998), 243, points out, the nowadays rather stilted literary expression *he aquí*, 'here is…'/'what follows is…' (French *voici*…) is not the imperative of *haber*: *he aquí un resultado cuidadosamente escondido* (*El País*, Ur.) 'this is a carefully concealed result'.

17.2.3 The *vos* imperative

The imperative form corresponding to *vos* (Argentina, Uruguay and also Central America) can usually be found by removing the *-r* from the infinitive; the final vowel is therefore usually stressed: *tener* > *tené, contar* > *contá, decir* > *decí*. Pronominal verbs take the pronoun *te*, so the imperative of *lavarse* is *lavate* (the standard form is *lávate*). Further examples, all from Argentina; the *tú* form is included for comparison. Stressed vowels are shown in bold:

Decile que pase (= *dile que pase*)	Tell him to come in
Vení cuando puedas (= *ven cuando puedas*. See 16.2.8 for *vení cuando podás*)	Come when you can
Levantate (= *levántate*)	Get up
Oíme, Pozzi (M. Puig, Arg.; = *óyeme*)	Listen, Pozzi
Escuchá esto (ibid.; = *escucha*)	Listen to this

17.2.4 The *vosotros* imperative

The European Spanish *vosotros*/*vosotras* imperative (used to address friends, relatives, children, animals) is formed by replacing the *-r* of the infinitive by *-d*. There are no exceptions:

ser to be: *sed*	*tener* to have: *tened*	*cantar* to sing: *cantad*
ir to go: *id*	*venir* to come: *venid*	

The *-d* is dropped in the pronominal ('reflexive') form: *dad + os = daos* as in *daos la mano* 'shake hands', *lavad + os = lavaos*: *lavaos el pelo* 'wash your hair'. There is one exception: *id + os = idos* 'go away!' from *irse*, although in everyday speech *iros* is nowadays much more usual.

(i) Latin-American language uses *ustedes* where Peninsular Spanish uses *vosotros/as*.

(ii) In informal speech in Spain this imperative is often expressed by the infinitive: *venid = venir*, *id = ir*, *daos = daros*, *veníos = veniros*, *lavaos las manos* 'wash your hands' = *lavaros las manos*, etc. Although it apparently has a long history, this construction is considered slovenly by some speakers. Example: *tener* (for *tened*) *cuidado con Socorro que ya se ha cargado tres matrimonios* (E. Arenas, Sp., dialogue) 'watch out for Socorro—she's already messed up three marriages'.

Formal and written styles require the forms in *–d*. For further remarks on the use of the infinitive as an imperative, see 17.9.

17.2.5 The *usted/ustedes* imperative

The pronouns *usted* and *ustedes* have no independent imperative forms: they use the third-person singular or plural present subjunctive endings respectively: *dígame* 'tell me', *tenga* 'take' / 'have', *empiecen* 'begin', *díganme (ustedes)*, 'tell (plural) me', etc. *Ustedes* forms are used for both polite and informal address in Latin America: Latin Americans address children and even animals as *ustedes*, which sounds strange to Spaniards. *Vosotros* forms of the verb are unfamiliar to most Latin Americans:

Vaya a descansar. Preséntese aquí a las 11 (M. Vázquez Montalbán, Sp.)	Go and rest. Be here at 11 o'clock
¡Ayúdeme, doctora! (M. Vargas Llosa, Pe.)	Help me, doctor!
Perdone si parezco impertinente (L. Ortiz, Sp.)	Excuse me if I seem impertinent

For the position of the pronouns and the popular Latin-American form *?siénte(n)sen*, see 17.4.

17.2.6 The imperative of *estar*

For the affirmative imperative of *estar* 'to be' the pronominal (i.e. 'reflexive') form is frequently (but not exclusively) used: *estate quieto* 'be still/'stop fidgeting', *estense listas para las ocho* 'be ready by eight'. This is more common with the *tú* imperative because the non-pronominal form is easily confused with the third-person present singular, *está*:

No esté tan segura de que era un miedo distinto (C. Martín Gaite, Sp., dialogue)	Don't be so sure that it was a different fear
—Esté tranquila —le dijo . . .si se mueve le va mal, así que estese tranquila (G. García Márquez, Col., dialogue)	'Keep calm', he told her. . . 'if you move it'll go badly for you, so keep calm'

But the pronominal construction is not universal: the following example would have been expressed *estate lista* in Spain: —*Paso a cambiarme como a las ocho. Por favor, está lista* (C. Fuentes, Mex., dialogue) 'I'll be home around eight to get changed. Please be ready'.

NB: Should one write *estate* or *estáte*, *estese*/*estense* or *estése*/*esténse*? Both forms are seen in print, and the Academy does not seem to have pronounced clearly on the matter, although the *GDLE* writes *estáte*. We use the unaccented forms on the grounds that the accent is unnecessary: one does not write **deténlo* for *detenlo* 'arrest him', even though the form without a pronoun is *detén*.

17.3 Negative forms of the imperative

To express a negative imperative, the present subjunctive must be used:

Affirmative imperative		**Negative imperative**	
canta	sing	*no cantes*	don't sing
vete	go away	*no te vayas*	don't go away
(usted) levántese	stand up	*no se levante*	don't stand up
(vosotros) sentaos	sit down	*no os sentéis*	don't sit down
(ustedes) dénselo	give it to him/ her/them	*no se lo den*	don't give it to him/ her/them

No vuelvas antes de las 9 (I. Grasa, Sp.)   Don't come back before 9
Oye, no lo tomes a mal, sobrino (M. Vargas   Listen, nephew, don't get me wrong
  Llosa, Pe., dialogue)

(i) The Argentine *vos* forms obey the same rules, and foreign students should use the standard subjunctive forms with them for the reasons explained at 16.2.8: *levantate* > *no te levantes* (*no te levantés* is a shade too popular for some Argentines).

(ii) Affirmative forms of the imperative are occasionally used in the negative in popular speech in Spain, e.g. ?*no rechistad* 'don't answer back!' for *no rechistéis*. This should not be imitated.

17.4 Position of object pronouns with the imperative

When an imperative form is used with an object pronoun, the following rules apply:

(a) If the imperative is affirmative, the pronouns are attached to the verb in the normal order (shown at 11.12):

(Tú) dame la mano	Hold my hand
(Tú) ponte la chaqueta (Arg., [*vos*] *ponete el saco*)	Put your jacket on
(Usted) démelo	Give it to me
(Vosotros/as) dádmelo	Give it to me
(Vosotros) despertaos (colloquial *despertaros*; see 17.2.4)	Wake up
(Ustedes) dénnoslo	Give it to us
Dime lo que sea, venga (C. Martín Gaite, Spain, dialogue)	Tell me, whatever it is. Come on
Déjamelo ver, déjamelo ver (A. Mastretta, Mex., dialogue; or *déjame verlo*)	Let me see it, let me see it

(b) If the imperative is negative, the pronouns precede it in the normal way, as shown at 11.12:

No me des la lata (tú)	Stop pestering me
No te pongas la chaqueta (tú)	Don't put your jacket on
No me lo dé (usted)	Don't give it to me
No os quejéis (vosotros)	Don't complain
No se lo enseñen (ustedes)	Don't show it to him/her/them
Es una chica que trabaja conmigo no te vayas a creer (C. Martin Gaite, Sp., dialogue)	She's a girl who works with me — don't get the wrong idea

(i) When a pronoun ending in a vowel is attached to an affirmative *ustedes* imperative there is a widespread tendency in popular Latin-American speech either to repeat the plural *-n* at the end of the word or to shift it to the end of the word: *?levántensen* or *?levántesen* (for *levántense*) 'get up', *?desen cuenta que está por pasar lo más terrible aquí en nuestro país* (reader's letter, *Foros Latinos*, Ve.; Sp. *dense cuenta de que*) 'be aware that the most terrible thing is about to happen here in our country', etc. In some places these forms are heard even in spontaneous educated speech, but only in sub-standard or dialect speech in Spain, and they are banned from Latin-American written styles.

(ii) In parts of northern Spain, popular language puts the pronouns before an affirmative imperative verb and uses a redundant pronoun even for a direct object (this construction should not be confused with imperatives preceded by *que*, discussed at 17.6): *?¡le dé el juguete al niño!* (for *dele el juguete al niño!*) 'give the toy to the child!', *?las riegue las plantas* (for *riegue las plantas*) 'water the plants'. This construction is often stigmatized as uneducated and should not be imitated.

(iii) Uncertainty surrounds the correct spelling of the *usted* imperative of *dar* (*dé*) when one pronoun is attached: *dele* or *déle* for 'give him'? Since the accent merely distinguishes *dé* 'give' from *de* 'of', it is not really needed on an unambiguous form like *dele, denos*.

17.5 First-person plural imperatives

The present subjunctive can be used to make a first-person plural imperative, e.g. 'let's go!', 'let's begin'. If the verb is pronominal ('reflexive'), the final *-s* is dropped before adding *-nos*:

Empecemos	Let's get started
Asegurémonos primero de la verdad de los hechos	Let us first assure ourselves of the truth of the facts
No nos enfademos (Lat. Am. *no nos enojemos*)	Let's not get angry/Don't let us get angry

(i) *Ir* forms its first-person plural imperative irregularly: *vamos, vámonos* 'let's go'. The expected form *vayámonos* is nowadays virtually extinct and *vayamos* is used as an imperative only in set phrases, e.g. *vayamos al grano* 'let's get to the point'.

(ii) With the exception of *vámonos* 'let's go', informal spoken language tends to avoid this construction. This is usually done by using *ir a* or sometimes simply *a* and an infinitive, e.g. *vamos a sentarnos* 'let's sit down', *bueno, a levantarse* 'OK, let's get up' (note third-person pronoun), *vamos a verlo/a ver* 'let's have a look'/'let's see'. Thus *no nos enfademos* 'let's not get angry' may be expressed by *no nos vamos a enfadar, no vamos a enfadarnos*. However, *no nos enfademos* is perfectly acceptable in spoken language.

(iii) Double *s* is not found in Spanish, so one *s* is dropped in cases like the following: *digámoselo* 'let's tell it to him/her/them (not *digámosselo*), *démoselos* 'let's give them to him/her/them'—although such forms are uncommon for the reason given in note ii.

17.6 Third-person imperatives

Third-person imperative forms consisting of *que* + a subjunctive are common. They are usually translatable by some formula like 'let him/her/them...', 'tell him/her/them to...':

—*Que llaman preguntando por su marido.*	'There's a phone call for your husband.'
—*Pues que le/lo llamen a la oficina*	'Then tell them to call him at his office'
Que nos cuente qué política económica querría que hiciéramos (El País, Sp.)	Let him tell us what economic policy he'd like us to follow (lit 'make')
Que ella los bañara, los vistiera, oyera sus preguntas, los enseñara a rezar y a creer en algo (A. Mastretta, Mex., dialogue)	[As far as I was concerned] let her bathe them, clothe them, listen to their questions, teach them to pray and believe in something

See 33.4 for further remarks on the use of the conjunction *que*.

Third-person imperatives without *que* are found in set phrases: *¡Dios nos coja confesados!* (archaic or humorous) 'Good God!'/'Heavens above!' (lit. 'may God take us after we've confessed!'), *¡sálvese quien pueda!* 'every man for himself!' (or woman: the Spanish is not sexist), *¡viva/muera el presidente!* 'long live/death to the president!'

17.7 Second-person imperatives preceded by *que*

An imperative can be formed from a second-person subjunctive preceded by *que*. This makes the order more emphatic or presents it as a reminder:

¡Que tengas un buen fin de semana!	Have a good weekend
¡Que no pierdas el dinero!	Don't lose the money!
¡Que se diviertan!	Have a good time! (*ustedes*)

17.8 Impersonal imperatives (passive *se* imperatives)

It is possible to form an imperative with passive *se*, the resulting construction having no exact equivalent in English. It is used in formal written Spanish to give instructions without directly addressing the reader:

Rellénese en mayúsculas	Fill out in capital letters (lit. 'let it be filled out...')
Tradúzcanse al castellano las siguientes frases	Translate the following phrases into Spanish
No obstante, permítansenos aquí algunas palabras (C. Sánchez López in *GDLE*)	However, let us be allowed to say a few words here
Cuézanse las patatas durante 15 minutos, córtense en rodajitas, déjense enfriar y cúbranse con mayonesa	Boil the potatoes for 15 minutes, cut them into slices, leave them to cool and cover them with mayonnaise

As the last two examples show, the verb agrees in number with the logical object of the verb (in these cases with *palabras* and *patatas*). There is a modern tendency to prefer the infinitive to this impersonal imperative. See the next section.

17.9 The infinitive used as an imperative

The infinitive can sometimes be used as an imperative:

(a) In spoken European Spanish as a familiar alternative to the standard affirmative *vosotros* imperative ending in *-d*: *decirme la verdad = decidme la verdad* 'tell me the truth'. This is discussed at 17.2.4.

(b) Everywhere, as a brief, impersonal alternative to the *usted/ustedes* imperative, useful for public notices or instructions, e.g. in technical manuals or cookery books. Its growing popularity seems to be due to a feeling that the impersonal imperative described at 17.8 is very formal or slightly old-fashioned:

Empujar (notice on doors)	Push
Poner los medallones en un plato, salsearlos, y acompañarlos con las bolitas de papa, zanahorias y un ramito de brócoli (*La Reforma*, Mex. Papas = *patatas* in Spain; *salsear* = *sazonar*)	Put the medallions (of beef) on a plate, season them and serve them with the potato balls, carrots and a broccoli floret
Descolgar y esperar. Percibirá una señal acústica continua y uniforme. No demorar el marcar (phone book, Sp.; *marcar* = *discar* in Lat. Am.)	Lift receiver and wait. You will hear a continuous even tone. Do not delay dialling/US dialing.

This use of the infinitive instead of the *usted(es)* form is controversial. Some grammarians reject it for affirmative commands and admit only negative forms like *no fumar* 'no smoking', *no tocar* 'don't touch', *no fijar carteles* 'no bill-sticking', *no asomarse a la ventanilla* 'do not lean out of the window'; but affirmative forms are nowadays seen everywhere.

In speech, use of the infinitive for an imperative when speaking directly to someone may sound sub-standard: María Moliner says that *callarse todos* for *cállense todos* 'everybody be quiet' is not acceptable.

(i) *Haber* plus the past participle is often used to make a sarcastic, wise-after-the-event suggestion:—*Me arrepiento de haberla llamado. —Bueno, no haberlo hecho...* '"I regret calling her." "Well, we shouldn't have done it, should we?"', —*Me he pegado una mojadura. —Haber traído el paraguas* '"I've got soaked." "You should have brought your umbrella, shouldn't you?"' This construction is called the *imperativo retrospectivo* in Spanish.

(c) With the preposition *a*, the infinitive may be used to give orders in informal styles:

—*Todavía está sucio. —Bueno, a lavarlo otra vez* (sounds uneducated without the *a*)	'It's still dirty.' 'Well wash it again.'
—*¡No tengo novio todavía! —Las ganas no te faltan. ¡A buscarlo!* (A. Arrufat, Cu., dialogue)	'I haven't got a boyfriend yet!' 'You're keen enough. So look for one!'
¡Todos a callar!	Be quiet everybody!
¡A dormir inmediatamente!	Go to sleep right now!

This type of imperative may sometimes include the speaker: *bueno, ahora a trabajar* 'OK, now let's get to work'.

(**d**) In Spain an infinitive is nowadays often used to introduce the last point in radio or TV news items. This is surely not an imperative but an abbreviation of some phrase like *sólo/solo nos queda. . .* or *sólo/solo falta. . .* 'all that remains is to. . .': *y finalmente, añadir que ésta no es la primera vez que el autor recibe un importante premio literario* 'and finally, we should add that this isn't the first time that the author has received an important literary prize'.

17.10 The present indicative used as an imperative

The present indicative is sometimes used as an imperative in spoken Spanish, just as in English; cf. 'you're getting up right now and going to school'. In both languages this tends to be a no-nonsense imperative and it can be brusque to the point of rudeness:

Si tienes dinero, me lo das	If you've got money, give it to me
De acuerdo. No te guardo el sitio para mañana, pero pasado me haces dos páginas (C. Rico-Godoy, Sp., dialogue)	OK. I won't keep the space for you tomorrow, but the day after you do two pages for me (editor to journalist)
Nomás que oscurezca te vas por la carretera y tiras en una barranca el cuerpo de una muchacha que se murió (J. Ibargüengoitia, Mex., dialogue; *nomás que = en cuanto* or *nada más. . .* in Spain)	As soon as it gets dark, you go down the road and you throw the body of a girl who died into a ravine

17.11 Ways of mellowing the imperative

There are numerous ways of making a request sound friendly, although in any language a politely worded request can sound rude if the intonation is abrupt or irritable. Some ways of making a request sound more mellow are to:

(**a**) Use the conditional or imperfect of *poder*:

¿Podrían/Podían hacer menos ruido (por favor)?	Would you mind making less noise?/ Could you make less noise?
¿Podrías hacerme el favor de no fumar?	Would you mind not smoking?

(**b**) Use *querer*. The conditional makes the imperative even milder:

¿Quieres decirme la verdad?	Would you mind telling me the truth?
¿Querrías (hacerme el favor de) darle un recado a Pedro?	Would you mind giving a message to Pedro?

(**c**) Use the phrase *a ver* 'let's see. . .':

A ver si vienes a verme más a menudo	Try to come and see me more often
A ver si me devuelves el dinero que te presté	Perhaps you could give me back the money I lent you

(**d**) Turn the request into a question:

¿Me pasas el agua (por favor)?	Pass the water please
¿Me pone con el 261-84-50 (por favor)? (See 10.17 for how to say telephone numbers)	Can you connect me to 261 8450 please?

(e) In Spain, use *tú* instead of *usted*, even to strangers:

This is very widespread in Spain and appropriate between young people (say under forty) even when they are strangers, but it sounds over-familiar when said to older persons or to people in authority. In Latin America *tú* is used much less frequently between strangers.

(f) Add a diminutive suffix to the direct object noun:

This is a common way of making a request sound friendly. Compare *deme una barra de pan* 'give me a loaf of bread' and *deme una barrita de pan* 'I'll just take a loaf of bread, please'. The diminutive does not necessarily imply smallness in this construction; it simply makes the tone friendlier, as in *espere un momentito* 'just a second, please' (see 38.2.2 for more details).

(g) Add some tag like *¿eh?*, *¿puedes?*:

Vamos al cine, ¿quieres?/¿vale?	Let's go the cinema, okay?
¿Abre la puerta, ¿puedes?	Open the door would you/US Do you want to open the door?
No chilles, ¿eh?	Stop screaming

NB: Constant use of *vale* 'fine'/'OK', is noted by Latin Americans as being typical of Peninsular Spanish.

17.12 Miscellaneous imperative constructions

Oye/Oiga (usted) (por favor)	Excuse me!/Pardon me! (lit. 'hear!')
No lo vuelvas a hacer/No vuelvas a hacerlo	Don't do it again
Mira lo que he comprado	Look what I bought
Fíjate lo que me ha pasado	Look what happened to me
Imagínate qué disgusto	Imagine how upset I was (lit. 'imagine what displeasure')
Ténmelo/Téngamelo preparado	Have it ready for me'
Trae que te lleve la bolsa (colloquial, Sp. only?)	Let me carry your bag
Trae aquí (colloquial, Sp. only?)	Give it here/Let me take it
No se te ocurra hacer eso	Don't even think of doing that
No dejes de llamarme/No se te olvide llamarme	Don't forget to call me
Vete a saber	Goodness knows/Heaven knows why
No me digas (incredulous tone)	You don't say!
Vayan entrando	Start coming in
Vete poniendo la mesa mientras yo acabo en la cocina	Start laying the table while I finish in the kitchen

(i) In Spain the word *venga* has become a largely meaningless catch-phrase: *venga, dáselo a papá* 'come on, give it to daddy', *venga, vámonos* 'ok, let's go', *venga, te llamo mañana* 'ok, I'll call you tomorrow'.

(ii) English allows passive imperatives (normally only in the negative): 'don't be scared by him'. A different solution must be found in Spanish: *no te dejes engañar por lo que dice* 'don't be deceived by what he says', *no dejes que te hagan cantar a la fuerza* 'don't be bullied into singing', *no dejes que te mangoneen/no te dejes mangonear* 'don't let yourself be pushed around'.

18

The infinitive

The main points discussed in this chapter are:

- Verb + infinitive, e.g. *quiero ir, dice saber, trató de pasar*, etc. (Section 18.2)
- *La vi entrar, los oí decir*, etc. (Section 18.2.5)
- Infinitive after prepositions and subordinators (Section 18.3)
- *Antes de hacerlo* compared with *antes de que lo haga* (Section 18.3.2)
- *Comimos al llegar, al darnos cuenta…*, etc. (Section 18.3.3)
- Infinitive used in place of finite forms (e.g. —*¿Qué hacemos?* —*Esperar; cualquier cosa menos casarse*, etc.) (Section 18.4)
- Possible passive meaning of the Spanish infinitive (Section 18.5)
- The infinitive as a noun and the definite article with the infinitive (Sections 18.6–7)
- *Es difícil de hacer* compared with *es difícil hacerlo* (Section 18.10)
- *Total a pagar, un punto a tener en cuenta* (Section 18.11)

18.1 Summary

Spanish infinitives end in *-ar, -er* or *–ir*, e.g. *hablar, comer, vivir*. A few infinitives, e.g. *freír, reír, sonreír*, have an accent on the *i*. These are listed at 13.1.4f.

The infinitive may act as a verb or noun. In the latter case it is masculine and usually singular: *fumar es malo para la salud* 'smoking is bad for the health'. One must not use the gerund to translate this kind of English sentence: **fumando es malo para la salud* is definitely not Spanish.

The Spanish infinitive (unlike the French) can sometimes have a passive meaning: in *tres cartas sin terminar* 'three unfinished letters' the letters are not finishing anything; they have not been finished.

The Spanish infinitive often takes suffixed personal pronouns, e.g. *antes de hacerlo* 'before doing it', cf. French *avant de le faire*. When the infinitive is governed by a finite verb, position of the pronouns is often optional, as in *quiero verlo* and *lo quiero ver* 'I want to see it': see 11.14.4 and below at 18.2.3.

For the use of the infinitive as an imperative see 17.9. For *de* + infinitive to mean 'if…', see 25.8.3.

18.2 Infinitive governed by a verb

This section refers to constructions like *sabe nadar* '(s)he can swim', *te desafío a hacerlo* 'I challenge you to do it', etc. These have many parallels in English, but there are some surprises. Foreign learners of English are faced with an unpredictable choice between the infinitive and the -ing form, as in 'he claimed **to have** done it' and 'he remembered **having** done it'. In Spanish only an infinitive can be used after a preposition, so the problem does not arise: *pretendía haberlo hecho, se acordaba de haberlo hecho* (never **se acordaba de habiéndolo hecho*, which is emphatically not Spanish).

18.2.1 Replacement of finite subordinate verbs by an infinitive

If the subject of the verb in a main clause and the verb in a subordinate clause share the same subject, the finite verb in the subordinate clause is usually replaced by an infinitive. This is obligatory in most cases, as can be seen from the following pairs (the subjunctive construction is discussed at 16.5):

Él quiere que lo haga (different subjects)	He wants him/her (someone else) to do it
Él quiere hacerlo (same subjects)	He wants to do it
Prefiero que tú lo abras	I prefer you to open it
Prefiero abrirlo yo mismo	I prefer to open it myself

Some verbs always take an infinitive because they can only have one subject: *se obstinaba en hacerlo* '(s)he insisted on doing it', *tienden a abstenerse* 'they tend to abstain'; these verbs are listed at 18.2.3.

In the case of some other verbs, either an infinitive or *que* + finite verb is allowed when the subjects are the same, e.g. *Juan niega haberlo hecho* or *Juan niega que lo hiciera/hiciese/haya hecho* 'Juan denies having done it' / 'Juan denies that he did it'. In such cases, use of the infinitive makes the sentence unambiguous in the third person, whereas *Juan niega que lo hiciera* could mean '...denies that (s)he (i.e. some other person) did it' or ...'you did it', as well as 'he (himself) did it': Compare these pairs:

Desmintieron que hubieran/hubiesen lanzado el misil	They denied that they'd launched the missile (i.e. themselves or someone else)
Desmintieron haber lanzado el misil (note use of *haber*)	They denied launching the missile
Afirmaba que era francés	He claimed he was French (himself or someone else)
Afirmaba ser francés	He claimed to be French

and similarly with *confesar/admitir* 'to admit', *reconocer* 'to recognize', *recordar/acordarse de* 'to remember', *ocultar* 'to hide' (in newspaper styles), *olvidar* 'to forget'. This construction is used with more verbs in Spanish than in English. See the next section.

18.2.2 Infinitive construction with certain verbs of saying, believing, affirming, etc.

Spanish allows an infinitive construction with a number of verbs of saying, believing, affirming, etc. This may seem bizarre to English-speakers since one cannot say ***'he says to be tired' for 'he says that he's tired'. As was mentioned earlier, the infinitive construction eliminates the ambiguity of *dice que lo sabe* '(s)he says (s)he knows it', which may refer to a fourth person. Despite this advantage, the infinitive construction tends to be confined to formal styles and the ambiguous construction with *que* is much more usual in everyday language. Further examples:

Creo tener razón/Creo que tengo razón	I think I'm right
Dijo llamarse Simón. . .tener 42 años, ser casado, mexicano y estar radicado en el Salto de la Tuxpana (J. Ibargüengoitia, Mex.; imitates police report language)	He said he was called Simón, was 42, married, Mexican and lived in Salto de la Tuxpana
Había creído volverse loco, pensado en matarse (M. Vargas Llosa, Pe.)	He had imagined he was going mad, thought about killing himself
Los oceanógrafos estiman haber descubierto una variedad no registrada a la fecha (El País, Ur., Sp. *...hasta la fecha*)	Oceanographers consider they have discovered a hitherto unrecorded variety
La información. . .revela ser falsa (C. Fuentes, Mex., dialogue)	The information turns out to be false
Dudo poder hacerlo/Dudo que pueda hacerlo	I doubt I can do it

(i) In written language an infinitive may appear in relative clauses when the subjects refer to different things and the clause includes a verb of saying or believing. This avoids the use of two *ques*: *las tres muchachas, que él creía ser hijas de don Mateo* (rather than *que él creía que eran. . .*) 'the three girls, whom he believed to be the daughters of Don Mateo'.

(ii) The past equivalent of the infinitive is made with *haber* + past participle: *dice haberlo comprado hace meses* '(s)he says that (s)he bought it months ago'.

18.2.3 Verbs followed by the infinitive

The following list shows some common verbs that are followed by an infinitive. French equivalents are supplied in some cases to remind students of that language to avoid all-too-frequent blunders like **se acercó de él* for *se acercó a él* (French *il s'est approché de lui*). Where no preposition is shown the verb is followed by an infinitive alone, as in *anhelaban hacerlo* 'they longed/yearned to do it'. Where 'see 16.5.2' appears, the verb may be used either with the infinitive or with a subjunctive, as explained in that section.

Verbs that are asterisked are followed by an infinitive even when the subject of this infinitive is different from the subject of the finite verb, as in *acusó a Miguel de haberlo hecho* '(s)he accused Miguel of having done it'. In other cases the infinitive construction requires that the subjects be identical, as in *me abstuve de hacer un comentario* 'I refrained from commenting'.

Verbs (plus prepositions) followed by infinitive
(Verbs marked § allow pronoun shifting. See note i)

abstenerse de to refrain from
acabar de§: acabo de verla 'I've just seen her'
acabar por to end by
acercarse a to approach (Fr. *s'approcher de*)
aceptar to accept
acertar a§ to manage to/to succeed
aconsejar§ to advise (Fr. *conseiller de*) (see 16.5.2)
acordar§ to agree to
acordarse de to remember (cf. *recordar*, see note iv)
acostumbrar a§ to be accustomed to (or 'to make someone accustomed to...')

acusar de* to accuse of
afanarse por to do one's best to
afirmar to claim/to state
alcanzar a§ to manage to: *es todo lo que alcancé a ver* 'it's all I managed to see'
amenazar (con) to threaten to (Fr. *menacer de*): *amenazó matarle* or *con matarle*
anhelar§ to long to
animar a to encourage to; see 16.5.2
ansiar§ to long to
aparentar§ to seem to
aprender a§ to learn to
apresurarse a to hasten to

arrepentirse de to regret/to repent
arriesgarse a to risk
asegurar§ to assure
atreverse a to dare to (cf. Fr. *oser faire*)
autorizar a to authorize to; see 16.5.2
avergonzarse de to be ashamed of
ayudar a§ to help to; see 16.5.2
bajar a to go down to
brindarse a to offer to
buscar to seek to (Fr. *chercher à*)
cansarse de to tire of
ceñirse a to limit oneself to
cesar de§ to cease from
comenzar a§ to begin to
comenzar por to start by
comprometerse a to undertake to
conceder to concede to
condenar a to condemn to; see 16.5.2
conducir a to lead to
confesar§ to confess
conseguir§ to succeed in
consentir en to consent to (Fr. *consentir à*)
consistir en to consist of
contribuir a to contribute to
convenir en to agree to
convidar a to invite to; see 16.5.2
creer§ to believe
cuidar de to take care to
culpar de* to blame someone for
deber§ must (see 21.3)
decidir§ to decide to (Fr. *décider de*)
decidirse a to make up one's mind to
decir tell (i.e. order; Fr. *dire de*); also 'say';
   see 16.5.2 and 18.2.2
declarar to declare
dedicarse a to dedicate oneself to
dejar§* to let/to allow: *le dejó hacerlo* or
   se lo dejó hacer '(she)he let him/
   her do it'; see 16.5.2
dejar de§ to leave off/to give up
demostrar§ to demonstrate (more usually
   with *que* + finite verb)
desafiar a to challenge to (Fr. *défier de*);
   see 16.5.2
desear§ to desire/to wish to
desesperar de to despair of
desvivirse por to do one's utmost to
dignarse to deign to
disponerse a to get ready to
disuadir de* to dissuade from
divertirse en to amuse oneself by (usually
   with gerund; Fr. *s'amuser à*)
dudar en to hesitate over (Fr. *hésiter à*)
echar(se) a to begin to
elegir to choose to
empeñarse en to insist on
empecinarse en to insist on

empezar a§ to begin to
empezar por to start by
encargarse de to take charge of
enseñar a§ to show how to/teach; see 16.5.2
enviar a to send to; see 16.5.2
escoger to choose
esforzarse por/en to strive to (Fr. *s'efforcer de*)
esperar§ to hope/to expect/to wait to
evitar§ to avoid (Fr. *éviter de*)
excitar a to excite to; see 16.5.2
figurarse to imagine
fingir to pretend to
forzar a§ to force to; see 16.5.2
guardarse de to take care not to
gustar de to like to (but usually *le*
   gusta fumar, etc.)
haber que: *hay que hacerlo* 'it has to be done'
habituarse a to get used to
hacer§ to make (*la hizo callar*, etc.); see 16.5.2
hartarse de to tire of/have enough of
imaginar to imagine
impedir§ to prevent from (Fr. *défendre de*);
   see 16.5.2
impulsar a to urge to see 16.5.2
incitar a to incite to; see 16.5.2
inclinar a to incline to; see 16.5.2
inducir a to induce/to persuade to; see
   16.5.2
insistir en to insist on (Fr. *insister pour*)
instar a to urge to; see 16.5.2
intentar§ to try to (Fr. *essayer de*)
interesarse en (or *por*) to interest in
   (Fr. *s'intéresser à*)
invitar a to invite to; see 16.5.2
ir a§ to go to (*esto va a hacerse pronto* 'this is
   going to be done soon')
jactarse de to boast of
jurar§ to swear to
juzgar to judge (but usually with *que...*)
lamentar to regret to
limitarse a to limit oneself to
llegar a to become/to go so far as to...
llevar a to lead to; see 16.5.2
lograr to succeed in
luchar por struggle to
mandar§ to order to (Fr. *ordonner de*);
   see 16.5.2
mandar a to send to (do something); see
   16.5.2
manifestar to state/to declare (usually
   with *que...*)
maravillarse de to marvel at (see also 16.6)
merecer to deserve to (usually with *que*)
meterse a to start to
molestarse en to bother to
mover a to move to
necesitar§ to need to

negar to deny (*negarse a* refuse to); see
   18.2.2
obligar a§ to oblige to (Fr. *obliger de*);
   see 16.5.2
obstinarse en to insist obstinately on (Fr.
   s'obstiner à)
ofrecer to offer (usually with *que…*)
oír§ to hear (see 20.7)
olvidar, to forget; infinitive *olvidar, olvidarse*
   de, olvidársele; see 26.7.26
optar (usually *optar por*) to opt to/for
ordenar§ to order to (Fr. *ordonner de*);
   see 16.5.2
parar de§ to stop
parecer§ to seem to; see 18.2.2
pasar a§ to go on to
pasar de to be uninterested in
pedir to ask to (Fr. *demander à, demander*
   de); see 16.5.3
pensar§ pienso hacerlo'I plan to do it'
pensar en to think of (Fr. *penser à*)
permitir§ to allow to (Fr. *permettre de*);
   see 16.5.2
persistir en to persist in (Fr. *persister à*)
persuadir a to persuade to (Fr. *persuader*
   à quelqu'un de faire…); see 16.5.2
poder§ to be able to
ponerse a to start to
precipitarse a to rush to
preferir§ to prefer to
prepararse a to get ready to
presumir de to boast about
pretender§ to claim to/to try to
proceder a to proceed to
procurar§ to try hard to

prohibir§ to prohibit from (Fr. *défendre de*)
   16.5.2
prometer§ to promise to (Fr. *promettre de*)
quedar en to agree to
querer§ to want to (see 21.5)
reconocer to acknowledge (more usually
   with *que*)
recordar§ to remember to (see note iv)
rehuir to shun/to avoid
rehusar§ to refuse to (Fr. *refuser de*)
renunciar a§ to renounce
resignarse a to resign oneself to
resistirse a to resist
resultar to turn out to be
resolver§ to resolve to (Fr. *résoudre de*)
saber§ to know how to (see 21.2)
sentir to regret/to be sorry for (see 16.6)
soler: solía hacerlo§ '(s)he habitually did it'
   (see 21.6)
solicitar§ to apply to; see 16.5.2
soñar con to dream of (Fr. *rêver de*)
tardar en to be late in/to be a long time
   in (Fr. *tarder à*)
temer§ to fear to
tender a§ to tend to
tener que§ to have to; see 21.3
tentar a to tempt to; see 16.5.2
terminar de§ to finish
tratar de§ try to
vacilar en to hesitate over
venir de to come from…
ver§ to see (see 20.7)
ver de to try to
volver a (hacer)§ to (do) again (see 32.6a)
votar por to vote for

(i) Verbs followed by § allow pronoun shifting, i.e. one can say *acabo de hacerlo* or *lo acabo de hacer, pienso mudarme mañana* or *me pienso mudar mañana* 'I'm thinking of moving tomorrow'. Doubtful verbs, e.g. *fingir, afirmar,* are not marked. Pronoun shifting is discussed in detail at 11.14.4.

(ii) Verbs of motion, e.g. *salir, bajar, ir, volver, entrar, acercar(se),* always take *a* before an infinitive: *bajó a verla* '(s)he went down to see her', *entraron a saludar al profesor* 'they went in to say hello to the teacher', etc. When the subjects are not identical, *a que* or *para que* + subjunctive is required: *bajó a/para que la vieran/viesen* 'she went down so they could see her'.

(iii) For the use of the infinitive as a noun, e.g. *es bueno jugar al tenis* 'it's good to play tennis'/'playing tennis is good', see 18.6–7.

(iv) The construction is *me acuerdo de haberla visto* or *recuerdo haberla visto* 'I remember seeing her'. *Recordarse* can only mean 'to remember oneself', as in *me recuerdo como un niño muy tímido* 'I remember myself as a very timid child'. However *recordarse* for 'to remember' is common in familiar Latin-American speech, although it is avoided in careful styles and is considered incorrect in Spain.

18.2.4 Verbs of permitting and forbidding, and other verbs constructed with an indirect object

Most (but not all) verbs that can be constructed with an indirect object, e.g. *les permití hacerlo/les permití que lo hicieran* 'I let them do it', allow either a subjunctive or an infinitive construction. They are discussed at 16.5.2.

It is worth repeating here that when used with the infinitive, verbs of obliging, prohibiting and permitting can appear without an object in Spanish but not in English: *esto prohíbe pensar que. . .* 'this prohibits us/one from thinking that...'. See 16.5.2 note (i).

18.2.5 Infinitive after verbs of perception

The infinitive is used after verbs like *ver, oír, sentir* to denote a completed action; an incomplete action is indicated by the gerund. English makes the same distinction: compare *le/lo vi fumar un puro* 'I saw him smoke a cigar' (and finish it) and *le/lo vi fumando un puro* 'I saw him smoking a cigar'. See 20.7 for more examples.

The word order with an intransitive verb is Infinitive-Subject: *vi entrar a María* 'I saw María come in', not **vi a María entrar*. But with transitive verbs the order is Subject-Infinitive-Direct Object: *vi a María fumar un puro* 'I saw María smoke a cigar':

Te vi entrar	I saw you come in
Se lo oí decir	I heard her/him/you (*usted*) say it
Te lo vi firmar	I saw you sign it
Vimos llegar el avión	We saw the plane arrive
No he oído nunca aullar a un lobo, pero sé que era un lobo (J. L. Borges, Arg., dialogue)	I've never heard a wolf howl, but I know it was a wolf
Ya estoy harta de oírlo hablar como si en América latina todo fuera de extrema izquierda (A. Bryce Echenique, Pe., dialogue)	I'm fed up with hearing you talk as though everything in Latin America was extreme left-wing
Marés sentía desintegrarse día a día su personalidad (J. Marsé, Sp.)	Marés felt his personality disintegrate day by day

(i) The Spanish infinitive can be active or passive in meaning, so a passive may be required in the English translation: *nunca la oí nombrar* 'I've never heard her mentioned', *vio matar a varios prisioneros* '(s)he saw several prisoners killed'. This occasionally causes ambiguity: *vi matar a dos leones* could, out of context, mean either 'I saw two lions killed' or 'I saw two lions kill'. The first meaning is more likely.

18.3 Infinitive after prepositions and subordinators

18.3.1 Infinitive after prepositions

The infinitive is used after prepositions and prepositional phrases: *fue la primera en enterarse* 'she was the first to find out', *estoy harto de decírtelo* 'I'm tired of telling you', *reprende a la banca por arriesgarse* (*El País*, Sp.) 'he reproaches the banks for taking risks', *un líquido para quitar las manchas* 'a liquid to remove stains', *un abrigo sin estrenar* 'an unworn coat', etc. Prepositions are never used before a Spanish gerund: **estoy harto de diciéndotelo* is definitely not Spanish (for an archaic exception to this rule see 20.5).

Some prepositional phrases may need to be followed by *que* + a subjunctive, e.g. *a cambio de que lo hagas tú* 'in return for you doing it', *para que él lo haga* 'in order for him to do it'. See the next section.

18.3.2 Choice between the infinitive and *que* + finite verb

An infinitive construction is possible after the subordinators listed at 16.12.2, e.g. *hasta* 'until', *para* 'in order to', *sin* 'without', *nada más* 'as soon as', and those consisting of phrases that require the word *de que* before a finite verb, e.g. *antes de (que)* 'before', *después de (que)* 'after', *el hecho de (que)* 'the fact that', etc.

Foreign students should apply the following rule: use the infinitive with these subordinators only if the subject of the following verb is the same as the main verb's, as in *lo hice antes de salir* 'I did it before I went out/before going out'.

If the subjects are different, the subjunctive or indicative must be used (although the rule is applied loosely with *antes de* and *después de*), the choice being determined by the rules laid at out at 16.12.1. Compare *lo haré nada más acabar esto* 'I'll do it as soon as I've finished this' and *lo haré nada más que acabe esto* 'I'll do it as soon as *this* finishes'. The latter sentence could also, however, mean 'as soon as I finish this' or 'as soon as (s)he finishes/you finish...'. Further examples:

Lo haré después de comer/de que coma	I'll do it after I've had lunch
Lo haré después de que hayáis comido	I'll do it after you've had lunch
Entré sin verte	I entered without seeing you
Entré sin que tú me vieras/vieses	I entered without you seeing me
Se fue antes de contestar	(S)he left before (s)he answered
Se fue antes de que yo contestase/contestara	(S)he left before I answered
Enfermó (Lat. Am. se enfermó) por no comer	(S)he fell sick from not eating

Spontaneous language often uses an infinitive construction with these subordinators even when the subjects are not identical. Thus *vino a los tres días de que te fueras tú* '(s)he arrived three days after you left' is correct, but *vino a los tres días de irte tú* (A. Buero Vallejo, Sp., dialogue) is constantly heard. The *GDLE* 27.2.1 describes *no es conveniente marcharte sin desperdirte* as 'careless' for *no es conveniente que te marches sin despedirte* 'it's not right for you to leave without saying goodbye'. Further examples:

?Le miraba sin él darse cuenta (J. Marsé, dialogue: *sin que él se diese/diera cuenta*)	He watched him without him realizing
?¿Te voy a ver antes de irte? (Spanish informant, i.e. ... *antes de que te vayas*)	Am I going to see you before you go?
¿Me podés comprar postales para mandar yo? (Argentine informant, i.e. *para que yo las mande*; Sp. *puedes* for *podés*)	Could you buy me some postcards for me to send?

(i) If the infinitive construction is used, the best order is preposition + infinitive + subject, as in *me fui antes de llegar tú* 'I left before you arrived'. One hears the order preposition + subject + infinitive in very informal speech, as in *?para él hablar así, tenía que estar borracho* 'he must have been drunk for him to talk like that' (from *GDLE* 36.3.4), *?es decir que había comprado marfil para usted vender* (*Vindicación de Cuba*, Cu., dialogue, for... *para que usted lo vendiera/vendiese*) 'in other words he'd bought ivory for you to sell'. But this is is not universally accepted. DeMello (1995, 2) reports this order to be commoner in Caracas and San Juan (Puerto Rico) than elsewhere, and generally more usual with *de* or *para* than with other prepositions.

18.3.3 *Al* + infinitive

In theory, *al* + infinitive ought also probably to be used only when the subjects are the same, as in *al despedirme le dije a uno de los dos...* 'as I said goodbye I said to one of the two of them...'. But sentences like *al despedirme uno de los dos me dijo* (J. L. Borges, Arg., dialogue, different subjects) 'as I left one of the two said to me' are universally common. Further examples:

Se enfadó al enterarse	(S)he got angry when (s)he found out
Se hace camino al andar (A. Machado, Sp.)	One makes one's path as one goes along
Al fumarlo los indios experimentaban una especie de éxtasis (El País, Sp.)	When they smoked it the Indians experienced a sort of ecstasy
Al terminar el bachillerato Gladys pasó a un organismo estatal (M. Puig, Arg.)	After finishing her baccalaureate Gladys moved to (a job) in a government organization

This construction can also mean 'because': *al encontrarse enfermo el conferenciante, se aplazó la conferencia* 'because the lecturer was sick, the lecture was postponed'; *una tecnología que no representa ningún riesgo para la población y el entorno, al no producir residuos* (Granma, Cu.) 'technology that presents no risk to the population or environment since it produces no waste'.

18.4 Replacement of finite forms by the infinitive

The infinitive rather than a finite verb may be used in the following circumstances:

(**a**) To give an abrupt response to a question (as one does when the answer is obvious):

—*¿Qué hacemos ahora?* —*Esperar*	'What do we do now?' 'Wait'
—*¿Pero se puede saber que está usted haciendo?* —*¡Sacar a mi mujer!* (E. Arenas, Sp., dialogue)	'But do you mind saying what you're doing?' 'Getting my wife out!'
—*¿Y ahora qué vas a hacer, Martín?* —*Entrar por la puerta principal* (A. Bryce Echenique, Pe., dialogue)	'And what are you going to do now, Martín?' 'Go in through the front door'

(**b**) After *más que, menos, excepto:*

Yo siempre sospeché que había algo después de la muerte. Más que sospecharlo, lo sabía, casi con seguridad (J. de Jesús Martínez, Panama, dialogue)	I always suspected that there was something after death. More than suspect it, I knew it, almost as a certainty
...ojos que más que mirar, retan (E. Arenas, Sp.)	...eyes that rather than look, challenge
...todo, menos/excepto volver a escribirlo	...anything, except write it again

(**c**) For naming or listing actions, as in:

...y esto es lo que hacen los campesinos: arar, plantar, podar, regar	...and this is what peasants do: ploughing/US plowing, planting, pruning, watering
¿Sabéis lo que yo hago después de que vosotros os habéis ido a casa? Trabajar	Do you know what I do after you've gone home? Work

(**d**) In indignant or sarcastic statements and questions like *¿para qué servirle carne a un vegetariano?* 'what's the point of serving meat to a vegetarian?' See 18.9.

18.5 Infinitive: passive or active?

The Spanish infinitive may have a passive meaning, especially after *sin, por, a* and *para*:

Esto aún está por ver	This is still to be seen
una cerveza sin abrir	an unopened beer
Los republicanos llegan a la convención. . . con las tácticas electorales sin decidir (El País, Sp.)	The Republicans are arriving at the Convention . . . with their electoral tactics undecided
Pasaba el tiempo sin sentir (C. Martín Gaite, Sp.)	Time passed unnoticed
En su recámara había cuatro maletas a medio hacer (A. Mastretta, Mex., dialogue; *recámara = dormitorio* in Spain)	In her bedroom there were four half-packed suitcases
Transcurrieron años sin tener noticias de lo ocurrido	Years passed without (lit. 'without having') news of what had happened being received
. . .trabajos para hacer por el estudiante	…work to be done (lit. 'to do') by the student

18.6 Infinitive as a noun

The infinitive may function as a noun, in which case it is sometimes translated by an English *-ing* form. Used as a noun, an infinitive is always masculine and usually singular:

Mañana me toca lavar el coche	It's my turn to wash the car tomorrow
Votar Comunista es votar contra el paro (election poster)	To vote Communist is to vote against unemployment
aquel fluir movedizo de los colores. . . (C. Martín Gaite, Sp.)	that shifting flow of the colo(u)rs…
Mejor no hacerlo	Best not do it
Odio ordenar	I hate sorting/tidying
un atolondrado ir y venir	a mad coming and going
Contemplar en vídeo el sufrimiento auténtico de algún semejante es mucho peor que infligirlo uno mismo (E. Lynch, Arg.)	Watching the actual suffering of another human being on video is much worse than actually inflicting it on them

18.7 Definite articles before the infinitive

The definite article is used before the infinitive:

(**a**) in the common construction *al* + infinitive: *tómese una pastilla al acostarse* 'take a pill on going to bed'. See 18.3.3 for more examples.

(**b**) When the infinitive is qualified by an adjective or by a noun phrase joined to the infinitive, often by the preposition *de*:

Oyó el agitado girar de una cucharilla contra un vaso (L. Goytisolo, Sp.)	He heard the agitated grating of a teaspoon against a glass
Cristina escuchó el percutir de las gotas de la ducha sobre los azulejos (L. Otero, Cu.)	Cristina listened to the splatter of drops from the shower on the tiles
con el andar de los años	as the years passed by

(**c**) Note that the definitive article can be used to attribute an idea to someone else, cf. *vivir separados cuesta más* 'living apart costs more' and *el vivir separados fue cosa de él* 'living apart was *his* idea'.

(**d**) In other cases when the infinitive is used as a noun, the definite article seems to be optional, although it is much less common in informal styles. The article is, however, quite often retained when the infinitive is the subject of a verb. In all the following examples the definite article before the infinitive could be omitted, although in the attributed examples it was in fact used. Omission would make the style slightly less literary:

Paula no pudo evitar (el) reírse (J. J. Plans, Sp.)	Paula couldn't help laughing
¿Por qué no se lo deja permanentemente aquí y se evita así (el) estar trayéndolo y llevándolo? (J. de Jesús Martínez, Panama, dialogue)	Why don't you leave it here for him permanently? That way you'll avoid fetching it and taking it away (again).
Esto permite a los robots (el) ser reprogramados para... (*Cambio16*, Sp.)	This allows robots to be reprogrammed to...

(**e**) The article is required in some constructions involving *en*:

La moda en el vestir influye en la moda del maquillaje	Fashion in dressing influences fashion in make-up
Algunos españoles son un poco enfáticos en el hablar	Some Spaniards are rather ponderous in their manner of speaking
Le conocí en el andar	I recognized him from his way of walking

(**f**) The indefinite article *un* is also found before a qualified infinitive:

en un abrir y cerrar de ojos	in the wink of an eye
Después de dos años de un agitado avanzar por el camino de la libertad...	after two years of agitated progress (lit. 'agitated progressing') along the road to liberty...

18.8 Infinitive as an imperative

The use of the infinitive as an imperative form is discussed at 17.9.

18.9 'Rhetorical' infinitive

The infinitive may be used in rhetorical questions or to express disbelief, indignation or sarcasm:

¡Pagar yo cien mil por eso!	What! Me pay 100,000 for that!
¡Enamorarme yo a mis años!	Me fall in love at my age!
Pero, ¿cómo abrirlo sin llave?	But how do you open it without a key?
¿Por qué condenar el proyecto estrella de toda una gestión presidencial? (*Vértice*, El Salvador)	Why condemn the star project of a whole presidential initiative?

and also after words like *¿dónde?* and *¿para qué?*: *¿(a)dónde ir?* 'where on earth shall we go?', *¿para qué insistir?* 'why insist?'

18.10 Adjective + *de* + infinitive

Es difícil aprender español 'it is difficult to learn Spanish' differs from *el español es difícil de aprender* 'Spanish is difficult to learn'. In the first sentence the subject of *es* is *aprender*, and *de* is not used when the infinitive is the subject: it means 'to learn Spanish is difficult'. Examples: *no es fácil creerlo* 'it isn't easy to believe it', *parece difícil solucionar tal problema* 'it seems difficult to solve such a problem', *resulta imposible comprobar que. . .* 'it turns out to be impossible to prove that. . .'.

But when the infinitive is not the subject, *de* must be used (subject in bold, but it may be implicit in the Spanish verb): (*eso*) *es difícil de averiguar* 'that is difficult to check', *para este Día del Padre sorprenda a papá con* **un delicioso menú** *fácil y rápido de elaborar* (*La Reforma*, Mex.) 'for today, Father's Day, surprise father with a delicious menu that's easy and quick to prepare', *resulta difícil de definir* '**it** turns out to be difficult to define', **ciertos movimientos** *difíciles de imitar* 'certain movements (that it was/is) difficult to imitate'.

18.11 Infinitive preceded by *que*

The following constructions must be noted, particularly by students of French: cf. *j'ai beaucoup à faire, il n'y a rien à manger*, etc.:

Tengo mucho que hacer/decir	I've got a lot to do/say
Voy a comprar algo que/para leer	I'm going to buy something to read
Dame algo que/para hacer	Give me something to do
Eso nos ha dado bastante que hacer	This has given us enough to do
Te queda mucho que sufrir en este mundo	You've a lot left to suffer in this world

But this construction with *que* cannot be used with verbs of needing, requesting, searching:

Necesito algo para comer	I need something to eat
Quiero algo para beber	I want something to drink
Pidió algo para (or *con que*) *calmar su dolor de muelas*	(S)he asked for something to soothe his/her toothache
Busco algo para. . .	I'm looking for something to. . .

The construction with *que* must be distinguished from the following similar construction with *qué* (stressed word) 'what'/'anything': *no tengo* **qué** *comer* 'I haven't got anything to eat', *no sabemos* **qué** *pensar* 'we don't know what to think'.

18.12 *El problema a resolver, un argumento a tener en cuenta*, etc.

This combination of a noun + *a* + an infinitive is a fashionable alternative way of saying 'the problem to be solved', etc. It causes controversy. *El País, Libro de estilo* 2002, 12.9, says it must be avoided. Seco (1998), 5, welcomes its brevity and points out that it is not identical to *por* + infinitive: *cosas por hacer* = 'things still to be done', *cosas a hacer* = 'things to do'. The Academy's *Esbozo. . .*, 3.11.5, tolerates certain set expressions used in commerce and finance, e.g. *total a pagar* 'total payable', *cantidades a deducir* 'amounts deductible', *asuntos a tratar* 'business pending'/'agenda', but notes that the Academies of all Spanish-speaking countries condemn such sentences as *tengo terrenos a vender* 'I've got land to sell' (for *que/para vender*), *personas a convocar* 'people to call/summon' (for *que convocar*), etc. Nevertheless, we find *es un dato a tener en cuenta* 'it is a point to be borne in mind' in the Academy's *GDLE*, p. 1785.

The construction with *a* is more widely accepted in Latin America; cf. *los uniformados presentaron hace poco un nuevo texto a ser considerado* (*Abc Color*, Par.) 'the military recently presented a new text for consideration'.

19

Participles

The main points discussed in this chapter are:

- Main uses of the past participle (Section 19.1)
- Forms of regular and irregular past participles (Section 19.2)
- Participle clauses (e.g. 'the dinner **having finished**, they left') (Section 19.3)
- Adjectival or present participles ending in -*ante*, -*(i)ente*, e.g. *perteneciente* 'belonging', *inquietante* 'worrying' (Section 19.4)

19.1 Past participles: general

The past participle has several uses:

(**a**) It is used with *haber* to form the compound tenses of verbs: *ha hablado* '(s)he has spoken', *yo la había visto* 'I had seen her'. See 14.8 for discussion.

(**b**) It is occasionally used with *tener* or *llevar* to emphasize the idea of acquiring or accumulating things or actions, as in *tengo compradas las entradas* 'I've bought the entrance tickets', *llevo tomados tres somníferos* 'I've taken three sleeping tablets'. See 14.8.3 for discussion.

(**c**) It is used to form the passive: *fue impreso/a* 'it was printed', *fueron observados/observadas* 'they were observed'. The passive is discussed in Chapter 28.

(**d**) It functions as an adjective, in which case it agrees in number and gender like any adjective: *una exagerada reacción* 'an exaggerated reaction', *un argumento improvisado* 'an improvised argument', *una desesperada tentativa* 'a desperate attempt', etc. These adjectival past participles can often be converted into nouns by the use of a determiner (see Glossary): *un muerto* 'a dead person', *ese herido* 'that wounded person', *¿qué dirán por su parte los censurados?* 'what will those who have been censured have to say for themselves?', *varios condenados* 'several condemned persons'. Such forms provide neat translations of English relative clauses: *nunca olvidaremos a los desaparecidos* 'we'll never forget those who disappeared', *¿dónde están los recién llegados?* 'where are the ones who've just arrived?'

Many words ending in -*ado*, -*ido* are used only as adjectives, e.g. *adecuado* 'appropriate'/'adequate', *desgraciado* 'unhappy', *desmesurado* 'disproportionate', *indiscriminado* 'indiscriminate', *descarado* 'shameless', etc. But the majority can function either as verbal participles, e.g. *había alarmado a sus colegas* '(s)he had alarmed his/her colleagues', or as adjectives: *la cara alarmada de sus colegas* 'his/her colleagues' alarmed faces'.

Most past participles that can function as adjectives can appear with *ser* without creating a passive sentence: *su reacción era exagerada* 'his reaction was exaggerated', *mi llanto era desesperado* 'my weeping was desperate', *su cara me era desconocida*, 'her/his face was unknown to me'. Verbal participles form passive sentences when used in the same way: *la ciudad fue destruida* 'the city was destroyed', *eran persegui- dos* 'they were being persecuted/pursued'. In the latter case it may be possible to make the verbal participle into an adjective by using *estar*, e.g. *la ciudad estaba destruida* 'the city was in a state of destruction'. See 28.2.5 for details.

(e) Some adjective/participles ending in *–do* confuse foreign learners since they seem to have two meanings. *Reducido* is notorious: *una cantidad reducida* = 'a *small* quantity', not a 'reduced' quantity, but *la cantidad ha sido reducida* = 'the quantity has been reduced'. Other examples are *acusado* 'clearly visible' or 'accused', *ajustado* 'tight' or 'adjusted', *alargado* 'long' or 'lengthened', *alejado* 'remote' or 'distanced', *aprovechado* 'opportunistic' or 'made use of', *cuidado* 'careful'/'painstaking' or 'looked after', *elevado* 'high' (e.g. number, quantity) or 'raised', *honrado* 'honest' or 'hono(u)red', *recogido* 'timid' or 'picked up', *retirado* 'remote' or 'withdrawn'/'retired'. *Prolongado* 'prolonged' and *aislado* 'isolated' have the same meanings as in English.

(f) The *GDLE* 4.4.1.2 notes survivals of older participle forms, e.g. *pago* 'paid', *calmo* 'calm(ed), *canso* 'tired', *nublo* 'cloudy', nowadays replaced by *pagado*, *cal- mado*, *cansado*, *nublado*. These older forms are still heard in some rural areas and are found in Golden-Age literature.

19.2 Past participles: forms

19.2.1 Regular and irregular past participles

The past participle is formed in most cases by replacing the *-ar* of an infinitive by *-ado*, and *-er* and *-ir* by *-ido*: *hablar/hablado, tener/tenido, construir/construido* (no accent!), *ir/ido, ser/sido*, etc. There are a few common irregular forms:

absolver (& all verbs ending in *-solver*): absuelto	*imprimir*: *impreso* (see note ii)
	morir: *muerto* (see note i)
cubrir (& all verbs ending in *-cubrir*): cubierto	*poner* (& all verbs ending in *–poner*): puesto
decir (& all verbs ending in *–decir*§): dicho	*romper roto*
	ver (& compounds like *prever*): *visto*
escribir (& all verbs ending in *-scribir*): escrito	*volver* (& all verbs ending in *volver*): vuelto
freír: *frito* (see note ii)	
hacer: *hecho*	
§See the next list for *maldecir*.	

A few have separate adjectival and verbal participles, cf. *está **despierto** porque lo/le he despert**ado*** 'he's awake because I've woken him', *ahora que han **soltado** a los animales andan **sueltos*** 'now they've released the animals they're wandering around free', *el agua que ha **bendecido** un cura se llama agua **bendita*** 'the water that a priest has blessed is called Holy Water'. In the following list the verbal participle is shown first:

absorber: *absorbido/absorto* absorbed
bendecir: *bendecido/bendito* blessed
confesar: *confesado/confeso* confessed
confundir: *confundido/confuso* confused
despertar: *despertado/despierto* woken up
elegir: *elegido/electo* elected
maldecir: *maldecido/maldito* cursed
prender: *prendido/preso* pinned on (see
   note iii)

presumir: *presumido/presunto*
   vain/presumed
proveer: *proveído/provisto* equipped
   with
soltar: *soltado/suelto* released
suspender: *suspendido/suspenso* failed
   (e.g. exams)/hanging

(i) *Muerto* is often used in literary styles as the passive past participle of *matar* 'to kill' when applied to human beings: *con el tiempo sería muerto por la Gestapo* (Ernesto Sábato, Arg., interview; ordinary language *sería matado/lo mataría*) 'he was later to be killed by the Gestapo', but *unos bandidos habían **matado** a su padre* 'some bandits had killed his father'.

(ii) *Freído* and *imprimido* are archaic verbal participles of *reír* and *imprimir*, still occasionally used by older speakers. *Frito, impreso* are usual nowadays.

(iii) *Prender* has numerous meanings, e.g. 'to capture', 'to pin on', 'catch fire' and, in Latin America, 'to switch on' lights, etc.; Spain *encender*. *Preso* often means a prisoner or detainee.

19.2.2 Irregular past participles in Latin America

A number of scholarly irregular adjectival participles are more widely used in Latin America than in Spain, and especially in Argentina. These forms are either obsolete in Spain or are used only in set phrases, e.g. *el presidente electo* 'the president elect'; but they are used in Latin America not only as adjectives but also to form passives, e.g. *resultó electo candidato a la presidencia* (A. Mastretta, Mex.) 'he was elected as presidential candidate', Spain *salió elegido*. In the following list the standard form appears first:

convencer: *convencido/convicto* convinced
corromper: *corrompido/corrupto* corrupt
describir: *descrito/descripto* described
dividir: *dividido/diviso* divided

inscribir: *inscrito/inscripto* entered (a
   written item)
prescribir: *prescrito/prescripto* prescribed

*Ocurre en las regiones antárticas descriptas
   con extraordinaria vividez...* (J. L. Borges,
   Arg.; Sp. *descritas*)
*Incluye todos los shampoos prescriptos por
   médicos* (Gente, Arg.; Sp. *recetados/
   prescritos*)
*...escritores que fueron conservadores
   convictos* (M. Vargas Llosa, Pe.; Sp.
   convencidos. Convicto = 'convicted')

It happens in the Antarctic regions
   described with extraordinary
   vividness...
It includes all the shampoos prescribed
   by doctors

...writers who were convinced
   conservatives

Latin Americans may reject the use of the regular participles in such sentences.

NB: Both *una sociedad corrompida* and *una sociedad corrupta* 'a corrupt society' are heard in Spain. *Corrupto* is usual in Latin America, but cf. *...los congresistas son corrompidos* (El Tiempo, Col.) 'the Congressmen are corrupt'.

19.3 Participle clauses

Participle clauses (see Glossary) are common. They often have exact English counterparts, but slight differences occur between the two languages (see also 31.3.4 for sentences like *aceptó irritada* 'she accepted irritably'):

Me fui, convencido de que él no sabía nada	I left, convinced he knew nothing
José González, nacido el 23 de marzo	José González, born on 23 March
¿Dónde vas? preguntó alarmado	Where are you going, he asked in alarm
su padre, muerto en 1956. . .	his father, who died in 1956. . .
. . .preguntado qué le había gustado de ella, contesta con un gruñido (G. García Márquez, Col.)	. . .asked what he had liked about her, he replies with a grunt

Spanish allows certain participle clauses, especially in literary language, that have no exact equivalents in English:

Llegados a Madrid, se alojaron en el mejor hotel	Having arrived in Madrid, they stayed at the best hotel
Concluidas las primeras investigaciones, la policía abandonó el lugar de autos	The initial investigations having been concluded, the police left the scene of the crime
. . .por fin, transcurridos siete años desde la publicación de su primera novela. . .	. . .at last, seven years having passed since the publication of his first novel. . .
Después de vendida la casa, nos arrepentimos (from Seco, 1998, 334)	Once the house was sold, we regretted it
Arrasado el jardín, profanados los cálices y las aras, entraron a caballo los hunos en la biblioteca monástica (J. L. Borges, Arg.; very literary)	Having demolished the garden and profaned chalices and altars, the Huns rode into the monastery library

Llegar seems to be the only verb of motion that allows this construction. One cannot say **entrada en el agua se puso a nadar* 'entering the water she began to swim': *cuando entró en el agua se puso a nadar*, or **bajados del tren* for *cuando bajaron del tren* 'when they got out of the train'.

19.4 Participles in *-ante*, *-iente* or *-ente*

Adjectival present participles may be formed from many verbs, but by no means from all. Such participles function like the English adjectival forms in -ing: 'Sleeping Beauty' = *La Bella Durmiente*. New coinages appear constantly, many of them inspired by English adjectives ending in -ing.

Adjectival participles are formed thus:

(i) *-ar* conjugation: replace the *-ar* of the infinitive by *-ante*: *alarmar > alarmante* 'alarming' *inquietar > inquietante* 'worrying';

(ii) *-er* conjugation: replace the *-er* of the infinitive by *-iente* or, in a few cases, by –*ente*;

(iii) *-ir* conjugation: replace the *-iendo* of the gerund by *-iente* or *-ente*, the choice being unpredictable.

Examples from the *-er* and *-ir* conjugations:

crecer: *creciendo-creciente* growing
proceder: *procediendo-procedente*
   proceeding
sorprender: *sorprendiendo-sorprendente*
   surprising
tender: *tendiendo-tendente* tending (to)
concernir: *concerniendo-concerniente*
   concerning
conducir: *conduciendo-conducente* leading
   (to)
existir: *existiendo-existente*
   existing/extant

dormir: *durmiendo-durmiente* sleeping
herir: *hiriendo-hiriente* wounding
producir: *produciendo-producente*
   producing (*contraproducente*, counter-
   productive)
reír: *riendo-riente* laughing
salir: *saliendo-saliente* outgoing, etc.
seguir: *siguiendo-siguiente* following
sonreír: *sonriendo-sonriente* smiling

There are a few irregular forms (the gerund is shown in brackets):

convencer: (*convenciendo*) *convincente*
   convincing
convenir: (*conviniendo*) *conveniente* suitable

fluir: (*fluyendo*) *fluente* flowing/fluent
provenir: (*proviniendo*) *proveniente de*
   coming from

Forms in *-nte* cannot be made from all verbs and they should be learned separately from the dictionary, especially in view of the remark in note (ii). They are often used in written, mainly journalistic style instead of relative clauses in the same way as English uses the *–ing* form:

una situación cambiante/estresante	a changing/stressful situation
el ministro saliente/entrante	the outgoing/incoming minister
condiciones vinculantes (*El País*, Spain)	binding conditions
resultados sobresalientes	outstanding results
el millón y medio restante	the remaining 1.5 million
157.000 personas, pertenecientes a diferentes clases sociales y procedentes de lugares muy distintos de nacimiento... (*El País*, Sp.)	157,000 people, belonging to various social classes and originating from widely different places...
...en fin, todo conducente a la violencia obtusa... (*Triunfo*, Sp.)	...in short, anything leading to brute violence...

(i) The gerund in *-ando* or *-iendo* could not be used instead of the *-nte* form in any of these examples. See 20.3 for discussion.

(ii) One cannot predict which verbs have present participles, and English-speakers often invent non-existent words like **moviente* for 'moving': *piezas movibles* = 'moving parts', *espectáculo conmovedor* = 'moving spectacle'. Also *mesa plegable* 'folding table', *agua potable* 'drinking water', *confiado/crédulo* = 'trusting', *planta trepadora* = 'climbing plant', *resultados satisfactorios* 'satisfying results', *hechos reveladores* 'revealing facts', *un libro aburrido* 'a boring book', *es cansado* 'it's tiring', and many others.

(iii) Many forms in *-nte* are not strictly speaking participles but non-verbal adjectives, e.g. *brillante* 'shining', *corriente* 'current'/'ordinary', *aparente* 'apparent', *reciente* 'recent', etc.

(iv) With the exception of a few slang or popular words, e.g. *dominanta* 'bossy' (of a woman), *currante-curranta* (familiar Peninsular Spanish for 'hard-working'), *atorrante-atorranta* (Lat. Am.) 'slacker'/'layabout', *golfante-golfanta* popular Peninsular Spanish for 'rascal'/'good-for-nothing', neither participles nor adjectives ending in *-nte* have a separate feminine form. However, a few nouns in *-nte* make their feminine with *-nta*. See 1.2.5.

20

The gerund

The main points discussed in this chapter are:

- Forms of the gerund (Section 20.2)
- 'A box containing books', 'a girl speaking French' (Section 20.3)
- Main uses of the gerund (Section 20.4)
- 'I imagined her dancing', 'I heard them talking', etc. (Sections 20.6–7)
- Gerund with *andar, ir, llevar, quedarse, salir, venir, acabar, terminar* (Section 20.8)
- Translating the English –ing form (Section 20.9)

For the use of the gerund to form the continuous aspect of verbs, e.g. *estoy hablando* 'I'm talking', *estaba diciendo* '(s)he was saying', etc., see Chapter 15. For the tendency of English to avoid relative clauses by simply joining nouns with prepositions – 'the meeting *in* the church *by* the supermarket *at* the crossroads' – see the introduction to Chapter 34, note (iii).

20.1 General

The gerund is the verb form that ends in –*ando* or –*iendo*: *andando, respondiendo, diciendo*, etc. It is invariable in form, but pronouns are sometimes attached to it. This may be obligatory, as in *contestó riéndose* '(s)he replied (by) laughing', or optional as in *estaba esperándolos* or *los estaba esperando* '(s)he was waiting for them'. See 11.14.5 for details.

The Spanish gerund is quite unlike the English -ing form ('walking', 'replying', 'saying', etc.), which can function as a gerund, a present participle, a noun or an adjective; and it is also unlike the French form ending in –*ant*, which covers the functions of both the Spanish gerund and the adjectival form in -*ante*, -*(i)ente* discussed at 19.4.

The Spanish gerund is theoretically a kind of adverb and it should not modify nouns. ?*Una caja conteniendo libros* 'a box containing books' is therefore not good Spanish. See 20.3 for detailed discussion.

Except in one archaic construction described at 20.5, the Spanish gerund is *never* preceded by a preposition, so *estoy harto de diciéndolo* is definitely not Spanish for *estoy harto de decirlo* 'I'm tired of saying it'. Nor can the gerund ever be used as a noun, so *fumando destruye los pulmones* is absolutely wrong for *(el) fumar destruye los pulmones* 'smoking destroys the lungs'.

20.2 Forms of the gerund

(a) All verbs of the -*ar* conjugation, including radical-changing verbs: replace the -*ar* of the infinitive by -*ando*: *hablar* 'to speak' *hablando*, *dar* 'to give' *dando*.

(b) Verbs of the -*er* and -*ir* conjugations: replace the infinitive ending with -*iendo*: *temer* 'to fear' *temiendo*, *vivir* 'to live' *viviendo*, *producir* 'to produce' *produciendo*.

Irregular verbs form the gerund in the same way: *ser-siendo*, *tener-teniendo*, with the following exceptions:

decir and its compounds: *diciendo*
dormir, morir: *durmiendo, muriendo*
erguirse: *irguiéndose*

ir: *yendo* (regular despite appearances)
oír and its compounds: *oyendo*
poder: *pudiendo*
traer, caer and compounds: *trayendo, cayendo*
venir and its compounds: *viniendo*

verbs ending in –*llir*: *bullendo*
verbs ending in -*ñir* or –*ñer*: *tañendo*
verbs like *construir*: *construyendo, huyendo*
verbs like *pedir*: *pidiendo*
verbs like *poseer*: *poseyendo, leyendo*
verbs like *reír*: *riendo, sonriendo*
verbs like *sentir*: *sintiendo, riñendo*

20.3 'A box containing books' 'a girl speaking French', etc.

English and French regularly avoid relative clauses by using the -*ing* or the -*ant* form of the verb:

We need a girl who speaks French
He had a box that contained several books
C'est là une réponse qui équivaut à un refus
(That's a reply that amounts to a refusal)

We need a girl speak**ing** French
He had a box contain**ing** several books
*C'est là une réponse équival**ant** à un refus*

Since the Spanish gerund can strictly speaking modify only verbs and not nouns, such sentences must usually be translated by a relative clause:

Necesitamos una chica que hable francés
(not **hablando francés*)
Tenían una caja que contenía varios libros
(not **conteniendo varios libros*)
Esa/Ésa es una respuesta que equivale a una negativa (not **equivaliendo a*)

We need a girl who speaks French

They had a box containing several books

That's a reply amounting to a refusal

The gerund is possible only when there is a verb in the main clause to which it can refer, e.g. *me escribió pidiéndome que fuera a verla* '(s)he wrote a letter asking me to go and see her'. *El cartero trajo una carta pidiendo dinero* 'the postman brought a letter asking for money' is therefore correct only if *pidiendo* refers to *trajo*... and not to *carta*, i.e. only if the postman is asking for money. But this rule is broken:

(a) In captions to pictures:

Dos 747 siendo preparados para el despegue
El Avante publicó mi foto quitándome los aretes (A. Mastretta, Mex., dialogue)

Two 747s being prepared for take-off
Avante published a photo of me taking off my earrings (lit. ear 'hoops')

(b) After verbs meaning 'hear', 'imagine', 'see', 'find', usually to show that the action is actually in progress. See 20.7 for more details.

(c) In the exceptional cases of the adjectives *ardiendo* 'burning' and *hirviendo* 'boiling'. See 4.4 for discussion.

(**d**) In official and administrative documents: *una ley decretando. . .* (= *una ley por la que se decreta* 'a law decreeing. . .'. This construction, sometimes called the *gerundio curialense* or 'lawyers' gerund', is deeply entrenched in certain documents, e.g. the *Boletín Oficial del Estado* (where Spanish laws are published), but Seco (1998, 228) condemns it, as does the Academy's *Esbozo. . .*, 3.16.8.

(**e**) Occasionally by writers whose style is presumably above reproach, as in *el propósito de Probo, el hombre solo afrontando a la multitud, no se pudo realizar* (Seco, 1998, xvii) 'it was not possible to realize the goal of Probus, the man alone confronting the multitude', despite his absolute condemnation of this very construction (*Diccionario de dudas. . .*, 1998, 228).

(**f**) Constantly in spontaneous speech and informal writing:

. . .luego ya en mi habitación, recién limpia y oliendo a ambientador de flores (C. Martín Gaite, Sp.)	. . .then back in my room, (which was) recently cleaned and smelling of flower-scented air-freshener
Tenía mi edad y un hijo viviendo con su mamá (A. Mastretta, Mex., dialogue)	She was my age and had a son living with her mother
el tenue ruido de un cuerpo moviéndose con sigilo (L. Sepúlveda, Ch.)	the faint sound of a body moving stealthily
. . .con la luna ahí colgando para nosotros (A. Bryce Echenique, Pe.)	. . .with the moon hanging there for us
Hombres trabajando a 400m (Mexican road-sign)	Men working at 400 metres/US meters

Foreign learners should probably imitate only the possibilities listed at (**a**), (**b**) and (**c**). However, the grammarians' wholesale condemnation of (**d**), (**e**) and (**f**) seems excessive, since these constructions are clearly sometimes acceptable to careful native speakers.

(i) The participle form ending in *-nte* may sometimes be used like the English -ing form: *. . .personas pertenecientes a diferentes clases sociales* '. . .people belonging to different social classes'. This uncommon construction, possible only with a limited number of verbs, is discussed at 19.4.

(ii) French allows the *–ant* form to refer to a subject different to that of the main clause: *la pluie tombant à verse, le voyageur s'arrêta sous un hangar.* The gerund cannot be used here: *ya que llovía a cántaros, el viajero se detuvo bajo un granero*, 'since it was pouring, the travel(l)er stopped under a barn' (not **lloviendo a cántaros. . .*).

20.4 Main uses of the gerund to modify the main verb in the sentence

20.4.1 Gerund used to indicate simultaneous actions:

The gerund is used to indicate an action happening at the same time as the action of the main verb:

Se fue gritando	(S)he went off shouting
Nos recibió bañándose	She received us while she was having a bath
Me bajé del caballo queriendo un zumo de naranja (A. Mastretta, Mex.)	I got down from my horse as I wanted (lit. 'wanting') an orange juice

> ...*y en el séquito se habían metido Ariel y Remesa, siendo el editor el que tenía que cambiar el paso constantemente* (M. Vázquez Montalbán, Sp.)
>
> ...Ariel and Remesa had joined the gang/retinue, it being the publisher who had to make an effort to keep up

(i) The action denoted by the gerund and the main verb should be simultaneous. *?El ladrón huyó volviendo horas más tarde* 'the thief fled, returning hours later' should be *el ladrón huyó y volvió horas más tarde*. *?Abriendo la puerta, entró en la casa* (better *abrió la puerta y entró en la casa*) is less acceptable in Spanish than 'opening the door, (s)he entered the house'. The Spanish gerund should also not be used to describe an action that is the result of a previous action: one says *el edificio se hundió y mató a varias personas* not *?se hundió matando a varias personas* 'the building collapsed killing several people', although journalists and TV and radio announcers constantly break this rule in Spanish.

(ii) With the verbs *ser* and *estar* the gerund can translate 'when' or 'while', a construction strange to English-speakers: *estando en París, me enteré de que su padre había muerto* 'while I was in Paris, I found out that his father had died', *le conocí siendo yo bombero* 'I met him while I was a fireman', *te lo diré, pero no estando aquí esta señora* 'I'll tell you, but not while this lady is here'.

20.4.2 Gerund used to indicate method

The gerund may indicate the method by which an action is performed. English usually requires the preposition 'by':

> *Hicieron su fortuna comprando acciones a tiempo*
> They made their fortune (by) buying shares at the right time
>
> *Hacéis divinamente no teniendo niños* (Antonio Gala, Sp., dialogue)
> You're doing just the right thing by not having children
>
> *Estás obligado a escribir otra novela. No publicando ésta/esta te he hecho un favor* (M. Vázquez Montalbán, Sp., dialogue)
> You're obliged to write another novel. I've done you a favo(u)r by not publishing this one
>
> *Conozco mucha gente que trabajando logró lo que quería* (A. Arrafut, Cu., dialogue)
> I know a lot of people who got what they wanted by working

This construction often expresses a condition: *apretando/si lo aprietas de ese modo lo vas a romper* 'you'll break it if you squeeze it/by squeezing it like that', *poniéndose/si se pone así conmigo usted no conseguirá nada* 'you'll get nowhere if you get like that with me'.

20.4.3 Gerund used to express purpose (= para + infinitive)

This construction occurs with verbs of communication:

> *Me escribió diciéndome/para decirme que fuera/fuese a verle*
> (S)he wrote telling me to come and see him
>
> *Nos llamó pidiendo/para pedir dinero*
> (S)he rang us asking/to ask for money
>
> *Letonia y Estonia han aprobado leyes privando a la población rusa del derecho de ciudadanía* (El País, Sp.)
> Latvia and Estonia have passed/ published laws depriving their Russian population of citizenship

20.4.4 Gerund used to indicate cause (= *ya que..., puesto que...* + finite verb)

Siendo estudiante, tendrá usted derecho a una beca	Since you're a student, you'll be entitled to a grant
Tratándose de usted, no faltaba más	Since it's you, there's no need to mention it
Confieso que, a mí, siendo editor, lo único que me preocupa es que no lean (*Cambio16*, Sp.)	I admit that, being a publisher, the only thing that worries me is that they don't read
No queriendo molestar me fui	Not wanting to be a nuisance, I left
Un día, no teniendo nada que hacer, fue a verla	One day, not having anything to do, (s)he went to see her

20.4.5 Gerund used to express concession (= *aunque* + finite verb)

The Spanish gerund occasionally signifies 'although', often in combination with *aun* 'even':

Siendo inteligente como es, parece tonto	Although intelligent, he looks stupid
Llegando tarde y todo, nos ayudó mucho	Although (s)he arrived late, (s)he helped us a lot
Es probable que este servicio no se ofrezca en su provincia o que, aun existiendo, no se haya anunciado (*Yellow Pages*, Sp.)	It is probable that this service is not available in your province or, even if it exists (lit. 'even existing'), it has not been advertised
Usted, siendo católica, parece ignorar que los católicos peruanos también dependemos de Roma (A. Bryce Echenique, Pe., dialogue)	Even though you are a Catholic, you seem not to know that we Peruvian Catholics also depend on Rome

20.4.6 Gerund preceded by *como* as an equivalent of *como si*

Me miró como calculando mi edad (S. Puértolas, Sp.; = *como si estuviera calculando...*)	She looked at me as though calculating my age
Julio se rascaba la cabeza, como diciendo... (A. Bryce Echenique, Pe.)	Julio was scratching his head, as if saying...

20.5 *En* + gerund

In older language and in some dialects this is an equivalent of *al* + infinitive: *en llegando al bosque = al llegar al bosque* 'on arriving at the woods' (cf. French *en arrivant à*). This construction seems to be extinct in modern Spanish. *Al* + infinitive is discussed at 18.3.3.

The use of *en* + the gerund to indicate conditions, as in *en sabiendo que están bien y contentos, ya tengo bastante* 'as long as I know they're well and happy, that's enough for me' is mentioned in *GDLE* 10.8.5, but it seems to be virtually extinct in modern Spanish.

20.6 Gerund used to qualify the object of a verb

Like the English -ing form, the Spanish gerund can also indicate an action performed by the direct object of certain kinds of verb:

(a) With verbs of 'perception' like 'see', 'hear', 'observe': see 20.7 for details.

(b) With verbs like *coger, pillar* ('to catch'), *arrestar* 'to arrest', *dejar* 'to leave', *encontrar* 'to find', *sorprender* 'to surprise':

La cogió/pilló robando	(S)he caught her stealing
Me sorprendí repitiendo entre dientes... (C. Martín Gaite, Sp.)	I caught myself repeating between my teeth... (i.e. 'muttering')
Dejamos a Andrés durmiendo (A. Mastretta, Mex., dialogue)	We left Andrés sleeping

(c) With verbs of representation like 'paint', 'draw', 'photograph', 'show', 'describe', 'imagine', 'represent', etc.:

La pintó tocando el clavicémbalo	(S)he painted her playing the harpsichord
Esta fotografía muestra al rey bajando del avión	This photo shows the King getting out of the plane
Se la imaginó recogiendo sus enseres (C. Carmen Gaite, Sp.)	She pictured her gathering together her belongings
Me los describió cazando leones	(S)he described them to me hunting lions
Por eso los recuerdo siempre bebiendo (A. Bryce Echenique, Pe., dialogue)	That's why I remember them always drinking

Captions under photos or other pictures fall into this category. See 20.3a above.

20.7 Gerund after verbs of perception ('see', 'hear', etc.)

Commonly after the verb *ver* 'to see', and occasionally after *oír* 'to hear', *recordar* 'to remember', *olvidar* 'to forget' and *sentir* 'to feel'/'to hear', the gerund may be used to qualify the object of the main verb, as in *abrimos el periódico y vemos a niños muriéndose de hambre* (*El País*, Sp.) 'we open newspapers and see children dying of hunger'. Usually the infinitive is also possible in this construction, the difference being that the infinitive indicates a completed action and the gerund an action that is or was still in progress. Compare *la vi fumando un cigarrillo* 'I saw her (while she was) smoking a cigarette' and *la vi fumar un cigarrillo* 'I saw her smoke a cigarette' (see 18.2.5 for the infinitive). There is usually a colloquial alternative to the gerund using *que* + a finite verb: *la vi que fumaba un cigarrillo* 'I saw that she was smoking a cigarette'. Further examples:

No se me olvida mi hijo bailando con ella	I can't forget my son dancing with her
Me gustaba sentir la lluvia azotando los avellanos de la huerta (C. Martín Gaite, Sp.)	I liked to hear the rain lashing the hazelnut trees in the garden
Cuando Félix divisó al doctor leyendo una revista política... (C. Fuentes, Mex.)	When Felix caught sight of the doctor reading a political magazine...

(i) With verbs of motion the gerund is not usually possible: 'I saw him coming towards me' is *lo/le vi venir hacia mí* or *lo/le vi que venía hacia mí* but not **lo/le vi viniendo hacia mi*.

(ii) *Oír* 'hear' may take a gerund, as in *desde allí oíamos al niño jugando en su cuarto* 'from there we could here the child playing in his/her room', but it appears more often with either the infinitive or with *que* and a finite verb: *oí entrar a alguien/que alguien entraba* I heard someone come in; see 18.2.5 for examples. The infinitive is safest for foreigners, since a gerund could be taken to refer to the subject of the main verb, e.g. *?la oí entrando* could mean 'I heard her while (I was) entering'.

However, the gerund is common when its subject is non-living: *cuando el sargento oye la corneta tocando la retirada* (M. Vargas Llosa, Pe.) 'when the sergeant hears the trumpet sounding the retreat', *...la voz del propio comandante saludando por la megafonía* (M. Torres, Sp.) '...the voice of the commander himself greeting us over the speakers'.

20.8 Other uses of the gerund

20.8.1 Gerund with *andar*

This translates the English 'to go around doing something', often with the same implication of pointless activity. *Ir* can usually replace *andar* in this construction:

Siempre anda/va buscando camorra	(S)he always goes round looking for trouble
Era profesor de geografía, y siempre anduvo solicitando traslados (C. Martín Gaite, Sp.)	He was a geography teacher, and was always applying for transfers (to other schools)
Anduve maldiciendo todo el jueves (A. Mastretta, Mex., dialogue)	All that Thursday I went around swearing

Spoken (not written) Mexican often uses *andar* for *estar* to form the continuous: *¿andas trabajando?* (for *¿estás trabajando?*) 'are you working?'; see 15.5.

20.8.2 Gerund with *ir*

(a) Expresses slow or gradual action:

Nos vamos haciendo viejos	We're (gradually) getting older
Ella se fue doblando hasta caer al suelo (*Cambio16*, Sp.)	She gradually doubled up until she fell to the ground
Así ha ido perdiendo todos los clientes, por estar pensando en otra cosa (M. Puig, Arg., dialogue)	That's how he's been losing all his customers, through thinking about other things
Poco a poco el consumidor ha ido descubriendo que las frutas de Cuba están a punto aunque sean de color amarillo verdoso (interview in *Granma*, Cu.)	Gradually the consumer has discovered that fruit from Cuba is ripe even if it is greenish yellow in colo(u)r

Spoken Mexican Spanish also uses this construction to express an action that is just finishing (examples from J. M. Lope Blanch, 1991, 16): *espera un momento; voy acabando ya* (Sp. *estoy acabando ya/estoy a punto de acabar*) 'wait a moment, I'm just finishing', *voy llegando ahorita* (Sp. *acabo de llegar*) 'I've only just arrived'.

(b) To express careful or laborious actions:

Ya puedes ir preparando todo para cuando lleguen	You can start getting things ready for when they arrive
Ve escribiendo todo lo que te dicte	Write down everything as I dictate it to you
Gano lo necesario para ir tirando	I earn enough to get by

20.8.3 Gerund with *llevar*

This provides a neat translation of 'for' in time expressions: *llevo dos meses pintando esta casa* 'I've been painting this house for two months'. This is discussed at 32.3.1.

20.8.4 Gerund with *quedarse*

This translates the idea of 'to continue to do something':

Me quedé ayudándolos un rato	I stayed on for a while to help them
Se quedó mirándome	(S)he remained staring at me

20.8.5 Gerund with *salir*

Usually translates English phrases involving 'come out'/'go out':

Salió ganando	(S)he came out the winner
Era lo único que quería: salir volando por la ventana (C. Martín Gaite, Sp., dialogue)	It was all I wanted to do—fly out of the window

20.8.6 Gerund with *seguir* and *continuar*

Seguir and *continuar* with the gerund translate 'to go on ...-ing', 'to continue to...'. See 32.8. for discussion.

20.8.7 Gerund with *venir*

To express an action that accumulates or increases with time. It sometimes conveys mounting exasperation:

Hace años que viene diciendo lo mismo	(S)he's been saying the same thing for years
La sensación de aislamiento en la Moncloa viene siendo progresiva (*Cambio16*, Sp.)	The sensation of isolation at the Moncloa (the Spanish Prime Minister's residence) is steadily growing
Los programas que se vienen ejecutando en el campo de la cardiología infantil (*Granma*, Cu.)	the program(me)s that have been carried out in the field of child cardiology

The following construction is typically Mexican: *¿Qué, no lo viste? Ah, claro: tú vienes llegando apenas* (Sp. *apenas acabas de llegar*) 'What? Didn't you see it? Oh, of course, you've only just arrived' (from J. M. Lope Blanch, 1991, 17).

20.8.8 Gerund with *acabar, terminar*

These verbs with the gerund mean 'end by':

Siempre acaba enfadándose	(S)he always ends by getting mad
Acabarás haciendo lo que ella diga	You'll end by/up doing what she says
...porque con el tiempo terminaríamos no viéndonos nunca (A. Bryce Echenique, Pe.)	...because with time we'd end by not seeing one another at all

Acabar por + infinitive is an equivalent and is more common in negative statements: *acabarás por no salir nunca de casa* 'you'll end by/up never going out of the house'.

20.9 Translating the English -ing form

The following examples consist mainly of cases where the English -ing form may not be translated by the Spanish gerund.

20.9.1 When the -ing form is the subject of a verb

This is normally translated by an infinitive or by a suitable noun:

Eating too much butter is bad for the heart	*Comer demasiada mantequilla es malo para el corazón*
No smoking	*Prohibido fumar*
Skiing is expensive	*Esquiar/El esquí cuesta mucho*
Salmon fishing is an art	*La pesca del salmón es un arte*

20.9.2 When the -ing form is the object of a verb

In this case there are two possibilities:

(**a**) When the same subject performs both actions, use an infinitive or a noun:

(S)he dreads having to start	*Teme tener que empezar*
I like swimming	*Me gusta nadar/Me gusta la natación*
(S)he gave up gambling	*Dejó de jugar/Dejó el juego*
Try calling him	*Intenta llamarlo/le*
There's nothing I like better than working in the garden	*No hay nada que me guste más que trabajar en el jardín*

(**b**) When the actions are performed by different subjects, use a clause or noun. The subjunctive must be used when required by the rules given in Chapter 16:

I can't stand Pedro singing	*No puedo ver que Pedro cante*
I didn't mind him/his living here	*No me importaba que viviera/viviese aquí*
I recommended promoting her	*Recomendé su ascenso/que la ascendiesen/ ascendieran*
I approve of you(r) getting up early	*Me parece bien que te levantes temprano*

Some verbs allow the gerund. See 20.7.

20.9.3 The -ing form used in a passive sense

Care is needed when the English -ing form replaces a passive infinitive, cf. 'your hair needs cutting' (= 'your hair needs to be cut'). In the Spanish translation an infinitive or a clause must be used:

Your hair needs cutting	*(Te) hace falta que te corten el pelo* or *que te cortes el pelo*
This needs attending to	*Hace falta cuidarse de esto/Hay que atender a esto*
You're not worth listening to	*No vale la pena escucharte*
It wants/needs polishing	*Hace falta sacarle brillo*

20.9.4 The -ing form preceded by prepositions

Unless the preposition is 'by' (see 20.4.2) an infinitive or clause must be used:

I'm looking forward to seeing you	*Tengo ganas de verte*
I prefer swimming to running	*Prefiero nadar a correr*
He was punished for being late	*Lo/Le castigaron por llegar tarde*
This is a good opportunity for showing what you mean	*Ésta/Esta es una buena oportunidad para demostrar lo que quieres decir*

You get nothing in life without working	*No se consigue nada en esta vida sin trabajo/sin trabajar*
He was furious at being mistaken for his/her brother	*Le enfureció que le/lo confundieran/ confundiesen con su hermano*

20.9.5 The -ing form before nouns

(a) If the -ing form is itself a noun, translation is usually by an infinitive or a noun:

driving licence/US permit	*el carnet/el permiso de conducir*
dancing shoes	*los zapatos de baile*
fishing rod	*la caña de pescar*

(b) If the -ing form is a participle (adjective) then a relative clause may be used, unless a participle in *-ante*, *-(i)ente* exists (see 19.4):

the chiming bells	*las campanas que tañen/tañían* (*tañente does not exist)
a worrying problem	*un problema inquietante*
a flying object	*un objeto volante*
a convincing reply	*una respuesta convincente*

But often an idiomatic solution must be sought in either case:

flying planes	*aviones en vuelo*
turning point	*el punto decisivo/la vuelta de la marea*
steering wheel	*el volante*
dining room	*el comedor*

For the exceptional use of *hirviendo* 'boiling' and *ardiendo* 'burning' as adjectives, see 4.4.

21

Modal auxiliary verbs

The main points discussed in this chapter are:

- *Poder hacer algo* and *saber hacer algo* (Section 21.2)
- *Deber, deber de* and *tener que hacer algo* (Section 21.3)
- *Haber, haber de, haber que* (Section 21.4)
- *Querer* (Section 21.5)
- *Soler* (Section 21.6)
- *Ha debido/podido hacerlo* or *lo ha debido/podido hacer*? (Section 21.7)
- Translating 'would', 'shall', 'will' and 'need to' (Section 21.8)

21.1 General

'Modal auxiliary verbs' are verbs like *poder, saber, deber, hay que, soler, tener que* or 'would', 'may', 'might', 'can', 'could', 'should', 'ought to', 'to have to', that express various shades of meaning, usually when combined with an infinitive, as in *podría llover* 'it may/might rain', *deberían hacerlo* 'they ought to do it'.

21.2 *Poder* and *saber* 'to be able to'/'to know how to'

21.2.1 *Poder* and *saber* contrasted

Both verbs often translate 'can' or 'could', but their meanings are slightly different: *saber*, as well as 'to know', means 'to know how to do something', and *poder* means 'to be able to do something'/'to be allowed to do something'. Sometimes the meanings overlap:

¿Sabes nadar?	Can you swim? (do you know how to?)
¿Puedes nadar hoy?	Can you swim today? (are you able to/are you allowed to?)
Nunca podía salir con sus amigas	She could never/was never allowed to go out with her girlfriends
Soy libre. Puedo hacer lo que quiero	I'm free. I can do whatever I want
Mi madre sabe guisar muy bien cuando quiere	My mother can cook very well when she wants to
Se sabe ganar/Sabe ganarse las simpatías de todo el mundo	She knows how to win people's affections

(i) Since 'can' and 'could' have no infinitives or participles in English, *poder* is translated by 'to be able to'/'to be allowed to' in compound and future tenses: *nunca había podido descifrarlo/nunca podrá descifrarlo* '(s)he had never been able to decipher it/(s)he'll never be able to decipher it'.

(ii) *No poder (por) menos de* means the same as *no poder evitar* + infinitive: *no podré (por) menos de decírselo* 'I won't be able to stop myself from telling him/her'. The Latin-American equivalent is *no poder menos que*.

(iii) Idioms with *poder*: *no puedo más, estoy harta* 'I can't go on, I'm fed up', *al menos en ese terreno la vida no ha podido conmigo* (C. Martín Gaite, Sp.) 'in this area at least, life hasn't got the better of me'.

21.2.2 Preterite and imperfect of *poder* and *saber*

The preterite tense refers to one occasion, the imperfect to a period of time usually made clear by the context. The preterite of *poder* often means 'to manage to', and the preterite of *saber* usually means 'to find out' as opposed to 'know':

No pudo escaparse	(S)he couldn't escape (…didn't manage to)
No podía escaparse	(S)he couldn't escape (at that time; no information about whether (s)he eventually did)
No me pudo ver porque estaba ocupada	S)he didn't get to see me because she/I was busy
No podía verme porque estaba siempre ocupada	(S)he couldn't see me because she/I was always busy
Yo ya sabía la verdad	I already knew the truth
cuando supe la noticia de su muerte…	when I heard the news of his/her death…

(i) Strangely, the positive preterite of *poder* can also mean the opposite of 'manage to', i.e. 'could have done but didn't'. See 21.2.3c.

(ii) 'Can you see the stars?', 'I *can* see it', etc., are usually expressed *¿ves las estrellas?*, *lo veo. No la/lo* (or *le*) *puedo ver* may mean 'I can't stand her/him' as well as 'can't see…'.

21.2.3 *Poder* to express possibility and suggestions

Poder is usually translated by 'could' or 'may'. Either the imperfect or the conditional can be used:

(a) Possibility/suggestions

Podía/Podría no haberla visto	(S)he may not have seen her
Lo que podíamos/podríamos hacer es tirar este tabique	What we could do is to knock down this partition wall
Puedes/Podías/Podrías venir a comer mañana	You could come to lunch tomorrow
Puede/Podría/Podía haberle ocurrido algo	Something may/could have happened to him

Pudiera could be also for *podría*, but it is less usual in spoken language.

(b) Polite requests

The conditional is perhaps more usual than the imperfect in polite requests, but both are heard:

¿Podría/Podía usted abrir la ventana?	Could you open the window?
¿Podrías/Podías decirle al jefe que estoy enfermo?	Could you tell the boss I'm ill/sick?

(c) The positive preterite indicative may sometimes express something that could have happened but didn't:

El día que pudo estallar la Tercera Guerra	The day World War III could have
Mundial (Cambio16, Sp.)	broken out
...pensando en lo que pudo haber sido y no	...thinking of what might have been
fue (J. Marsé, Sp.)	and wasn't
Pudo haberte demorado el amor, pero unos	Love could have delayed you, but
amigos te esperaban en el centro	some friends were waiting for you
(P. Armando Fernández, Cu.)	in the centre/US center

Paradoxically, the preterite may also mean 'could and *did*', as in *pudo abrir la puerta* '(s)he managed to open the door'. The negative preterite means 'couldn't and didn't': *no pudo hacerlo* '(s)he didn't manage to do it'.

(d) The imperfect indicative (not the conditional) can also be used to reproach somebody for something done or left undone in the past:

Me lo podías haber dicho	You could have told me
Podías haber puesto algún adornito de	You could have put up some Christmas
Navidad (C. Rico-Godoy, Sp., dialogue)	decorations

(i) *Puede ser, podría/pudiera ser, podría/pudiera haber sido* are equivalent to 'it could be', 'it could have been'; *pudiera* is less common in the spoken language: *aun en el caso de que nuestro viejo profesor se hubiera muerto, que bien pudiera ser...* (C. Martín Gaite, Sp.) 'even if our old teacher has died, which could well have happened'.

In answers, *puede ser* can be abbreviated to *puede:* —*¿Vas a pescar mañana?* —*Puede* '"Are you going fishing tomorrow?" "Perhaps/Maybe...".'

For the use of *poder que* with the subjunctive, see 16.3.1.

21.2.4 *Poder* used in speculations

As in English, *poder* can be used to speculate about something: *ha llamado alguien. ¿Quién puede/podrá haber sido/ha podido ser?* 'Somebody called. Who could it have been?', *podría ser tu tía* 'it could be your aunt'.

21.3 *Deber, deber de* and *tener que*

21.3.1 *Deber* to express obligation

Deber + infinitive translates 'must' in the sense of 'is obliged to':

Su hijo debe trabajar más si quiere aprobar	Your/His/Her son must work harder if
el examen (in Latin America *pasar un*	he is to pass the examination
examen is common)	
El presidente y el ministro de Economía	The President and the Minister for the
debieron intervenir personalmente en las	Economy were obliged to intervene
últimas horas (La República, Ur.)	late in the day
Hubo un verano en el que el marido debió	There was a summer when her husband
ausentarse de más por razones	had to be away more often than usual
profesionales (J. Marías, Sp.)	for professional reasons

In these three examples *tener que* could have been used instead to strengthen the obligation, i.e. *tiene que trabajar, tuvieron que intervenir, tuvo que ausentarse*.

(i) The degree of obligation is reduced by using the conditional or, less often, the *-ra* form of *deber*. Since the imperfect is often colloquially used as a conditional (see 14.5.4b), *deberías hacerlo, debías hacerlo* and *debieras hacerlo* can therefore all mean 'you ought to do it', although *debiera* is more literary.

(ii) *No tener más remedio que* is a variation of *tener que* often used in everyday language to express strong obligation: *no tengo más remedio que despedirla* 'I've got no choice but to fire her'.

(iii) *Deber* **de** must not be used to express obligation. **Debes de hacerlo ahora* is bad Spanish for *debes hacerlo ahora* 'you've got to do it now'. This mistake is not uncommon in popular speech on both continents and even in writing, cf. *si desea hacer alguna rectificación en la libreta electoral, debe de acreditarlo con documentación* (Peruvian official document) 'if you wish to make any change in the Electoral Register, you must provide documentary support'. See the next section for the correct use of *deber de*.

21.3.2 *Deber (de)* to express probability or supposition

Deber de can only express probability or supposition, although *deber* alone is nowadays also used with this meaning:

Debiste (de) llegar tarde	You must have arrived late
Debe (de) haber sido muy guapa	She must have been very beautiful
Deben (de) ser las cinco	It must be five o'clock
Mi madre debió de pensar que había que confiar en el destino (S. Puértolas, Spain)	My mother must have thought that she had better put her trust in fate
En verano debía de ser una bella alameda (L. Sepúlveda, Ch.)	In summer it must have been a fine tree-lined avenue
Debió ser vergüenza (J. Madrid, Sp.; better *debió de ser…*)	It must have been shame

The modern tendency to use *deber* both for obligation and supposition (*deber de*) creates ambiguities. Use of *deber de* to translate 'must' would have clarified the following examples:

Debió hacerlo Juan	John ought to have done it (on that occasion)/John must have done it
Debía hacerlo Juan	John used to have to do it/John ought to do it/John must have done it

(i) Mexican Spanish constantly uses *haber de* to express suppositions. See 21.4.1b.

(ii) Like 'got to' in English, *tener que* can also indicate a strong supposition, as in *búscalo bien, tiene que estar ahí* 'check thoroughly, it's *got* to be there'.

21.3.3 Preterite, conditional and imperfect of *deber*

The preterite expresses something that should have been done; the negative something that should not have been done. The conditional and the imperfect express something that should be done.

Debió decírtelo antes	(S)he ought to/should have told you before
Debía/debería decírtelo antes	(S)he ought to/should tell you before
No debiste hacerlo	You shouldn't have done it
En ese momento debí desconfiarme, pero no lo hice (J. Ibargüengoitia, Mex., dialogue)	At that moment I ought to/should have been suspicious, but I wasn't
Volvió al sitio del que nunca debió salir (E. Arenas, Sp., dialogue)	He went back to the place he ought never to have left/should never have left
Debieron llamarla PDUSA, no PDVSA (*Rebelión*, Ven.)	They should have called it [Venezuela Oil inc.] PDUSA, not PDVSA

However, when it is used to express suppositions, the preterite of *deber* may also indicate an assumption or guess so strong as to be a virtual certainty: *lo que ella le dijo debió convencerlo, ya que al día siguiente le dio cien mil dólares* 'what she told him must have convinced him since he gave her 100,000 dollars the following day'. One should say *debió **de** convencerlo*, as explained at 21.3.2, but there is an unfortunate universal tendency to omit the *de*.

21.4 *Haber*

Haber is the modal auxiliary used for forming compound tenses, e.g. *he visto* 'I have seen', *habían vuelto* 'they had returned'. This use is discussed at 14.8.

Haber, with the special present tense form *hay*, is used to translate 'there is', 'there are', 'there were', etc., as in *hay cincuenta* 'there are fifty', *hubo una explosión* 'there was an explosion'. This is discussed in Chapter 30.

21.4.1 *Haber de*

Haber de has the following uses:

(**a**) It expresses mild obligation or future certainty. This usage is nowadays literary and faintly archaic, at least outside Catalonia:

He de hacerlo cuanto antes	I have to do it as soon as possible
si su compañía tiene bancos de datos que han de ser accesibles desde varias sedes... (computer manual, Sp.)	If your company has data banks that are to be accessed from several sites...
Hubo de repetir el experimento (J. Marías, Sp.)	(S)he had to repeat the experiment
las dos tendencias, centralista y federalista, que habían de marcar la historia de Colombia (*Promocomercio*, Col.)	the two tendencies, centralist and federalist, that were to leave their imprint on Colombian history

Catalans often use this construction in Castilian to express obligation since their own language uses *haver de* for obligation.

(**b**) It may express probability or suppositions:

Ha de haberle dicho todo	(S)he must have told her/him everything

This construction is also nowadays rare and literary except in Mexico, where it is very common, e.g. *para terminar, el capitán ha de haberse quejado de su soledad. Serafina ha de haberlo compadecido* (J. Ibargüengoitia, Mex.) 'eventually, the Captain must have complained about his solitude. Serafina must have taken pity on him'; Spain *debió (de) haberse quejado, debió (de) haberlo/le compadecido.*

(c) In the conditional or imperfect forms it translates an indignant or mystified 'should...'. This usage is normal, at least in Spain:

¿Por qué habría/había de ofenderse si yo no dije nada? (or, more colloquially, *iba a ofenderse*)	Why should (s)he get offended if/when I didn't say anything?

21.4.2 *Haber que*

Haber que means 'to be necessary to...'. In this construction the verb is used only in the third-person singular. The present-tense form is *hay que*:

Hay que darles tiempo	One has to give them time/It's necessary to give them time
A los muertos hay que dejarlos irse (C. Martín Gaite, Sp.)	The dead must be allowed to depart
No había que hacer autopsia (G. García Márquez, Col.)	There was no need to do an autopsy
Hubo que llamar a los bomberos (with the implication 'and that's what we did')	It was necessary to call the firemen

21.5 *Querer* 'to want to'

This verb must not be confused with *querer* 'to love'. In the latter meaning it cannot precede an infinitive or a noun referring to something non-living: *me encanta nadar* 'I love swimming', *me encanta/adoro el helado de vainilla* 'I love vanilla ice-cream'.

(a) The imperfect of *querer* with an infinitive simply means 'wanted to' and does not tell us whether you did or not: *quería hablar con José* 'I wanted to talk to José (and may or may not have succeeded)'.

(b) The preterite of *querer* plus an infinitive is peculiar in that out of context it is ambiguous. It may mean 'wanted to and failed': *quise hablar con José* 'I wanted/tried to talk to José (but failed)'. But in other contexts, and less commonly, it may mean 'wanted to and did', especially when the speaker is being very assertive: *lo hice porque quise* 'I did it because I wanted to (and that's that!)'.

(c) The negative preterite usually means 'to refuse to'. Compare *no quiso hacerlo* '(s)he didn't want to do it' (and didn't) and *no quería hacerlo* '(s)he didn't want to do it' (no information about whether (s)he did it or not). But it can also imply 'didn't mean to' when something unintended happened: *no quise ofenderte* 'I didn't mean to upset you'.

(d) The *-ra* imperfect subjunctive form can be used for the conditional: *no querría/quisiera volver a nacer* 'I wouldn't like to be born again'. The imperfect indicative can also be used instead of these two tenses in polite enquiries or requests: *querría/quisiera/quería hablar con el encargado* 'I would like to speak to the manager'.

21.6 *Soler*

Soler translates the idea of 'usually', 'to be used to'. It is not used in the future, conditional or preterite tenses:

Los zapatos de tacón alto suelen ser incómodos	High-heeled shoes are usually uncomfortable
Solía hablar solo	He used to talk to himself
Ha solido portarse/acostumbrado a portarse bien conmigo	(S)he's usually behaved well towards me
El crecimiento afectó especialmente a las ciudades más importantes de cada país, que solían ser una o dos (*Artehistoria*, Ven.)	Growth especially affected the major cities in each country, of which there were usually one or two

(i) *Acostumbrar a* 'to be in the habit of' may be used for *soler* when conscious habits are involved (so not **acostumbraba a hablar solo*): *no acostumbro a/suelo beber* 'I don't usually drink'. *Acostumbrar* (no *a*) used to be usual in Spain and is still used in Latin America: *se dirige al rancho de un morador, donde acostumbra pernoctar* (M. Vargas Llosa, Pe.; Sp. *rancho = choza, casucha*) 'he makes for the hut of a local inhabitant, where he usually spends the night'.

(ii) In some spoken varieties of Latin-American Spanish, notably in the Southern Cone, *saber* is used for *soler*: *sabe levantarse a las ocho* for *suele levantarse a las ocho* '(s)he usually gets up at eight'. This usage is, however, popular or provincial.

21.7 *Deber, poder* and *tener que*: **alternative construction with compound tenses**

Deber and *poder* allow a variety of constructions in compound tenses, i.e. tenses based on *haber* and a participle. The option of pronoun shifting (discussed at 11.14.4) doubles the number of possibilities:

Ha debido hacerlo/Lo ha debido hacer *Debe haberlo hecho/Lo debe haber hecho*	(S)he must have done it
Ha podido hacerlo/Lo ha podido hacer *Puede haberlo hecho/Lo puede haber hecho*	(S)he could have done it
Habían debido hacerlo/Lo habían debido hacer *Debían haberlo hecho/Lo debían haber hecho*	They must have done it (before)
Habían podido hacerlo/Podían haberlo hecho *Podían haberlo hecho/Lo podían haber hecho*	They could have done it (before)
Habría debido hacerlo/Lo habría debido hacer/Debería haberlo hecho/Lo debería haber hecho (*debiera* can be used for *debería* here)	(S)he ought to have done it

and also *habría podido hacerlo, podría haberlo hecho*, etc. '(s)he might have done it'.

    Tener que may also appear in the same alternative constructions: *ha tenido que hacerlo/tiene que haberlo hecho/lo tiene que haber hecho* '(s)he had to do it' / '(s)he must have done it', etc.

21.8 Translation of miscellaneous English modal verbs: 'would', 'shall', 'will' and 'need'

(**a**) 'Would'. This may form a conditional: 'it would be better' *sería mejor.* In English narrative it is often means 'used to' and must then be translated by the imperfect: 'every morning he would leave/he left/he used to leave at seven' *todas las mañanas salía a las siete.*

(**b**) 'Should'. This usually means 'ought to', in which case the conditional of *deber* is the translation: 'this should work now' *debería funcionar ahora.* In older English it may mean the same as the conditional 'would' 'I should/would be very angry if you did it' *me enfadaría mucho si lo hicieras.*

(**c**) 'Ought to'. The conditional or imperfect of *deber* is the likely equivalent: 'you ought to eat less meat' *deberías/debieras/debías comer menos carne.* When it refers to the past, the preterite of *deber* is a common translation: *debiste hacerlo antes* 'you ought to have done it sooner'.

(**d**) 'Got to'. This may imply a strong obligation: 'you've got to work harder' *tienes que trabajar más.* In both American and colloquial British English it may also express a strong supposition: 'it's got to/must be a lie' *debe (de) ser mentira/tiene que ser mentira.*

22

Personal a

The main points discussed in this chapter are:

- Use of personal *a* before direct objects referring to living things (Section 22.2)
- *Me trató **como a** una reina*, etc. (Section 22.3)
- Personal *a* before pronouns (Section 22.4)
- Personal *a* before personified nouns (Section 22.5)
- Personal *a* with *tener* and *querer* (Section 22.6)
- Personal *a* before collective nouns (Section 22.9)
- Personal *a* before non-living direct objects (Section 22.10)
- Use of the preposition *a* with other verbs (Section 22.11)

22.1 Personal *a*: general

The use of the preposition *a* before certain kinds of direct object is so important in Spanish that it deserves a special chapter.

The basic rule is that identified or particularized human (and most other animal) direct objects are preceded by *a*, e.g. *vi a tu hermana* 'I saw your sister'. Compare *vi tu coche* 'I saw your car' (non-human). However, 'personal' *a* is a rather inaccurate label since the same *a* also sometimes appears with non-living direct objects, particularly, but not only, whenever there might be doubt about which is the subject and which the object in the sentence.

NB: The words 'identified' or 'particularized' are important here. Grammar books sometimes imply that human direct objects always require personal *a*, but as the following section shows, this is not true.

22.2 Personal *a* before direct objects denoting human beings or animals

Personal *a* is required before a direct object which denotes a known or identified human being or an animal such as a pet or some other familiar creature.

Before a direct object which is a personal name or title—*Pedro, el jefe, mamá*—personal *a* is never omitted: *conozco a tu madre* 'I know your mother', *vi a Mario y a Elena* 'I saw Mario and Elena', *no aguantan al nuevo jefe* 'they can't stand the new boss'.

With animals, use of personal *a* depends on the extent to which the creature is humanized. Pets virtually always take personal *a*, but in other cases use of *a* depends on factors of emotion or context: the more familiar the language, the more likely the use of *a*. At the zoo one is likely to say *vamos a ver a los monos* 'let's go and see the monkeys' but, probably, *vamos a ver los insectos* 'let's go and see the insects', monkeys being more loveable than cockroaches. Clinical or scientific language would naturally use personal *a* much more sparingly.

In the following examples personal *a* is obligatory:

No conozco a Feliciano	I don't know Feliciano
La policía busca a un individuo con una cicatriz en la cara	The police are seeking an individual with a scar on his face
Llevó a las niñas al zoo	(S)he took the girls to the zoo
¡Mira a los turistas!	Look at the (i.e. those) tourists!
No me importa que encuentre al o a los asesinos (L. Sepúlveda, Ch., dialogue)	I don't care whether you find the murderer or murderers
Admiran mucho al cámara (cf. *admiran la cámara* 'they admire the camera')	They admire the cameraman a great deal
¿Quieres pasear al perro?	Do you want to take the dog for a walk?
Dejad de atormentar al gato	Stop tormenting the cat

Compare the following sentences in which the object of the verb is not individually particularized:

Busco un marido que me ayude en la casa	I'm looking for a husband who will help me in the house (any one will do)
No conozco un solo farmacéutico en todo Bruselas (A. Bryce Echenique, Pe.)	I don't know a single pharmacist in the whole of Brussels
Veía un chico que jugaba en silencio (E. Sábato, Arg.)	I saw a child playing in silence
Los universitarios eligieron una reina de belleza (I. Allende, Chi.)	The university students elected a beauty queen
Amenazaron con no dejar un terrorista vivo en todo el país	They threatened not to leave a single terrorist alive in the whole country
Mira los turistas, siempre gastando dinero	Look at tourists (for example), always spending money
Utilizaron un perro lobo para el experimento	They used an Alsatian dog for the experiment

(i) A proper name may occasionally denote a non-living thing, in which case personal *a* is not used: *dice conocer todo Shakespeare* '(s)he says (s)he knows the whole of Shakespeare' (i.e. the works), *van a subastar un Turner* 'they're going to auction a Turner', *procura tomar la reina* 'try to take the queen' (in chess).

(ii) The *GDLE*, Chapter 28, notes that with some verbs personal *a* is used even with unidentified persons: *encarcelaron a un narcotraficante* 'they jailed a drug-pusher', not **encarcelaron un*…. Likewise *insultar* 'to insult', *curar* 'to cure', *emborrachar* 'to make drunk', *sobornar* 'to bribe', *golpear* 'to hit', *odiar* 'to hate', *hacer* + infinitive 'to make …', etc.

Matar is a special case: *mataron (a) un transeúnte* 'they killed a passer-by' implies accidentally without the *a*, deliberately with it (based on *GDLE* 28.2.1).

22.3 Personal *a* with nouns linked by *como*

A noun linked by *como* to a previous noun which itself has a personal *a*, or to a pronoun standing for such a noun, usually also takes personal *a* (although it is often omitted colloquially if there is no ambiguity):

Tuve que recoger a mi hermana como a un fardo	I had to pick my sister up as though she were a bundle
Su reacción fue una de las primeras cosas que delató a Adriano Gómez como a un ser peligroso (J. Donoso, Ch.)	His reaction was one of the first things to expose Adriano Gómez as a dangerous person
Me trataba como a una reina (A. Mastretta, Mex., dialogue)	He treated me like a queen

?*Tuve que recoger a mi hermana como un fardo* sounds like ?'I had to pick up my sister as if I were a bundle'.

22.4 Personal *a* before pronouns

22.4.1 Before pronouns other than relative pronouns

When a pronoun refers to a person it takes personal *a*. These pronouns include *alguien, alguno, uno, ambos, cualquiera, nadie, otro, ninguno, este, ese, aquel, quien, todo, él, ella, usted* and other personal pronouns, except *me, te, se, nos, os, le, la, lo*. See next section for discussion of the use of personal *a* in relative clauses:

He visto a alguien en el pasillo	I've seen someone in the corridor
Aunque yo no conozco a nadie de la gente que viene aquí… (C. Martín Gaite, Sp.)	Although I don't know anyone among the people who come here…
Era capaz de insultar a cualquiera	(S)he was capable of insulting anybody
¿A quién has visto?	Who(m) did you see?
La persona a quien yo más echaba de menos	The person I missed most
A ése/ese es al que quiere, no a ti	He's the one (s)he loves, not you
Conocen a todo el mundo	They know everyone

Pronouns like *alguien, nadie, cualquiera* are unusual in that they take personal *a* even though they do not refer to specific individuals.

22.4.2 Personal *a* before relative pronouns

Personal *a* may appear before a direct object relative pronoun that refers to a human being, in which case the form of the relative pronoun will be *a quien, al que* or *al cual* (see 35.4.1 for discussion). If personal *a* is not used, *que* is the usual relative pronoun.

Personal *a* is not usual when the clause is clearly restrictive (as defined at 35.1.2). But if it is non-restrictive it must be used, though the difference is occasionally elusive. Peninsular informants generally insisted on *a* in the following examples:

Tengo un profesor al que/a quien han nombrado miembro de la Academia	I have a teacher whom they've appointed as a member of the Academy
Hace unos días, en el puerto, me dijiste que yo era la primera persona a la que habías querido (E. Sábato, Arg., dialogue)	A few days ago, at the harbour, you told me I was the first person you had loved
Plutón, esposo de Proserpina, a la que/a quien/a la cual robó	Pluto, the husband of Proserpine, whom he carried off

(i) The word *único* generates disagreement. One hears *tú eres el único que quiero* 'you're the only one I love', some prefer ...*al que quiero*, others accept both.

(ii) *El que* or *quien* are obligatory in all types of clause if *que* alone creates ambiguities, as it quite often does when it refers to a human being: *ése/ese es el autor que siempre ataca* 'that's the author whom (s)he always attacks' or 'that's the author who always attacks'. *Al que* or *a quien* clearly mean 'whom (s)he always attacks'.

(iii) Personal *a* is rare before relative pronouns referring to non-human objects, but it is found: *hemos encontrado enormes listas de coches* **a** *los que tenían controlados* (*Cambio16*, Sp.) 'we have found enormous lists of cars that they had under surveillance'.

22.5 Personal *a* before personified nouns

A personified noun usually requires personal *a*. The decision whether a noun is personified or not is, however, dependent on complex factors of context:

A lo que yo temo es a la maldita casualidad (A. Buero Vallejo, Sp., dialogue)	What I'm scared of is damned random chance
Se iba feliz a su casa para no seguir desafiando al azar (G. García Márquez, Col.)	He went off happily to his home so as not to go on tempting fate
Los cazas llevan bengalas para confundir a un misil dirigido (*Cambio16*, Sp.)	The fighters carry flares to confuse a guided missile

The last example shows how certain verbs, e.g. *confundir* 'confuse', *criticar* 'criticize', *temer* 'to fear', *satirizar* 'satirize', *insultar* 'insult', etc., tend, by their meaning, to personify their object because they suggest a human-like reaction. They therefore quite often appear with personal *a* even before non-living things, which explains—but does not excuse—sentences like ?*criticaba a las novelas de fulano* '(s)he criticized so-and-so's novels' (better without the *a*).

22.6 Personal *a* after *tener, querer*

These verbs may change their meaning when used with personal *a*:

Tengo un hijo y una hija	I've got a son and a daughter
Tenemos una asistenta griega	We have a Greek maid

but

Así tiene al marido y a los hijos, a base de bocadillos, latas y congelados	That's how she keeps her husband and children—on sandwiches, tins/cans and frozen food
Tengo a mi tío como fiador	I've got my uncle to act as guarantor
La humedad de la noche... tiene a las veredas resbaladizas y brillosas (M. Vargas Llosa, Pe., in Sp. *acera* for 'pavement', *brillantes* for *brillosas*)	The dampness of the night ... makes the pavements slippery and shiny
querer una mujer	to want a woman
querer a una mujer	to love a woman

22.7 Omission of personal *a* before numerals

Nouns preceded by a number tend to be unspecified or unidentified and personal *a* is often omitted before them:

Reclutaron (a) doscientos jóvenes	They recruited 200 young people
Bayardo San Román. . .vio las dos mujeres vestidas de negro (G. García Márquez, Col.)	Bayardo San Román ... saw the two women dressed in black
Sólo/Solo conozco un hombre capaz de componer esta emboscada maestra (...a un hombre also possible)	I only know one man capable of organizing this brilliant ambush

A clearly particularized or identified personal noun will, however, take personal *a*: *yo conocía personalmente a sus tres hijas* 'I knew his three daughters personally'.

22.8 Personal *a* combined with dative *a*

Ambiguity may arise when two *a*s occur in the same sentence, e.g. *?presenté a mi marido a mi jefe* 'I introduced my husband to my boss' or '...my boss to my husband'. The usual solution is to omit personal *a* and place the direct object before the indirect object:

Presenté mi marido a mi jefe	I introduced my husband to my boss
Denuncié el ladrón al guardia	I reported the thief to the policeman
Mande el paciente al especialista	Send the patient to the specialist
Yo prefiero Dickens a Balzac	I prefer Dickens to Balzac

22.9 Personal *a* before collective nouns

Personal *a* is normally used before collective nouns when these refer to human beings:

Sir Walter Raleigh enriqueció a la enclenque corte inglesa (*Cambio16*, Spain)	Sir Walter Raleigh enriched the feeble English court
No conocía al resto del grupo	I/(S)he didn't know the rest of the group
...un paso que podría poner a Estados Unidos en una posición delicada (*La Prensa*, Arg.)	...a step which could put the United States in a delicate position
Admiro al pueblo cubano	I admire the Cuban people

A is obligatory in all these examples, but in the following sentences *pueblo* and *Rusia* do not refer to people but to places: *pintó el pueblo* '(s)he painted the village', *Hitler invadió Rusia* 'Hitler invaded Russia'.

(i) Before words like *país, nación, partido, movimiento*, when these words refer to people, *a* seems to be optional: *criticó duramente al/el movimiento anarquista* '(s)he criticized the anarchist movement severely', *será imposible gobernar a Euskadi* (*Cambio16*, Sp.; omission possible) 'it will be impossible to govern the Basque country', *Luis García Meza, quien gobernó el país entre julio de 1980 y agosto de 1981* (*El País*, Sp.; al possible) 'Luis García Meza, who governed the country between July 1980 and August 1981'.

(ii) Seeing, visiting, leaving, picturing or painting a place do not call for personal *a*: *estamos deseando ver Lima* 'we're longing to see Lima', *se negó a visitar Rumanía* '(s)he refused to visit Romania', *quería pintar Toledo* '(s)he wanted to paint Toledo', *abandonaron Madrid* 'they left Madrid'. The Academy used to maintain that *a* was necessary in such sentences, and DeMello, (2000),1, shows that it is still quite often used in spontaneous speech, although omission is the norm in writing.

22.10 Personal *a* before non-living direct objects

Personal *a* cannot appear before a noun denoting an non-living direct object in straightforward sentences of the following kind:

He comprado un sacacorchos	I've bought a corkscrew
Escribe poesía	(S)he writes poetry
Tus palabras delataban tu derrotismo	Your words betrayed your defeatism

But, despite its name, personal *a* is used before non-living objects:

(a) When there is likely to be uncertainty about which is the subject and which the direct object of a verb. This often happens in relative clauses, where the verb often precedes the subject:

Este producto es el que mejor impermeabiliza al algodón	This product is the one that best waterproofs cotton
La trama conceptual que subyace a esta obra	The network of concepts underlying this work
Es difícil saber en qué medida afectó esto a la economía cubana (M. Vargas Llosa, Pe.)	It is difficult to know to what extent this affected the Cuban economy
una organización que protege a su coche (advertisement, Cambio16, Sp.)	an organization which protects your car
A tres Autos y un Comercio quemaron (Latin-American headline, strange to Peninsular speakers)	Three Cars and Store Burnt

A sentence like *es difícil saber en qué medida afectó esto la economía cubana* could be ambiguous: '...this affected the Cuban economy' or '...the Cuban economy affected this'. Personal *a* makes it clear which is the direct object.

(b) *A* also sometimes appears before non-living direct objects when both subject and object are non-living, even though there is apparently no danger of ambiguity.

It seems that this occurs only in those sentences in which the subject is also the true agent of the action. In a sentence like *la piedra rompió un cristal*, 'the stone broke a pane of glass' or *la novela causó una sensación* 'the novel caused a sensation', it can be argued that the agents of the action are the person who threw the stone or wrote the novel; *piedra* and *novela* are merely instruments, and for this reason personal *a* is impossible. However, if the non-living subject really performs the action, personal *a* may optionally appear before the direct object:

Ambos creían que los astros regían a las pasiones (Octavio Paz, Mex.)	Both believed the stars ruled the passions
Este morfema nominal concretiza al semantema (F. Abad Nebot, Sp.)	This nominal morpheme makes the semanteme specific
El suicidio de la muchacha... excitó a la opinión pública (M. Vargas Llosa, Pe.)	The girl's suicide... stirred public opinion
el artículo 516 del código penal, que considera a la homosexualidad como un delito (La Hora, Ec.)	article 516 of the Penal Code, which views homosexuality as a crime

A could in fact be omitted in all these examples.

(**c**) *A* regularly appears after impersonal *se* so as to show that the *se* is indeed impersonal *se* and not any other kind of *se* such as reflexive *se* or passive *se*:

. . .*la plataforma, como se llama a los andenes en Inglaterra* (J. Marías, Sp.)	. . .the 'platform', as they call the *andén* (of a railway station) in England
En España se llamaba a la plata (Sp. *dinero*) *de los cohechos y sobornos "unto de México"* (O. Paz, Mex.; cf. *la plata se llamaba* 'money was called. . .')	In Spain they used to call the money from bribery and graft 'Mexican grease'
La inversión es indispensable si se quiere convertir al sistema ferroviario en un sector atractivo para los inversionistas (*La Hora*, Ec.)	Investment is essential if one wishes to turn the railroad system into an attractive sector for investors

22.11 A obligatory or preferred with certain verbs

Some verbs always take the preposition *a*, e.g. *agarrarse a* 'to hold on to', *asociarse a* 'to associate oneself with', *seguir a* 'to follow', *suceder a* 'to follow', *sustituir a* 'to substitute', *renunciar a* 'to renounce', *ayudar a* 'to help', *gustar/agradar* 'to please', etc. However, this *a* is usually not personal *a* but some other manifestation of the preposition *a*:

Considera que la opción más sabia es renunciar gradualmente a la energía nuclear (*El País*, Sp.)	He considers that the wisest option is to gradually give up nuclear energy
Esto obedece a unas normas de comportamiento	This obeys certain norms of behaviour
Le gustaba todo lo que le gustara a su mujer, pero no que su mujer les gustara tanto a los hombres (M. Vázquez Montalbán, Sp.)	He liked everything his wife liked but not the fact that men liked his wife so much
Este nuevo producto ayuda al cabello a recobrar su brillo natural	This new product helps the hair recover its natural shine
Los historiadores británicos llaman "guerra peninsular" a lo que nosotros denominamos guerra de la independencia	British historians give the name 'Peninsular War' to what we call the War of Independence
Estas ventajas permiten al Volkswagen superar a sus rivales	These advantages allow the Volkswagen to beat its rivals
. . .*y cuántas lágrimas de hiel tuvo que derramar para sobrevivir a su desastre íntimo* (G. García Márquez, Col.)	. . .and how many bitter tears (lit 'tears of bile') he had to shed in order to survive his intimate personal disaster

Other similar verbs are: *acompañar a* 'accompany', *afectar a* 'to affect', *atender a* 'to pay attention to', *asentir a* 'to agree with', *asistir a* 'to be present at', *combatir a* 'to combat', *contestar a* 'to reply to', *contribuir a* 'to contribute to', *corresponder a* 'to correspond to'/'to reciprocate', *equivaler a* 'to be equivalent to', *reemplazar a* 'to replace', *sucumbir a* 'to succumb to', *sustituir a* 'to replace'.

23

Negation

The Spanish negative words discussed in this chapter are:

no (Section 23.2)
'Redundant *no*' (Section 23.2.4)
nomás (Section 23.2.5)
Double negatives (Section 23.3)
The use of negative words in positive
　sentences (Section 23.4)*
nada and *nadie* (Section 23.5–3)

ni (Section 23.5.4)
ninguno (Section 23.5.5)
nunca/jamás (Section 23.5.6)
apenas (Section 23.5.7)
en mi vida, etc. (Section 23.5.8)
en absoluto (Section 23.5.8)
tampoco (Section 23.5.9)

*E.g. in sentences like 'bigger than **ever**', 'it's imposible to see **anything**', 'why blame **anybody**?', where the words in bold type are translated by *nunca, nada* and *nadie*.

23.1　General

Matters that cause problems for English-speakers are: the use or non-use of the double negative, e.g. *no lo he visto nunca/nunca lo he visto* 'I've never seen it/him', sentences like *¿quién ha dicho nunca eso?* 'who ever said that?', and the use of redundant *no*, e.g. *¡cuántas veces no te habré dicho!* 'how many times must I have told you!' (see 23.2.4).

23.2　*No*

23.2.1　Use and position

No means both 'no' and 'not': this chapter is concerned with the latter meaning. *No* usually precedes the word that it negates, but object pronouns are never separated from a verb: *no dije* 'I didn't say', but *no se lo dije* 'I didn't say it to him/her/you/them':

Mario no estaba	Mario wasn't there
No perdamos tiempo	Let's not waste time
No todos son capaces de aprender idiomas	Not everyone is capable of learning languages
Arguyen—y no sin razón—que. . .	They argue—and not without reason—that. . .
No intentabas verla	You weren't trying to see her
Intentabas no verla	You were trying not to see her

If a verb has been deleted, *no* retains its position: *bebe cerveza pero no bebe vino > bebe cerveza, pero no vino* '(s)he drinks beer but not wine', *—¿Sabéis nadar? —Yo sí, pero él no* '"Can you swim?" "I can, but he can't".' But in emphatic denials it may follow a noun or pronoun: *¡bases nucleares no!* 'no nuclear bases!', *ah no, eso no. . .* 'oh no, not that. . .', *aquí puede entrar todo el que quiera, pero borrachos no* (or *pero no borrachos*) 'anyone who wants to can come in here, but not drunkards'.

(i) Compound tenses do not allow participle deletion in Spanish. In other words, the answer to *¿lo has visto?* 'have you seen him/it?' is *sí* or *sí, lo he visto*, or *no* or *no, no lo he visto*, but not **no, no lo he. . .* (compare English 'no, I haven't. . .'): —*¿Has sido tú? —No, no he sido yo* '"Was it you?" "No, it wasn't"', —*¿Se lo has dado? —No, no se lo he dado* '"Did you give it to him/her/them?" "No, I didn't".' This rule is occasionally broken with the pluperfect: see 14.8.2 for an example.

(ii) Deletion of a gerund or infinitive is, however, possible: —*¿Estabas comiendo* (Lat. Am. *almorzando)? —No, no estaba* '"Were you having lunch?" "No I wasn't"', —*¿Quieres venir? —No, no quiero* '"Do you want to come?" "No I don't"'.

(iii) If it means 'non-' or 'un-', *no* precedes the noun or adjective: *yo estoy por la no violencia* 'I support non-violence', *la política de la no intervención* 'the non-intervention policy', *es la única imagen no real en todo el libro* (J. Marsé, Sp.) 'it's the only non-real image in the whole book'.

23.2.2 'No' and *no* contrasted

The English word 'no' may require translation in various different ways:

Look, no hands!	*Mira, ¡sin manos!*
'What's the problem?' 'No money.'	—*¿Cuál es el problema? —No tengo/ tiene/tenemos/tienen* (etc.) *dinero*
no petrol/US gas	*No hay gasolina*
no smoking	*prohibido fumar/no fumar*
no way!	*¡ni hablar!*
no kidding?!	*¿en serio?*
There's no need for arguments	*No hay por qué discutir*

23.2.3 *No* as a question tag

¿No? at the end of a statement implies that the asker already knows the answer, cf. 'isn't it?', 'do you?':

Usted habla inglés, ¿no?	You speak English, don't you?
Mejor tarde que nunca, ¿no?	Better late than never, don't you think?

A reply to a negative question is handled as in English: i.e. *no* confirms the negative. There is no equivalent of the contradicting 'yes' of French (*si*) or German (*doch*): —*¿No vienes?—No* '"Aren't you coming?" "No (I'm not)"', —*¿No cerraste con llave el armario? —Sí* '"Didn't you lock the cupboard?" "Yes. I did".'

23.2.4 'Redundant' *no*

An apparently superfluous *no* is inserted in certain types of sentence:

(a) Colloquially and optionally, to avoid two *que*s side by side:

Más vale que vengas conmigo que (no) que te quedes solo aquí (or *. . . a que te quedes solo. . .*)	Better come with me than stay here alone

(**b**) In informal language redundant *no* is often unnecessarily used in comparisons, especially before an infinitive:

Mejor gastar cien mil ahora que (no) tener que comprar un coche nuevo para el verano	Better spend one hundred thousand now than have to buy a new car by summer
La obra de R. vale más para un conocimiento de la derecha que no para conocer la República (M. Tuñón de Lara, Sp.)	R.'s work is more useful for learning about the Right than the Republic
. . .con los ojos más luminosos, más tristes y más agradecidos que ella no le vio nunca. . . (G. García Márquez, Col.)	. . .with the most luminous, saddest and most grateful eyes she had ever seen in him. . .

(**c**) Optionally in interjections involving *cuánto* or *qué de* 'how much', 'how many'. Use of *no* is rather literary nowadays:

¡Cuántas veces no lo había soñado en los últimos tiempos! (L. Goytisolo, Sp.)	How often he had dreamt of it lately!
¡Qué de angustias (no) habrán pasado!	What anguish they must have suffered!
¡Cuántas veces (no) te lo habré dicho!	How many times must I have told you!

The *no* makes it clear that the sentence is an exclamation, not a question: cf. *¿cuántas veces te lo he dicho?* 'how many times have I told you?' This type of *no* seems to be rare in Latin-American texts.

(**d**) Optionally after *hasta* and *a menos que* in negative sentences:

Adolfito, hasta que no te tomes el bocadillo no te vas a jugar (E. Arenas, Sp., dialogue)	Adolfo, you're not going out to play until you finish your sandwich
No cobrarás hasta que (no) encuentre trabajo	You won't get the money until (s)he finds work
No era noticia hasta que no la publicaba Abc (Cambio16, Sp.)	It wasn't news until *Abc* published it

But *no* is not used if the main clause is positive: *siguieron sin hacer nada hasta que llegó el capataz* 'they carried on doing nothing until the foreman arrived', *me quedaré aquí hasta que se ponga el sol* 'I'll stay here until the sun sets'.

(**e**) In literary usage, after expressions of fear. The *no* does not alter the sense. Note that *que* is used if the *no* is removed:

Temo no le haya sucedido/Temo que le haya sucedido alguna desgracia	I'm worried (s)he may have suffered some misfortune
Tenía miedo no (or *tenía miedo de que*) *le/lo vieran desde arriba*	He was afraid that they would see him from above

23.2.5 *Nomás* (occasionally written *no más*)

Throughout Latin America this word has a variety of meanings in colloquial language. It is not used in Spain:

—*¿Donde está el hospital?* —*En la esquina nomás* (Spain *justo en la esquina*)	'Where's the hospital?' 'Right on the corner'
La vi ayer nomás (Spain *lo/le vi ayer mismo*)	I saw her only yesterday
Pase nomás (Spain *pase, pase*, etc.)	*Do* come in, please

nomás que venga. . .(en cuanto venga)	as soon as s(h)e arrives…
El gringo viejo se murió en México. Nomás porque cruzó la frontera (C. Fuentes, Mex.)	The old gringo died in Mexico. Just because he crossed the frontier
Una invitación del señor Presidente nomás no se rechaza (idem, dialogue)	You don't turn down an invitation from the President himself

On both continents, *no. . . más que* means 'only' and must be distinguished from *no. . . más de* 'not more than'; see 5.5.

23.3 Double negatives

One may say *nadie vino* or *no vino nadie* 'no one came'. As the second example shows, if a negative follows a verb a negative must also precede the verb. Moreover, if a word is negated, all the following words in the sentence must be negated, if possible: *pero una no debe esperar nunca nada de un hombre sino malas noticias* (Carmen Rico-Godoy, Sp.) 'but one (fem.) should never expect anything from a man except bad news', *nunca hay nada nuevo en ninguna parte* (C. Solórzano, Mex., dialogue) 'there's never anything new anywhere'. The difference between a double and a single negative, e.g. between *nunca viene* and *no viene nunca*, is sometimes merely stylistic. References under the individual items give guidance on this subject:

Double negatives

No dice nada	(S)he says nothing
Nadie dijo nada	No one said anything
Apenas come nada	(S)he scarcely eats anything
Tampoco vino nadie	Nor did anyone come
Nunca trae ninguno	(S)he never brings a single one
Pero no había ningún otro síntoma (E. Lynch, Arg.)	But there was no other symptom
No sabe ni latín ni francés	(S)he knows neither Latin nor French
No la he visto nunca con nadie	I've never seen her with anyone

Single negatives

Tampoco vino	(S)he didn't come either
Apenas habla	(S)he scarcely talks
Nadie cree eso	No one believes that
Ninguna era más guapa que ella	No woman was more beautiful than her
Jamás/Nunca la volvería a ver	(S)he was never to see her again
Ni él ni ella podían decir si esa servidumbre recíproca se fundaba en el amor o la comodidad (G. García Márquez, Col.)	Neither he nor she could have said whether this mutual servitude was based on love or convenience

(i) The double negative can be ambiguous, although intonation or context usually make the meaning clear: *lo que dice no es nada* 'what (s)he says is nothing' (i.e. worthless) or 'what (s)he says isn't nothing' (i.e. it is something); *no llora por nada* '(s)he doesn't cry over nothing'/'(s)he doesn't cry over anything'; cf. *llora por nada* '(s)he cries over nothing'. *No llora sin motivo* expresses the first idea unambiguously.

(ii) One preceding negative word is enough in Spanish: compare French ***personne ne*** *savait la vérité* and *nadie sabía la verdad* 'no one knew the truth', never **nadie no* *sabía la verdad*; or *de ninguna manera pensaban hacerlo* 'in no way were they thinking of doing it', never **de ninguna manera no pensaban.* ...

An exception is the double preceding negative *nunca nadie*: *nunca nadie ha dicho eso* 'no one has ever said that', *nunca nadie supo decirle el porqué de ese Ynés con i griega* (J. Marsé, Sp.) 'no one was ever able to tell him the reason for that "Ynés" with a "y"'. The same idea can be expressed by *nadie ha dicho eso nunca*, or *nunca ha dicho eso nadie*, or *no ha dicho eso nunca nadie*.

A compound preceding negative linked with *y* is also possible, at least in literary styles, as in *en ningún momento y en ninguna parte había visto que volara/volase un elefante* 'never and nowhere had (s)he seen an elephant fly'/'(s)he had never seen anywhere that an elephant could fly'.

23.4 *Nada, nadie, nunca, jamás, ninguno* in sentences that are positive in form or meaning

These words can have the meaning of 'anything', 'ever', 'anyone', 'anything' in the following contexts:

(**a**) After comparisons:

Más que nada, es taimado	More than anything, he's cunning
Salió más temprano que nunca (A. Mastretta, Mex., dialogue; *jamás* not possible)	She went out earlier than ever before
En España son muchos los que se precian de asar el cordero mejor que nadie (*Cambio16*, Sp.)	There are many in Spain who pride themselves on roasting lamb better than anyone else
...y allí un capataz, el mejor que jamás hubiera (M. Puig, Arg., dialogue)	...and a foreman there—the best that ever was
Este libro es más complicado que ninguno de los que yo he leído	This book is more complicated than any I've read
Es más inteligente que ninguna de las otras	She's more intelligent than any of the other girls/women

NB: *Demasiado* and *poco* behave similarly: *es demasiado perezoso para que nadie quiera casarse con él* 'he's too lazy for anyone to want to marry him'; *pocos libros dirían nada semejante* 'few books would say anything similar'.

(**b**) In sentences which involve expressions of doubt, denial, abstention, impossibility, etc.:

Es dudoso que nadie pueda pasar por nativo en más de tres idiomas	It's doubtful whether anyone can pass as a native in more than three languages
Se negó siquiera a hablar a nadie de la emisora (G. Cabrera Infante, Cu.)	He even refused to talk to anyone from the radio station
Es imposible ver nada de lo que está sucediendo	It's impossible to see anything of what's going on
Es horrible contar todo esto a nadie	It's horrible to tell all this to anyone
Yo no sé dónde está nada en esta maldita casa	I don't know where anything is in this damned house

(**c**) In questions or exclamations that expect a negative answer:

¿A usted cuándo le han preguntado nada?	When did anyone ask you anything?
¿Quién ha visto a nadie que trabaje más que él?	Who has ever seen anyone who works more than he does?
¿Para qué despedirme de nada ni de nadie? (A. Gala, Sp.)	Why say goodbye to anyone or anything?
¿Quién puede pensar en nada cuándo se está rodeado de idiotas? (C. Solórzano, Mex., dialogue)	Who can think of anything when one's surrounded by idiots?
¿Quién hubiera pensado nunca/jamás que se casaría con Josefa?	Who would ever have thought he'd have married Josefa?

(d) After *antes de*, *antes que*, and *sin*

He venido sin nada	I've come without anything
sin nadie que lo/le cuidara/cuidase	without anyone to look after him
Al otro día me levanté antes que nadie (J. Cortázar, Arg., dialogue)	The next day I got up before everyone else (lit. 'before anyone')
Esto hay que hacerlo antes de empezar nada	This must be done before starting anything else

(i) Statements of emotion involve a subtlety: *me sorprendería que nadie me llamara/ que no me llamara/nadie* 'I'd be surprised if nobody rang me', *me sorprendería que me llamara/llamase nadie* 'I'd be surprised if anyone rang me'; *sentiría que nadie me viera así/que me viera/viese así nadie* 'I'd be sorry if anyone sees me (looking) like this', *sentiría que nadie me viera/viese así/sentiría que no me viera/viese así nadie* 'I'd be sorry if no one sees me (looking) like this'.

(ii) In sentences in which English allows 'something' after 'without' Spanish allows *algo*: *. . .sin que nadie pudiera hacer algo para impedirlo* (L. Spota, Mex.; *hacer nada* also possible) '…without anyone being able to do anything/something to stop it', *no podía dormir sin que algo* (not *nada*) *la despertara/despertase* 'she couldn't sleep without something waking her up'.

23.5 Further remarks on individual negative words

23.5.1 *Nada, nadie*

(a) When *nada* or *nadie* are a direct object or a predicate, or follow a preposition, they usually appear in the double negative construction in ordinary language:

No sé nada	I know nothing/I don't know anything
No sé nada de nada	I don't know anything about anything
No conozco a nadie	I don't know anyone
No hay nada/nadie	There's nothing/nobody
No lo haría por nada/nadie	I wouldn't do it for anything/anyone
Porque la palabra "felicidad" no era apropiada para nada que tuviera alguna vinculación con Alejandra (E. Sábato, Arg.)	Because the word 'happiness' was not appropriate for anything linked to Alejandra

But in literary or emotive styles they may precede the verb:

. . . nada prometen que luego traicionen (L. Cernuda, Sp., poetry)	…they [i.e. violets] promise nothing that they then betray
Desde hace tiempo para nadie es desconocido que el Sol emite rayos ultravioletas (*Granma*, Cu. Sp. *rayos ultravioleta*)	For some time now no one has been unaware of the fact that the sun gives off ultraviolet rays

A nadie conozco más apto para esta labor literaria	I know no one more suited for this literary task
Por nada del mundo quisiera perderme eso (set phrase in everyday use)	I wouldn't miss that for anything in the world
...como esos hombres silenciosos y solitarios que a nadie piden nada y con nadie hablan (E. Sábato, Arg.)	...like those silent and solitary men who ask nothing from anyone and speak to no one

In all these cases the double negative would have been plainer style, e.g. *no prometen nada..., no conozco a nadie..., no quisiera perderme eso por nada..., ...que no piden nada a nadie y no hablan con nadie.*

(b) When *nada, nadie* are the subject of a verb they usually precede it:

Nada parece cierto en todo esto	Nothing seems sure in all this
Dentro de la pensión reinaba el silencio, como si nadie la habitara (J. Marsé, Sp.)	Inside the boarding-house silence reigned, as if no one were living in it
Nada en el mundo nos podrá separar (A. Arrafut, Cu., dialogue)	Nothing in the world will be able to separate us
Nada en la pieza es histórico (M. Vargas Llosa, Pe.)	Nothing in the play is historical
Nadie quiso creerle que era honrado... (ibid., dialogue)	No one was willing to believe he was honest...
Nadie cree eso ya	No one believes that any more

(c) But a double negative construction is usual in questions: *¿no ha venido nadie?* 'hasn't anyone come?', *¿no llueve nunca aquí?* 'doesn't it ever rain here?'/'does it never rain here?'

23.5.2 *Nada* as intensifier

Nada may be used as an adverb meaning 'not at all':

Manuel no trabaja nada	Manuel does absolutely no work
No hemos dormido nada	We haven't slept a wink
La separación de su marido no había sido nada dramática (S. Puértolas, Sp.)	The break from her husband had not been at all dramatic
No me gusta nada lo que acabas de decir (A. Bryce Echenique, Pe., dialogue)	I really don't like what you just said

23.5.3 Further remarks on *nadie*

Nadie takes personal *a* if it is the object of a verb:

Apenas conozco a nadie	I hardly know anybody
No se veía a nadie en la playa	There was no one to be seen on the beach

Nadie de should not be followed by a plural noun or pronoun: *nadie de la clase* but *ninguno de los alumnos* 'none of the students', *ninguno de ellos* 'none of them', *ninguno de nosotros salimos* 'none of us went out'.

23.5.4 *Ni*

'Nor', 'neither'. As with other negative words, if *ni* follows the verb, the verb must itself be negated: compare *ni tú ni yo lo sabemos* 'neither you nor I know (it)' and *no lo sabemos ni tú ni yo*. Constructions like **ni tú ni yo no lo sabemos* are considered archaic or incorrect.

Unlike 'nor', *ni* is usually repeated before each member of a list: *no han llegado (ni) Antonio, ni Pilar, ni Ana, ni Marta* 'neither Antonio, Pilar, Ana nor Marta has arrived' (first *ni* optional). Examples of the use of *ni*:

Ya no eres joven ni atropellado ni inexperto (E. Lynch, Arg.)	You're no longer young, hasty or inexperienced
Ni fumo ni bebo/No fumo ni bebo	I neither smoke nor drink
No hubo tiempo ni de llamar a una ambulancia (C. Martín Gaite, Sp.)	There wasn't even time to call an ambulance
Ni con ella, ni con nadie, me puedo comunicar (M. Puig, Arg., dialogue)	I can't communicate with her or with anybody
Ya no puede uno llorar ni en los entierros (A. Mastretta, Mex.)	One can't even cry at funerals any more

(i) *Ni* commonly translates 'not even'. It can be reinforced by *siquiera*: *ni (siquiera) en mis peores momentos soñé que esto pudiera/pudiese suceder* 'not even in my worst moments did I dream this could happen', *eres un inútil, no puedes ni (siquiera) freírte un huevo* 'you're useless, you can't even fry yourself an egg', *...experiencia que no les sirvió ni para enfrentarse con un puñado de bandidos* (M. Vargas Llosa, Pe., dialogue) '...an experience that didn't even help you take on a handful of bandits', *¡ni se te ocurra (siquiera) venir a verme!* 'don't even get the idea of coming to see me!'

(ii) Before a noun it may be an emphatic denial: *—¿Sabes quién es? —Ni idea* '"Do you know who it is?" "No idea"', *—¿Cuánto ganabas? —Ni (siquiera) un céntimo* '"What were you earning?" "Not a cent".'

(iii) *Ni* is required after *sin*: *vivía sin dinero ni ganas de tenerlo* '(s)he lived without money or the urge to have it', *sin mujer ni hijos* 'without wife or children', *el buque seguía aquellas vueltas y recodos sin vacilar ni equivocarse nunca* (from Ramsey & Spaulding, 11.45) 'the vessel followed those turns and bends without ever hesitating or making a mistake'.

(iv) The following Latin-American sentence, *si no te gusta lárgate que ni haces falta* (A. Mastretta, Mex., dialogue) 'if you don't like it go away, because you're not even wanted' would be expressed in Spain by *...ni falta que haces*.

23.5.5 *Ninguno*

'No', 'none', 'nobody' (cf. French *aucun*, German *kein*). The double negative rule applies: if *ninguno* follows the verb, the verb must be negated: *ninguno de ellos lo sabe/no lo sabe ninguno de ellos* 'none of them knows it', *nunca compra ninguno* '(s)he never buys a single one'. In certain types of sentences it may be an equivalent of 'any': see 23.4 for examples.

It may be either adjectival or pronominal. As an adjective it loses its final *-o* before a masculine noun or noun phrase: *en ningún momento pensé que...* 'at no point did I think that...', *en ningún miserable pueblo costero...* 'in no wretched coastal village...', but *no aceptaremos ninguna solución parcial* 'we will accept no partial (or 'biased') solution'.

It is usually pronounced 'ningún' before feminine nouns beginning with stressed *a-* or *ha-*, but it should be written in full, e.g. *ninguna arma nuclear*. Seco (1998), 307, rejects written forms like ?*ningún arma*.

The plural *ningunos/ningunas* is rare since one rarely needs to mention more than one of something that does not exist. But it occurs with nouns that are always plural: *ningunas vacaciones en Cataluña son completas sin una excursión al Pirineo* 'no holiday/vacation in Catalonia is complete without a trip to the Pyrenees', *total, tenía 18 años y ningunas ganas de volver al pueblo* (A. Mastretta, Mex., dialogue) 'in short/in a word, he was eighteen and had no desire to go back to the village'. Further examples:

(a) Pronominal forms

Ninguno de los que hablan un idioma está libre de dudas... (M. Seco, Sp.)	None of those who speak a language is free of doubts...
O se lleva todos, o ninguno	Either you take/(s)he takes them all, or none
pues ninguno tiene menos de un noveno grado (Granma, Cu.)	since none is lower than the ninth grade (at school)
Si he sido insincero con ninguno/alguno de vosotros, decídmelo (*ninguno* is more literary)	If I have been insincere with any of you, tell me so

(b) Adjectival forms

¡Ningún gobierno puede sentirse estable sin una oposición poderosa! (El Nacional, Ven.)	No government can feel secure without a powerful opposition!
Tampoco recibimos ninguna contestación/recibimos contestación alguna	Neither did we receive any reply
—Si es molestia, puedo esperar. —Molestia ninguna/Ninguna molestia	'If it's a nuisance I can wait.' 'No nuisance at all'
Había llegado al climaterio con tres hijas y ningún varón (G. García Márquez, Col.)	She had reached the menopause with three daughters and no male (offspring)

(i) *Alguno*, placed after the noun, may be used as an emphatic alternative to *ninguno*. See 9.4.1a for details.

(ii) When *ninguno* is the subject of a verb, person and number agreement seems to be optional when a pronoun appears: *ninguna de nosotras tiene/tenemos marido* 'none of us women has/have a husband', *ninguno de vosotros habéis/ha traído el libro* 'none of you has/have brought the book'.

If the pronoun is omitted, the verb ending must make the meaning clear: *ninguno hemos dicho eso* 'none of us said that', *¿no salisteis ninguna anoche?* 'didn't any of you girls/women go out last night?' (compare *¿no salió ninguna anoche?* 'didn't any of the girls/women go out last night?').

(iii) If *ninguno* is a direct or indirect object and is placed before the verb, the redundant pronoun (explained at 11.16) agrees with the accompanying noun or pronoun: *a ninguno de ellos los conozco* 'I don't know any of them', *a ninguno de nosotros nos quiere dar el dinero* '(s)he doesn't want to give the money to any of us'.

23.5.6 *Nunca* and *jamás*

Both mean 'never' or, in certain sentences, 'ever'. *Jamás* is somewhat stronger and less common than *nunca*. It is usually identical in meaning to *nunca*, but see note (i). The combination *nunca jamás* is strongly emphatic, but it can only refer to the future: *nunca más te lo volveré a decir* 'I'll never tell you again'.

Both require a double negative construction when they follow the verb phrase to which they refer: *nunca viene = no viene nunca* '(s)he never comes', *nadie viene jamás* 'no one ever comes'. When placed before the verb, they are stronger in meaning: *nunca he oído cosa/nada semejante* 'I *never* heard anything like that', *nunca se sabe muy bien por qué ni para qué pasan las cosas* (L. Silva, Sp.) 'one *never* really knows why things happen and to what purpose':

Yo nunca/jamás conocí a nadie que hablase/hablara tan bien (el) español	I've never met anyone who spoke Spanish so well
No sale nunca/jamás de casa	(S)he never goes out of the house

(i) *Jamás* cannot appear after comparisons, i.e. after *más que* or *menos que*: *ahora más que nunca* 'now more than ever', *trabaja menos que nunca* '(s)he's working less than ever'.

(ii) In rhetorical questions inviting the answer 'no' *jamás/nunca* means 'ever': *¿se vio jamás/nunca tal cosa?* 'was such a thing ever seen?', *¿se ha oído jamás/nunca que un hombre mordiera a un perro?* 'who ever heard' (lit. 'was it ever heard') that a man bit a dog?' Compare the non-rhetorical question: *¿has estado alguna vez en Madrid?* 'have you ever been in Madrid?'

23.5.7 *Apenas* and other words meaning 'scarcely', 'hardly', 'as soon as'

The variant *apenas si* is much used for the meanings 'only' and 'scarcely'; Seco (1998), 51, says it is especially common in literary styles. It is not used in time statements or when *apenas* follows the verb.

The subjunctive is required when the action is or was still in the future, as in *lo haré apenas lleguemos a casa* 'I'll do it as soon as we get home'; see 16.12.7. The *pretérito anterior* (*hubo llegado*, etc.) may be used in literary styles to denote a completed past action in conjunction with words meaning 'scarcely', but it is very rare in speech. See 14.10.4 for discussion.

No te conozco apenas	I hardly know you
Apenas (si) te conozco	I hardly know you
En una semana apenas si cambió dos palabras con su tío (J. Marsé, Sp.)	In the course of a week she barely exchanged two words with her uncle
Apenas llegamos/habíamos llegado/hubimos llegado/cuando empezó a llover	We had scarcely arrived when it started raining
hace apenas seis años	barely six years ago
Apenas tengo lo suficiente para pagar la cena	I've barely got enough to pay for supper

(i) *No bien* (*ni bien* in Argentina and perhaps elsewhere in Latin America) is an alternative: *no bien se hubo marchado/se marchó cuando. . .* '(s)he'd barely left when. . .', *no bien algo me produce una tristeza infinita, me convierto en un hombre de izquierda* (A. Bryce Echenique, Pe.) 'as soon as something produces an infinite sadness in me, I turn into a man of the Left' (i.e. politically). *Nomás* (see 23.2.5) may also be used in Latin America to mean 'as soon as'.

(ii) *Nada más* is a colloquial alternative in time statements: *nada más llegar, pasé por su despacho* 'as soon as I arrived, I dropped in at his office', *lo haré nada más llegue* 'I'll do it as soon as I arrive' (or 'as soon as he/she/it arrives/you arrive').

23.5.8 *En mi vida, en toda la noche, en absoluto*

The phrases *en mi vida/en la vida*, 'in my life', *en toda la noche* 'in the whole night', *en absoluto* 'absolutely not' are occasionally used as negatives: e*n mi vida lo/le he visto* (or *no lo/le he visto en mi vida*) 'I've never seen him in my life', *en toda la noche he podido dormir* 'I've not been able to sleep the whole night', *en mi vida he visto nada más francés ni más bonito que tú* (A. Bryce Echenique, Pe.) 'I've never in my life seen anything more French or prettier than you', —*¿Te molesta?* —*En absoluto* '"Does it bother you?" "Absolutely not/not at all".'

En toda la noche as a negative phrase is rather old-fashioned: *no he podido dormir en toda la noche* is more normal.

23.5.9 *Tampoco*

'Not...either', 'nor', 'neither' (cf. French *non plus*): it is the opposite of *también* 'also'. As with other negative particles, it requires a double negative construction if it follows a verb phrase: *tampoco creo en los ovnis = no creo en los ovnis tampoco* 'nor do I believe in UFOs'/'I don't believe in UFOs either'. *Tampoco* is common on both continents:

—*¿Tienes la llave?* —*No.* —*Yo tampoco...*	'Do you have the key?' 'No.' 'Nor do I...'
Tampoco pienso decir a qué me dedico (L. Silva, Sp., dialogue)	Nor am I planning ro say what I do for a living
Tampoco dice nada a nadie	Nor does (s)he say anything to anyone
Ellos tampoco hicieron ningún comentario	They didn't make any comment either

(i) *Ni* or *y* can precede *tampoco*: *me dijo que no le gustaba el vino, y/ni tampoco la cerveza* '(s)he told me (s)he didn't like wine or beer'. As this example shows, *ni* can only be combined with *tampoco* if a negative statement precedes.

(ii) *Tampoco* is much used colloquially, especially in in Spain, to reduce the importance of a preceding remark, usually a negative one: —*Estoy furioso.* —*Hombre, tampoco es para que te pongas así/tampoco es para tanto* '"I'm furious." "Come on, there's no need to get like that/it's not such a big deal"', —*Me han dicho que no pagaban sus impuestos.* —*Sí, tampoco es gran cosa* '"They told me that they didn't pay their taxes." "Right, but that's not so unusual".'

24

Interrogation and exclamations

The following words are discussed in this chapter:

¿cómo? how? (Section 24.7)
¿cuál? which?/what? (Section 24.3)
¿cuándo? when? (Section 24.8)
¿cuánto? how many/much?
   (Section 24.6)

¿dónde? where? (Section 24.9)
¿para qué? what for? (Section 24.10)
¿por qué? why? (Section 24.10)
¿qué? what? (Section 24.4)
¿quién? who? (Section 24.5)

Frequent mistakes made by foreigners in interrogative or exclamatory sentences are: confusion between *qué* and *cuál*, failure to write accents on interrogative or exclamatory pronouns and adverbs, omission or wrong position of the upside-down question mark and exclamation mark, mistakes in the choice between *qué* and *lo que* in indirect questions (see Glossary for 'indirect question'). For the use of the Spanish signs ¿ and ¡ see 39.4.5.

24.1 Spelling

Spanish question-words are written with an accent: *ahora hay más muertos y ni siquiera hay acuerdo entorno a **cuántos** son y **cómo** murieron* (*La Reforma*, Mex.) 'now there are more dead and there isn't even any agreement about how many and how they died', *no sabemos ni **quién** es usted ni **cuál** es su juego* (L. Sepúlveda, Ch., dialogue) 'we don't know who you are or what your game is'.

The accent shows that these words are stressed in speech, and this can radically alter the meaning. Compare *yo sé que piensan* 'I know that they think' and *yo sé qué piensan* 'I know *what* they think', or *quien sabe francés…* 'the person who knows French…' and *¿quién sabe francés?* '*who* knows French?'

24.2 Word order in questions and exclamations

When a sentence or clause begins with one of the words listed above, the order Verb-Subject is used:

¿Qué hizo usted? — What did you do?
¿Cómo se llama tu hermana? — What's your sister called?
¿A qué viene la pregunta? (G. García Márquez, Col., dialogue) — What's the question for?
¿Desde cuándo no fuma tu marido? — How long is it since your husband hasn't smoked?

Word order in interrogative sentences is discussed more fully at 37.2.2.

NB: In Caribbean Spanish constructions like *¿qué usted hizo?* are common. See 37.2.2 note (ii).

24.3 *Cuál*

24.3.1 Basic uses of *cuál*

This word is a pronoun whose basic meaning is 'which one?' of a set of things:

¿Cuál prefieres?	Which one do you prefer?
¿A cuál prefieres?	Which of them (refers to persons) do you prefer?
¿A cuál de los tres se refiere usted?	To which of the three are you referring?
Dime cuál debo elegir	Tell me which (one) I should choose

However, when persons are referred to, *quién* is preferred: *han venido algunos de tercero, pero no sé quiénes* (rather than *cuáles*) 'some of the third year have come, but I don't know which/who'.

(i) *Cual* (no accent) is an archaic alternative for *como* 'like', occasionally revived for literary effect: *se mantiene a su lado cual guardaespaldas* (E. Poniatowska, Mex.) 'he stays at her side like a bodyguard'. *Cual si* is archaic for *como si*: *arrimada a las paredes cual si la atosigara el miedo* (E. Tusquets, Sp.) 'clinging to the walls, as if fear were harrying her', *uno espera ese vistazo cual si fuera una maravilla* (M. Benedetti, Ur.) 'one awaits that spectacle as though it were a miracle'.

24.3.2 Translating 'what is/are/were?', etc.

The usual translations of the phrase 'what is..?' is *¿cuál es?*: *¿cuál es/era el motivo/la diferencia?* 'what is/was the motive/difference' (cf. *¿qué motivo/diferencia hay/había?* 'what motive/difference is/was there?'). *¿Qué es?* literally means 'what *thing*?' or 'what kind of thing?', and it is used ask the definition of something's nature, as in *¿qué es la democracia/un agujero negro?* 'what (kind of thing) is democracy/a black hole?' Examples:

¿Cuál es el problema?	What's the problem?
¿Cuál es su impresión de los acontecimientos?	What is your impression of the events?
Ya hay bastante desolación como para poder ver cuáles son los deberes del hombre (E. Sábato, Arg.)	There is already enough desolation for us to be able to see what man's duties are

Compare

¿Qué es la vida?	What is life?
¿Qué hora es?	What's the time?
¿Qué es su hermana?	What is his/her sister? (i.e. what does she do?)
¿Qué griterío es ése/ese?	What's that shouting?

(i) It is possible to say *ninguno de ellos sabe siquiera cuál es mi nombre* (L. Otero, Cu., dialogue) 'none of them even knows what my name is', but far more usual is *...ninguno sabe cómo me llamo*. One says *¿a qué fecha estamos?* / *¿a cuántos estamos?* for 'what's the date today?' or *¿qué fecha es hoy?* Compare *¿cuál es la fecha de la Batalla de Waterloo?* 'what's the date of the Battle of Waterloo?'

24.3.3 *Cuál:* dialect differences

In Spain and in some parts of Latin America, *cuál* is almost never used adjectivally (i.e. directly before a noun): one says *¿qué chicas vienen esta noche?* 'which girls are coming tonight?', not *¿cuáles chicas vienen esta noche?* However, sentences like the latter are common in many parts of Latin America, including Mexico:

¿Gatos? ¿Cuáles gatos? (C. Fuentes, Mex., dialogue; Sp. *¿qué gatos?*)   Cats? What cats?

¿Cuál vida me improviso para ustedes? (L. Rafael Sánchez, Puerto Rico, dialogue; Sp. *¿qué vida?*)   What life should I take on (i.e. 'act out', 'invent') for you?

Sentences like *¿cuál sombrero prefieres?* may occasionally be heard in Spain, but learners of European Spanish should say *¿qué sombrero prefieres?* or *¿cuál **de** los sombreros prefieres?*, or simply *¿cuál prefieres?*

24.4 Qué

For the conjunction *que* (as in *dice que viene*) see 33.4. For the relative pronoun *que* (as in *el libro que estoy leyendo*), see Chapter 35.

24.4.1 Basic uses of *qué*

¿Qué? means 'what?', 'what sort of?', but not in sentences like *¿cuál es el problema?* 'what's the problem?', for which see 24.3.2. It is also used in exclamations like *¡qué inteligente es!* 'isn't (s)he intelligent!' See 24.4.4.

(a) *Qué* as a pronoun

No sé qué decirte	I don't know what to say to you
De qué estás hablando?	What are you talking about?
Discutían sobre qué iban a decirles	They were arguing about what to tell them
No recuerdo ya qué fue de Antonio	I can't remember what became of Antonio
Nunca voy a tener con qué pagarte (A. Mastretta, Mex.)	I'll never be able to repay you (lit. 'I'll never have anything to pay you with')

(b) *Qué* as an adjective (see 24.3.3 for the Latin-American use of *cuál* in this context)

¿A qué párrafo te refieres?	Which paragraph are you referring to?
¿Qué animales prefieren fotografiar?	What animals do they prefer to photograph?
¿Con qué medios podemos contar?	What means can we count on?
Me pregunto en qué situación estará ahora	I wonder what situation (s)he's in now

(i) *¿Qué?* is a familiar alternative for the more refined *¿cómo?/¿cómo dices?* when a repetition is requested: —*María es muy respondona.* —*¿Qué?* (polite *¿cómo?*, Mex. *mande*) '"Maria answers back a lot." "What?"' (i.e. 'what did you say?').

(ii) *El qué* may occasionally be used as an interrogative, presumably to make clear that 'what?' is meant rather than 'I beg your pardon': —*Eso es extraño.* —*¿El qué?* '"That's odd." "What is?"', —*Se le olvidó traer el Malibu.* —*¿El qué?* '"(S)he forgot to bring the Malibu." "The what?"'

(iii) In the following sentence the word *que* is an unstressed conjunction and therefore does not take an accent: *¡que me llamen a las cinco!* 'let them call me at five o'clock!'/'tell them to call me at five!'.

24.4.2 *Qué* and *lo que* in indirect questions

Either *qué* or *lo que* are possible in indirect questions (see Glossary), except immediately before an infinitive, when *qué* is required and *lo que* may sound uneducated:

Sé de lo que te hablo (C. Fuentes, Mex., dialogue; or *qué*)	I know what I'm talking to you about
Ni sé qué piensa y tampoco sé lo que pienso yo (E. Sábato, Arg., dialogue)	I don't know what he thinks, and I don't know what I think either
No sé lo que/qué voy a hacer	I don't know what I'm going to do
Pregúntale qué/lo que tiene	Ask him/her what (s)he's got
No sé qué hacer (not **no sé lo que hacer*)	I don't know what to do

24.4.3 *Qué:* idiomatic uses

¿Qué tal estás? (= *¿cómo estás?*)	How are you? How are things?
¿Qué te parece?	What do you think of it?
¿A santo de qué haces eso?	What on earth are you doing that for?
¿A mí qué?/¿y qué?	What do I care?/So what?
A qué viene esta compra? (J. Aldecoa, Sp., dialogue)	What's the point of this purchase?

NB: Compare the colloquial *a que*, as in *¡a que llueve esta tarde!* 'I bet you it rains this afternoon!'

24.4.4 Translating 'What a...!'

Qué is used without a following article to translate 'what a...!' in exclamations:

¡Qué vida!	What a life!
¡Qué día más/tan hermoso!	What a lovely day!
¡Qué cara! (Spain, familiarly, *¡qué morro!*)	What a nerve/cheek!

A following adjective is preceded by *más* or *tan*:

¡Qué pareja más/tan moderna!	What a modern couple!
¡Qué libro más/tan aburrido!	What a boring book!
¡Qué nevera más/tan estúpida ésta/esta!	Isn't this a stupid refrigerator!

(i) Before a verb phrase it may optionally be followed by *que*: *¡qué guapa (que) es tu hermana!* 'isn't your sister good-looking!', *¡qué bien que lo han hecho!* 'they've really done it well!'

(ii) Use of *cómo* before adjectives is found in Latin America but is archaic in Spain: *¡cómo somos desgraciadas las mujeres!* (Sp. *¡qué desgraciadas somos las mujeres!* 'how unhappy we women are!', *¡cómo es difícil vivir!* (= *¡qué difícil es vivir!*) 'how difficult living is!'; (Argentine and Uruguayan examples from Kany, 342–3), *cómo es díscola alguna gente* 'how unruly some people are' (A. Mastretta, Mex., dialogue; Sp. *qué díscola es...*). J. M. Lope Blanch (1991), 13, notes that *cómo* is used thus by all social classes in Mexico.

The colloquial *cómo... de* is common on both continents: *¡cómo estás de guapa!* 'aren't you looking attractive!', *pero ¡cómo está de gordo!* 'wow, isn't he fat!'

(iii) *Qué de...* is a rather old-fashioned alternative for *cuánto* in exclamations: *¡qué de cosas/cuántas cosas tengo que contarte!* (familiarly *¡la de cosas que tengo que contarte!*) 'what a lot of things I've got to tell you!'

24.5 *Quién*

For *quien* as a relative pronoun see Chapter 35. For *quien* as a nominalizer (e.g. *quien dice eso...* 'people who say that...') see Chapter 36. *Quién/quiénes* translates 'who'/'whom' in direct and indirect questions:

¿Quién ha sido?	Who was it?
¿Quién iba a pensar que era médico?	Who would have thought he was a doctor?
Sabes en quién estoy pensando ahora?	Do you know who(m) I'm thinking of now?
No sé quién va a estar	I don't know who is going to be there

(i) Historically *quien* had no plural (it descends from a Latin singular form *quem*), and popular speech still often uses the singular for the plural, e.g. *¿y todas esas con quien has salido?* (A. Buero Vallejo, Sp., dialogue) 'and all those girls you've been out with?' (for *con quiénes*). This construction, frequent in older literature, should not be imitated.

(ii) *Quién* plus the imperfect subjunctive translates 'if only...'. See 16.15.2.

(iii) The following construction is common: *yo no soy quién para aconsejar* (A. Buero Vallejo, Sp., dialogue), 'I'm not the right person to give advice', *tú no eres quién para criticar* 'you're no one to criticize'/'you've got no right to criticize'.

24.6 *Cuánto*

Cuánto may function as a pronoun, adjective or as an adverb. In the former two cases it agrees in number and gender with the noun; in the latter case it is invariable.

(a) 'How much', 'how many'

¿Cuánto es?	How much is it?
¿Cuánta mantequilla queda?	How much butter is left?
¿Cuántos vienen?	How many are coming?
¿Cuánto han trabajado?	How much/long have they been working?

(b) In exclamations, 'how much!', 'what a lot!'

¡Cuántas veces (no) te lo habré dicho!	How many times have I told you!
¡Mira cuánta nieve!	Look at all that snow!
¡Cuánto pesa esta mochila!	Is this rucksack heavy!
¡Cuánto más trágico!	How much more tragic!
¡Cuánto mejor estarías así!	How much better you'd be like that!

In exclamations *cuánto* is shortened to *cuán* before adverbs or adjectives other than *más, menos, mayor, menor, mejor, peor*. However, although it is not yet quite extinct in educated speech, *cuán* is nowadays usually found only in flowery styles, and *qué*, or *lo* + adjective or adverb (the latter discussed at 7.2.2) are more usual:

Ella misma se sorprendió de cuán lejos estaba de su vida (G. García Márquez, Col., or *...de lo lejos que estaba de su vida*)	She herself was surprised at how distant he was from her life
Melania insistió tosiendo un poquito para demostrar cuán mal estaba (J. Donoso, Chi.; usually *...lo mal que estaba*)	Melania insisted, coughing slightly to demonstrate how ill she was

Cuán in questions like *¿cuán apoyado te sientes por tu familia?* 'how supported do you feel/to what extent do you feel supported by your family?' is apparently normal in Puerto Rico and in some other parts of Latin America (*GDLE* 35.6.2), but it is archaic elsewhere. Usually one says *¿hasta qué punto te sientes apoyado?* . . .

(i) In the comparative phrases *cuanto más/menos. . . más/menos* 'the more. . . the more' 'the less. . . the less', *cuanto* is not used exclamatorily, is not stressed, and does not take an accent. See 5.11 for further discussion of this construction.

(ii) *Cuanto* may be used as a relative pronoun equivalent to *todo lo que*: *tengo cuanto necesito* (A. Buero Vallejo, Sp., dialogue) = *tengo todo lo que necesito* 'I have all I need'.

(iii) Exclamatory *cuánto* may optionally be followed by *que* before verbs: *¡cuánto (que) te he extrañado!* 'I've missed you so much!' (example from *GDLE* 31.3.12).

24.7 *Cómo*

'How' in direct and indirect questions and in exclamations. Sometimes it means 'why?', and in this case it is more formal than the English 'how come?' (for *como* = 'as', 'since', see 33.5.2; for *como* + subjunctive = 'if' see 25.8.2):

¿Cómo te llamas?	What's your name?
¿Cómo quieres que me peine?	How do you want me to do my hair?
No sé cómo hacerlo	I don't know how to do it
¡Cómo llueve!	Look how it's raining!
¿Cómo/Por qué no me llamaste ayer?	Why didn't you ring me yesterday?
¿Cómo le dejas ir solo al cine a ese niño?	How can you let that child go to the cinema on his own?
...su ignorancia sobre el cómo y el porqué... (J. Aldecoa, Sp.)	...his ignorance about the how and why...
¿Cómo de inteligente es tu cuñado?	How intelligent is your brother-in-law?

¿Cómo? Or *¿cómo dice (usted)?* (Mex. *mande*) are polite ways of requesting a repetition of something misheard or misunderstood (politer than *¿qué?*).

24.8 *Cuándo* 'when'

Little need be said about this word in direct questions, e.g. *¿cuándo fue eso?* 'when was that? and in indirect questions: *no sé cuándo llegarán* 'I don't know when they'll arrive'.

When it is not a question word, *cuando* (no accent) may introduce relative clauses (see 35.12); or it may be a subordinator, often requiring the subjunctive (see 16.12.7). For 'whenever' see 16.13.6. For the use of *cuando* in cleft sentences, e.g. *fue entonces cuando. . .* 'it was then that. . .' see 36.2.

It may also occasionally function as a preposition meaning 'at the time of': *nos casamos cuando el terremoto* 'we got married at the time of the earthquake'.

NB: Foreign students sometimes wonder why the subjunctive is not used after *cuándo*, e.g. **no sé cuándo 'lleguen'*; but the subjunctive is not used after interrogative words (i.e. accented words like *cuándo, dónde*). See 16.12.1 for more details.

24.9 *Dónde* 'where'

This word behaves predictably in direct questions, e.g. *¿dónde viven?* 'where do they live?' and indirect questions: *no sé dónde viven* 'I don't know where they live'.

Dónde should be differentiated from *¿adónde?*, which means 'where to?' and is optionally used with verbs of motion: *¿adónde/dónde van ustedes?* Only *¿dónde?* can be used when no motion is involved: *¿dónde estamos?*, not **¿adónde estamos?*

When it is not a question word, *donde* (no accent) may introduce relative clauses (see 16.14.4 and 35.10), where the difference between *donde*, *adonde* and *a donde* is discussed. For 'wherever' see 16.13.8. For *donde* in cleft sentences, e.g. *fue allí donde. . .* 'it was there that. . .' see 36.2.

Donde may also mean 'at the house of' in some countries, especially Chile, Peru, Ecuador and Central America: *voy donde Miguel* = *voy a casa de Miguel*; this construction is also heard in regional speech in Spain. *Lo de* has the same meaning in Argentina: *voy a lo de Miguel*.

24.10 *Por qué, para qué*

Por qué 'why' (stressed *qué*) must be distinguished in spelling and pronunciation from *porque* 'because'. *¿Para qué?* 'what. . .for?' must be distinguished from *para que* 'in order to'.

In questions *para qué* emphasizes intention, *por qué* emphasizes cause, and the difference is the same as between 'what *for*?' and 'why?': *¿para qué* (or *¿por qué*) *vamos a cambiarlo si todo está bien?* 'what are we changing it for if everything's OK?' Statistically *por qué* is much more frequent and can often be used instead of *para qué*, but not always: *¿por qué se incendió la casa?* 'why did the house catch fire?' (not *para qué* or 'what for?').

25

Conditional sentences

Apart from the types of conditional sentence listed in the next section, the following topics are discussed in this chapter:

- The use of the imperfect for the conditional (Section 25.5)
- The uses of *si* (= 'if') (Section 25.8)
- *Como* + subjunctive instead of *si* (Section 25.8.2)
- *De* + subjunctive instead of *si* (Section 25.8.3)
- Other ways of expressing conditions (Section 25.9)
- Miscellaneous translation problems involving conditions (Section 25.10)

25.1 General

The commonest types of conditional sentences are:

(**a**) Open conditions (Section 25.2)

Si viene me quedo/quedaré	If (s)he comes I'll stay
Si han llegado, me quedaré	If they have arrived, I'll stay

(**b**) Remote conditions (Section 25.3)

Si yo tuviera/tuviese cien mil dólares, lo compraría	If I had $100,000 I would buy it

(**c**) Unfulfilled conditions (Section 25.4)

Si yo hubiera/hubiese tenido cien mil dólares, lo habría comprado	If I had had $100,000 I would have bought it

(**d**) Fulfilled conditions (Section 25.7)

Si no salía, era porque prefería quedarse en casa	If (s)he didn't go out, it was because (s)he preferred staying at home
Si llegaba temprano comíamos a las doce	If (s)he arrived early we had lunch at twelve

One point can hardly be over-emphasized: *si*, in the meaning of 'if', is *never* followed by the present subjunctive except in one rare construction. See 25.8.1 for details.

NB: The *–ra* form and *–se* form of the imperfect subjunctive are interchangeable in conditional sentences, although the *–ra* form is much more common. See 16.2.3.

25.2 Open conditions

So called because fulfilment (US fulfillment) or non-fulfilment of the condition is equally possible. The subjunctive is not used in open conditions and the tense pattern is the same as in English:

(a) *Si* + present + present

Si tenemos que pagar tanto no vale la pena	If we have to pay so much it isn't worth it
Sólo concibo escribir algo si me divierto,	I can only contemplate writing something
y sólo puedo divertirme si me intereso	if I enjoy it, and I can only enjoy it if I'm
(J. Marías, Sp.)	interested
Si (el elitismo) significa que selecciona sus	If elitism means they select their members
miembros en razón de su aptitud, todas	according to their ability, every
las universidades del mundo son elitistas	university in the world is elitist
(M. Vargas Llosa, Pe.)	

(b) *Si* + present + future (or present with future meaning)

Si el contrato no está mañana en Londres,	If the contract isn't in London by
no hay/habrá trato	tomorrow, there will be no deal
Si llueve me quedo/quedaré en casa	If it rains I'll stay at home
Si te oye tu papi se muere (A. Mastretta,	If daddy hears you he'll die (figuratively
Mex., dialogue)	or literally)

(c) *Si* + past tense + present or future, normally only possible when the subject of the verb in the main clause is not yet sure about the facts described in the if-clause.

Si han contestado ya, no les escribiré	If they've already answered, I won't write to them
Si llevaba minifalda su madre estará	If she was wearing a miniskirt her mother
enfadadísima (Lat. Am. *enojadísima*)	will be really cross

(d) *Si* + present + imperative

Si queréis ver el desfile salid al balcón	If you want to see the parade go out on to
(Lat. Am. *si quieren... salgan...*)	the balcony

(e) In reported speech referring to the past, the imperfect or pluperfect indicative appears in the if-clause, and the conditional (or colloquially the imperfect indicative) in the main clause: *me dijo que me pagaría si había terminado* '(s)he told me he'd pay me if I'd finished'. This reports the actual words *te pago si has terminado* 'I'll pay you if you've finished'. Likewise *el médico dijo que la operarían si tenía algún hueso roto* 'the doctor said that they'd operate on her if she had any broken bones'. This construction is also very common in stream-of-consciousness style, i.e. when the text reports someone's unspoken thoughts.

Si la policía la detenía, ya escarmentaría	If the police arrested her, that would
(M. Vázquez Montalbán, Sp.;	teach her a lesson
unspoken thoughts)	
Si no actuaba pronto, Gianni terminaría	If she didn't act promptly Gianni would
por resquebrajarse (S. Pitol, Mex.)	break down
Me pareció que si me mostraba disponible	I thought that if I showed I was available
te ibas a cansar (M. Puig, Arg.,	you'd get tired of me
dialogue)	

The frequent occurrence of this type of construction in indirect speech encourages students to assume that the pattern *si* + imperfect indicative + conditional is the usual way of making remote conditions in Spanish, as it is in French and English, e.g. 'if I had money'/*si j'avais de l'argent* ... The next section should correct this assumption.

25.3 Remote conditions

In 'remote' conditions the verb in the if-clause is in the imperfect subjunctive (*-ra* or *-se* form). The verb in the other clause is usually in the conditional.

There are two types, which correspond to the English sentences 'if you paid now it would cost less' and 'if I were rich I'd buy you a house'. The first is fulfillable and is merely a slightly hypothetical variant of an equivalent open condition: there is little difference between *si pagaras ahora, costaría menos* 'if you **paid** now it would cost less' and *si pagas ahora, costará menos* 'if you **pay** now it will cost less'.

In the second type the condition is contrary to fact and the subjunctive construction is the only possible one: *si yo fuera/fuese rico, te compraría una casa*, 'if I were rich, I'd buy you a house (but I'm not)'. As was mentioned at 25.2(e), English and French-speaking students must avoid using the imperfect indicative in the if-clause (cf. *si j'**étais** riche...*):

Si supieras hacer el nudo como todos los chicos de tu edad, no te tendrías que quejar (I. Aldecoa, Sp., dialogue; *supieses* also possible)	If you knew how to make a knot like all the boys of your age, you wouldn't have to complain
Si pagaran más las labores me convendría tomar una sirvienta con cama (M. Puig, Arg., dialogue)	If the needlework was better paid it'd be worth my while getting a live-in maid
Si por lo menos se pudiera limitar el contrabando de cocaína, se ahorrarían muchas muertes (M. Vargas Llosa, Pe., dialogue; or *pudiese*)	If one could at least cut back on the cocaine smuggling, a lot of deaths would be avoided

(i) Use of the conditional in the if-clause is regional or sub-standard, but it is common in Navarre, the Basque Provinces and nearby parts of Spain, and in popular Argentine speech, e.g. ?*si no estaría preso, no lo habrían soltado* 'if he wasn't arrested they wouldn't have let him go' (M. Puig, Arg., dialogue; for *estuviera/estuviese*). This should not be imitated.

(ii) For use of the *-ra* subjunctive form as an alternative for the conditional, see 25.6 and 14.7.5.

25.4 Unfulfilled conditions

These indicate a condition in the past that was not fulfilled. The verb in the if-clause is in the pluperfect subjunctive (*hubiera/hubiese hablado*, etc.) and the verb in the main clause is usually in the perfect conditional (*habría/hubiera hecho*, etc.):

Si él hubiera/hubiese tenido dinero, hubiera/habría saldado la cuenta	If (s)he'd had money (s)he'd have settled the bill
Si no hubiera sido por las contracciones del estómago, se habría sentido muy bien (J. Cortázar, Arg., dialogue)	If it hadn't been for the stomach cramps, he'd have felt fine

(i) A number of simpler ways of making unfulfilled conditions are heard in spontaneous speech but are banned from careful language and are a shade too informal for most foreign learners: *si lo llego a saber, te habría llamado* 'If I'd found out, I'd have rung you', *si llegas a estar más rato, te juro que entro a cobrarles algo...* (C. Martín Gaite, Sp., dialogue) 'if you'd stayed there any longer, I swear I'd have gone in and charged them some money...', *si sé que estás enfermo, no vengo* 'if I'd known you were ill, I wouldn't have come', *di un tropezón y si me descuido, me caigo* 'I slipped and I'd have fallen down if I hadn't taken care'.

(ii) *Si* + imperfect + imperfect is widespread but defined as 'sub-standard' by the *GDLE* 57.2.3.3: *si me tocabas, te mataba con mi cuchillo* (E. Sábato, Arg., dialogue) 'if you'd touched me, I'd have killed you with my knife'. One also hears *si* + imperfect + conditional in Argentina: *si hace unos años yo veía* (for *hubiera visto*) *en la playa a alguien con esto, hubiera pensado: ese tipo es loco* (Mafalda cartoon, Arg.; Sp. *está loco*) 'if I'd seen someone wearing that on the beach a few years ago, I'd have thought: the guy's crazy'.

25.5 Imperfect indicative for conditional

The imperfect indicative is frequently used instead of the conditional tense in spontaneous speech on both sides of the Atlantic (the subject is further discussed at 14.5.4). This is perfectly acceptable in relaxed European Spanish but it is not allowed in formal styles. We are not sure of the extent of its use in Latin America:

Desde luego, si yo fuera hombre, no me casaba ... (L. Goytisolo, Sp., dialogue)	Of course, if I were a man I wouldn't get married...
Si no fuera por vosotros iba yo a aguantar a vuestro padre... (Sp. set expression: *iría* not used)	If it weren't for you, would I put up with your father?
¡Si yo fuera hombre, qué extraño, qué loco, tenaz vagabundo que había de ser! (poem by J. de Ibarbourou, Ur.)	If I were a man, what a strange, wild, ceaseless wanderer I'd be!

25.6 -ra forms instead of the conditional

The imperfect subjunctive in *-ra* (but not, at least in careful language, the *-se* form) is a very common alternative for the conditional of the auxiliary verb *haber* and also of some other verbs: *con él o sin él, hubiera/habría sido igual* 'with him or without him, it would have been the same'. See 14.7.5 for detailed discussion.

25.7 Fulfilled conditions

These are not really conditions at all but merely an elegant way of saying 'the reason why'/'just because'/'whenever'. The verb is never in the subjunctive:

Si me estaba contando todos aquellos proyectos era porque inexorablemente pensaba realizarlos (F. Umbral, Sp.)	If he was telling me about all those plans it was because he was inevitably intending to carry them out
Si he tenido suerte, la culpa no es mía	It's not my fault if I've been lucky
Si teníamos dinero, íbamos al teatro	If (i.e. 'whenever') we had any money we used to go to the theatre
Si te traje a la playa es para que vigilaras a Alvarito y no para que te pusieras a leer (S. Vodanovic, Ch., dialogue)	If I brought you to the beach it's so you can keep an eye on little Álvaro, not so you could start reading

25.8 *Si* 'if'

25.8.1 *Si*: general

Si is never followed by the present subjunctive, except occasionally after *saber*: *no sé si sea cierto* 'I do not know whether it be true' for *no sé si es cierto*; *no sé si en este estado pueda continuar* (L. Rafael Sánchez, Puerto Rico, dialogue) 'I don't know if I can go on in this condition'.

Ser cannot be deleted after *si*: *si es urgente* 'if urgent', *ven antes si es posible* 'come earlier if possible'; cf. also French *si nécessaire* 'if necessary', *si es/fuera/fuese necesario*.

Si sometimes merely has an emphatic meaning: *pero, ¡si tiene más de cincuenta años!* 'but he's more than fifty years old!': see 31.4.8. In the phrase *apenas si* it has no function: *apenas (si) la conocía* 'I/he/she/you barely knew her'.

25.8.2 *Como* = *si* 'if'

In informal language in type 1 (open) conditions, *como* with the present or imperfect subjunctive may be used instead of *si*. This tends to be confined to threats and warnings and is found on both continents, as the Cuban example shows; but Lope Blanch, 1991, (146), says that the construction is unknown in Mexican Spanish:

Como vuelvas a hablarme de mala manera, me voy	If you talk to me in a nasty way again, I'm going
Me dijo que como no se lo pagara/pagase, se lo llevaba/ llevaría	(S)he told me that if I didn't pay her/him, for it, (s)he would take it away
—*¿Está enfermo su hijo?* —*Enferma me pondrá a mí como lo deje* (A. Arrufat, Cu., dialogue)	'Is your son sick?' 'He'll make *me* sick if I let him'

Como with the indicative means 'since' and is discussed at 33.5.2, e.g. *como no me lo has pagado, me lo llevo* 'since you've not paid me for it, I'm taking it away'.

25.8.3 *De* + infinitive = *si* + finite verb

De plus an infinitive may be used for *si* and a finite verb in an if-clause, although this is not particularly common. This construction is best restricted to sentences in which the verb in the if-clause and the verb in the subordinate clause are in the same person. One can say *de llover, lloverá mucho* 'if it rains it'll rain a lot' (both third-person), but not **de llover, me quedo en casa* 'if it rains I'm staying at home' (*si llueve me quedo/quedaré en casa*). This rule is by no means always applied, but foreigners should probably observe it:

Se me ocurrió que, de estar viva, la mujer me habría parecido más vieja y más digna (A. Martín, Sp., dialogue)	It occurred to me that, had she been alive, the woman would have seemed older and more dignified to me
Un experimento...que, de confirmarse, supondría el hallazgo de la fuente de energía más buscada por los científicos (Granma, Cu.)	An experiment which, if confirmed, would mean the discovery of the energy source most sought after by scientists

> *De no haberse hecho la cirugía estética. . . se le arrugaría la nariz* (J. Asís, Arg.; Sp. *se le habría arrugado*. Different subjects)

> If she hadn't had plastic surgery her nose would have become wrinkled

When used thus *de* must have an unfulfilled or future meaning. One can say *de llover, lloverá mucho* 'if it rains it'll rain a lot', or *de haberlo sabido, habríamos…* 'had we known, we would have…' (unfulfilled), but not **de ser guapa, es mi novia* 'if she's beautiful, she's my girlfriend' (timeless statement: *si es guapa…*). *De* cannot therefore be used in type 4 (fulfilled) conditional sentences (25.7).

25.9 Other ways of expressing conditions

(**a**) The gerund may sometimes have a conditional force: *hablando de esa manera no consigues nada* 'you'll get nowhere by talking like that' = *si hablas de esa manera . . .* 'if you talk like that'. See 20.4.2 for more examples.

(**b**) A negative if-clause may be introduced by some phrase meaning 'unless', e.g. *a menos que, a no ser que* (see 16.12.8b): *debe estar en casa, a no ser que/a menos que haya ido al bar con sus amigos* '(s)he must be at home, unless (s)he's gone to the bar with his/her friends'.

(**c**) 'If' may be expressed by some phrase meaning 'on condition that', e.g. *con tal (de) que, a condición de que* (see 16.12.8a): *compraré los riñones, con tal (de) que estén frescos* 'I'll buy the kidneys provided they're fresh'.

(**d**) *Al* + infinitive (see 18.3.3) properly means 'on . . .-ing', but is sometimes seen with a conditional meaning: *?al ser verdad esta afirmación se tendrá que repensar todo* 'if this claim is true, everything will have to be rethought'. This should not be imitated.

(**e**) *A* + infinitive can have a conditional meaning in a few cases:

> *a juzgar por lo que dicen. . . (= si se juzga por lo que dicen. . .)*

> to judge by what they say …

> *A decir verdad, no me cae bien (= si digo la verdad . . .)*

> To tell the truth, I don't like him/ her/you

(**f**) *Por si. . .* forms conditionals of the sort translated by 'in case. . .' or some similar phrase:

> *Me asomé a la ventana por si venía*

> I looked out of the window in case he was coming

> *Compramos otra botella por si acaso*

> We'll buy another bottle just in case

> *Por si esto fuera poco, también me han robado el reloj*

> As if that weren't enough, they've stolen my watch too

NB: Note the phrase, much used in familiar Peninsular Spanish, *por si las moscas* 'just in case'.

25.10 Miscellaneous examples of conditional sentences

The following are translations of typical English conditionals:

> Had he known, he wouldn't have protested

> *Si lo hubiese/hubiera sabido no habría/hubiera protestado* (or *De haberlo sabido . . .*)

Were that the only reason, there'd be no problem	*Si ésa fuera/fuese la única razón, no habría problema*
If possible, come earlier (not **si posible …*)	*Si es posible, ven antes*
I won't compromise, even if he offers / were to offer me money	*No transijo, incluso/aun si me ofrece/ofreciera/ofreciese dinero*
It'll be impossible unless you change your attitude	*Será imposible, a menos que/salvo que/a no ser que cambies de actitud*
Provided no objection is raised, the meeting will be held here	*Con tal (de) que no haya ninguna objeción, la reunión se celebrará aquí*
Should it turn out to be true, things will be different	*Si resulta ser verdad, las cosas serán distintas*

25.11 Translating 'if I were you…'

If I were you, I'd keep quiet	*Yo de usted/Yo que usted/Si yo fuera usted, me callaría/callaba*

Yo que tú/usted is the older Peninsular formula. *Yo de ti/usted* is a Catalanism which is now widespread in Spain, although it is censured by manuals of good usage (e.g. Santamaría et al. 1989, 309): *yo de ti lo dejaba* 'if I were you I would leave it', *yo de Ana no lo haría* 'if I were Ana I wouldn't do it'.

26

Pronominal verbs

The main points discussed in this chapter are:

- The reflexive meaning of pronominal verbs (e.g. *lavarse, matarse*) (Section 26.2)
- Reciprocal meaning ('they love one another', etc.) (Section 26.3)
- Intransitive meaning of pronominal verbs (e.g. difference between *casar* and *casarse*) (Section 26.4)
- *Se de matización* (i.e. *se* used to add a shade of meaning) (Section 26.5–8)
- Possible meanings of sentences like *se abrió la puerta* (Section 26.10)
- Obligatory use of *uno* where two *se*'s would occur side-by-side (Section 26.11)

26.1 General

Pronominal verbs (called 'reflexive' verbs in most traditional grammar books) are those which are accompanied by an object pronoun (i.e. *me, te, se, nos, os* or *se*) which is of the same person and number as the verb's subject: *yo me lavo* 'I'm washing (myself)', *nos acostamos* 'we're going to bed', *os cansaréis*/Lat. Am. *ustedes se cansarán* 'you'll get tired', *(él) se ha marchado* 'he's gone/left'. The usual object pronouns are used with these verbs except in the third person (*usted, ustedes* included), which uses the invariable pronoun *se* for singular and plural. Common forms of a typical pronominal verb are:

Infinitive *sentarse* 'to sit down'	**Gerund** *sentándose*
Imperative *(tú) siéntate, (vosotros/as) sentaos, (usted) siéntese, (ustedes) siéntense*	
(see 17.2 for details about these imperative forms)	
Present indicative *(yo) me siento*	*(nosotros/nosotras) nos sentamos*
(tú) te sientas	*(vosotros/vosotras) os sentáis*
(él/ella/usted) se sienta	*(ellos/ellas/ustedes) se sientan*

A very large number of Spanish verbs can be pronominalized, even intransitive verbs like 'to be' and 'to die'. It is misleading to give the name 'reflexive' to such verbs. 'Reflexive' refers to just one of the *meanings* that a pronominal verb can have, i.e that the subject performs an action on or for him/herself, as in 'I'm washing myself', 'they give themselves airs', etc. The range of meanings expressed by pronominal verbs is much wider than this, and the relationship between them is sometimes subtle:

Possible meanings of Spanish pronominal ('reflexive') verb forms
(based on Moreira and Butt, 1996, p. 3.)

Name	Example	Singular or plural verb?	Person of verb	Living or non-living subject?	Where discussed
1. Reflexive	*me lavo, me calzo*	either	any	living	26.2
2. Reciprocal	*nos queremos, os habláis*	plural	any	living	26.3
3. Intransitive	*me irrito, se abrió*	either	any, if living; third if non-living	either	26.4
4. *Se de matización*	*se fue, se murió, te bajaste, me lo esperaba, se lo cree,* etc.	either	any	either	26.5–7
5. 'Total consumption'	*se bebió un litro de vino*	either	any	living	26.8
6. Passive *se*	*se construyó el puente*	either	third only	non-living, with few exceptions	Chapter 28
7. 'Special construction'	*se arrestó a tres personas*	singular	third only	human, with a few exceptions	Chapter 28
8. Impersonal *se*	*en España se vive bien, en general se come demasiado*	singular	third only	human	Chapter 28

Constructions 6, 7 and 8 are discussed under Passive and Impersonal Sentences in Chapter 28.

In the following analysis it must be remembered that the meanings of pronominal verbs are often ambiguous, e.g. *se critican* could mean 'they criticize themselves', 'they criticize one another', or 'they are criticized' (passive *se*: Chapter 28). The context of the sentence or the meaning of the verb nearly always removes these ambiguities.

26.2 Reflexive meaning of pronominal verbs

This meaning is very common, but it is not the most frequently encountered, even though it is traditionally the first one studied, probably because it was the basic meaning of pronominal verbs in Classical Latin. It indicates that an action is done by the subject to or for him/herself: *se está duchando* '(s)he's having a shower', *os alabáis mucho* 'you praise yourselves a lot' (or 'you praise one another a lot'; see next section), *me voy a comprar otro traje* 'I'm going to buy (myself) another suit'. Four important features of this reflexive meaning are:

(a) The subject is always living, since doors or stones don't usually do things to themselves.

(b) The pronoun may stand for the direct or the indirect object: *se está afeitando* 'he's shaving' (*se* = direct object), *me estoy quitando la camisa* 'I'm taking my shirt off' (*me* is the indirect object; *la camisa* is the direct object).

(**c**) The action can be deliberate or accidental, and in a few cases may actually be done by someone else: see note (iii).

(**d**) The original verb is always transitive. If the original verb is intransitive then the pronominal form cannot have a reflexive meaning, cf. *dormir* 'to sleep'(intransitive) – *se durmió* '(s)he went to sleep' (*se de matización*, not 'reflexive').

Examples of the reflexive meaning of pronominal verbs:

Se está lavando	(S)he's washing
Me corté con una lata	I cut myself on a tin
Se ha roto una pierna	(S)he's broken a leg
¡Qué bien te peinas!	How well you do your hair!
¡Cuidado, que te vas a salpicar!	Careful, you're going to get splashed!
la fuerte resolución 1441 que instó a Iraq a mostrar que se ha desarmado (*La Reforma*, Mex.)	the strongly-worded Resolution 1441 that required Iraq to show that it had disarmed (itself)
Se daban crema para el sol	They were putting sun-cream on (or reciprocal 'they were putting sun-cream on each other')
Esto me lo pido, esto me lo pido … (children overheard in a toyshop at Christmas)	I'm asking for this… and this…
Se mató en un accidente (see note v)	(S)he got killed in an accident

(i) The subject can be emphasized by using subject pronouns, sometimes reinforced by the appropriate form of *solo* 'alone' or *mismo*. This construction also makes it unambiguously clear that the meaning is reflexive: *primero vistió a la niña y luego se vistió ella* 'first she dressed the child, then she dressed herself', *no eches la culpa a nadie, te has perjudicado tú solo/mismo* 'don't blame anyone else, you harmed yourself', *la niña se pone los zapatos ella sola* 'the little girl puts on her shoes all by herself'.

If a preposition is used (including personal *a*), emphasis is given by using the appropriate prepositional form of the personal pronoun (*mí/ti/sí/nosotros/vosotros/ sí*) plus the correct number and gender of *mismo*: *se decía a sí misma que tenía que hacerlo* 'she told herself she had to do it', *me odio a mí mismo/misma* 'I hate myself', *nos mentimos a nosotros mismos con frecuencia* 'we lie to ourselves frequently'. *Mismo* is not used if the preposition is *para*: *se decía para sí que no valía la pena* '(s)he told her/himself that it wasn't worthwhile'.

(ii) Verbs expressing hurt take either the prepositional or non-prepositional form: *se hace daño él mismo/a sí mismo* 'he's hurting himself', *te perjudicas tú mismo/a ti mismo* 'you (masc.) are damaging yourself'.

(iii) With a few common verbs the reflexive meaning may also include 'to get or have something done for oneself': *Ana se va a hacer un abrigo rojo* 'Ana's going to make herself a red coat'/'Ana is going to get a red coat made', *se han construido un chalet* 'they have built themselves a house (either themselves or to their specifications)', *me voy a cortar el pelo* 'I'm going to get/have my hair cut', *¿dónde te vistes?* 'where do you get you clothes from?' (also 'where do you get dressed?'). Ambiguity can be removed by the appropriate use of the personal pronoun followed by *mismo* or *solo*, e.g. *me voy a cortar yo mismo el pelo* 'I'm going to cut my hair' (myself). See also note (i).

This interpretation of the reflexive meaning is not possible in all Latin-American varieties of Spanish, in which cases *mandar* or *hacer* are used, e.g. *mandó construir un palacio* or *hizo construir un palacio* '(s)he had a palace built'; both of these constructions are also used in Spain.

In a few cases it is unlikely that the action will actually be performed by the subject: *inyectarse contra el cólera* 'to get injected against cholera', *me voy a operar de cataratas* 'I'm going to be operated on for cataracts', *si te duele esa muela, debías sacártela* 'if that tooth's aching you ought to have it out' (less likely, 'you ought to take it out'), *no me gusta nada ese corte que tienes en la mano. Debes ir a vértelo* (colloquial, Sp.) 'I really don't like the look of that cut on your hand. You ought to go and get it looked at'.

(iv) In colloquial language in Spain, but not in Latin America, the reflexive meaning of a few verbs may imply that the action concerns or is important for the subject only and no one else: *tú sabrás lo que te dices* 'I guess *you* know what you're talking about (i.e. I don't)', *yo me entiendo* 'I know what I'm referring to'/'I know what I'm talking about', *yo sé lo que me hago* 'I know what I'm doing' (i.e. even if *you* don't).

(v) *Se mató* can imply accidental death or suicide. If the death was accidental, it means that the subject was performing the action that killed him/her. *Se mató en un accidente de coche* implies that (s)he was driving, but one cannot say **se mató en una riña* *'*(s)he killed him/herself in a fight': *le/lo/la mataron en una riña*, since someone else is responsible.

26.3 Reciprocal meaning of pronominal verbs

Plural pronominal verbs with human or animal subjects can have a reciprocal meaning, i.e. they may show that an action is done to or for one another. *El uno al otro/los unos a los otros* can be added to make clear that this is the meaning:

Nos escribimos periódicamente	We write to one another regularly
Hace años que no se hablan	They haven't been talking to one another for years
Pasó mucho tiempo sin que nos viésemos/viéramos	We didn't see one another for a long time
Os conocisteis en Córdoba	You met (for the first time) in Cordoba
Los guardianes parecían vigilarse los unos a los otros (G. García Márquez, Col.)	The guards seemed to be watching one another
Se hacen la compra los unos a los otros	They do one another's shopping
Siempre se ponen pegas (*el uno al otro*)	They're always finding fault with one another

If both female and male subjects are involved, masculine pronouns are used: *Pedro y María se quieren mucho el uno al otro* 'Pedro and María love one another a lot' (*el uno a la otra* in such sentences might eliminate the idea of reciprocity, i.e. suggest that he loved her but not vice versa).

26.4 Pronominal verbs and intransitivity

26.4.1 General remarks on pronominal verbs and intransitivity

One important use of pronominal verbs is to show that a verb is intransitive. English does not always differentiate transitive from intransitive verbs: cf. 'I've finished the dinner'/'the dinner has finished', 'I boiled it'/'it boiled'. But with a few important exceptions, Spanish marks the intransitive meaning of an otherwise transitive verb by making it pronominal: Compare:

Transitive	Intransitive
abrir to open (but see 26.7.1)	*abrirse* to open (intransitive)
acabar to finish (transitive and intransitive)	*acabarse* to end (intransitive)
acostar to put someone to bed	*acostarse* to go to bed
casar to marry someone off (also intransitive in archaic or regional styles)	*casarse* to get married
cerrar to close	*cerrarse* to close (intransitive)
despertar to wake someone up (also intransitive)	*despertarse* to wake up (intransitive)
divorciar to divorce	*divorciarse* to get divorced
dormir to put somebody to sleep (also 'to sleep')	*dormirse* to go to sleep
enamorar to make someone fall in love	*enamorarse de* to fall in love with
involucrar to implicate	*involucrarse* to be implicated
meter to put in	*meterse* to get in, to interfere
perder to lose	*perderse* to get lost
preocupar to worry somebody	*preocuparse* to worry
presentar to introduce people	*presentarse* to appear unexpectedly
terminar (see *acabar*)	*terminarse* (see *acabarse*)
tirar to throw/pull	*tirarse* to jump

NB: An intransitive pronominal verb does not have a reflexive meaning: *se abrió la ventana* 'the window opened' does not mean 'the window opened **itself**'.

Intransitive pronominal verbs are so numerous in Spanish that beginners sometimes conclude that all intransitive counterparts of transitive verbs must be pronominal. But a number of non-pronominal verbs have both a transitive and an intransitive meaning. Thus we can say *lo/le suspendieron en francés* 'they failed him in French' and *suspendió en francés* '(s)he failed in French'; *su cabeza asomaba por la ventana* 'his/her head was sticking out of the window' and *asomaba la cabeza por la ventana* '(s)he was sticking his/her head out of the window'; *desconectó la radio* '(s)he disconnected the radio' and *en clase siempre desconecta* 'in class (s)he always switches off' (i.e. 'daydreams'); *lo empezó* '(s)he/you began it' and *empezó* '(s)he/it/you began'.

The following are other common examples (there is also a list of non-pronominal intransitive verbs denoting change of state at 27.2):

acabar to end (see 26.7.2)	*enfermar* to get ill/to make ill (*enfermarse* = 'to get ill/sick' in Latin America)
aflojar to loosen	
aprobar to approve/to pass (an exam)	
aumentar to grow bigger/to make bigger	*mejorar* to improve (see 26.7.23)
bajar to go down/to lift down	*oscurecer* to darken
comenzar to begin	*resucitar* to resuscitate
conectar to connect	*sangrar* to bleed
despertar to wake up	*subir* to go up/to lift up
empeorar to worsen	*terminar* to end
	vestir to wear

Sometimes the pronominal form of the verb is radically different in meaning:

cambiar to change	*cambiarse de* to change clothes/house
correr to run	*correrse* to be ashamed/to 'come' (sexually, vulgar, Spain only)

desenvolver to unwrap	*desenvolverse* to get ahead/to be good at something
despedir to see someone off/to fire/sack	*despedirse de* to take one's leave/say goodbye
empeñar to pawn/pledge	*empeñarse en* to insist on doing something
gastar to spend	*gastarse* to wear out
llevar to take/to wear	*llevarse* to take with one/to steal
mudar to change bedclothes	*mudarse* to move house/to change one's clothes
negar to deny	*negarse a* to refuse to do something
oponer to contrast two views	*oponerse* to oppose
valer to be worth	*valerse de* to make use of/to have recourse to

(i) Some pronominal intransitive verbs have no transitive counterparts, at least in normal language, e.g. *acatarrarse/constiparse* 'to catch a cold', *aferrarse a* 'to clutch on to', *arrepentirse* 'to repent', *abstenerse* 'to abstain', *apropiarse de* 'to take possession of', *atenerse a* 'to limit oneself to', *atragantarse* 'to choke', *atreverse a* 'to dare', *comportarse* 'to behave', *contonearse* 'to swing one's hips', *dignarse* 'to deign to', *encaramarse a* 'to climb up', *equivocarse* 'to make a mistake', *inmiscuirse* 'to interfere', *jactarse* 'to boast', *obstinarse en* 'to insist on', *quejarse* 'to complain', *suicidarse* 'to commit suicide', etc. All of these appear only in the pronominal form.

(ii) Some pronominal verbs may be transitive, as in *se bebió un litro de vino* '(s)he drank a litre/US liter of wine', or *me la conozco* 'I know her only too well'. See 26.9 for examples.

(iii) Some pronominal verbs are being replaced by the non-pronominal form, e.g. *entrenar* for *entrenarse* 'to train', which has spread despite grammarians' complaints (*entreno mañana en el gimnasio* 'I'm training tomorrow at the gym'), or *encarar* for *encararse con* 'to face up to (a problem)': *Arco 93 trata de encarar la crisis del mercado de arte* (*El País,* Spain) 'Arco 93 is trying to face up to the economic crisis in the art market'.

26.4.2 Pronominal and non-pronominal verbs denoting emotional reactions

A word is needed about two different types of impersonal verbs and phrases that express emotional reactions. The non-pronominal verbs and non-verbal expressions in List A (not exhaustive) are followed only by *que*, e.g. *le enfada **que** el perro no deje de ladrar* 'it annoys him/her that the dog won't stop barking'. These verbs do not appear—at least in educated usage—in the pronominal form with *de que*: one does not say *?se enfada de que....* If they are used pronominally ('reflexively') *porque* should follow: *se enfada porque...* + indicative.

The verbs in List B (also not exhaustive) have pronominal counterparts followed by *de que*. In these cases one can either say *le aburre que* + subjunctive 'it bores him/her that...' or *se aburre de que* + subjunctive '(s)he is bored by the fact that...'.

List A Emotional reactions and value judgements followed by *que*
(and **not** by *de que*)

apenarle a alguien que	to pain someone that...
darle lástima a alguien que	to fill someone with pity that...

deprimirle a alguien que	to depress someone that…
encantarle a alguien que	to enchant someone that…
enfadarle/enojarle a alguien que	to anger someone that…
extrañarle a alguien que	to puzzle someone that…
fastidiarle a alguien que	to bother someone that…
gustarle a alguien que	to like: *me gusta que canten* 'I like them to sing'
importarle a alguien que	to matter to someone that…
irritarle a alguien que	to irritate someone that…
parecerle bien/mal a alguien que	to seem good/bad to someone that…
satisfacerle a alguien que	to satisfy someone that…

List B Emotional reactions followed by *de que*
(see 16.6.2 for further remarks on these verbs)

aburrirle a alguien que/aburrirse de que	to bore someone that/to be bored by the fact that…
alegrarle a alguien que/alegrarse de que	to cheer someone that/to be happy that…
asustarle a alguien que/asustarse de que	to frighten someone that/to be frightened that…
avergonzarle a alguien que/avergonzarse de que	to shame someone that/to be ashamed that…
dolerle a alguien que/dolerse de que	to hurt someone that/to be hurt that…
emocionarle a alguien que/emocionarse de que	to excite someone that/to get excited by the fact that…
entristecerle a alguien que/entristecerse de que	to sadden someone that/to be saddened that…
entusiasmarle a alguien que/entusiasmarse de que	to make someone enthusiastic that/to be enthusiastic that…
horrorizarle a alguien que/horrorizarse de que	to horrify someone that/to be horrified that…
indignarle a alguien que/indignarse de que	to make someone indignant that/to be indignant that…
sorprenderle a alguien que/sorprenderse de que	to surprise someone that/to be surprised that…

Further examples of both types of construction:

Me molesta que te quejes tanto	It annoys me that you complain so much
Me importa un bledo que se celebre o no se celebre	I couldn't care less whether it takes place or not
Se aburre de que Gene Kelly baile siempre con Cyd Charisse (G. Cabrera Infante, Cu., dialogue)	He gets bored with the fact that Gene Kelly always dances with Cyd Charisse
El catedrático de portugués se sorprendió mucho de que yo me sorprendiera cuando me contó que este año sólo tenía un estudiante (M. Vargas Llosa, Pe.)	The professor of Portuguese was very surprised that I was surprised when he told me that he only had one student this year

26.5. *Se de matización*: general

(The term *se de matización* is taken from Moreira & Butt (1996). It is, however, inaccurate in the sense that such verbs appear in any person and number, e.g. *me voy, te duermes, nos trajimos, os creéis*, etc.)

Se de matización (lit. '*se* that adds a shade of meaning') refers to the use of the pronominal form to modify the meaning of the original verb in some often unpredictable way. Compare *bajó del árbol* and *se bajó del árbol* '(s)he came down from the tree' (the difference between the two is barely translatable), or *salió del cine* '(s)he left the cinema' and *se salió del cine* '(s)he walked out of the cinema'. Several points must be made about this construction:

(**a**) It is confined to a limited and apparently closed series of common transitive and intransitive verbs. The fact, for example, that *volver* 'to return' has a pronominal counterpart *volverse* 'to return before time'/'to turn back' (not to be confused with *volverse* 'to become' or 'to turn round') does not mean that *regresar* 'to return' also has a pronominal counterpart *regresarse* (the latter form is, however, much used in Latin America); nor does *descender* 'to descend' have a form **descenderse*, despite the fact that *bajar* has the form *bajarse*. For this reason these verbs must be learned separately. The most common verbs that take *se de matización* are:

abrir	correr	entrar	llevar	pasear	sonreír
acabar	crecer	envejecer	marchar	pensar	subir
aguantar	creer	escapar	mejorar	probar	suponer
aparecer	decidir	esperar	merecer	quedar	temer
bajar	dejar	estar	montar	regresar	traer
caer	desayunar	figurar	morir	reír	venir
callar	despertar	guardar	olvidar	resbalar	ver
cambiar	devolver	imaginar	oscurecer	resistir	volar
cerrar	empeorar	ir	parar	salir	volver
coger	encontrar	leer	parecer	saltar	
conocer	enfermar	llegar	pasar	sentir	

Only a selection of these is discussed in detail below. The rest should be sought in a good dictionary.

(**b**) Some of the pronominalized forms described below are more characteristic of spoken language, and the simple form is used in formal styles. Thus only *morir* 'to die' is used in formal Spanish, whereas both *morir* and *morirse* are heard in everyday speech, with a subtle difference of meaning.

(**c**) The majority, but not all, of these verbs are used in Latin America. There are some pronominal verbs of this type, e.g. *regresarse/devolverse* 'to return', *robarse* 'to steal', that are heard in all or parts of Latin America but not in Spain. See 26.8.

Our Latin-American examples are often taken from very colloquial sources, since these verbs are rare in formal written styles.

(**d**) The nuance added by pronominalization is sometimes very subtle. The ability to distinguish correctly between pairs like *bajar/bajarse* 'to descend'/'to get down/out', *llegar/llegarse* 'to arrive'/'to approach' or *traer/traerse* 'to bring' is the mark of the true master of idiomatic Spanish.

(**e**) The possibility of *se de matización* does not eliminate the possibility that the verb can be pronominalized for one of the reasons discussed elsewhere in this chapter. Out of context a form like *se encontraban* can therefore mean 'they found by chance', 'they found themselves', 'they found one another' or 'they were found': context usually clarifies the meaning. Pronominalized verbs of motion tend to share common features of meaning, so they are discussed separately at 26.6. Other examples of *se de matización* are discussed at 26.7.

26.6 Verbs of motion and *se de matización*

Many common verbs of motion acquire an extra nuance in the pronominal form. The pronominal form may:

(**a**) Draw attention to the point of departure as opposed to the destination, cf. *ir* 'to go somewhere', *irse* 'to go *away from* somewhere'.

(**b**) Suggest that an action is untimely, accidental or unplanned, e.g. *caer* 'to fall', *caerse* 'to fall over/down'; *salir* 'to leave'/'to come out', *salirse* 'to leave unexpectedly'/'to leak' (liquids, gases). Sometimes both nuances are combined.

26.6.1 *Bajar/bajarse* 'to go down'; *subir/subirse* 'to go up'

As far as 'getting on/into' and 'getting off/out of' some kind of vehicle is concerned, the forms are usually interchangeable, although informal language strongly prefers the pronominal form:

Iba a bajar(me) en la Plaza de la Revolución, pero me voy a bajar aquí	I was getting out a Revolution Square, but I'm going to get out here
Vino hacia ellos sonriente tan pronto se bajaron del coche (M. Delibes, Sp.)	He came towards them, smiling, as soon as they got out of the car
Yo me bajo sola —le dijo—. Dígame qué hago (G. García Márquez, Col., dialogue)	'I'll get out on my own,' she said. 'Tell me what to do.'

In these examples the non-pronominal form could have been used. Ordinary going up and down (e.g. stairs, lifts) requires the non-pronominal form unless reference is made to a whole set of stairs (see 26.9. for a more detailed discussion of the latter construction):

Espérame abajo/arriba que bajo/subo enseguida	Wait for me downstairs/upstairs – I'll be down/up in a minute
Subía siempre las escaleras lentamente	(S)he always used to go upstairs slowly
(Se) subió las escaleras de un tirón (the whole flight of stairs; see 26.9)	(S)he rushed upstairs without stopping

Other meanings require the pronominal form:

Se subieron a la tapia de un salto	They jumped on top of the garden wall
Súbase por los andenes, como sea, pero arranque (G. García Márquez, Col., dialogue; Sp. *los andenes = las aceras*)	Drive on the pavements/sidewalks, anything you like, but get moving!
Se subía por las paredes	(S)he was climbing up the wall (with rage, not literally)

(i) *Bajar(se)/subir(se)* can also be used colloquially as transitive verbs meaning 'to take up', and 'to take down': *bája(te) estos tiestos al jardín* 'take these flowerpots down to the garden'.

(ii) The non-pronominal form is used for 'to increase', 'to diminish': *los precios suben/bajan* 'prices go up/down'.

26.6.2 *Caer/caerse*

The non-pronominal form can emphasize either the point of departure or arrival: *el meteoro cayó del cielo* 'the meteor fell from the sky', *el tigre cayó sobre su presa* 'the tiger fell on its prey', *el avión cayó aquí* 'the plane fell here'. It is also used when the point of departure is taken for granted: *caía una lluvia fuerte* 'heavy rain was falling'. The non-pronominal form is also reserved for the following figurative meanings:

Cayó en la guerra	(S)he fell (was killed) in the war
El Gobierno ha caído	The government has fallen/has been toppled
Esa calle cae lejos de aquí	That street lies far from here
caer en la tentación	to fall into temptation
Ya caigo	I get it/I understand

Caerse suggests accidental falling ('falling over', 'falling down'):

(Se) cayó de la mesa	It fell off the table (accidentally)
¡Que no se te caiga el paquete!	Don't drop the parcel!
Ella resistió hasta donde pudo, se cayó, se hizo un raspón en una pierna (García Márquez, Col.)	She struggled as much as possible, fell over, scraped her leg
Se le cayó el alma a los pies (figurative)	(S)he suddenly became intensely depressed (lit. 'his/her soul dropped to his/her feet')

26.6.3 *Entrar/entrarse*

Entrar 'to enter' is by far the more common form. The status of *entrarse* is problematic: most Peninsular speakers reject it altogether, although it is sometimes heard in popular speech and is quite common in Latin America to emphasize point of departure:

Salió al balcón pero volvió a entrar(se) porque hacía frío (many Peninsular speakers reject *entrarse* as sub-standard)	(S)he went out on to the balcony but came in again because it was cold

Se impersonal with *entrar* is common: *se entra por aquí* 'one goes in through here'.

26.6.4 *Escapar/escaparse*

The pronominal form is the more usual. The non-pronominal form is used only for figurative meanings: *escapar con vida* 'to escape with one's life', *escapar del peligro* 'to escape danger', *escapar a la justicia* 'to escape justice', *escapar a la calle* 'to take to the street'. But *los prisioneros se escaparon* 'the prisoners escaped', *no me digas que otra vez se escaparon las pupilas* (M. Vargas Llosa, Pe., dialogue) 'don't tell me the girls at the convent have escaped again'.

26.6.5 *Ir/irse*

The difference between the two generally coincides with the difference between 'to go' and 'to go away', French *aller/s'en aller*, Italian *andare/andarsene*:

Vamos a casa de Pepe (destination stressed)	We're going to Pepe's house
Me voy a casa de Pepe (departure stressed)	I'm off to Pepe's house
Se casaron en el tren y se fueron de luna de miel a Bariloche (*Río Negro*, Arg.)	They got married on the train and left on their honeymoon to Bariloche
Vete (point of departure stressed)	Go away
Este avión va a Caracas (destination stressed)	This plane's going to Caracas
¡Voy! (destination stressed)	I'm coming!/I'll be right there!

26.6.6 *Llegar/llegarse*

Llegar means 'to arrive' and is by far the more common form. *Llegarse* means 'to approach' 'to pop over to', 'to get as far as':

Llegamos a Madrid	We arrived in Madrid
Llégate/Acércate a la tienda de enfrente	Go over to the shop/US store opposite
Se llegaron a la reina	They approached the Queen
Se tomaron un colectivo y se llegaron hasta la casa de unos parientes de Pablo (*Lugcos*, Arg.)	They took a 'collective' (bus) and went as far as the house of some of Pablo's relatives

26.6.7 *Marchar/marcharse*

Marchar means 'to march' and *marcharse* means 'to leave a place', but in León and in much of western Spain *marchar* may have the same meaning as *marcharse*:

¡Mira cómo marchan los soldados!	Look at the soldiers marching!
Me marcho/Me voy	I'm leaving
El tren ya se marchó/ya salió	The train's already left
50% de los jóvenes y 51% de la clase media, manifiestan el deseo de marcharse del país (*Mundo Laboral*, Ve.)	50% of young people and 51% of middle classes say they want to leave the country

26.6.8 *Pasar/pasarse*

As a verb of motion, both forms mean 'to pass'/'to pass by'/'to pass over'. (For *pasar* as a transitive verb meaning 'to pass time', see 26.7.30.) *Pasar* suggests normal motion (it is also used during card games: *paso* 'I pass'):

Cuando pasó la frontera	When (s)he crossed the frontier
La carretera pasa por el pueblo	The road goes through the village

Pasarse suggests unwanted or illegal passage:

Se pasó de la raya	(S)he went beyond the mark/overdid it
No te pases	Don't go too far/Don't overdo it
¡No te pases de sol! (*Mujer a Mujer*, Col.)	Don't overdo (exposure to) the sun!

Pasárselo bien/mal is 'to have a good/bad time, e.g. *pásatelo bien* 'have a good time' (sometimes *pasársela* in Latin America). Note also *no les pasa ni una* '(s)he doesn't let them get away with a thing', *pasa de todo* '(s)he doesn't care about anything'.

26.6.9 *Salir/salirse*

Salir means 'to go out' / 'to leave' without further implications. *Salirse* implies untimely or unexpected departure or, applied to liquids or gases, accidental leakages or escapes:

Salimos del cine cuando terminó la película (as expected)	We left the cinema when the film ended
Nos salimos del cine porque la película era muy violenta (unexpected)	We left the cinema (before the end) because the film was very violent
Salí del convento a las cinco (intended)	I left the convent at 5 o'clock
Me salí del convento a los treinta años (unexpected)	I left the convent at the age of thirty
El agua sale por aquí (intended)	The water comes out here (where it should)
El grifo se sale (accidental)	The tap's leaking
El FMI se salió de las normas (*Clarín*, Arg.)	The IMF (International Monetary Fund) has exceeded its powers

26.6.10 *Saltar/saltarse*

Saltar is the normal word for 'to jump'. It can also mean 'to jump over', but *saltarse* is replacing it in informal language in this meaning. *Saltarse* is used for illegal jumps, e.g. traffic lights or starting signals:

Saltaban de alegría	They were jumping for joy
Nunca se había saltado un semáforo en rojo en toda su vida (L. Sepúlveda, Ch., dialogue)	He had never jumped a red light in his life
Te saltaste la pistola de salida	You jumped the starting pistol
Se saltó la hoguera	(S)he jumped over the bonfire

26.6.11 *Subir/subirse* (see *bajar/bajarse*)

26.6.12 *Venir/venirse*

Venirse suggests 'to come away from somewhere' either permanently or for a long time. Applied to inanimates it implies accidental or unexpected coming. *Venir* simply means 'to come to a place':

Ha venido de París a pasar unos días (destination stressed)	(S)he's come from Paris to spend a few days
Se ha venido de París porque no aguanta la contaminación (point of departure stressed)	(S)he's come here from Paris because (s)he can't stand the pollution
¿Por qué no vienes conmigo? (destination stressed)	Why don't you come with me?
¿Por qué no te vienes conmigo? (point of departure stressed)	Why don't you (leave him/her/this place and) come with me?
Véngase para acá y conversamos (G. García Márquez, Col., dialogue)	Come over here and let's talk
cuando las Torres Gemelas se vinieron abajo... (idem)	when the Twin Towers collapsed...
Mira la tormenta que se nos viene encima (accidental)	Look at the storm that's going to hit us (lit. 'that's coming down on us')

In Latin America caution is required since *venirse* also has the same sexual meaning as 'to come'.

26.6.13 *Volver/volverse;* Latin American *regresar/regresarse*, also *devolverse*

Volver means 'to return'. It is also used for intangible things, e.g. happiness, summer, fine weather. *Volver a* + infinitive is also the most usual way of saying 'to do something again'. It is discussed at 32.6a.

Nunca volveré a aquella casa	I'll never return to that house
Has vuelto muy moreno	You've come back very suntanned
No vuelvas tarde	Don't come back late
Fue a París, se entrevistó con el presidente, y volvió a Londres	(S)he went to Paris, talked to the President and returned to London
Vuelve la primavera	Spring returns

Volverse may mean 'to turn back half-way', 'to return before time' (unplanned return):

Se volvió hacia ella	(S)he turned to (to face) her
Me volví antes de llegar	I turned back before arriving
Nos hemos vuelto porque no paraba de llover	We've come back (ahead of time) because it didn't stop raining
Vuélvanse a Montevideo que yo en 15 días estoy allá (Tenfield Digital, interview, Ch.)	Go back to Montevideo. I'll be there in 15 days

(i) In Latin America, as well as *volver(se)*, *regresar(se)* is much used for 'to return', with the same difference between the two forms (*regresarse* is not used in Spain): *Helen se había regresado a Puebla* (A. Mastretta, Mex., dialogue; Sp. *se había vuelto* or *había regresado*). Some countries, e.g. Colombia, also use *devolverse* for 'to return': *pero se había devuelto del Camino Real* (G. García Márquez, Col.) 'but he'd turned back on the highway'. *Devolver* (transitive) means 'to give back' or 'to throw up' (i.e. vomit) in Peninsular Spanish and in many Latin-American countries.

(ii) *Volverse* has other meanings everywhere, e.g. 'to become' (see 27.3.2) or 'to turn round' as in *se volvió hacia ella* '(s)he turned towards her'. 'To make a U-turn' in a vehicle is *dar la vuelta*.

26.7 *Se de matización* with miscellaneous verbs

Pronominalization adds nuances to a number of other verbs, of which the following are frequently encountered:

26.7.1 *Abrir/abrirse* and *cerrar/cerrarse*

Abrir 'to open' is used when the verb is transitive: *abrimos la puerta* 'we opened the door'. *Abrirse* is used when the verb is intransitive: *la puerta se abrió* 'the door opened'. However, *abrir* is also used intransitively for the scheduled opening of establishments: *¿cuándo abre el restaurante?* 'when is the restaurant opening?', *el museo abre de martes a domingo en el horario de 8:00 am-6:00pm* (website, Cu.) 'the museum opens from Tuesday to Sundays, 8 a.m. to 6 p.m.'.

Cerrar 'to close' behaves in the same way: *la puerta se cerró* 'the door closed' (on its own) but *el único cine del pueblo ha cerrado* 'the only cinema in the village/town has closed down', *mañana cierra el banco francés* (*Seprin.com*, Arg.) 'French bank closes tomorrow'.

26.7.2 *Acabar/acabarse*

Acabar can be used transitively and intransitively, like its English translation 'to finish': *han acabado el proyecto* 'they've finished the project', *el proyecto ha acabado* 'the project's finished'. *Acabarse* is common in informal styles for the intransitive meaning. It is also much used to mean 'to run out': *se ha acabado la cerveza* 'the beer's run out', *¡bueno, esto se ha acabado* 'this is the last straw!'/'this is the end!', *Puntocom, se acabó la fiesta* (*¿Qué Pasa?*, Ch.) 'Dotcoms – the party's over'.

26.7.3 *Aguantar/aguantarse*

The basic meaning of *aguantar* is 'to tolerate'/'to bear': *este puente aguanta pesos muy fuertes* 'this bridge supports very heavy weights', *no puedo aguantarlos* 'I can't stand them'. *Aguantarse* is intransitive and means 'to stand upright'—*la abuela ya no se aguanta sola* 'grandmother can't stand on her own any more'— or 'to put up with something': *si te duele esa muela tendrás que aguantarte hasta el lunes* 'if that tooth aches, you'll have to put up with it until Monday'; *bueno, a aguantarse* 'oh well, we'll just have to put up with it', *le disgustaban algunos comentarios de F. S. pero se aguantaba* (*Jornada*, Mex.) 'he disliked some of F.S.'s remarks but he put up with it'.

26.7.4 *Aparecer/aparecerse*

Aparecer means 'to appear' without further nuances. *Aparecerse* is used of apparitions:

La revista aparece todos los días	The journal appears every day
La Virgen de Guadalupe se apareció al indio Juan Diego (www.guadalupe.com, Mex.)	The Virgin of Guadalupe appeared to the Indian Juan Diego

In Latin America *aparecerse* is often used of people turning up unexpectedly: *en vez de despedirla, como Flora temía, se apareció, contrito, en la covacha de la rue du Foarre* (M. Vargas Llosa, Pe.) 'instead of dropping her, which is what Flora feared, he turned up, full of remorse, at the hovel on the rue du Foarre'.

26.7.5 *Callar/callarse*

Callar/callarse are in theory interchangeable, except when the subject is non-living, in which case the pronominal form is less usual: *la música calló de repente* 'the music suddenly stopped'. When the subject is human or animal, either form can be used, the pronominal form being more informal: *el niño (se) calló en cuanto le dieron el biberón* 'the little boy stopped crying as soon as he was given a bottle'.

26.7.6 *Cambiar/cambiarse*

Cambiar means 'to change' in the sense of 'to alter': *la situación ha cambiado* 'the situation has changed', *Ángela ha cambiado desde que va a la universidad* 'Angela has changed since she's been going to university'. The most usual meaning of *cambiarse* is 'to get changed' or 'to move on': *tengo la ropa mojada: me voy a cambiar* 'my clothes are wet: I'm going to get changed', *me cambié de trabajo* (*Prensa Gráfica*, El Salvador) 'I changed jobs'.

26.7.7 *Coger/cogerse*

Coger is used for physical catching or grasping hold of: *coger un tren/autobús/una pelota/un ladrón/una flor* 'to catch a train/bus/ball/thief', 'to pick a flower', etc. The pronominal form is rare (at least in standard Peninsular language), but it is found in colloquial phrases referring to drunkenness: contrast *coger un catarro* 'to catch a cold' and *cogerse una borrachera* 'to get drunk'.

    Coger is used everywhere in Latin America and is an obscene or very familiar word for the sex act, so some regions, e.g. Argentina, prefer *agarrar* for 'to catch' (Sp. 'to clutch', 'to seize', but also used for emphasis, as in *he agarrado una gripe de cuidado* 'I've got a terrible attack of flu').

26.7.8 *Conocer/conocerse*

Conocer covers all meanings of the French *connaître* 'to know a person/place' (cf. *saber* 'to know a fact/the truth/a language', etc.). It can also mean 'to meet for the first time': *la conocí en Madrid* 'I met her in Madrid'. The pronominal form, as well as meaning 'to know oneself', may imply total knowledge and can add a sarcastic note: *se conoce todo Madrid* '(s)he knows the whole of Madrid' (but not **se conoce Madrid*), *me la conozco…* 'I know her (and her little tricks…)', *me los conozco de arriba a abajo* (*Río Negro*, Arg.) 'I know them from top to bottom'.

26.7.9 *Correr/correrse*

Correr is overwhelmingly the more frequent form and is used for meanings including 'to run', 'to flow', 'to hurry' (even for drivers of vehicles: *no corras tanto* 'don't go so fast'). The only use of the pronominal form in respectable language is to mean 'to shift over', 'to move over' (intransitive): *córrete hacia acá para que el señor pueda sentarse* 'move over this way so the gentleman can sit down', *Lula se corre más a la derecha* (*Prensa Obrera*, Arg.) 'Lula is shifting to the right'. Foreigners should be careful since in Spain it also has the sexual meaning of 'to come' (Latin America *venirse*).

26.7.10 *Crecer/crecerse*

Crecer means to grow in size. *Crecerse* means to grow in worth or value:

La hierba crece mucho con tanta lluvia	The grass grows quickly with so much rain
¡Ya crezcan idiotas! (graffiti in Mexico City. In Spain *crecer* implies physical growth)	Grow up, you idiots!

Hay personas que se crecen con el peligro	There are people who grow stronger/more confident when they are in danger

In parts of Latin America *crecerse* means 'to be brought up': *yo me crecí* (Sp. *me crié*) *en Bolivia* 'I was raised in Bolivia'.

26.7.11 *Creer/creerse*

The non-pronominal form translates most meanings of 'to believe'/'to think that…'. *Creer en* 'to believe in' appears only in the non-pronominal form. The pronominal form usually implies unfounded belief, although its use is often optional:

Creo que han llegado	I think they've arrived
Creo en ella	I believe in her
Ése/Ese(se) cree que habla francés	He thinks he speaks French
(Se) cree todo lo que le dicen	(S)he believes everything they tell her/him
Yo (me) creía que él había llegado	I thought he had arrived
La gente se cree todo lo que ve en la tele (interview, popular Mexican press)	People believe everything they see on TV

Creerse can also emphasize unbelief: *no me creo todavía que se haya muerto* 'I still can't believe that (s)he's dead'.

(i) Idiom: *se lo tiene creído* '(s)he has a high opinion of him/herself', (British) '(s)he fancies him/herself'.

(ii) *Pensar/pensarse* 'to think' is used colloquially like *creer/creerse*, although good style respects the difference between *creer* 'to believe'/'to have an opinion' and *pensar* 'to think', i.e. indulge in thinking activity, as in *es un escritor que piensa mucho* 'he's a writer who thinks a lot'. *Pensarse algo* means 'to think something through carefully'.

26.7.12 *Decidir/decidirse*

Decidir can be used transitively in the sense of 'to make up someone's mind'/'to decide the outcome': *lo que me decidió fue el estado del presupuesto* 'what made up my mind was the state of the budget', …*lo que decidió el resultado del partido…* 'what decided the outcome of the game…'. Used with a living subject, the verb means 'to decide': *ha decidido dejar el trabajo* '(s)he's decided to leave work'. The pronominal form implies a decision taken after hesitation and effort, cf. 'to make up one's mind': *a ver si te decides de una vez* 'make up your mind, for Heaven's sake!', *el primer paso para realizar comercio electrónico, es decidirse a hacerlo* (advertisement, Mex.) 'the first step towards getting into electronic trading is making up one's mind to do it'.

26.7.13 *Dejar/dejarse*

Dejar translates 'to let' and 'to leave' (in the sense of 'abandon'). *Dejarse* emphasizes accidental leaving behind, but it can also have the reflexive meaning 'to let oneself go' (i.e. physically, morally):

Deja tu maleta aquí	Leave your suitcase here
cuando dejó el ejército...	when (s)he left the army...
Me he dejado el dinero en casa	I've left my money at home

This use of *dejarse* is apparently confined to Spain. Latin-American informants said *dejé la plata...* 'I left my money...' (in Spain *la plata* = 'silver' and *el dinero* = 'money'), which in European Spanish would imply deliberate leaving. *Dejarse* is used on both continents in sentences like *déjate de tonterías* 'stop the nonsense!'

26.7.14 Desayunar/desayunarse

Desayunar is nowadays overwhelmingly the more common form in Spain and may be intransitive or transitive: *desayuno fruta y cereales* 'I have fruit and cereals for breakfast', *¿a qué hora desayunaste?* 'what time did you have breakfast?' The older form *desayunarse con* does, however, occur in Spain, *me desayuno con fruta* 'I have fruit for breakfast', and is widespread in Latin America: *desayúnese con nosotros, con nuestro humeante y sabroso café, las medialunas recién horneadas* (advertisement, Ur.) 'have breakfast with us, with our steaming, delicious coffee and freshly baked croissants' (*croissants* in Spain).

26.7.15 Despertar/despertarse

Despertar is used transitively: *me despertó la tormenta* 'the storm woke me up'. Either form can be used intransitively, the non-pronominal form being rather more formal: *(me) desperté a las cinco* 'I woke up at five o'clock', *se despertó el fantasma de la derecha en Europa* (*Clarín*, Arg.) 'the spectre of the [political far] Right has awoken in Europe' (personification). The imperatives *despierta* and *despiértate* are used interchangeably.

26.7.16 Encontrar/encontrarse

The transitive form means 'to find', the pronominal form 'to find something by chance' (but the reflexive meaning of *encontrarse*, 'to be found'/'to be located', is also very common):

Encontré el libro que buscaba	I found the book I was searching for
Me encontré una moneda de oro	I found a gold coin
Me encontré a Pepe	I ran into Pepe (by chance)
Me encontré con que no me quedaba nada de sal	I found that I didn't have any salt left
Todo el dinero es igual. Yo lo agarro de donde me lo encuentro (A. Mastretta, Mex., dialogue; Spain *yo lo cojo/agarro donde lo encuentro*)	All money's the same. I grab it where I find it

26.7.17 Enfermar/enfermarse

Enfermar is used intransitively in Spain, where one says *enfermó de bronquitis* '(s)he fell ill with bronchitis', the pronominal form being sub-standard or popular. In Latin America the pronominal form is universally used: *el pirulo animal se enfermó de la guatita* (*La Cuarta*, Ch.) 'the super-elegant animal went down with a stomach bug' (refers to a famous model's poodle. Sp. *pirulo = pijo, guatita = barriga* or *tripas*).

26.7.18 *Esperar/esperarse*

Esperar translates 'to wait for'. Both *esperar* and *esperarse* are used for 'to expect' and 'to wait':

¿(A) qué estás esperando?	What are you waiting for?
Te estamos esperando	We're waiting for you
Eso no (me) lo esperaba yo	I wasn't expecting this
No me esperaba este 5–0 (*Terra*, Col.)	I wasn't expecting this 5–0 win (in soccer)
Hay que esperar(se) a que te atiendan	One has to wait to be served

Espera/espere and *espérate/espérese* seem to be interchangeable in the imperative. The pronominal imperative is common everywhere.

26.7.19 *Estar/estarse*

Estar means 'to be', and its use is discussed in Chapter 29. The pronominal form *estarse* is used:

(**a**) To form the imperative of *estar*: *¡estate quieto!* 'sit still!, *¡estese tranquilo!* 'stay calm!/don't worry!' See 17.2.6 for details.

(**b**) To express obligatory or deliberate being in a place. The translation is usually 'to stay':

Antes se estaba usted en la finca, y nosotras aquí tranquilitas (A. Buero Vallejo, Sp., dialogue)	You used to stay on the estate, and we women were so peaceful here
Me estuve estudiando toda la noche (from María Moliner)	I stayed up all night studying
He tenido que estar(me) a la cola todo el día	I had to queue/US stand in line all day
. . .y aquí que se esté para lo que se ofrezca (A. Mastretta, Mex., dialogue)	. . .and let him remain here in case anything turns up

Quedarse would have been possible in all these examples.

26.7.20 *Ganar/ganarse*

Ganar is used in the phrase *ganar mucho/poco dinero* 'to earn a lot'/'very little money', *¿cuánto ganas?* 'how much do you earn?' It also means 'to win'. *Ganarse* can sometimes add more emphasis to the amount earned. It is also used for metaphorical meanings or when the way of earning one's living is mentioned:

(Se) gana diez mil euros todos los meses	(S)he earns 10,000 euros every month
Ellos saben que yo me gano la vida trabajando por ahí con los campesinos (*Río Negro*, Arg.)	They know I earn my living working there with the peasants
Se gana el cariño de todos	(S)he gains/wins everybody's affection
Nos ganó cien mil pesos al póker	(S)he won 100,000 pesos off us at poker
Me ganas en fuerza pero no en inteligencia	You are stronger than me but not more intelligent

26.7.21 *Imaginar/imaginarse*

Imaginar is a transitive verb meaning 'to conceive of' / 'invent a new idea'. *Imaginarse* means 'imagine' in the sense of 'suppose', 'guess' or 'picture':

Imaginó un nuevo modo de hacerlo	(S)he thought of a new way of doing it
Te puedes imaginar lo que yo estaba pensando	You can imagine what I was thinking
Me los imagino divirtiéndose	I imagine them amusing themselves
Pues no me imaginaba qué locura se les podía ocurrir (Terra, Col.)	Because I couldn't imagine what crazy idea they might get

Figurarse means the same as *imaginarse*: *me figuro que ya se ha marchado* 'I guess he must have gone already'. The non-pronominal form means 'to figure as an item': *no figura en el índice* 'it doesn't appear in the index'.

26.7.22 *Llevar/llevarse*

Llevar means 'to wear', 'to take' or 'to carry'. *Llevarse* means 'to take away':

Voy a llevar el traje al tinte	I'm going to take my suit to the cleaner's
No se te olvide llevarte los libros	Don't forget to take the books with you
Llevaba un abrigo negro	She was wearing a black coat
Trae que te lleve ese paquete (the *trae* is a colloquial Peninsular interjection)	Here, let me carry that parcel for you
La crisis se llevó lo poco que quedaba (Río Negro, Arg.)	The crisis took away the little that was left

26.7.23 *Mejorar/mejorarse*

Mejorar as a transitive verb means 'to make better', as an intransitive verb it means 'to improve'. *Mejorarse* means 'to get better' from an illness and is not used everywhere in Spain, but it is common in Latin America, to judge by electronic greeting-card websites:

La situación ha mejorado	The situation has improved
(Se) ha mejorado mucho/Está mucho mejor (but only *ha mejorado mucho en español* '(s)he's improved a lot in Spanish')	(S)he's a lot better (in health)
¡Mejórate!/¡Que te mejores!	Get better soon!

26.7.24 *Morir/morirse*

Both translate 'to die', but the pronominal form denotes natural death, especially (but not exclusively) a gradual death: *su madre se murió de cáncer* 'his mother died of cancer'. *Morir* is generally used for accidental or deliberate death: *(se) murió de un ataque al corazón* 'she died from a heart attack', *murió en un accidente de avión* '(s)he died in a plane accident' (not *se murió…*). In formal written Spanish *morir* is used for all kinds of death. In colloquial Spanish *morirse* is especially used for the death of relatives and friends:

Ha muerto el primer ministro (formal style)   The Primer Minister has died
La propia Tránsito Arias se murió   Tránsito Arias herself died convinced
    convencida de que. . . (G. García   that. . .
    Márquez, Col.)
Yo lloré al contarle que casi se nos había   I cried when I told him how he had
    muerto esa noche (M. Puig, Arg.,   nearly died that night
    dialogue)

26.7.25 *Ocurrir/ocurrirse*

Ocurrir means 'to happen'. *Occurírsele a alguien algo* means 'to occur to one', 'to have a sudden idea':

Esto lleva ocurriendo desde hace algún   This has been happening for some
    tiempo   time
Se les ocurrió tocar la puerta de las   They had the idea of knocking on the
    habitaciones de hotel a las tres de la   hotel-room doors at 3 a.m.
    mañana (*Reforma*, Mex.; Sp. *tocar* here
    = *llamar a*)

26.7.26 *Olvidar/olvidarse(de)/olvidársele algo a uno*

The verb means 'to forget', and there are four possibilities: *olvidar algo, olvidarse algo, olvidarse de algo* and *olvidársele algo a alguien*.

(a) When deliberate forgetting is implied, the first form is rather formal and is usually replaced in colloquial styles by *olvidarse de*: *no puedo olvidarla/no puedo olvidarme de ella* 'I can't forget her'.

(b) For absent-minded forgetting *olvidar* and *olvidársele* can be used, the former again being rather formal: *he olvidado mi agenda/se me olvidó la agenda* 'I've forgotten my diary', *se le olvidaban los otros compromisos, se le olvidaba todo menos ella* (G. García Márquez, Col.) 'he forgot his other commitments, he forgot everything except her'. In the latter construction the thing forgotten is the subject of the verb: *se me olvidaron las flores* 'I forgot the flowers' (lit. 'the flowers forgot themselves "on" me').

(c) *Olvidarse algo* (without the *de*) is colloquial and is censured by some grammarians, including Manuel Seco. Foreigners should probably say *me he olvidado de ella* or *la he olvidado* and not *?me la he olvidado*. It can, however, be used colloquially for the accidental forgetting of objects: *me he olvidado el libro/se me olvidó el libro* 'I've forgotten the book' (but, since this is absent-minded forgetting, not *me he olvidado del libro*). *Olvidarse algo* is also common in Latin America.

26.7.27 *Oscurecer/oscurecerse*

The pronominal form means 'to get darker' (e.g. colo(u)rs). *este amarillo se ha oscurecido* 'this yellow has got darker', *el cielo se oscureció* 'the sky darkened', *los mayas se sentían atemorizados cuando el Sol se oscurecía parcialmente* (www.yucatan.com, Mex.) 'the Mayas grew afraid when the Sun was partially darkened'. The non-pronominal form may be transitive—'to make darker'— or it may have the special meaning of 'to grow dark' (i.e. at dusk): *está oscureciendo* 'night is falling' / 'it's growing dark', *siempre oscurecía temprano. Fuese invierno, fuese verano* (J. F. Alburqueque, Pe.) 'it always grew dark early, whether it was winter or summer'.

26.7.28 *Parar/pararse*

Both verbs translate 'to stop' on both continents, but they are not usually interchangeable. The non-pronominal form indicates scheduled or planned halts, e.g. buses at bus-stops, trains in stations: *el tren expreso para en Montera* 'the express train stops at Montera'. The pronominal form suggests unexpected stops, i.e. at traffic lights or because of breakdown: *el motor se ha parado* 'the motor's stopped', *me tuve que parar en un semáforo* 'I had to stop at the lights'.

When the subject is human, the pronominal form often suggests that the subject is personally moving, i.e. walking or running, and the non-pronominal form that (s)he is driving a car: *me paré delante de la tienda* 'I paused in front of the shop', *paré delante de la tienda* 'I stopped (the car) in front of/outside the shop'. *Parar* can also be used as a transitive verb: *¡para esa máquina!* 'stop that machine!'.

Pararse is also much used in Latin America, but not in Spain, to mean 'to stand up': *párate derecho* = Sp. *ponte derecho* 'stand up straight'.

26.7.29 *Parecer/parecerse*

Parecer means 'to seem', *parecerse a* means 'to look like': *parece cansada*, 'she seems/looks tired'; *se parecen a su madre* 'they look like their mother', *la película no se parece a ninguna otra* (*¿Qué Pasa?*, Ch.) 'the movie is like no other'.

26.7.30 *Pasar/pasarse*

For the use of these two as verbs of motion, see 26.6.8. *Pasar* also means 'to spend time somewhere' or 'to pass' time:

Miguel pasó la noche en casa de su hermano	Miguel spent the night in his brother's house
Pasaron tres horas	Three hours passed

Pasarse means 'to spend time doing something':

Se pasa horas mirando por la ventana	(S)he spends hours gazing out of the window
Podíamos pasarnos la vida sin verlos (A. Mastretta, Mex., dialogue)	We could spend our lives without seeing them

NB: *Pasar un examen* is heard in Latin America, but in Spain *aprobar un examen* is more usual.

26.7.31 *Probar/probarse*

Probar means 'to prove', 'to test', 'to sample': *prueba este vino* 'try this wine', *eso no prueba nada* 'that proves nothing'. The pronominal form is used for the special meaning 'to try on': *se pasa horas en las tiendas probándose todo* '(s)he spends hours in the shops trying on everything', *la mejor hora para probarse zapatos es por la tarde o durante la noche* (*Impulso*, Mex.) 'the best time to try on shoes is in the evening or at night'.

26.7.32 *Quedar* and *quedarse*

Quedar basically means 'to remain'. With participles, adjectives and a few adverbs, it therefore tends to indicate a more or less permanent outcome of some action:

Queda por ver si lo hará	It remains to be seen whether (s)he'll do it
Queda bien/mejor/mal/feo	It looks nice/better/bad/ugly
La casa les ha quedado bien (more or less permanent result)	You/They have decorated the house very nicely
Tuvo un accidente y quedó cojo	He had an accident and became lame as a result

Quedar en means 'to agree to do something'. Compare also *he quedado con él a las siete* 'I've agreed to see him at seven'.

The basic meaning of *quedarse* is 'to stay', but with adjectives and participles it often means 'to become', and usually focuses on the change itself rather than on the state arising from it: compare *la casa se quedó vacía* 'the house emptied' and *la casa quedó vacía*, which suggests 'the house remained empty':

Me quedaré unos días contigo	I'll spend a few days with you
Yo me quedé de pie ante él (C. Martín Gaite, Sp.)	I remained (i.e. stayed) standing in front of him
Por no salir a tiempo hombre se quedó encerrado en un banco (headline, *Terra*, Col.; Sp. *un* hombre se quedó…)	Man locked in bank after failing to leave in time
Había que quedarse quietos durante unos segundos (E. Lynch, Arg.)	One had to stay still for a few seconds
Se quedó embarazada	She became pregnant

NB: Also *quedó embarazada* in northern Spain and perhaps elsewhere, and in formal written styles. *Quedarse* is normal in Madrid and Latin America.

(i) *Quedarse (con) algo* 'to keep something' (e.g. change, a book; the preposition is often dropped in modern speech, at least in Spain: *quédatelo* 'keep it'). For other meanings of *quedar(se)* see 27.3.6 (= 'to become') and 28.2.6a.

(ii) *Quedarse* is not common with non-living subjects: *la casa quedó destruida* 'the house was destroyed', not **se quedó*. The pronominal form can optionally be used, however, to emphasize a result or outcome: *el barco (se) quedó varado en el viejo puerto* 'the boat finally ran aground in the old harbour' (from *GDLE* 38.3.41).

26.7.33 *Reír/reírse*

Both mean 'to laugh'. *Reírse* is the more common form; *reír* is rather literary. However *reírse* implies spontaneous laughter, so it is not used when the cause of merriment comes from outside, as in *el gas me hizo reír* 'the gas made me laugh', *ya los haré reír* 'I'll make them laugh'. 'To laugh at' is *reírse de*:

Se rió de su propia risa (G. García Márquez, Col.)	She laughed at her own laughter
Todos se reían de él	They all made fun of him

26.7.34 *Temer/temerse*

Temer usually means 'to be afraid' in the literal sense of 'to fear', especially with a direct object; *temerse* can mean the same, but often simply means 'to suspect', 'to be worried that'. See 16.9, especially note (ii).

26.7.35 *Traer/traerse*

Traer is the normal word for 'to bring', but it seems to us that in modern spoken usage *traerse* is increasingly used with the same meaning as *traer*, cf. *trae a tu marido/tráete a tu marido* 'bring your husband with you', *y tráete a los otros a mi casa* (M. Vargas Llosa, Pe., dialogue) 'and bring the others to my house'.

    Traer can also mean 'to wear', at least in Spain: *traía/llevaba un traje precioso* 'she was wearing a lovely suit/dress'. *Traerse* is used in phrases implying shady business: *yo creo que no es por ella, sino por su tío y los asuntos que os traéis entre manos* (J. Marsé, Sp., dialogue)'I think it has nothing to do with her but with her uncle and the things you're getting up to between you', *¿qué se traen entre manos las grandes de la tecnología de la información?* (*El Universal*, Ve.) 'what are the big IT companies up to?'

26.8 *Se de matización* in **Latin America**

Most of the uses of *se de matización* heard in Spain are also normal in Latin America, but a few constructions accepted in Latin America sound strange or plain wrong to Spaniards. The following selection, not exhaustive, includes verbs discussed elsewhere, and not all the forms are current in educated speech in all countries. Peninsular equivalents are shown in brackets:

crecerse to be brought up (*criarse*)
desayunarse to have breakfast (*desayunar*)
devolverse to return (particularly in Col.; elsewhere *volver, regresar*)
enfermarse to get ill/US sick (*enfermar*)
heredarse to inherit (*heredar*); see note (i)
lloverse to leak (of roofs: rural Argentina)
prestarse to borrow (*pedir prestado*); see note (ii)

recordarse remember (*recordar, acordarse*; see 18.2.3, note iv)
regresarse to return (*volverse*)
robarse to steal (*robar*)
soñarse con to dream of (*soñar con*)
verse to look (i.e. *parecer*)/to seem: see note (iii)
vomitarse to vomit (*vomitar, devolver*)

(i) In some parts of Latin America, e.g. Mexico, *heredar* can mean 'to leave to someone in a will' (Spain *dejar*): *estaba seguro de su alcurnia y pudo heredársela entera a su hija* (A. Mastretta, Mex.) 'he was sure of his pedigree and managed to bequeath it intact to his daughter'.

(ii) In Argentina the popular word for 'to borrow' is *emprestar*. This verb is heard in Spain and elsewhere, but it is considered sub-standard.

(iii) In Latin America *verse* is used to refer to personal appearance: *te ves muy guapa* (A. Mastretta, Mex., dialogue; Sp. *qué guapa estás*. . .) 'you look very pretty', *y tú no te ves nada mal con esa tenida* (S. Vodanovic, Ch., dialogue: Sp. *no estás nada mal; la tenida = el traje*) 'and you don't look at all bad in that outfit'.

26.9 **Pronominal verbs of consumption, perception, knowledge**

A curious optional function of the pronominal form of these transitive verbs is to emphasize the totality of an act of consuming, perceiving or knowing. Thus one says *como pizza* (no quantity specified), but, optionally —though usually— *me comí una pizza* 'I ate a (whole) pizza'. The verb must have a direct object which must refer to a specific item or quantity:

Bebe mucho vino	(S)he drinks a lot of wine
Se *bebió un litro de vino*	(S)he drank a litre/US liter of wine
Nos *liquidamos las dos un par de Viña Tondonias y* **nos** *comimos un par de bolsas King size de patatas fritas* (C. Rico-Godoy, Sp.)	The two of us women finished off a couple of bottles of Viña Tondonia and ate a couple of king-size bags of crisps/US chips
No deberías fumar	You shouldn't smoke
(Se) fuma tres paquetes al día	(S)he smokes three packets a day
Ando mucho	I walk a lot
(Me) anduve cincuenta kilómetros	I walked 50 km
Aprendo francés	I'm learning French
(Me) aprendí todo el capítulo en una hora	I learnt the whole chapter in an hour
Sabe mucho	She knows a lot
¿(Te) sabes los verbos irregulares?	Do you know the irregular verbs?
Conozco Valencia	I know Valencia
(Me) conozco Valencia de cabo a rabo	I know Valencia inside out
Toma somníferos para dormir	(S)he takes sleeping pills to sleep
Tóma(te) un somnífero	Take a sleeping pill
Trago mal	I can't swallow properly
(Se) lo ha tragado	(S)he's swallowed it
Vi a tu cuñada	I saw your sister-in-law
(Se) vio todo el museo en diez minutos	(S)he saw the whole museum in ten minutes
Lee muchas novelas	She reads a lot of novels
Vas a tener que releerte las obras completas [de Shakespeare] para que nos entendamos (C. Fuentes, Mex., dialogue)	You're going to have to reread the complete works of [Shakespeare] so that we can understand one another
Piénsalo	Think about it
Piénsatelo	Think it through (completely)
Tómate tus vacaciones y pásatelo bien (S. Puértolas, Sp., dialogue)	Go ahead and have your holiday and have a good time
Gasta mucho	(S)he spends a lot
Se gasta todo lo que gana	(S)he spends everything (s)he earns

NB: A similar construction is also heard in colloquial Italian—*mi sono mangiato una pizza*— and in southern dialects of French—*je me suis mangé une pizza*— but not in standard French. It is not used in Portuguese.

26.10 Interpretation of pronominal verbs with inanimate subjects

A third-person pronominal verb may also be interpreted as a passive: *se construyó en España* means the same as *fue construido en España* 'it was built in Spain' (see 28.4 for more details).

A difficulty therefore sometimes arises with sentences containing pronominal verbs, for example *se abrió la puerta*: is this to be understood as intransitive, i.e. 'the door opened', or passive, 'the door **was** opened'? Likewise, does *se hundió el barco* mean 'the boat sank' or 'the boat was sunk'? This problem only arises with certain verbs which have well-established pronominal intransitive forms, e.g. *abrir/abrirse* 'to open', *cerrar/cerrarse* 'to close', *encontrar/encontrarse* 'to find'/'to be located', *esconder/ esconderse* 'to hide' and others which will be found in good dictionaries. Most transitive verbs, e.g. *construir* 'to build', *derribar* 'to fell', *operar* 'to operate', do not have intransitive counterparts, so confusion is hardly possible.

The general rule for clarifying which sense is intended is as follows: if a pronominal verb has an established intransitive meaning, e.g. *abrirse* 'to open', *encenderse* 'to light up'/'to switch on', it will usually precede the subject if the passive meaning is intended, although this position does not preclude a pronominal interpretation. Thus *la puerta se abrió* usually means 'the door opened', but *se abrió la puerta* may mean either 'the door opened' or 'the door was opened'. Similarly:

Las luces se encienden a las nueve	The lights come on at nine
Se encienden las luces a las nueve	The lights are lit/come on at nine
Tres ventanas se rompieron durante la tormenta	Three windows broke in the storm
Se rompieron tres ventanas durante la manifestación	Three windows were broken in the demonstration

In the second of each of these examples the passive is the more likely meaning. If the verb has no intransitive possibility, then only a passive meaning is possible:

Se derribaron tres árboles/Tres árboles se derribaron	Three trees were felled
Los motivos se ignoran/Se ignoran los motivos	The motives are unknown

The foregoing points hardly constitute a hard and fast rule, and it must be remembered that complex word order rules, discussed in Chapter 37, affect the choice between sentences like *los motivos se ignoran* and *se ignoran los motivos* 'the motives are unknown'.

26.11 Obligatory use of *uno* as impersonal pronoun with pronominal verbs

Uno/una must be used to give an impersonal meaning to a pronominal verb since two *se*s cannot occur with the same verb:

Se moría de frío en esa casa (morirse)	(S)he/It was/You were dying from the cold in that house
Se moría uno de frío en esa casa	One died from the cold in that house
Cuando está así, se irrita fácilmente por cualquier cosa	When (s)he's like that, (s)he gets easily irritated over anything
Cuando se/uno está así, se irrita uno fácilmente por cualquier cosa	When one is like that, one gets easily irritated over anything
Con estas cosas se cansa mucho	(S)he gets very tired with these things
Con estas cosas se cansa uno mucho	One gets very tired with these things

For more details about the pronoun *uno* see 28.7.1.

27

Verbs of becoming

Matters discussed in this chapter are:

- Verbs like *cansarse, indignarse, aumentar,* etc. (Section 27.2)
- *Ponerse* (Section 27.3.1)
- *Volverse* (Section 27.3.2)
- *Hacerse* (Section 27.3.3)
- *Llegar a ser, pasar a ser* (Section 27.3.4)
- *Convertirse en* (Section 27.3.5)
- *Quedar(se)* (Section 27.3.6)

27.1 General

There are basically two ways in Spanish of expressing the idea of 'to become': either use one of the many verbs derived from adjectives to indicate a change of state, e.g. *enfermó* (Lat. Am. *se enfermó*) *de bronquitis* '(s)he became ill/sick with bronchitis', *se entristeció* '(s)he became sad'; or use one of the several verbs that mean 'to become', e.g. *ponerse, volverse, hacerse, llegar a ser, convertirse, quedarse*. One can therefore also say *se puso enfermo* 'he became ill/sick', *se puso/se quedó triste* '(s)he became sad'. The tendency in everyday spoken Spanish is to prefer the latter type of construction.

27.2 Special verbs denoting change of state

These are numerous in Spanish. Many of them are pronominal verbs (i.e. 'reflexive' verbs; the term is explained in Chapter 26). The following is only a small selection:

aburrirse (de) to get bored	*enredarse* to get entangled
alegrarse (de) to cheer up/to be happy about something	*extrañarse (de)* to be puzzled at
	fastidiarse to get annoyed
asustarse (de) to get frightened	*indignarse* to get indignant
cansarse (de) to get tired	*irritarse (por)* to get irritated
deprimirse to get depressed	*marearse* to feel sick
divertirse to be amused	*molestarse (por)* to be bothered
endurecerse to grow hard/to harden	*vaciarse* to become empty
enfadarse (Lat. Am. *enojarse*) to get angry	

(i) Not all verbs that express changes of state are pronominal. 'To go mad' is *enloquecer* (also 'to send mad'); **enloquecerse* is not used. Some other common cases of intransitive, non-pronominal verbs denoting 'to become…'/'to get…' are:

agonizar to be dying
aclarar to brighten/lighten/, e.g. after a storm
adelgazar to lose weight
amanecer to dawn
anochecer: anochece night is falling
aumentar to increase
cambiar to change (*cambiarse* = to change clothes)
clarear to grow bright
crecer (for *crecerse* see 26.7.10) to grow
disminuir to diminish
empeorar (Lat. Am. *empeorarse*) to get worse
enfermar (Lat. Am. *enfermarse*) to get ill
encoger to shrink
enflaquecer to lose weight

enfriar to grow cold
engordar to get fat
enmudecer to be silent/to lose one's voice
ennegrecer to go black
enrojecer to go red
ensordecer to go deaf
envejecer (also *envejecerse*) to age, but compare *rejuvenecerse* to grow young again
hervir to boil
mejorar§ to improve
nacer to be born
oscurecer to get dark (but *el cielo se oscurece* the sky grows dark)
palidecer to grow pale
resucitar to come back to life

§ For *mejorarse* 'to recover' (from an illness) see 26.7.23.

(ii) *Amanecer* can also be used with living subjects: *amanecí detestando mi color de pelo, mis ojeras, mi estatura* (A. Mastretta, Mex.) 'I woke up (lit. 'I dawned') hating the colour of my hair, the bags under my eyes, my height'. *Anochecer* and *amanecer* can also be used impersonally with object pronouns, as in *me anocheció/amaneció en medio de la carretera* 'night/morning found me on the road'.

27.3 Special verbs meaning 'to become'

Apart from the use of the pronominal forms discussed in the previous section, the following verbs, most, but not all, themselves pronominal verbs, are also used with various shades of meaning. Spanish thus resembles English in having several words meaning 'to become': cf. 'to *grow* old', 'to *get* cold', 'to *go* mad', 'to *turn* nasty', 'to *become* senile', etc. French and Italian make much use of one word, *devenir* and *diventare* respectively. The Spanish verb *devenir* 'to become' is virtually never used outside academic or philosophical texts. Its infinitive means 'the process of becoming'.

27.3.1 *Ponerse* 'to become', 'to get'

Ponerse is used to indicate changes of mood, physical condition and appearance which are usually short-lived, e.g. *ponerse enfermo/frenético/cabizbajo* 'to get ill/frantic/preoccupied', *ponerse contento* 'to become pleased'; although there are exceptions. Thus there is a contrast between *se ha puesto muy pesado* 'he's become boring' (temporarily) and *se ha vuelto muy pesado* 'he's become a bore'. There is sometimes some overlap with *quedarse*, e.g. *quedarse delgado* 'to become thin', 'to lose weight'; see 27.3.6, and with *volverse* (see the examples). There are often pronominal verbs of equivalent meaning: see 27.2.

Ponerse can have living subjects and also certain kinds of non-living subjects, e.g. prices, foodstuffs, situations and, in some cases, weather conditions.

Cuando se enteró se puso muy contenta/ triste/de mal humor/enfadada (se entristeció, se enfadó could also be used)	When she heard about it she became very happy/sad/bad-tempered/ cross
Se puso/Se quedó ronco/Enronqueció de tanto hablar	(S)he got hoarse from talking so much
El FMI se puso duro (Clarín, Arg.; Sp. *se ha puesto)*	The IMF has got tough
Se puso/Está mejor/Mejoró de su enfermedad (but not **la enfermedad se puso mejor)*	(S)he's better from his/her illness
En estos últimos años se me ha puesto el pelo rizado	My hair has got curly in recent years
La situación se ha puesto/vuelto insoportable	The situation has become unbearable
El tiempo se está poniendo/volviendo frío	The weather is getting cold
El pescado se ha puesto malo	The fish has gone bad
Esto se está poniendo color de hormiga (M. Vargas Llosa, Pe., dialogue. The phrase was used until recently in Madrid)	Things are looking bad (lit 'things are turning ant-coloured')

(i) *Ponerse* is often used with children to indicate that they are looking bigger or handsomer than ever: *¡pero qué guapo/grande se ha puesto este niño!* 'hasn't this child got handsome/big!' It may also imply deliberate effort: *mi madre se ha puesto guapa* 'my mother's made herself attractive'.

(ii) *Ponerse a* + infinitive means to begin, i.e.: *se puso a llorar/correr/trabajar/escribir*, etc. '(s)he began to cry/started running/working/writing, etc., *nos pusimos a hablar de la muerte* (C. Rico-Godoy, Sp.) 'we started talking about death'.

27.3.2 *Volverse*

This usually translates 'to become'/'to go', as in 'to go mad', and implies involuntary mental or psychological change when applied to living subjects. It can also be used with some non-living subjects, but not as often as *ponerse*. The change is felt to be more permanent than with *ponerse*: compare *se puso malhumorada* 'she got into a bad mood' (for a while) and *se volvió malhumorada* 'she became a grumpy person'.

Con la edad nos vamos volviendo más de derechas	We get more right-wing with age
Últimamente todo se vuelven complicaciones, dificultades y disgustos (see 2.3.3 for agreement of *vuelven*)	Recently everything has become complications, difficulties and upsets
¿Dónde se volvió asesino ese chico? (M. Puig, Arg., dialogue)	Where did that boy learn to be a murderer?
La peor pesadilla para una madre en esta época es que sus hijos vuelvan un día de la escuela y anuncien que se han vuelto vegetarianos (Terra, Ve.)	The worst nightmare for a mother these days is for her children to come home from school one day and announce they've become vegetarians
Durante un rato el cielo se volvió anaranjado (A. Mastretta, Mex.; or *se puso*)	The sky turned orange for a while

See 26.6.13 for other meanings of *volver(se)*.

27.3.3 *Hacerse* 'to become'

This often implies voluntary or deliberate changes and it is usual for religious, professional or political conversions. It can also occasionally be used of circumstances:

Se hizo católico/Se convirtió al catolicismo	He became a Catholic
Para hacerte arquitecto necesitas saber dibujo	You need to know how to draw to become an architect
¿Qué se hicieron los ídolos? (*La Prensa,* Panama.; Sp. *se hizo de...*)	What became of (our) idols/heroes?
Emigró a México, se hizo inmensamente rico (A. Grandes, Sp.)	He emigrated to Mexico and became immensely rich
La situación se está haciendo/poniendo/ volviendo difícil	The situation is getting difficult
...como volutas de humo que se hace progresivamente más espeso (C. Martín Gaite, Sp.)	...like columns of smoke growing progressively thicker
Se me hace cuesta arriba tener que levantarme temprano	It's turning into a chore (lit 'uphill') for me to have to get up early

(i) There is no difference between sentences like *se está haciendo cada vez más vaga* and *se está volviendo cada vez más vaga/perezosa* 'she's getting lazier and lazier'.

(ii) Idioms: *hacerse tarde* 'to get late', *hacerse de miel* 'to become so soft that people can take advantage of one', *hacerse humo* (Lat. Am.) 'to vanish', lit. 'to become smoke'; *no te hagas el tonto* 'stop pretending you don't understand'.

(iii) 'To become' with the meaning of 'to be appointed' is translated into Spanish as *nombrar* or *hacer*: *le/lo han nombrado/hecho ministro* 'he's become a Minister'.

27.3.4 *Llegar a ser, pasar a ser*

Llegar a ser is used to indicate the result of a slow and sometimes difficult change, i.e. 'to manage to become'/'to become eventually'. It is only occasionally used with non-living subjects, as in *la situación llegó a ser imposible* 'the situation (eventually) became impossible':

Trabajó mucho y con el tiempo llegó a ser alguien/director general/una persona importante	He worked hard and in due time he became someone/general manager/ an important person

Pasar a (ser) means 'to go on to be' but it does not imply difficulty or lapse of time:

De secretario pasó a (ser) jefe	From being a secretary he went on to become the boss
Pasó a ser uno de los partidos políticos del mundo con el porcentaje más alto de afiliados (*La República,* Ur.)	It became one of the world's political parties with the highest percentage of members
De hija pasé a ser esposa (C. Rico-Godoy, Sp.)	From being a daughter I went on to being a wife

27.3.5 *Convertirse en* 'to become/change/turn into'

This verb precedes noun phrases but not adjectives. The change can be due to external circumstances:

Nada más tocarlo/le el hada con la varita el príncipe se convirtió en rana	As soon as the fairy touched him with her wand, the prince turned into a frog
Se ha convertido en un drogadicto/un criminal	He's become a drug addict/a criminal

Tu socarronería ha dejado de ser irónica para convertirse en vitriólica (C. Martín Gaite, Sp.)	Your sarcasm has stopped being ironic; it's become vitriolic
El golf se convirtió en pasión de multitudes (*Río Negro*, Arg.)	Golf has become a mass craze
La silla se convierte fácilmente en una escalera	The chair turns easily into a step-ladder

'To convert to' a new belief is *convertirse a*; see also *hacerse*, 27.3.3: *no todos los que se convierten a una religión se vuelven buenos* 'not everybody who is converted to a religion becomes good'.

27.3.6 *Quedarse* and *quedar*

The relationship between *quedarse* and *quedar* (when they are used as verbs of becoming, i.e. are followed by an adjective or participle) is affected by regional considerations that make it difficult to be precise about usage. In general, it seems to us that *quedarse* as a verb of becoming is the most common form in Madrid speech, while *quedar* has a literary or regional character.

NB: Both verbs have other meanings not discussed here: *quedarse* = 'to stay'; *quedar* can mean 'to agree' or 'to be situated' (as in *queda lejos* 'it's a long way away'). Also *quedarse con alguien* (Sp.) 'to tease someone'.

(**a**) In many cases, *quedarse* implies loss, incapacity or disadvantage:

Se quedó ciego/mudo/impedido/sordo	He became blind/dumb/disabled/deaf
Se quedó soltera/viuda	She never married/She became a widow
Se quedó solo en el mundo	He was left alone in the world
¡Qué delgado te has quedado!	Haven't you got thin!
Me he quedado helado esperándote	I've got frozen waiting for you
El mundo se me ha quedado pequeño	The world has got too small for me

(**b**) In a few other cases it does not imply loss or disadvantage See 26.7.32 and 28.2.6 for more remarks about *quedar(se)*:

¿Te has quedado contento?	Are you satisfied now?
Me quedé convencido de que era verdad	I became convinced that it was true
Se quedó embarazada	She became pregnant

(i) *Quedarse helado* can also apply to shock: *cuando se lo dijeron se quedó helada/de piedra/de una pieza* 'she had a terrible shock when they told her'/'she froze when they told her'.

(ii) In some Spanish regions and in literary styles *quedar* can be used instead of *quedarse* in the first four examples of (**a**) and also in *quedarse embarazada*. *Quedar embarazada* is not accepted in Madrid.

28

Passive and impersonal sentences

This chapter discusses:

- The passive with *ser* (Section 28.2)
- Passive *se* (*se pasivo*) Section (28.4)
- *Se vio a tres personas/Se les vio* (Section 28.5)
- Impersonal *se* (Section 28.6)
- Other impersonal pronouns (*uno/una, tú, ellos*) (Section 28.7)

28.1 General

In impersonal sentences the agent of the action is either unknown or irrelevant, as in 'the fire was started accidentally' (we don't know by whom) or 'they drink vodka in Russia' (the exact identity of 'they' is irrelevant).

Spanish is rich in impersonal constructions, and it is not always easy to distinguish between them. The following chart lists the constructions. Students who know French may find the comparisons helpful:

Construction	Example	English	French	Section
Passive with *ser*	*el libro fue publicado*	the book was published	*le livre a été publié*	28.2
Passive *se*	*se publicó el libro* *se come mucho*	the book was published a lot **of it** is eaten	*le livre s'est publié* *on **en** mange beaucoup*	28.4
Impersonal *se* with personal *a*	*se recibió a los embajadores* *se les recibió*	the ambassadors were received they were received	*les ambassadeurs ont été reçus/on a reçu les ambassadeurs* *on les a reçus/ils ont été reçus*	28.5
Impersonal *se*	*se entra* *se come mucho*	one goes in people eat a lot	*on entre* *on mange beaucoup*	28.6
uno/una	*uno debería hacerlo así*	one should do it this way	*on devrait le faire comme ça*	28.7.1
Impersonal *tú* (informal styles)	*cuando te quejas de todo no te pasa nada bueno*	when you complain about everything nothing good happens to you	*quand on se plaint de tout, il ne vous arrive rien de bon*	28.7.2
Impersonal 3rd person	*dicen que es verdad*	they say it's true	*on dit que c'est vrai*	28.7.3

Passive with *ser* differs from the constructions with *se* in that the agent of the action can be mentioned: *el libro fue publicado **por** el autor* 'the book was published by the author'. In this case it is no longer an impersonal construction.

As can be seen from the chart, Spanish lacks an exact equivalent of the French *on*, German *man*. Medieval Spanish once used the word *hombre* as an impersonal pronoun, cf. *como hombre es mujer y vieja, no hacen caso de hombre* 'since one's a woman and old, they don't pay any attention to one' (from G. Correas, *Vocabulario de refranes y frases populares*, quoted Kany, 1970, 179). When this useful construction became extinct, some of its functions were transferred to the already overburdened pronoun *se*.

28.2 Passive with *ser*

28.2.1 General

The passive with *ser* is formed from the appropriate tense and person of *ser* 'to be' and the past participle, which agrees in number and gender with the subject of *ser*:

Active	**Passive**
Solucionaron los problemas	*Los problemas fueron solucionados*
They solved the problems	The problems were solved
Manuel escribió la respuesta	*La respuesta fue escrita por Manuel*
Manuel wrote the reply	The reply was written by Manuel

There are several points to be made about this construction:

(a) In English an indirect object can become the subject of the verb in a passive sentence: '**she** was sent a letter', '**they** were told a tall story'. This is impossible in Spanish. See 28.2.2.

(b) Passive and impersonal *se* constructions (sections 28.4–6) are heard in ordinary speech, but passive with *ser* is more typical of written or non-spontaneous language. Some grammarians claim that the passive with *ser* is never found in spontaneous speech, but this is not true, assuming that the following extracts really reflect spontaneous speech:

Ese jardín es alemán, y la película se ve que fue hecha en Alemania (M. Puig, Arg., dialogue)	That garden's German, and you can see the film was made in Germany
...la mujer "esposa de" que llevas dentro de ti y para lo que fuiste educada (R. Montero, Sp., dialogue)	...the 'wife-woman' that you carry inside you and you were brought up to be
Los derechos de filmación del fin del mundo ya fueron vendidos a la televisión norteamericana (L. Rafael Sánchez, Puerto Rico, dialogue; Sp. *...ya han sido vendidos*)	Film rights for the end of the world have already been sold to US television

However, such examples seem more common in the dialogue of Latin-American novels than in Spain. In informal speech impersonal 'they' (28.7.3) is much more common than the passive, e.g. *la película se ve que **la hicieron** en Alemania*.

(c) The passive with *ser* is common in written Spanish everywhere, especially in newspapers, for the reasons given at 28.2.7. It seems to be more common than fifty years ago: sentences like *estos ejemplos son vistos como logros enormes* (C. Fuentes,

Mex.) 'these examples are seen as enormous successes' would almost certainly have been written . . .*se ven como logros enormes* in the recent past, and may still surprise Peninsular speakers. But the passive with *ser* is not a modern invention: it is common in medieval and Golden-Age Spanish, e.g. in *Don Quixote*, and even in dialogues: *nunca fui desdeñado de mi señora —respondió don Quijote* '"never was I spurned by my lady," Don Quixote replied'.

English uses the passive constantly – 'he was seen by the police', 'my car was wrecked by a falling tree', 'you've been swindled' – with the result that English-speaking students constantly over-use it in spoken Spanish. The result may not always be ungrammatical, but it usually sounds pedantic and awkward.

(**d**) If no agent is mentioned, the passive with *ser* is often identical in meaning with passive *se* (explained at 28.4): *encontraron dos cargas explosivas que fueron desactivadas* and *encontraron dos cargas explosivas que se desactivaron* both mean 'they found two explosive charges which were defused', although the first is unambiguous whereas the second could conceivably be read as '. . .which defused themselves'. But there is often a difference of nuance which may become crucial. The passive with *ser* is less impersonal than the *se* construction in the sense that the latter completely eliminates information about the agent from the message, whereas the former does not. Thus it is probably more usual to say *el acusado fue sentenciado* 'the accused was sentenced' than *se sentenció al acusado*, since the agent (the judge) is obviously implicitly involved in the message: *se sentenció. . .* almost implies 'someone sentenced the accused'. But *en Inglaterra se habla inglés* 'English is spoken in England' is much more normal than . . .*el inglés es hablado* because the subject, 'people', is too obvious to be worth mentioning.

Por should not be used with passive *se*: **el latín se hablaba por los romanos* is generally considered to be bad Spanish for *los romanos hablaban latín*. This constraint reflects the impersonality of *se* and may partly explain the increasing popularity of the passive with *ser*. See 28.4.1, note (iii) for more on this point.

(**e**) The passive with *ser* is more common with the preterite, future, perfect, pluperfect tenses and with the infinitive than with the imperfect, present and continuous tenses: *fue entrevistado ayer* is normal written style for 'he was interviewed yesterday', but *Mario es entrevistado con frecuencia por periodistas de la prensa amarilla* 'Mario is frequently interviewed by journalists from the gutter press/US yellow press' is less usual. However, passive sentences in which the verb is timeless or habitual are nowadays increasingly common in writing and non-spontaneous speech, and more so in Latin America than Spain:

Basta saber que un hombre es buscado para que todos lo vean de manera distinta (C. Fuentes, Mex., dialogue)	It's enough to know a man's being sought for everyone to look at him in a different way
Algunos de ellos recuerdan que no hace mucho eran corridos por la Policía (*Cambio16*, Sp.)	Some of them remember that not so long ago they were being chased by the police
El parlamento gibraltareño tiene 17 miembros, de los que 2 son puestos por el Gobierno inglés (*El País*, Sp.)	The Gibraltarian parliament has 17 members, two of which are appointed by the British Government

Most Peninsular informants found these sentences unnatural and preferred a *se* construction or, where the agent is mentioned, an active sentence, e.g. *basta saber que a un hombre se le busca. . ., recuerdan que no hace mucho la Policía les corría. . ., dos de los cuales los pone. . . .* The fact that the example mentioning Gibraltar sounds natural if one substitutes *impuestos* 'imposed' for *puestos* indicates the difficulties surrounding the whole question of when to use passive with *ser*.

Further examples of the passive with *ser* (colloquial alternatives are shown in the unattributed examples):

Han sido detenidos por la Guardia Civil (*los ha detenido la Guardia Civil*)	They've been arrested by the Civil Guard
Las muestras les serán devueltas (*se les devolverán las muestras*)	The samples will be returned to you
El hijo de Pilar Ternera fue llevado a casa de sus abuelos (G. García Márquez, Col.; *llevar* cannot form a passive with *ser* if it means 'to wear' or 'to hold')	Pilar Ternera's son was taken (i.e. carried) to his grandparents' house

The difference between the passive with *ser la ciudad fue destruida* 'the city was destroyed' (action) and *la ciudad estaba destruida* 'the city was in a state of destruction' is discussed at 28.2.5.

28.2.2 Constraints on the passive with *ser*

Students should observe the following rules about the use of the Spanish passive with *ser*:

(a) The passive must not be used when the subject of the passive sentence would be an indirect object: 'she was sent a letter' must be *le fue enviada una carta* or *le enviaron una carta*. **Ella fue enviada una carta* is neither Spanish nor intelligible, and *fue enviada una carta* can only mean 'a letter was sent'. This is a common mistake among English-speaking beginners.

Nor can the passive with *ser* be used when the object of the verb in the active sentence takes the third-person pronouns *le* or *les*. One can transform *su marido la abandonó* into *fue abandonada por su marido* 'she was deserted by her husband', but *su marido **le** pegó* 'her husband beat her' cannot be transformed into **fue pegada por su marido*. Section 12.6.4 includes a list of verbs similar to *pegar*. The verbs *pagar*, *preguntar* and *obedecer* are exceptions to this rule:

Los ministros fueron preguntados. . . (El País, Sp.)	The ministers were asked...
Serás pagado por la Secretaría del Trabajo (J. Marías, Sp., dialogue)	You'll be paid by the Labour/US Labor Ministry
Por la contundencia de su voz deduje que estaba acostumbrada a ser obedecida (A. Gala, Sp., dialogue)	From her no-nonsense voice I inferred that she was used to being obeyed

But such sentences cannot include a direct object: one cannot say **fui preguntado una pregunta* for 'I was asked a question' (*se me hizo una pregunta/me hicieron una pregunta*) or **fui pagado el dinero* for 'I was paid the money' (*el dinero me fue pagado/ se me pagó el dinero/me pagaron el dinero*).

(b) The passive is not usual when the subject of *ser* has no article: *se venden naranjas aquí* 'oranges for sale' but not **naranjas son vendidas aquí* 'oranges are sold here'. However, sentences like *en el mercado antiguo eran vendidas manzanas y otras frutas* 'in the old market apples and other fruits were sold' may be found, especially in literary Latin-American Spanish; ...*se vendían manzanas y otras frutas* is more normal.

(**c**) The passive is rarely used with a present or imperfect tense to denote a single action. The Academy (*Esbozo*, 3.12.9c) says that *la puerta es/era abierta por el portero* 'the door is/was opened by the doorman' can only refer to a habitual or timeless event. This rule does not apply to all styles. Journalists sometimes use the imperfect for single events (usually for disasters)—*momentos después era asesinado por un terrorista* 'seconds later he was murdered by a terrorist' (see 28.2.1e and 14.5.8 for discussion)—and the historic present may denote a single past action, as in *el 22 de junio de 1941 la Unión Soviética es invadida por ejércitos alemanes* 'on 22 June 1941 the Soviet Union was (lit. 'is') invaded by German armies'.

(**d**) The passive is not used in reciprocal constructions. One can say *se vieron el uno al otro* 'they saw one another', but never **fueron vistos el uno por el otro* *'they were seen by one another'. This explains why, in both languages, *ver* 'to see' can only be used in the passive with a non-reciprocal meaning. *Fue vista por Mark cuando salía del restaurante* 'she was seen by Mark when she was leaving the restaurant' is possible (at least in journalese or official language) since she didn't know Mark was watching; but one can only say *Mark la vio anoche—fueron juntos a un restaurante* 'Mark saw her last night (i.e. they saw one another)—they went to a restaurant'.

(**e**) A phrase consisting of preposition + noun or pronoun cannot become the subject of a Spanish passive sentence. In this respect Spanish differs markedly from English: one can translate 'this bed has been slept **in**' only by *alguien ha dormido en esta cama*, never by the incomprehensible **esta cama ha sido dormido en*. Spanish sentences never end with prepositions.

(**f**) The Spanish passive cannot be used in constructions that involve verbs of seeing, hearing, etc., followed by an infinitive: *vi estrellarse el avión* 'I saw the plane crash' can be made passive in English 'the plane was seen to crash', but **el avión fue visto estrellarse* is not Spanish. A *se* construction must be used: *se vio cómo se estrellaba el avión*.

(**g**) Unattributed beliefs or opinions of the sort 'it is said that...', 'it is believed that', 'people thought that' are translated by a *se* construction: *se dice que, se cree que, se pensaba que*.

(**h**) The passive is not used with a large number of verbs, and for no obvious reason. These are more numerous than in English, which has similar constraints, e.g. 'the window was broken by Jill' but not ***'the stairs were descended by Jill'. Only familiarity with the language will eliminate such malformations as **fueron esperados por sus padres* 'they were expected by their parents', **fue permitido hacerlo* 'he was allowed to do it', both of them sentences which should be expressed in the active form or, in the second example, by impersonal *se*: *se le permitió hacerlo* (but *le fue permitido hacerlo* is possible).

 Likewise, one can say *la casa fue destruida por una bomba* 'the house was destroyed by a bomb', but not **la ventana fue rota por una piedra* 'the window was broken by a stone', which, curiously, is difficult to translate into Spanish: *esta ventana la han roto* *de una pedrada*. The *GDLE*'s explanation, 26.3.12, is that bombing is 'intentional' but a stone has no 'intention'; but where is the 'intention' in *el cráter fue producido por un meteoro* 'the crater was produced by a meteor'?

Sometimes the passive is wrong with a personal pronoun, but acceptable with other types of agent: *él era admirado por todos* 'he was admired by everybody', but not *?él era admirado por mí* 'he was admired by me' (*yo lo/le admiraba*).

It would be beyond the scope of this grammar to establish a comprehensive list of verbs which do not allow the passive with *ser*. As a general rule it seems that verbs commonly used in everyday conversation are less likely to appear in the passive form than verbs usually associated with formal or written language.

28.2.3 Ways of avoiding the passive

English-speaking students constantly over-use the Spanish passive. It can be avoided by the following stratagems:

(**a**) Make the sentence active—the simplest solution, but stylistically awkward if overdone:

Los críticos le/lo alabaron (= fue alabado por los críticos)	The critics praised him
Suspendieron la sesión (= la sesión fue suspendida)	The session was suspended

(**b**) Use passive *se* (discussed at 28.4).

The following typical piece of journalese . . .*su bufete privado es utilizado con frecuencia para asuntos propios del Gobierno* (*El País*, Sp.) 'his private office is often used for government business' could be neatly rephrased as . . .*su bufete privado se utiliza con frecuencia....* But passive *se* should only be used if the agent of the action is not included in the sentence. See 28.4.1 note (iii) for details.

(**c**) Since one function of the passive is to turn the object of the active sentence into the topic of a sentence—compare 'he preferred Jane' and '**Jane** was preferred by him'—the effect of an English passive can often be reproduced in Spanish by putting the direct object before the verb, e.g. *la explicación hay que buscarla en otra parte* 'the explanation must be sought elsewhere'. A redundant object pronoun then usually becomes necessary (see 11.16.1 and 37.5.1 note ii for details).

28.2.4 Passive meaning of the infinitive

The distinction between active and passive is often blurred in infinitive constructions:

un partido heterogéneo y sin estructurar	a heterogeneous and unstructured political party (lit. 'without structuring')
Vi matar a dos zorros	I saw two foxes kill**ed**

The last of these sentences is in fact ambiguous: it could mean 'I saw two foxes kill', but 'killed' is the more likely reading. See 18.2.5 and 18.5 for further examples.

28.2.5 Comparison between *fue convencido* and *estaba convencido* (also mentioned at 19.1)

The passive with *ser* denotes an action; the participle with *estar* usually describes a state arising from an action—i.e. it is not dynamic (see Glossary). Compare *la puerta fue abierta* 'the door was open**ed**' and *la puerta estaba abierta* 'the door was **open**'. The possibility of making this contrast is normally confined to verbs with a dynamic meaning, i.e. ones that describe actions, not states. The participle of a non-dynamic verb will probably denote only a state and therefore may only allow *estar*, cf. *estoy acostumbrado* 'I'm used to', *estás deprimido* 'you're depressed' (*ser* impossible).

In some cases a special participle is used with *estar*: cf. *estaba **despierto** porque había sido **despertado** por una voz de hombre* 'he was awake because he had been woken by a man's voice'. See 19.2.1 for a list of these participles. Examples:

La ciudad fue destruida	The city was destroyed
La ciudad estaba destruida	The city was in ruins
Fui detenido/Yo estaba detenido	I was arrested/I was under arrest
La reunión fue aplazada (action)	The meeting was postponed
Cuando llegué me encontré con que la reunión estaba aplazada (state)	When I arrived I found the meeting was postponed
[El libro] estaba muy leído, subrayado en algunos pasajes, e incluso con notas al margen (C. Martín Gaite, Sp.)	[The book] had been read a lot, underlined in some places, and even had notes in the margins
Los hechos históricos no están gobernados por leyes (O. Paz, Mex.)	Historical facts are not governed by laws

NB: Since literary Latin-American Spanish quite often uses the passive with *ser* to express habitual actions, the last sentence might well have been expressed as *son gobernados*. *Están gobernados* would be more normal in Spain.

(i) The '*estar* passive' is not used with the perfect (compound) tenses: **la ciudad ha/había estado inundada* is not Spanish. It is also rare with the preterite: *la ciudad estuvo inundada* (possible in sentences like *...estuvo inundada durante cuatro días* '...was flooded for four days').

28.2.6 Alternatives to *ser* to express passive meaning

Several other verbs may be used instead of *ser* in the passive construction. They usually add nuances which can barely be translated into normal English:

(a) *Quedar*

When it is used to form the passive, *quedar* emphasizes a condition that has arisen from some event, rather like the popular English 'ended up':

Queda dicho al principio de este párrafo que... (Academy, *Esbozo...*)	It was stated at the beginning of this paragraph that...
...mientras su colega quedó herido (El Correo, Pe.)	...while his colleague was injured

NB: *Quedarse* is not used in these passive constructions.

The use of *quedar/quedarse* with adjectives and participles is further discussed at 26.7.32 and 27.3.6.

(b) *Resultar*

Resultar also emphasizes the idea of a condition arising from an event. It is used on both continents:

Una veintena de personas resultaron heridas	About twenty people were injured (as a result)

(c) *Verse*

Verse is quite often used with a participle in literary styles, even with non-living subjects, and especially in the phrase *verse afectado*:

Mis ingresos eran reducidos, ya que se veían afectados por la piratería informática (letter in *El País*, Sp.)	My earnings were low, as they were affected by software piracy
...esos individuos que se ven proyectados de golpe a la condición de clase dominante (E. Lynch, Arg.)	...those individuals who are suddenly catapulted into the ruling classes

(d) *Venir*

Use of *venir* emphasizes that a condition has arisen from some previous event. Again, it is confined to literary styles and it is particularly commonly used when quoting some previous statement:

...como viene dicho en el párrafo anterior...	...as was stated in the previous paragraph...
En el caso de producirse omisiones y errores en la guía, la Compañía Telefónica vendrá obligada a corregirlos (Spanish phone book)	If omissions or error should appear in the directory, the telephone company shall be obliged to correct them

This construction seems to be less widespread in Latin America.

28.2.7 *Fue arrestado* or *se le arrestó?*

Learners are often obliged to choose between the passive with *ser* and one of the *se* constructions described at 28.3–6, a choice that normally only arises in writing since the passive with *ser* is avoided in spontaneous speech.

The passive with *ser* seems to be preferred in news reports or other impersonal styles to the construction *se + a +* human direct object described at 28.5: *varias personas fueron arrestadas* is probably more usual in newspapers than *se arrestó a varias personas*. It seems that this is due to the fact that the passive with *ser* tends to ascribe an action to some named or unnamed agent, whereas constructions with *se* may suggest that anyone might do the same. Compare *las patatas se fríen en aceite* '(the) potatoes are fried in oil' (the normal practice, so the sentence could appear in a cookery book) and *las patas habían sido fritas en margarina* 'the potatoes had been fried (by someone or other) in margarine', which is not normal. Compare also *se aplaudió mucho a las niñas* 'the girls were applauded warmly' but *las niñas fueron asesinadas* 'the girls were murdered', a repugnant action that we want to ascribe to some specific though unnamed individual.

The fact that, in the view of most grammarians, *por* should not be used with passive *se* also accounts for the frequent use in written language of the passive with *ser*: *varias personas fueron arrestadas por la policía* is the passive version of *la policía arrestó a varias personas* 'the police arrested several people', not **se arrestó a varias personas por la policía*, which is generally considered incorrect.

28.3 General remarks about passive and impersonal *se*

There are three types of passive and impersonal construction that use *se*:

(a) *Se pasivo* or 'passive *se*' (28.4). This is found only with transitive verbs in the third person, singular or plural: *se vendió la casa* 'the house was sold', *se debatieron varios problemas* 'several problems were discussed'.

(b) The 'mixed' construction *se* + transitive verb + *a* (28.5). The verb is always singular: *se detuvo a tres narcotraficantes* 'three drug-dealers were arrested', *se llama a los perros con un silbido* 'dogs are called by whistling'.

(c) *Se impersonal* or 'impersonal *se*' (28.6). This is found with intransitive verbs, e.g. *se vive mejor aquí* 'one lives better here', and also with 'objectless' transitive verbs, as in *en España se come mucho* 'people eat a lot in Spain' (no mention of what they eat).

28.4 Passive *se*

28.4.1 Basic rules

Passive *se* can only be used with third-person transitive verbs, and usually only with non-living nouns and pronouns so as to avoid clashes of meaning with other uses of *se* (see 28.5 for discussion). It is normally equivalent in meaning to passive with *ser*, but it is much more common in ordinary speech, more 'impersonal' than the passive with *ser* (see 28.2.1 and 28.2.7) and it should not be used when the agent of the action is mentioned; see note (iii):

Los cangrejos se cuecen en vino blanco	(The) crabs are boiled in white wine
El vino se le sirvió en copas de cristal (M. Vázquez Montalbán, Sp.)	The wine was served to him in wine glasses
Nunca se oyeron y leyeron en el Perú tantas definiciones de la libertad de información (M. Vargas Llosa, Pe.)	Never were there heard and read in Peru so many definitions of freedom of information
Es una zona de mucha sequía, así que no se ven muchos árboles (M. Puig, Arg., dialogue)	It's a very drought-ridden area, so you don't see many trees/not many trees are to be seen
Se reparan relojes	Watches mended
Estos errores podrían deberse a…	These errors could be due to…
Se acababan de promulgar varias leyes	Several laws had just been published
Que se sepa	As far as is known
Eso no se hace	That sort of thing isn't done
Se dice que va a dimitir (see note vii)	They say/It's said that (s)he's going to resign

(i) For a comparison of this construction with the true passive—*el problema se solucionó/el problema fue solucionado* 'the problem was solved'—see 28.2.1(d) and 28.2.7.

(ii) *Vendieron los libros* 'they sold the books' can be transformed into the sentence *se vendieron* 'they were sold', but not into *se los vendió*. See 28.5.2 for discussion.

(iii) Passive *se* should not be followed by *por* and the real agent of the verb: **la decisión se tomó por el presidente* is bad Spanish for *la decisión fue tomada por el presidente* 'the decision was taken by the President'. Cf. *?la decisión de irnos se tomó conjuntamente y por personas de la misma línea política* (F. Ordóñez in *Cambio16*, Sp.) 'the decision to leave was taken jointly and by persons sharing the same political line', *?el terrorismo no debe atacarse aisladamente por las naciones que lo padecen* (Felipe González in *El País*, Sp.) 'terrorism must not be combated individually by those nations that suffer from it'.

These blunders could have been avoided either by use of passive with *ser*, or by a simple active construction. It must be admitted that this use of *se* with *por* is sometimes seen in modern written texts, and it was also common in Golden-Age writing (16–17th centuries). The *GDLE* notes contexts in which it is more acceptable than in others but declares the phenomenon to be uncommon (26.3.3). Sentences like *?*se construyó el puente por los militares* are vehemently rejected by most literate Spanish-speakers in favour of *el puente fue construido por los militares*, and the *GDLE*, 26.1.1.2, notes that **se pasaron los trabajos a ordenador por Sandra* 'the work was typed into the computer by Sandra' is ungrammatical.

(iv) Passive *se* may be used to form a passive imperative, useful for footnotes, written instructions and so on: *no se crea que* 'let it not be believed that', *téngase presente que* 'let it be borne in mind that...' See 17.8.

(v) It must be remembered that as far as form is concerned there is no difference between this passive *se* construction and reflexive or reciprocal *se*. In other words, only common sense tells us that the first example does not mean 'the crabs cook themselves in white wine' or 'cook one another...'.

(vi) French passive *se*, as in *cela ne se dit pas* (= *eso no se dice* 'that isn't said'/'one doesn't say that') is more restricted in use and tends to be reserved for timeless statements.

(vii) *Se dice que...* This can be interpreted either as passive *se* or as impersonal *se*; see 28.6. The old-fashioned form *dícese que* is probably the origin of a colloquial form, very widespread in Latin America in various guises, e.g. *isque*, *dizque*. It is often sarcastic: *a los seis años de andar dizque* (Sp. *según dicen*) *gobernando se puso enfermo* (A. Mastretta, Mex.) 'after six year of "governing" (so they say) he fell ill'.

(viii) Passive *se* must not be confused with intransitive *se*, described at 26.4.1. The *GDLE*, 26.2.1.1, gives two examples in which context alone differentiates the meaning of *se*: *en verano los bosques se queman fácilmente* 'in summer the forests burn easily' (intransitive) and *se quemaron los bosques para acabar con la plaga* 'the forests were burnt to exterminate the infestation' (passive *se*).

28.4.2 Agreement of the verb with passive *se*

In theory, any verb used with *se* must agree with the logical subject. This applies to all constructions with reflexive, reciprocal and passive *se*. Compare *los niños se están lavando* (reflexive) 'the children are washing' or '...are washing one another' and *las tuercas se quitan con llave, no con martillo* (passive *se*) 'bolts are removed with a spanner/US wrench, not with a hammer'. Further examples of the agreement of the verb with passive *se*:

Se mezclan en el turmix los tomates sin pepitas y sin piel	The tomatoes, with skins and pips removed, are mixed in the liquidizer
Se enviaron los hombres y las armas necesarios para concluirla (i.e. *la lucha*: Fidel Castro, Cu., speech)	The men and weapons necessary to finish it [the fight] were sent
...aquellos reportajes en que se veían los fusilamientos de los campesinos (R. Arenas, Cu.)	...those news items in which one could see the executions of the peasants

In constructions involving passive *se*, the rules of agreement are always respected when a plural noun precedes the verb: *los libros se vendían a diez euros* 'the books were being sold at ten euros', never **los libros se vendía a diez euros*.

However, when the verb precedes a plural noun, popular language sometimes breaks the rules of agreement: ?*se compra objetos usados* 'used articles bought' for *se compran objetos usados*. This phenomenon raises problems for an impartial grammarian, since whereas some speakers find ?*se compra objetos...* quite illiterate, others, including a few grammarians, accept it on the grounds that this is really an impersonal construction. Plural agreement seems overwhelmingly to be the norm on both continents (see DeMello 1995 (1) for a survey), and foreigners should probably observe it; but it should be noted that in some contexts, especially advertisements of the type *se necesita camareros* 'waiters needed', singular agreement is more tolerated. For more on this problem, see 28.5.2.

The following forms may therefore be unacceptable to many speakers:

?*Y nunca más se **ha** tenido noticias de su paradero* (*Abc*; for *se han tenido...*)	No further news has been received of his whereabouts
?*Se necesita agallas para hacer eso* (Spanish informant overheard: *se necesitan agallas*)	You need 'guts' to do that
?*Se les **dio** varios premios* (for *se les dieron...*)	Several prizes were given to them
?*Se vende máquinas de coser usadas* (street sign in Mexico)	Used sewing machines sold

(i) The last example must be exceptional if we are to believe the claim of J. M. Lope Blanch (1991), 12, that Mexican Spanish preserves, 'casi con exclusividad, la construcción pasiva refleja del tipo "se rentan departamentos" (Sp. *se alquilan pisos*) sin dar entrada a la construcción activa impersonal del tipo "se vende botellas", relativamente frecuente en el habla española'.

(ii) When passive *se* is followed by the interrogative words *cuánto, qué, cuál* or *quién* the verb is singular: *se calculó cuántos kilos había* 'it was calculated how many kilos there were', *se averiguó qué existencias quedaban* 'a check was made of what stocks remained', *no se sabe quiénes son* 'it is not known who they are'.

(iii) When a verb which is not a modal verb (see next section) precedes an infinitive whose direct object is plural, agreement is in the singular: *se intentó solucionar varios problemas* 'an attempt was made to solve several problems', *se decidió tomar estas medidas...* 'it was decided to take these measures...'. Other similar non-modal verbs are: *tratar de* 'to try', *necesitar* 'to need', *esperar* 'to hope'. Incorrect plural agreement is, in fact, quite often seen: see 28.4.3, note (ii).

(iv) With verbs of perception followed by an infinitive, both singular and plural agreement seem equally acceptable: *se veía(n) caer gotas de agua* 'drops of water could be seen falling'.

(v) The verb *tardar* is a special case. It is always singular in this construction: *se tardó varias horas en llegar a un acuerdo* 'it took several hours to reach an agreement' (lit. 'several hours were taken to reach…').

28.4.3 Agreement of passive *se* with modal verbs

Agreement with plural nouns is required with modal verbs (*poder, saber, tener que, haber de, querer, soler*) when they precede the infinitive of a transitive verb. In this case *se* can be suffixed to the infinitive or it can precede the modal verb:

Se tienen que resolver varios problemas/ Tienen que resolverse varios problemas	Several problems must be solved
Se deben limpiar bien las verduras antes de cocerlas (= *deben limpiarse*)	Vegetables should be washed well before boiling
…*cosas que no se quieren hacer/cosas que no quieren hacerse*	…things one doesn't want to do
¿Se pueden prevenir las várices? (*El Comercio*, Pe.; Sp. usually *las varices*)	Can varicose veins be prevented?
En Londres por la calle se pueden observar los tipos de personas más extrañas (*Cosmopolitan*, Sp.)	In London one can observe the strangest sorts of people in the streets

See 11.14.4 for further discussion of the position of pronouns with the infinitive.

(i) Singular agreement with modal auxiliary verbs is generally considered to be incorrect, but it is commonly seen and heard, cf. *?se puede imprimir textos con más rapidez con un procesador de textos* (*Ordenador Personal*, Sp., for *se pueden*) 'texts can be printed more rapidly with a word processor', *?la Ley prohíbe que se pueda transferir fondos de un programa a otro* (*La Prensa*, Panama) 'the Law prohibits the transfer of funds from one programme to another' (for *se puedan transferir*).

(ii) There is, however, a contrary tendency, deplored by grammarians, to pluralize non-modal verbs preceding an infinitive whose object is plural, cf. *se necesitan resolver muchos problemas* 'many problems have to be resolved', *cuando se tratan de estudiar los hallazgos de tiempos pasados* (*Abc*, Sp.) 'when an attempt is made to study the discoveries of the past', *y en el ministerio de Obras Públicas (MOP) también se esperan firmar otros contratos* (*El Comercio*, Ec.) 'and in the Ministry of Public Works it is also hoped that other contracts will be signed'. These verbs should be singular.

28.5 *Se* + transitive verb + personal *a*

28.5.1 General

This special type of construction has evolved to eliminate some of the ambiguities surrounding the overworked pronoun *se*.

Passive *se* as described at 28.4 is usually unambiguous if there is no noun in the sentence that could be understood to be the subject, as is usually the case when talking about non-living things: *los platos se lavan* 'the plates are washed' is unlikely to mean 'the plates wash themselves', which could be said *los platos se lavan a sí mismos/los platos se lavan solos*. However *se* may be intolerably ambiguous with nouns referring to creatures that can do things to themselves: *se mataron dos ingleses* could mean 'two Englishmen killed themselves' as well as 'killed one another'. Spanish has developed a way of avoiding this problem by marking the direct object by the preposition *a*: *se mató a dos ingleses*. Three points must be remembered about this construction:

(**a**) The verb is always singular: **se mataron a dos ingleses* for *se mató a…* is a bad mistake.

(**b**) In this construction the word *se* always implies an unidentified *human* agent, in which respect it resembles English 'one', French *on*, German *man*. In other words, one could not say *se mató a dos ingleses* if the Englishmen were killed by a falling tree or a bolt of lightning, in which case one would say *murieron dos ingleses* or *dos ingleses resultaron muertos*.

(**c**) The noun can be replaced by an object pronoun: *se **me** había reconocido* 'I had been recognized', *se **les** reconoció* 'they were recognized'.

Examples of *se* + verb + personal *a*:

Se persiguió y encarceló a millares de creyentes (El País, Sp.)	Thousands of believers were persecuted and jailed
Se incitaba a las muchachas a trabajar más que los muchachos	The girls were encouraged to work harder than the boys
¿Se puede destrozar a una persona de esa manera porque se la ama de esa manera…? (A. Bryce Echenique, Pe.)	Can one destroy a person that way because one loves them that way…?
No se te paga tan mal, entonces, si puedes comprarte tus revistas (S. Vodanovic, Ch., dialogue)	You're not that badly paid if you can afford to buy your magazines

(i) When a pronoun replaces the noun in this type of sentence, many speakers, including Latin Americans, prefer *le/les* to *lo/la/los/las*, despite the fact that the pronouns are the direct object of the verb and may also be feminine: …*hasta que se **les** pueda evacuar* (El País, Sp.) '…until they can be evacuated', *se **le** veía nerviosa* 'one could see she was nervous'. This is discussed in more detail at 12.6.3.

(ii) As was mentioned, the verb must be singular in this construction. **Se les notaban cansados* is an error sometimes heard and seen in Spain and rather more often in Latin America (see 28.4 for examples like *se pueden ver los árboles desde aquí*, which is passive *se*).

(iii) The construction discussed here seems to be a relatively recent innovation. Before the 18th century, *Juan y Antonio se vieron* could also mean 'Juan and Antonio were seen'. Nowadays it is taken to mean 'saw one another' or 'saw themselves', and *se vio a Antonio y Juan* (or, in written styles, *Antonio y Juan fueron vistos*) would be used for the passive. In modern journalisam passive with *ser* is in fact increasingly preferred to the construction with *se + a*. See 28.2.7.

28.5.2 **Difference between the construction *se* + verb + *a* and passive *se***

Foreign students (and, it must be admitted, quite a few native speakers too) have difficulty distinguishing between the construction just described and passive *se*, especially when pronouns replace nouns, as in *se le/la nota cansada* 'one can see she's tired'.

In theory, and also in practice as far as most careful speakers and writers are concerned, passive *se* is used only when the direct object of the equivalent active sentence refers to something non-living, and *se* + *a* is reserved for cases in which it refers to an identified human being or, less commonly, an animal. This should be clear from the difference between the following sentences:

*A Eugenio d'Ors se **lo/le** lee poco*	Eugenio d'Ors isn't read much
Los libros de Eugenio d'Ors se leen poco (se pasivo)	Eugenio d'Ors's books aren't read much
*Se **lo/le** lee poco* (refers to a male author)	**He** isn't read much/people don't read him much
Se lee poco (refers to a book: *se pasivo*)	**It** isn't read much
*Se **le/la** admira mucho* (i.e. a woman)	**She**'s admired a lot
Se admira mucho (e.g. some non-living thing: *se pasivo*)	**It**'s admired a lot
*Se **las/les** criticó duramente* (i.e. some women)	They were strongly criticized
Se criticaron duramente (i.e. some non-living things: *se pasivo*)	They were strongly criticized

These examples show that true passive *se* constructions cannot contain a direct object pronoun other than *se* itself. In *se los envió*, *se* cannot be the direct object, which is *los*, so it cannot be passive *se*. So the sentence must mean one of two things:

(1) '(S)he sent them to her/him/you' (active sentence, *se* stands for *le* or *les*). This is the likely reading; or

(2) it is an example of *se* + *a* + transitive verb, so *los* refers to human beings and it means 'they (the students/the people, etc.) were sent to him/her/you/them'.

It cannot mean 'they were sent' if 'they' refers to something non-living like 'books': the latter can only be *se enviaron* (or *fueron enviados*).

The passive *se* construction is, however, allowed with human beings when the latter are unidentified, as in *se necesitan secretarias* 'secretaries needed', *se ven muchos turistas en la playa* 'a lot of tourists are seen on the beach; compare *desde aquí se ve a muchos turistas alemanes durmiendo en la playa* 'from here you can see a lot of German tourists sleeping on the beach' (identified or specified as German tourists).

(i) It must be acknowledged that impersonal *se* does appear with a non-living direct object, as in *el ascensor subía por dentro de las barandillas y se **le** oía chirriar desde todas las habitaciones de la casa* (C. Martín Gaite, Sp.) 'the lift went up on the inside of the banisters, and one could hear it squeaking from every room in the house'. Lack of space precludes a lengthy discussion of this possibility, but two points must be made:

(**a**) some speakers, and even some grammarians, accept sentences like ?*se vende manzanas* as grammatical whereas the majority reject them, as we do, since in our view this is passive *se* so one should say *se venden manzanas* for the reasons given at 28.4.2. The *GDLE*, 26.3.2.2, notes that singular agreement with passive *se* has featured sporadically in Spanish for many centuries: 'su uso parece haberse extendido en los últimos tiempos, especialmente en el español de América, aunque sin llegar nunca a generalizarse';

(**b**) Spanish-speakers seem to be very sensitive to the possibility of a reflexive or reciprocal meaning of some verbs used with *se*, so they may prefer impersonal to passive *se* whenever the danger of ambiguity arises. This probably explains the following sentences: *hay que cruzar el río Tajo, y **se le cruza** por el puente llamado del Cardenal* (M. de Unamuno, Sp.) 'one has to cross the river Tagus, and one crosses it over the bridge called the Cardinal's Bridge'; *en la obra de la santa de Ávila **se ve** esas dulces huertas interiores de esta tierra* (ibid.) 'in the work of the saint of Avila [Teresa] one can see those gentle interior gardens typical of this land'; *su extensión* [i.e. *de esta pauta*] *es muy reducida, pues **se la ha señalado** para el oeste de Panamá* (*GDLE*, p. 1411) 'its scope [i.e. of this grammatical tendency] is very limited, since it has been noted in the west of Panama'. Presumably the nature of the verbs persuaded the writers against *se cruza*, which can mean 'cross over itself', *se ven*, which in a writer addicted to personification can mean 'see themselves', and *se ha señalado* which can mean 'has stood out'. Thus *los metales blandos se derriten con facilidad* means 'soft metals melt easily', but *se derrite los metales blandos con facilidad* means 'soft metals are easily melted' (impersonal *se* because *se derriten* is ambiguous). This is a peculiarity of *derretir*, but it does not justify sentences like *?se debatió varios temas* for *se debatieron*, since no reflexive meaning is possible here. The example with *derretirse*, but not the explanation, is inspired by *GDLE* 23.3.2.3.

   Personal *a* may appear in sentences that use impersonal *se* with a lifeless object, for example *se ha comparado **a** los ordenadores* (Lat. Am. *las computadoras* or *los computadores*) *con el cerebro humano* 'computers have been compared with the human brain'. 22.10c discusses this phenomenon.

28.6 Impersonal *se*

28.6.1 General

Spanish also uses *se* with third-person verbs as an equivalent of the English 'one'/'people', French *on*, German *man*. Impersonal *se*, like English 'one' and French *on*, refers to an unidentified *human* agent: this is demonstrated by the peculiarity of *?*es difícil dormir por las noches porque se ladra mucho* ?'it's difficult to sleep at night because one barks a lot'.

   Impersonal *se* most commonly occurs with intransitive verbs: *se está mejor aquí* 'one's better off here' (French *on est mieux ici*), *se entra por aquí* (French *on entre par ici*) 'one goes in this way', etc. But impersonal *se* can also be used with transitive verbs, as in *en este país se lee poco* 'in this country people don't read much'. See 28.6.3.

28.6.2 Impersonal *se* with intransitive verbs

The following examples show impersonal *se* used with intransitive verbs. The verb is always singular. In some cases, explained in note (iii), *uno* could be used instead of *se*:

No se puede entrar	Entrance forbidden
Siempre se vuelve a los sitios a los que se pertenece (Antonio Gala, Sp., dialogue; or *uno vuelve…uno pertenece*)	One always returns to the places one belongs to
O se va a referéndum, o habrá guerra civil	Either a referendum is held, or there will be a civil war
¿Quién puede pensar en nada cuándo se está rodeado de idiotas? (C. Solórzano, Mex.)	Who can think of anything when one's surrounded by idiots?
…que en vez de ser pobre, se es rico; que en vez de ser nadie, se es alguien… (S. Vodanovic, Ch., dialogue; or *uno*)	…that instead of being poor, one's rich, that instead of being nobody, one's somebody…
A las tres de la madrugada pareció llegarse a un acuerdo tácito para descansar (J. Cortázar, Arg.)	At three in the morning it appeared that a tacit agreement was reached to get some rest
Se cruza si el semáforo está en verde y se espera si está en rojo (*El País*, Sp.; or *uno cruza…uno espera*)	One crosses if the lights are green and one waits if they are red

(i) Impersonal *se* cannot be used with a verb that already has *se* or some other reflexive pronoun attached to it: one cannot say **se se lava mucho* for 'people wash themselves a lot': *la gente se lava mucho*. See 26.11.

(ii) As with most sentences involving *se*, common sense and context often clarify the meaning. Thus *se iba al teatro* may mean '(s)he was going to the theatre' (*irse* is also a pronominal verb meaning 'to go away') or 'people used to go to the theatre' (impersonal *se*).

(iii) In some cases *uno* can be used instead of impersonal *se*. This is possible when *se* includes the speaker, as in *nunca escuchaba cuando se le hablaba/cuando **uno** le hablaba* '(s)he never listened when one spoke to him/her/when he/she was spoken to'. But when the speaker excludes him/herself, *uno* is not possible, as in *éste/este es un país donde se fuma y se bebe* (or *donde fuman y beben*) *mucho* 'this is a country where people smoke and drink a lot'.

(iv) Impersonal *se* may even appear in combination with the passive with *ser*, although this is rare: *no se debe hablar más que con personas a las que **se ha sido ya presentado*** 'one must only talk to people one has been introduced to' (C. Rico-Godoy, Sp.).

(v) The use of *se* with intransitive verbs has no counterpart in French, which uses *on*. Italian impersonal *si* is constructed differently from its Spanish counterpart, cf. *si è **contenti*** and *se está **contento*** 'one's content'/'people are content' (adjective always singular in Spanish).

28.6.3 Impersonal *se* with transitive verbs

Impersonal *se* can also be used with transitive verbs, in which case the verb is always singular and no direct object appears:

En España se come mucho	People eat a lot in Spain (in general; does not refer to any specific food)
Sí, se habla, se habla…	Yes, people talk and talk…
Es difícil vender periódicos en un país donde se lee poco (cf. *se leen poco*, passive *se*: 'they aren't read much')	It's difficult to sell newspapers in a country where people don't read much
Se critica mucho pero se alaba poco	People criticize a lot but don't praise much

Students, and not a few native speakers, find it difficult to distinguish between this construction and passive *se*. The difference depends on whether the context refers to a direct object, explicit or implicit: if it does then the construction is passive *se*; if not, it is impersonal *se*. Thus if we are talking about garlic, the sentence *en España se come mucho* is taken to mean 'a lot **of it** is eaten in Spain' (passive *se*, underlying object 'garlic'/*ajo*; French *on* **en** *mange beaucoup*). If the conversation is simply about quantities eaten, the same sentence means 'people eat a lot in Spain' (no underlying object, French *on mange beaucoup*) and the *se* is impersonal *se*.

(i) If a direct object pronoun appears in this construction it can usually refer only to a human being: *se le considera útil* '(s)he is considered useful/you're considered useful', but not '**it** is considered useful', which is *se considera útil* (passive *se*): see 28.5.2.

If the object pronoun is an indirect object, the construction is likely to be impersonal *se* with an intransitive verb, as in *se* **le** *rompió la taza* 'the cup "broke itself" on him/her' (i.e. (s)he accidentally broke the cup, intransitive verb *romperse* 'to break'), or passive *se* with a non-living underlying object: *se* **le** *dio un regalo* (passive *se*) 'a present was given to him'/her/'(s)he was given a present'.

28.7 Other impersonal constructions

28.7.1 *Uno/una* as a pronoun

This is similar to the English 'one' in that it can be a modest way of saying 'I' or 'we'. A woman uses *una* if the pronoun refers to herself, but *uno* if no self-reference is intended. Its object forms are *lo/la/le*. For many Latin Americans *uno* is the only form used, even by women, but the examples from Vargas Llosa, Arrufat and Benedetti show that this is not universal. *Uno/una* is often interchangeable with impersonal *se*:

Bueno, si no le dicen a una como hay que hacerlo… (woman speaking, or *si no se le dice a una*)	Well, if they don't tell one how to do it…
Uno no hace mal a la gente que le es indiferente (E. Sábato, Arg., dialogue, woman speaking; or *no se hace mal a. . .*)	One doesn't do harm to people one is indifferent to
En ese tiempo una no hablaba de eso con las amigas (M. Vargas Llosa, Pe., dialogue, woman speaking; or *no se hablaba de eso*)	In those days one didn't talk about those things with one's women friends
Con tal de salirse con la suya, la llevan a una a la tumba (A. Arrufat, Cu., dialogue; mother complaining about her children)	As long as they get their own way, they'll put you in your grave

Cuando una se lava las manos en los aeropuertos quedan bastante más limpias pero arrugaditas (M. Benedetti, Ur., little girl speaking)	When one washes one's hands at airports they come out quite a lot cleaner but all wrinkly

(i) *Uno* must be used to make an impersonal expression from a verb that already has *se* (since two *ses* cannot occur with the same verb): *en este pueblo **se** aburre **uno** mucho* 'in this village one gets bored a lot'. See 26.11 for discussion.

(ii) Colloquially *uno/una* may mean 'someone'. See 9.3 note (iv).

28.7.2 Impersonal *tú*

The second-person singular is often used impersonally, much the same as in English. *Uno* or *se* may be preferred when one is on very formal terms with the hearer, but impersonal *tú* is quite common in Spain (not in Latin America) even when the speakers are using *usted* to one another (see DeMello 2000, 2):

Yo nunca voy allí porque te cobran más que en otra parte (le cobran a uno más)	I never go there because they charge you more than elsewhere
Es increíble, si lo piensas (si uno lo piensa)	It's incredible if you think of it
Es que no se tiene conciencia de que pasa el tiempo cuando eres joven (Queen Sofía in *El País*, Sp. Mixed pronouns, common in informal styles)	It's that **one** isn't conscious of time passing when **you**'re young

28.7.3 Impersonal third-person plural

As in English, the third-person plural is constantly used impersonally when the speaker does not include him/herself or the hearer in the reference:

Dicen que las zanahorias son buenas para los ojos (= *se dice que…*)	They say carrots are good for the eyes
Parece que hablan más despacio en Estados Unidos que en Inglaterra (= *que se habla*)	It seems that they speak more slowly in the United States than in England

29

Ser *and* estar

For the conjugation of *ser* see 13.3.45, and of *estar* see 13.3.21.

The main topics discussed here are:

- The uses of *ser* (Section 29.2)
- The uses of *estar* (Section 29.3)
- When *ser* and *estar* are more or less interchangeable (Section 29.4)
- *Estar* used to mean 'seem', 'taste', etc. (Section 29.4.3)
- *Ser* or *estar* used to change the meaning of adjectives (Section 29.4.4)

29.1 General

Ser and *estar* both translate the English 'to be', but the difference between the two Spanish words is fundamental and sometimes subtle.

Basically *ser* is used to answer questions about who or what something or someone is, whereas *estar* answers questions about where, how or in what condition something is: *soy español, pero estoy en Londres* 'I'm Spanish, but I'm in London'; *es callado* 'he's the quiet type', *está callado* 'he's keeping silent (at the moment)'; *puede que sea así* 'perhaps he/she/it is like that', *puede que esté así* 'perhaps that's the condition/situation he/she/it's in'.

It is usually true that *ser* indicates permanent features and *estar* temporary conditions, but this is contradicted by *está muerto* 'he's dead' or *durante varias horas fue feliz* 'for several hours (s)he was happy', or by the fact that one can say either *soy calvo* or *estoy calvo* 'I'm bald'. Nor is a characteristic expressed by *ser* necessarily permanent: a brunette can change the colour of her hair and say *antes era morena pero ahora soy rubia* 'I was a brunette before, but now I'm a blonde': each colour is considered, at the time, to be a typical feature of the woman, not a temporary state.

Ser is also often used with a few adjectives that indicate what can be thought of as states, e.g. *feliz* 'happy', *desgraciado* 'unhappy', *pobre* 'poor', *rico* 'rich', *consciente* 'conscious', but these are probably best treated as exceptions: cf. *está deprimido* 'he's depressed', *está contento* 'he's happy'/'content', *está animado* 'he's full of life' (*estar* obligatory).

Some adjectives, e.g. *gordo* 'fat', *divorciado* 'divorced', *casado* 'married', may be used with either *ser* or *estar* with hardly any significant change of meaning.

Estar before a noun phrase can normally only denote location: compare *¿es el jefe?* 'is (s)he/are you the boss?' with *¿está el jefe?* 'is the boss in?'

Learners constantly forget that *ser* must be used for the location of events as opposed to people or things: *¿dónde es la fiesta?* 'where's the party?', but *¿dónde está el libro?* 'where's the book?'

Ser is used to form the passive: *fue criticado* 'he was criticized'; see Chapter 28. *Estar* is used to form the continuous aspect of verbs: *está hablando* 'he's talking'; see Chapter 15.

Both *ser* and *estar* are often echoed or 'resumed' by *lo*, as in —*Ana parece sueca.* —*Lo es* '"Ana looks Swedish." "She is."'. See 7.4.1 note (i).

29.2 Uses of *ser*

29.2.1 In equational sentences of the sort A = B

Ser is used to link elements in statements of the type 'A = B', where A and B are nouns or pronouns:

París es la capital de Francia	Paris is the French capital
Es médico/abogado/bibliotecario	He's a doctor/lawyer/librarian
Es un estafador/Esto es una estafa	He's a swindler/This is a swindle
Es la una/Son las doce	It's one o'clock/twelve o'clock
Ha sido un año/verano frío	It's been a cold year/summer
Esto es lo que me fastidia	This is what I find annoying
La confrontación de culturas en el siglo XXI puede ser sangrienta, vaticina Umberto Eco (El Mundo, Sp.)	Umberto Eco predicts that culture clashes in the 21st century may be bloody

(i) *Estar* cannot appear before nouns or pronouns unless the latter are its subject: **yo estoy maestro* is emphatically not Spanish for 'I'm a schoolteacher': *soy maestro.*

Exceptions to this rule are very rare, and include ranking, as in *el Barcelona está/es el segundo en la clasificación* 'Barcelona is second in the league table' (from *GDLE* 37.6.3), *estar pez*, e.g. *estoy pez en historia* 'I'm a complete dunce in history' (colloquial and Spain only?), and weather expressions like *está un día magnífico* 'it's a lovely day'. Many speakers accept only *hace un día magnífico* or *es un día magnífico*, etc., but all Spanish informants accepted *está un día que da gusto salir a la calle* 'it's one of those days when you like going out into the streets'. With an adjective *estar* is used in weather expressions—*está lluvioso* 'it's rainy'—but with certain nouns *hacer* is used: *hoy hace frío/calor/viento* 'it's cold/hot/windy today'; but *hay niebla/helada* 'it's foggy/frosty'.

29.2.2 *Ser* with adjectives

Ser is used with adjectives or adjectival phrases which indicate identity or nature, i.e. physical, moral and mental characteristics, as opposed to conditions or states:

—*¿Quién eres?* —*Soy Carlos*	'Who are you?' 'I'm Carlos'
—*¿Cómo eres?* —*Soy, alto, moreno y delgado*	'What are you like?' 'I'm tall, dark and slim'
El cobre es ideal para los cables	Copper is ideal for cables
Esa chaqueta es bien bonita	That jacket is very nice
Así soy de testarudo (G. Cabrera Infante, Cu., dialogue)	That's how stubborn I am

Hacer is used in statements about the weather that involve certain nouns: see 29.2.1 note (i). One uses *tener frío/calor* for sensations: compare *tiene frío* '(s)he feels cold' and *es muy frío* 'he is very cold' (i.e. emotionless). *Estar caliente* means 'to be hot' applied to lifeless things, 'to be sexually excited' applied to humans.

29.2.3 *Ser* with certain adjectives apparently denoting states

Ser is normally used with *pobre* 'poor', *feliz* 'happy', *desgraciado* 'unhappy', *inocente* 'innocent', *culpable* 'guilty', *consciente* 'aware', despite the fact that they may be thought of as conditions:

Ahora que el precio del petróleo ha bajado, este país es pobre	Now that the price of oil has gone down, this country is poor
El acusado dijo que era inocente	The accused said he was innocent
Hay muchos que no se sienten culpables aunque lo sean	There are many people who don't feel guilty even though they are
Soy consciente de mis limitaciones	I'm conscious of my limitations
Pocas veces fue tan feliz como en las horas que precedieron a la entrevista con Bordenave (E. Sábato, Arg.)	He was seldom so happy as during the hours before his interview with Bordenave
Yo sólo quiero que sea feliz (A. Mastretta, Mex., dialogue)	I only want her to be happy
—Soy tan desgraciada —me dijo (G. Cabrera Infante, Cu.)	'I'm so unhappy,' she told me

(i) *Estar rico/pobre/feliz* is sometimes heard in Spain when describing a transitory state, although many Spaniards reject *estar* with these adjectives, except in the phrase *estoy feliz y contento* 'I'm happy and satisfied'. Latin Americans frequently use *estar* with *feliz*: *estaban tan felices que me dieron envidia* (A. Mastretta, Mex.) 'they were so happy that they filled me with envy', *acaban de ganar las elecciones y están felices* (A. Bryce Echenique, Pe., dialogue) 'they've just won the elections and they're happy'.

Estar rico generally means 'to be tasty' / 'to taste nice' in Spain; see 29.4.4; but not necessarily in Latin America: *Andrés acompañó al padre José que estaba riquísimo y lo oyó jurar por la Virgen de Covadonga que no tenía un centavo* (A. Mastretta, Mex.) 'Andrés accompanied Father José, who was extremely rich, and he heard him swear by the Virgin of Covadonga that he didn't have a cent'.

(ii) Peninsular usage differentiates *ser consciente (de)* 'to be aware/conscious of' and *estar consciente* 'to be conscious' (i.e. awake). In Latin America the distinction is not always made: *quienes no están conscientes de su libertad no son libres* 'those who are not aware of their freedom are not free' (E. Poniatowska, Mex., dialogue; but in the same novel *tú eres muy consciente...* 'you're clearly aware...').

29.2.4 *Ser de*

Ser can be followed by *de* + noun or by *de* + *un* + adjective to denote identity, nature, origin or the material something is made of:

—¿De dónde eres? —De Londres	'Where do you come from?' 'London'
La situación era de risa	The situation was extremely funny
Es de día/noche	It's day/night

—¿De qué es la mesa? —Es de madera	'What's the table made of?' 'Wood'
Era una película de guerra	It was a war film/movie
Esa chica es de miedo	That girl is tremendous
Tú eres de prontos impetuosos (C. Martín Gaite, Sp.)	You're given to hasty decisions

29.2.5 *Ser* and *estar* in impersonal statements

As stated at 29.2.1, *ser* is used before nouns and noun phrases:

Es verdad/mentira/una tontería/una pena/una lata	It's true/a lie/nonsense/a pity/a bore, etc.

Phrases based on adverbs take *estar*, e.g. *está bien/mal/estupendamente* 'It's/(s)he's fine/bad/great'. See 29.3.4. With adjectives, *ser* is the usual verb, but there are apparent exceptions:

Es triste/trágico/increíble que haya muerto tan joven	It's sad/tragic/incredible that (s)he died so young
es evidente/obvio que...	it's clear that...
es necesario/imposible/probable/dudoso	it's necessary/impossible/probable/ doubtful
está visto que...	it's evident that...
claro está...	clearly.../of course...

Es claro is common in Latin America: *es claro que, cuando eso acaba, debe quedarle a uno un sentimiento de dignidad* (M. Benedetti, Ur., dialogue) 'it's obvious that when that sort of thing ends one must be left with a feeling of dignity'.

29.2.6 *Ser* to denote possession

Estar cannot be used with possessive adjectives :

Todo esto es mío, el día de mañana será tuyo	All this is mine, tomorrow it'll be yours
El piso es de mi yerno	The flat/apartment belongs to my son-in-law

29.2.7 *Ser* to denote impressions

Me es/resulta simpática	I find her likeable
Esto me es/resulta molesto	This is uncomfortable for me
Todo le era distinto (A. Carpentier, Cu.)	Everything seemed different to her

29.2.8 *Ser* of events

If 'to be' means 'to be held' or 'to happen' it must be translated by *ser*:

La fiesta es/se celebra en su casa	The party is at his place
Hay un incendio en el edificio pero no sé en qué piso es	There's a fire in the building but I don't know which floor it's on
¿Dónde es la manifestación?	Where is the demonstration?
El entierro sería a las cinco (G. García Márquez, Col.)	The funeral was to be at five

Use of *estar* may imply a physical object. Compare *¿dónde es la conferencia?* 'where's the lecture (being held)?' and *¿dónde está la conferencia?* 'where's the lecture?' (i.e. the lecture notes or typescript). Note also *el jarro es/va encima del aparador* 'the vase belongs/goes on top of the sideboard', as opposed to *...está...* 'is on...'.

29.3 Uses of estar

29.3.1 *Estar* to describe state as opposed to identity or nature

Estar is used with adjectives that indicate mood, physical condition, temporary physical appearance or other non-characteristic features. Note the difference between *es guapa* 'she's good-looking' and *está guapa* 'she's looking good/attractive', *eres inaguantable* 'you are unbearable (by nature)' and *estás inaguantable* 'you're being unbearable':

Está más bien triste	(S)he's rather sad
Estuvo enferma una temporada	She was ill/US sick for a time
Hoy no estoy muy católico	I don't feel too great today (lit. 'I'm not feeling too Catholic')
Estaba roja de vergüenza	She was red with shame
El agua que se añada tiene que estar caliente	The water to be added has to be hot
El televisor está estropeado	The television doesn't work
Está parado desde febrero	He's been out of work since February
Estuvo callado todo el tiempo	He was silent all the time
Nueva York está llena de ventanas (J. Aldecoa, Sp.)	New York is full of windows

(i) The pervasive use of the passive with *ser* in written Latin-American Spanish, especially to denote habitual or continuous actions, may produce sentences that require *estar* in Spain. This seems to be particularly frequent in Mexico: *una de las mesas era ocupada por el doctor Bernstein* (C. Fuentes, Mex.'; Sp. *estaba ocupada*) 'one of the tables was occupied by Doctor Bernstein'.

(ii) *Ser hecho de* for *estar hecho de* sounds poetic or archaic: *¡y cuán frágil el barro de que somos hechos!* (R. del Valle-Inclán, Sp., 1890s) 'and how frail the clay of which we are made!'

29.3.2 *Estar de*

Estar de + adjective or noun to indicate mood, temporary employment or situation:

Está de buen/mal humor	(S)he's in a good/bad mood
Está de camarera en Inglaterra	She's working as a waitress in England
Están de veraneo/de viaje	They're taking their summer vacation/trave(l)ling
Estamos de charla/de bromas	We're having a chat/fooling around

Colloquially:

Estás de un guapo subido/de un antipático...	You're looking really good /You're in a really bad mood

29.3.3 *Estar con*

Estar followed by *con* + noun:

Está con gripe	(S)he's got the flu
Estaba con una cara malísima	(S)he looked terrible
Estaba con un traje de chaqueta muy bonito	She was wearing a beautiful suit

29.3.4 *Estar* + adverb

Estar followed by an adverb or an adjective used as an adverb:

—*¿Cómo estás?* —*Estoy bien/mal*	'How are you?' 'I'm well/not well'
El nombre está mal. Se llamaba Luis José (*Cambio16*, Sp.)	The name is wrong. His name was Luis José
Los trenes están fatal	The trains are in a dreadful state

Adverbs are invariable in form, e.g. *estamos mal* 'we're in trouble'/'we're in a bad way', *están mejor/peor* 'they're feeling /looking better/worse' (*mejor* and *peor* are here the comparative forms of the adverbs *bien* and *mal*).

29.3.5 *Estar que*

Está que muerde	(S)he's in a lousy mood (lit. 'ready to bite')
Hoy estás que no hay quien te aguante	You're unbearable today

29.3.6 *Estar* to indicate location

(For *ser* used for the location of events see 29.2.8.)

Segovia está en España	Segovia is in Spain
No está (en casa)	(S)he's not at home
Está encima de todo	It's on top of everything
Yo soy el que esta ahí (L. Silva, Sp., dialogue)	I'm the one who's on the spot (lit. 'who's there')

But with nouns that are permanent fixtures or features there is a colloquial tendency to use *ser*:

¿Dónde es la casa de tu amigo?	Where's your friend's house?
Aquí era la plaza de las Carretas (J. L. Borges, Arg., dialogue)	This is where Carretas Square used to be
Turku es en Finlandia, ¿no?	Turku is in Finland, isn't it?

Estar would also be correct in these three sentences.

29.3.7 *Estar* meaning 'to suit', or 'to fit'

Este traje te está muy bien	This dress suits you
El abrigo te está corto	The coat is too short for you
El puesto de ministro le está grande	The ministerial job is too big for him

For *estar* with *por* and *para* see 34.14.8.

29.3.8 Idiomatic use of *andar*, *encontrarse* and *hallarse* for *estar*

Andar 'to walk' is sometimes used in colloquial language instead of *estar* when the subject is human. This is only possible when the phrase refers to some kind of activity or to dress or attitude: one could not say **ando calvo* for *estoy calvo* 'I'm bald':

Miguel dice que andan recelosos y no le falta razón (M. Delibes, Sp., dialogue)	Miguel says they're suspicious, and he's right
Andan muy atareados estos días	They've got a lot of work these days
¿Cómo andas? (= *¿cómo estás?*)	How are things?/How are you doing?
tantos niños y jóvenes que andan perdidos por causa de la adicción (*Tiempos del Mundo*, Nicaragua)	so many children and adolescents who are lost because of addiction

¿Dónde andas? is a good question to ask someone answering from a mobile phone.

Andar is also sometimes used colloquially (at least in Spain) to refer to non-living things that can easily be moved about, e.g. *Dios sabe dónde andarán mis gafas* 'God knows where my glasses have got to', *¿dónde anda el coche, tú?* (M. Delibes, Sp., dialogue) 'Hey, whereabouts is the car?'

(i) *Encontrarse* can mean the same as *estar*: *¿dónde se encuentra el museo?* 'where's the museum?', *¿qué tal te encuentras?* 'how are you/how do you feel?', *nuestros servidores se encuentran conectados a 6 proveedores de backbone* (advert., Arg.) 'our servers are linked to six backbone service providers', *no me encuentro con fuerzas para seguir* 'I'm not strong enough to go on'. *Hallarse* is used in formal or literary language: *me hallo enfermo y fatigado* 'I'm feeling ill and tired'.

29.4 *Ser* or *estar*?

29.4.1 *Ser* and *estar* more or less interchangeable

(a) With words indicating marital status:

Sale con una chica que es/está divorciada	(S)he's going out with a girl who's divorced
Tiene que mantener a su madre que es/está viuda	(S)he has to keep his/her widowed mother
Pero si es casado debe estar cenando en casa a estas horas (M. Puig, Arg., dialogue; or *está casado*)	But if he's married (i.e. 'a married man') he must be at home having his supper at this time of day

One would usually ask as stranger *¿es usted casado?* 'are you married?' (or *está*), but two friends meeting again after some time would say *¿estás casado?* or *¿todavía estás soltero?* 'are you married?' or 'are you still single?' because the enquiry is about a change since the last meeting.

(b) With *calvo*, *gordo* and *delgado*, *estar* is always used when there has been a change of state. Elsewhere the two verbs are practically interchangeable except in generalizations, when *ser* is required:

¡Mujer, pero qué delgada estás!	Good heavens, haven't you lost weight!
Siempre ha sido calvo/gordo, pero ahora está más calvo/gordo que nunca	He's always been bald/fat but now he's balder/fatter than ever

> *Dentro de cien años todos seremos calvos*   We'll all be bald in a hundred years
>   (L. Rafael Sánchez, Puerto Rico)
> *La novia de mi primo parece simpática*   My cousin's girlfriend seems nice but
>   *pero está/es muy delgada*   she's very thin
> *Las mujeres de esa tribu son muy gordas*   The women of that tribe are very fat
>   (generalization)

(c) With adjectives describing social manner when 'to be' = 'to behave':

> *Estuvo/Fue muy cortés conmigo*   (S)he was very courteous towards me
> *Siempre está/es cariñosa*   She's always affectionate
> *Tienes que estar/ser más amable con él*   You must be kinder to him

But *hoy has sido bueno* 'you've behaved well today' because *estar bueno* means 'tasty', 'appetising' and therefore also sexually attractive (at least in Spain). Note, however *¡hoy has estado bueno!* 'you had a good day today!' (ironic, i.e. 'I don't think...').

  Estar is not used for general statements about behaviour: *antes los ingleses eran muy corteses* 'formerly the English were very courteous'.

(d) With adjectives applied to events and with *vida* and *situación*:

> *La conferencia fue/estuvo muy interesante* . The lecture was very interesting
> *La situación es/está caótica*   The situation is chaotic
> *La fiesta fue/estuvo muy animada*   The party was very lively
> *La vida es/está cara hoy día*   Life is expensive nowadays

But *la vida es difícil/maravillosa/amarga* 'life is difficult/wonderful/bitter' can only be general comments on life. *La vida está difícil* means 'life is difficult now'.

NB: Note how *ser* can be used to make it clear that a situation is being talked about: *ahora era mucho más serio y ella estaba más seria* (S. Puértolas, Sp.) 'now it (the situation) was more serious and she was more serious'.

(e) With adjectives referring to weather applied to *día* and *tiempo*:

> *El día es/está bueno*   The weather is nice today
> *Es/Está un tiempo soleado, agradable*   The weather is sunny and pleasant
> (but see 29.2.1, note i for *estar* before noun phrases)

29.4.2 *Ser* and *estar* with prices and quantities

Ser is obligatory when the price or quantity is fixed:

> *¿Cuánto (es lo que) le debo?*   How much do I owe you?
> *¿Cuántos somos hoy para comer?*   How many are we for lunch today?
> *Somos doce en mi familia*   There are twelve of us in my family
> *Los sobrevivientes fueron pocos*   Few people survived

But either can be used for fluctuating prices:

> *¿Cuánto/A cuánto/A cómo son/están las uvas?* How much are the grapes?
> *Son/Están a un euro con veinte el kilo*   They're €1.20 a kilo
> *¿A cuánto/A cómo están esas acciones?*   What are those shares at?

29.4.3 *Estar* implying impression or change of condition

When *estar* denotes impression, sensation or appearance, it often calls for translation by a special verb in English, e.g. 'to look', 'to taste', 'to feel' or 'get'. Use of *estar* rather than *ser* often shows there has been a change of condition. Compare:

Es muy guapa/Está muy guapa	She's very good-looking/She's looking very attractive
Este niño es muy alto/Está muy alto	This child is very tall/He's grown very tall
Este sillón es ya viejo/Está ya viejo	This armchair is old/It's getting old
El pollo es riquísimo/Está riquísimo*	[The] chicken is very good/It tastes delicious
El café es horrible/Está horrible*	(The) coffee is horrible/It tastes awful
Tráelo como sea/Tráelo como esté	Bring it any way you can/Bring it as it is
Eres muy española/Estás muy española	You're very Spanish/You're looking very Spanish/acting very Spanish

The examples marked with an asterisk are ambiguous: *el pollo es riquísimo* is either a general statement about chicken or it could mean 'the chicken (uncooked) is very good quality'. *Estar* could only mean 'to taste'.

(i) Note *tú eres/tú estás viejo para estas cosas* 'you're old/getting old for these things' (there is a slight difference of meaning in both languages). But one says *tú eres demasiado joven para estas cosas*.

29.4.4 *Ser* and *estar* involving change of meaning

There are some words whose meaning is radically affected by choice of *ser* or *estar*. The following list is not exhaustive:

ser aburrido	boring	*estar aburrido*	to be bored
ser atento	courteous	*estar atento*	attentive
ser bueno		*estar bueno*	(see 29.4.1 c)
ser cansado	tiresome	*estar cansado*	tired
ser católico	catholic	*no estar católico*	unwell
ser decidido	resolute	*estar decidido*	decided
ser consciente		*estar consciente*	(see 29.2.3)
ser despierto	sharp/alert	*estar despierto*	awake
ser un enfermo	be an invalid	*estar enfermo*	be ill
ser interesado	self-seeking	*estar interesado*	interested
ser listo	clever	*estar listo*	to be ready
ser (un) loco	scatterbrained	*estar loco*	mad
ser malo	bad	*estar malo*	ill
ser negro	black	*estar negro*	very irritated
ser orgulloso	proud (pejorative)	*estar orgulloso*	proud (of something/someone)
ser rico		*estar rico*	(see 29.2.3 note i)
ser torpe	slow-witted	*estar torpe*	clumsy, moving with difficulty
ser verde	green/smutty	*estar verde*	unripe
ser violento	violent/embarrassing	*estar violento*	embarrassed
ser vivo	sharp/alert	*estar vivo*	alive
(*ser un vivo*	to be sly)		

30

Existential sentences

The main points discussed in this chapter are:

- The forms and uses of *haber/hay* (Section 30.2.1)
- *Lo hay, la hay,* etc. (Section 30.2.2)
- *Hay* and *estar* compared (Section 30.3)

30.1 General

'Existential sentences' refer to the existence of things: 'there's bread', 'there are several possibilities', 'God exists'/'there is a God'. In Spanish such sentences usually involve the special verb *haber* (present indicative *hay*), which means 'there is/are'. However, the picture is complicated by the existence of another verb, *estar*, which often means 'to be located'/'to be present'. For the much more specific spatial words *allí/allá* 'there' (Fr. *là*) see 31.6.1.

30.2 *Haber (hay)*

For the conjugation of *haber* see 13.3.22.

30.2.1 Basic uses

Haber has two uses: (**a**) as an auxiliary used to form perfect tenses, e.g. *han dicho* 'they've said' (discussed at 14.8); (**b**) as a verb meaning 'there is'/'there are', cf. French *il y a*, German *es gibt*.

In the latter sense the verb occurs only in the third-person singular (see notes i & ii for popular or colloquial exceptions). It is conjugated exactly like the third-person singular of the auxiliary *haber*, except that its present indicative is *hay*, not *ha*. In this chapter, *haber* in the sense of 'there is/are' is referred to as *hay* to avoid confusion with the auxiliary verb.

Hay can occur in any non-continuous tense form. However, it does not mean '...is/are/were *there*' = *está/están/estaban* (*ahí/allí*): the relationship between *hay* and *estar* is discussed further at 30.3. Examples of *hay*:

Había muchas chicas de mi edad y más jóvenes (J. Marías, Sp.)	There were many girls of my age and younger
Hay casos peores, hay quienes no pueden volver del exilio (A. Mastretta, Mex.)	There are worse cases, there are people who can't return from exile
—¿Qué hay?) (¿Qué hubo?/¿Quiubo? in (Colombia and surrounding areas)	'What's happening/How're things?'

Hubo muchas noches que salíamos a recorrer su barrio (G. Cabrera Infante, Cu. dialogue)	There were many nights when we went out for a walk round her part of town
había una vez…/érase una vez… (*érase* is here a grammatically unusual set formula)	once upon a time there was…

(i) *Hay* has no plural in standard Peninsular speech and in written Spanish everywhere: **había** *tres chicas* 'there were three girls', not ?*habían tres chicas*; **hubo** *clases de italiano el año pasado* 'there were Italian classes last year', not ?*hubieron clases de italiano*. The plural construction is considered incorrect by most Spaniards, but it is very common in the Castilian spoken in Catalonia, even by educated speakers. In the Americas the plural is very common in spontaneous, even educated, speech, but it is not found in formal written language, cf. *dijeron que había muchos liberianos entre los combatientes* (*El Norte*, Ve.) 'they said there were many Liberians among the fighters'.

(ii) It is used only in the third person: *hay cinco* 'there are five', but *somos cinco* 'there are five of us', *ustedes son cinco* 'there are five of you', also *son cinco* 'there are five of them'.

A first-person plural construction, e.g. ?*habemos cinco* = *somos cinco* 'there are five of us' (n.b. not the usual form *hemos*) occurs in rustic speech in Spain and is more common in popular Latin-American speech, cf. ?*pues bien, habemos algunos que no queremos estar con ellos ni con el terrorismo* (reader's letter, *Contracultural*, Arg. for *hay algunos que no queremos…*) 'well, there are some of us who don't want to back them or terrorism'. This is rejected by educated speakers.

(iii) *Hay* is not followed by the definite article, except when it means 'to exist', in which case *existir* is more commonly used: *ha venido el médico* (not *hay el médico) 'there's the doctor! (i.e. he's arrived)', but *también hay/existe la posibilidad de. . .'* the possibility also exists of…' ?*Hay el cartero* for *ha venido el cartero* 'the postman's there'/'the postman's come' are typical Catalanisms.

(iv) For *hay que* 'it is necessary to' see Chapter 21.4.2.

30.2.2 Direct object pronouns and *hay*

Hay functions like a transitive verb, and since transitive verbs in Spanish must usually have a direct object, an object pronoun is normally used before *hay* to indicate the presence of a deleted noun:

No hubo presiones, ni las hay, ni las habrá (interview in *El País*, Sp.)	There wasn't any pressure, there isn't any and there won't be
El cochero quiso asegurarse de que no había ningún error. No lo había (G. García Márquez, Col.)	The coach driver sought reassurance that there was no mistake. There wasn't
Incluso los hay que tienen la desfachatez de retratarse en sus propios anuncios (E. Lynch, Arg.)	There are even some people who have the cheek to put pictures of themselves in their own advertisements

(i) The pronoun is not used when answering questions about the existence of non-countable things (bread, water, justice, etc.): *—¿Hay azúcar? —Sí, hay* '"Is there any sugar?" "Yes, there is"', *—¿Hay mucho que hacer? —Sí hay, sí.* '"Is there a lot to do?"

"Yes, there is."' Compare this reference to countable items: —*¿Hay problemas?* —*Los hay y muchos* '"Are there any problems?" "There are. Plenty"'. See 7.4 for resumptive pronoun with *ser, estar, parecer*.

(ii) The use of the echoing pronoun to some extent compensates for the absence in Spanish of a pronoun like the French *en*, Italian *ne* found in phrases like *il n'y en a pas, non ce n'è* 'there isn't *any*'.

30.3 *Hay* and *estar* in existential sentences

Estar has many other uses, discussed in detail in Chapter 29.

As far as its relationship with *hay* is concerned, *está* basically means '. . .is somewhere' and *hay* means 'there is/are. . .' (exists). In certain cases the meanings overlap, as in —*¿El Sr. Ramírez?. —No está. –¿Y su mujer? —No está nadie/No hay nadie* '"Mr Ramírez?" "He's not in." "And his wife?" "There's no one in."' On entering an empty building, one shouts *¿hay alguien?* 'is there any one around?'/ 'is anyone there?'

30.3.1 Uses of *estar* and *hay* with defined nouns

Nouns accompanied by the definite article, by a possessive adjective or by a demonstrative (*ese, este, aquel*) normally require *estar*. *Hay* used with such noun phrases is restricted in its meaning to 'exists', as explained at 30.2.1 note (iii). *Estar* takes for granted that the subject exists and tells us about its location or availability:

Hay un gerente en la compañía	There's a manager in the company (i.e. 'a manager exists')
Está el gerente	The manager's there/here/in
No hay dinero	There's no money (anywhere)
No está el dinero/El dinero no está	The money isn't here/there
¿Hay tortilla española?	Do you have Spanish omelette/(US omelet)?
¿Está la tortilla española?	Is the Spanish omelette/omelet on the list?/Is the Spanish omelette ready?
Por un lado hay las grandes fiestas, y por el otro, las distracciones institucionales (*Cambio16*, Sp.; = *existen*))	On the one hand there are the major fiestas, and on the other hand institutionalized amusements
No se pueden subir ni perros ni cosas. . . para eso está el montacargas (E. Arenas, Sp., dialogue)	You can't take up dogs and things. The service lift is there for that
Las mujeres no estaban para hablar de temas que no fueran domésticos (A. Mastretta, Mex.)	The women weren't there to discuss non-domestic subjects

In this last example, *no había mujeres para hablar. . .*would have meant 'there were no women there to talk about. . .'.

(i) In relative clauses, *hay* and *estar* seem to be interchangeable: *tropecé con la silla que estaba/había en el dormitorio* 'I tripped over the chair that was in the bedroom', *. . .del espejo que había sobre la chimenea* (C. Martín Gaite, Sp.; or *está*) '. . .from the mirror hanging over the fireplace', *el sitio estratégico es la mesa que hay al lado de la cristalera que da a la calle* (E. Arenas, Sp., dialogue; or *está*) 'the strategic place is the table next to the window looking out onto the street'.

(ii) In this exchange, —*¿Qué hay en este pueblo?* —*Hay/Está* **la** *iglesia. . .* '"What is there in this village?" "There's the church. . ."', *hay* is possible with the definite article because it answers the question 'what things exist?' However, Latin Americans may insist on *está* in this sentence.

30.3.2 *Estar* for mobile things

As we have said, *estar* implies that a thing is present in a certain place, *hay* merely that it exists. For this reason, words like 'problem', 'question', 'atmosphere', 'accident' can only appear with *hay* since they do not refer to locatable or moveable things:

Ha habido un accidente	There's been an accident
Ha habido aquí tres presidentes	There have been three presidents here/ We've had three presidents (in this country)
Han estado aquí tres presidentes	Three presidents have been here/have visited here

30.3.3 *Hay* used before partitive nouns and numbers

Before partitive nouns (quantities, parts of a whole), only *hay* can be used:

Hay leche	There's (some) milk
Había gente	There were (some) people

Since *hay* can be used only in the third person (see 30.2.1, note ii), *ser* or *estar* must be used for other persons. This construction occurs with numbers:

Había cuarenta personas en la fiesta	There were forty people at the party
Éramos cuarenta en la fiesta	There were forty of us at the party
Vais (Lat. Am. *van*) *a ser cuarenta en la fiesta*	There will be forty of you at the party
Estábamos más de quince personas encerradas en el ascensor	There were more than fifteen of us shut in the lift

30.4 Miscellaneous English sentences whose translation requires *hay* or *estar*

If there hadn't been a doctor (available), he'd have died	*Si no hubiera habido (un) médico, habría muerto/De no haber habido (un) médico, habría muerto*
If the doctor hadn't been **there**, he'd have died	*Si no hubiera **estado** el médico, habría muerto*
There's no such thing as fairies	*Las hadas no existen/No hay hadas/No existen las hadas*
There have always been economic crises	*Siempre ha habido crisis económicas*
Horchata available/*Horchata* sold here	*Hay horchata* (a cold drink made from crushed tiger nuts or *chufas*)
There's a book on the table	*Hay un libro encima de la mesa*
The book isn't there any more	*El libro ya no está ahí*

31

Adverbs

The main points discussed in this chapter are:

- Adverbs ending in *–mente* (Section 31.2)
- Adverbs of manner not ending in *–mente* (Section 31.3)
- Adverbial use of adjectives and nouns (Section 31.3.3–7)
- Intensifiers and moderators (*muy, algo, increíblemente*, etc. (Section 31.4)
- *Aquí, ahí, allí, allá* (Section 31.6.1–4)
- *Dentro/adentro, fuera/afuera* (Section 31.6.5)
- *Abajo, debajo de, arriba, encima, detrás, delante, adelante* (Section 31.6.6–8)
- Adverbs of time (*ya, recién, todavía, aún, luego, entonces*, etc.) (Section 31.7)
- Words meaning 'even' (*incluso, aun, hasta*, etc.) (Section 31.8)

31.1 General

Spanish adverbs and adverb phrases can be divided into two large classes: (1) adverbs formed from adjectives by adding the suffix -*mente* to an adjective and (2) invariable words and phrases. Examples of the former type are *tranquilamente* 'tranquilly', *violentamente* 'violently', *naturalmente* 'naturally'. Examples of the latter are *mal* 'badly', *ayer* 'yesterday', *adrede* (familiar *aposta*) 'on purpose', *en serio* 'seriously' (i.e. not jokingly), *aquí* 'here', etc.

A few adjectives can also function as adverbs: *hablaban fuerte* 'they were talking loudly'; see 31.3.3. More common in Spanish than in English is the use of an adjective where English uses an adverb: *el rey los recibió agradecido* 'the King received them gratefully', *vivían felices* 'they lived happily'. See 31.3.4.

31.2 Adverbs in *-mente*

Adverbs formed by adding -*mente* to an adjective are very numerous but there are apparently arbitrary constraints on its use:

Lo del médico había sido sencillamente horrible (A. Grandes, Sp.)	The business with the doctor had been simply dreadful
Pero en el futuro no estamos solamente vos y yo (M. Benedetti, Ur., dialogue; Sp. *tú y yo*)	But it won't be just you and me in the future
...muy inteligente, buen abogado, pero sumamente peligroso (G. García Márquez, Col., dialogue)	...very intelligent, a good lawyer, but extremely dangerous

31.2.1 Formation

If the adjective has a separate feminine form, *-mente* is added to it. Otherwise it is added to the invariable singular form:

Masc. singular	Fem. singular	Adverbial form	
absoluto	*absoluta*	*absolutamente*	absolutely
cansado	*cansada*	*cansadamente*	in a tired way
evidente	*(evidente)*	*evidentemente*	evidently
leal	*(leal)*	*lealmente*	loyally
tenaz	*(tenaz)*	*tenazmente*	tenaciously

31.2.2 Accent rules for adverbs in *-mente*

Adjectives that have an accent on one of their vowels make adverbs in *-mente* that have two stress accents, one on the vowel that carries the written accent (which is retained), another on the penultimate syllable (audible, but not shown in writing): *crítico/críticamente* 'critical'/'critically', *electrónico/electrónicamente* 'electronic'/'electronically', *hábil/hábilmente* 'skilful'/'skilfully'. Pronunciation of such words with penultimate stress only should be avoided.

31.2.3 Consecutive adverbs in *-mente*

If more than one adverb in *-mente* is joined by a conjunction (e.g. *y, ni, o, pero*, etc.), *-mente* is dropped from all but the last:

ni intelectual, ni política, ni económicamente se puede mantener tal postura (El País, Sp.)	and neither intellectually, nor politically, nor economically can such a position be sustained
Ellos mataron a muchos indios, directa o indirectamente (L. Sepúlveda, Ch., dialogue)	They killed a lot of Indians, directly or indirectly
Significa mucho personalmente, pero también cultural e intelectualmente (Granma, Cu.)	It means a lot personally, but also culturally and intellectually

The rule is also applied in comparative phrases like *más ampulosa que profundamente* 'more pompously than profoundly', *lo explicó tan clara como sinceramente* '(s)he explained it as clearly as (s)he did sincerely'.

(i) This is an important rule of written Spanish, although often ignored in spontaneous speech. It is not applied when there is no joining conjunction: *y así, separados por el muro de vidrio, habíamos vivido ansiosamente, melancólicamente* (E. Sábato, Arg.) 'and thus, separated by the wall of glass, we had lived anxiously, melancholically'.

31.2.4 Limits on the use of the suffix *-mente*

-mente cannot be added to all adjectives, although there is no accounting for experiments like Julio Cortázar's invention *pelirrojamente* 'red-hairedly' in his novel *Rayuela*.

  With a few exceptions (cf. *difícil/ difícilmente* 'difficult'/'with difficulty', *lleno* 'full', but 'fully' = *plenamente*; *inclusive* 'including' – see 31.8), the set of Spanish adjectives that take *-mente* corresponds to the set of English adjectives that end in *-ly*. These are chiefly adverbs of manner or behaviour, so the following do not take *-mente* (at least in normal styles):

(a) Adjectives denoting physical appearance: *rojo* 'red', *negro* 'black', *calvo* 'bald', *gordo* 'fat', *cojo* 'lame', *viejo* 'old'/'aged', etc.

(b) Adjectives denoting origin, nationality, religion: *cordobés* 'Cordoban', *argentino* 'Argentine', *protestante* 'Protestant', *musulmán* 'Muslim', etc. Two exceptions are *católicamente* and *cristianamente*: *tienes que educar a tus hijos católicamente* 'you must bring up your children in the Catholic way'.

(c) Ordinal numbers, e.g. *segundo* 'second', *quinto* 'fifth', *vigésimo* 'twentieth'. Exceptions: *primeramente* 'chiefly'/'firstly' and *últimamente* 'lately'/'lastly'. *En segundo lugar* = 'secondly'.

(d) Some adjectives, for no obvious reason, e.g. *vacío* 'empty', *lleno* 'full' (*plenamente* = 'fully'), *importante* 'important', and most adjectives in *-ón*, cf. *mandón* 'bossy', *peleón* 'aggressive'/'prone to start fights'.

(e) Many verbal participles which cannot, because of their meaning, function as adverbs, e.g. *roto* 'broken', which has no corresponding adverb **rotamente* 'brokenly'.

However, some Spanish participles take *-mente*: the following are some of the many examples. They all refer to behaviour or manner:

abatido: abatidamente downcast	*equivocado: equivocadamente* mistaken(ly)
abierto: abiertamente open(ly)	*exagerado: exageradamente* exaggerated(ly)
acentuado: acentuadamente marked(ly)	*irritado: irritadamente* irritated(ly)
atrevido: atrevidamente daring(ly)	*perdido:* ('lost') *perdidamente* hopeless(ly)
debido: debidamente due/duly	(e.g. in love)
decidido: decididamente decided(ly)	*reiterado: reiteradamente* repeated(ly)
deliberado: deliberadamente deliberate(ly)	*resuelto: resueltamente* resolute(ly)

31.2.5 Popular forms

Popular forms like *buenamente* and *malamente* are occasionally heard in familiar speech with specialized meanings:

Lo terminamos, pero malamente	We finished it, but it was rushed
Hazlo buenamente cuando puedas	Do it in your own time when you can

The forms ?*mayormente* 'especially' (more acceptable in Latin America), *otramente* 'otherwise' (= *de otra manera*) and ?*mismamente*, cf. ?*mismamente el cura* 'the priest himself', are considered substandard or popular.

31.2.6 Equivalents of adverbs in *-mente*

The existence of an adverb in *-mente* does not mean that the adjective from which it is derived cannot also function as an adverb, or that there does not exist an adverbial phrase with the same or a similar meaning. Constant reading and dictionary work are the only solution to this problem, e.g.:

en vano/vanamente	in vain
de inmediato/inmediatamente	immediately
directo/directamente	directly
Siempre obra locamente/a lo loco	(S)he always acts wildly/in a mad way

NB: One says *locamente/perdidamente enamorado* 'madly in love', not *a lo loco*....

31.2.7 Too many adverbs in -*mente*

It is bad style to include too many adverbs ending in -*mente* in a single paragraph: the final syllables set off ugly rhymes. The horrible sentence *evidentemente, todas las lenguas evolucionan constantemente, y sería totalmente absurdo pretender detener arbitrariamente su crecimiento* makes passable English in literal translation—'clearly, all languages evolve constantly, and it would be totally absurd to attempt to arrest their growth arbitrarily'—but must be recast in Spanish along the lines of *es evidente que todas las lenguas están en constante evolución, y sería totalmente absurdo pretender detener de manera arbitraria su crecimiento.*

Nor can an adverb ending in –*mente* be used to modify another: **increíblemente rápidamente* for 'incredibly quickly' is not Spanish. See 31.4.3.

A form in -*mente* can usually be replaced by *con* + an abstract noun or by some other adverbial phrase, e.g. *alegremente = con alegría* or *de un modo* (or *manera*) *alegre,* 'incredibly quickly' = *con una rapidez increíble, ferozmente = con ferocidad* or *de un modo feroz.* The sentence *vivían de un modo tranquilo, feliz y libre* 'they lived quietly, happy and free' is much better Spanish than *vivían tranquila, feliz y libremente.* For a selection of adverbial phrases, see 31.3.2.

31.2.8 -*ísimamente*

The suffix -*ísimo* (see 4.9.1) may be added (judiciously) to adverbs of manner, and time. The result is very emphatic:

claramente	*clarísimamente*	extremely clearly
intensamente	*intensísimamente*	extremely intensely
recientemente	*recientísimamente*	extremely recently
urgentemente	*urgentísimamente*	extremely urgently

More common alternatives exist, e.g. *con gran claridad, con enorme intensidad, con gran urgencia,* etc. *Lejos* and *cerca* can also have -*ísimo* added to them: *lejísimos* (note the final *s*) and *cerquísima.* (Colloquially *lejotes* can be used to denote uncomfortable distance, often preceded by *allá/allí: esa casa está allí lejotes* 'that house is miles off/away'.)

31.2.9 Adverbs in -*mente* to mean 'from a...point of view'

Adverbs in -*mente* are freely used to indicate point of view, a common construction in journalistic styles:

Económicamente, este país va a la ruina	Economically, this country is heading for ruin
Personalmente, lo dudo	Personally, I doubt it
Editorialmente, lo apruebo	From a publishing point of view, I approve

31.3 Adverbs of manner not ending in -*mente*

31.3.1 General

These include words like *bien* 'well', *mal* 'badly', *despacio* 'slowly', *pronto* 'quickly', *adrede/aposta* 'on purpose', *igual* 'the same'. There are regional differences of usage, e.g. *deprisa* 'quickly' in Spain and *aprisa* in Latin America: the latter is considered popular by some speakers in Spain, but *quiero ir muy aprisa* (A. Mastretta, Mex., dialogue; Sp. *deprisa*) 'I want to go very fast'. *De prisa* is possible for *deprisa*, but see note (ii).

There are countless adverbial phrases: *a propósito* 'deliberately', *en balde* 'in vain', *a contrapelo* 'unwillingly', *en serio* 'seriously'. A selection appears at 31.3.2.

These adverbs of manner (and also those ending in *–mente*) can modify verbs, participles, adjectives or other adverbs:

Hable despacio	Speak slowly
Lo quieren así	They want it that way
Esto está mal hecho	This is badly made/This is the wrong thing to do
Está bien	It/He/She's OK/You're OK
Me da igual	It's all the same to me
Aquí estamos mejor/peor	We're better/worse (off) here
Infórmese gratis (advert., Sp.)	Get information free

A few can even modify nouns:

¿No te das cuenta que una mujer así no puedeser aristócrata? (S. Vodanovic, Ch., dialogue; Sp. usually *cuenta de que*)	Don't you realize that a woman like that can't be an aristocrat?
una niña bien (pejorative)	a 'nice' girl/a girl from a 'respectable' family
Dos coñacs con hielo, y dos cafés igual	Two cognacs with ice, and two coffees the same way

(i) *Bien* and *así de* can intensify adjectives when they are used as intensifiers. See 31.4.9.

(ii) *Deprisa* can be spelled *de prisa*; Santillana (1995), 129, prefers the former spelling.

31.3.2 Adverbial phrases of manner

These are numerous, and they often provide an elegant alternative to an unwieldy adverb in *-mente*. The following is a small sample:

a buen paso at a smart pace	*(llorar) a lágrima viva* to shed floods of tears
a caballo on horseback	
a ciegas in the dark	*a mano* by hand
a conciencia conscientiously	*a máquina* machine-made/by machine
El agua sale a chorros The water is pouring out	*a matacaballo* at breakneck speed
	a medias by halves
a destiempo inopportunely	*a oscuras* in the dark
entrar a empujones to push one's way in	*a quemarropa* point-blank
a escondidas secretly/clandestinely	*a regañadientes* reluctantly/unwillingly
a fuego lento on a low flame	*a sabiendas de que* …fully aware that …
a hurtadillas by stealth	*a tiempo* in time (e.g. for the train)
al alimón together by turns/jointly	*a tientas* by touch/by feel
a la carrera at full speed	*a traición* treacherously
a la fuerza by force/under obligation	*al raso* in the open/out of doors
a la ligera hastily/without proper thought	*al sereno* in the open/'under the stars'
	bajo cuerda on the sly/in an underhand way
a las claras clearly (i.e. without beating about the bush)	*con delirio/locura* madly/passionately

con frecuencia/a menudo frequently	*(leer algo) de un tirón* to read something
de balde free (= without paying, i.e.	in one sitting/straight through
gratis)	*de verdad* really/genuinely
de continuo continuously	*en balde* in vain/pointlessly
de corrido at one go/straight off	*en cambio* on the other hand
de costumbre usually	*en confianza* confidentially
de golpe suddenly	*en cueros (vivos)* stark naked
de improviso unexpectedly	*en el acto* on the spot
(saberse/aprenderse) de memoria (learn) by	*en lo sucesivo* from now on/hereafter
heart	*(hablar) por los codos* to talk too much
de ordinario normally/usually	(lit. 'through the elbows')
de puntillas on tiptoe	*sin empacho* coolly/unconcernedly
de rodillas kneeling	*sin reserva* unreservedly
de seguro for certain/sure	*sin ton ni son* willy-nilly/thoughtlessly
de sobra in excess/more than enough	

31.3.3 Adverbs derived from adjectives and participles

A few adverbs are identical in form to masculine singular adjectives (like all adverbs, their form is invariable). They are used only with certain verbs, e.g. *hablar/pronunciar claro* 'to speak/pronounce clearly' but only *expresarse claramente/con claridad* 'to express oneself clearly':

Hablan alto/bajo	They talk loudly/softly
Lo hemos comprado barato/caro	We've bought it cheap/dear
El tren va directo a Tuy	The train goes direct to Tuy
Hay que tirar fuerte	You have to pull hard
Se me apiló firme (J. Cortázar, Arg.,	He pushed himself tight up against me
dialogue; Sp. *se me arrimó*)	
Anda rápido que vamos a llegar tarde	Walk fast or we'll arrive late
(see 31.3.6 for *rápido*)	
Respiraba hondo	(S)he was breathing deeply
Me sienta fatal	It doesn't suit me/agree with me at all
Él no juega limpio	He doesn't play fair
Me casé enamorada (J. Madrid, Sp.,	I was in love when I married
dialogue)	

The following are typical of familiar speech and are not to everyone's taste:

Lo hemos pasado estupendo/fantástico/	We had a tremendous/fantastic time
bárbaro	
La chaqueta le sienta bárbaro a Mariluz	The jacket looks terrific on Mariluz
Eso se hace fácil	That's dead easy/That's a cinch
tomar somníferos seguido (familiar, esp.	to take sleeping pills continuously
Lat. Am. = *continuamente*)	

Colloquial Latin American provides numerous examples unacceptable in Spain but admitted in informal styles in the Americas: ...*un gran número de mexicanos que piensan distinto que el PRI* (*Excelsior*, Mex.) '...a large number of Mexicans who think differently from the PRI', *inicialmente pensé que podíamos haber conseguido unos dólares fácil, sin problemas para la revolución* (*Vindicación de Cuba*, Cu.) 'initially I thought we could easily have got a few dollars, without any problems for the Revolution', *¡qué bonito baila!* (A. Mastretta, Mex.; Sp. *¡qué bien baila!*) 'how beautifully she dances!'

31.3.4 Adjectives used to modify both subject and verb

Spanish often uses adjectives in combination with verbs to produce an effect more easily expressed by an adverb in English: the adjective agrees with the number and gender of the subject. This construction is restricted in the spoken language to a limited range of verbs and adjectives. It makes the adjective act both as an adverb and an adjective, i.e. it modifies both the verb and the subject of the verb. Sometimes the construction is obligatory: *las niñas cansadas dormían* 'the tired girls were sleeping' is not the same as *las niñas dormían cansadas* which is most nearly translated as 'the girls were tired and asleep' or 'sleeping in their tiredness'. But one could hardly say ?*las niñas dormían cansadamente* ?'the girls were sleeping wearily', which modifies 'sleep' but not 'girls'!

This construction is obviously limited to adjectives that can equally well apply to a noun and an action, e.g. *inocente* 'innocent', *confuso* 'confused', *feliz* 'happy'; but not adjectives like *harapiento* 'ragged' or *azul* 'blue', which can hardly describe an action:

Sonrió tranquila (J. Marsé, Sp.)	She smiled gently
Javier miraba atónito desde el vagón vacío (M. Benedetti, Ur.)	Javier gazed in surprise from the empty carriage
Me extendió un papel que leí asombrado (A. Bryce Echenique, Pe.; same as *...leí con asombro*)	He handed me a paper that I read in amazement
Viven felices (normal style)	They live happily

31.3.5 Nouns used adverbially

For familiar constructions like *llover cantidad, divertirse horrores* see 31.4.7.

31.3.6 *Rápido*

Rápido is an adjective, and it is correctly used in phrases like *tren rápido* 'fast train', *comidas rápidas* 'fast food'. As an adverb it is, like 'quick', familiar; *con prisa, deprisa* (see 31.3.1. *Aprisa* is considered popular in Spain), *rápidamente* or *pronto* are correct adverbial forms: *¡rápido (deprisa/pronto), que se va el tren!* 'quick, the train's going!', *¡fuera! ¡Rápido!* 'get out! Quick!' *Rápido* sounds too colloquial to Peninsular ears in this sentence from *El Tiempo*, Colombia: *que juzguen rápido a los narcotraficantes* 'let them bring the drug-peddlers to justice quickly'. Spaniards would probably write *rápidamente*.

31.3.7 *A la* and *a lo*

Both may form adverbial phrases of manner, but *a la* followed by a feminine adjective is much more common than *a lo*, which is probably nowadays confined to set phrases, usually of a derogatory nature:

tortilla a la francesa	plain omelette
lenguado a la normanda	sole à la normande
despedirse a la francesa	to leave without saying goodbye

Viven todavía a la antigua	They still live in the old style
Ando un poco a la defensiva (C. Martín Gaite, Sp., dialogue)	I'm feeling a bit on the defensive
a lo tonto/a lo bruto/a lo salvaje, etc.	crazily/by force/savagely, etc.

En plan. . . is familiar, like '-style': *viajar en plan hippy* 'to travel rough/hippy-style', *hablar en plan Tarzan* 'to talk Tarzan-style'.

31.3.8 Note on position of adverbs of manner (see also 37.2.6 and 37.4)

An adverb of manner usually follows an intransitive verb:

Trabaja intensivamente en una segunda novela	(S)he is working very hard on a second novel
Este problema está íntimamente ligado al problema del paro	This problem is intimately linked to the problem of unemployment
Esa cara de asco que parece ser habitualmente la suya	That look of disgust which seems habitually to be his/hers

But, less commonly, an adverb may precede the verb to add emphasis:

Tu vida inevitablemente se dispone a recorrer el tramo final de la parábola (J. Marías, Sp.)	Your life is inevitably getting itself ready for the last lap (lit. 'to run the last section of the parabola')

In a transitive sentence, an adverb may follow the object—*habla griego correctamente*—or the verb—*habla correctamente **el** griego* '(s)he speaks Greek perfectly/ without making mistakes'; there is no noticeable change of meaning here. But strictly speaking an adverb that follows the object modifies the whole verb phrase, whereas an adverb that precedes the object modifies only the verb. Thus *robaba dinero con frecuencia* '(s)he frequently stole money', but *robaba con frecuencia dinero. . .* '(s)he frequently stole money. . .' is the appropriate order if more items, e.g. watches, jewels, follow.

31.4 Intensifiers and moderators

31.4.1 General

Intensifiers and moderators strengthen or weaken the force of a verb, adverb, adjective and, occasionally, noun. Typical intensifiers are *muy* 'very', *mucho/poco* 'much'/'little', *intensamente* 'intensely', *extremadamente* extremely', *algo/más bien* 'rather', *increíblemente* 'incredibly', *sobremanera* (literary) 'exceedingly'. Many intensifiers have other functions, and are dealt with elsewhere, e.g. *algo* and *más bien* at 9.2, *demasiado* at 9.9, *mucho* and *poco* at 9.12.

New colloquial intensifiers appear and vanish as fashion dictates. *Requete-* used to be a popular suffix and has created permanent expressions in Spain like *requeteguapo/a* 'really good-looking' and *requetebién* 'really well done'. *Archi-* can still be found in *archiconocido/archisabido* 'very well known'. Nowadays, at least in Spain, any adjective can be reinforced in colloquial styles by *super-*: *supertonto/superinteligente* 'really stupid silly'/'really intelligent'.

31.4.2 *Muy*

Muy 'very' is originally an abbreviated form of *mucho*, and the full form should be used in isolation:

Es muy inteligente	(S)he's very intelligent
—¿Es inteligente? —Sí, mucho	'Is (s)he intelligent?' 'Yes, very'

NB: *Muy* cannot be used with *más* 'more', *menos* 'less', *mejor* 'better' or *peor* 'worse'. One uses *mucho más/menos/mejor/peor*. For more about *mucho más/menos* see 9.12b note i. *Muy mucho* is humorous.

31.4.3 Intensifiers in *-mente*

There are numerous intensifiers ending in *–mente*, e.g. *sumamente* 'exceedingly', *increíblemente* 'incredibly', *tremendamente* 'tremendously', *fenomenalmente* 'phenomenally', etc. These cannot modify another adverb in *-mente*, i.e. '(s)he speaks English incredibly fluently' cannot be translated **habla inglés increíblemente corrientemente* but must be recast, e.g. *habla inglés increíblemente bien/con una soltura/facilidad increíble*:

Ha actuado con admirable honradez	(S)he's acted admirably honestly
Lo hicieron con una prisa absurda	They did it absurdly quickly/with absurd haste
Le voy a hablar con una franqueza total	I'm going to talk to you totally frankly

31.4.4 *Más* and *menos*

(For the use of *más* and *menos* in comparisons, see Chapter 5.) *Más* is used as an intensifier in familiar speech, without any comparative meaning:

Es que eres más tonto...	Heavens, are you stupid!
Está más borracho ...	Is he drunk!

31.4.5 *Lo* as an intensifier

For *lo* in sentences like *cuéntale lo bien que canta* 'tell her/him how well he/she sings', *camina lo más lentamente/despacio que puedas* 'walk as slowly as possible' see 7.2.1.

31.4.6 *Qué* and *cuán* as intensifiers

Exclamatory *qué* is discussed at 24.4, *cuán(to)* at 24.6.

31.4.7 Nouns used as intensifiers

Familiar speech uses some nouns as intensifiers—not to every taste, as the translations show:

Lo pasamos bomba (now old-fashioned?)	We had a terrific time
Canta fenómeno	(S)he's a smashing singer
Para los setenta y cinco años que traía a cuestas...¡estaba fenómeno! (S. Galindo, Mex., dialogue)	For her seventy-five years (lit. 'for the seventy-five years she was carrying on her back'), she looked great!
Nos aburrimos cantidad/Nos reímos cantidad	We were bored stiff/Did we laugh!

31.4.8 *Sí* and *si* as intensifiers

Sí, which means 'yes', and *si*, which usually means 'if', can both also be used as intensifiers.

Sí (with an accent) is used to assert a fact that the speaker thinks has been contradicted or doubted, or for purposes of contrast: —*María no vendrá.* —*Sí que vendrá. Me lo prometió* '"María won't come." "She *will* come. She promised me"', *una respuesta que esta vez sí me irritó* 'a reply that *did* annoy me this time', *entonces me entró cierta impaciencia por conocer un país que sí pudo llevar a cabo su cambio* (M. Benedetti, Ur., dialogue) 'then I felt a certain impatience to get to know a country that actually did complete its process of change'.

Si (no accent) is often used as an intensifier in spoken language, usually preceded by *pero*. It emphasizes the following statement, often with an indignant or insistent tone, *¡(pero) si te oí la primera vez!* 'but I heard you *first* time!!', *pero si vivimos muy bien. No necesitamos nada* (Soledad Puértolas, Sp., dialogue) 'but we really *do* live well. We don't need anything', *pero si mañana me voy al Perú y no vuelvo más* (A. Bryce Echenique, Pe., dialogue; Sp. *a Perú*) 'but tomorrow I'm going to Peru and I'm not coming back'.

For *apenas si* 'scarcely' see 23.5.7.

31.4.9 *Bien* and *así de* as intensifiers

Both of these words are occasionally used colloquially before adjectives:

Es bien lista	She's pretty clever
Bien bueno que está, ¿eh?	Great, isn't it (sarcastic)?
¿Adónde vas así de guapa? or *. . .vas tan guapa?*	Where are you off to looking so pretty?

Bien = 'very' is more common in Latin America than in Spain: *es bien simpática* (Chilean informant) 'she's very pleasant', *¡si está bien viejo para ti!* (popular Mexican, from Arjona Iglesias, 1991, 78) 'he's really/pretty old for you!'

31.5 Adverbs of doubt

Words meaning 'perhaps', 'probably', 'possibly' may call for the subjunctive and are discussed under 16.3.

31.6 Adverbs of place

31.6.1 *Aquí, ahí, allí*

It is important to distinguish carefully between *ahí* and *allí*: they tend to sound similar in some varieties of Spanish. These adverbs are closely linked in meaning to the demonstratives:

este this near me/us	*aquí* here near me/us
ese that	*ahí* (just) there
aquel that further away	*allí* there further away

In other words, *aquí* indicates somewhere near the speaker, *ahí* points to space near the hearer, and *allí* to something distant from both. One can therefore say on the telephone to someone far away *¿qué tal tiempo hace ahí?* 'what's the weather like there?' However, misuse of *ahí* to refer to something distant from the hearer produces a bizarre effect: to ask people from another country *¿qué tal se vive ahí?* 'what's it like living just there?' instead of *allí* prompts them to look under their chairs.

Pero otras veces me siento aquí también un exiliado (M. Benedetti, Ur., dialogue)	But sometimes I feel like an exile here too
Aquí construiremos la casa, ahí el garaje, y allí al final del jardín, la piscina	We'll build the house here, the garage there, and the swimming pool there at the bottom of the garden
Deja la linterna ahí a tu lado	Leave the torch/US flashlight there next to you
Sería interesante visitar Groenlandia, pero no quisiera vivir allí	It would be interesting to visit Greenland, but I wouldn't like to live there

If the place referred to is out of sight, *ahí* is generally used if it is nearby or in the same town, *allí* for more remote places:

—*Lo he comprado en esa tienda.* —*Ah, sí, yo compro siempre ahí*	'I bought it in that shop.' 'Oh yes, I always shop there'
Ya están ahí monsieur Fréjus y monsieur Bebé, y quieren cocktails (J. Cortázar, Arg., dialogue; note *están ahí* = 'have arrived')	M. Fréjus and M. Bebé are here, and they want cocktails
Ismael detestaba la canción española. Ahí es donde le traicionaba (M. Torres, Sp.)	Ismael hated Spanish songs. There's where I let him down
Mi hermana nació en Caracas, y yo también nací allí	My sister was born in Caracas, and I was born there too
El rock les entra por un oído, les deteriora un poco el tímpano pertinente y se les queda allí, en el cerebro (M. Benedetti, Ur.; *ahí* could have been used)	Rock goes in one of their ears, does a bit of damage to the relevant eardrum and stays there, in their brains

When there is more than one verb it is important to place *allí* and *ahí* near the verb that they qualify:

Allí/Ahí me dijo que nos casaríamos	(S)he told me there that we would get married
Me dijo que nos casaríamos allí/ahí	She told me we would get married there

Native speakers may use *ahí* for *allí* (but not vice versa) if they feel emotionally close to the place they are talking about: *¿conoces la iglesia a la entrada del pueblo? Pues ahí/allí se casaron mis padres* 'do you know the church on the way in to the village? Well, that's where my parents got married', —*Y al fin llegué a Manaos. De ahí era fácil pasar a Iquitos.* —*Y ¿ahí fue donde conociste al señor Julio Reátegui?* (M. Vargas Llosa, Pe., dialogue) '"And I eventually got to Manaos. From there it was easy to cross to Iquitos." "And was that where you met Sr Julio Reátegui?"', *ahí está, dijo, y ahí estaba porque él lo conocía . . .* (G. García Márquez, Col., dialogue, pointing to a comet in the sky; or *allí*) '"There it is," he said, "and there it was because he was familiar with it."'

31.6.2 *Acá, allá*

In the Southern Cone and in many other parts of Latin America, *acá* is much more common than *aquí* in all styles: *acá en la Argentina si querés una taza de té, tenés que beber mate* = in Peninsular Spanish *aquí en Argentina, si quieres una taza de té, tienes que beber mate* 'here in Argentina if you feel like a cup of tea you have to drink mate'.

In Spain, *acá* and *allá* are much less common than *aquí, ahí* and *allí*, and denote vague or non-specific location or, most commonly, movement (often with the preposition *para*):

Ven acá/aquí, que te voy a contar una cosa	Come here, I'm going to tell you something
Íbamos allá/hacia allí cuando nos lo/le encontramos	We were on the way there when we ran into him
Que se venga para acá en cuanto pueda	(S)he must come here as soon as (s)he can

(i) *Allá* is often used of large distances in Latin America and occasionally in Spain. It can also in both regions express vague yearnings. In time phrases it emphasizes remoteness and may be obligatory: *allá/allí en (la) Argentina tenemos mucha familia* (*allí* in Spain) 'we have a lot of family out there in Argentina', *nos casamos allá en los años veinte* (not *allí*) 'we got married some time in the twenties', *el sur era y es acentuadamente indio; allá la cultura tradicional está todavía viva* (O. Paz, Mex.) 'the south was and is markedly Amerindian; (down) there traditional culture is still alive'.

(ii) *Acá* and *allá* can take an intensifier, unlike *aquí, ahí, allí*: *más allá del sistema solar* 'beyond the solar system', *más allá de la realidad y el sueño* (L. Mateo Díaz, Sp.) 'beyond reality and dreams', *más acá de la frontera* 'on this side of the frontier', *un poco más acá del horizonte* (M. Benedetti, Ur.) 'just on this side of the horizon', *¡un poquito más acá!* 'this way a bit!', *lo más acá/allá posible* 'as far over here/there as possible'. *El más allá* is 'the Beyond' of science fiction and the occult.

(iii) *Allá* with a pronoun translates 'let him/her get on with it', 'it's your look-out', etc.: *allá él si hace tonterías* 'if he wants to fool about, that's his affair', *bueno, allá tú si no me haces caso* 'well, if you don't pay any attention to me, it's your problem'.

(iv) *Acá* is sometimes used in time expressions in informal language, though it sounds a little old-fashioned (at least in Spain), and *desde* on its own is normally used: *¿de cuándo acá no se dice hola a los amigos?* (*desde cuándo...*) 'since when have people not been saying 'hello' to their friends?', *desde las elecciones (acá), este país ya no tiene remedio* 'since the elections, this country's been beyond hope', *de un tiempo acá se le nota cansada* (*desde un tiempo a esta parte...*) 'she's been looking tired for some time now'.

31.6.3 Use of adverbs of place as pronouns

One hears uneducated speakers use *aquí/ahí/allí* for *éste/ése/aquél*: *aquí me dice* = *éste me dice* 'this one here says to me' (itself very familiar). The same phenomenon occurs in Latin America, and also with *acá/allá*.

31.6.4 Adverbs of place with prepositions

All the adverbs of place can be preceded by *de, desde, hacia, hasta, por* and, less commonly, *para* (for which see *acá/allá*).

Los melocotones de aquí son mejores que los de Estados Unidos	The peaches (from) here are better than the ones from the United States
Mira el sombrero que lleva la señora de allí	Look at the hat that lady over there is wearing
Desde aquí se ve el mar	You can see the sea from here
Se sale por aquí	This is the way out

31.6.5 *Dentro/adentro, fuera/afuera*

'Inside' and 'outside', respectively. In Spain *dentro* and *fuera* are preferred after prepositions (except perhaps *para*) and also to form prepositional phrases when followed by *de*. *Afuera* and *adentro* strictly speaking denote motion *towards* and should be used only in this sense, although they are occasionally found in isolation with the meaning of *fuera*, *dentro*. European Spanish:

Por dentro era negro, y por fuera blanco	On the inside it was black, on the outside white
Dentro había flores en macetas	Inside there were flowers in pots
Dentro de la caja había otra	Inside the box was another
Ven (a)dentro y te lo explicaré	Come inside and I'll explain it to you
Vamos a cenar fuera	We're eating out (tonight)/We're having dinner outside
El gas tiende a escaparse hacia fuera	Gas tends to escape outwards
He estado fuera unos días	I've been away for a couple of days
¡Las manos fuera de Cuba!	Hands off Cuba!
Su ocurrencia ha estado fuera de lugar	His witty remark was out of place
Las luces de fuera (C. Martín Gaite, Sp.)	The lights outside
Afuera quedaba el domingo de verano, despoblado y soso (F. Umbral, Sp. Poetic: *fuera* is more normal)	Outside was the summer Sunday, empty (lit. 'depopulated') and lifeless

In Latin-America *afuera* and *adentro* tend to be used in all circumstances. *Adentro de* and *afuera de* are also used as prepositional phrases, this usage being considered normal in Argentina and colloquial in most other republics. Only *fuera de* and *dentro de* are allowed in Spain:

Afuera hacía calor porque empezaba enero (J. Cortázar, Arg.; Sp. *fuera*)	Outside it was hot because January was beginning (Argentina is in the southern hemisphere)
fuera en el parque, y adentro, por la casa entera seguían los disparos (José Donoso, Ch.; Sp. *fuera, dentro*)	Outside in the park, and inside, throughout the house, the shooting continued
Adentro de Aqueronte hay lágrimas, tinieblas, crujir de dientes (J. L. Borges, Arg., Sp. *dentro de*)	Within Acheron there are tears, darkness, gnashing of teeth
nuestros treinta años adentro de Abc Color (*Abc Color*, Par.)	…our thirty years (working) at *Abc Color*

However, *dentro de* is used in Latin America, as in Spain, in time phrases of the sort *dentro de una semana* 'in a week's time' (often *en una semana* in Latin America).

31.6.6 *Abajo, debajo de, abajo de, arriba, encima*

For the prepositions *bajo*, *debajo de* see 34.3. For *encima de* see 34.9 and 34,17.

Abajo means 'down' or 'downstairs', and *arriba* means 'up' or 'upstairs':

Te espero abajo/arriba	I'll wait downstairs/upstairs
Caminaba calle abajo/arriba	(S)he walked up/down the street

Abajo de is often used in Latin America, but not in Spain, for 'underneath':

¿Chofi guarda las quincenas abajo del colchón? (A. Mastretta, Mex.; Sp. *debajo de.* Quincenas = wages paid every two weeks)	Does Chofi keep her wages under the mattress?
La nevera está abajo del bar (C. Fuentes, Mex., dialogue; Sp. *debajo de*)	The fridge is under the bar

The difference between *arriba* and *encima* is basically the same as between 'up' and 'on top':

Ponlo encima de la mesa	Put it on (top of) the table
Ponlo ahí encima	Put it there on top
Ponlo ahí arriba	Put it up there
El avión pasó por encima del pueblo	The plane flew over the village

Encima can also be used figuratively: *les dije que se lo daría y encima se quejan* 'I told them I would give it to them and on top of that/even then they complain'.

Arriba de for *encima de* in the meaning of 'above' is heard in Latin America.

31.6.7 *Detrás*, *detrás de* and *atrás*

Atrás 'behind/backwards' denotes motion backwards, whereas *detrás* and the prepositional phrase *detrás de* 'behind' denote static position:

dar un paso atrás	to move a step backwards
Ella subió las escaleras sin siquiera mirar hacia atrás (G. Cabrera Infante, Cu.)	She went up the stairs without even looking back
Ponte detrás	Stand behind
detrás de mí/detrás de la mesa	behind me/the table

In Latin America *atrás de* is often used: *las demás me veían desde atrás de la mesa* (A. Mastretta, Mex.; Sp. *desde detrás de la mesa*) 'the others looked at me from behind the table'.

31.6.8 *Delante*, *delante de* and *adelante*

In Spain *delante* 'in front' and the prepositional phrase *delante de* 'in front of' denote place, *adelante* 'forward(s)/onward(s)' denotes motion forward:

Yo iba delante	I was walking ahead
Delante de ti no hablará	(S)he won't say anything in front of you
Sigue adelante que yo te alcanzaré	Go on ahead. I'll catch you up

In colloquial Latin-American Spanish *adelante de* is often used for 'in front of', but this is not heard in Spain: *vio a Federico que, unos cuantos pasos adelante de él, se detenía y agachaba a tomar una piedra* (S. Galindo, Mexico; Sp. *delante de él*) 'he saw Federico, who was stopping and bending down to pick a stone a few paces in front of him'.

(i) Only *adentro, afuera, abajo, arriba, atrás, delante* and *adelante* can be intensified: *más adentro/abajo/arriba/atrás* 'further inside/down/up/back', *más afuera* or *más hacia fuera* 'more to the outside', *más hacia delante* 'further forwards'. *Más adelante* means 'later on', e.g. *ya hablaremos más adelante* 'we'll talk later on'.

(ii) Omission of *de* in the prepositional phrase, common in Latin America, occasionally heard in Spain, is considered incorrect in careful language: *dentro de mi corazón, fuera de la casa*.

(iii) *Fuera de* can mean *aparte de*, 'apart from' but is rather colloquial: *fuera de él no hay nadie en que yo pueda confiar* 'apart from him, there's no one I can trust' (some grammarians prefer *excepto él/aparte de él*).

(iv) *Atrás* is also used in the time phrases *años/meses/días atrás* 'some years/months/days ago' See 31.6.2 note (iv).

(v) *De...en adelante* is used in time phrases and in quantities: *para esto necesitas de un millón en adelante* 'for this you'll need a million or more', *de ahora en adelante no lo vuelvo a hacer* 'from now on I won't do it again'.

31.7 Adverbs of time

31.7.1 *Ya, ya no*

Ya has a wide variety of uses. In many common constructions its meaning is determined by the tense of the verb which it modifies:

Vienen ya	They're coming right now
Ya llegarán	They'll arrive, for sure
Ya han llegado	They've already arrived
Ya llegaron (Latin America)	They already arrived (US)
Ya no vienen	They're not coming any more
Ya no llegarán	They won't be arriving any more
(but *aún/todavía no han llegado*	they haven't arrived yet)

Further examples:

Ya no soy el de antes	I'm not the man I was
¿Quién se acuerda ya de lo que era el Charleston?	Who can remember any more what the Charleston was?
Ya no tengo edad para trabajar (J. Madrid, Sp., dialogue)	I'm no longer of an age to be working/I'm too old to work
Estaba perdido, extraviado en una casa ajena donde ya ni nada ni nadie le suscitaba el menor vestigio de afecto (G. García Márquez, Col.)	He was lost, adrift in a strange house where nothing and nobody aroused the slightest trace of affection in him any more

But *ya* has many idiomatic uses which do not always appear in the dictionaries. It can indicate impatience, accumulating frustration, fulfilled expectations, resignation, certainty about the future, incredulity or, in negative sentences, denial of something expected:

Iros, iros a la playa, que ya me quedo yo aquí a lavar la ropa (Carmen Rico-Godoy in *Cambio16*; *iros* is familiar Peninsular usage for *idos*. See 17.2.4 for discussion)	Go on, off you go to the beach while I stay here washing the clothes (martyred tone)
Lleva seis meses en cama. Si eso no es grave, pues ya me dirás	(S)he's been in bed six months. If that's not serious, then you tell me what is

Porque la tarea que tenemos planteada es casi una tarea de titanes. Pero el país puede resolverla. Ya verán (Cambio16, Sp.)	Because the task confronting us is almost a task for Titans. But the country can solve it. You'll see
Sirve ya la cena, que hemos esperado bastante	Serve supper now, we've waited long enough
Por mí, que se vaya ya	(S)he can go right now, as far as I'm concerned
Ya le pasaré la cuenta cuando gane el gallo (G. García Márquez, Col., dialogue; ya here makes a promise more certain)	I'll send you the bill when your cockerel wins
¡Basta ya! ¡Calla ya!/¡Ya está bien!	That's enough! Not another word!/ Enough!
Bueno, eso es el colmo ya	Well, that *is* the limit!
Ya puedes tener buen olfato con la nariz que tú tienes	You bet you've got a good sense of smell with the nose you've got!
Ya quisiera la Diana Ross para sus días festivos ser tan linda como tú (L. Rafael Sánchez, Puerto Rico, dialogue; Sp. para sus días de fiesta)	Diana Ross on a good day (lit. 'on her holidays') wouldn't mind being as pretty as you
Por mí, ya puede llover, que tenemos tienda de campaña	As far as I'm concerned, it can go ahead and rain—we've got a tent
Hitler habría sido todavía peor—y ya es decir—si a su criminal racismo hubiera juntado un fanatismo religioso (Abc, Sp.)	Hitler would have been even worse—and that's saying something—if he had added religious fanaticism to his criminal racism
cuando ya acabemos de limpiar la casa...	when we finally finish cleaning the house...
No, no, ya te digo que él no sabía nada de todo aquello	No, no, I'm *telling* you he knew nothing about all that
¡Ya tuviste que contarme el final!	You *would* have to tell me the ending!
Ya lo sé	I already know/I *know*
Ya empezamos...	(Oh dear) here we go again...
Ya era hora	It's about time...
Ya siéntate y deja de interrumpir (A. Mastretta, Mex., dialogue; Sp. siéntate ya)	Sit down and stop interrupting
—¿No ves lo inteligente que soy? —Ya, ya...	'Don't you see how intelligent I am?' 'Sure, sure...' (ironic)
—El jefe quiere hablar conmigo. Está muy enfadado. —Ya será menos	'The boss wants to talk to me. He's very angry.' 'Come on, it won't be that bad.'
Ya ves	There you are/Didn't I say so? (confirms something that the speaker had predicted)

(i) *Ya . . .ya* is a literary alternative for *o . . .o* 'either...or': *ya porque la idea del matrimonio acabara/acabó por asustarle, ya porque no pudiera/podía olvidar a María, no apareció en la iglesia* 'either because the idea of marriage eventually frightened him or because he couldn't forget Maria, he didn't appear at the church'. The indicative is more colloquial. *Bien...bien...* with the indicative can also be used.

(ii) *Ya* may be an abbreviation of *ya lo sé* 'I know', or *ya entiendo* 'I understand': *—Cuando veas la luz verde pulsa el botón rojo. —Ya* '"When you see the green light, push the red button." "Right/OK."'

(iii) *Desde ya* 'straightaway' is an expression from the Southern Cone which seems to have spread to Spain, where *desde ahora ya* or *enseguida* are more usual.

31.7.2 *Recién*

In Spain *recién* can only appear before participles, e.g. *recién pintado* 'newly painted', *recién casado* 'newly wed', *recién divorciado* 'recently divorced', *un chico recién salido del colegio* 'a boy who has recently left school'. Its use before other parts of speech is very rare.

The use of *recién* as a free-standing adverb of time is one hallmark of Latin-American Spanish everywhere and in all styles. It has two basic meanings:

(**a**) 'Right now' or 'just now':

Recién lo vi (Spain *le acabo de ver*)	I've just seen him
—¿Cuándo lo dijo? —Recién (Sp. *ahora mismo*)	'When did he say it?' ' Just now'

(**b**) 'Only', as in 'only now', 'only this year'. This usage is colloquial in some regions:

recién en los últimos siete años (Sp. *sólo en* or *solamente en…*)	only in the last seven years
Recién entonces me di cuenta (Sp. *sólo entonces*)	Only then did I realize
Recién mañana llegará (Sp. *no llegará hasta mañana*)	(S)he won't be here till tomorrow
Y él recién entonces se da cuenta de que está herida (M. Puig, Arg., dialogue; Sp. *…sólo entonces se da cuenta…*)	And only then he realizes that she's injured
Por eso es que recién ahora se descorre el velo sobre el déficit real de la administración Vázquez (*El País*, Ur.; Sp. *por eso es por lo que, …sólo ahora*)	This is why the veil concealing the real deficit accrued by the Vázquez administration is being lifted only now

Used thus, *recién* precedes the word or phrase it modifies.

31.7.3 *Todavía, aún*

Todavía and *aún* both mean 'still'/'yet' and are synonymous. With words like *menos*, *más*, *menor* and *mayor* they are translated as 'even'. *Aún* 'still' must be distinguished from *aun* meaning 'even'; the latter discussed at 31.8:

Todavía/Aún están aquí	They are still here
No han venido aún/todavía	They haven't come yet
Su cara puede verse menos bonita aún, se lo aseguro (C. Fuentes, Mex., dialogue; or *todavía menos/menos bonita todavía*)	I can assure you, your face can look even less pretty
Es todavía/aún/incluso/hasta más difícil de lo que yo pensaba (not *aun….* See next section)	It's even more difficult than I thought

31.7.4 *Luego* and **entonces**

Both words are translatable as 'then', but they usually mean different things.

(**a**) As time words, *entonces* means 'then'/'at that moment' whereas *luego* means 'afterwards'/'later on'. *Luego* in this sense is stressed: **luego** *viene/viene* **luego** '(s)he's coming later'. If the *luego* is not stressed here, it means 'so'/'in that case':

Abrí la puerta, y entonces me di cuenta de lo que había pasado (*luego* here would mean *después* 'afterwards')	I opened the door, and realized then what had happened
Entonces supe que Mario había mentido (*luego* would mean 'later on')	I realized then that Mario had lied
Desde entonces soy feliz	From that time on I have been happy
Recuerdo que los cines de entonces siempre apestaban a agua de colonia	I remember that cinemas at that time always stank of eau de Cologne
el entonces catedrático de griego	the professor of Greek at that time / the then professor of Greek
—¿Quién es? —Te lo diré luego	'Who is it?' 'I'll tell you later'
hasta luego (cf. *hasta ahora*, 'see you in a minute')	see you later / goodbye
Según dice mamá, que luego estuvo seis años liada con Tey (J. Marsé, Sp.)	According to mother, who later on was involved with Tey for six years

Luego de hacerlo (literary) = *después de hacerlo* 'after doing it'.

31.7.5 *Antes* 'before', *después* 'afterwards'

(**a**) *Antes* must be distinguished from the entirely separate word *ante* 'in the presence of'/'in front of', discussed at 34.2:

Antes prefería hablar contigo	First I'd like to talk to you
Ella llegó mucho antes	She arrived much earlier / long before
Después Dios dirá	In the long run (lit 'afterwards') only God knows (lit. 'will say')

For the subordinators *antes de que* and *después de que* see 16.12.7 and 18.3.

(**b**) Both *entonces* and *luego* may mean 'in that case'. In this meaning *luego* is not stressed:

—En Madrid hace 40 grados, en Sevilla 38. —Entonces hace más calor en Madrid que en Sevilla (or *Luego, hace...*)	'In Madrid it's 40 degrees, in Seville 38.' 'In that case it's hotter in Madrid than in Seville'
Es mi secreto. Entonces ya me lo contarás. Los secretos siempre se cuentan (A. Buero Vallejo, Sp., dialogue; *luego* not possible in conjunction with *ya*)	'It's my secret'. 'Then you'll soon tell me. Secrets always get told'
Pienso luego existo (set phrase)	I think, therefore I am

(i) Use of *luego* to mean 'straightaway'/'immediately' is a regionalism in Spain, but it is common in certain Latin-American countries.

(ii) The following words also convey the idea of 'then': *después*, 'after', *acto seguido* 'next/immediately after', *a continuación* 'next/immediately after', *en seguida/enseguida* 'immediately'/'straightaway'.

31.8 *Incluso* (inclusive), *hasta, aun, siquiera*

All these words may translate the English 'even' in such sentences as 'she even speaks Russian and Greek', 'even in England the sun shines sometimes'. *Incluso* and *aun* are synonyms, but nowadays *incluso* is more often used:

Incluso/Aun hoy día algunas personas siguen creyendo en las hadas	Even today some people still believe in fairies
Incluso/Aun si le das dinero, no lo hará do it	Even if you give him money he won't do it

NB: Before or after comparative adjectives and adverbs (including *más* and *menos*), 'even' is translated by *todavía*, *aún* or *incluso*, but not by *aun*: *todavía/incluso/aún más inteligente* 'even more intelligent', *menos probable aún/todavía* 'even less probable'.

Inclusive is much used in Latin America where Peninsular Spanish uses *incluso*:

Para que una persona con un malestar llegue a un bienestar, debe pasar inclusive por un malestar peor que el que ya tenía (interview in *Cuba Internacional*; Sp. *malestar* = 'discomfort', 'indisposition', 'economic embarrassment')	For people with troubles to get out of them (lit. 'to arrive at well-being'), they have to pass through even worse troubles than they already had
... e inclusive con un pequeño superávit (*El País*, Ur.)	...and even with a slight surplus

NB: In Spain *inclusive* is used thus: *te mando las revistas, el último número inclusive* (*inclusive* follows the noun) 'I'm sending you the magazines, including the latest number', *hasta el domingo inclusive* 'up to and including Sunday'; *inclusivamente* is hardly ever used. However, use of *inclusive* for 'even' is deep-rooted in Latin America in all styles.

Hasta, literally 'until', may also mean 'even':

Ha llovido tanto que hasta/incluso/aun los patos están hartos	It's rained so much that even the ducks have had enough
...y un día hasta me dijeron que usara el teléfono cuando quisiera (A. Bryce Echenique, Pe., dialogue)	...and one day they even told me to use the phone whenever I liked

Siquiera means 'at least':

Dame siquiera cien euros	Give me a hundred euros at least
Yo creo que si se mete uno a eso de las caridades, tiene que ser a lo grande, siquiera quedar como San Francisco (A. Mastretta, Mex., dialogue)	I think that if one's going to go into charity work, one's got to do it in a big way, at least be like St Francis
Siquiera el General es generoso. Mira el coche que me regaló (ibid.)	At least the General is generous. Look at the car he gave me

Ni siquiera translates 'not even':

Bueno, los ingleses...los autos por la izquierda...ni siquiera han aceptado el sistema métrico (C. Catania, Arg., interview; Sp. *los autos* = *los coches*)	Well, the English ... cars on the left-hand side of the road ... they haven't even accepted the metric system

32

Expressions of time

The main points discussed in this chapter are:

- Tenses in sentences like 'I've been here three days', 'it's the first time that…' (Section 32.2)
- Ways of saying 'for six months', 'I've waited (for) two hours', etc. (Section 32.3)
- Uses of the following words to express duration of time:

llevar (32.3.1)	*durante* (32.3.4)	*para* (32.3.6)
hace…que (32.3.2)	*por* (32.3.5)	*desde* (32.3.7)

- Translating 'ago' (Section 32.4)
- Translating 'in three days', etc. (Section 32.5)
- Translating 'again' (Section 32.6)
- Translating 'still' (Section 32.8)
- Translating dates (Section 32.9)
- Telling the time and miscellaneous time expressions (Section 32.10)
- Translating 'next' (Section 32.11)
- Expressions of age (Section 32.12)

32.1 General

This chapter is divided into two parts. Section 32.2–8 covers such matters as the expression of duration, e.g. 'for *n* days', 'since…', 'during…', 'still'. Sections 32.9–32.10 contain translations of a number of useful expressions connected with the clock, dates and similar matters.

32.2 General remarks on tenses used in expressions of duration and other expressions of time

English-speakers tend to use the wrong tense in Spanish for sentences like 'I have been learning Spanish for three years', 'it's the first time I've seen her for months'. Unlike English, European Spanish often uses—and Latin-American Spanish normally uses—the present tense to indicate events that are still in progress or are likely to recur: *estudio español desde hace tres años* 'I've been learning Spanish for three years' (not *he estudiado…*), *desde que te conozco es la primera vez que te oigo decir algo que no debías* (G. García Márquez, Col., dialogue) 'it's the first time since I've known you that I've heard you say something that you shouldn't have said'.

If the event was continuing in the past, European Spanish often uses—and Latin-American normally uses—the imperfect tense where English uses the pluperfect: *estudiaba español desde hacía tres años* 'I/(s)he had been learning Spanish for three years', *desde que llegó a Europa por primera vez andaba a todas partes en el landó familiar* (G. García Márquez; Sp. *iba a todas partes/había ido a todas partes. . .*) 'since he'd first arrived from Europe he had been driving around in the family landau'.

English speakers often use the compound tenses (perfect and pluperfect) for both completed and incomplete events. This may confuse Spaniards since the perfect tense is, in Spain, a past tense: *¿cuánto tiempo has estado en Nueva York?* implies—for Spaniards—that the hearer's stay in New York is over, i.e. it means much the same as *¿cuánto tiempo estuviste en Nueva York?* 'how long were you/did you stay in New York?', except that the preterite suggests a more remote event. The present tense would be used if the hearer is still there: *¿cuánto tiempo hace que estás en Nueva York?* or *¿cuánto tiempo llevas en Nueva York?* French and Italian have similar rules: *vous êtes ici depuis combien de temps?* 'how long have you been here?', *da quando sei a Roma?* 'how long have you been in Rome?'

(i) Students of Latin-American Spanish should read the previous paragraph in conjunction with 14.9.8, since the perfect tense is notoriously variable in meaning in Latin America. In some places, e.g. Mexico, it implies that an event is continuing in the present.

32.3 Duration

There are various possibilities, not all of them interchangeable, e.g. *llevar. . ., hace. . ., desde hace. . ., desde, durante, en, por, para.*

32.3.1 *Llevar*

This verb provides the best translation of sentences like 'I've been doing something for *n* hours/days/months/years', but it can only be used when the event is or was still in progress. One cannot say *llevo seis meses en España* 'I've been in Spain for six months' after one has left the country for good; one says *he estado/estuve seis meses en España.*

It can appear before various types of phrase, including participles and gerunds, but the latter cannot be negative: **llevo años no fumando* is not a possible translation of 'I haven't been smoking for years': *hace años que no fumo/llevo años sin fumar/no fumo desde hace años.* Examples:

Llevamos cinco años viviendo juntos (C. Rico-Godoy, Sp.)	We've been living together for five years
¿Cuánto (tiempo) llevas en este trabajo?	How long have you been in this job?
El ascensor lleva estropeado dos meses (ibid.)	The lift/elevator has been broken for two months
Llevo diez años sentada aquí esperando que me lo preguntes (G. García Márquez, Col., dialogue)	I've been sitting here for ten years waiting for you to ask me that
Se comprende que llevan un buen tiempo apostados allí (E. Lynch, Argentina)	As one can see, they've been waiting there for some time (*apostar* = 'to post a sentry'/'set up a guard')

If the event or state *was* still in progress at the time, the imperfect of *llevar* is used (*he llevado. . .* is not possible in this construction):

Llevabas años diciéndolo	You had been saying it for years
Ya llevaba varios meses en Montevideo	He had already been in Montevideo
(M. Benedetti, Ur.)	for several months

(i) This construction with *llevar* is very common in speech in Spain, but less common in writing than the construction using *hace. . ./hacía. . .* described in the next section.

In Latin America *tener* is often used, and *tener de* + infinitive before verbs: *tengo dos años aquí*, 'I've been here for two years', *tenía pocos meses de gobernar cuando logró el cambio* (A. Mastretta, Mex., dialogue) 'he'd only been acting as Governor for a few months when he managed to bring about the change'; Kany, 273–4, quotes examples from all parts of the continent. This is also found in formal styles: *aunque tengan muchos años de vivir allí. . .nadie los confundiría con los norteamericanos auténticos* (Octavio Paz, Mex.) 'although they've been living there for years, no one would take them for true North Americans'.

(ii) The following idioms with *llevar* are noteworthy: *esto me va a llevar mucho tiempo* 'this is going to take me a long time', *Ana me lleva tres años* 'Ana's three years older than me'.

(iii) Earlier editions of B&B wrongly stated that *llevar* is not used for momentary duration, but *solamente llevo aquí unos segundos* is in fact correct for 'I've only been here a couple of seconds'.

32.3.2 *Hace/hacía/hará...que...*

Hace dos años que estoy en Madrid means the same as *llevo dos años en Madrid* 'I've been in Madrid for two years' (and I'm still there). *Hace* in this construction is followed by a simple present tense when the following verb indicates an action that is still in progress.

If the sentence is negative, the perfect tense is, however, also often found in Spain: *¿cuántos años hace que no le has visto?* (J. Marsé, Sp., dialogue) 'how long has it been since you last saw him?' Use of the perfect tense instead of the present in this type of sentence is rejected by many Latin Americans (and by some Spaniards, particularly northerners) and should probably be avoided by learners of Latin-American Spanish, although there is much regional variation in this matter.

Hacía + *que* translates 'for' in past time and is followed by the imperfect to denote an action that was still in progress: *hacía tiempo que nos veíamos* 'we had been seeing one another for some time'. In this case the pluperfect changes the meaning: *hacía tiempo que nos habíamos visto* 'it had been some time since we had seen one another'. But Peninsular Spanish often uses the pluperfect in negative sentences in the same way as English: *hacía siete años que Juan de Dios no había visto a su hijo mayor* (M. Vázquez Montalbán) 'Juan de Dios hadn't seen his oldest son for seven years'. Some informants from northern Spain thought this should have been expressed *...que no veía a su hijo mayor*.

Hará. . .que + the present tense and *haría* + the imperfect are commonly used in suppositions or approximations: *hará dos años que no la veo* (Sp. also *...no la he* *visto*) 'it must be two years since I've seen her'. Further examples (affirmative sentences):

Me dijo que la señorita Brines hacía más de un mes que venía merodeando por el edificio (A. Bryce Echenique, Pe., dialogue)	She told me that Ms Brines had been lurking around the building for more than a month
Hacía tiempo que la cosa andaba mal (M. Benedetti, Ur.)	Things had been going badly for some time
Haría dos semanas que no nos veíamos	It must have been two weeks since we'd seen one another

Negative sentences:

Hacía años que no veía a David (J. Aldecoa, Sp., dialogue)	I hadn't seen David for years
No los veo hace mil años (A. Bryce Echenique, Pe., dialogue)	I haven't seen them in a thousand years
...como no bebo hace tiempo... (M. Vargas Llosa, Pe., dialogue)	...since I haven't been drinking for some time...

(i) One cannot use the present tense if no preposition is used. One can say *he estado tres horas aquí* 'I've been here three hours', but not **estoy tres horas aquí*. If one intends to remain one must say *llevo tres horas aquí/hace tres horas que estoy aquí/estoy aquí desde hace tres horas*.

(ii) The verb *hacer* does not appear in the plural in this construction: **hacían años que no hablaban de otra cosa* 'they hadn't talked of anything else for years' is bad Spanish for *hacía años que*... This is a common error of popular speech.

(iii) The imperfect tense may be used in negative sentences with a change of meaning. *Hace años que no tomábamos café juntos* 'we haven't had coffee together for years' differs from *hace años que no tomamos café juntos*. The former is appropriate while one is actually drinking coffee with the friend; the latter suggests that it would be a good idea to have coffee together.

(iv) *En* may be used in the same way as the English 'in' in negative sentences, e.g. 'I hadn't seen her in/for three days'; see 32.5.

32.3.3 Translating 'for' when the event is no longer in progress

Verb in a past tense and no preposition:

Estuvo una temporada en Guatemala, y luego se volvió a California	(S)he was in Guatemala for a while and then (s)he returned to California
Trabajé varios años en Madrid	I worked in Madrid for several years
Trabajábamos sin pausa tres o cuatro horas	We used to work non-stop for three or four hours
Esperamos cinco minutos en la parada	We waited at the stop for five minutes
Cuánto tiempo ha estado usted/estuvo en Madrid? (addressed to someone whose stay is over)	How long were you in Madrid?
...la clase de clínica, que dictó todos los días hasta el día de su muerte (G. García Márquez, Col.)	...the class in clinical techniques he gave every day until the day of his death

Sentences like 'I haven't seen him for years', 'she hasn't smoked for years' can be thought of as 'non-events' that are still in progress. For this reason they are discussed at 32.3.2. *Hace. . .que* with a preterite tense means 'ago' and is discussed at 32.4.

32.3.4 *Durante*

The basic meaning of *durante* is 'during': *durante el siglo veinte* 'during the twentieth century', *durante los tres meses que estuvo aquí* 'in the three months he was here'. Unlike 'during' it is regularly used before plural nouns to mean 'for' a specific period of time: *durante años* 'in years', *durante muchos siglos* 'for/in many centuries'. When the event lasted throughout the whole of the period mentioned, the verb is in the preterite tense: see 14.4.1.

(i) Spanish uses the preterite continuous (*estuve hablando, estuvo leyendo,* etc.) to emphasize that an event continued uninterrupted throughout a period of time: *estuve leyendo durante tres horas* 'I read/was reading for three hours', *durante un cuarto de hora estuvo mirándote* (L. Spota, Mex., dialogue) 'he was staring at you for a quarter of an hour'.

(ii) *En* may be used for *durante* in Latin America: *Olga no habló en varios minutos* (L. Spota, Mex.) 'Olga didn't speak for several minutes'.

(iii) Use of *en* may, on both continents, also correspond to English 'in' in negative sentences like 'I haven't smoked in/for years'; see 32.5 note (ii).

(iv) *En* may also, especially in Latin America, be an alternative for *dentro de* in sentences like *te veo dentro de/en cinco minutos* 'I'll see you in five minutes'. See 32.5 for discussion.

32.3.5 *Por* meaning 'for' in time phrases

Por is used 'for' when referring to brief moments of time (seconds, minutes, etc.), when the speaker emphasizes the shortness of the period. The preposition may in some cases be omitted altogether:

Entraré sólo/solo (por) un momento	I'll come in just for a moment
Me ha prestado el coche sólo/solo (por) tres días	(S)he lent me the car for three days only
Por un momento, Bernardo estuvo a punto de ocultar los motivos de la visita (J.-M. Merino, Sp.)	For a moment Bernardo was about to conceal the reasons for his visit
Por un instante, Félix sintió que una pantalla plateada los separaba a él y a Mary (C. Fuentes, Mex.)	For a moment Félix felt that a silver screen was separating him and Mary

(i) *Por* and *para* are interchangeable in time expressions fixing the duration of some future need (see also 32.3.6 for *para* in time phrases): *sólo/solo queremos la habitación por/para unos días* 'we only want the room for a few days'.

(ii) When longer periods are involved, Latin Americans may use *por* where Peninsular speakers use nothing or *durante*: *por cuatro o cinco años nos tuvieron acorralados*

(M. Vargas Llosa, Pe., dialogue; Sp. *durante...*) 'they had us cornered for four or five years', *mi viejo sombrero, que ha soportado soles y lluvias por más de tres años* (J. J. Arreola, Mex., dialogue; Sp. *durante*) 'my old hat, that has put up with rain and sun for more than three years', *ahí permaneció por casi dos semanas* (L. Sepúlveda, Ch.; Sp. *durante...* or no preposition) 'there he stayed for nearly two weeks'.

32.3.6 *Para* in expressions of duration

Para is used to translate the idea of 'for' a specified period of time in the future:

Tenemos agua para tres días	We've enough water for three days
Necesito el coche para tres días	I need the car for three days
Vamos a tener lluvia para rato	We're going to have rain for some time

Ir para is a colloquial translation of 'for nearly...': *va para cinco años que trabajo aquí* 'I've been working here for nearly five years'/'it's getting on for five years that I've been working here'.

32.3.7 *Desde*

Desde translates 'since' or, sometimes, 'for'. *Desde que* is used before verb phrases, *desde* before singular noun phrases, and *desde hace/hacía* before plural nouns. *Desde* can be used in a way unfamiliar to English-speakers: *desde niña hablo catalán* 'I've spoken Catalan since I was a girl'.

Correct choice of the tense is important, especially in Latin-American Spanish. Events that are still in progress usually require the present tense, especially in Latin America. But in Spain, the perfect may optionally be used:

Mi marido está parado desde hace dos años (A. Buero Vallejo, Sp., dialogue.; still in progress)	My husband's been out of work for two years
Te he estado esperando desde antes de la una (or Sp. *te estoy esperando*)	I've been waiting for you since before one o'clock
La administración de la televisión pública ha sido un desastre desde siempre (*Tribuna*, Sp.; or *es*)	The administration of public television has been a disaster from the start (lit. 'since always')
Desde entonces nada le ha durado mucho (J. Marías, Sp.; or *...nada le dura*)	Since then nothing has lasted long for him
Lo sé desde que te vi en el hospital (G. García Márquez, Col., dialogue; or Sp. *lo he sabido*)	I've known it since I saw you in the hospital
lo que está pasando desde julio del pasado año (*Granma*, Cu.; or Sp. *ha estado pasando*)	what has been happening since July last year

Events that *were* in progress are expressed by the imperfect tense: *desde la gran crisis dormían en habitaciones separadas* (S. Pitol, Mex., Sp. also *habían dormido*) 'since the great crisis they had been sleeping in separate rooms'.

Events that are or were no longer in progress require a past tense, normally the compound tense (perfect, pluperfect) in Spain or the preterite in much of Latin America:

He fumado tres veces desde octubre/Había fumado tres veces desde entonces	I have smoked three times since October/I had smoked three times since then
Desde que se casó con el millonario ese, Julia ya no se habla con los amigos (not in progress)	Since she married that millionaire Julia doesn't talk to her friends any more
Claro que he vuelto a hacerlo/volví a hacerlo desde entonces (preterite preferred in Latin America)	Obviously I've done it again since then
Ayer te estuve esperando desde antes de la una	I was waiting for you yesterday from before one o'clock

Desde hace/desde hacía are required before plural nouns, before specified periods of time and before numbers. The compound tenses are possible in Peninsular Spanish:

Me tranquilizo pensando que todos los adolescentes se han comportado exactamente igual desde hace tres mil años (C. Rico-Godoy, Sp.; *se comportan* possible in Spain, normal in Latin America)	I console myself by thinking that all adolescents have acted the same way for three thousand years
Desde hacía tiempo sospechaba que Tita deseaba que ella desapareciera de este mundo (I. Esquivel, Mex.)	She had been suspecting for a long time that Tita wanted her to disappear from this world
Eso es un campo de batalla desde hace un año (M. Vargas Llosa, Pe., dialogue; Sp. also *ha sido*)	That's been a battlefield for a year now

Colloquial speech sometimes omits the *desde* from this phrase. This is considered careless by many speakers, but it may be more acceptable in Latin America, cf. *hace treinta años estoy sentado frente a una máquina de escribir* (*Abc Color*, Par.) 'for thirty years I've been sitting in front of a typewriter' (for *desde hace treinta años*), *somos República hace ocho años* (M. Vargas Llosa, Pe., dialogue) 'we've been a Republic for eight years' (*desde hace ocho años*).

(i) When the preterite is expected (event not still in progress), literary styles (especially in Spain) often use a *-ra* or *-se* form of the verb after *desde*: *ésta/esta es la primera vez que menciona el asunto desde que ingresara/ingresase/ingresó en la cárcel* 'this is the first time he has mentioned the matter since he entered prison'. See 14.10.3 for discussion.

(ii) 'Since' may sometimes need to be translated by *hace que.../hacía...que* with a past tense: *hace ya ocho años que nos casamos* 'it's eight years since we married/got married/we got married eight years ago'.

(iii) *Desde* is sometimes used in Mexican speech and elsewhere in Latin America simply to emphasize the moment at which something was done: *desde el martes llegó mi hermano* 'my brother already arrived—on Tuesday'.

32.4 Translating 'ago'

Hace/hacía with a preterite or pluperfect (or, in Spain, a perfect tense if the event is recent; see 14.9.3) is the usual formula:

Lo/Le vi hace años	I saw him years ago
Lo/Le habíamos visto hacía años	We'd seen him years ago/before then
Hace ya algún tiempo dijiste que...	Some time ago you said that...
La vi hace cosa de dos meses	I saw her a couple of months ago
La he visto (Lat. Am. *la vi*) *hace un momento* (Sp. perfect of recency)	I saw her a moment ago

Atrás is sometimes used in literary styles: *lo repararon tiempo atrás* 'they mended it/fixed it some time ago', *lo/le conocí días atrás* 'I met him some days ago'.

Use of the verb *haber* for *hacer* in this construction (with the present-tense form *ha*) is now archaic in Spain, but survives in some colloquial varieties in Latin America: *ha mucho que él perdió a su madre* (M. Puig, Arg., dialogue = *hace mucho*) 'he lost his mother a long time ago'.

32.5 'In n days/weeks', etc.

Foreign students often misuse *dentro de* when translating the English 'in'. *Dentro de* can only refer to the future or the future in the past. One cannot say **lo hice dentro de un año* 'I did it in one year' (*lo hice en un año*):

—¿Cuándo empieza? —Dentro de tres días	'When does it start?' 'In three days' time'
Dentro de tres meses, el Gobierno iniciará la construcción de la autopista del Coral (Presidential website, Dominican Republic)	The government will start work on the Coral motorway/US freeway in three months
de hoy en ocho días	in eight days' time
Me faltan/quedan tres días para irme	I'm going in three days' time

(i) Use of *en* to mean *dentro de* is common in Latin America; much less common in Spain: *no te preocupes, vuelvo en un rato* (A. Mastretta, Mex., dialogue) 'don't worry, I'll be back in a minute'. Seco (1998), 186, says that this use of *en* is an Anglicism and is obscure since it can also mean 'in the space of': *lo haré en una hora* is more likely to mean 'it'll take me an hour do it'.

(ii) *En* can mean the same as the English 'in' in negative sentences like 'I've not been there in/for years': *sabe usted que no nos hemos visto en doce años* (C. Fuentes, Mex., dialogue) 'you know that we haven't seen one another in/for twelve years'.

32.6 'Again'

There are numerous ways of translating 'again':

(a) *Volver a. . . .* This is probably the most usual construction before a verb:

Han vuelto a hacerlo	They've done it again
Cuando cerró la puerta volví a llorar (A. Mastretta, Mex., dialogue)	When he shut the door, I started crying again
Como me vuelvas a hablar de esa manera... (this use of *como* is discussed at 25.8.2)	If you talk to me like that again...

(b) *Otra vez*:

Hazlo otra vez/Vuelve a hacerlo/Hazlo de nuevo	Do it again
No te lo digo otra vez/No te lo vuelvo a decir/No vuelvo a decírtelo	I won't tell you again
Otra vez más vuelve a subir la bencina (*Primera Línea*, Ch., Sp. *la gasolina*)	Petrol/US Gas up again

(c) *De nuevo* is more literary than *otra vez*:

De nuevo volvieron las suspicacias y los recelos	Once again suspicion and distrust returned
De nuevo vuelven inspecciones en Iraq (*Nación*, Costa Rica)	Inspections resume in Iraq

32.7 *Tardar*

Tardar, as well as meaning 'to be late' (*no tardes* 'don't be late'), may translate 'to take' in expressions of time:

Tardó un año en escribirnos	(S)he took a year to write to us/(S)he didn't write to us for a year
Poco tardaron en vengarse (*Crónica*, Arg.)	They soon got their own back
Se tarda media hora andando	It takes half an hour to walk it

Llevar may also be used in certain expressions: *eso te llevará horas* 'that'll take you hours', *me llevó días* 'it took me days'; but *el viaje duró varias horas* 'the journey took several hours'.

32.8 'Still'

(*Todavía* and *aún* are discussed at 31.7.3.) A very frequent construction is *continuar* or, more commonly, *seguir* followed by the gerund (**continuar a hacer algo*, 'to continue to do something' is not Spanish). *Seguir* is used before adjectives and participles, i.e. one says *sigue enfermo* 'he's still ill' rather than *continúa enfermo*:

Te has dado cuenta de que sigues llevando puesta la chaqueta del pijama (J.-M. Merino, Sp., dialogue)	You've realized that you're still wearing your pyjama/US pajama jacket
Continuaban/Seguían viéndose	They went on seeing one another
Pero yo seguía preguntándome cómo demonios podía vivir una familia así (A. Bryce Echenique, Pe.)	But I went on wondering how the devil a family like this could live
Pero ella sigue soltera (C. Fuentes, Mex., dialogue)	But she's still unmarried

32.9 Dates

32.9.1 Saying and writing dates

Months are not written with a capital letter in Spanish. The usual way of saying dates is *quince de mayo de dos mil siete* 'fifteenth of May 2007', *dos de abril de dos mil cuatro* 'April the second 2004', i.e. the ordinal numbers are not used. The only exception is *primero de...* 'the first of'. The form *el uno de...* is increasingly common, and although it is criticized by strict grammarians, Manuel Seco does not object.

The format used for dates in Spain is the same as in most of Europe: dd-mm-yy, e.g. *17 de junio de 2015, 17-VI-2015 or 17-06-2015*. In Latin America the North-American format mm-dd-yy is often used, as in *junio 17 de 2015, 06-17-2015*.

Typists often use a point after the thousands when writing years, e.g. 1.999, but grammarians, including Manuel Seco and *El País*, condemn this.

NB: 'On the nth of m' is translated without a preposition: *salimos de Montevideo el veinticinco de febrero* 'we left Montevideo on 25 February'. But cf. *estamos al veinticinco de febrero* 'today is 25 February'.

32.9.2 Decades

Seco, 1998, 150, says that *una década* is a decade, which can only start in a year that is a multiple of ten, e.g. 2020–30. *El decenio* simply means any period of ten years. *El País, Libro de estilo*, 2002, 266, takes the opposite view: *los años cincuenta* = 'the fifties', *los años noventa* 'the nineties'. One can also say *la década de los cincuenta*, but Seco considers this long-winded. *El decenio 1950–1960* is a rather literary alternative. The formula *los cincuentas* 'the fifties', *los noventas* 'the nineties' is sometimes found, but is condemned by Seco as an Anglicism.

32.10 Miscellaneous time expressions

32.10.1 Telling the time

Except where specified, the following examples reflect Peninsular usage. Several variations may be heard in the various Latin-American republics.

(**a**) Asking the time (12-hour clock):

¿Qué hora es? (Lat. Am. *¿Qué horas son?*)	What time is it?
¿Qué hora tiene?	What time do you make it?
¿Qué hora será?	I wonder what time it is
¿A qué hora viene/empieza?	What time is (s)he coming/does it start?

(**b**) Telling the exact time:

Es *la una (en punto)*	It's one o'clock (exactly)
Son *las dos, las tres*, etc.	It's two o'clock, three o'clock, etc.
Es la una de la mañana/de la tarde	It's one in the morning/afternoon
Son las cuatro y cinco (Mex. also *son las cuatro con cinco minutos*)	It's five (minutes) past/after four
Son las cinco y cuarto/y media	It's five fifteen/thirty
Son las siete y veinticinco	It's seven twenty-five/twenty-five past seven
Son las ocho menos cuarto	It's seven forty-five
Son las nueve menos diez (also *diez minutos para las nueve* in parts of Latin America)	It's ten to nine
Son y media/cuarto	It's thirty/fifteen minutes past
Son menos diez/y cinco	It's ten to/five past
Empezará a las diez de la noche	It'll begin at ten p.m.
Falta poco para las cuatro	It's nearly four o'clock

Los autobuses salen a menos veinte	The buses leave at twenty to
Van a dar las doce	It's just coming up to twelve
Acaba de dar la una	The clock has just struck one
Acaban de dar las dos	The clock has just struck two
Cuando daba la última campanada de las cuatro	On the last stroke of four
La consulta es de nueve a once/desde las nueve hasta las once	The doctor's surgery is from nine to eleven
Al filo de la medianoche (poetic)	At exactly midnight

(c) Approximate time

(Ya) han dado las siete	It's already gone seven
Son las ocho más o menos	It's about eight o'clock
Son pasadas las ocho (not **después de las ocho*)	It's gone eight/past eight
Son las tres y poco/algo	It's just after three
Son las tres como mucho	It's three o'clock at the latest
Son cerca de las nueve	It's nearly nine o'clock
Deben de ser las/cerca de las nueve (or *serán las nueve*)	It must be nine o'clock/nearly nine o'clock
Llegaré a eso de/sobre las dos de la mañana	I'll be there around two a.m.
Serían las siete de la tarde	It must have been seven p.m.
No acabaré hasta después de las tres/ hasta pasadas las tres	I won't finish until after three

32.10.2 The 24-hour clock

El tren sale a las quince horas	The train leaves at fifteen hundred
El avión llegó a las diecisiete (*horas*) *quince minutos/y quince*	The plane arrived at seventeen-fifteen

32.10.3 Times of the day

a primera hora de la mañana/por la mañana temprano	early in the morning
por la mañana (Lat. Am. *a/en la mañana*)	in the morning
a media mañana	in the middle of the morning
a mediodía	at noon
a la hora de comer/almorzar	at lunchtime (2–4 p.m. in Spain)
a la hora de la merienda	at teatime (i.e. around 4 p.m.)
a la hora de cenar	at dinner time (9–11 p.m. in Spain)
después de comer/cenar 'to have lunch' = *almorzar* in Latin America)	after lunch/dinner
por la tarde	in the afternoon (midday until about 8 p.m.)
al atardecer/anochecer	in the evening
por la noche	at night
a (la) medianoche	at midnight
al amanecer/de madrugada	at dawn
Ven esta noche/a la noche	Come tonight
Ven por la noche	Come during the night/by night

32.10.4 Greetings associated with different times of the day

buenos días	good morning (greeting)
buenas tardes (midday to 8 p.m.)	good afternoon/evening (greeting)
buenas noches	good evening/goodnight (greeting and goodbye; used after about 8 p.m.)

32.10.5 Frequency

dos veces a la semana/al día	twice a week/a day
cada media hora/dos o tres días	every half hour/every two or three days
todos los días	every day
Cada día que amanece nos trae más problemas	Each day that dawns brings us more problems
El sábado/Los sábados no trabajo	I don't work on Saturdays
todos los días entre semana	every day from Monday to Friday

For *cada día* and *todos los días* see 9.6.

32.10.6 Miscellaneous expressions

—*¿Qué (día) es hoy?* —*Domingo*	'What day is it today?' 'Sunday'
Hoy es lunes, martes, etc.	Today's Monday, Tuesday, etc.
Hoy es el/estamos a 28 de marzo	Today it's the 28th of March
¿A cuántos estamos (¿Qué fecha es hoy)?	What's the date today?
a 17 de enero de 2010	the 17th of January, 2010
Estamos a mediados/principios/finales/ últimos/de este mes	We're at the middle/beginning/end of this month
el 5 del corriente (business language)	the 5th of this month/'the fifth inst.'
Saldremos el viernes 28 (veintiocho) al mediodía	We'll leave on Friday the 28th at midday
la semana/el mes/el año pasado	last week, month, year
Se casaron el 20 de julio pasado	They got married on the 20th of last July
Nació en (el mes de) abril del año pasado	(S)he was born in February last year
al cabo de un año	a year later
a los 5 minutos quería irse	after 5 minutes (s)he wanted to leave
al día siguiente	the following/next day
de hoy en ocho días	a week today
ayer/anteayer	yesterday/the day before yesterday

32.11 Translating 'next'

The word *próximo* means 'coming', so it can only refer to the future: *el año próximo/ que viene* 'next year', *la próxima parada* 'next stop'. But when 'following' could replace 'next' in English, *siguiente* must be used: *al día siguiente* (not *próximo*) *volvieron a casa* 'the next/following day they returned home', *me bajé en la parada siguiente* 'I got out at the next stop':

el/al año/mes/la semana que viene (but *que viene* is not used with the names of months: *el próximo julio* 'next July')	next year/month/week
la próxima vez que lo hagan	the next time they do it

32.12 Age

The word *años* cannot usually be omitted when talking about age, at least on the first mention of the topic: *al año andaba, a los dos hablaba dos idiomas, a los tres leía* '(s)he was walking by the time (s)he was one, speaking two languages at two and reading at three'.

A los 15 años se mudó a La Habana (*Latina*, New York)	At fifteen she moved to Havana
—¿Cuántos años tienes? —Veinte (the word *años* can be omitted only when answering this question)	'How old are you?' 'I'm twenty'
Mi hermano tiene quince años	My brother is fifteen
¿A qué edad andan los niños?	At what age do children walk?
Acaba de cumplir los cincuenta años	(S)he has just turned fifty
Andará por los cuarenta (*años* can be omitted)	(S)he must be around forty
a los cuarenta años	at the age of forty

32.13 Omission of preposition before certain expressions of time

There is no preposition before some words and expressions. These are:

(a) Days of the week, and weeks: *nos vemos el lunes/el viernes* 'we're meeting on Monday/Friday', *fuimos la semana pasada* 'we went last week.

(b) Dates: *nos vemos el trece de abril* 'we're meeting on 13 April'.

(c) With a demonstrative + *año/día/mañana/tarde/noche/vez*: *aquel día/año llovió mucho* 'it rained a lot that day/year', *lo/le vi esta mañana* 'I saw him this morning'.

In informal Latin-American Spanish prepositions are omitted before some other words, as in *la ocasión que te vi* (Spain ...*en que te vi*) the occasion I saw you', *cuando la mañana siguiente me anunció que...* (A. Mastretta, Mex.; Sp. *a la mañana siguiente*) 'when he announced to me the following morning that...', ...*los funcionarios destituidos injustamente los últimos 18 meses* (*La Prensa*, Panama) 'State employees unfairly dismissed during the last 18 months', more formally *durante/en los últimos 18 meses*, ...*murieron la tarde de ayer en un accidente automovilístico* (*La Prensa*, Honduras = *murieron ayer por la tarde*) '...died yesterday afternoon/evening in a car accident'.

33

Conjunctions and connectors

This chapter discusses the following words:

pero, sino, mas but (Section 33.1)
o/u or (Section 33.2)
y/e and (Section 33.3)
que, de que that (Section 33.4)
porque/pues/como and other words
    meaning 'because', 'since...'
    (Section 33.5.1)
ya que/puesto que/como and other
    words meaning 'since'/'seeing
    that' (Section 33.5.2)
aunque, y eso que and other words
    meaning 'although' (Section 33.6)

con tal de que, a menos que and other
    expressions of condition and
    exception (Section 33.7)
words indicating purpose
    (Section 33.8)
de modo/manera que and other
    words expressing result
    (Section 33.9)
Discourse markers (e.g. 'however',
    'nevertheless', 'on the other
    hand', etc.) (Section 33.11)

Many Spanish subordinating conjunctions, e.g. *cuando, sin que, después de que, antes de que, para que*, etc., may be followed by the subjunctive and these are also discussed in Chapter 16. They are merely noted in the appropriate section of this chapter.

33.1 *Pero, sino, mas*

All of these translate 'but'. *Mas* (no accent) is virtually extinct, but it is occasionally found in flowery written language and in the Spanish of students influenced by French or Portuguese.

The distinction between *pero* and *sino* is crucial:

(a) *Sino* almost always occurs in statements of the type involving a correction, e.g. 'not A but B', and it is especially common in the formula *no sólo/solo...sino (que)...* 'not only...but...'. Before a verb phrase *sino que* must be used. Examples:

No quiero pan, sino vino	I don't want bread, but wine
no tú, sino él, no éste/este sino ése/ese	not you, but him, not this one but that one
No sólo se produce adentro sino también afuera de nuestro país (El Universal, Ve.; Sp. *dentro de..., fuera de...*)	It occurs not only inside but also outside our country
No ponía, sino que arrojaba las tazas sobre la bandeja (C. Rico-Godoy, Sp.)	She was not so much putting as flinging the cups on the tray

Pero is not possible in any of the above examples, but it translates 'but' in all other cases:

Habla francés, pero mal	(S)he speaks French, but badly
No se produce dentro de nuestro país, *pero se produce fuera de él* (the first statement is not being corrected)	It doesn't happen inside our country, but it does outside
Pero ¿es posible?	But can it (really) be possible?

(i) *Sino* often means 'except', especially in questions: *¿qué puedo decir sino que lo siento?* 'what can I say but/except that I'm sorry?', *¿por quién sino por ti habría subido las escaleras cantando a gritos 'aprendimos a quererte'?* (A. Bryce Echenique, Pe.) 'for whom except you would I have gone up the stairs singing "we learnt to love you" at the top of my voice?', *ni él pudo entenderlo sino como un milagro del amor* (G. García Márquez, Col.) 'even he couldn't understand it except as a miracle of love'.

(ii) *No...sino* may translate 'only' or 'just': *yo no podía sino dar gracias a Dios...'* I could only thank God', *el pueblo mexicano...no cree ya sino en la Virgen de Guadalupe y en la Lotería Nacional* (O. Paz, Mex.) 'the Mexican people now believe in nothing but the Virgin of Guadalupe and the National Lottery', *pero esa sabiduría no te tranquiliza ni reconforta sino todo lo contrario* (E. Lynch, Arg.) 'but that wisdom doesn't calm you down or comfort you—just the opposite'.

(iii) *Sino* must not be confused (as it sometimes is in older or badly written texts) with *si no* 'if not'.

33.2 O

'Or'. It is written and pronounced *u* before a word beginning with *o-* or *ho-*: *hombres o mujeres* 'men or women', but *mujeres **u** hombres*. Spoken language often neglects to use *u*, and *o* is also sometimes retained if it is the first word in a sentence.

  O...o translates 'either...or': *o lo sabe o no lo sabe* 'either he knows it or he doesn't', *os digo que u os apartáis, u os araño* (dialogue in a popular novel, Sp.) 'I'm telling you, either you get out of my way or I'll scratch you'.

  O is often written with an accent when it appears alongside a number to avoid confusion with zero: *4 ó 5* '4 or 5'. However, *El País* insists on *4 o 5* on the grounds that confusion with *405* is unlikely – which may be true in print, but not in handwriting.

33.3 Y

'And'; used much like its English equivalent. It is written and pronounced *e* before a word beginning with a pure *i* sound, e.g. *Miguel **e** Ignacio, padre **e** hijos*, but not before a *y* sound—*carbón y hierro* 'coal and iron'—and not when it means 'what about?': *¿Y Ignacio?* 'what about Ignacio?' Substitution of *e* for *y* is not always made in spontaneous speech. The use of *y* differs from the English 'and' in a few other respects:

  As was mentioned earlier, it often means 'what about?': *¿y el perro?* 'what about the dog?', *¿y la democracia?* 'what about democracy?', *¿y qué?* 'so what?/who cares?'

33.4 *Que*

Que is an overworked word: it has at least four separate uses in Spanish:

(**a**) As the most common relative pronoun: *la mujer que vi* 'the woman that/whom I saw', *el año en que nací* 'the year I was born in'. This use is discussed in Chapter 35. For sentences like *llovía que daba miedo* see 35.2 note (iii).

(**b**) *Qué* with an accent means 'what' and is best thought of as an entirely different word. It is discussed at 24.4.

(**c**) *Que* may mean 'than' in comparisons: see Chapter 5.

(**d**) As a subordinating conjunction: see the next section.

33.4.1 *Que* as a subordinating conjunction

Que introduces clauses in the same way as the English conjunction 'that'. It differs from the latter in that it cannot be omitted (see 33.4.6 for rare exceptions):

Dice que viene	(S)he says (that) (s)he's coming
Cree que no ha pagado	(S)he thinks (that) (s)he hasn't paid
Parece que va a llover	It seems (that) it's going to rain

However, the absence of a personal infinitive construction in Spanish makes this use of *que* much more common than the English 'that':

Te aconsejo que no lo hagas	I advise you not **to do** it
Quiero que vengas	I want you **to come**
Les pidió que no firmasen/firmaran	(S)he asked them not **to sign**

Statements followed by *que* that require the subjunctive, for example *quiero que...* 'I want...', *es necesario que...* 'it's necessary that...', are discussed in Chapter 16.

33.4.2 *De* before *que*

In certain circumstances a subordinate clause must be introduced by *de que*. This is necessary:

(**a**) After noun phrases, when *que* is a conjunction and not a relative pronoun. English does not differentiate between 'that' as a relative pronoun and 'that' as a subordinating conjunction, so 'the idea that he liked...' is ambiguous out of context. If 'which' could replace 'that' in the English translation, *que* alone is possible in Spanish, otherwise *de que* is used:

This is the idea that (= which) (s)he likes	*Ésta/Esta es la idea* **que** *le gusta* (relative pronoun; *de que* impossible)
The idea that (s)he likes her/him is absurd (that <> which)	*La idea de que le gusta es absurda* (subordinating conjunction)
Se dio cuenta de que ya no llovía	(S)he realized that it was no longer raining
Me desesperaba ante la idea de que mi madre debía morirse un día (E. Sábato, Arg.)	I despaired at the idea that my mother would have to die one day
tengo ganas de que...	I feel like...
tengo la certeza de que...	I'm certain that...

tenía miedo de que...	(S)he was afraid that...
el argumento/la creencia de que...	the argument/belief that...
la causa de que no llegara a tiempo	the cause of his/her not arriving on time

(b) After a number of common verbs that require the preposition *de*

me acuerdo de que...	I remember that...
me olvidaba de que...	I was forgetting that...
se convenció de que...	(s)he became convinced that...
se lamentaba/quejaba de que...	(s)he was bewailing the fact that.../ complaining that...
se trata de que...	it's about.../it's a question of...

and similarly after a number of verbs denoting mental or emotional states such as *aburrirse de que* 'to be bored that', *cansarse de que* 'to get tired of...', etc. For a selection see 26.4.2.

For *informar de que, hablar de que, dudar de que, advertir de que* and *avisar de que*, see the notes to 33.4.3.

(c) After certain adjectives and adverbial phrases that are normally followed by *de*:

estoy seguro/convencido de que...	I'm sure/convinced that...
estamos contentos de que...	we're pleased that...
estoy cansado/harto de que...	I'm tired/fed up with...
soy consciente de que...	I'm aware that...
estoy hasta la coronilla de que...	I'm sick to death with...

(d) After subordinators that include *de*:

antes de que/después de que llegara/ llegase	before/after (s)he arrived
a condición de que...	on condition that...
a cambio de que...	in exchange for...

and also *a pesar de que* 'despite the fact that', *con tal de que* 'provided that', *en lugar de que* 'instead of', *con el objeto de que* 'with the object of...'.

(i) There is a colloquial tendency, much stronger in Latin America than in Spain, to drop the *de* in these constructions: *Wenceslao se había dado cuenta **que** la maniobra de Juvenal era extraviar a sus primos* (J. Donoso, Ch.) 'Wenceslao had realized that Juvenal's manoeuvre was (designed) to lead his cousins astray', *pero estoy segura **que** es lo que haces...* (L. Goytisolo, Sp., dialogue) 'but I'm sure that that is what you're doing', *para que te convenzas **que** la dignidad no se come* (G. García Márquez, Col., dialogue) 'to convince you that (lit. 'so you convince yourself') that one can't eat dignity'. Peninsular speakers may find this careless, but it is found even in the Academy's publications, e.g. *...tenemos la impresión que...*, GDLE, p. 2188. It is common among speakers of Catalan or Valencian, since these languages do not use *de que*.

(ii) *Antes que* 'before' may, however, be used instead of *antes de que* in many regions, cf. *venda ese gallo antes que sea demasiado tarde* (G. García Márquez, Col., dialogue) 'sell that cockerel before it's too late', *lo conozco desde antes que tú nacieras* (M. Vargas Llosa, Pe., dialogue) 'I've known him since before you were born', *antes que te cases, mira lo que haces* (Spanish proverb) 'before you marry, look what you're doing'. *Antes que. . .* is more common in Latin America, though *antes de que* is frequent, especially in writing. *Antes que* is accepted in Spain, but is much less common than *antes de que*.

Antes que. . . also means 'rather than' everywhere: *cualquier cosa antes que eso* 'anything but/rather than that', *. . .para evitar que resulte un nuevo problema antes que la solución deseada* (*El Comercio*, Ec.) '. . .so as to avoid it becoming a another problem rather than the desired solution', *. . .el aprecio por las cosas bellas antes que por las que tienen éxito* (A. Mastretta, Mex.) '. . .the appreciation of beautiful things rather than successful ones'.

33.4.3 *Dequeísmo*

There is a growing tendency on both continents to insert *de* before *que* after verbs other than those mentioned above, especially *decir* 'say', *afirmar* 'claim', *creer* 'believe', *sostener* 'maintain', *negar* 'deny', *pensar* 'think', *ser* 'to be', *resultar* 'to turn out to be', *confesar* 'confess', *argüir* 'argue', etc. Examples (a question mark denotes sentences that are widely rejected as sub-standard): *?dice de que no viene* (for *dice que no viene*) '(s)he says (s)he's not coming', *lo curioso es de que* (for *. . .es que*) 'the strange thing is that, *?creo de que no es verdad* (for *creo que no es verdad*) 'I think it isn't true'.

This use of *de que* for *que* (called *dequeísmo*) is vehemently rejected by educated speakers and should be avoided by foreigners. It is very frequent in some regions, notoriously Peru, where it is constantly heard on radio and TV.

(i) *Hablar de que* is correctly used for 'to talk *about. . .*' in sentences like *cuando hablábamos de que no sabemos cómo somos* (A. Buero Vallejo, Sp., dialogue) 'when we were talking about our not knowing what we are like'.

(ii) *Dudar de que* is a permitted variant of *dudar que* 'to doubt': *nadie dudó (de) que dijera la verdad* 'no one doubted that (s)he told the truth', *ni a nosotros se nos ocurría dudar de que él abandonase su camino* (S. Puértolas, Sp.) 'it didn't even occur to us to doubt that he would abandon his vocation (lit. 'way')'. Note also *dudo de tus intenciones* 'I have my doubts about your intentions'.

(iii) *Informar a alguien de algo* 'to inform someone of something' is correct, so *La OMS informa **de** que han sido registrados 2.270 casos de neumonía atípica* (*El Mundo*, Sp.) 'WHO reports that 2,270 cases of "atypical pneumonia" (SARS) have been registered'. *Informar que* is also used, especially in Latin America, but *El País, Libro de estilo*, 2002, 152, condemns it. The construction *te lo informaré, nos lo informaron* is heard in Latin America, but not in Spain.

(iv) *Advertir que* means 'to notice that'. *Advertir de* means 'to inform', so *nos advirtieron de que había retrasos* 'they informed/warned us there were delays'. However, for explicit threats one uses *advertir que*: *te advierto que, si no trabajas, no cobras* (not *de que. . .*) 'I'm warning you that if you don't work you won't get paid' (example from *GDLE* 34.1.5.2).

The construction with *avisar* 'to inform'/'to warn' is with *que* or *de que*. 'To advise' is *aconsejar*; *un aviso* is 'a warning', 'a notice' or, in Latin America, 'an advertisement' (Sp. *un anuncio*).

33.4.4 *Que* at the head of a phrase

Que may appear at the head of a sentence or clause, especially in speech. Its main functions are:

(**a**) To reinforce the idea that what follows is something expected, something repeated or something that is being insisted on. In this case some verb like *decir* or *preguntar* may have been omitted:

¿Que cómo se llama mi película?	(did you ask) What's my film called?
¿Que por qué no van obreros al teatro?	(you're asking me) Why don't workers go to the theatre/US theater?
Que no quiero verla	(I said that) I don't want to see her/it
Oye, que aquí pone que no hay que abrirlo	Listen, it says here that it mustn't be opened
¡Que sí! ¡Que no!	Yes! No! (impatient repetition)
¡Socorro! ¡Que me ahogo!	Help! I'm drowning!

(**b**) As a colloquial subordinator of cause. It is often used to connect one idea to another where English uses a pause represented in writing by a dash:

¡Rápido! ¡Rápido! ¡Que se va!	Quick! Quick! It's going! (e.g. the train)
Eso dijo, que lo oí yo con mis propios oídos	That's what (s)he said—I heard it with my own ears
¡¿Dónde está mi marido que lo degüello?!	Where's my husband—I'm going to slaughter him!
No te cases con tu novio, que ése va a por tu dinero (A. Grandes, Sp., dialogue)	Don't marry your boyfriend—he's after your money
No lo inclines tanto, que se caen los papeles (J. de Jesús Martínez, Panama, dialogue)	Don't tilt it so much—the papers will fall off

(**c**) Colloquially, to show that the truth has dawned after some doubt:

¡Ah! Que usted es el fontanero (Lat. Am. *plomero*)	Ah—so you're the plumber, then
Que tú eres entonces el que lo hizo	So you're the one who did it, then
¿Que no quieres ir conmigo?	You mean you don't want to go with me?

(**d**) To translate 'that' in colloquial sentences meaning 'it was so…that…':

Tengo un sueño que no veo	I'm so tired I could drop (lit. 'that I can't see')
Estaba la habitación que no cabía un alfiler	The room was so packed you couldn't get a pin in it

(**e**) With the subjunctive in commands, exhortations and wishes, e.g. *que venga en seguida* 'tell him/her to come/have him/her come immediately', *que te acuerdes de escribirnos* 'remember to write to us'. See 17.6 for details.

(**f**) To mean 'the fact that', in which case it is likely to take the subjunctive. See 16.10.1 for further discussion.

(**g**) Occasionally in very colloquial (never in written) Peninsular Spanish, as a substitute for *si* 'if': *que no quiere venir, me lo dices* (better *si no quiere venir…*) 'if (s)he doesn't want to come, tell me'.

33.4.5 *Que* in indirect questions

Decir que may mean 'to ask'. *Que* is also used optionally after *preguntar* 'to ask':

—¿*Sabes lo que me dijo este animal de bellota?* —*Te dijo que si estaba la cena lista* (C. Rico-Godoy, Sp., dialogue complaining about husbands)	'Do you know what this pig (lit. 'acorn animal') said to/asked me?' 'He asked you if dinner/supper was ready'
Yo me pregunto (que) dónde estará ella estudiando	I wonder where she's studying
Le pregunté (que) qué hacía allí	I asked him/her what (s)he was doing there

33.4.6 Omission of conjunction *que*

Que is occasionally omitted, but much less often than the English 'that':

(**a**) if the following verb is in the subjunctive, and especially with the verb *rogar que* 'to request'. This construction is practically confined to business letters and other official language, but it is also found in sub-standard language. Foreigners should probably avoid it:

Les ruego envíen más información sobre la máquina de escribir ES 3 (advert., Sp.)	Please send more information about the ES 3 typewriter
No importa le tilden de bufón (popular press, Sp.; better *no importa que le tilden…*)	It doesn't matter if they dub him a clown
Solicitan se les solucione la deuda que mantiene el Estado con ellos (*La Prensa*, Panama)	They are requesting settlement of the debt the State has incurred towards them

(**b**) In relative clauses introduced by *que* so as to avoid excessive use of *que*. This is probably confined to written language (# marks the point of omission):

desde este punto de vista, que pienso # comparten muchos españoles	from this point of view, which I think many Spaniards share
Me contestó con una serie de argumentos que supongo # están de moda hoy día	(S)he replied with a series of arguments which I suppose are fashionable nowadays

33.4.7 Replacement of subordinating *que* by an infinitive

For a discussion of sentences like *dice estar enferma* 'she says she's ill' (for *dice que está enferma*) see 18.2.2.

33.4.8 Miscellaneous examples of *que*

The bracket indicates that the *que* is optional:

Qué bien (que) lo hemos pasado (the redundant *que* sounds uneducated)	What a nice time we've had
y él habla que habla (colloquial)	and he kept talking on and on
Yo venga a pedirle el divorcio y él que no (*venga a* is a colloquial Peninsular form suggesting constant repetition)	I kept on asking him for a divorce and he wouldn't have it/kept saying no

> *Lucho por conseguir comprensión, (que) no amor*
> I'm struggling to get understanding, not love
> *¡Tonto! Eran monos, (que) no alienígenas*
> Fool! They were monkeys, not aliens
> *¡Cuidado que sois pesados!*
> Heavens, are you a nuisance!

33.5 Causal conjunctions

The most common are:

porque because	*ya que* since	*en vista de que* in view
como since, as	*puesto que* since	of the fact that
pues for (= 'because')		

33.5.1 *Porque*

Porque means 'because'; *por qué*, spelt and pronounced differently (the *qué* is stressed), means 'why'. The noun *el porqué* means 'the reason why'. *Porque* may occasionally require the subjunctive: see 16.12.4b. The difference between *porque* 'because' and *por qué* 'why' is crucial:

> *No saben porque llegaron tarde*
> They don't know because they arrived late
> *No saben por qué llegaron tarde*
> They don't know why they arrived late

(i) *Porque* may be used as an alternative to *para que* after those words which allow *por*, e.g. *esforzarse por* 'to make an effort to...', *tener prisa por...* 'to be in a hurry to...' (see the section on *por* and *para*, 34.14). For the difference between *por qué* and *para qué* 'why' see 24.10.

(ii) *Por* is intimately associated with the idea of cause, e.g. *te lo mereces, por tonto* 'serves you right for being stupid', *se perdieron por no haber comprado un mapa* 'they got lost as a result of not having bought a map'. See 34.14.4 for more examples.

(iii) *Porque* and *por qué* can never be used to translate 'that's why' or 'that's the reason why'; see 36.2.4.

33.5.2 *Como, ya que, puesto que, que, en vista de que*

All of these may mean 'since', i.e. 'in view of the fact that'. *Que* is discussed under 33.4.

> *Puesto/Ya que quieres que me vaya, me voy*
> Since you want me to go, I'm leaving
> *La reunión se aplazó en vista de que no vino casi nadie*
> The meeting was postponed in view of the fact that hardly anybody turned up

When *como* is used to mean 'since'/'because' it can appear only at the head of the phrase it refers to. **Yo no comía como no tenía apetito* is not Spanish, but *como no tenía apetito, yo no comía* 'as I had no appetite, I didn't eat' is correct. Compare also *no lo hice como me dijiste* 'I didn't do it the way you told me to', and *no lo hice, como me lo dijiste* (from *Libro de estilo de El País*) 'I didn't do it, just as you told me' (i.e. 'because you told me not to'). Further examples:

Es de peor educación todavía insinuar que, como soy una mujer, se supone que no soy nadie (C. Rico-Godoy, Sp., dialogue)	It's even more ill-mannered to hint that, since I'm a woman, it's assumed that I'm nobody
Como se sentía cansado y no quería que le molestaran, les ordenó que escribieran una composición (S. Galindo, Mex.)	As he was feeling tired and didn't want them to bother him, he told them (the schoolchildren) to write an essay

(i) *Desde que* is found in Latin America with the meaning *ya que*. Its standard meaning is 'since' as in *desde que los vi* 'since (the moment when) I saw them'.

(ii) The form *como que* for *ya que* 'since'/'as', when placed before the main verb, should generally be avoided. Seco (1998), 118, censures it as a Catalanism; *como* alone should be used: *como no es posible no podemos hacerlo*, 'since it is not possible, we cannot do it', not ?*como que no es posible*…. Placed after the main verb it is, however, found on both continents as an alternative to *como* = 'since': *ella lo siguió encontrando todo muy natural y como que empezó a tomarme afecto*... (A. Bryce Echenique, Pe.) 'she continued to find everything very natural, and since she had started to grow fond of me...'.

However, when used emphatically it may, in colloquial Spanish and usually with an ironic tone, introduce an explanation of a fact: *claro que es verdad. ¡Como que lo he dicho yo!* 'of course it's true. *I* said it!'

(iii) *Como* with the subjunctive translates 'if' in conditional sentences; see 25.8.2. Occasionally *como* meaning 'since' occurs with a *–ra* verb form, as in —*Quizá —dijo Víctor. Y como Arturo no replicara, añadió—: Bueno, me subo* (M. Delibes, Sp.) '"Perhaps," Victor said. And as Arturo didn't reply, he added '"OK, I'm getting in"' (i.e. *ya que…/puesto que… + replicó*).

(iv) *Comoquiera* is occasionally used in literature to mean 'since'/'as': *Lucrecia se detuvo para observar mi reacción. Comoquiera que yo permanecía impasible, prosiguió…* (L. Silva, Sp.) 'Lucrecia paused to watch my reaction. As I remained impassive, she continued…'.

33.5.3 *Pues*

Pues has numerous uses.

(**a**) *Pues* meaning 'because':

Just as 'for' is a flowery variant for 'because' in English, *pues* may be an elegant written variation on *porque* when used by a stylist: *la voz no se sabe si es femenina o de hombre, pues es aguda, verdaderamente penetrante* (J.-M. Arguedas, Pe.) 'one can't tell whether the voice is a woman's or a man's, for it is high-pitched, truly piercing'. But non-natives should stick to *porque, ya que* or *puesto que*: Gili y Gaya (1972), 15, warns that 'discovery of causal *pues* as a way of adding a certain literary flourish to one's style is typical of writing between childhood and adolescence. This phase does not usually last long'.

(**b**) 'In that case...'. This use is very frequent in everyday speech:

—*No queremos comer ahora.* —*Pues, cuando ustedes quieran...* (or *entonces/en ese caso*)	'We don't want to eat now.' 'In that case, whenever you like...'
—*No quiero estar aquí.* —*Pues vete*	'I don't want to be here.' 'Go away, then'

(c) Like the English 'well', it may tone down an answer to a question, adding a modest or tentative note or perhaps showing that the speaker has thought for a moment before answering:

—*¿En qué situación se encuentran las* 'What is the state of the negotiations
  negociaciones entre los dos gobiernos? between the two governments?'
—*Pues, el hecho es que no hay* 'Well, the fact is, there are no
  negociaciones (Cambio16, Sp.) negotiations'
—*¿Quiénes estaban? —Pues... Manuel,* 'Who was there?' 'Er... Manuel,
  Antonio, Mariluz... Antonio, Mariluz...'

(d) It may add emphasis or a note of contradiction:

—*Yo creía que estaba enfermo. —Pues no* 'I thought he was ill.' 'Well he isn't'
No, si ya me figuro dónde está ¡Pues me No, I can well imagine where she is.
  va a oír! (A. Buero Vallejo, Sp., Well, she's going to hear what I've
  dialogue) got to say!

(i) In some parts of Latin America and Northern Spain, conversation is sprinkled with *pues*: *oye pues, vámonos pues,* etc.

(ii) Students of French should not confuse *pues* with *puis,* which means *después, entonces* or *luego.*

33.6 Concession

33.6.1 Phrases that introduce concessions ('although', etc.)

The main ways of introducing a concession are as follows (forms marked with a dagger are typical of literary language):

aunque/bien que/y eso que/así/aun cuando/ although/even though/even in the
  si bien event that
a pesar de que/pese a que†/por más que/a despite the fact that
  despecho de que
por mucho que however much

All of these, except *y eso que* and *si bien,* may appear with the subjunctive and are discussed at 16.12.9. *Por mucho que* is discussed at 16.13.2.

33.6.2 *Y eso que* and *si bien*

Y eso que 'although', does not take the subjunctive. It can only refer to events that are realities, i.e. it means 'despite the fact that': *no la reconocí, y eso que la había visto dos días antes* 'I didn't recognise her although/despite the fact that I'd seen her two days before':

...y eso que no leo novelas eróticas (A. ...despite the fact that I don't read
  Bryce Echenique, Pe.) erotic novels
—*Qué paz se respira aquí —dijo* 'It's so peaceful here,' she said.
—*Y eso que es el gran pueblo de la* 'Despite the fact that it's the main
  comarca —anoté (L. Silva, Sp., town of the region,' I added
  dialogue)

Y eso que cannot come before the main clause: **y eso que es profesora, no sabe contar* 'despite the fact that she's a teacher, she can't count' is wrong. *A pesar de ser profesora, no sabe...*or *no sabe contar, y eso que es profesora.*

Si bien is rather literary in style and is used like *y eso que* to refer only to an established fact (i.e. it cannot refer to the future). Unlike *y eso que*, *si bien* can, however, appear at the start of a sentence:

Si bien la lluvia es frecuente, el verano inglés es a menudo agradable	Despite the fact that rain is frequent, the English summer is often pleasant
Si bien el Programa de Riesgos Profesionales muestra un superávit de 150 millones de dólares... (*La Prensa*, Panama)	Despite the fact that the Professional Indemnities programme has 150 million dollars in reserve...

The commonest word for 'although' is *aunque*, discussed at 16.12.9.

33.7 Condition and exception

(a) The main conjunctions of condition are (all can be translated as 'provided that'/'as long as'):

con tal (de) que	*siempre que*	*como*
a condición de que	*siempre y cuando*	
bajo (la) condición de que	*mientras (no)*	

All of these require the subjunctive and are discussed under 16.12.8a.

(b) The main conjunctions of exception are:

a menos que	*a no ser que*	*fuera de que*
excepto que/salvo que	*como no*	*si no* (if not)

All of these mean 'unless' and are discussed at 16.12.8b since they may require the subjunctive.

33.8 Subordinating conjunctions of purpose and aim

The most common are:

(a) 'in order that'/'so that'

para que	*de modo que*[†]	*a fin de que*
de manera que[†]	*a que*	*con el objeto de que*
porque	*de forma que*[†]	

(b) lest/in order that not...

no sea que...	*no fuera que.../no fuese que...*

All conjunctions of purpose require the subjunctive and are discussed under 16.12.3. Those marked with daggers may also indicate result and are then followed by the indicative. See 16.12.5 for discussion.

33.9 Subordinating conjunctions of result

Subordinators that express manner can denote either a result or an aim; in the latter case they take the subjunctive. *Conque* and *así que* indicate results: *conque ha sido ella* 'so it was her', *así que no he vuelto* 'so I haven't gone back'. *De modo que*, *de manera que*, *de forma que* can express results or aims; in the latter case they take the subjunctive. All are discussed under 16.12.5, but it should be noted that the phrases *de **tal** modo que, de **tal** manera que, de **tal** forma que* can only express result, not purpose: *gritó de tal modo/manera/forma que todos los vecinos se asomaron a la ventana* '(s)he shouted in such a way that all the neighbo(u)rs leaned out of their windows'.

33.10 Subordinating conjunctions of time

These include such words and phrases as:

a la vez que at the same time as	*antes de que* before	*nada más que* as soon as
a partir del momento en que from the moment that	*apenas* scarcely	*no bien (que)* scarcely
	así que as soon as	*siempre que* whenever/as long as
a poco de que shortly after	*cada vez que* every time that	*tan pronto como* as soon as
al mismo tiempo at the same time as	*cuando* when	*una vez que* once/as soon as
	después de que after	
al poco rato de que shortly after	*en cuanto* as soon as	
	en tanto que as long as	
	hasta que until	
	mientras while/as long as	

All subordinators of time require the subjunctive in certain circumstances (*antes de que* always takes the subjunctive). They are discussed at 16.12.7. For further remarks on *cuando* 'when' see 24.8.

33.11 Discourse markers

Discourse markers (called 'connectors' in the previous edition of this book) are words used to link what has been said to what is about to be said. The colloquial variants listed below reflect Peninsular usage, and the list is not exhaustive. Many conjunctions mentioned in the first part of this chapter and in Chapter 16 could have been included here but are dealt with elsewhere. These are:

antes que rather than (16.12.7)	*conque* so...(16.12.5a)
a pesar de, pese a in spite of (16.12.9)	*o/u* or (33.2)
aunque, y eso que, si bien although, even though (16.12.9, 33.6.2)	*pero, sino, mas* but (33.1)
	porque, pues, como because (33.5.1, 16.12.4)
con tal de que, bajo la condición de que and similar phrases, 'provided that' (33.7, 16.12.8)	*que/de que* that (33.4)
	y/e and (33.3
a menos que unless (16.12.8b, 25.9b)	*ya que, puesto que* since (33.5.2)

33.11.1. Afterthoughts

The standard ways of introducing an afterthought or some apparently digressive remark are *a propósito* and *por cierto*, which both mean 'by the way'/'incidentally': *a propósito/por cierto vi a tu madre ayer* 'by the way, I saw your mother yesterday'. *Por cierto* is slightly more colloquial than *a propósito*; it does not mean 'for certain'. *A propósito* can also mean *adrede* 'on purpose'.

A todo esto is another, colloquial, equivalent of 'incidentally'.

33.11.2. Addition

There are several sentence-openers that indicate the speaker's intention of adding new information, e.g. *además*, *es más* 'moreover', *encima* 'moreover' / 'on top of that', *por lo demás* 'apart from that':

Por lo demás no tengo más que decirte	Apart from that, I haven't got anything else to tell you
Es más, también se lo dije a su hermano	Moreover, I also told his brother
Además, mi mujer era mecanógrafa (G. Cabrera Infante, Cu., dialogue)	Moreover, my wife was a typist
Encima no nos han dado el contrato	On top of everything they haven't given us the contract

33.11.3 Qualification, reservation

There are a number of ways of indicating that what precedes is not a complete explanation of the facts or is not the whole truth:

(**a**) *Sin embargo* 'nevertheless' / 'still…' / 'however' / 'in spite of that' occurs in speech and in writing. *No obstante* means the same thing, but is confined to writing. *Empero* also means 'nevertheless', but is highly literary, even archaic.

Sin embargo a los extranjeros, y especialmente a los españoles, les gusta Montevideo (M. Benedetti, Ur.)	Nevertheless foreigners, and especially Spaniards, like Montevideo
Estaban muy cansados. Sin embargo/no obstante tenían que acabarlo	They were very tired. Nevertheless/in spite of that they had to finish it
Empero lo más importante es que se inicia un proceso para eliminar "la joroba de pagos" (*La Reforma*, Mex.)	Nevertheless, the most important thing is that a process is being initiated to eliminate the debt burden (lit. 'payments hassle')

(**b**) In colloquial language, the word *bueno* is much used to express scepticism when combined with a sceptical intonation, e.g. 'that's as may be, but…': —*Es que no pude venir a clase ayer porque tenía gripe* —*Bueno, te has recuperado muy rápidamente…* 'I couldn't come to class yesterday because I had the flu.' 'Well, you got over it pretty quickly.'

(**c**) A colloquial way of saying 'however' is *pero, bueno…*: *no tenemos mucho dinero, pero, bueno, tenemos que pagar nuestras deudas* 'we don't have a lot of money, but still, we have to pay our debts'.

(**d**) Colloquially, *mira que* can express the idea of 'nevertheless': *las asistentas siempre se me van, y mira que las trato bien* 'My home-helps always walk out on me, despite the fact that I always treat them well'. The phrase is quite strong: 'but I'm telling you' or 'and mind you…' might be better translations.

33.11.4 Dismissing or downgrading information

Words meaning 'anyway' essentially indicate that the speaker has chosen to disregard some aspect of the previous information. They express some variant on the theme 'it doesn't matter…'.

Phrases like *de todas formas/maneras*, *sea como sea*, are usual in all styles; *sea como fuere* is very literary. Colloquially, 'anyway' can be expressed by *bueno*, which has numerous uses as a discourse marker, most of them differentiated by intonation. *Nada*, sometimes combined with *bueno*, is also much used in spoken Peninsular Spanish to discount information previously received: *(Bueno,) de todos modos/de todas formas, llámame mañana* 'anyway, call me tomorrow', *—Es que nunca está aquí los viernes. —(Bueno,) nada, volveré el lunes* '"(S)he's never here on Fridays." "Never mind, I'll come back on Monday".'

33.11.5 Resumption

The effect of these words is to carry on or draw a conclusion from what has previously been said.

(a) The most common are *de modo que, de manera que, de forma que, así que, conque* (colloquial), *o sea que*. They all mean 'so' in the sense of 'carrying on from what I just said', 'as a result' or 'in other words' (especially *o sea que*):

De modo/forma/manera que, como íbamos diciendo…	So, as we were saying…
De forma que lo extraordinario se ha convertido en ordinario (M. F. Álvarez, Sp.)	So the extraordinary has become ordinary
Así que/O sea que, en lugar de dejarlo allí, te lo llevaste	So/In other words, instead of leaving it there, you took it with you
Conque lo que pasó fue eso…	So what happened was that…

(b) *Bueno*, without a sceptical intonation, is much used in spoken, but not written Spanish, to show that the speaker has taken previous remarks into account before continuing. Its rough equivalent is 'right…'/'OK…'/'fine…': *bueno, yo no sabía todo eso, y si las cosas están así, me voy…* 'right/OK/fine, I didn't know all that, and if that's the way things are, I'm going…', *—Es que no he podido terminarlo. —Bueno, tendrás que dejarlo para mañana* '"I wasn't able to finish it…." "Right/OK, you'll have to leave it until tomorrow".'

33.11.6 Emphasis and insistence

There are various ways of driving home a point.

(a) *En realidad, realmente* are like the English 'really' or 'actually': they indicate that the speaker is about to reveal the 'real' facts: *en realidad/realmente este tipo de argumento no viene al caso* 'in fact/in reality/to tell the truth, this type of argument is irrelevant'.

(b) *De hecho* means 'the fact is': *de hecho es como si fuera mi padre* 'in fact it's just as if he were my father'.

(c) *Ahora bien* is like the English 'now' used to insist on the following statement as something that may not yet have been fully taken into account. It is used more than its English equivalent: *ahora bien, hay que insistir en que los ejércitos de la Monarquía Católica estaban integrados por soldados de muy diversas nacionalidades* (M. Fernández Álvarez, Sp.) 'now, it must be stressed that the armies of the Catholic Monarchy consisted of soldiers of different nationalities'.

(**d**) Colloquially, Spanish makes much use of the formula *es que...* which conveys the idea of 'the fact is...' but is used mainly when offering expanations: *—Te llamé pero no contestaste.—Es que/El hecho es que no dormí en casa* '"I called you but I couldn't get an answer." "The fact is/The thing is that I didn't sleep at home".'

33.11.7 Summing up

There are several ways of summarizing the previous information.

(**a**) *En resumen* and *en suma* are literary phrases meaning 'in short'/'to sum up...':

En suma, todo cuanto pueda hacerle ganar en prestigio lo cuidará al máximo (M. Fernández Álvarez, Sp.)	In short, he'll be extremely careful about anything that can enhance his prestige
En resumen, las cifras de este año son marcadamente inferiores a las del año pasado	To sum up, this year's figures are markedly lower than last year's

(**b**) *Total* can be thought of as a colloquial equivalent of *en resumen*. It indicates that the speaker has decided to get to the point. English often uses a slightly impatient 'anyway' in a similar way: *total, se levanta y se va* 'to cut a long story short/anyway, (s)he gets up and walks out', *total, has metido la pata* 'in a word, you've put your foot in it'.

(**c**) *En fin* is constantly used, but its meaning is, like *total*, rather indefinable. It means 'well' when this introduces a conclusion arrived at after a certain amount of thought. There are several English possibilities:

En fin, a mí me sigue pareciendo que es como si Sherlock Holmes resolviera sus casos acudiendo a la Interpol (J. A. Marina, Sp., dialogue)	Well, it still seems to me like Sherlock Holmes solving his cases by calling in Interpol
En fin, lo que me estás diciendo es no que has perdido el dinero sino que te lo has gastado	OK/Right, what you're telling me is that you haven't lost the money but you've spent it

33.11.8 Contradiction

These words show that the speaker does not agree with the previous information:

(**a**) *Por el contrario, al contrario* are standard equivalents of 'on the contrary'. *Por el contrario* is rather literary: *—¿Te encuentras mal? —Por el/Al contrario, estoy estupendamente* '"Are you feeling ill?" "On the contrary, I feel great".'

(**b**) *Qué va* is a colloquial phrase expressing strong disagreement: *—Es que es riquísima —Qué va, no tiene donde caerse muerta* '"She's really rich." "The heck she is. She hasn't got a cent"' (lit. 'she hasn't got anywhere to drop dead on').

(**c**) *De ninguna manera* expresses strong refusal, and is common in all styles. *De eso nada* is a colloquial phrase that conveys the same idea (cf. 'no way...'): *—¿Puedo pagarte por/a plazos? —De ninguna manera/De eso nada* '"Can I pay you by installments?" "Certainly not."'

(d) *Oye* (*oiga* to a stranger or person held in special respect) is commonly used colloquially, above all in Spain, to reject an implication: *oye, si ya lo he pagado* '(I'm telling you) I've already paid'. It is constantly put at the end of statements in familiar speech (at least in Spain), *(si) ya lo he pagado, oye*, but some informants said this sounds 'common'.

¡Oye! (or, respectfully, *¡oiga!*) can also be used to call someone's attention, and it is not rude if the intonation is friendly—at least in Spain. But it may sound abrupt to Latin Americans.

(e) The word *si*, which usually means 'if', is much used on both continents to disapprove of previous information (see also 31.4.8): *—Te tienes que levantar. —¡Si sólo son las cinco y media!* '"You've got to get up." "It's only five-thirty, for heaven's sake!"'

(f) *Tampoco* is often used colloquially to play down certain types of statement, as in *tampoco es para tanto* 'come on, it's not such a big deal'. See 23.5.9 note (ii).

(g) The words *ca* or *quia* used to be used, in Spain, until the late 1940s, to mean 'certainly not'. They now seem to be all but extinct.

33.11.9 Contrast

Various words and phrases imply contrast, like the English 'on the other hand'.

Por otra parte is one equivalent of 'on the other hand': *por otra parte es posible pensar que tiene razón* 'on the other hand, it's possible to think that (s)he's right'.

En cambio/Por el contrario can have a similar meaning but are more often used to express difference or contrast: *Ella le/lo adora, en cambio/sin embargo/por el contrario, él no la puede ver* 'she adores him; on the other hand/however, he can't stand her', *en cambio, cabe suponer que nunca hubo vida en Marte* 'on the other hand, there is room to suppose that life never existed on Mars'.

33.11.10 Consequence and result

These words and phrases show that what follows is the result of what preceded.

(a) *Por (lo) tanto, por consiguiente, en/como consecuencia* all mean 'as a result' and are all typical of formal styles: *por lo tanto, estamos ante otro instrumento de la Monarquía de los Austrias* (M. Fernández Álvarez, Sp.) 'here we have, therefore, another of the tools used by the (royal house of the) Austrias', *la inflación sigue aumentando. Por (lo) tanto/Por consiguiente/Como consecuencia, habrá que pensar en un incremento de los tipos de interés* 'inflation continues to rise. As a result, it will be necessary to think of an increase in interest rates'.

(b) *Por ende* 'hence' is archaic, but is occasionally resurrected for stylistic effect. It could have replaced *por consiguiente* in the previous example, but the result would have sounded pompous.

(c) *De modo que, de forma que, así que, con que*, can all also mean 'hence', 'as a result'. They are discussed above at 33.11.5.

(**d**) *Por eso...* 'that's why...' is much used in everyday language in all styles: *por eso las generalizaciones no sólo son absurdas y peligrosas, sino indefectiblemente inexactas* (J. Marías, Sp.) 'that's why generalizations are not only absurd and dangerous, they are also inevitably inaccurate'. *Por esta razón* 'that's why' has the same meaning.

(**e**) *Entonces*, as well as meaning 'then' in the sense of 'just after', is much used to introduce a conclusion: *¿te gusto entonces?* (G. Cabrera Infante, Cu., dialogue) 'do you like me then?', *entonces ¿estamos de acuerdo?* 'so, are we in agreement?'.

(**f**) *Pues* is discussed elsewhere, and it can mean 'because' in literary language; see 33.5.3. It is constantly used in colloquial language to introduce conclusions: *—No me gusta la forma. —Pues cámbialo* '"I don't like the shape." "Then change it"', *pues eso mismo te iba a decir* 'that's just what I was going to tell you'.

33.11.11 Agreement

There are numerous ways of agreeing with the previous information or of asserting something as self-evident.

(**a**) *Claro* is probably the most common, and is found in all styles, although it is slightly colloquial: *claro, no me avisaste con tiempo, no pude ir* 'of course you didn't warn me in time, I couldn't go', *claro que si no quieres venir, no vengas* 'obviously if you don't want to come, don't come'. Sometimes it makes *sí* 'yes' unnecessary: *—¿Puedo pasar unos días en tu casa? —Hombre, claro, cuando quieras* '"can I stay a few days with you?" "Yes, of course, any time you want"'.
   Está claro (Latin America *es claro*) is discussed at 29.2.5.

(**b**) *Desde luego* means 'of course' and is in daily use, at least in Spain: *desde luego, si quieres entrar tendrás que pagar* 'obviously, if you want to go in you'll have to pay'.

(**c**) *En efecto* and *efectivamente* both signify agreement with what has preceded: *en efecto/efectivamente todos estaban de acuerdo conmigo* 'they were indeed all in agreement with me'. *—Bueno, estamos fastidiados. —Efectivamente/En efecto* '"Well, we've had it/we're in trouble." "You're right."'

(**d**) *Ya* has many uses, listed at 31.7.1. It is often used to indicate agreement with the previous statement, although spoken sarcastically it can mean the exact opposite: *—Es que hay que darle un nombre al fichero antes de guardarlo. —Ya* '"You have to give the file a name before saving it." "Right/OK/I see"', *—Es que soy más listo que tú —Ya, ya...* '"I'm smarter than you." "Yeah, sure..."'.

(**e**) *De verdad* insists on the truth of a statement, rather like *en serio* 'seriously': *de verdad te lo digo que estoy loca por él* 'I'm telling you, I'm really mad about him'. *A decir verdad* 'to tell the truth...' has a similar meaning.

34

Prepositions

In this chapter prepositions are treated in alphabetical order and special emphasis has been given to aspects of prepositional usage likely to be unfamiliar to English-speakers. The following prepositions are discussed:

a 'to', 'at' 34.1	*contra* 'against' 34.6	*hacia* 'towards' 34.11	*sin* 'without' 34.16
ante, delante de 'in front of', 'faced with' 34.2	*de* 'of', 'from' 34.7 *desde* 'from' 34.7.5	*hasta* 'until', 'as far as' 34.12	*sobre* 'over', 'on', 'about' 34.17
bajo, debajo de 'beneath', 'underneath' 34.3	*durante* 'during' 34.8	*mediante* 'by means of' 34.13	*tras, detrás de* 'after', 'behind' 34.18
cabe (archaic) 'next to' 34.4	*en* 'in', 'on', 'at' 34.9	*para* & *por* 'for', 'because of', etc. 34.14	
con 'with' 34.5	*entre* 'between', 'among' 34.10	*según* 'according to' 34.15	

Many of these can be combined with other words to form prepositional phrases such as *debajo de* 'underneath', *frente a* 'opposite', *a razón de* 'at the rate of', etc. A list of common prepositional phrases is included at 34.19.

Spanish prepositions call for a number of general remarks.

(i) They appear only immediately before noun phrases (nouns, adjectives plus nouns, pronouns, infinitives: *en la casa, con muchos amigos, sin ella, para la que…, de fumar*, etc.). This makes English structures like 'which shop did you buy that **in**?' impossible in Spanish: *¿en qué tienda compraste eso?*, never ***¿qué tienda compraste eso en?*; *la película de la que estoy hablando* 'the film I'm talking **about**', never ***la película que estoy hablando de.*

Grammarians therefore dislike sentences like ?*la cerámica es hecha por y para los mismos habitantes del pueblo* 'the pottery is made by and for the villagers themselves', since the *por* stands in front of a conjunction, *y*: they prefer *…es hecha por los habitantes del pueblo y para ellos mismos.* Similarly, 'I'll go with or without you' is *iré contigo o sin ti*, not **iré con o sin ti.* But this rule is broken in many phrases, e.g. *el tráfico aéreo desde y hacia Madrid* 'air traffic to and from Madrid'. The 'correct' *tráfico aéreo hacia Madrid y desde él* is hopelessly long-winded.

On the other hand, omission of prepositions should be avoided: **personas acusadas de pertenecer y colaborar con el movimiento terrorista* 'persons accused of belonging and collaborating with the terrorist movement' sounds bad in both languages: *…acusadas de pertenecer al movimiento terrorista y de colaborar con él* is correct, *…pertenecer a y colaborar con el movimiento terrorista* may offend purists. However, *entraban y salían del edificio* 'they entered and left the building' is nowadays usual, and, as García Yebra (*Claudicación en el uso de las preposiciones*, Madrid, Gredos, 1988, 243ff) points out, no one would say **un billete de ida a Segovia y de vuelta de ella* for *un billete de ida y vuelta a Segovia* 'a round trip to Segovia'/'a return ticket to Segovia'.

(ii) English is very precise about location and direction; Spanish is often quite vague. The subtle differences between colloquial English prepositions of space, as in 'I'm going to/across to/round to/down to/up to/over to the shops' are virtually untranslatable: *voy a las tiendas*.

(iii) English constantly joins nouns by prepositions as a way of avoiding relative clauses: '*the train to New York* has arrived' is short for 'the train (that is) going to New York has arrived', 'I've read *the book on the table*' = '...the book that is on the table'.

English-speakers therefore write and say things like ?*el tren a Nueva York ha llegado*, ?*he leído el libro en la mesa*; but this usually makes poor Spanish unless there is a verb to support the preposition, as in **iba** en el tren **a** Madrid, **puse** el libro **en** la mesa. Lack of space prevents a more detailed discussion of this complex topic, but the best rule for beginners is: when an English phrase consisting of a noun + preposition + noun could be expressed by a relative clause, use a relative clause in Spanish unless the preposition is *de*:

Good Spanish	**Compressed English equivalent**
La casa que está en la colina es de mi madre (or *la casa de la colina es...*)	The house on the hill is my mother's
El avión que va a Lima ha salido ya (or *el avión para Lima...*)	The plane to Lima has already left
El hombre que iba en el coche era mi tío	The man in the car was my uncle
He leído el libro que está en la mesa	I've read the book on the table
Los hombres de Ruritania son muy guapos	The men in Ruritania are very good-looking
El perro que está debajo de la mesa es del vecino	The dog under the table is the neighbo(u)r's

These are much better Spanish than ?*la casa en la colina...*, ?*el avión a Lima...*, ?*el hombre en el coche...*, ?*...el libro en la mesa*, ?*los hombres en Ruritania...*, ?*El perro debajo de la mesa...*. However, when the preposition does not indicate the place where something is located, the construction often makes perfectly normal Spanish: *un café con leche, un viaje a la Luna, gasolina sin plomo* 'unleaded petrol/US gas', *los pasajeros sin billete* 'passengers without tickets'. Further remarks are included under the individual prepositions discussed in this chapter.

34.1 A

This very common preposition has many uses. Apart from the problems they have with personal *a* before certain kinds of direct object (discussed in Chapter 22), English-speakers tend to misuse it when translating phrases like 'at the dentist's', 'at Cambridge', 'at the station'. See (**c**) for discussion.

(**a**) Motion, to, at, up, down, etc.

Almost any verb or noun indicating motion is likely to be followed by *a*. As a result its meaning includes 'on', 'into', 'onto', 'down', 'up', as well as 'to' and 'at':

Por fin llegaron a Managua	They finally got to Managua
Fui a/para que me diera hora	I went to make an appointment
Se acercó al buzón	(S)he approached the letter box
Me subí al coche/al tren	I got into the car/on the train
El gato se subió a un árbol	The cat ran up a tree
Lanzaban piedras a/contra las ventanas	They were throwing stones at the windows
Arrojó la espada al aire	(S)he hurled the sword into the air
Salieron a/para dar batalla	They went out to do battle
He venido a/para/por hablar con usted	I've come to talk to you
Lo pegó al/en el sobre	(S)he stuck it on the envelope
Cuélgaselo al cuello	Hang it round his neck
(cf. *cuélgalo **en** la pared*	hang it on the wall)
Cayó al suelo/al mar	It fell to the ground, into the sea
una expedición a Marte	an expedition to Mars
salida a la calle	way out to the street
tiro al blanco	target shooting

(i) *A* is omitted after verbs of motion before *aquí, acá, ahí, allí, allá*: *ven aquí/ven acá/ven para acá* 'come here', *allá voy/voy para allá* 'I'm going there'.

(ii) Spain *entrar en el cuarto*, Latin America *entró **al** cuarto* '(s)he entered the room', the latter sometimes heard also in Spain. The noun *entrada* (and *salida*) takes *a*: *entrada a la galería* 'entrance to the gallery', *salida a la calle* 'exit to the street'. Spain also prefers *en* with *penetrar* 'penetrate', *ingresar* 'to join (club, etc.)', *introducir* 'to insert', but *a* is common in Latin America, cf. *ingresa como adepto laico a la orden* (J. L. Borges, Arg.) 'he entered (historic present) the order as a lay follower'.

(iii) *A* should not be used to join nouns when motion is implied: *el tren que va a Madrid*, not ?*el tren a Madrid* (see the introduction to this chapter, iii), unless the noun itself implies motion, as in *un viaje a la Luna* 'a journey to the Moon', *vuelos a La Paz* 'flights to La Paz'.

(**b**) Direction 'at':

Mira al techo y no te entrará agua en los ojos	Look up at the ceiling and you won't get water in your eyes
Apunta a la bombilla	Aim at the light bulb

Spanish differentiates *mirar a* 'to look towards/in the direction of' and *mirar* 'to look at', cf. *mira este cuadro con detenimiento* 'look at this painting attentively' and *mira a la derecha/a la izquierda* 'look to the right/to the left'.

(**c**) After verbs of giving, sending, informing, etc.:

Dáselo a papá	Give it to father
Le envié cien dólares a mi hijo	I sent my son $100
Comunicaremos los datos a los aseguradores	We will inform the insurers of the details

(**d**) Place (static):

The use of the preposition *a* to indicate 'at' or 'in' a place is limited in Spanish. English-speakers—particularly those who know French, German or Italian—must not use *a* in sentences like *estoy haciendo mis estudios en Cambridge* 'I'm studying *at* Cambridge', *te esperaré en la estación* 'I'll wait for you *at* the station (cf. *à la gare, am Bahnhof, alla stazione*, etc.), *vive en Londres* '(s)he lives in London' (*il habite à Londres*), etc. Apart from set phrases like *al lado de* 'at the side of', *a la luz de* 'in the light of', *a* can only be used with a few nouns like *vuelta*, 'turn', 'return' (*a mi vuelta de* 'on my return from'), *salida* 'exit', *entrada* 'entrance' which denote actions or moments in time rather than places. *Os esperaré a la salida* is best thought of as 'I'll wait for you on the way out' rather than 'at the exit', which is *en la salida*.

In phrases like *estaba asomado a la ventana* 'he was leaning in/out of the window' *asomar* is a verb of motion: *estaba en la ventana* is, however, safer than *estaba a la ventana* '(s)he was at the window'. Similarly, *fue a estudiar a Oxford* is only a variant of *fue a Oxford a estudiar* '(s)he went to Oxford to study': it does not mean '(s)he went to study *at* Oxford' – ...*en Oxford.*

A is used to translate 'at' in a number of situations involving close proximity to an object, e.g. *a la barra* 'at the bar', *a la mesa* 'at table'; but note *se sienta en una mesa de la calle y pide una cerveza* 'he sits down *at* a table in the street and asks for a beer' (J. Cortázar, Arg.).

Vivo a la vuelta	I live round the corner
a orillas del mar	on the seashore
Oí pasos a mi espalda	I heard footsteps at my back
Se pasa horas sentada al ordenador	She spends hours sitting at the computer
Se arrodilló a los pies de la Virgen	(S)he knelt at the feet of the Virgin
Está con el agua al cuello	(S)he's up to his neck (in troubles: *hasta* implies real water)
a la izquierda/derecha de	to the left/right of (cf. *a diestro y siniestro* 'to right and left', i.e. 'on all sides')
a lo lejos/en la distancia	in the distance
Se sentaron al sol/a la luz/al calor del fuego/a la sombra/al amparo de un roble	They sat in the sun/light/warmth of the fire/shade/in the shelter of an oak

Compare:

*Espérame **en** la parada del autobús*	Wait for me at the bus stop
*Estaba parado **en** un semáforo*	He was waiting at a traffic light
*Mario está **en** el banco*	Mario is at/in the bank
*Los niños están **en** el colegio*	The children are in/at school
(cf. *mi hijo todavía no va **al** colegio*)	my son isn't at school yet, (i.e. doesn't go yet)
...*para que el coche no estuviera tanto tiempo estacionado en la puerta* (G. García Márquez, Col. Refers to a horse-drawn carriage)	...so the carriage wouldn't be parked so long at the door

(i) *A la puerta* is also good Spanish for 'at the door', although we found that some Latin-American informants preferred *en*—but compare *Morelli habla del napolitano que se pasó años sentado a la puerta de su casa* (J. Cortázar, Arg.) 'Morelli speaks of the Neapolitan who spent years sitting at the door of his house'.

(ii) Spanish therefore has no prepositions that can differentiate 'he's at the hospital' and 'he's in (the) hospital': verbs are used instead—*ha ido al hospital* and *está en el hospital.*

(e) Manner (adverbial phrases of manner with *a* are numerous):

a pie/a mano/a lápiz	on foot/by hand/in pencil
a golpes/a tiros/a patadas	with blows/by shooting/with kicks
Pedía socorro a gritos	(S)he/I was shouting for help
un documento escrito a máquina	a typed document
El servicio es a voluntad del cliente	Service charge at the customer's discretion

Las patatas están a punto	The potatoes are done
Le cortaron el pelo al rape	They cropped his hair short
Estoy a dieta	I'm on a diet
a la buena de Dios	any old how/willy-nilly
a oscuras/a la luz del día	in the dark/by daylight
Las verduras se pueden guisar al vapor	Vegetables can be steamed
a la manera de Dickens	in the style of Dickens

The construction with *a* found in *sois dos a ganar* 'there are two of you earning', *ahora son cuatro a dormir* (J. Cercas, Sp.) 'there are four of them sleeping there now', may perhaps be included under this heading.

(f) In certain time phrases:

a las diez/a medianoche	at 10 o'clock/at midnight
Se cansa a los cinco minutos	(S)he gets tired after five minutes
Bonos del Estado a diez años	ten-year Government Bonds
Se casaron a los/con veinte años	They got married at the age of twenty
al día siguiente/al otro día	on the following day
a la mañana siguiente	the following morning
a la caída de la noche/al alba	at nightfall/at dawn
al mismo tiempo	at the same time
A su recepción pagaré la cantidad estipulada	On receipt I shall pay the stipulated amount
Estamos a miércoles/a quince	it's Wednesday/the fifteenth
tres veces al/por día	three times a day
Se enfada a/por la menor provocación	(S)he gets angry at the slightest provocation

A is particularly common in the construction *al* + infinitive, e.g. *al ver* 'on seeing', *al volverse* 'as (s)he turned round/back'. See 18.3.3.

A is also used to indicate a stage in some process, as in *a la segunda taza no aparece ya tan malo* (E. Tusquets, Sp.) 'it doesn't taste so bad by the time you get to the second cup', *a la tercera llamada del teléfono* 'when the phone rang for the third time'.

(i) One can say *a su muerte se dividió el reino en tres partes* 'at his death the kingdom was divided into three parts', but only *cuando nació. . .* 'at his birth. . .'.

(ii) Note the construction *ya deben estar al llegar* 'they must be about to arrive'.

(g) To translate 'of' or 'like' after verbs meaning 'smell', 'taste', 'sound', and also after the nouns derived from some of these:

Me suena a cuento chino	It sounds like a tall story to me
Esto sabe a pescado	This tastes of fish
Había un leve olor a fritura y a crema bronceadora (F. Umbral, Spain)	There was a faint smell of frying and suntan cream

and similarly after *oler a* 'to smell of' (*huele a quemado* 'there's a smell of burning'), *apestar a* 'to stink of'.

NB: In this construction two nouns can be joined by *a*, as in *sabor a ajo* 'taste of garlic'.

(h) 'Fitted with', 'propelled by':

Many grammarians have criticized *a* as a Gallicism in the following constructions, but most are normal in everyday language:

olla a presión/caldera a/de gas-oil	pressure cooker/oil-fired boiler
un suplemento a color (El País, Sp.; also *en color*)	a colo(u)r supplement

un avión a/de dos motores	a twin-engine plane
un coche que va a/por metanol	a methanol-powered car

The use of *a* before ingredients is occasionally seen in advertising language but it should not be imitated: *crema bronceadora a lanolina* 'suntan cream with lanolin' (better, and more usually nowadays, *con lanolina*).

(i) Rate, measure, speed, amount, distance:

Se vende a mil pesos el metro	It's on sale at 1000 pesos a metre
¿A cómo están las peras?	How much are the pears?
Volaba a más de dos mil kilómetros por hora	It was flying at more than 2000 km per hour
cambiar a razón de dos por uno	to change at the rate of two for one
Está a cinco manzanas (Lat. Am. *cuadras*)	it's five blocks away
si Vd. tiene un 80386 a 20 Mhz y un módem a 28.800 bps...(computer manual, Sp.)	if you have a 20-megaherz 80386 (computer) and a 28,800 bit-per-second modem...
a montones	in heaps
Trabaja a ratos/a veces	(S)he works now and again/sometimes

(j) It translates 'from' after a number of words with such meanings as 'steal', 'confiscate', 'buy', and after *oír* 'to hear':

Le robaron una sortija a mi tía	They stole a ring from my aunt
Le compró un coche a su vecino	(S)he bought a car from his/her neighbo(u)r
una banda de traficantes de drogas, a los que aprehendieron trece kilos de cocaína (*La Vanguardia*, Sp.)	a gang of drug-peddlers, from whom thirteen kilos of cocaine were confiscated
Eso se lo has oído a tu padre	You've heard that from your father

and similarly after *quitar* 'take away', *sustraer* 'steal', *confiscar* 'confiscate', *llevarse* 'take away', *sacar* 'to take out/remove', etc. However, *recibir* 'to receive', *adquirir* 'to acquire' and *aceptar* 'to accept' take *de*: *aceptar algo de alguien* 'to accept something from someone'.

(k) Before certain types of direct object (the so-called 'personal *a*', e.g. *vi al gitano* 'I saw the gypsy'). See Chapter 22 for detailed discussion.

(l) After verbs meaning 'begin', 'start', 'get ready to...':

Rompió a llorar/Echó a correr	(S)he burst into tears/(S)he broke into a run
El cielo empezaba a despejarse	The sky was beginning to clear

and after *comenzar a* 'to begin', *ponerse a* 'to start to', *prepararse a* 'to get ready to', *disponerse a* 'to prepare oneself to', *meterse a* 'to take up...', as in *no te metas a (p)sicoterapeuta con él, porque solamente complicarás las cosas* 'don't get into being a psychotherapist with him, because you'll only complicate things'.

(m) After numerous verbs, adjectives and adverbs which must be learned separately:

Aspiraba a hacerse médico	He was aiming to become a doctor
Acostumbraban a hacerlo	They habitually did it
Tienes que hacerte al trabajo	You have to get used to the work
Prefiero una vida mediocre a ser héroe	I prefer a mediocre life to being a hero
El viejo argumento de que la religión sirve de freno a los instintos	The old argument that religion serves as a curb on the instincts

Pude salvarme agarrándome a/de un árbol	I managed to save myself by clinging to a tree
No hay otro igual a él	There is no other equal to him
Tenía el jersey liado en torno a la cintura	(S)he had his/her jersey tied round his/her waist
Tendían emboscadas al enemigo	They were laying ambushes for the enemy

and other verbs, listed at 18.2.3 and 22.11.

(**n**) To link two nouns whenever ambiguity might arise from the use of *de*: *el amor de Dios* = 'God's love' or 'love of God' and *el amor a Dios* = only 'love for God'; often either preposition is possible. *A* is also often used to link two nouns when a common verbal phrase exists which also requires *a*, e.g. *les tiene miedo a los toros* '(s)he's afraid of bulls', *su miedo a los toros* 'his fear of bulls':

el abrazo de un padre a su hijo	the embrace that a father gives to his son
el amor a la patria	love for one's home country
el respeto a la autoridad	respect for authority
Lo denunciaron como traidor a/de su clase	They denounced him as a traitor to his class
La Casa Blanca confirmó el boicot a los Juegos de Moscú (*Cambio16*, Sp.)	The White House confirmed the boycott of the Moscow Games
Insinué algo en el prólogo al libro de Lafaye. . . (O. Paz, Mex.; *del* possible)	I hinted something in the prologue to Lafaye's book. . .
Espero que no sea una referencia a mí	I hope it's not a reference to me
El culto al sol tendría sus ventajas	Sun-worship would have its advantage
El departamento se encargará de la protección a/de la carretera	The department will take over responsibility for protecting roads

With words like *miedo* 'fear' or *amor* 'love' one can use either *a* or *de* if no ambiguity arises, cf. *así que tiene miedo de las cucarachas* (C. Martín Gaite, Sp., dialogue; or *a*) 'so you're afraid of cockroaches…'.

34.2 *Ante* and *delante de*

'Before' (i.e. 'in front of') or 'in the presence of' and, like the English 'before', it can in literary (not spoken) Spanish mean the same as *delante de*: *me eché en la cama ante la televisión* (J. Marías, Sp.) 'I lay down on the bed in front of the television', *ante el negro y el niño había dos tazas de chocolate* (J. L. Borges, Arg.) 'in front of the black man and the child were two cups of chocolate'. *Ante* is, however, very common in the figurative meaning of 'faced with', 'in the face of'. It must not be confused with the entirely separate word *antes* 'before' (in time). Examples:

Tuvo que comparecer ante el tribunal	(S)he had to appear before the court
Ellas presumían de parienta famosa ante las otras viejas (M. Torres, Sp.)	They boasted of having a famous female relative in the presence of the other old women
ante este dilema/insulto/problema	faced with this dilemma/insult/problem
ante tantas posibilidades	faced with so many possibilities
Ante todo, quisiera agradecer al organizador	Above all, I'd like to thank the organizer

(i) *Delante de* makes it clear that physical location rather than figurative 'presence' is implied, cf. *justificarse ante Dios* 'to justify oneself before God', but *arrodillarse delante de la Virgen* 'to kneel before (a statue of) the Virgin'. For more about *delante de*, see 31.6.8.

(ii) *Frente a* for *ante* in phrases like *frente a estos problemas* 'faced with these problems' is very widespread.

(iii) *Ante* and *delante de* should not be used to join nouns, as explained in note (iii) of the introduction to this chapter: *el coche que está delante de la casa es mío*, not **el coche delante de la casa es mío*.

34.3 *Bajo* and *debajo de*

Bajo means 'beneath' or 'under'. It may be a literary variant of *debajo de* 'underneath' (discussed at 31.6.6), but in this sense it is spatially less specific (like 'under' compared with 'underneath'): *se resguardaron bajo un haya* 'they sheltered under/beneath a beech tree' but *enterró el botín debajo de un roble* '(s)he buried the loot underneath (i.e. under the roots of) an oak tree'.

Carnicer notes that for those educated speakers who use *bajo*, the difference is that it implies 'a good distance under' or 'under but not close to or touching': *bajo una masa de nubes* 'under a mass of clouds', *no me quedo ni un minuto más bajo este techo* 'I'm not staying one more minute under this roof'. *Debajo de* implies 'underneath and close to whatever is on top': *hay mucho polvo debajo de la alfombra* 'there's a lot of dust underneath the carpet'. *?El perro está bajo la silla* 'the dog's beneath the chair' sounds affected in both languages: ...*debajo de la silla* 'under(neath) the chair'.

Bajo must be used in the figurative sense of 'under' in phrases like *bajo el gobierno de* 'under the government of', *bajo ciertas condiciones* 'under certain conditions', *funciona bajo Windows 2000* 'it works under Windows 2000', etc.

bajo las estrellas/la lluvia/un cielo azul	beneath the stars/in the rain/beneath a blue sky
bajo tierra (or *debajo de la tierra*)	underground
bajo los efectos de la anestesia	under the effects of the anaesthetic
bajo la monarquía/la república/el socialismo	under the monarchy/republic/socialism, etc.
Bajo la máscara se percibe el lento trabajo de la verdad (M. Torres, Sp.)	Beneath the mask the slow workings of truth are visible

(i) *Abajo de* is often heard for *debajo de* in Latin America: see 31.6.6.

(ii) *Bajo* and *debajo de* should not be used to join nouns, as explained in note (iii) of the introduction to this chapter; but there are set phrases like *temperaturas bajo cero* 'sub-zero temperatures', *declaraciones bajo juramento* 'statements under oath'.

34.4 *Cabe*

An archaic or rustic equivalent of *junto a/cerca de* 'by/near' still occasionally found in Latin-American authors.

34.5 *Con*

(a) In many contexts it coincides with the English 'with', but it is used more widely than the latter. English speakers often misuse it when translating phrases

like 'the boy with the blue Mercedes': *el chico **del** Mercedes azul*. But if temporary
wearing or carrying are implied, *con* is usual: *nunca te he visto con gafas* 'I've never
seen you with glasses'. *De* implies something typical: *¿te acuerdas del viejo del imper-
meable que venía todos los días?* 'do you remember the old man with/in the raincoat
who used to come every day?'

Fui a la reunión con Niso	I went to the meeting with Niso
Llegaron dos policías con perros	Two policemen with dogs arrived
No podía quitarlo con una llave normal	I couldn't get it off with a normal spanner
con lo enferma que está...	and with her being so ill...
té con miel/café con leche	tea with honey/coffee with milk
Se levantó con el sol	(S)he got up with the sun
con la llegada del otoño	with the arrival of autumn

Con cannot be used in combination with the nominalizer *el*: contrast *el chico con/de
la americana blanca* 'the boy with the white jacket' and *el de la americana blanca* 'the
one (masc.) with/in the white jacket'. Phrases like **el con gafas* for 'the one with
glasses' are not Spanish.

(**b**) After phrases meaning 'to show an attitude towards' *con* alternates with *para
con*, much as 'with' alternates with 'towards': *es muy cariñoso (para) con su mujer*
'he's very affectionate towards/with his wife', *su amabilidad es igual (para) con todos*
'her kindness is the same towards all'. But if the object of the attitude does not
benefit by it, *para* is not used:

Es muy crítico con su hijo	He's very critical with/towards his son
Eres muy cruel con tu novia	You're very cruel to your girlfriend
Es poco confiada con sus colegas	She's not very trusting with his/her colleagues

(**c**) It may be used with expressions signifying meeting, encounter, collision,
'facing up to', 'struggle with', etc.:

Me encontré/Tropecé hoy con tu jefe	I ran into/met your boss today
Ha vuelto con su marido (*ha vuelto a* is not used in this sense)	She's gone back to her husband (or 'she's come back with her husband')
Tengo que vérmelas con el vecino	I'll have to have it out with the neighbo(u)r (i.e. have a frank talk with)
Iba en la moto y me di un golpe con/contra un poste	I was on my motorbike and I crashed into a post
Se enfrentaron con los guerrilleros/con el problema	They clashed with the guerrillas/faced up to the problem
Contactó con/a su padre	(S)he contacted his/her father
Te paso con María	I'm handing the phone over to Maria

(**d**) It may—strangely to English-speakers—mean 'containing':

un vaso con/de agua, un saco con/de patatas	a glass of water/sack of potatoes
Llevaba una cesta con pan, huevos, uvas y vino (*de* is not possible here)	(S)he was carrying a basket of bread, eggs, grapes and wine
una jeringa con morfina	a syringe full of morphine

This use eliminates the ambiguity of *de*, which either means 'full of'—*una cesta de
huevos* is 'a basketful of eggs'—or denotes the container and not the contents, cf.
una botella de coñac 'a bottle of cognac' or 'a cognac bottle'; but *una botella con coñac*
'a bottle with cognac in it'.

(**e**) 'Despite' or some similar phrase (*a pesar de* is often an equivalent):

Con ser inteligente y rico nunca llegó a nada	Despite being intelligent and rich, he never came to anything
Con todo, la vida no es tan terrible	Despite everything, life isn't so awful
con lo guapa que estarías con el pelo recogido. . .	to think how attractive you'd look with your hair up...

(**f**) *Con* plus an infinitive may, like the gerund, have a conditional sense:

Con hacer (or *haciendo*) *lo que yo os digo, todo irá bien*	Provided you (pl.) do what I say everything will go well
Sólo/Solo con pulsar una tecla el ordenador almacena los datos	If you simply press a key the computer stores the data

A subjunctive may also follow *con* in this conditional meaning but *con que* must then be used. This must not be confused with the conjunction *conque* or with *con* plus a relative pronoun:

Con que me pagaran mis gastos me conformaba	I'd be happy if they paid my expenses

(**g**) It may mean 'as a result of', like the gerund (see 20.4.2):

Se nos ha ido la tarde con hablar/hablando	The afternoon's gone with all this talking
Con cambiar/Cambiando de empleo no resuelves nada	You'll solve nothing by changing jobs

(**h**) It may indicate the cause or origin of a condition:

Estamos muy entusiasmados/ilusionados con la perspectiva de un nuevo gobierno	We're very excited about the prospect of a new government
Está muy preocupado con sus negocios	He's very busy with his business affairs

Compare *me preocupo por ellos* 'I worry about them', and *me preocupo de hacer todo lo posible* 'I take care to do everything possible'.

Se puso enferma con paludismo/malaria (or *enfermó de*, Lat. Am. *se enfermó de*)	She fell ill with/from malaria
Se mareó con el vaivén del tren	(S)he felt sick/US nauseous because of the swaying of the train
Se alegró con/de la noticia del nacimiento de su nieto	(S)he cheered up at the news of his/her grandson's birth

(**i**) It is used with *soñar* 'to dream', e.g. *soñar con algo/alguien*, 'to dream of something/someone'. Compare *pensar en algo/alguien* 'to think of something/someone'.

(**j**) Miscellaneous examples of *con* used in ways unfamiliar to English speakers: *hace años que él se escribe con ella* 'he and she have been writing to one another for years', *murió con más de setenta años* 'she died aged more than seventy', *usted fue el último que lo/le vio con vida* 'you were the last one to see him alive', *voy a verme con ella esta noche* 'I'm seeing her tonight'.

34.6 *Contra*

A close equivalent of 'against', but it may mean 'at' after verbs meaning firing, throwing, launching, etc. *En contra de* is an equivalent of *contra* when the latter means 'in opposition to'. It becomes *en contra de que* before a verb:

una campaña contra/en contra de la corrupción	a campaign against corruption
Contra lo que creen algunos...	Despite/Contrary to what some believe...
Apoya tu pala contra el árbol	Lean your spade against the tree
En ese caso optarían por lanzar un misil contra el enemigo	In that case they would opt for launching a missile at the enemy
Lanzó la piedra contra el árbol	(S)he threw the stone at the tree (intending to strike it)
(cf. *se la lanzó al árbol*	(S)he threw it up at the tree (e.g. a lasso or rope))
inyectarse contra la hepatitis/la rabia (not *inyectarse para...*)	to get injected against hepatitis/rabies
¿Está usted en contra de que lo hagan ellos?	Are you against them doing it?

(i) For *contra mí, en contra tuya*, etc. 'against me'/'against you' see note to 8.7.

(ii) For the dialectal use of *contra* for *cuanto* in phrases like *cuanto más trabajas, más te dan* 'the more you work, the more they give you', see 5.11.

(iii) *Contra* can join nouns if the meaning of the first noun invites its use, as in *la guerra contra la corrupción*. But not *?la moto contra la pared es mía* 'the motor-bike against the wall is mine': *la moto que está apoyada contra la pared...*. See introduction to the chapter, note (iii).

34.7 De

34.7.1 General uses

Section (a) covers those uses of *de* which correspond to the English 'of' or to the possessive ending *'s*: these sentences should give English speakers no great problems. French speakers must resist the temptation to replace *de* by *a*: *c'est à vous?* = *¿es de usted?* 'is it yours?'

(**a**) 'Of', 'belonging to':

la matrícula del coche	the car number plate/US license-plate
las bisagras de la puerta	the hinges of/on the door
el primero/uno de mayo	the first of May
¿De quién es esto?	Whose is this?

(**b**) To create 'compound' nouns, usually—but not always— expressed in English by joining nouns. Note that *de* in such cases is not followed by a definite article:

un traje de baño	a swimsuit
un reloj de pulsera	a wristwatch
unos recortes de prensa	some press-cuttings

This is the usual way of forming the equivalents of English compound nouns, but there are other methods, e.g. *un año luz* 'a light year' or *la industria hotelera* 'the hotel industry' mentioned at 2.1.7b and 4.12 respectively.

NB: This way of creating compound nouns can create ambiguities in Spanish: *un vaso de whisky* is both 'a whisky-glass' and 'a glass of whisky'. See 34.5d.

(**c**) Origin (see 34.7.5 for the difference between *de* and *desde*):

Soy de México	I'm from Mexico
un ser de otro planeta	a being from another planet
un vino de solera	a vintage wine
un dolor de cabeza	a headache

(i) English-speakers tend use *en* to join nouns to indicate belonging to or originating from a place. Spanish strongly prefers *de*: *los hombres de Grecia* 'the men in Greece' (= Greek men), *las flores de los Andes* 'the flowers in (= of) the Andes', *las colinas de tierra adentro son más verdes* 'the hills in the interior/inland are greener'. The temptation is particularly strong after a superlative: *éste es el mejor restaurante de Madrid* 'this is the best restaurant in Madrid', *el mejor momento de mi vida* 'the best moment in/of my life'.

Mexican Spanish often uses *en*: *el plan más ambicioso en el mundo* (Mexican TV) 'the most ambitious plan in the world', *el mejor surtido en México* 'the best range in Mexico' (advert.).

(ii) *Viene de Toledo* normally only means '(s)he's coming from Toledo'; *es de Toledo* = '(s)he's from Toledo'.

(**d**) 'Made of', 'consisting of':

una estatua de oro macizo	a solid gold statue
un manuscrito de pergamino	a parchment manuscript
Tiene una voluntad de hierro	(S)he has an iron will
Este yogur es de leche de oveja	This is ewe's-milk yoghurt

(**e**) 'About' in the sense of 'concerning':

De is much used for 'about' after verbs like *hablar, quejarse de, protestar de* and after nouns like *carta* 'letter'. It implies something different from *sobre*: *una carta de amor* 'a love letter' is not a *una carta sobre el amor* 'a letter about love':

No quiero hablar de mis problemas personales	I don't want to talk about my personal problems
Esta noche va a hablar sobre problemas personales	Tonight (s)he's talking on/about 'personal problems'
Es que yo quería hablar con usted de mi salario (in Spain *sueldo* = salary and *salario* = weekly wages)	Actually I wanted to talk to you about my wages
¿De qué va la cosa?	What's it all about?

(**f**) 'Costing':

Las naranjas de mil pesos son las mejores	The 1000-peso oranges are the best
Han comprado una casa de un millón de libras	They've bought a million-pound house

(**g**) Emotions arising from something:

Tengo miedo del agua (see note)	I'm afraid of the water
el respeto de/a los derechos humanos	respect for human rights
Me da pena de él	I'm sorry for him
la obsesión del/por el golf	the golf craze/the golf bug

And similarly *el horror de/a/hacia una cosa* 'horror towards/about a thing'. However, after *sentir, experimentar* and similar verbs the following words take *por* or *hacia*: *compasión* 'pity', *simpatía* 'affection'/'liking', *admiración* 'admiration', *desprecio* 'contempt', *odio* 'hatred', etc.

NB: Note also *le tengo miedo al agua, tengo miedo de/le tengo miedo a todo.* See 34.1(n).

(h) In certain adverbial phrases of manner:

Lo escribió de manera que nadie pudiera *leerlo*	(S)he wrote it in such a way that no one could read it
Me puse a pensar de qué modo podría *ayudarlos*	I set about thinking how I could help them
Le ha venido de perlas	It suited him/her just right
Sólo/Solo he estado en Sevilla de paso	I've only been in Seville on the way to somewhere else
Intentaron entrar de balde	They tried to get in free/without paying
Sale todos los sábados de juerga	(S)he goes out on the town every Saturday
Estuvimos de bromas hasta las tres de la *mañana*	We were up until three telling jokes/fooling around

(i) Condition (English 'as', 'in'):

This construction is closely related to the previous one:

De niña me gustaba mucho coser (M. Arrafut, Cu., dialogue)	As a child I really used to like sewing
Trabajó dos meses de camarero	He worked as a waiter for two months
—¿De qué vas al baile? —De obispo	'What are you going to the ball as?' 'As a bishop'
Tú aquí estás de más	You're not needed here
Vi a una criada de blanco paseando *al niño*	I saw a maid in white taking the child for a walk
una chica joven de vaqueros y chaqueta de hombre (C. Martín Gaite, Sp.)	a young girl in jeans and a man's jacket

De + an adjective is a common colloquial way of describing the condition something is in, especially when the condition is in some way extreme or surprising:

La cesta de costura casi no cierra de puro *llena* (C. Martín Gaite, Sp.)	The sewing basket almost won't shut because it's so full
De puro ansioso, Javier había bostezado (M. Benedetti, Ur.)	Javier was so anxious that he yawned

(j) To mean 'if': for *de* plus the infinitive used for *si* in the if-clause of a conditional sentence, see 25.8.3.

(k) Age, measurements:

un hombre de cuarenta años	a man aged forty
Esta soga tiene tres metros de largo	This rope is three metres long
Tiene más de seiscientos metros *de profundo*	It's more than 600 metres deep

(l) *De* is used in certain circumstances with adjectives before an infinitive. Compare: *su conducta es difícil de comprender* 'his/her behavio(u)r is difficult to understand', and *es difícil comprender su conducta* 'it's difficult to understand his/her behavio(u)r'. See 18.10 for further examples and discussion.

(m) *De* is used after *más* and *menos* before numerals and quantities: *los cojinetes necesitan menos de medio litro de aceite* 'the bearings need less than half a litre of oil'. See 5.5 for further discussion.

(n) *De* is used and not *que* in comparisons involving a clause: *es más listo de lo que parece* 'he's cleverer than he seems', *no uses más de los que necesites* 'don't use more than those you need'. See 5.6 for discussion.

(o) *De* alternates with *para* in sentences of the type 'his attitude is not to be copied', 'his stories aren't to be believed':

Sus excusas no son de/para creer	His/Her excuses aren't to be believed
Su veracidad no es muy de recomendarse	One can't recommend his truthfulness
(J. J. Arreola, Mex., dialogue; not *para*)	very much
Su habilidad no es de/para subestimar	His/Her skill shouldn't be
	underestimated

(p) After certain verbs meaning 'to take by', 'seize by', 'pull on', etc.:

La cogió de la mano/Me tiraba de la manga	(S)he took her by the hand/(S)he was
	pulling my sleeve
El profesor lo/le asió de una oreja	The teacher took him by an ear

(q) To denote the agent in some types of passive construction and to indicate the author of a work or the main actor in a film or play:

acompañado de su esposa	accompanied by his wife
un viejo acompañado de un perro	an old man accompanied by a dog
(M. Benedetti, Ur.)	
un cuento de Borges	a short story by Borges

See 34.14.4 note (ii) for a discussion of participle + *de*.

(r) In certain set time phrases: *de día/de noche* 'by day/by night', *se levantó muy de mañana* '(s)he got up very early in the morning'.

(s) In constructions of the type *pobre de ti* 'poor you', *ese tonto de John* 'that fool John', etc.:

Tendrás que habértelas con el gandul de	You'll have to tackle that lay-about
Fulano	So-and-So
¿Sabes lo que ha hecho la pobre de su mujer?	Do you know what his poor wife has
	done?

(t) Partitive *de:*

De is occasionally used before adjectives—particularly demonstrative adjectives—to mean 'some of', 'one of': *hay de todo* 'there is a bit of everything':

Puedes comprar de todo	You can buy a little of everything
Tráiganos de ese vino que nos sirvió ayer	Bring us some of that wine you served
	us yesterday

(u) After numerous verbs which must be learned separately, e.g. *acordarse de* 'to remember', *apoderarse de* 'to get hold of', *calificar/tachar/tildar de* 'to describe/label as', *compadecerse de* 'to take pity on', *culpar de* 'to blame for', *encargarse de* 'to take charge of, *jactarse de* 'to boast of', *librarse/deshacerse de* 'to get rid of', *burlarse de* 'to mock', *reírse de* 'to laugh at', and many more.

(v) In some cases *de* can replace relative clauses:

Hace unos guisos sabrosos de mucho llenar	She makes delicious, really filling stews
(C. M. Gaite, Sp.; *...que llenan mucho*)	
Es hombre de poco comer/que come poco	He isn't a big eater/He doesn't eat a lot

34.7.2 Deber or deber de?

For the choice between *debe hacerlo* and *debe de hacerlo* see 21.3.

34.7.3 De before que

Some verbs, all verbal phrases involving a noun or adjective, and some adverbial phrases must be followed by *de que* when they introduce a clause: *nos dimos cuenta de que ya no llovía* 'we realized that it was no longer raining'. See 33.4.2 for discussion.

34.7.4 Dequeísmo

For the popular and spreading tendency to use *de que* instead of *que* after verbs of belief and communication, e.g. ?*dice de que no viene* for *dice que no viene* 'she says she isn't coming', see 33.4.3.

34.7.5 Desde, and de with the meaning of 'from'

The existence of two Spanish words which both mean 'from' is a source of confusion; nor is the distinction always strictly observed by native speakers. *Desde* emphasizes the idea of movement or distance more than *de*. It is therefore appropriate when motion 'from' a place requires some unusual effort or when the point of origin is mentioned but not the destination, as in *os veo desde mi ventana* 'I can see you from my window'. It is also freely used in time phrases to mean 'since': see 32.3.7.

Desde nuestro balcón se divisa la cima de Mulhacén	From our balcony one can make out the summit of Mulhacén
Desde aquí el camino es muy bueno	From here the road is very good
Avanzó desde la puerta con un cuchillo en la mano	(S)he moved forward from the door with a knife in his/her hand
He venido andando desde el centro	I've walked all the way from the centre
Y entonces una soga lo atrapó desde atrás (J. Cortázar, Arg.)	Then he was caught from behind by a rope
Desde hoy/A partir de hoy tienen que llegar a tiempo	From today you must arrive on time
Los tenemos desde cincuenta centavos hasta cinco pesos	We have them from 50 centavos to 5 pesos
Desde siempre oí que ella era perfecta (A. Mastretta, Mex., dialogue)	I had always heard that she was perfect

(i) If *a, hasta* or some other preposition of destination appears, *desde* is often interchangeable with *de*: *de/desde aquí a/hasta el centro las calles son muy estrechas* 'from here to the centre the roads are very narrow', *de/desde aquí a la cima mide diez mil metros* 'from here to the summit it measures 10,000 metres', *¿desde/de 1922 a 1942 estuve en Colombia* 'from 1922 to 1942 I was in Colombia'.

If no such prepositional phrase of destination occurs *desde* is usually the safer option, though usage is fickle: *las partículas subatómicas que llegan desde/de otras galaxias* 'subatomic particles arriving from other galaxies', *¿desde dónde hablas?* 'where are you talking from?', *desde entonces no lo/le he vuelto a ver* 'since then I haven't seen him'.

In the following types of sentence only *de* is possible: *yo soy de Madrid* 'I'm from Madrid', *las hojas caen ya de los abedules* 'the leaves are already falling from the birches', *sacó tres diamantes de la bolsa* '(s)he took three diamonds from the bag', *pasó de secretaria a jefe en tres meses* 'she went from secretary to boss in three months', *hizo un modelo de un trozo de madera* '(s)he made a model from a piece of wood', *del techo pendía una enorme araña de luces* 'from the ceiling hung an enormous chandelier', *se ha venido de España a vivir en Inglaterra* '(s)he's come from Spain to live in England', *sólo/solo la veo de Pascuas a Ramos* 'I only see her once in a blue moon' (lit. 'from Easter to Palm Sunday').

(ii) *Desde ya* is commonly found in the River Plate region (and increasingly in Spain, according to Manuel Seco) with the meaning of 'right away'; *desde ahora ya* is more common in Spain. *Desde luego* means 'of course' on both continents.

(iii) *Desde* should not be used to join nouns unless the meaning of the noun justifies its use: *la vuelta desde Madrid* for 'the return from Madrid' is possible, but **el tren desde Madrid* should be rephrased *el tren que viene de Madrid/el tren de Madrid*.

34.8 *Durante*

This word, which means 'during', 'for...' a period of time, and other ways of saying '*for* a period of time' is discussed at 32.2 and 32.3.4.

34.9 *En*

En often seems vague to English-speakers since it combines the meanings of 'in' and 'on' (French *sur* and *dans*), as well as 'at', 'into' and 'onto': *en la caja* 'in the box', *en la mesa* 'on/at the table', *está en la comisaría* '(s)he's in/at the police station'. Spanish-speaking learners of English have problems in differentiating 'in', 'on' and 'at'. For the relationship between *en* and 'at' in sentences like 'at the station', 'at Cambridge', see 34.1(d).

When it means 'on a horizontal surface', it alternates with *sobre* (see 34.17) and also sometimes with *encima de* 'on top of'. One can say *en/sobre/encima de la mesa* 'on the table', but *mi hijo duerme en mi cama* 'my son sleeps in my bed', since 'inside' is implied. *En* may be replaced by *dentro de* if the idea of 'inside' needs to be emphasized.

(a) As an equivalent of 'in', 'on' or 'at':

Tus camisas están en el cajón	Your shirts are in the drawer
Cuelga el cuadro en la pared	Hang the picture on the wall
Dio unos golpes discretos en la puerta	(S)he tapped discreetly on the door
La llave está en la puerta	The key's in the door
Gasto mucho dinero en juegos de azar	I spend a lot of money on gambling
...sentado a/en una mesa (see note i)	...sitting at a table
El agua ha penetrado en las vigas	The water has soaked into the joists
Uno de mis pendientes se me ha caído en el agua (see note ii)	One of my earrings fell off in the water (note translation)
Propusieron convertirlo en sanatorio	They suggested turning it into a sanatorium
en otoño/primavera/1924	in autumn/spring/1924
En las mañanas salíamos a montar a caballo (A. Mastretta, Mex.; Sp. *por las mañanas*)	In the mornings we used to go riding
Todavía está en proyecto	It's still at the planning stage
Te da ciento y raya en latín	(S)he's miles better than you in Latin

(i) Compare *se sentó a la mesa* '(s)he sat down at table' with *siempre se comporta bien en la mesa* '(s)he always behaves well at table'. See 34.1(d) for discussion.

(ii) The example suggests the wearer was already in the water, e.g. swimming. If trajectory down to the water is meant, *a* is more usual: *se tiró al río* '(s)he jumped into the river', *el avión cayó al mar* 'the plane fell into the sea'.

(iii) *Entrar* and similar verbs take *en* (often *a* in Latin America, and occasionally in Spain): *entró en el cuarto* '(s)he entered the room'.

(iv) For the translation of phrases like 'the men in Mexico', 'the books in the drawer', see 34.7.1(c) and the introduction to this chapter.

(**b**) To express the thing by which something else is judged or estimated:

El tipo oficial quedó fijado en 151,93 por dólar (*El País*, Sp.)	The official rate was fixed at 151.93 to the dollar
Lo vendieron en/por un millón de euros (*por* is more usual)	They sold it for a million euros
Te tenía en más estima	I thought higher of you
El progreso logrado en esta investigación es computable en cero	The progress achieved in this investigation can be reckoned as zero
Me lo presupuestaron en cien mil	They gave me an estimate of 100,000 for it
Lo/Le conocí en el andar	I recognized him from the way he walked

(**c**) In a number of adverbial phrases:

Lo tomaron en serio	They took it/him seriously
en mangas de camisa/en cueros/en broma/en balde	in shirtsleeves/naked/as a joke/ pointlessly
en fila/en seguida (or *enseguida*)	in a row/straight away
Estoy en contra	I'm against

(**d**) To mean 'as'

Como is much more usual nowadays in the following sentences:

Hablar de esa manera, en/como ser superior, es absurdo	To talk like that, as a superior being, is absurd
Ve tú en mi representación (A. Buero Vallejo, Sp., dialogue; *como* not possible)	You stand in for me/represent me

(**e**) After a number of common verbs, and in several miscellaneous constructions:

Pensé mucho en usted	I thought of you a lot
Se fijó en él	(S)he noticed him
Tardaron cinco semanas en reparar el coche	They took five weeks to mend the car

Also *quedar en* 'to agree to', *vacilar/dudar* en 'to hesitate over', *empeñarse/insistir/ obstinarse en* 'to insist on', *abdicar en* 'to abdicate in favo(u)r of', *interesarse en/por* 'to be interested in', *ser el primero/último en* 'to be the first/last to…'.

See 18.2 for further remarks about prepositional usage with verbs. For the obsolete construction *en* + gerund see 20.5.

34.10 *Entre*

Both 'between' and 'among'. *Entre* also has a number of uses unfamiliar to English speakers.

Prepositional pronoun forms are not nowadays used after *entre*: *entre Juan y tú recogeréis los papeles* 'you and John will pick up the pieces of paper between you' (not **entre Juan y ti*). But the prepositional form *sí*, from *se*, is used after *entre*. See section (c) below.

(a) 'Between':

Estábamos entre la espada y la pared	We were between the sword and the wall (i.e. 'we had our backs to the wall')
...constantemente entre la excitación y la depresión (M. Vázquez Montalbán, Sp.)	...constantly between excitement and depression
Cuestan entre mil y dos mil	They cost between one and two thousand
entre tú/usted y yo...	between you and me...
Entre todos rehabilitaremos Madrid (poster)	Together we'll modernize Madrid
Lo terminaron entre María y su hermana	Maria and her sister finished it between them

The last example is a construction unfamiliar to English speakers: *llenan el pantano entre cuatro ríos* (from María Moliner, I, 1146) 'four rivers combine to fill the reservoir', *trozos de una novela rosa que fuimos escribiendo entre las dos* (C. Martín Gaite, Sp.) 'bits of a romantic novel we were writing between the two of us'.

(b) 'Among':

It is used with a wider range of nouns than its English equivalent, e.g. *entre la niebla* 'in the mist', *encontraron la sortija entre la arena* 'they found the ring in the sand':

Vivió diez años entre los beduinos	(S)he lived for ten years among the Bedouins
La perdí de vista entre la muchedumbre	I lost sight of her in the crowd
...y entre el ruido de la lluvia se escuchaba el ladrido de los perros (L. Sepúlveda, Ch.)	...and through/above the noise of the rain the barking of the dogs could be heard
Entre la niebla se percibía una masa inquieta (L. Mateo Díez, Sp.)	A restless mass/shape could be seen in the fog

(c) 'Among themselves', 'one from the other':

In the second of these two meanings *entre* is used in a way unfamiliar to English-speakers. It is especially liable to appear with the pronoun *sí* (discussed in detail at 11.5.3):

En casa hablan castellano entre sí (or *entre ellos*)	At home they speak Spanish among themselves
Es más fácil que dos personas vivan en armonía cuando se respetan entre sí	It's easier for two people to live in harmony when they respect one another
Enseguida notamos el recelo manifiesto que se dispensan entre sí (E. Lynch, Arg.; one can also write *en seguida*)	We immediately noticed the obvious distrust they felt among themselves

(d) It can translate the English phrase 'what with':

Entre los niños y el estruendo de los albañiles, me estoy volviendo loca	What with the children and the din of the builders, I'm going mad
entre pitos y flautas...	what with one thing and another (lit. 'what with whistles and flutes')

(e) In certain phrases, in a way strange to English speakers:

Van como ovejas al matadero, decía entre sí	They're going like lambs to the slaughter, (s)he said to her/himself
Decía entre mí. . .	I said to myself. . .
El museo está abierto entre semana	The museum is open Monday to Saturday
Tengo un asunto entre manos	I've got some business in hand

34.11 *Hacia*

(a) A close equivalent of 'towards', but rather wider in application since it also translates the English suffix *-ward/-wards*:

El satélite viaja hacia Venus	The satellite is travel(l)ing towards Venus
Señaló hacia el este	(S)he pointed to the east
La actitud de la ONU hacia tales problemas parece ambigua	The attitude of the UN towards such problems seems ambiguous
El incidente ocurrió hacia las tres de la tarde	The incident occurred towards three in the afternoon
El coche rodaba hacia atrás	The car was rolling backwards

In time phrases *hacia* can less commonly be replaced by *sobre*: *sobre finales de agosto* 'around the end of August', *sobre las tres de la tarde*, 'around 3 p.m.', or, with dates, by *para*: *para octubre* 'towards/around October'.

(b) Emotions, attitudes 'towards':

Por, con and *para con* are also possible, but not always interchangeable. Deep emotions such as love or hatred prefer *hacia* or *por*; attitudes (e.g. kindness, severity, irritability) prefer *hacia* or *con*. For *para con* see 34.5(b).

mi profundo amor hacia/por/a todo lo andaluz	my deep love for everything Andalusian
Mostraba una indiferencia total hacia/por las críticas	(S)he displayed total indifference towards criticisms
la simpatía de los insurgentes hacia/por el modelo cubano	the insurgents' sympathy for the Cuban model

34.12 *Hasta*

(a) 'As far as', 'until', 'up to':

hasta ahora	until now/up to now
Llegaron hasta el oasis	They got as far as the oasis
No nos vamos hasta el día trece	We're not leaving until the thirteenth
Siguió leyendo hasta que no había luz	She kept reading until there was no light
Bailaron hasta no poder más	They danced until they were exhausted
Estoy de exámenes hasta la coronilla (or *hasta las narices*)	I've had enough of exams (I'm sick to death of exams)
hasta luego	goodbye/see you later

From Mexico to Colombia *hasta* has acquired the meaning of '*not* until': *perdona que te llame hasta ahora* (C. Fuentes, dialogue), 'sorry for not ringing you before now', *bajamos hasta la Plaza de la Independencia* 'we're not getting off until Independence Square', *hasta entonces me di cuenta* 'I realized only then' or 'I didn't realize until then'.

(b) *Hasta que no*: see 23.2.4d for this construction.

(c) For *hasta = incluso* 'even', see 31.8.

34.13 *Mediante*

'By means of' some instrument, argument or device:

Es inútil intentar abolir el abuso del alcohol mediante/por decreto/con decretos	It is useless to try to abolish alcohol abuse by decree
Lograron abrir la caja mediante/con una antorcha de butano	They managed to open the safe by means of a butane torch

34.14 *Para* and *por*

34.14.1 The difference between them

Para and *por* are both often translatable as 'for' although they nearly always mean different things. They have many different uses, so generalizations are unhelpful, but one basic distinction between them when they seem to mean 'for' is that *para* expresses purpose or destination and *por* cause or motive. This is clear from the two sentences *hago esto para ti* 'I'm **making** this for you (to give to you)' and *hago esto por ti* 'I'm **doing** this because of you/on your behalf'.

English-speakers are usually confused by sentences like 'this fence is for the rabbits': this obviously means 'because of the rabbits', so one says *esta valla es por los conejos*. The Spanish Civil Guards' motto *Todo por la Patria* 'Everything for our Country' means 'everything we do is done for our country'. *Todo para la Patria* would mean 'everything we possess or make is for our country'.

It is useful to recall that if 'for' can be replaced by 'out of' or 'because of' then *por* may be the correct translation, but not *para*: *lo hizo por amor* '(s)he did it for (out of) love', *lo hago por el dinero* 'I do it for (because of) the money':

Llevo el abrigo por/a causa de mi madre	I'm wearing this coat because of my mother (she'll be cross/worried if I don't)
Llevo este abrigo para/a mi madre	I'm taking this coat to my mother
Han venido por ti	They've come to get you/come because of you/come instead of you
Han venido estos paquetes para ti	These parcels have come for you
Lo has conseguido por mí	You've got it through me
Lo has conseguido para mí	You've got it for me

Particularly troublesome is the fact that *por* and *para* can mean almost the same thing in some sentences involving intentions, e.g. *ha venido por/para estar contigo* '(s)he's come to be with you', whereas in others only *para* is possible. This problem is discussed at 34.14.7.

(i) The form *pa* is substandard for *para*. It is accepted in a few humorous familiar expressions used in Spain (and possibly elsewhere), e.g. *es muy echao palante* 'he's very forward', *estoy pal arrastre* 'I'm all-in/exhausted', *pal gato* 'worthless' (literally 'for the cat').

34.14.2 Uses of *para*

Para is used:

(**a**) To indicate purpose, object or destination, e.g. *¿para quién es esto?* 'who(m) is this for?', *¿para qué es esto?* 'what's this for?', *trabaja para ganar dinero* '(s)he works to earn money', etc. (but see 34.14.7 for the possible use of *por* in certain contexts):

Una mesa para dos, por favor	A table for two, please
Se preparó para saltar	(S)he got ready to jump
Un coche hecho para durar (advert., Sp.)	A car made to last
Estudia para médico	(S)he's studying to become a doctor
Para manzanas, Asturias	For apples, Asturias (i.e. if you want apples go to Asturias)

(i) *Para* can also express ironic purpose, like the English 'only to': *corrió a casa para encontrarse con que ya se habían marchado* '(s)he hurried home only to find that they'd already left'.

(ii) The following construction may also be thought of as expressing the object or purpose of something: *sus historias no son para/de creer* 'his/her stories aren't to be believed' (lit. 'aren't for believing'), *no es para tanto* 'it's not that serious/it doesn't call for that much fuss'. Linked to this is the meaning 'considering...' in sentences like *sabe mucho de política argentina, para ser extranjera* 'she knows a lot about Argentine politics considering she's a foreigner'.

(iii) For the difference between *¿por qué?* 'why?' and *¿para qué?* 'what for?', see 24.10.

(**b**) Direction after verbs of motion:

Íbamos para casa cuando empezó a llover	We going home when it started raining
La secretaria ya ha salido para Burgos	The secretary has already left for Burgos
Ya va para viejo	(S)he's getting old now
Va para ministro	He's on the way to becoming a minister

(i) *Para* can link to nouns where we would use 'to': *ha llegado el tren para/de Madrid* 'the train to Madrid has arrived'. See introduction to this chapter, (iii).

(**c**) To indicate advantage, disadvantage, usefulness, need:

Fumar es malo para la salud	Smoking is bad for the health
La paciencia es un requisito indispensable para los profesores	Patience is an indispensable requirement for teachers
Tú eres para él lo más importante	You're the most important thing to/for him

(**d**) Reaction, response, mood:

Esto para mí huele a vinagre/Esto a mí me huele a vinagre	This smells of vinegar to me
Yo no tengo amigos. Para mí, que mi mujer los espanta	I haven't got any friends. If you ask me, my wife scares them away
Para su padre es un genio	(S)he's a genius in his/her father's eyes

(i) For *para con* in sentences like *es muy atento para con los invitados* 'he's very courteous towards guests', see 34.5(b).

(ii) *Para* can also translate 'not in the mood for': *no estoy para bromas* 'I'm not in the mood for jokes'.

(e) To translate 'for' when it means 'considering', 'in view of':

Está muy alto para su edad	He's very tall for his age
Estás muy viejo para esos trotes	You're very old for all that nonsense
Es poco dinero para tanto trabajo	It's not much money for so much work

(f) 'To' in certain reflexive expressions:

Me lo guardo para mí	I'm keeping it to/for myself
Esto acabará mal, me decía para mí/entre mí	This will end badly, I said to myself
Murmuraba para/entre sí	(S)he was muttering to himself/herself

(g) 'About' in the meaning of 'on the point of':

Ya deben estar para/al llegar	They must be about to arrive
La leche está para/ a punto de hervir	The milk's about to boil
—Pues yo estoy para cumplir treinta	Well, I'm going to be thirty-five
y cinco la semana que viene (E. Arenas, Sp., dialogue)	next week

In Latin America *estar por* is used: *en 1942, cuando volvió definitivamente, estaba por cumplir veinte años* (S. Pitol, Mex.) 'in 1942, when he came back for good, he was on the verge of his twentieth birthday', *oye bien. Un pájaro está por cantar* (J. L. Borges, Arg.) 'listen. A bird is about to sing'. In Spain *estar por* means 'to be in favo(u)r of'/'to be thinking about doing something'.

34.14.3 *Para* in time phrases

(a) To translate 'by':

Lo tendré preparado para las cinco	I'll have it ready by/for five o'clock
Para entonces ya estaremos todos muertos	We'll all be dead by then
Si ensayamos fuerte durante todo el año, para el verano estaremos en condiciones de actuar (S. Puértolas, Sp., dialogue)	If we rehearse hard all year we'll be in a condition to perform by summer

(b) 'For':

Para sometimes expresses the idea of 'for *n* days/weeks/years'. See 32.3.6 for further discussion.

(c) 'Around', 'towards':

El embalse estará terminado para finales de noviembre	The dam will be finished around the end of November
Volveremos para agosto	We'll return around August

(i) In the last example *para* is more precise than *hacia* and *por* and less precise than *en*.

(ii) *Ir para* is a colloquial translation of 'for nearly...' in time phrases: *va para cinco años que trabajo aquí* 'I've been working here for nearly five years'.

(d) 'Not enough to', 'considering how much':

No había tomado suficientes pastillas como para matarse (M. Vázquez Montalbán, Sp.)	She hadn't taken enough pills to kill herself
...un matrimonio rápido, bastante rápido para lo mucho que siempre se dice que hay que pensárselo (J. Marías, Sp.)	...a quick marriage, pretty quick, considering how much they always say one ought to think it over

34.14.4 Main uses of *por*

(a) *Por* often means simply 'because of', as in *¿por qué?* (two words!) 'why?' (i.e. 'because of what?') and *porque* 'because':

No pudimos salir por/a causa de la nieve	We couldn't go out because of the snow
la razón por la que me voy	the reason for my leaving
muchas gracias por el regalo	many thanks for the present
Me pusieron una multa por aparcar en el centro	They fined me for parking in the centre
Te ha pasado por tonto	It happened to you because you're a fool
Las críticas de la izquierda vienen por/a causa de tres temas	Criticism from the left arises on three grounds (lit. 'from three topics')
El profesor la calificó con un cero por no saber la lección (M. Puig, Arg.)	The teacher gave her a zero because she didn't know the lesson
Las empresas navieras sufren un descalabro importante por la situación actual del mercado (*Abc*, Spain)	Shipping firms have suffered significant losses due to the present state of the market

Por may thus indicate the origin or inspiration of an emotion or mental state:

No lo/le puedo ver por lo engreído que es	I can't stand him because of his conceitedness
Nuestro amor por/hacia/a nuestros hijos	our love for our children
su fascinación por los Estados Unidos	his/her fascination with the USA
Siento una enorme curiosidad por saber si ésta/esta es la única vida	I feel enormous curiosity to know whether this is the only life
No por previsible la foto anual dejaba de ser un acontecimiento excepcional (E. Lynch, Arg.)	Predictability did not stop the annual photograph from being an exceptional event

Note the idiom, common to Spain and Latin America, *darle a uno por* 'to take up', 'to get keen on', e.g. *a Carlos no le interesan estas cosas; le ha dado por el arte* (L. Otero, Cu., dialogue) 'Carlos isn't interested in those things. He's taken up art/He's developed a passion for art'.

(b) *Por* = 'by' in passive constructions:

Sus novelas fueron elogiadas por los críticos	His/Her novels were praised by the critics
La catedral fue diseñada por Gaudí	The cathedral was designed by Gaudí
Los campos estaban devastados por la sequía	The fields were devastated by drought
El suelo estaba cubierto por/de un lecho de hierba	The ground was covered by a bed of grass
Sociedad y economía aztecas por M. León-Portilla (see note ii)	*Aztec Society and Economy* by M. León-Portilla

(i) For *de* meaning 'by' to indicate the author of a work or the main actor in a film or play see 34.7.1q.

(ii) *De* is not nowadays used in passive sentences to mean 'by', except with certain verbs which are best learnt separately. Where there is a possibility of using either *por* or *de*, the former usually implies an active agent, the latter generally implies a state. *De* is therefore common when *estar* is used (see 28.2.5 for *estar convencido* contrasted with *ser convencido*): *me sentía tentado de tomar el atajo* 'I felt tempted to take the short cut', *Jesús fue tentado por el Diablo* 'Jesus was tempted by the Devil'; *María dijo algunas palabras en voz muy baja. . .seguidas de un ruido de sillas* (E. Sábato, Arg.) 'Maria said a few words in a very low voice ... followed by a noise [i.e. scraping] of chairs'; *en todas partes era seguido por una muchedumbre de admiradores* (*le seguía una muchedumbre* is more natural) 'he was followed everywhere by a crowd of admirers'; *el formulario debe estar acompañado de dos fotos* 'the form must be accompanied by two photos'; *las zonas pantanosas suelen estar plagadas de mosquitos* 'marshy zones are usually plagued with mosquitoes'; *en verano las vacas están atormentadas por las moscas* 'in summer the cows are tormented by flies'.

(iii) Phrases like *Hamlet por William Shakespeare* are seen and heard, perhaps with increasing frequency, but *Hamlet de W.S.* is the time-honoured construction.

(**c**) 'Runs *on*', 'works *by*'; 'by means of':

El sistema de alarma funciona por rayos infrarrojos	The alarm system works by infra-red rays
El tratamiento por/con rayos X ha producido resultados animadores	Treatment by X-rays has produced encouraging results
un coche que marcha por/con/a gas-oil	a car which runs on diesel oil
Se puede pagar por/con cheque bancario	Payment by cheque/US check accepted
[el Buda] enseñaba la aniquilación del dolor por la aniquilación del deseo (J. L. Borges, Arg.)	[the Buddha] taught the extinction of suffering by the extinction of desire

(**d**) 'In support of', 'in favour of', 'on behalf of', 'for …'s sake':

Yo voté por que tu libro fuera premiado (R. Arenas, Cu.)	I voted in favour of your book getting the prize
¿Estás tú por la violencia?	Do you support violence?
Encuentro de Escritores por la Paz	Conference of Writers for Peace (i.e. who support peace)
Es senador por Massachusetts	He's Senator for Massachusetts
Aprendió a tocar el piano por sí misma/ella sola	She learned to play the piano by herself
Siéntese por Dios (a polite request in Spanish)	Please do sit down

(**e**) Exchange *for*, substitute *for*, distribution *per*:

Te lo cambiarán por uno nuevo	They'll change it for a new one for you
Ahora daría lo que no tengo por oírla (C. Martín Gaite, Sp.)	Now I'd give everything I haven't got (for the chance) to hear her (voice)
Te han dado gato por liebre	They've served you cat for hare (i.e. swindled you)
¿Por quién me toma usted?	Who do you take me for?
Lo doy por supuesto/sentado	I take it for granted
Él dará la clase por mí	He'll give the class instead of me
Comes por tres	You eat enough for three
tres raciones por persona	three helpings per person
cien kilómetros por hora	100 km an hour
40 horas a la/por semana (*a* is more usual)	40 hours a week
la media anual por español	the annual average per Spaniard
El dos por ciento es protestante/son protestantes	Two per cent are Protestants

(**f**) Prices, amounts of money:

un cheque por/de cien dólares	a cheque/US check for 100 dollars
Compró una casa por un millón de dólares	(S)he bought a house for one million dollars

Por is used with *pagar* only when the latter already has a direct object in the form of a quantity of money: *he pagado mil libras por este ordenador* (Lat. Am. *por esta computadora*) 'I paid 1000 for this computer', *he pagado mucho por él* 'I paid a lot for it', but *yo lo pagué la semana pasada* 'I paid for it last week'.

(g) 'To judge *by*':

...por las señas que me ha dado...	...from the description (s)he's given me...
por lo que tú dices...	...from what you say...
por lo visto	apparently
Evidentemente, por su voz, por su aspecto, por su ropa era una persona decente (G. Cabrera Infante, Cu.)	Clearly, to judge by his voice, looks and clothes, he was a decent person
Por mí haz lo que quieras	As far as I'm concerned, do what you like

(h) 'In search *of*':

Peninsular speech prefers *a por*, a construction rejected by the Academy and by Latin Americans, but approved by *El País* and by Manuel Seco on the grounds that *fui por ella* could also mean 'I went instead of her/on her behalf', whereas *...a por ella* is only 'to look for her':

Voy al baño a por Kleenex (C. Rico-Godoy, Sp.; Lat. Am. *por Kleenex*)	I'm going/I go to the bathroom/toilet to fetch a tissue
Fui por mi abrigo (A. Mastretta, Mex.; Sp. *a por*)	I went for my coat/I went to get my coat

(i) 'Through' (= 'by means of'):

Conseguí el empleo por/a través de mi tío	I got the job through my uncle
Me enteré por un amigo	I found out through/from a friend

(j) *Por* in adverbial phrases of manner:

por correo/avión/mar (but *en tren, en coche, en bicicleta, a pie*)	by mail/air/sea
Los denuncio por igual	I denounce both/all sides equally
por lo general/generalmente	generally
por lo corriente/corrientemente	usually
Me lo tendrás que decir por las buenas o por las malas	You'll have to tell me one way or another
Es agrimensor, o algo por el estilo	He's a surveyor, or something like that

and numerous others, which must be learned from the dictionary.

(k) 'However...' in concessions (see 16.13):

Por más inteligente que seas, no lo vas a resolver	However intelligent you may be, you won't solve it
Era la verdad por dura que me pareciera (M. Torres, Sp.)	It was the truth, however hard it seemed to me

(l) 'Multiplied by':

Cinco por tres son quince	5 times 3 equals 15
Mide 7 por 5	It measures 7 by 5

(m) With numerous verbs, e.g.:

afanarse por to strive to	*luchar por* to struggle to
apurarse por§ get anxious about	*molestarse por* to bother about
asustarse por/de get frightened about	*optar por* to opt for
decidirse por to decide on	*preguntar por* to ask about/after
desvelarse por to be very concerned about	*preocuparse por* to worry about
disculparse por to apologize for	*rezar por* to pray for
esforzarse por to make an effort to	*tomar por* to take for
interesarse por to be interested in	*votar por* to vote for
jurar por swear by/on	

§*Apurarse* means 'to hurry' in Latin America.

34.14.5 *Por* in time phrases

(a) *Por* = 'in', but less precise than *en* where the latter is also possible:

Debió ser por mayo	It must have been some time in May
por aquellos días	in those days/during those days

(b) For 'just for', 'only for' and for more details on *por* in time phrases see 32.3.5.

(c) Latin Americans sometimes use *por* where Spaniards use *durante*. See 32.3.5(ii).

34.14.6 *Por* as a preposition of place

(a) 'All over', 'throughout':

He viajado por Latinoamérica	I've travel(l)ed around Latin America
Había muchos libros desparramados por el suelo	There were many books scattered over the floor
Oye, ¿me das crema por/en la espalda?	Could you please put cream on my back?

(b) 'In': less precise than *en* and often implying motion:

La vi por/en la calle	I saw her in the street
Creo que las mujeres andan por Europa (M. Benedetti, Ur., dialogue)	I think the women are somewhere in Europe
Debe estar por el jardín	It must be somewhere in the garden
Yo no sabía por dónde empezar (M. Torres, Sp.)	I didn't know where to begin

(c) 'Up to':

El agua le llegaba por la cintura	The water was up to his waist
Me llegas por los hombros	You reach my shoulders (e.g. to a growing child)

(d) 'Through', 'out of', 'down':

Me tiré por la ventana	I threw myself out of the window
Entró por la puerta	(S)he came through the door
Se cayó por la escalera	(S)he fell down the stairs
Salía agua por el/del grifo	Water was coming out of the tap
El tren pasó por/a través del túnel	The train went through the tunnel
por Madrid	through/via Madrid

(e) In conjunction with adverbs of place, to denote direction or whereabouts:

por aquí	this way/around here
por delante/detrás	in front/from behind
por entre	in between

34.14.7 *He venido* por *hablarle* or para *hablarle*?

Both prepositions may translate 'to' or 'in order to' in sentences like 'I've come to talk to you'. In some cases they are virtually interchangeable:

¿Para qué has venido?	What have you come for?
¿Por qué has venido?	Why have you come?
Estoy aquí para/por verle/lo	I've come to see him
...todo cuanto ella hacía por hacerlo feliz (G. García Márquez, Col., or *para*)	...everything she did to make him happy
Ella le habría vendido el alma al Diablo por casarse con él (ibid.)	She'd have sold her soul to the Devil to marry him
...el esfuerzo por conservarse bien	...the effort to look after oneself

A useful rule seems to be: if the English sentence can be rewritten using a phrase like 'out of a desire to' or 'from an urge to', then *por* can be used. If not, *para* is indicated; i.e. *por* refers to the mental state of the subject, *para* to the goal of his/her action. Thus, *me dijeron que estabas en Madrid y he venido por verte de nuevo* 'I heard you were in Madrid and I've come to (out of an urge to) see you again' is possible (*para* could be used). But **el fontanero ha venido por reparar el grifo* is as absurd as 'the plumber has come out of an urge to mend the tap'. Another example may clarify the point: —*¿Para qué salgo a cenar contigo?* —*Para comer* (not *por*) '"What am I going out to dinner with you for?" "(In order) to eat"', —*¿Por qué salgo a cenar contigo?* —*Por/Para estar conmigo* '"Why am I going out to dinner with you?" "To be with me".'

After some words *por* is required: *teníamos prisa por verla* 'we were in a hurry to see her', *el celo por la reforma* 'eagerness for reform', *el anhelo por la gloria* 'longing for glory'.

34.14.8 Some vital differences between *por* and *para*

Tengo muchas cosas por/sin hacer	I have a lot of things still to do
Tengo muchas cosas para hacer	I have many things to do
Estoy por hacerlo	I feel inclined to do it
Estoy (aquí) para hacerlo	I'm here in order to do it
Estaba para hacerlo (Lat. Am. *por*)	I was about to do it
Está por/sin acabar	It isn't finished yet
Está para acabar	This has to be finished
Está para (Lat. Am. *por*) *acabar de un momento a otro*	(S)he/It's about to finish at any moment

34.14.9 'For' not translated by *por* or *para*

la razón de mi queja	the reason for my complaining
Bebía porque no tenía otra cosa que hacer	(S)he drank for want of something else to do
Los días eran cortos pues era ahora noviembre	The days were short, for it was now November
el deseo de fama	the desire for fame

Lloró de alegría	(S)he wept for joy
Es una buena secretaria a pesar de lo que gruñe	She's a good secretary, for all her grumbling
No dijo una palabra durante dos horas	(S)he didn't say a word for two hours
No lo/le he visto desde hace meses	I haven't seen him for months
Llevamos tres semanas sin que recojan la basura	They haven't collected our rubbish/ US trash for three weeks
Estuvimos horas esperando	We waited for hours
Se podía ver muy lejos	You could see for miles
ir a dar un paseo	to go for a walk
irse de vacaciones	to go for a holiday/vacation
Me voy a Madrid unos días	I'm going to Madrid for a few days

34.15 *Según*

'According to', 'depending on'. As with *entre*, a following pronoun appears in the subject form: *según tú* 'according to you', not *según ti*:

según el parte meteorológico	according to the weather report
Según tú, se debería abolir la televisión	According to you, television should be abolished
Iremos modificando el programa de estudios según el tipo de estudiante que se matricule	We'll modify the syllabus according to the type of student that signs on
Los precios varían según a qué dentista vayas (or *según el dentista al que vayas*)	The prices vary according to which dentist you go to
Me decidiré luego, según cómo salgan las cosas	I'll decide later, depending on how things turn out

(i) As the examples show, *según* often functions as an adverb: —*¿Vas tú también?* —*Según* '"Are you going too?" "It depends"', *la policía detenía a los manifestantes según iban saliendo del edificio* 'the police were arresting the demonstrators as they came out of the building', *lo haremos según llegue papá* (*en cuanto llegue* is more usual) 'we'll do it as soon as father arrives', *según llegábamos al aparcamiento. . .un automóvil abandonaba un lugar grande y espacioso* (C. Rico-Godoy, Sp.) 'just as we were arriving at the parking lot … a car was leaving a large and roomy parking space', *según dicen. . .* 'according to what they say…'.

(ii) The following are colloquial or dialect: *dirías que es un millonario según habla* (*por la manera en que habla*) 'you'd think he was a millionaire from the way he talks', *a mí, según qué cosas, no me gusta hacerlas* (regional for *ciertas cosas. . .*) 'there are certain kinds of thing I don't like doing', the latter example being typical of eastern Spain.

34.16 *Sin*

'Without'. *Sin* raises few problems for the English-speaker, except when it appears before an infinitive, in which case it sometimes cannot be translated by the English verb form ending in -ing: cf. *dos Coca-Colas sin abrir* 'two Coca-Colas, unopened' (or 'not opened'). See 28.2.4.

No subas al tren sin billete	Don't get on the train without a ticket
Como vuelva a verte por aquí te echo sin contemplaciones	If I see you around here again I'll throw you out on the spot
Fumabas sin cesar	You were smoking ceaselessly

sin nadie que me ayude	without anyone to help me
Está más guapa sin peinar	She's more attractive without her hair done

Sin can be used to create a new noun, e.g. *los sin casa* 'the homeless'. *Sin* exists as a prefix in a few words, like *sinnúmero* 'vast abundance', *sinrazón* 'insanity'/'absurdity', *sinvergüenza* 'shameless person'.

34.17 *Sobre*

This preposition combines some of the meanings of the English words 'on', 'over', 'on top of' and 'above'.

(**a**) As a preposition of place:

It is an equivalent of *en* in the sense of 'on': *en/sobre la mesa* 'on the table', *en/sobre la pared* 'on the wall'; it is rather more literary than *en*. *Encima de* is also used of horizontal surfaces: *encima de la mesa* 'on (top of) the table'. However, where 'on top of' is impossible in English *encima de* is impossible in Spanish: *los hinchas se encuentran todavía en/sobre el terreno* 'the fans are still on the field/British 'pitch'.

Querían edificar sobre estos terrenos un hotel nuevo	They wanted to build a new hotel on this land
Este neumático tiene poco agarre sobre mojado	This tyre has poor grip on wet surfaces
Los rebeldes marcharon sobre la capital	The rebels marched on the capital
El castillo está edificado sobre un pintoresco valle	The castle is built overlooking a picturesque valley
Dios vela sobre sus hijos	God watches over his children
Un árbol agita unas hojas secas sobre sus cabezas (J. Cortázar, Arg.)	A tree is waving a few dry leaves over their heads
Un sol de fuego caía sobre los campos	A fiery sun fell on the plains

Compare *sobre*, *encima de* and *por encima de* in the following examples:

El rey está por encima de/sobre todos (rest, not motion)	The King is above everyone
Mi jefe siempre está encima de mí	My boss is always breathing down my neck
La bala pasó por encima de su cabeza, rozándole el pelo (motion)	The bullet passed over his/her head, just touching his/her hair
El avión voló por encima de/sobre la ciudad (motion: *sobre* implies height and is often more literary than *encima de*)	The plane flew over the city

(**i**) *Sobre*, when used as a spatial preposition, should not be used to join nouns in the way described in the introduction to this chapter: *?el libro sobre la mesa es mío* should be *el libro que está sobre la mesa es mío*.

(**b**) Approximation (especially with time phrases):

Llegaremos sobre las cinco de la tarde	We'll arrive around 5 p.m.
Tenía sobre cuarenta años (*unos 40 años* is more usual)	(S)he was around forty years old
Costó sobre cien mil (= *unos/unas 100.000*)	It cost around 100,000

(c) 'About' (= 'on the subject of')

In this sense, *sobre* implies formal discourse 'about', i.e. 'on the subject of' something. Informal discourse usually requires *de*, cf. *no he venido a hablar de tus problemas* 'I haven't come to talk about your problems' (not *sobre*), but *la OMS advierte sobre el peligro del uso de tranquilizantes sin receta médica* 'the WHO (World Health Organization) warns about the use of tranquillizers without medical prescription'. See 34.7.1e.

(d) Centre of rotation:

El mundo gira sobre su eje polar	The world spins about its polar axis
Las puertas se mueven sobre bisagras	Doors turn on hinges
Dio media vuelta sobre el pie izquierdo	(S)he did a half-turn on her/his left foot

(e) Superiority or precedence 'over':

El triunfo de los conservadores sobre la izquierda	The victory of the conservatives over the Left
Sobre todo, quisiera agradecer a mi mujer...	Above all, I would like to thank my wife...
Y, sobre cualquier escrúpulo, estaba mi hijo (A. Gala, Sp., dialogue)	And over and above any scruples there was my child (not 'son' here, since it was still unborn)
El crecimiento, en términos reales, supera el 50% sobre enero de 1983 (El País, Sp.)	In real terms, the growth in exports is 50% higher than January 1983
impuestos sobre la renta	income tax

34.18 *Tras*

'Behind', 'after'. It is an equivalent of the more usual *detrás de* 'behind' (location) and *después de* 'after' (time). Its brevity makes it popular with journalists (especially in Spain), but it is very rare in everyday speech. *Tras de* is an equally literary variant.

Dos siluetas deformes se destacaron tras el vidrio esmerilado (L. Goytisolo, Sp.)	Two distorted outlines loomed through/behind the frosted glass (i.e. semi-opaque ground glass)
un generoso proyecto tras el cual se esconden intenciones menos altruistas	a generous project behind which less generous intentions lurk
Me oculté tras el marco de la puerta (G. Cabrera Infante, Cu.)	I hid behind the door frame
Una banda de gaviotas venía tras el barco	A flock of gulls was following the boat

Detrás de could be used in all the above examples.

Así, tras de los duros años de 1936 a 1939... (popular press; *después de* possible)	So, after the hard years between 1936 and 1939...
Los cazadores denuncian "intereses políticos" tras las críticas de un grupo ecologista andaluz (El Mundo, Sp.)	Hunters denounce 'political interests' after criticisms by an Andalusian ecologist group

(i) Occasionally *tras* is unavoidable: *siguieron el mismo ritmo de trabajo, año tras año/día tras día* 'they followed the same work-pace, year after year/day after day', *...una beca para primer año, que será renovado para segundo...y así año tras año* (M. Puig, Arg., dialogue) '...a grant for the first year, which will be renewed for the second … and so on year after year', *han puesto un detective tras sus pasos* 'they've put a detective after him/on his trail'.

(ii) Note also the following construction: *tras de tener él la culpa, se enfada* (or *encima de tener él…*) 'not only is it his fault; he has the nerve to get angry', *tras ladrones, bufones* (*BCB*, Col.) 'as well as thieves, they're clowns'.

34.19 Prepositional phrases

The following is a list of common prepositional phrases. They can appear before nouns and, if their meaning is appropriate, before pronouns and infinitives. They should generally not be used to join nouns in the way described in the introduction to this chapter: **los senadores a favor de este proyecto* is bad Spanish for *los senadores que apoyaban/estaban a favor de este proyecto* 'the senators in favo(u)r of this project'.

a base de based on/consisting of (see note i)
a bordo de on board (of)
a cambio de in exchange for
a cargo de in charge of
a causa de because of
a costa de at the cost of
a despecho de in spite of
a diferencia de unlike
a disposición de at the disposal of
a distinción de unlike
a espaldas de behind the back of
a excepción de with the exception of
a expensas de at the expense of
a falta de for lack of/for want of
a favor de in favour of
a fin de with the aim of
a finales/fines de towards the end of
a flor de flush with/at…level (used with *piel* 'skin', *agua* 'water', *tierra* 'ground')
a fuerza de by dint of
a guisa de (literary) = *a modo de*
a gusto de to the taste of
a juicio de in the opinion of
a la hora de at the moment of/when it comes to…
a la sombra de in the shadow of
a la vera de (literary) = *al lado de*
a lo largo de throughout/along
a más de as well as
a mediados de towards the middle of
a modo de in the manner of
a partir de starting from
a pesar de despite
a por see 34.14.4h
a principios de towards the beginning of
a prueba de -proof, e.g. *a prueba de incendios* 'fireproof'

a punto de on the verge of
a raíz de immediately after/as an immediate result of
a razón de at the rate of
a riesgo de at the risk of
a sabiendas de with the knowledge of
a través de through/across
a vista de in the sight/presence of
a voluntad de at the discretion of
a vuelta de e.g. *a vuelta de correo* by return of post
abajo de (Lat. Am. only) underneath; see 34.3, 31.6.6
además de as well as
adentro de (Lat. Am. only) inside; see 31.6.5
afuera de (Lat. Am. only) outside; see 34.18, 31.6.6
al alcance de within reach of
al amor de in the warmth of (e.g. a fire)
al cabo de at the end of
al contrario de contrary to
al corriente de au fait with/informed about
al estilo de in the style of
al frente de at the head/forefront of
al lado de next to
al nivel de at the level of
al tanto de = *al corriente de*
alrededor de around
atrás de (Lat. Am. only) behind; see 31.6.7
bajo (la) condición de que on condition of
bajo pena de on pain of
cerca de near
con arreglo a in accordance with
con miras a bearing in mind/with a view to

con motivo de on the occasion of (an anniversary, etc.)

con objeto de with the object of

con relación a in respect of/in relation to

con respecto a with respect/reference to/in comparison to

con rumbo a in the direction of (i.e. moving towards)

con vistas a with a view to/bearing in mind

de acuerdo con in accordance with

de regreso a on returning to

debajo de see 34.3, 31.6.6

delante de see 34.2, 31.6.8

dentro de see 31.6.5

después de after (time); see 14.10.3

detrás de behind; see 34.18, 31.6.7

en atención a in consideration of

en base a see note (i)

en busca de in search of

en caso de in case of

en concepto de as/by way of e.g. *este dinero es en concepto de ayuda* 'this money is by way of assistance'

en contra de against

en cuanto a as for.../concerning

en forma de in the shape of

en honor de in honour of (but *en honor a la verdad* 'strictly speaking')

en lugar de instead of (+ noun or pronoun)

en medio de in the middle of

en pos de (literary) in search of/(also = *tras de*)

en pro de (literary) = *a favor de*

en torno a around (the subject of)/concerning

en vez de (+ infinitive) instead of ...-ing

en vías de on the way to: *país en vías de desarrollo* 'developing countries'

en vísperas de on the eve of

en vista de in view of

encima de see 34.9, 34.17

enfrente de opposite

fuera de see 31.6.5

lejos de far from

luego de (Lat. Am.) after; see 14.10.3

mas allá de beyond

no obstante (literary) notwithstanding

por causa de = *a causa de*

por cuenta de = *a mis/tus/sus/nuestras expensas*

por encima de over the head of/against the will of

por parte de on the part of

por razón de = *a causa de*

sin embargo de (literary) notwithstanding

so pena de (literary) = *bajo pena de*

so pretexto de (literary) on the pretext of

tras de see 34.18

(i) *El País, Libro de estilo,* 2002, 158, says of the phrase *?a base de*: 'En lugar de este horrible latiguillo y barbarismo de políticos y abogados, escríbase "a partir de", "basado en"'.

35

Relative clauses and relative pronouns

The main topics discussed in this chapter are:

- Forms of relative pronouns (Section 35.1.1)
- Definition of 'restrictive' and 'non-restrictive' relative clauses (Section 35.1.2)
- The uses of *que* as a relative pronoun (Section 35.2)
- Relative pronouns in non-restrictive relative clauses (Section 35.3)
- Relative pronouns after prepositions (35.4)
- Remarks on individual relative pronouns:

  El cual (35.5)   *Lo cual* and *lo que* (35.6)   *Cuyo* (35.7)

- *Donde*, *como* and *cuando* used to form relative clauses (Sections 35.10–12)

35.1 General

There are five relative pronouns in Spanish: *que, quien(es), el que, el cual* and *cuyo*. These introduce relative clauses, like the English relative pronouns 'that', 'who(m)', 'which' and 'whose' in 'the book that I read', 'the woman that/who(m) we saw', 'the book that/which I'm talking about', 'the students whose books are on the table', etc. Spanish relative pronouns are *never* written with an accent.

35.1.1 Forms of relative pronouns

El que and *el cual* agree in number and gender with the noun or pronoun that they refer to. *Quien* has no separate feminine form. *Que* is invariable. *Cuyo* 'whose' is discussed at 35.7.

	Singular		Plural	
Masculine	*el que*	*el cual*	*los que*	*los cuales*
Feminine	*la que*	*la cual*	*las que*	*las cuales*
	quien		*quienes*	
	que			

When it is used as a relative pronoun, *el que* is found only after prepositions (it has other uses as a nominalizer, explained in Chapter 36). Foreign students often neglect the more usual *el que* and *quien* in favour of *el cual*, which tends nowadays to be confined to formal styles.

Cuando, donde and como may also introduce relative clauses:, e.g. *la calle donde/en la que la vi* 'the street I saw her in/where I saw her'. See 35.10–35.12 for discussion.

35.1.2 Restrictive and non-restrictive relative clauses

This chapter occasionally refers to a distinction between restrictive and non-restrictive clauses.

Restrictive clauses limit the scope of what they refer to: *dejamos las manzanas que estaban verdes* 'we left the apples that were unripe'. This refers only to the unripe apples and therefore implies that some of them were ripe.

Non-restrictive clauses do not limit the scope of what they refer to: *dejamos las manzanas, que/las cuales estaban verdes* 'we left the apples, which were unripe'. This sentence indicates that all the apples were unripe. In writing non-restrictive clauses are typically marked in both languages by a comma, and in speech by a pause. English does not allow the relative pronoun 'that' in such sentences, and Spanish allows *el cual*, at least in formal styles.

A relative clause which refers to the whole of a unique entity is bound to be non-restrictive: *las pirámides egipcias, que/las cuales son uno de los monumentos más visitados por los turistas* 'the Egyptian pyramids, which are one of the monuments most visited by tourists'.

35.1.3 English and Spanish relative pronouns contrasted

Spanish relative clauses differ from English in five major respects:

(a) English constantly separates prepositions from relative pronouns: 'the path (that/which) we were walking **along**'. This is never possible in Spanish: *el camino **por el que** caminábamos*. Sentences like **el camino que caminábamos por*, sometimes heard in the Spanish of beginners, are almost unintelligible.

(b) A relative pronoun cannot be omitted in Spanish: 'the plane I saw' = *el avión que (yo) vi*.

(c) English and French constantly express relative clauses by using a gerund or participle: 'a box containing two books'/*une boîte contenant deux livres*. This is usually impossible in Spanish: *una caja que contiene/contenía dos libros*. The subject is discussed in detail at 20.3.

English goes further by simply using prepositions: 'the shirt on the chair is mine' = *la camisa **que está** en la silla es mía*. This is often impossible in Spanish: see introduction to Chapter 34, note (iii).

(d) Spanish does not allow a relative pronoun to be separated by a verb phrase from what it refers to. The type of sentence sporadically heard in English like ?'the man doesn't exist whom/that I'd want to marry', for the more normal 'the man (whom/that) I'd want to marry doesn't exist', cannot be translated by **el hombre no existe con el que/con quien yo quisiera casarme*. The correct translations are *no existe el hombre con el que/con quien yo quisiera casarme* or *el hombre con el que/con quien yo quisiera casarme no existe*. The first of these two translations is preferable, and this has important consequences for the word order of Spanish sentences containing relative clauses. See 37.2.1 for discussion. Further examples:

Acudieron corriendo los vecinos, que/quienes/los cuales no pudieron hacer nada (not **los vecinos acudieron corriendo, que. . .*)	The neighbo(u)rs came running, but could do nothing (literally, 'who could. . .')
Han vuelto las cigüeñas que hicieron su nido en el campanario el año pasado (not **las cigüeñas han vuelto que. . .*)	The storks that made their nest in the bell-tower last year have returned

(e) *Me voy a casar con un hombre que **tiene** dinero* and *me voy a casar con un hombre que **tenga** dinero* are both translatable as 'I'm going to marry a man who has money', but they mean very different things. See 16.14 for this crucial point.

35.2 The relative pronoun *que*

Que is by far the most frequent relative pronoun and may be used in the majority of cases to translate the English relative pronouns 'who', 'whom', 'which' or 'that'. However, there are certain cases in which *el que*, *quien* or *el cual* must be used, especially after prepositions. See 35.4 and 35.5 for further discussion. Examples of *que* as a relative pronoun:

los inversionistas que se quemaron los dedos	the investors who burnt their fingers
las hojas que caían de las ramas	the leaves (which were) falling from the branches
el libro que compré ayer	the book (that/which) I bought yesterday
las enfermeras que despidieron el año pasado (see 22.4.2 for use of personal *a* in this type of sentence)	the nurses (that/whom) they fired/ sacked last year
Le decía a cada momento que era diferente a todos los hombres que había conocido (S. Pitol, Mex.)	She told him constantly that he was different from all the men (whom/ that) she had known

(i) The word *todo* requires the pronoun *el que*: *todos los que dicen eso. . .* 'all who say that. . ./everyone who says that. . .'.

(ii) *Quien/quienes* are not used in restrictive clauses unless they follow a preposition (see the next two sections). Incorrect forms like **la chica quien viene*, **los hombres quienes dijeron eso* are heard in the Spanish of English-speakers, but *la chica que viene. . .* 'the girl who's/that's coming', *los hombres que dijeron eso*, 'the men who/that said that. . .', are the only possibilities.

(iii) In some very colloquial sentences *que* can have a verb or verb phrase as its antecedent (see Glossary): *llovía que daba miedo* 'it was raining enough to scare you witless', *da unos cortes que lo deja a uno patidifuso* (Sp.; from *GDLE* 7.4.1.1) '(s)he comes out with some really embarrassing things that knock you sideways!' (note singular form *deja*).

35.3 Use of *que*, *quien*, *el cual* in non-restrictive relative clauses

When no preposition appears before the relative pronoun and the relative clause is non-restrictive (see 35.1.2 for definition), *que*, *quien* or *el cual* may be used. *Quien* is nowadays used only for human beings, and *el cual* is emphatic and tends to be restricted to formal language (see 35.5 for discussion):

Fueron a hablar con José, que/quien/el cual estaba de buen humor	They went to talk to José, who was in a good mood
los Líderes Agropecuarios del Grupo Cairns, el cual incluye 18 países exportadores (advert., Arg.)	the leaders in Agriculture and Fisheries in the Cairns Group, which includes eighteen exporting countries
Nadie miraba al párroco, quien, sentado en la primera banca, había abierto los ojos (M. Vargas Llosa, Pe.)	No one was looking at the parish priest who, sitting in the front pew, had opened his eyes

El cual or *quien* is more likely to be used whenever the relative pronoun is separated from what it refers to or from the verb of which it is the subject or object, or after a heavy pause. *El cual* is discussed further at 35.5.

(i) Only *que* can be used after personal pronouns: *yo que me preocupo tanto por ti...* 'I who worry so much about you...', *...y ahora, hablando con ella, que tenía el sol de la tarde en el rostro* (F. Umbral, Sp.) '...and now, talking to her, who had the evening sun on her face', *él, que en el fondo es muy clase media, vive en una casita nada suntuosa de el Prado* (M. Benedetti, Ur.) 'he, who is at heart very middle-class, lives in a in a by no means sumptuous little house in El Prado'.

(ii) In 'cleft' sentences (discussed at 36.2) a nominalizer, e.g. *el que* or *quien*, must be used: *soy consciente de que tengo que ser yo misma **la que/quien** resuelva el problema* (female speaking) 'I'm aware that I must be the one to solve the problem myself', *dice que fue su marido quien lo mató* (A. Grandes, Sp., dialogue; or *el que*) 'she says it was her husband who killed him'.

(iii) *El que* also translates 'the one who/which' and is discussed under nominalizers at 36.1: *aquella chica es Charo—la que lleva el chándal rojo* 'that girl over there is Charo—the one wearing the red tracksuit'. This is not a relative clause but a phrase in apposition (see Glossary); *el que* is used as a relative pronoun only after prepositions (see 35.4). However, *GDLE* 7.5.1.4 notes the occurrence in Argentina of examples like *ahogada en un mar de sellos y de rúbricas, **los** que se repiten...* 'drowning in a sea of rubber stamps and signatures repeating themselves...' where standard language uses *...que se repiten*.

35.4 Relative pronoun after prepositions

35.4.1 After prepositions *el que, quien* or *el cual* are used

The relative pronouns required are:

(a) Non-human antecedents (see Glossary): *el que* (or *el cual*).

(b) Human antecedents: *el que, quien* (or *el cual*). *Quien* is slightly more formal than *el que*:

la amenaza de guerra bajo la que vivimos	the threat of war we're living under
la puerta tras la que se escondió	the door behind which she hid
comunicados en los que se recuerda la ilegalidad de las acciones propuestas (*Abc*, Sp.)	communiqués recalling the illegality of the actions proposed

la calle desde la que/desde donde he venido andando	the street I've walked from
Hay gente con la que la vida se ensaña (A. Mastretta, Mex., or *con quien*)	There are people that life has it in for
¿y todas. . .ésas con quien has paseado? (A. Buero Vallejo, Sp., dialogue; *quien* for *quienes* is popular style; *las que* possible)	and what about all those… women you've walked out with?

(i) If the gender of a human antecedent is unknown or irrelevant, the genderless *quien* must be used: *no hay nadie con quien hablar* 'there's no one to talk to', *busca a alguien de quien te puedas fiar* 'look for someone you can trust', *como se ayuda a alguna persona a quien se quiere* (J. J. Arreola, Mex.) 'as one helps some person whom one loves'.

(ii) To refer to neuter words like *algo, nada* and *mucho, lo que* or *que* are used: *no hay nada con (lo) que puedas sacarle punta* 'there's nothing you can sharpen it with', *esto es algo sobre lo que tenemos que reflexionar* (J. Caro Baroja, Sp.) 'this is something we have to reflect on', *iba a morir allí, no por algo en lo que creía, sino por respeto a su hermano mayor* (M. Vargas Llosa, Pe.) 'he was going to die there, not for something he believed in, but out of respect for his elder brother'.

(iii) *Quien(es)* was often used for non-living antecedents before the 18th century, e.g. *un monasterio en quien era priora una su hermana* (*Don Quijote*) 'a convent in which a sister of his was prioress', nowadays *en el que* or *donde*, and *una hermana suya*.

(iv) Popular speech says things like *?la chica que fui con ella* for *la chica con la que fui*. See 35.8b.

35.4.2 Relative pronoun *que* after a preposition

Que alone is preferred as a relative pronoun after prepositions in certain circumstances difficult to define (as *GDLE* 7.5.1.3 acknowledges), but most often when the antecedent is definite, e.g. preceded by the definite article:

(a) After *a* (when it is not personal *a*), after *con* and after *de*—unless the latter means 'from'. Use of *que* alone is especially common after abstract nouns:

la discriminación a que están sometidas nuestras frutas y hortalizas (El País)	the discrimination which our fruits and vegetables are subject to
la notoria buena fe con que Collazos expone sus dudas y sus convicciones (M. Vargas Llosa, Pe.)	the well-known good faith with which Collazos expounds his doubts and convictions
los litros de tónico capilar con que se bañaba la cara cada día (L. Sepúlveda, Ch.)	the litres of hair tonic he bathed his face with every day
la aspereza con que la trataba (S. Pitol, Mex.)	the harshness with which he treated her
Suspiraba con la misma compasión con que le habían oído en los sueños (L. Mateo Díez, Sp.)	He sighed with the same compassion that they had heard him sigh with in their dreams

El/la/los/las que would be possible, though less elegant, in the foregoing examples, except the last.

(b) Frequently after *en* when precise spatial location is not intended. Compare *la caja en la que encontré la llave* 'the box I found the key in', but *la casa en que/donde vivo* 'the house I live in', not **'the house **inside which** I live':

el desierto humano en que ella estaba *perdida* (F. Umbral)	the human desert she was lost in
Me gustaría vivir en un sitio en que/ *donde no hubiera coches*	I'd like to live in a place where there were no cars
las formas racionales en que se basa la *vida social* (M. Vargas Llosa, Pe.)	the rational forms on which social life is based

If precise spatial location is intended *el/la/los que* is needed: *trenzó primero su melena en la que se le habían multiplicado las canas* (A. Mastretta, Mex.) 'she first plaited her hair, where grey/US gray hairs had multiplied'.

En que is also preferred when the preceding noun is a period of time. After *día, semana, mes, año, momento* the *en* is also often omitted. In the following examples *el que* is not possible:

una noche en que iba a buscarla (F. Umbral)	one night (when) I went to fetch her
el día que te vi	the day I saw you
el único día que se produjeron diferencias *de importancia fue el jueves* (*La Nación,* Arg.)	the only day on which any important differences were recorded was Thursday
el año que nos casamos	the year we got married
el mes que llovió tanto	the month it rained so much
en los meses que estuvo Edwards en Cuba (M. Vargas Llosa, Pe.)	during the months Edwards spent in Cuba
durante el año y medio que he estado en el *cargo*	in the year and a half I've been in the job

35.5 *El cual*

In general *el cual* is more formal than *el que* or *quien*: foreigners spoil much good Spanish by over-using it. But it may be preferred or obligatory in the following contexts:

(a) After *según* when this word means 'according to' rather than 'depending on':

el argumento según el cual...	the argument according to which...
José Carlos Mariátegui, según el cual "el *marxismo leninismo es el sendero* *luminoso de la revolución"* (M. Vargas Llosa, Pe.)	J. C. Mariátegui, according to whom 'Marxist Leninism is the shining path to revolution'

As an example of *según* meaning 'depending on', cf. —*¿Qué precio tienen? —Según los que quiera* '"What's their price?" "It depends on which ones you want".'

(b) It is often preferred after prepositions of more than one syllable like *para, sobre, contra, entre, mediante,* and after prepositional phrases, e.g. *a pesar de* 'despite', *debajo de* 'underneath', *delante de* 'in front of', *frente a* 'opposite', *en virtud de* 'by reason of', etc.:

...una formación profesional mediante la *cual los funcionarios de grado medio* *estén capacitados para...* (*Cambio16,* Sp.)	...professional training whereby middle-grade government employees will be equipped to...
Hay seres con atmósfera propia, dentro de la *cual es bueno vivir* (F. Umbral, Sp.)	There are beings with their own atmosphere, within which it is good to live

However, *el que* is nowadays found even in these contexts:

El otro fue alcanzado por ocho balazos, a consecuencia de los que moriría minutos más tarde (El País, Sp.)	The other one received eight bullet wounds, as a consequence of which he was to die a few minutes later
mi pobre y sucio uniforme de enfermero, sobre el que me había puesto un veterano jersey (L. Silva, Sp.)	my poor and dirty nurse's uniform, over which I had put an ancient jersey

(**c**) *El cual* is also especially favoured when the antecedent (see Glossary) is separated from the relative pronoun by intervening words, or when the relative is separated from its verb:

*un gran árbol, en cuyo tronco algunos muchachos vagos han pintado ciertas palabrotas u obscenidades, pero en **el cual** no deja de circular la vida que proviene de la savia* (La Prensa, Nicaragua)	a great tree, on whose trunk some idle boys have painted swearwords or obscenities, but in which the life coming from its sap is still flowing

A statistical survey of spoken Spanish (DeMello, 1994, 3) amply confirms this tendency.

(**d**) *El cual* is used after *algunos de...*, *todos...*, *la mayoría de...*, *parte de...* and similar phrases:

los jóvenes españoles, la mayoría de los cuales son partidarios del divorcio	young Spaniards, the majority of whom are in favour of divorce
La selección chilena marcó diecisiete goles, once de los cuales fueron de Jorge Toro (L. Sepúlveda, Ch.)	The Chilean selection scored seventeen goals, eleven of which were by Jorge Toro
la revolución social, parte integrante de la cual era la emancipación de la mujer	the social revolution, of which an integral part was the emancipation of woman
Corren por Madrid muchos rumores, algunos de los cuales vamos a recoger aquí	Many rumours are circulating in Madrid, some of which we shall report here

(**e**) As the subject of a verb, *el cual* seems to be obligatory after a heavy pause such as a sentence break:

*Fueron a hablar con su tío, un setentón de bigote blanco y acento andaluz, que hacía alarde de ideas muy avanzadas. **El cual**, tras un largo silencio, contestó...*	They went to talk with his uncle, a seventy-year-old with a white moustache and an Andalusian accent who boasted of very advanced ideas. Who, after a long silence, replied...

(i) Despite all these remarks, a survey of the corpus of educated spoken Spanish by DeMello (1994), 2, reveals that *el cual* is the favoured form after prepositions in spontaneous speech in Buenos Aires, Santiago de Chile, Lima, Bogotá and Caracas. *El que* was preferred in Mexico, Havana, Madrid and Seville.

35.6 *Lo cual* and *lo que*

These are used when the relative pronoun refers not to a noun or pronoun but to a whole sentence or to an idea, which, being neither masculine or feminine in gender, require a neuter pronoun. Since the clause is always non-restrictive, *lo cual* is common, especially in writing. Compare: *Juan trajo una lista de cifras que explicaba su inquietud* 'Juan brought a list of figures which (i.e. the list) explained his anxiety', and *Juan trajo una lista de cifras, lo cual/lo que explicaba su inquietud* 'Juan brought a list of figures, which (i.e. the fact he brought it) explained his anxiety'. Further examples:

En un primer momento se anunció que los misiles eran americanos, lo cual fue desmentido en Washington (El País, Sp.)	Initially it was stated that the missiles were American, which was denied in Washington
Se declara agente de compras de Marroquinerías Brunni, lo cual ponía en evidencia la complicidad de esa empresa (L. Sepúlveda, Ch., dialogue)	He admits he is a buyer for Brunni Leather Goods, which proved that company's complicity

For *lo que* as a nominalizer (= 'the thing that...'), see 36.1.5.

35.7 Cuyo

Cuyo has the following forms:

	Masculine	Feminine
Singular	*cuyo*	*cuya*
Plural	*cuyos*	*cuyas*

It translates 'whose', and is often an elegant alternative for an otherwise tortuous relative clause. It agrees in number and gender with the following noun, but if there is more than one noun it agrees only with the first: *una mujer cuyas manos y pies estaban quemados por el sol* 'a woman whose hands and feet had been burnt by the sun':

la Asamblea Constituyente, cuyos miembros serían elegidos en diciembre (G. García Márquez, Col.)	the Constituent Assembly, whose members would be elected in December
un reptil cubierto completamente de plumas y cuyas extremidades evolucionaron en alas (Granma, Cu.)	a reptile completely covered in feathers, and whose limbs evolved into wings

(i) Grammarians condemn such sentences as *?se alojó en el Imperial, en cuyo hotel había conocido a su primera mujer* 'he stayed at the Imperial, in which hotel he had met his first wife': better *...el Imperial, hotel donde/hotel en el cual había conocido a su primera mujer*. But this construction is allowed with *caso*: *es posible de que todos los hoteles estén completos, en cuyo caso la reunión será aplazada* 'it is possible that all the hotels may be full, in which case the meeting will be postponed'.

(ii) *Del que/de quien* are occasionally used for *cuyo*, although this is criticized by Seco (1998), 143: *un torero, de quien alabó el tesón y el valor a toda prueba* (i.e. *cuyo tesón y valor alabó...*) 'a bullfighter, whose indefatigable steadfastness and courage he praised', *Alidio era un preso del que nunca se supo con exactitud su delito* (L. Mateo Díez, Sp., i.e. *cuyo delito nunca se supo...*) 'Alidio was a prisoner whose crime was never precisely known'.

(iii) *Cuyo* is rare in spontaneous speech and virtually unheard in popular styles. See 35.8c.

(iv) There used to be an interrogative form *cúyo*, but it is no longer used except in some local Latin American dialects, e.g. rural Colombia. One now says *¿de quién es esa mochila?* 'whose rucksack is that?', not **¿cúya mochila es ésa/esa?*

35.8 Relative clauses in familiar speech

Students will encounter a number of popular or familiar constructions that should probably be left to native speakers.

(a) There is a colloquial tendency, which may sound uneducated, to insert a redundant pronoun in relative clauses: *dicen cosas que nadie (las) entiende* 'they say things no one understands'. See 11.16.5.

(b) Popular and very relaxed informal speech often avoids combining prepositions and relative pronouns by a type of construction banned from writing:

?*en casa de una mujer que yo vivía con ella (con la que yo vivía)*	in the house of a woman I was living with
?*Te acuerdas del hotel que estuvimos el año pasado? (. . .en el que estuvimos. . .)*	Do you remember the hotel we stayed in last year?
?*Soy un emigrante que siempre me han preocupado los problemas de la emigración (. . .al que siempre han preocupado los problemas) (reader's letter in El País, Sp.)*	I am an emigrant who has always been concerned with the problems of emigration

This construction is not uncommon in Golden-Age texts, but it should not be imitated by foreign learners.

(c) *Cuyo* is rare in spontaneous speech (*GDLE* 15.5 says that it is virtually extinct in Mexico). There are many correct alternatives, e.g. *las mujeres cuyo marido las ayuda en casa* 'women whose husbands help them in the house' can be recast as *las mujeres que tienen un marido que las ayuda en casa*. However, popular speech often uses a construction called *quesuismo* which is generally stigmatized: *los alumnos que sus notas no están en la lista (cuyas notas no están. . .)* 'the students whose marks aren't on the list'. This construction quite often slips into educated speech, as DeMello (1992), 5, shows.

35.9 *Cartas a contestar...*, etc.

The following construction is nowadays common in journalism, official documents or business letters: *un libro y una tesis **a tomar** muy en serio por estudiosos y ciudadanos en general* (*Cambio16*, Sp., for *que deben ser tomados en serio. . .*) 'a book and a thesis to be taken very seriously by students and citizens in general'. See 18.12 for a discussion.

35.10 *Donde, adonde, en donde* as relatives

Donde is commonly used as a relative, especially after *hacia, a* (in the meaning of 'towards'), *desde, de* meaning 'from', *por* meaning 'along'/'through', *en* meaning 'place in', etc. As a relative its use is rather wider than the English 'where':

Lo recogí en la calle donde te vi	I picked it up in the street where I saw you
Perquín, la ciudad donde impera la limpieza (*La Prensa*, El Salvador)	Perquín, the city where cleanliness rules
Ése/Ese es el cajón de donde sacó los papeles	That's the drawer from which (s)he took the papers

In all the above restrictive clauses, *el que* or *el cual* could be used with the appropriate preposition. However, in the following non-restrictive clause only *donde* is possible (just as 'where' is in English): *volvieron a encontrarse en París, donde se habían conocido veinte años antes* 'they met again in Paris, where they had met for the first time twenty years before'.

(i) *Adonde* is not the same as *a donde* or *adónde*.

(1) **Adonde** is a relative used before verbs of motion and and it refers to some clearly identified place, e.g. *el pueblo adonde yo iba* (relative) 'the village I was going to'.

(2) **A donde** is an adverb used with verbs of motion when no noun of place appears, as in *fueron a donde no debían ir* 'they went where they shouldn't have gone'.

(3) **Adónde** is found in direct or indirect questions, as in *¿adónde va usted?* 'where are you going?', *¿adónde habrán ido rodando las pastillas de Optalidón?* (C. Martín Gaite, Sp.) 'where can the Optalidon tablets have rolled to?' (direct questions), and *me dijiste no saber adónde iban a parar* (A. Buero Vallejo, Sp., dialogue) 'you said you didn't know where they'd end up' (indirect question).

In carelessly written texts these three forms are constantly confused.

(ii) *En donde* is spatially more specific than *donde*, and is rather literary: *hay una tienda pequeña en Westwood en donde venden infinidad de camisetas con letreros increíbles* (C. Rico-Godoy, Sp.) 'there's a little store in Westwood where they sell a vast range of T-shirts with fantastic things written on them' (...*Westwood donde venden*... would have come to the same thing), *los cajones en donde el tío guardaba sus útiles de trabajo* (M. Torres, Sp.) 'the drawers where my uncle kept his tools'.

(iii) *Donde* is sometimes used colloquially in Mexico (and possibly elsewhere in northern Latin America) to mean a nervous 'what if?' In this context Peninsular Spanish uses *anda que si* + indicative or *anda que como* + subjunctive : *no digas, estoy muy espantada, donde a la pobre criatura le salga la nariz de este hombre* (A. Mastretta, Mex., dialogue; Sp. *anda que como le salga*...) 'don't even mention it, I'm really terrified. What if this poor little thing gets this man's nose?!', *no sé cómo se van a casar. Donde estén igual de ignorantes en lo demás* (ibid. Sp. *anda que como estén*..., *anda que si están*...) 'I don't know how they're going to get married. What if they're just as ignorant about all the other things?!'

(iv) For *donde* meaning 'at the house of', see 24.9.

35.11 *Como* as a relative

Como is officially recommended after *la manera* and *el modo*, although *en que* is used after *forma*, and usually after the other two as well:

La manera como un país se fortalece y desarrolla su cultura es abriendo sus puertas y ventanas (M. Vargas Llosa, Pe.)	The way a country strengthens and develops its culture is by opening its doors and windows
...y la manera en que nos adorábamos (A. Bryce Echenique, Pe.)	...and the way we adored one another
...la forma en que los países tratan a su propia gente (*La Nación*, Arg.)	...the way countries treat their own people

35.12 *Cuando* as a relative

Cuando occurs only in non-restrictive clauses: *en agosto, cuando les den las vacaciones a los niños, nos iremos al campo* 'in August, when the children have their holidays/vacation, we'll go to the countryside', *incluso en nuestros días, cuando nadie cree ya en las hadas* 'even in our day, when no one believes in fairies any more'; but *solamente puedo salir los días (en) que no trabajo* (restrictive) 'I can only go out on the days I'm not working'.

(i) *Cuando* is used with *apenas, aún, todavía, entonces, no, no bien*: *apenas había aparcado el coche cuando se acercó un policía* '(s)he had hardly parked the car when a policeman came up', *aún/todavía no había empezado a estudiar cuando le dieron un empleo* '(s)he hadn't yet started studying when they gave him/her a job'. Compare the following restrictive clauses: *en un momento en que...* 'at a moment when...', *en una época en que...* 'in a period when...', *en un año (en) que...* 'in a year when...', etc.

(ii) *Que* is used in the following phrases: *ahora que usted sabe la verdad* 'now (that) you know the truth', *luego que haya terminado* 'as soon as (s)he's finished', *siempre que haya bastante* 'as long as there's enough', *cada vez que me mira* 'whenever (s)he looks at me', *de modo que/de manera que* 'so that'.

In cleft sentences *donde, como* or *cuando* may be obligatory and *que* disallowed (especially in Peninsular Spanish): *es así como hay que hacerlo* 'this is how it must be done', *fue entonces cuando lo notó* 'it was then that (s)he noticed it'. See 36.2 for discussion.

35.13 Relative clauses after a nominalizer

A nominalizer (e.g. *el que* meaning 'the one who/which') cannot be followed by the relatives *el que* or *el cual*. The noun must be repeated or, in written language, *aquel* is used:

Se imagina un nuevo don Julián, una versión moderna de aquel al que rinde homenaje el título del libro (M. Vargas Llosa, Pe.; not *el al que...*)	He imagines a new Don Julian, a modern version of the one to whom the book's title pays homage
Traiga otro plato, que no me gusta comer en los platos en los que han comido otros (spoken language)	Bring another plate—I don't like eating off those that others have eaten off

(i) *Ese/este* cannot replace *aquel* in this construction: *los/aquellos que suspendan en junio deberán presentarse de nuevo en septiembre* (from *GDLE* 14.3.1), not *esos/estos que...* 'those who fail in June must sit the examination again in September'.

35.14 Miscellaneous examples of relative clauses

Falta saber las condiciones en que está	We have yet to know what conditions he is in
Falta saber en qué condiciones está	We have yet to know what conditions he is in
Falta saber en las condiciones que está	We have yet to know what conditions he is in
Según el cine a que vayas/Según al cine que vayas (four examples from M. Moliner)	Depending on what cinema you go to
Era la habitación más pequeña en (la) que jamás he estado	It was the smallest room I've ever been in
Era la habitación más pequeña de todas las que he estado (familiar spoken language)	It was the smallest room I've ever been in
¿Cómo se explica el fenómeno singular que fue la victoria de los liberales?	How does one explain the singular phenomenon of the liberals' victory?
el espectáculo conmovedor que son las ruinas de Machu Picchu	the moving spectacle of the Machu Picchu ruins

36

Nominalizers and cleft sentences

The main points discussed in this chapter are:

- *el de*, *los de*, etc. (= 'the one(s) from…') (Section 36.1.2)
- *lo de* (Section 36.1.3)
- *el que*, *los que*, etc. ('the one(s) that…') (Section 36.1.4)
- *lo que* (Section 36.1.5)
- *quien/quienes* when it means 'the person(s) who…' (Section 36.1.6)
- Cleft sentences (e.g. 'it was here that…', 'it was X that said it', etc.) (Section 36.2)
- Translating 'that's why…' (Section 36.2.4)

36.1 Nominalizers

36.1.1 General

'Nominalizers' are words or phrases that turn other words or phrases into noun phrases: *los que interrogan* 'those who interrogate' is close in meaning to *los interrogadores* 'the interrogators', *la de antes* 'the one (fem.) from before' to *la anterior* 'the previous one', *quien* (no accent) *es inteligente* 'someone who is intelligent' means more or less the same as *una persona inteligente* 'an intelligent person', etc.

For the use of *el que* and *quien* as relative pronouns (*el hombre con el que/con quien hablaba*, *la mesa en la que escribo*) see Chapter 35, especially 35.3 and 35.4. For *quién* in questions, see 24.5. For *el que* (invariable) + subjunctive meaning 'the fact that' (*el hecho de que*), see 16.10.1.

36.1.2 *El de*

'The one(s) belonging to', 'that/those of', 'the one(s) from', etc., French *celui de*, *celle de*, *ceux de*, *celles de*. *El de* agrees in number and gender with the noun it refers to:

De los alumnos, los de cuarto son los mejores	Of the students, the ones from the fourth year are the best
—Quién ha venido? —Las de siempre	'Who's come?' 'The same women/ girls as usual'
Así que eres la de la droguería (S. Puértolas, Sp., dialogue)	So you're the girl from the chemist's/ US drugstore
Espera cotejar el ADN de los restos hallados con los del familiar enterrado (Granma, Cu.)	She hopes to compare the DNA from the remains discovered with those of the buried family member

Translation by a Saxon genitive (i.e. apostrophe *s*) or by a compound noun is sometimes the solution:

Quita los de ayer y pon los de la semana pasada	Take away yesterday's and put last week's
Lo he hecho para aumentar la moral, sobre todo la de los escritores (J. M. Lara, Sp.)	I've done it to raise morale, especially writers'
la industria del petróleo y la del carbón	the oil and coal industries

La de can mean 'the amount of'/'how many' in colloquial language: *no sé la de temas que tengo apuntados* (C. Martín Gaite, Sp.) 'I don't know how many topics I've got jotted down', *me recordó la de veces que me he reído!* (*La Jornada*, Mex.) 'he reminded me how many times I've laughed...' See also 3.2.30.

(i) Note that *de* is the only preposition that can follow *el/la/los/las*. Mistakes like **los con coche* 'those with cars', **la para María* 'the one (e.g. *carta*) for Maria' are common among English-speakers; one says *los que tienen coche, la que es para María*, etc.

36.1.3 Lo de

This is the neuter version of *el de*. Like all neuter pronouns, it must be used if there is no noun to which it can refer, otherwise *el/la/los/las de* must be used. It is invariable in form.

Lo de usually means 'the business/affair of...' in such phrases as *lo del dinero perdido* 'the affair of the lost money':

Siempre está a vueltas con lo de que cuándo nos vamos a casar	(S)he's always coming back to/going on about (the issue of) when we're getting married
De lo de la abuela poco les debe quedar (C. Martín Gaite, Sp.)	They must have very little left of grandma's (things, money)
Cedí en lo de dejar el piso a Chule por tres días más (I. Merlo, Sp., dialogue)	I gave in about letting Chule have the flat for another three days
La primera vez que vi a Andrés furioso fue cuando lo de la plaza de toros (A. Mastretta, Mex., dialogue; for *cuando* here see 24.8)	The first time I saw Andrés furious was at the time of the bullring business
Todo lo del maldito telegrama se me vino a la memoria (A. Bryce Echenique, Pe.)	The whole business of the damned telegram came into my mind

(i) *Lo de* is common in the Southern Cone with the meaning *en casa de* 'at...'s house', cf. *la semana pasada tuvimos una reunioncita en lo del viejo Leandro* (M. Benedetti, Ur., dialogue) 'last week we had a get-together at old Leandro's house'.

36.1.4 El que

This translates 'the one(s) who/which', 'that/those which', etc. (Fr. *celui/celle/ceux/celles qui*). It agrees in number and gender with the noun it replaces:

la que está fuera	the one (fem.) who/that is outside
el que llegó ayer	the one (masc.) who/that arrived yesterday
los que dicen eso	the ones/those (masc.) who say that

la que fue considerada doctrina alternativa (*El País*, Sp.)	what was considered the alternative doctrine
Yo no soy el que fui (J. Marías, Sp., dialogue)	I'm not the person I was
Me atraían las que le tuvieron cariño, las que incluso le parieron hijos (A. Mastretta, Mex., dialogue)	I felt drawn to those women who had been fond of him, even to the ones who had given him children

(i) *El de* and *el que* can be combined: *la libertad de la televisión debería ser siempre la del que la contempla, no la del que la programa* (*El País*, Sp.) 'freedom in television should always belong to the person watching it, not to the person programming it'.

(ii) *La que* is often used on both continents instead of *lo que* in humorous warnings: *no sabes la que te espera* 'you don't know what's waiting for you...', *¡la que te tienen preparada!...* 'what they've got in store for you!...'

36.1.5 *Lo que*

The invariable neuter version of the above: it refers to no specific noun. It can normally be translated by the phrase 'the thing that...' or by the pronoun 'what' (cf. Fr. *ce qui/ce que*):

Lo que más me gusta es cuando haces versos (C. Martín Gaite, Sp., dialogue)	What I like best is when you make up rhymes
Octavia, un hombre es lo que siente (A. Bryce Echenique, Pe., dialogue)	Octavia, a man is what he feels
Tuvo bien acordarse de un chiste tras otro en lo que quedó de cena (A. Mastretta, Mex.)	He was so good as to remember joke after joke during what was left of dinner
La valla se prolonga todo lo que da de sí la vista	The fence stretches as far as the eye can see
Le pasa lo que a ti	The same thing happens to him as to you

Compare *por Rosario fue por la que se pelearon* 'Rosario was **the woman** they fought over', and *por Rosario fue por lo que se pelearon* 'Rosario was **what** (i.e. the issue/problem) they fought over'.

(i) *Cuanto* can be used pronominally as an equivalent of *todo lo que* 'everything that...': *se creen cuanto le dicen* = *se creen todo lo que le dicen* 'they believe everything they tell them'.

36.1.6 *Quien/quienes* as an equivalent of 'the one(s) who'

Quien/quienes (no accent, but see note ii) can optionally replace *el que* in many contexts provided it refers to a human being. Since *quien* is not marked for gender it is not an exact equivalent of *el que* and must be used when reference to a specific gender is to be avoided. Only *quien* is possible in the meaning of 'no one':

El que diga eso es un cobarde	The person who says that is a coward
Quien diga eso es un cobarde	(same, but rather literary)
Quienes/Los que no estén de acuerdo, que se vayan	Anyone not in agreement should go
Quien no es mala persona es el sargento	Someone who's not a bad guy is the sergeant

El coronel no tiene quien le escriba (G. García Márquez, Col., title; *el que* impossible here)	The colonel has no one to write to him
Escuchaba sin oír las conversaciones de quienes se cruzaban con nosotros (S. Puértolas, Sp.)	He listened absent-mindedly (lit. 'without hearing') the conversations of the people walking by us
Cada quien tiene sus ritos (A. Mastretta, Mex. Sp. *cada cual*)	Everyone has different rites/rituals

(i) Since it is indeterminate, *quien/quienes* cannot be used when the identity or sex of the person referred to is known and emphasized: *lo/le vimos con la que vive al lado* 'we saw him with the girl who lives next door' (**le/lo vimos con quien vive al lado* = ***'we saw him with whoever lives next door').

(ii) A common colloquial construction is *tú no eres quién para decirme eso* 'you're no one to tell me that'/'who are you to tell me that?' This seems to be the nominalizer *quien*, but it is usually written with an accent in this construction. Nominalizers do not normally have an accent.

36.2 'Cleft' sentences

36.2.1 General

These are sentences on which one of the elements is picked out and focused by using 'to be'. This can be done in one of two ways:

Simple sentence	*Cleft sentence*
The fire started here	It was here that the fire started/ Here was where the fire started
John said it	It was John who said it/ John was the one who said it
I cut it with this knife	It was this knife I cut it with/ This knife is the one I cut it with

The structure of such sentences differs in Spanish from their French and English counterparts, and there are important differences between Peninsular and Latin-American usage with respect to cleft sentences containing prepositions.

(i) In cleft sentences the tense of the two verbs should be the same (although the rule is sometimes ignored): *fue aquí donde la vi* 'it was here that I saw her', *ha sido aquí donde la he visto* (same meaning, but perfect of recency), *era aquí donde la veía* 'it was here that I used to see her'. One should not, for example, say *?era aquí donde la vi*, cf. English 'it is here that I saw her', although *es aquí donde la vi* 'it is here that I saw her' is heard.

When *ser* is in the future or conditional tense, the other verb is in the present subjunctive: *seré yo quien tenga que solucionarlo* 'it'll be me who has to solve it'. See 16.4.3.

36.2.2 'She is the one who...', etc.

English-speakers, especially those who know French, are tempted to link this type of cleft sentence by the word *que*, but only a nominalizer (*el que* or *quien*) can be used:

Es este coche el que compré	It's this car that I bought
Este coche es el que compré	This car's the one that I bought
Fue esa chica la que/quien lo hizo	It was that girl who did it
Esa chica fue la que/quien lo hizo	That girl was the one who did it
Esto es lo que más rabia me da	This is what makes me most furious
Lo que más rabia me da es esto	What makes me most furious is this
Porque nunca es ella, doña Pilar, la que aporta el dinero (interview, *Cambio16*, Sp.)	Because it's never Doña Pilar who brings in the money
No, eres tú el que no me entiende (J. Madrid, Sp., dialogue)	No, you're the one who doesn't understand me
El pelaje overo es el que prefieren los ángeles (J. L. Borges, Arg.)	Lamb's fleece is the one that angels prefer

The following is *not* a cleft sentence: *éstas son las niñas que me lo dijeron* 'these are the girls who told me'; but this is: *fueron estas niñas las que/quienes me lo dijeron* 'it was these girls who told me', and so is *estas niñas fueron las que/quienes me lo dijeron*. In other words, the English translation of the cleft sentence begins with 'it' or contains the pronoun 'the one(s)', as in 'these girls are the ones who told me'.

(i) Foreign students tend not to use nominalizers in cleft sentences. This produces bad Spanish like **fue él que me dijo* for *fue él quien/el que me dijo* 'it was he who told me', **fue esto que* (or even **qué*) *descubrió Darwin* for the correct *fue esto lo que descubrió Darwin / esto fue lo que descubrió Darwin* 'this is what Darwin discovered'. The question words *quién, qué, cuál, dónde, cómo*, are never used to join cleft sentences.

36.2.3 Cleft sentences involving prepositions or adverbs

(a) If the first half of a Spanish cleft sentence contains a preposition, the preposition must normally be repeated in the second half: Spanish says 'it's with her with whom you must speak', *es con ella con la que/con quien tienes que hablar; del que más se hablaba era de David Siqueiros* (E. Poniatowska, Mex.) 'the person most talked about was D. Siqueiros', *por lo que más se distinguía era por su incansable afición a molestar* (S. Puértolas, Sp.) 'what most distinguished him was his tireless delight in being a nuisance'.

However, when the cleft sentence begins with *ser*, informal Latin-American Spanish often uses *que* alone in a way similar to French or to the English 'that'. This tendency is vehemently rejected by many Spaniards, although it is heard increasingly among younger generations in Spain:

Sp. *Es desde esta ventana desde donde se ve el mar*	It's from this window that you can see the sea
Lat. Am. *Es desde esta ventana que se ve el mar*	
Desde esta ventana es desde donde se ve el mar (avoided in Latin America?)	This balcony is where you can see the sea from
Sp. *Fue por eso por lo que cambió de empleo*	That was why (s)he decided to change jobs
Lat. Am. *Fue por eso que cambió de empleo*	
Pero es con la Maga que hablo (J. Cortázar, Arg., dialogue; Sp. . . .*con la que/quien hablo*)	But it's Maga I'm talking to

No fue por el champagne que vine aquí día tras día (S. Pitol, Mex.; Sp. *por lo que*)	It wasn't because of the champagne that I came here day after day
Era para esto para lo que he tenido que esperar tanto (J. Madrid, Sp., dialogue; Lat. Am. *...esto que...*)	That was what I'd had to wait so long for

(**b**) If the first part of a cleft sentence contains an adverb or adverbial phrase of time, place or manner it must be joined to the second part by *cuando*, *donde* or *como*, respectively, although Latin Americans may use *que* if the cleft sentence begins with *ser*, especially in informal speech: Lat. Am. *fue ahí que la vi*, Sp. *fue ahí donde la vi* 'that's where I saw her':

Es en esta última novela donde se enfrentan los más verídicos tipos clericales trazados por Galdós (Ínsula, Sp.)	It is in this last novel where the most lifelike clerical figures drawn by Galdós confront one another
Fue en casa de ella que tuvo lugar aquel encuentro con Vallejos (M. Vargas Llosa, Pe.; Sp. *donde*)	It was in her house that this meeting with Vallejos took place
Sp. *Es así como hay que hacerlo*	This is how you have to do it
Lat. Am. *Es así que hay que hacerlo*	This is how you have to do it
Sp./Lat. Am. *Así es como hay que hacerlo*	This is how you have to do it
Fue entonces cuando, podríamos decir, comenzó la historia del automóvil (El País, Sp.)	It was then, we might say, that the story of the car began
Naturalmente tenía que ser en ese momento que sonara el timbre (J. Cortázar, Arg.; Sp. *cuando*)	Of course it had to be at that moment... that the bell rang

(i) If the original sentence contained *lo que*, this neuter pronoun is retained in the cleft sentence: *lo que me sorprende es su timidez* > *es su timidez lo que me sorprende* 'what surprises me is his/her shyness', *es la inseguridad lo que le hace reaccionar de esa forma* 'it's insecurity that makes him react like that', *ha hecho cine, teatro, televisión, pero es con la canción con lo que le gustaría triunfar* (Cambio16, Sp.) 'he has worked in cinema, theatre and TV, but it is in singing that he would like to make a success'.

Lo que is used when the thing referred to is non-specific. *Era un traje negro lo que llevaba* 'it was a black suit that (s)he was wearing' answers the question '*what* was (s)he wearing?', but *el que llevaba era el traje negro/era el traje negro el que llevaba* 'the one (s)he was wearing was the black suit' is an answer to '*which* suit (*el traje*, masc.) was (s)he wearing?'.

(ii) English makes the verb 'to be' singular when it is shifted to the head of a cleft sentence: 'the mosquitoes are what annoys him'/'it is the mosquitoes that annoy him'. In Spanish *ser* normally remains plural in such cleft sentences: *son los mosquitos lo que me irrita* 'the mosquitoes are what annoys me', *lo que me irrita son los mosquitos* 'what annoys me is the mosquitoes'.

The plural construction is apparently not universal: *en la terrible escasez que vive el país, lo único que no falta es cigarrillos* (M. Vargas Llosa, Pe.) 'amidst the terrible shortages the country is living through, the only thing that isn't lacking is cigarettes'.

(iii) Cleft sentences involving lengthy prepositional phrases may be connected by *que* in Latin American usage but are likely to be avoided by careful Peninsular speakers: *teniendo en cuenta que es gracias al número de parados que podemos mantener la inflación a nivel europeo* (*Triunfo*, Sp., Argentine writer) 'bearing in mind that it is thanks to the number of unemployed that we are able to keep inflation at European levels', *fue a causa de eso que lo hizo* (Lat. Am.) or, in Spain, *lo hizo a causa de eso, fue a causa de eso por lo que lo hizo* 'it was because of that that (s)he did it'.

(iv) The complexities of cleft sentences can be avoided by not using *ser* (which is what usually happens in ordinary conversation): *por eso te digo…, desde esta ventana se ve el* mar, *se pelearon por Pepita, no por Teresa*.

(v) The standard construction with repeated pronouns is often used in Latin America in formal styles, cf. *es por lo anterior por lo que nos gusta la idea de Ecopetrol* (*El Tiempo*, Col.) 'it is because of the previous point that we like the idea of Ecopetrol'. The construction with *que* alone seems to be more acceptable in writing in Argentina than elsewhere. The *GDLE*, 27.3.8, notes that the construction with repeated pronouns is usual in Mexico.

36.2.4 Translating 'that's why'

Porque means 'because' and it cannot be used to translate sentences like 'she's got the flu, **that's why** she didn't come to work'. A construction with *por* is called for: *tiene gripe, por eso no ha venido al trabajo/por eso es por lo que no ha venido al trabajo*:

Es por eso que no se había casado (A. Mastretta, Mex.; Sp . …*por lo que no…*)	That's why she hadn't got married
Es también por eso por lo que se traiciona a cualquiera (J. Marías, Sp.)	That's also why one betrays anyone

36.2.5 Agreement in cleft sentences

The view of María Moliner, confirmed by native informants, is that in the singular either *tú fuiste el que lo/le viste* or *tú fuiste el que le/lo vio* 'you're the one who saw him' is correct, with a preference for third-person agreement (*vio*). But strict agreement seems to be the only possibility in the plural: *vosotros fuisteis los que lo/le visteis/ ustedes fueron los que lo vieron* 'you were the ones who saw him'. Further examples:

Yo fui la que se lo bebió/la que me lo bebí	I was the one (fem.) who drank it
Soy yo quien no se soporta a sí misma (J. Madrid, Sp., dialogue)	It's me (fem.) who can't stand myself
Fui yo finalmente quien la convencí (G. Cabrera Infante, Cu., dialogue)	It was me who eventually convinced her
La que te equivocas, como casi siempre, eres tú (A. Gala, Sp., dialogue; or *que se equivoca*)	The one who's making a mistake, as is almost always the case, is you
Vos sos el que no me aguanta. Vos sos el que no aguantás a Rocamadour (J. Cortázar, Arg. dialogue; both constructions used. Sp. *tú eres* for *vos sos*, *aguantas* for *aguantás*)	You're the one who can't stand me. You're the one who can't stand Rocamadour
Somos los únicos que no tenemos ni un centavo para apostar (G. García Márquez, Col., dialogue)	We're the only ones who haven't got a *centavo* to bet

37

Word order

The main subjects discussed in this chapter are:

- Verb-Subject-Object order in sentence containing relative clauses (Section 37.2.1)
- Word order in questions and exclamations (Section 37.2.2–4)
- —*Gracias* —*dijo Juan* (not —*Juan dijo*) (Section 37.2.5)
- Verb-Subject order after adverbs (Section 37.2.6)
- Miscellaneous word order rules (Section 37.3)
- The position of adverbs and adverbial phrases (Section 37.4)
- Sentences like *tonta no es, dinero tiene*, etc. (Section 37.5.1)
- *Viene el profesor* or *el profesor viene*? (Section 37.5.2)
- *Ana leyó el libro, el libro lo leyó Ana*, etc. (Section 37.5.3)

37.1 General

Compared with English and French, word order in Spanish is pretty variable. Many adjectives may be placed before or after the noun that they modify: *en el pasado remoto/en el remoto pasado* 'in the remote past'; see 4.11 for discussion. A subject may follow or precede a verb: *Juan lo sabe/lo sabe Juan* 'Juan knows'. A direct object noun phrase may follow or precede the verb: *no tengo hambre/hambre no tengo* 'I'm not hungry'; and, as in English, adverbs and adverb phrases may occupy various positions in relation to the verb that they modify: *a veces llueve/llueve a veces* 'sometimes it rains' / 'it rains sometimes'.

Usually the factors that determine Spanish word order depend on considerations of style, context, emphasis and rhythm of the sort that few non-natives are sensitive to. In this respect Spanish word order can be as complex a question as intonation and word stress is in English.

Sections 37.2–37.4 deal with patterns of word order that can be explained in terms of more or less clearly definable rules. Sections 37.5 and 37.6 consider the more difficult questions of word order that depend on matters of focus and other features of discourse.

This chapter assumes—rather arbitrarily—that the 'normal' word order in Spanish sentences is Subject-Verb, e.g. *Mario llega hoy* 'Mario's arriving today', and Subject-Verb-Object, e.g. *Olivia come una manzana* 'Olivia is eating an apple', and that other arrangements of Verb, Subject and Object are departures from the norm. We are here discussing only plain, late 20th-century Spanish prose. In poetic styles, and in prose from earlier periods when Classical Latin influenced literary Spanish, word order is much freer.

37.2 General rules of word order

37.2.1 Verb-Subject order in sentences containing relative clauses

The two principles explained here account for one of the most common differences between Spanish and English word order.

(**a**) Word order in the Main Clause

When a sentence includes a relative clause, Verb-Subject order is very often preferred in the main clause to ensure that the relative pronoun is not separated by a verb phrase from what it refers to: *lo compró un señor que había estado en Venezuela* 'a man who had been in Venezuela bought it', not **un señor lo compró que había estado en Venezuela*. The latter incorrect sentence breaks the strong rule (also discussed at 35.1.3d) that a verb phrase (*lo compró*) cannot come between a noun phrase (*un señor*) and a relative pronoun that refers to it (*que*). Another example: *no existe todavía el coche que yo quiero comprar* 'the car that I want to buy doesn't exist yet', not **el coche no existe todavía que yo quiero comprar* ?'the car doesn't exist yet that I want to buy'. The second sentence is not Spanish and probably not English either.

 In both cases another more recognizably English order is also possible, e.g. *un señor que había estado en Venezuela lo compró* 'a gentleman who had been in Venezuela bought it', *el coche que yo quiero comprar no existe todavía* 'the car that I want to buy doesn't exist yet'. This order is usually less elegant in Spanish, especially when the verb is separated from its subject by many words. As a result, the verb in the main clause is usually put at the head of the sentence as explained earlier: *tienen suerte las mujeres cuyo marido siempre las ayuda en casa* 'women whose husbands always help them in the house are lucky', which is better than *las mujeres cuyo marido siempre las ayuda en casa tienen suerte. Me llama una chica que se llama América* (C. Rico-Godoy, Sp., dialogue) 'a girl called América rings me' is better than *una chica que se llama América me llama*. But there is no objection to this order if the verb does not come last in the sentence, as in *una chica que se llama América me llama para pedirme un favor*.

(**b**) Word order in the relative clause

Verb-Subject order is also strongly preferred in relative clauses to keep the verb close to the relative pronoun. Spanish dislikes sentences structured like 'that's the dog that my friend from Kansas City **bought**', best translated *ése/ese es el perro **que compró** mi amigo de Kansas City*, not *?ése/ese es el perro que mi amigo de Kansas City compró*. Examples:

Estas acciones han rendido más que las que compró tu madre	These shares have yielded more than the ones your mother bought
el carnaval de invierno que organiza el Departamento de Turismo (El Mercurio, Ch.)	the Winter Carnival that the Department of Tourism is organizing

 When rules (**a**) and (**b**) are combined, sentences are produced whose word order is very different from their English equivalents: *gana la que eligen los jueces* 'the winner is the girl/woman whom the judges choose', literally 'wins the one whom choose the judges'. Further examples of inversion in both main and relative clauses:

Así dice la carta que nos envió tu padre	That's what's in the letter your father sent (lit. 'thus says the letter that sent your father')
Son innumerables las dificultades que plantea la lucha contra el terrorismo (La Vanguardia, Sp.)	The difficulties posed by the struggle against terrorism are innumerable
Durante toda mi vida, ahí donde hubiese un duro, ahí estaba yo (interview, Sp.)	Throughout my life, wherever you could find five pesetas you'd find me (lit. '…wherever there was a five-peseta coin, there was I')

But set verb phrases like *tratar de, tener que*, are not divided unnaturally. See 37.3.2.

37.2.2 Word order in questions (direct and indirect)

Verb-Subject order is required when a question word opens the sentence. Verb-Subject order is also required in indirect questions in the clause following question words, i.e.:

¿cómo? how?	*¿cuánto?* how much/many?	*¿qué?* what?/which? (see note i)
¿cuál (de)? which (of)?	*¿dónde?* where?	*¿a quién?* whom?
¿cuándo? when?	*¿por/para qué?* why?	

Examples (subject in bold):

*¿Cómo va **una** a estar esperando y delgada?* (A. Mastretta, Mex., dialogue)	How is one going to be expecting a baby and (be) thin?
*¿Qué tal va **tu nuevo trabajo**?*	How's your new job going?
*¿A quién arrestó **la policía**?*	Who(m) did the police arrest?
*No recuerdo dónde vive **tu hermano***	I don't remember where your brother lives
*No me imagino qué pensaría **tu mujer** de todo esto*	I can't imagine what your wife would think about all this

As the examples show, direct objects precede the verb, as in English: *¿qué consejos me das?* 'what advice do you give me?, *¿cuántas naranjas has comido?* 'how many oranges have you eaten?' Verb-Object order can occasionally be used colloquially to express shock or incredulity: *¿has comido cuántas?. .* (more usually *¿cuántas dices que has comido?*) 'you've eaten *how many* (oranges)?'

However, when the sentence contains both an object and a subject there are three possibilities: (**1**) when the object is shorter than the subject Verb-Object-Subject order is usual. (**2**) When the subject is shorter, Verb-Subject-Object order is preferred. (**3**) When subject and object are of equal length, either order may be used. The objects are in in bold in these sentences:

*¿Dónde compran **drogas** los adolescentes?* (short object)	Where do young people buy drugs?
*¿A quién ha escrito **la carta** tu amigo Federico?* (short object)	Who(m) did your friend Federico write the letter to?
*¿Dónde compran los adolescentes **las drogas vendidas por los narcotraficantes**?* (long object)	Where do young people the drugs sold by drug-pushers?
*¿Cuándo va a incluir su revista **programas y artículos dedicados a ordenadores tales como los ya citados**?* (long object; reader's letter in El Ordenador Personal, Sp.; Lat. Am. *la computadora = el ordenador*)	When is your magazine going to include programs and articles devoted to computers like the ones mentioned above?

*¿Cuándo piensan hacer**lo** ustedes?/*	When are you thinking of doing it?
*¿Cuándo piensan ustedes hacer**lo**?*	
(equal length)	
*¿Dónde compra **pan** mamá?/¿Dónde*	Where does Mother buy bread?
*compra mamá **pan**?* (equal length)	

(i) A noun phrase introduced by *¿qué?* meaning 'which?' or by *¿cuál de?* 'which?' always appears before the verb: *¿qué programas han gustado más al público?* 'which programmes/US programs did the public like most?', *¿cuál de los aviones consume menos combustible?* 'which of the planes uses least fuel?', *¿qué frutas ha comprado Marta?* 'what fruits did Marta buy?', *¿cuál de los proyectos ha aceptado el comité?* 'which of the projects has the committee accepted?'

(ii) The Spanish of Cuba, Puerto Rico and the Dominican Republic is unusual in optionally retaining Subject-Verb order after question words (subject in bold): *¿cómo **usted** conoció que Tony tenía negocio de narcotráfico?* (*Vindicación de Cuba*; standard Spanish ...*se enteró **usted** de que...*) 'how did you find out that Tony had a drug-peddling business?, *¿en qué fecha **usted** ingresó en la Corporación CIMEX?* (ibid.; standard Spanish *ingresó **usted***) 'on what date did you join the CIMEX Corporation?', *¿qué **tú** crees del acto de hoy en el Teatro Oriente?* (L. Otero, Cu., dialogue) 'what do you think of the event today at the Oriente Theatre?'

37.2.3 Word order in questions that do not contain a question word

When no question-word is included in a question, Subject-Verb-Object order can be used, in which case question marks or, in speech, question (rising) intonation, are the only things that show that a question is intended:

¿Julia viene esta noche? (usually *¿viene Julia...?*)	Is Julia coming tonight?
¿Tú también notaste lo bonito que se ríe? (A. Mastretta, Mex., dialogue; Sp. *lo bonita que es su risa*)	Did you also notice how prettily she laughs?
¿El XIII [decimotercer] Congreso va a ser el de la desaparición de su partido? (interview in *Tribuna*, Sp.)	Is the 13th Congress going to be the one at which your party disappears?

But in such sentences Verb-Subject order is usual if there is no object: *¿ha llamado mi hermano?* 'has my brother called?'

If the sentence includes an object, Verb-Object-Subject order is usual if the object is shorter than the subject (object in bold) :*¿ha traído **flores** el vecino de tu suegra?* 'has your mother-in-law's neighbo(u)r brought flowers?' But if the object is longer than the subject, Verb-Subject-Object order is usual; and if they are of the same length, the order is optional (object in bold):

*¿Ha traído Miguel **las flores que encargamos ayer por la noche**?* (short subject, so not **¿Ha traído las flores que encargamos anoche Miguel?*)	Has Miguel brought the flowers we ordered last night?

but

*¿Ha traído **flores** Miguel?/¿Ha traído Miguel **flores**?* (same length)	Has Miguel brought (some) flowers?

(i) Words should not be inserted between the auxiliary *haber* and a past participle: never ** *¿ha Miguel traído flores?* 'has Miguel brought flowers?' See 14.8.1 for discussion.

37.2.4 Word order in exclamations

When one of the words listed at 37.2.2 introduces an exclamation, (Object-)Verb-Subject order is required:

¡Qué guapo es tu hermano!	Isn't your brother good-looking!
¡Cómo se parece Ana a su madre!	Doesn't Ana look like her mother!
¡Cuántos piropos te echa el jefe!	What a lot of flirtatious remarks the boss makes to you!

37.2.5 Inversion in dialogue identifiers

Verb-Subject order is required in writing in dialogue identifiers of the sort 'Mary said', 'John replied', when they follow the words quoted. Inversion in this case is nowadays optional in English and sounds old-fashioned:

—Está bien —dijo el presidente	'Fine,' the President said/said the President
—Lo dudo —contestó Armando	'I doubt it,' Armando replied/replied Armando

37.2.6 Verb-Subject order required after adverbs

Verb-Subject is very common when certain adverbs and adverbial phrases precede the verb.

When the verb is intransitive, inversion is usual. Speakers of either language would probably prefer sentences (**a**) to (**b**) (subjects in bold):

(**a**) *Delante de mí se levantaba **un enorme edificio***	Before me stood an enormous building
*Delante de ella aparecieron **dos hombres chillando y gesticulando***	Before her there appeared two men screaming and gesticulating
(**b**) *?Delante de mí **un enorme edificio** se levantaba*	?Before me an enormous building stood
*?Delante de ella **dos hombres chillando y gesticulando** aparecieron*	?Before her two men screaming and gesticulating appeared

When the verb has an object it seems that either word order is possible in Spanish (subject in bold): *delante de ella **dos mujeres** voceaban sus mercancías* 'before her two women were calling out their wares', or *delante de ella voceaban sus mercancías **dos mujeres***.

In the following examples, Subject-Verb order is not always impossible, but it is usually awkward (subject in bold):

*Siempre me dijeron **las brujas y echadoras de cartas** que mi número mágico era el tres* (C. Rico-Godoy, Sp.)	Witches and card-readers always told me that my magic number was three
*Siempre fue altanera **la Sofía*** (A. Mastretta, Mex., dialogue; see 3.2.21 for the *la*)	Sofia was always haughty/arrogant
*Nunca me hablaban **los vecinos***	The neighbo(u)rs never spoke to me

*Apenas salían **sus padres**, ponía música rock*	(S)he used to put on rock music as soon as his parents went out
*Bien saben **las autoridades** que...*	The authorities know very well that...
*Así dice **Platón***	This is what Plato says
*Todavía humeaban **algunos incendios***	Some fires were still smoking
*Para tales personas existen **las cárceles***	Prisons exist for such people

Adverbial phrases of place especially favour Verb-Subject order (subject in bold: see also 37.4 for further remarks about the position of adverbial phrases):

*Ahí vivo **yo***	That's where I live
*Aquí dejó la sangre **el muerto*** (J. Ibargüengoitia, Mex., dialogue)	The dead man left his blood here
*En su mirada veía **yo** con claridad que me estaba pasando de la raya* (C. Rico-Godoy, Sp.)	I could see clearly by his expression (lit. 'in his gaze') that I was overdoing it
*Junto a la puerta colgaba **una deshilachada toalla*** (L. Sepúlveda, Ch.)	Next to the door hung a frayed towel

(i) These are not rigid rules. Native speakers who have an ear for sentence structure will know when Subject-Verb order sounds right, as in *nunca los intereses publicitarios motivarán la publicación de un artículo o suplemento* (*Libro de estilo de El País*, Sp.) 'the publication of an article or supplement will never be motivated by publicity interests', rather than *nunca motivarán los intereses publicitarios. . . .*

37.3 Miscellaneous word order rules

This section includes a number of miscellaneous but important rules that explain various features of Spanish word order.

37.3.1 Prepositions stay with the word they modify

Spanish does not separate prepositions from the noun or pronoun that they modify. This rule is absolute in relative clauses: an English sentence like 'that's the hotel we're going **to**' must be expressed *ese/ese es el hotel **al que** vamos* 'that's the hotel to which we're going'.

In general, only *no* should separate a preposition from its infinitive:

*Su nombramiento se demoró **por estar** siempre la vacante ocupada* (not **por la vacante estar*)	His appointment (to the post) was delayed because the vacant position was always occupied
*La promesa de una vida de ocio fue frustrada **al negarse** el Fisco a devolverle el dinero* (not **al Fisco negarse*)	The promise of a life of leisure was frustrated when the Revenue Department refused to return the money to him

37.3.2 Set phrases are not broken up

Set phrases, particularly set verbal phrases like *tener que* 'to have to', *llevar a cabo* 'carry out', *hacer público* 'make public', *surtir efecto* 'produce an effect', *tener lugar* 'take place', *darse cuenta de que* 'realize', should not be broken up by the insertion of other words:

Probablemente las obras se llevarán a cabo para febrero (not *se llevarán probablemente a cabo. . .)	The work will probably be carried out by February
[Las maestras] no tienen la culpa: si no existiera la maldita instrucción primaria que ellas tienen que aplicar. . . (J. Cortázar, Arg.; and not *que tienen ellas que aplicar*)	[The schoolmistresses] aren't to blame: if the wretched primary education they have to administer didn't exist. . .
Por eso hacemos pública esta información (and not the typical English word order . . .*hacemos esta información pública*)	This is why we are making this information public

37.3.3 No insertion of words between *haber* and participles

As a rule, words should not be inserted between *haber* and a participle, e.g. *siempre he dicho* or *he dicho siempre* 'I've always said', but not *he siempre dicho (students of French take note: *j'ai presque toujours pensé que...* is *casi siempre he pensado que...* or *he pensado casi siempre que...*). This rule is occasionally broken: see 14.8.1 for discussion.

37.3.4 Unstressed object pronouns remain with their verb

Unstressed object pronouns (*me, te, se, la, lo, le, nos, os, los, las, les*) are never separated from their verb: *te lo diré luego* 'I'll tell you later', *sólo/solo te quiero a ti* 'I only love you'/'I love only you', etc. There are often optional positions when a finite verb governs an infinitive or gerund: *no debí decírtelo* or *no te lo debí decir, estoy haciéndolo* or *lo estoy haciendo* 'I'm doing it'. This is discussed at 11.14.4–5.

37.3.5 Adjectival phrases are kept close to the noun they modify

Spanish does not like to separate adjectival phrases (in bold) from the noun they modify:

*Regresó como a las seis y media con un ejemplar **arrugado y manchado de huevo** de las Últimas Noticias del mediodía* (C. Fuentes, Mex.)	He returned around 6.30 with a crumpled and egg-stained copy of the midday *Últimas Noticias*

This sentence would sound awkward, at least in careful styles, if the adjectival phrase were put at the end: *?. . .con un ejemplar de las Últimas Noticias del mediodía arrugado y manchado de huevo*. Compound nouns formed with *de* are not broken up. One says *un reloj de pared suizo* 'a Swiss wall-clock', not **un reloj suizo de pared*. See 4.11.5.

37.3.6 Keep verbs close to their subject

Verb-Subject order is commonly used to avoid separating a subject from its verb. Spanish does not like to leave a verb dangling at the end of a clause or sentence far from its subject. Compare the English and Spanish versions of this sentence:

> El tratamiento debe repetirse durante toda
>   la vida, salvo que **se realice** con éxito
>   un trasplante de riñón (Ercilla, Ch.;
>   rather than...un trasplante de riñón
>   se realice con éxito)

> The treatment must be repeated
>   throughout [the patient's] life,
>   unless a successful kidney
>   transplant **is performed**

37.3.7 Numerals are usually avoided at the beginning of sentences: see note to 10.16e for discussion

37.3.8 Word order in apposition

When two nouns are in apposition, nothing should separate them: one says *había muerto J. M., leyenda de la música rock de los años sesenta* 'J. M., legend of sixties rock music, had died', to keep *J. M.* and *leyenda* together, not *?J. M. había muerto, leyenda de la música rock....*

37.4 Position of adverbs and adverbial phrases

37.4.1 Adverbs and adverb phrases are kept close to the words they modify

Generally speaking, adverbials (i.e. adverbs, adverbial phrases and adverbial clauses) are placed either immediately before or, more usually, immediately after the word(s) that they modify. In this respect the *Libro de estilo* of *El País*, Sp., p. 134, specifically admonishes its journalists and editors against:

(a) separating adverbs from their verb: *el Rey ha inaugurado hoy...* 'the King today inaugurated...', not *hoy, el Rey ha inaugurado...*;

(b) breaking up verbal phrases by inserting adverbs in them: *el presidente está dispuesto claramente a dimitir* 'the president is clearly prepared to resign', not *el presidente está claramente dispuesto a dimitir* (see *Libro de estilo*, 2002, 155. This is the usual English order and, despite *El País*, very common in Spanish);

(c) beginning articles with an adverb other than *sólo/solo* or *solamente*, on the grounds that since adverbs modify other phrases the latter should precede them. But this rule applies only to formal writing.

37.4.2 Adverbs are not left at the end of sentences

English differs from Spanish in that it frequently puts adverbs and adverb phrases at the end of the sentence: 'I saw that lady who lives next door to your grandmother **yesterday**'. For the reason given at 37.4.1, Spanish puts 'yesterday' close to 'saw': *vi ayer/ayer vi a esa señora que vive al lado de tu abuela;* if the *ayer* ends the sentence it seems to modify *vive*. The Spanish requirement that adverbs should stay close to their verb therefore produces the un-English order Verb-Adverbial-Object (adverbial in bold):

> Besó **fervorosamente** la mano de su
>   anfitriona
> El tribunal fijará **discrecionalmente** la
>   duración de la fianza (Spanish legal
>   dictionary)

> (S)he kissed his/her hostess's hand
>   fervently
> The Court will fix the period of the
>   bail bond at its discretion

*Casi siempre **a la una** seguía en chanclas y bata* (A. Mastretta, Mex., dialogue; Sp. *chanclas = zapatillas*)	She was nearly always still in her slippers and dressing-gown/US bathrobe at one o'clock

Adverbials of time are very often put before adverbials of place: 'we went to grandma's house yesterday' = *ayer fuimos/fuimos ayer a casa de la abuela*.

Note particularly the position of the adverbials in bold in the following sentences (other orders are possible but are not shown here):

*Fue inútil que los párrocos advirtieran **en los pueblos** a las mujeres que sus maridos las abandonarían si llegaba la ley del divorcio* (*Cambio16*, Sp.)	It was no use the parish priests in the villages warning women that their husbands would leave them if the divorce law was introduced
*Parece que la habilidad más importante es la de memorizar información para **luego** escupirla en un examen* (Spanish popular press)	It seems the most important skill is memorizing information in order to churn (lit. 'spit') it out later in an examination
*Me di cuenta de que había estado **antes** en aquel sitio*	I realized I'd been in that place before
*¿Sabes que el presidente Romeo Lucas sufrió **ayer** un atentado? Estaba en su coche parado en un semáforo cuando **desde una bicicleta** le arrojaron un diccionario* (joke in *Cambio16*, Sp., about an illiterate Guatemalan dictator)	Do you know someone made an attempt on President Romeo Lucas's life yesterday? He was waiting in his car at some traffic lights when someone threw a dictionary at him from a bicycle

For further remarks about the position of adverbs see 37.2.6 and 31.3.8.

37.5 Word order not explainable by sentence structure

Even when all the foregoing more or less codifiable rules are taken into account, there are many cases in which word order is determined by less easily definable factors that reflect the information content of the sentence. It is never easy to explain these factors in grammar books which quote fragments of language out of context. There are also important differences between written and spoken language with respect to word order. The following remarks by no means exhaust the subject and they do not apply to questions or negative sentences.

37.5.1 The topic of a sentence may be put first

Utterances naturally consist of a 'topic'—something we want to say something about—and a 'comment'—what we say about the topic. In simple declarative sentences (i.e. ones which are neither questions nor orders) the subject of the main verb is usually also the topic of the sentence: '**Mary** hates strawberry yoghurt' is about Mary, '**polar bears** have amazingly thick fur' is about polar bears, and the usual order in such sentences in both English in Spanish is topic—comment: *María odia el yogur de fresa*, *los osos polares tienen un pelaje extraordinariamente espeso*.

However, the topic need not necessarily be the subject of the verb. It may be some adverbial phrase, as in '**on Fridays** I usually play bridge'/*los viernes suelo jugar al bridge*, or it may be the direct object of a transitive verb or the predicate of a verb like 'to be': '**pork** I'm not eating!' / *carne de cerdo no como*, '**stupid** she isn't' / *tonta no es*.

Since spoken Spanish makes less use of word stress and intonation than English, this device of shifting topics to the head is quite common, and regularly produces 'un-English' word order, as in a sentence like *me gusta la miel* 'I like honey', *a María le encanta el yogur de fresa* 'Mary loves strawberry yoghurt', where I and Mary are the topics of the utterance but happen to be grammatical objects in Spanish. But more unusual shifts are also found, especially in emotive colloquial language, and much more commonly than in English. In the following sentences the speakers emphatically 'declare' the topic they wish to raise, and then add a comment afterwards:

¡*De dinero* no quiero volver a oír ni una palabra!	About *money* I don't want to hear another word!
Trabajo le costó a Maruja convencerlo de que no (G. García Márquez, Col.)	It was really hard work for Maruja to convince him otherwise
Americano vino uno solamente (Cuban TV interview)	As for Americans, only one came
Como en la foto de la boda no creo que yo vuelva a estar	I don't think I'll be like I was in the wedding photo again
Muchas cosas he leído, *pocas* he vivido (J. L. Borges, Arg.)	I've read many things, but lived few

(i) When a direct object is placed before the verb, it is usually resumed or echoed by a pronoun: *al verano inglés debían llamarlo estación de las lluvias* 'the English summer ought to be called the rainy season', *estos/éstos los dejo aquí, los demás me los llevo* 'I'll leave these here, I'll take the others with me'. See 11.16.1 for details and exceptions.

(ii) One of the functions of the passive with *ser* is to make the direct object of the equivalent active sentence into a topic by putting it at the head of the utterance: *Miguel fue atropellado por un coche* 'Miguel was run over by a car' is more likely than ?*un coche atropelló a Miguel* ?'a car ran over Miguel'. Informal Spanish generally avoids the passive with *ser*, so placing the direct object at the head of the sentence is a good way of producing the same effect as a passive: *a Miguel lo/le atropelló un coche*.

(iii) Latin-American headline writers exploit the fact that the topic of an utterance can come first. This produces sentences in which a direct object, or the predicate of *ser* or *estar*, or sometimes a verb, is shifted to the head of the sentence for dramatic purposes: *a tres coches quemaron* (Colombian headline) 'three cars burnt', *ingeniero buscamos* (advert., Ven.) 'engineer sought', *signada por muchos altibajos estuvo la actividad bursátil* (headline in *La Nación*, Arg.; *signada* = *caracterizada* in Spain) 'Stock Exchange Activity marked by many rises and falls', *gigantesco tiburón de una especie desconocida capturó un pesquero frente a las costas del Chuy* (*El País*, Ur.) 'giant shark of unknown species caught by fishing boat off Chuy coast', *capturan la policía y el ejército a 23 miembros de Sendero Luminoso* (*UnomásUno*, Mex.) 'police and army capture 23 Members of "Shining Path"' (a Peruvian left-wing guerrilla organization). This word order sounds strange to Spaniards.

(iv) The topic may be specifically identified by some phrase like *en cuanto a* 'as for', *con respecto a* 'with regard to', *en/por lo que se refiere a…*'with reference to', 'as far as… is concerned', e.g. *por lo que se refiere a Pedro, no lo/le he visto* 'as far as

Pedro's concerned, I haven't seen him'. Use of such phrases is normal in written language: informal language might say *a Pedro no lo/le he visto*.

37.5.2 *El profesor viene* or *Viene el profesor?*

This section discusses sentences consisting only of a subject and verb. The principle explained at 37.5.1—that the topic of an utterance may precede the comment made about it—explains the difference between *Antonio viene* and *viene Antonio*, 'Antonio's coming', two sentences that can really only be differentiated by emphasis and intonation in English.

In a neutral statement, i.e. matter-of-fact declarations, the Subject is usually the Topic, so it comes first (when none of the factors listed in 37.2–37.4 operates): *el médico llega a las diez* 'the doctor arrives/is arriving at ten o'clock'. But the time could be the topic—*a las diez llega el médico*— and in some circumstances the verb is focused, for example when the doctor's arrival is feared, unexpected or hoped for. In this case Verb-Subject order is appropriate: *¡ha llegado el médico!* 'the doctor's arrived!'

But in most cases departures from Subject-Verb order are also influenced by factors of style and rhythm that cannot easily be explained in abstract terms. When it is not clearly called for, Verb-Subject order may produce a heavily literary, even 'Academic' tone, cf. *recordará el lector que los complementos directos. . .* (Royal Academy, *Esbozo. . .*, 3.7.3f) 'the reader will recall that direct objects. . .' where the order *el lector recordará que. . .* would have been less formal.

In the following examples, Subject-Verb order is preferred because the subject is also the topic:

Miguel *está leyendo* (answers the question 'what's Miguel doing?')	Miguel's reading
Bentley *se volvió*	Bentley turned round

In the following sentence, the verb is the topic; in other words, the sentences answers the question 'what happened?' rather than 'who did it?'

Ha muerto Franco (headline)	Franco is dead
Han vuelto a España ya muchos	Many have returned to Spain already
Se abrió la puerta y entró Juan	The door opened and John came in

37.5.3 Word order in sentences that include direct objects

A sentence consisting of a subject, verb and direct object can theoretically appear in Spanish in the following forms:

(**a**) *Ana leyó el libro*	Subject-Verb-Direct Object
(**b**) *El libro lo leyó Ana*	Direct Object-(redundant pronoun)-Verb-Subject
(**c**) *El libro Ana lo leyó*	Direct Object-Subject-(redundant pronoun)-Verb
(**d**) *Ana el libro leyó*	Subject-Direct Object-Verb
(**e**) *Leyó Ana el libro*	Verb-Subject-Direct Object
(**f**) *Leyó el libro Ana*	Verb-Direct Object-Subject

Of these possibilities, only the first three are at all common in ordinary language. (**d**) is very unnatural and might occur in songs or comic verse, and (**e**) and (**f**) are only found in archaic or very flowery literary styles, unless they are questions.

(**a**) is a neutral word order corresponding to an English sentence spoken with equal emphasis on 'Ana' and 'book'. Since, in neutral sentences, the subject of the verb tends naturally to be the topic, Subject-Verb-Object order is normal.

(**b**) clearly makes the direct object, the book, into the topic of the sentence, and then adds the comment about what Ana did to it: 'as for the book, Ana read it'. It also may emphasize Ana: 'Ana (not someone else) read the book'. See 11.16.1 for the use of the redundant pronoun here.

(**c**) is not particularly common. It would only appear at the beginning of a sentence that has to be completed, and is likely to occur when the whole statement is the topic of a sentence, and some comment is added that refers to the fact that Ana read the book, as in *el libro Ana lo leyó antes que su hermana, lo cual hizo que las dos se pelearan* 'Ana read the book before her sister, which made the two of them quarrel'. Another example: *la moto la compró mi marido porque nos habían robado el coche* 'the motor-bike was bought by my husband because they had stolen the car', literally, 'as for my husband's buying the motor-bike, he did it because they'd stolen our car'.

38

Diminutive, augmentative and pejorative suffixes

This chapter discusses:

- Diminutive suffixes like *–ito, –illo, –ín*, etc. (Section 38.2)
- Augmentative suffixes like *–ón, –azo, –ote, -udo* (Section 38.3)
- Pejorative suffixes like *–aco, –acho, –ajo, –uco, –ucho*, etc. (Section 38.4)

38.1 General

There are numerous suffixes that modify the emotional tone of a word, e.g. *-ito, -illo, -ón, -ote, -azo, -aco, -ejo*, etc. Their effect is very unpredictable. Sometimes they simply create new words without any emotional colouring at all: *ventana* = 'window', *ventanilla* = 'window of a vehicle'/'box office'; *la caja* = 'box', *el cajón* = 'drawer' (in furniture); *la botella* = 'bottle', but *un botellín* (Sp.) = a small bottle of beer; these words must be learned separately. But usually they add an emotional tone to a word or phrase, e.g. affection, contempt, irony, repugnance, and they may sound affected, effeminate, childish or too familiar if used wrongly. As a result, foreign learners are usually advised not to experiment with them, since inexpert use may produce unfortunate effects: *estarías mejor con el pelo recogido* means 'you'd look better with your hair up'; *estarías mejor con el pelo recogidito* means the same, but sounds like an adult talking to a little child; ??*estarías mejor con el pelito recogidito* sounds ludicrous.

In view of this and the fact that the forms and frequency of the suffixes differ widely from place, and also in some regions seem to be more common in women's speech than men's, the following account is very condensed. Except where indicated, the remarks in this chapter apply to educated usage in central Spain, but they should be checked against the speech habits of different Latin-American republics. For a detailed picture of usage in Spain see Gooch (1974), from which some of the following examples are taken.

38.2 Diminutive suffixes

Diminutive suffixes have various uses, described at 38.2.1–6. Although it is not always their effect, they often imply smallness, and a few words must be said about their relationship with the adjective *pequeño*. The following remarks apply to spoken rather than to formal written Spanish.

Pequeño means 'small', but it does not usually have the emotional overtones of the English word 'little'. It is used:

(**a**) to mean 'slight'/'unimportant' with abstract nouns: *un pequeño problema* 'a slight problem' (familiarly *un problemita*), *esas pequeñas complicaciones que mencionamos* 'those slight complications that we mentioned', *España era una pequeña potencia* 'Spain was a small/unimportant power'.

(**b**) To mean 'small' as opposed to 'large', without any warm overtones or implications of 'cute': *un ratón es más pequeño que una rata* 'a mouse is smaller than a rat', *una pequeña cantidad de azufre* 'a small quantity of sulphur', *un niño pequeño* 'a small child'. *Chico*, even more familiarly *chiquito*, is often used colloquially for *pequeño*, above all in Latin America, but it does not come before nouns: *mi carro (coche) es más chico que el tuyo* 'my car's smaller than yours'.

(**c**) The English combination of 'little' followed by a noun is, in spoken Spanish, most often expressed by a diminutive. One says *esta casa es pequeña* but, colloquially, *una casita* for a 'little house'; *un perrito* rather than *un pequeño perro* 'a little dog', *un pajarito* rather than *un pequeño pájaro* 'a little bird': *...desde la primera vez que la vio leyendo bajo los árboles del parquecito* (G. García Márquez, Col.) 'since the first time he had seen her reading under the trees in the little park', *conozco un barecito ahí en la calle del Pez* (J. Madrid, Sp., dialogue). 'I know a little bar near by in Pez street'. In more formal styles one would have said *el pequeño parque, un pequeño bar*.

(i) Sometimes abbreviations are used in familiar speech instead of suffixes, e.g. *mami* or *papi* for *mamá* or *papá*, which are in turn abbreviations for *madre* and *padre*; *cole* from *colegio* 'school', *tele* from *television*, *la peli* for *la película* 'film', etc. In Spain a little child is often affectionately called *el chiquitín, el nene, el pequeño, el pequeñín* or even *el peque*.

38.2.1 Formation of the diminutive

The following are found, *-ito* being the most common in central Spain and *-illo* used especially in the South. *-ico, -iño* and *-ín* have a northern flavour. The usual form is shown first, with variant forms in brackets:

-ito (-cito, -ecito, -ececito)	*-ete (-cete, -ecete)*
-illo (-cillo, -ecillo, -ececillo)	*-ín*
-ico (-cico, -ecico, -ececico)	*-iño*
-uelo (-zuelo, -ezuelo, -ecezuelo)	

All are marked for gender in the usual way: for the feminine a final vowel is replaced by *-a*; *-ín* makes its feminine *-ina*.

(i) Words of more than one syllable ending in *-n*, *-ol* or *-r*, and words ending in *-e* or having the diphthong *-ie* in their first syllable, usually take the form in *-c-*. The following forms were generated spontaneously by Peninsular informants, but not all are guaranteed to be in common use:

mujer woman: *mujercita*	*madre* mother: *madrecita*	*nieto* grandson: *nietecito*
mejor better: *mejorcito*	*padre* father: *padrecito*	*piedra* stone: *piedrecita*
mayor bigger: *mayorcito*	*cofre* case/box: *cofrecito*	*sueño* sleep/dream:
cajón drawer: *cajoncito*	*puente* bridge: *puentecito*	*sueñecito*

But note *el café* > *cafelito* or *cafetito* 'coffee'; *el cafecito* usually means 'a little café'. Also *el alfiler* > *alfilerito* 'pin', *la mano* > *la manita/la manecita* 'hand'.

(ii) Words of one syllable commonly take forms in -ec-, at least in Spain:

flor flower *florecita*	*rey* king *reyecito*	*voz* voice *vocecita*
pan bread *panecillo* bread roll	*tos* cough *tosecita/tosecilla*	*sol* sun *solecito/solito*
pez fish *pececito/pececillo*	*pie* foot *piececito* (?*piececillo*— rare)	

Note the following Latin-American forms: *tiene el vestido a florcitas verdes* (M. Puig, Arg., dialogue) 'she's got the dress with green flowers', *y el solcito está lindo* (M. Benedetti, Ur., dialogue) 'and the sun's lovely'.

(iii) Words ending in an unaccented vowel or diphthong lose their final vowel, but if the vowel is accented it may be preserved and its accent transferred to the *i* of *-ito*:

armario wardrobe *armarito*	*mamá* mummy *mamaíta* or *mamita*
estatua statue *estatuilla*	*papá* daddy *papaíto* or *papito*
silla chair *sillita*	*tío/tía* uncle/aunt *tiíto/tiíta*

(iv) Diminutive suffixes are not added to nouns of more than one syllable ending in –d like *la ciudad* 'city', *el césped* 'lawn'. But *la red* > *la redecita* 'net'.

38.2.2 Uses of the diminutive suffix -*ito*

The main effects of this suffix are:

(a) To give a friendly tone to a statement:

This very common use of the diminutive may simply give a warm tone to a remark. In a bakery one might say *deme una barrita de pan* 'give me a loaf of bread', which is merely a friendly equivalent of *deme una barra de pan*. This use of the diminutive does not imply smallness but merely signals the speaker's attitude to the hearer:

Dame un paquetito por ahora	Give me just one packet for now
Tómate un cafelito (J. Madrid, Sp., dialogue)	Have a coffee
Me tiras el vaso con el codo. A ver si tenemos más cuidadito...	You're knocking my glass over with your elbow. Let's see if we can't have a little bit more care ...
Voy a echar una siestecita	I'm going to have forty winks/a quick nap
Un momentito, por favor	Just a moment, please
¿Alguna cosita más? (often used in shops) (cf. *¿Alguna cosa más?*	Would you like anything else? Anything else?)
¿Te puedo coger una almendrita?	Can I have (just one) one of your almonds?

(b) To modify the meaning of adjectives and adverbs by adding a warm tone or, sometimes, by making them more precise—e.g. *ahora* 'now', *ahorita* (Mexican colloquial) 'right now':

cerquita de la catedral	just by the cathedral
Ahora mismito se lo sirvo	Don't worry, I'll bring it at once
Ya eres mayorcito	You're a big boy now

Está gordito/Está gordo	He's put on a bit of weight/He's fat
¡tontito!/¡tonto!	silly!/fool!

'Nice' or 'lovely' can be the English equivalent of some adjectival and adverbial diminutives in *-ito:¿un café calentito?* 'a nice cup of hot coffee?', *las empanadas están recientitas* 'the meat pies are lovely and freshly baked', *despacito* 'nice and slow/ take it slowly'.

(**c**) To denote endearment or affection: *hermanita* (lit. 'little sister') is often a term of endearment and does not necessarily imply that the sister is younger than the speaker. *Abuelita* 'grandma' is merely an affectionate form for *abuela* 'grandmother':

Vamos, m'hijito (Lat.-Am.; Sp. *vamos, hijo mío*)	Come on son
Se ha hecho daño en la patita	It's hurt its paw
¡Pobrecito! ¿Te has caído?	Poor little thing! Did you fall down?

(**d**) To denote smallness (see 38.2b):

el perro-el perrito dog-little dog/doggy	*el sillón-silloncito* armchair-little armchair
la puerta-la puertecita door-little door	*el coche-cochecito* car-little car/pram, buggy

Sometimes the diminutive is reinforced, as in *¿tienes un sobrecito pequeño?* 'Have you got a little envelope?' or —*¿quieres un poco? —Sólo/Solo un poquito. No tanto, un poquitín* '"Do you want a bit?" "Just a little bit. Not so much, just a tiny little bit".'

(**e**) Occasionally in an ironic way to emphasize largeness or grandeur: *¡menuda casita!* 'some house' (looking at a vast mansion), *¡mira el cochecito ese!* 'nice little car!'(pointing at a gold-plated Rolls Royce), *la cerebrito de tu hermana* (from *GDLE* 8.4) 'that genius of a sister of yours' (*el cerebro* = 'brain').

38.2.3 Diminutive suffix *-illo*

The suffix *-illo* is used:

(**a**) as a diminutive:

pan-panecillo	bread-bread roll
flor-florecilla	flower-little flower

(**b**) To downgrade the importance of something:

Tengo unas cosillas que hacer	I've got a few little things to do
Ahora sólo/solo queda el jaleíllo de las entradas (*jaleo* = row, fuss)	All that's left is the business of the entrance tickets
Hacía un airecillo agradable	There was a pleasant breeze
vulgar-vulgarcillo	vulgar-pretty vulgar/a bit coarse

(**c**) To soften a word that otherwise might sound too offensive:

mentirosillo	'fibber'
Es bastante dejadilla (*dejado* 'careless'/ 'sloppy')	She's pretty careless/She doesn't take a lot of care
Tú eres comiloncillo ¿eh?	You eat quite a lot/You sure like your food

(**d**) To give an affectionate tone:

> *Pero ¿qué haces, chiquilla?* But what **are** you doing, honey/darling?
> *He comprado un cachorrillo/cachorrito* I bought a little puppy

Diminutives in *-illo* are typical of Seville but they are also often used in central Spain.

(**e**) To give a specialized meaning to a word, cf. English 'book'-'booklet'. In some of these cases the diminutive ending has no diminutive function:

el palo-palillo stick-toothpick
la caja-cajetilla box-box for cigarettes, etc.
la vara-varilla (but *la varita mágica* 'magic wand') rod-thin stick, spoke, wand
la guerra-guerrilla war-guerrilla warfare
el cigarro-cigarrillo cigar-cigarette
la cama/camilla bed-stretcher
la manzana-la manzanilla apple/camomile (also a type of dry sherry)
la masa-la masilla dough/mass/putty
la ventana-la ventanilla window-vehicle window/ticket window
la bomba-la bombilla bomb-light bulb
la parra-la parrilla vine-grill
el bolso-el bolsillo bag/pocket

(**f**) To denote a combination of diminutive and pejorative:

la cultura-culturilla culture-'smattering of culture'
mujer-mujercilla woman-unimportant woman
listo-listillo clever-'know-all'

38.2.4 Diminutive suffix *-ín*

-ín is typical of Asturias, but it is used to express affection in many contexts in the rest of Spain:

> *¿Donde está el chiquitín?* Where's baby?/the little one?
> *¡chiquirriquitín!* my tiny little thing!
> *¡mi (niña) chiquitina!* (not *¡mi pequeña niña!*) my little girl!

and also to form new words:

la espada-el espadín sword-dress sword
el cerebro-el cerebrín brain-brainy person
la maleta-el maletín suitcase-briefcase
la tesis-la tesina thesis-dissertation
la silla–el sillín chair-saddle

38.2.5 Diminutive suffixes *-uelo, -eto, -ete*

(**a**) *-uelo* can denote a combination of diminutive and pejorative:

la calleja-callejuela alley-narrow little alley
el arroyo-arroyuelo stream-trickle/rivulet
el rey-reyezuelo king-petty king/princeling
tonto/tontuelo stupid-dumbo (affectionate)

It may also be used to form new words: *el paño/pañuelo* 'cloth/handkerchief'.

(**b**) *–eto/a, -ete/a* may add a specialized meaning:

el avión-la avioneta aircraft-light aircraft
el camión-la camioneta truck/van (or light truck)
el caballo-el caballete horse-easel

(c) *-ete* may add a humorous tone:

amigo-amiguete friend-pal   *gordo-regordete* fat-chubby

38.2.6 Diminutive forms in Latin America

In many areas of Latin America, especially Central America and Mexico, diminutive forms pervade everyday speech to an extent that amuses Spaniards:

Viene ya merito (Mex.; i.e. *ahora mismo*)	(S)he's coming right now
merito ayer no más (Mex., i.e. *ayer mismo*)	only yesterday
Ahorita lo voy a hacer (i.e. *ahora mismo/ahora mismito*)	I'll do it straightaway (in practice it usually means 'when I can...')
Clarito la recuerdo	I remember her vividly
Apártate tantito, que voy a saltar (Guatemala, from Kany, 385)	Get out of the way a bit, I'm going to jump
Reciencito llegó... (see 31.7.2 for *recién*)	(S)he arrived just a minute ago
Las caras de los gringos son todititas igualitas (C. Fuentes, Mex., dialogue)	Gringos' faces are all exactly the same

38.3 'Augmentative' suffixes

Typical, in order of frequency, are *-ón*, *-azo*, *-ote*, *-udo*.

(a) These are mainly used to denote intensity or large size, almost always with some associated pejorative idea of clumsiness, unpleasantness, awkwardness, excess, etc., as in *se me ha pegado un catarrazo* 'I've caught one heck of a cold' (*un catarro* = 'a cold'), *a través de la puerta, muchachones vestidos de negro y con el pelo al cero alborotaban* (J. Madrid, Sp.) 'on the other side of the door some young toughs in black with shaved heads were causing a din', *¿dónde compraste esas pezuñotas?* 'where did you buy those clodhoppers?' (i.e. enormous shoes/boots: *la pezuña* = 'hoof').

However, *-azo* can in some contexts imply admiration, as in *debes ser un profesorazo* 'you must be one heck of a teacher':

rico-ricachón rich-stinking rich, 'loaded'	*la broma-el bromazo* joke/joke pushed too far
pedante-pedantón pedant-insufferable pedant	*el coche-cochazo* car-'heck of a car'
el soltero-solterón bachelor-confirmed bachelor	*la ginebra-un ginebrazo* gin-an enormous shot of gin
contestón tending to answer back/cheeky	*el libro-librazo* book/tome
preguntón constantly asking questions	*el gringo-gringote* gringo-bloody gringo
cursi-cursilón affected-incredibly affected	*la palabra-la palabrota* word-swear word
fácil-facilón easy/facile	*el favor-favorzote* favour-'heck of a favour'

-azo is also much used to form nouns which denote a blow or flourish with some object:

el aldabón-aldabonazo	door knocker-thump with a door knocker/blow on door
el codo-codazo	elbow-dig with elbow
la bayoneta-el bayonetazo	bayonet-bayonet thrust

(**b**) To form an entirely new word. The suffix may then have no connotations of size or awkwardness and may even imply smallness:

la rata-el ratón rat-mouse (animal or computer)
la caja-el cajón box/drawer
la culebra-el culebrón grass-snake-soap opera (Sp. only? = *la telenovela*)

la cintura-el cinturón waist-belt
el fuego-el fogón fire-stove
la tela-el telón cloth-theatre curtain
la cuerda-el cordón string-shoelace

38.4 Pejorative suffixes

These are not particularly frequent. The words formed by them should be learnt as separate lexical items. Typical suffixes are *-aco, -arraco, -acho, -ajo, -astro, -uco, -ucho, -ejo* and a few others. They variously denote ugliness, wretchedness, squalor, meanness, etc.

el pájaro-pajarraco bird-sinister bird
el poeta-poetastro poet-rhymer/poetaster
el pueblo-poblacho village-'dump'/squalid village/dead-end town
el latín-latinajo Latin-Latin jargon/dog Latin

la casa-casucha house-pathetic little house
la palabra-palabreja word-horrible word
el hotel-hotelucho hotel-dingy hotel

Some of these suffixes can be used affectionately: *¿cómo va a poder estudiar con tres pequeñajas como ésas/esas?* 'how is she going to be able to study with three little terrors (i.e. children) like them?'

39

Spelling, accent rules, punctuation and word division

This chapter discusses the following points:

- Alphabet and spelling (Section 39.1)
- Use of the written accent (Section 39.2)
- Upper- and lower-case letters (Section 39.3)
- Punctuation (Section 39.4)
- Division of words (Section 39.5)

Spanish pronunciation is shown in this book by a system of phonetic transcription which offers only a rough guide to pronunciation and deliberately departs from the International Phonetic Alphabet, which is confusing for non-experts. The signs whose pronunciation is not self-evident are:

Symbol	Phonetic description	Remarks
β	voiced bilabial fricative	Air released steadily through lips held as for English **b**
χ	voiceless velar fricative	Like **ch** of German *lachen* or of Scottish 'loch'
γ	voiced velar fricative	Air released steadily through throat held as for English **g** of 'ago'
θ	voiceless interdental fricative	Like **th** of 'think'
ð	voiced interdental fricative	Like **th** of 'this'
ʎ	voiced palatal lateral	Palatalized **l**, as in Spanish *llamo*
rr	voiced alveolar trill	Rolled **r**, as in *perro*

Other signs should be given their usual Spanish pronunciation. *Y* in the transcriptions must always be pronounced like the y of English 'yes', never as a vowel; *aw* is similar to the ow in English 'cow'; *ay* is similar to the i in English 'high'.

39.1 Spelling

39.1.1 The *Nuevas normas* and the alphabet

The spelling rules of modern Spanish are laid down by the Academy in the *Nuevas normas de prosodia y ortografía* which came into official use in January 1959. This introduced several important changes, but more than forty years later pre-1959 spellings are still often used by persons not connected with the publishing world, and the *Nuevas normas* are by no means always obeyed by editors and publishers.

Among the more striking innovations of 1959 were the removal of the accent from the words *fui, fue, vi, dio, vio*, its adoption in words like *búho, rehúso, reúne, ahínca, aísla, prohíbe* (for the verbs affected see 13.2.3), and the decision to make the accent optional in the cases of the pronouns *éste, ése* and *aquél* (see 6.3), and on the word *sólo* = 'only' (see 9.15).

39.1.2 The Spanish alphabet

Until 1994, the Spanish alphabet had twenty-nine letters, since the signs *ch* and *ll* were treated as separate letters: *ch* or *ll* followed *c* or *l*, so in dictionaries *mancha* followed *mancornas* and *collado* followed *colza*, etc. This was very inconvenient for computerized sorting and out of line with other languages that use Latin letters, so in April 1994 the 10th Conference of Academies of the Spanish Language voted by a large majority to abolish *ch* and *ll* as separate letters. The position of the special letter *ñ* remained unchanged. The Spanish alphabet therefore now has twenty-seven letters:

a	*a*	h	*hache*	ñ	*eñe*	u	*u*
b	*be*	i	*i*	o	*o*	v	*uve*
c	*ce*	j	*jota*	p	*pe*	w	*uve doble*
d	*de*	k	*ka*	q	*cu*	x	*equis*
e	*e*	l	*ele*	r	*erre*	y	*i griega*
f	*efe*	m	*eme*	s	*ese*	z	*zeta* (less commonly *zeda*)
g	*ge*	n	*ene*	t	*te*		

NB: Double *r* (normally called *erre doble*) is a separate sound, but it is not treated as a separate letter of the alphabet.

(i) The Academy insists that accents should always be written on capital letters, a rule that printers often ignore since it creates letters that are too tall.

(ii) Letters of the alphabet are all feminine—*la cu, la uve*—and one says *la/una a, la/una hache*, despite the rule that singular feminine words beginning with a stressed *a* sound require the articles *el/un*, cf. *el/un arma* (fem.) 'the/a weapon': see 3.1.2 for discussion.

39.1.3 Relationship between sounds and letters

Spanish spelling is not entirely rational, but it is much more logical than French or English. Basically one sound corresponds to one letter, so one merely needs to hear words like *colocar* [kolokár] 'to place', *chaleco* [chaléko] 'waistcoat'/US vest, *calenturiento* [kalenturyénto] 'feverish', to be able to spell them correctly. However, the rule of one sound for one letter is broken in numerous cases:

(a) *H* is always silent except in some rural dialects, but it is common in writing, where it is merely a burden on the memory: *hacha* [ácha] 'axe'/US ax, *hombre* [ómbre] 'man', *Huesca* [wéska], *Honduras* [ondúras], *ahíto* [a-íto] 'gorged'/'satiated', etc. *H* had one useful function in the past: it showed that two vowels separated by *h* did not form a diphthong, as in words like *prohibe* [pro-íβe] 'prohibits' or *buho* [bú-o] 'owl'. In its wisdom the Academy abolished this rule in 1959, so one must now write *prohíbe, búho, rehíla, la retahíla*, etc.

The sound [w] at the beginning of a syllable is spelt *hu*: *huele* [wéle] 'it smells', *ahuecar* [awekár] 'to hollow out', *Náhuatl* [ná-watl] 'the Nahuatl language (of Mexico)', etc.

(b) Z is pronounced [θ] (like the th of 'think') in standard European Spanish, like the s of 'sit' throughout Latin America, in southern Spain and in the Canary Islands. The same sound is almost always written *c* before *i* or *e*: *cebra* [θéβra/séβra] 'zebra', *hacer* [aθér/asér] 'do', *nación* [naθyón/nasyón] 'nation', etc. For this reason, a verb like *realizar* 'attain'/'achieve'/'bring about' undergoes spelling changes: *realizo, realice, realicé, realizó*, etc. See 13.5.3 for the effect of these and other spelling rules on the verb system.

Z appears before *e* or *i* only in a handful of exceptional cases: *el eczema* (or *el eccema*) 'eczema', *la enzima* 'enzyme', *zeta* 'zed'/US 'zee', *Nueva Zelanda* (in Latin America *Nueva Zelandia*) 'New Zealand', *zigzag* (plural *zigzags*), *Zimbabue/Zimbabwe, zinc* (also *cinc*) 'zinc', *zipizape* 'rumpus'/'fuss'/'noisy quarrel'.

Spelling in Latin America and Andalusia is therefore much more troublesome than in central Spain since pairs of words like *haz* 'do' and *as* 'ace', *ves* 'you see' and *vez* 'time' (as in 'three times'), *Sena* 'the river Seine' and *cena* 'supper' sound the same.

(c) The sound of *c* in *cama* is written *qu* before *e* and *i*: *querer* [kerér] 'to want', *quiso* [kíso] 'wanted', *saque* [sáke] 'take out' (third-person present subjunctive of *sacar*), etc. The letter *k* is consequently not needed in Spanish and is found only in foreign words, for example measurements preceded by *kilo-*, or in *kantiano* 'Kantian', *krausismo*, 'Krausism', *el kiwi* [elkíβi] 'kiwi'/'kiwi fruit', *Kuwait* [kuβáyt] 'Kuwait', etc.

The sound [kw] is always written *cu*, e.g. *cuestión* [kwestyón] 'issue' (*la pregunta* = a question one asks), *cuáquero* [kwákero] 'Quaker' (students of Portuguese and Italian take note!).

(d) The sound [χ] (like *ch* in 'loch') is always written *j* before *a, o* and *u*, and is usually written *g* before *e* and *i*: *general* [χenerál], *Gibraltar* [χiβraltár], *rige* [rríχe] 'he/she/it rules', *rugir* [rruχír] 'to roar', etc. There are exceptions to the latter rule, e.g. iregular preterite and imperfect subjunctive forms of the type *dije/dijeron/dijera(n)/dijese(n)* 'said', *traje/trajeron/trajera(n)* 'brought', and all verbs whose infinitive ends in *-ducir* (see 13.3.37), and many other words, e.g.:

la bujía spark plug	*el jersey* jersey	*el paisaje* landscape
crujir to rustle/to crackle	*el jesuita* Jesuit	*el peaje* toll (on a road
dejé I left behind (from	*Jesús* Jesus	or bridge)
dejar)	*la jeta* thick lips/snout	*tejer* to weave
el equipaje luggage	*Jiménez* (a family name;	*el traje* suit
el garaje garage	also *Giménez*)	*el ultraje* outrage
la jeringa syringe	*la jirafa* giraffe	

(e) The sound of *g* in *tengo, hago* is written *gu* before *e* and *i*: *ruegue* [rrwéɣe] present subjunctive of *rogar* 'to request', *la guirnalda* [laɣirnálda] 'wreath'/'garland'. The silent *u* simply shows that the *g* is not pronounced like Spanish *j* [χ].

The syllables pronounced [gwe] and [gwi] are written *güe* and *güi*, e.g. *lingüístico* [lingwístiko], *el desagüe* [eldesáɣwe] 'drainage'/'water outlet', *averigüe* [aßeríɣwe] present subjunctive of *averiguar* 'to check', *nicaragüense* [nikaraɣwénse] 'Nicaraguan', *el pingüino* [elpingwíno] 'penguin'. This is the only use of the dieresis in the modern language.

(f) *B* and *v* sound exactly the same and are most often pronounced as a voiced bilabial fricative [β], although they both sound like the English *b* after *n* or *m* or after a pause. The English sound [v] as in 'vat' does not exist in Spanish, and English-speakers often make a false distinction between the pronunciation of the Spanish written signs *b* and *v*. For this reason they usually do not confuse these letters in writing.

Native speakers who are bad spellers make blunders like **la uba* for *la uva* [laúβa] 'grape', **Premio Novel* for *Premio Nobel* [prémyonoβél] 'Nobel Prize', mistakes which are at least the sign of a normal pronunciation.

(g) In Spain, *x* (*equis*) is often pronounced like *s* before a consonant: *extender* = [estendér] 'extend', *el extracto*, = [elestrákto] 'extract', etc. Seco (1998), 459, rejects the pronunciation of *x* as [ks] in this position as 'affected', but Latin Americans insist on it, and it is apparently becoming more common in Spain. For the pronunciation and spelling of the words *México, mexicano, Oaxaca* see 4.8.1, note (iv).

X is pronounced [s] at the beginning of words: *la xenofobia* [lasenofóβya] 'xenophobia', *el xilófono* [elsilófono] (colloquially *el xilofón* [elsilofón]) 'xylophone'.

The pronunciation [ks] is normal between vowels and at the end of words: *el examen* [eleksámen] 'examination', *el taxi* 'taxi' [eltáksi], *Xerox* [séroks]. Learners should avoid popular pronunciations like [esámen], [tási], often heard in Spain.

(h) *N* is pronounced *m* before *b, v, p*: *en Barcelona* = [embarθelóna/embarselóna] 'in Barcelona', *invitar* = [imbitár] 'to invite', *en París* = [emparís] 'in Paris'.

(i) *R* and *rr* represent a flapped and a rolled *r* ([r] and [rr]) respectively, and in a few words they indicate a difference of meaning, e.g. *pero* [péro] 'but', *perro* [pérro] 'dog'; *caro* [káro] 'dear', *carro* [kárro] 'car'/'cart'; *enteró* [enteró] '(s)he informed', *enterró* [enterró] '(s)he buried'.

But *r* is pronounced like *rr* when it is the first letter in a word, e.g. *Roma* [rróma], *la ropa* [larrópa] 'clothes', or when it occurs after *l, n* or *s*: *Israel* [isrraél], *la sonrisa* [lasonrrísa] 'smile', *alrededor* [alrreðeðór] 'around'.

When a prefix ending in a vowel is added to a word beginning with *r*, the *r* is doubled in writing and is therefore rolled in speech: *infra+rojo* = *infrarrojo* 'infrared', *contra+revolucionario* = *contrarrevolucionario* 'counter-revolutionary', *anti+republicano* = *antirrepublicano* 'anti-Republican'. Such words are not spelt with a hyphen in Spanish.

(j) *Ll* is properly a palatalized *l* [ʎ], but it is nowadays pronounced like the letter *y* by many speakers, to the dismay of purists. Poor spellers sometimes make mistakes like **cullo* for *cuyo* 'whose', **vállase* for *váyase* 'go away', and it is much better to pronounce it *y* than to pronounce it like the *lli* of 'million', which is written *li* in Spanish. *Polio* [pólyo] 'polio' and *pollo* [póʎo] 'chicken' sound quite different in Spanish.

(k) *M* is often pronounced *n* at the end of words by many, though not by all speakers: *el álbum* = [elálβun/elálβum] 'album', *el referéndum* = [elrreferéndun] 'referendum', *el ultimátum* = [elultimátun] 'ultimatum'.

(l) *Ps, mn* and *gn* at the beginning of words are pronounced *s, n* and *n* and may, since the Academy's reform of 1959, be spelled this way. But many, including *El País*, cannot bring themselves to write *la sicología* for *la psicología* 'psychology' or *la* *siquiatría* for *la psiquiatría* 'psychiatry', and very few would write *la nosis* or *nóstico* for *la gnosis, gnóstico* 'gnosis', 'gnostic'. The older spellings *ps-, gn-, mn-* are therefore still used—even by the Academy itself! *El seudónimo* 'pseudonym' is, however, universally used.

(**m**) The *p* in *septiembre* 'September' and *séptimo* 'seventh' is sometimes silent and may be dropped in writing according to the Academy. But many, including *El País*, find the forms *setiembre, sétimo* repugnant, so the forms with *p* are much more common.

(**n**) If the prefix *re-* is added to a word beginning with *e* one of the *es* may be dropped in writing: *re + emplazo > remplazo* or *reemplazo* 'replacement', *re + embolso > rembolso* or *reembolso* 'reimbursement', *reelige > relige* 're-elects'. The new spelling is frequently (but not universally) seen in Latin America, but the spelling with *ree-* is much more usual in Spain.

(**o**) The sound [y] (like the *y* in 'yacht') is always spelt *y* at the end of words: *Paraguay, convoy.*

39.1.4 *Trans-* or *-tras-*

Some uncertainty surrounds the spelling of words that begin with the prefix *trans-* or *tras-*. Educated usage, according to Seco (1998), 437, seems to be:

(a) usually *trans-*

transalpino	transatlántico	transbordar	transbordo
transcribir	transgresión	transpiración	transpirar
transcripción	transgresor	transpirar	transpirenaico
transcurrir	transmediterráneo	transpirenaico	transportar
transcurso	transmigración	transportar	transporte
transferencia	transmisión	transporte	transposición
transferir	transmitir	transposición	transversal
transformar	transmisión	transversal	
transformación	transparencia	transparentar	
transfusión	transparentar	transparente	
transgredir	transparente	transpiración	

(b) usually *tras-*

trascendencia	trascendente	trasponer	trasvasar
trascendental	trascender		

(c) always *tras-*

trasfondo	trasluz	trasplantar	trastornar
trashumancia	trasnochar	trasplante	trastorno
trashumante	traspapelar	traspunte	trastrocar
trasladar	traspasar	trasquilar	trastrueque
traslado	traspaso	trastienda	
traslucir	traspié	trastocar	

Seco notes that in the case of (**a**) and (**b**) the alternative spellings in *tras-* and *trans-* are 'tolerated' by the Academy but are not in general use.

39.1.5 Common non-Castilian forms

Words written in the other official languages of Spain are nowadays often seen in Spanish texts printed in Castilian. Common pronunciations are:

	Pronunciation
j (Catalan, Galician)	like s in 'pleasure'
j (Basque)	Spanish j
g before i, e (Catalan, Galician)	like s in 'pleasure'
g (Basque)	always like g in English 'get'
h (Catalan, Galician, Basque)	silent, as in Spanish
tx (Basque, Catalan)	like Spanish ch
ny (Catalan)	like Spanish ñ
l·l (Catalan)	double l (not as Spanish ll)
x (Catalan, Galician, Basque)	sh
tz (Basque)	ts
-aig, -eig, -oig, -uig (Catalan)	-ach, -ech, -och, -uch
z (Catalan)	like English z
z (Basque)	like Spanish s

Latin-American spellings sometimes reflect the sounds of native American languages. In many of these, notably Maya and Nahuatl, *x* is pronounced sh. This affects some Mexican place-names like Uxmal [ushmál], Tlaxcala [tlashkála], Xcaret [shkarét]. However, x is pronounced like Spanish j in some other Mexican place names, e.g. *México*, Oaxaca. See 4.8.1, note (iv).

Grammarians sometimes recommend that foreign words should be spelled according to their Spanish pronunciation, e.g. *güisqui* for *whisky*, *yip* for *jeep*, *yóquey* or *yoqui* for *jockey*, *tique* for *ticket*, etc. Such forms are sometimes seen, but since they imply ignorance of foreign languages they have a slightly embarrassing appearance for many people.

NB: One must use the right word for 'ticket' in Spain. *Un billete* is for train, bus or air journeys. *Una entrada* is for places of entertainment like museums, cinemas, theatres. *Un tique* or *un ticket* allows the holder to use facilities, e.g. for toll roads, car parks, cloakrooms, left-luggage offices. *El boleto* is universal for *el billete* in Latin America. Enquire locally for the other terms.

39.2 The written accent

The Academy and many Hispanic grammarians call both the curly sign over an *ñ* and the acute accent (´) *la tilde*, but in everyday language the latter usually means only the sign over *ñ*. *El acento* properly means 'stress' in linguistics, but in ordinary language it means 'written accent', specifically the acute accent.

39.2.1 General rules

Native Spanish-speakers are rather careless about the use of the written accent in handwriting, but in printing and formal writing the rules must be observed. The basic rules are as follows (note that these rules assume a correct pronunciation of Spanish):

(a) if the word ends in a consonant other than *n* or *s* and the stress falls on the last syllable no written accent is required: *contestad* 'answer!', *el coñac* 'cognac' / 'brandy', *Madrid*, *natural*, *Paraguay*, *hablar* 'to talk';

(b) if the word ends in a vowel or *n* or *s* and the stress falls on the last syllable but one, no written accent is required. Examples: *la calle* 'street', *el juego*, 'game', *hablan* 'they speak', *la imagen* 'image', *hablas* 'you talk', *Francia* 'France' (see 39.2.2b for diphthongs);

(**c**) in all other cases the position of the stress must be shown in writing by an acute accent. The following are therefore stressed irregularly and must have a written accent:

el álbum album	*difícil* difficult	*el rehén* hostage
alérgicamente allergically	*dirán* they will say	*la/las síntesis* synthesis/
contéstenles answer them	*fácil* easy	syntheses
(*ustedes* imperative)	*las imágenes* images	*las vírgenes* virgins
colocó (s)he placed	*la nación* nation	
decídmelo tell me it	*la química* chemistry	
(*vosotros* imperative)	*el récord* record (in sports)	

(i) It follows from these rules that all Spanish words stressed more than two syllables from the end must be written with an accent on the stressed vowel: *díganmelo*, *teléfono*, *la química*, etc.

(ii) Words ending in two consonants of which the second is *s* (all of them foreign words) are stressed on the last syllable: *Orleans*, *los complots* 'plots', *los cabarets* 'cabarets'. *El/los fórceps* 'forceps', *el/los bíceps* 'biceps', *el/los récords* are exceptions.

(iii) When, as happens in archaic or very flowery styles, an object pronoun is added to a preterite form, a written accent on a final vowel is usually retained: *acabó + se = acabóse* for *se acabó* 'it ended' (see 11.14.1 note ii for a discussion of this construction). This produces the anomaly of a predictably stressed vowel written with an accent, and the Academy's *Nuevas normas* of 1959 decreed that the accent should be removed. However, most people still write the accent, as did the Spanish *El País* until 2002. Its new *Libro de estilo*, 11.101, now recommends spellings like *acabose*, *pidiome*, which many find disconcerting.

When a pronoun is added to an imperative the accent is not written if it becomes unnecessary, e.g. *detén* 'stop' but *detenlos* 'stop them'. This rule is generally observed, but for *dele* or *déle* 'give him/her', see 39.2.6(i).

(iv) If a word bearing a written accent is joined to another to form a compound, the original written accent is discarded: *tío + vivo = tiovivo* 'merry-go-round', *balón + cesto = baloncesto* 'basketball', etc.

39.2.2 Diphthongs, triphthongs and the position of the stress

Spanish vowels are divided into two classes:

(1) Strong vowels
i when pronounced as in *ti*
u when pronounced as in *su, tú*
a, e, o in any position

(2) Semi-vowels
i when pronounced [y] as in *bien, voy*
u when pronounced [w] as in *bueno, causa*

Vowels may appear in combinations of two or three, e.g. *eai, au, uai, iai*, etc. An intervening *h* is disregarded, so that *au* and *ahu*, *eu* and *ehu*, *ai* and *ahi*, etc., are treated the same way—at least since the publication of the Academy's *Nuevas normas* in 1959.

(a) When two or more **strong** vowels appear side by side, they are, in careful speech, pronounced as separate syllables and do not form diphthongs or triphthongs:

leo [lé-o] I read	*moho* [mó-o] rust/mildew
créamelo [kré-amelo] believe me	*Seoane* [se-o-á-ne] (a surname)
pasee [pasé-e] subjunctive of *pasear*	*creí* [kre-í] I believed
'to go for a walk'	*aún* [a-ún] still/yet

(b) A combination, in either order, of a **strong vowel** and a **semi-vowel** creates a diphthong and is counted as a single vowel for the purpose of finding the position of the written accent. Therefore the following words are stressed predictably:

arduo [árðwo] arduous	*Francia* [fránθya/fránsya] France
continuo [kontínwo] continuous	*la historia* [laystórya] history/story
erais [érays] you were	*produjisteis* [proðuχísteys] you produced
la lengua [laléngwa] tongue/language	*hablabais* [aβláβays] you were speaking

and the following words have unpredictable stress and require a written accent:

amáis [amáys] you love	*hacías* [aθías/asías] you were doing
debéis [deβéys] you owe	*ella respondía* [eʎarrespondía] she was
volvió [bolβyó] he/she returned	answering
continúo [kontinú-o] I continue	

(c) If a semi-vowel is added to a diphthong, a triphthong is formed. Triphthongs are also counted as a single vowel for the purpose of determining where a written accent should appear:

continuáis [kontinwáys]	you continue (three syllables)
las vieiras [lasβyéyras]	scallops (Spain only; two syllables)
cambiáis [kambyáys]	you change (two syllables)

(i) Students of Portuguese should remember that Portuguese has the opposite rule and writes *colónia*, *história*, but *temia* (all stressed the same as Spanish *colonia*, *historia*, *temía*).

39.2.3 Written accent on stressed diphthongs and combinations of strong vowels

If one of a group of combined vowels is stressed, the written accent may or may not appear on it. There are three possibilities:

(a) If the combination is **strong vowel** and **semi-vowel** (in either order) the stress falls predictably on the strong vowel, so the following require no written accent:

vais [báys] you go (*vosotros* form)	*la ruina* [larrwína] ruin
el aire [eláyre] the air	*tiene* [tyéne] (s)he has (from *tener*)
el peine [elpéyne] comb	*luego* [lwéɣo] then/later
la causa [lakáwsa] cause	*la tiara* [latyára] tiara
Palau [paláw] (personal surname)	*acuoso* [akwóso] watery
Berneu [bernéw] (personal surname)	*vio* [byó] (s)he saw
alcaloide [alkalóyðe] alkaloid	*dio* [dyó] (s)he gave
fui [fwí] I was	*el pie* [elpyé] foot
huido [wíðo] fled (p.p. of *huir* 'to flee')	*la viuda* [laβyúða] widow

and the following are exceptions:

el país [elpa-ís] country	*reúne* [rre-úne] he reunites
el baúl [elβa-úl] trunk/large suitcase	*prohíbe* [pro-íβe] he prohibits
aún [a-ún] still/yet (pronounced	*heroína* [ero-ína] heroine/heroin
differently from *aun*, 'even')	*el arcaísmo* [arka-ísmo] archaism
reír [rre-ír] to laugh	*ahí* [a-í] there
reís [rre-ís] you (*vosotros*) laugh	*oís* [o-ís] you (*vosotros*) hear
el dúo [eldú-o] duet/duo	*ríe* [rrí-e] (s)he laughs (from *reír*)
el búho [elβú-o] owl	*se fía* [sefí-a] (s)he trusts (from *fiarse*)
frío [frí-o] cold	

(b) If the combination is **strong vowel** + **strong vowel** the two vowels form separate syllables, so the following are stressed predictably:

los jacarandaes [losχakarandá-es]	*feo* [fé-o] ugly
jacaranda trees (plural of *el jacarandá*)	*leen* [lé-en] they read
los noes [losnó-es] noes (plural of 'no')	*la boa* [laβó-a] boa (the snake may
el caos [elká-os] chaos	be *el boa* in Latin America)
	(see 39.2.2a for more examples)

and the following are exceptions:

aéreo [a-éreo] air (adjective)	*el deán* [elde-án] dean (ecclesiastical)
el león [elle-ón] lion	*el rehén* [elrre-én] hostage

(i) *Huido, construido* and other words ending in *-uido* are stressed regularly because the *ui* is a diphthong, but words like *creído* 'believed' (past participle of *creer*) and *reído* 'laughed' (past participle of *reír*) are written with an accent because they fall under the exceptions to (**a**), i.e. the *i* is not pronounced like 'y'.

(ii) Accented forms like *rió* [rri-ó] '(s)he laughed', *lió* [li-ó] '(s)he tied in a bundle', *huís* [u-ís] 'you (*vosotros*) flee', *huí* [u-í] 'I fled', etc. are apparently exceptions to the rule that the strong vowel is predictably stressed in the combination semi-vowel + strong vowel: compare *fui* 'I was', *fue* '(s)he was', *vio* '(s)he saw', *dio* '(s)he gave'. Words like *rió, lió, fió* are given a written accent to show that the two vowels are pronounced separately, whereas *vio, dio, fui* and *fue* are pronounced as monosyllabic words [byó], [dyó], [fwí], [fwé]. Compare the pronunciation of *pie* 'foot' [pyé] with *pié* [pi-é], first-person preterite of *piar* 'to cheep' (like a bird).

(iii) As mentioned in 39.2.2c, a triphthong is treated like a single vowel for the purpose of determining the position of the stress, so that *continuáis* [kontinwáys] (from *continuar* 'to continue') is in fact an exception and must be written with the accent.

39.2.4 Written accent: some common doubtful cases

The following forms are recommended (where *el/la* precedes the noun the latter may refer to a male or a female; when no accent is written the stressed vowel is shown in bold):

la acrobacia acrobatics	*el/la chófer* driver (see note i)
afrodisiaco aphrodisiac	*el cóctel* cocktail
amoniaco ammonia	*demoniaco* or *demoníaco* demonic; likewise
austriaco Austrian	other words ending in *-iaco/íaco*, the
cardiaco cardiac	unaccented form being more common

la dinamo dynamo (see note ii)
disponte familiar imperative of
   disponerse 'get ready' (see
   note iii)
el electrodo electrode
etíope Ethiopean
la exégesis or *la exegesis* exegesis
el fríjol bean (see note iv)
el fútbol soccer (see note v)
el géiser geyser (geological)
hipocondríaco hypochondriac (see
   demoniaco above)
ibero (less commonly *íbero*) Iberian
el láser laser
la metempsicosis metempsychosis
el meteoro meteor
el misil (less commonly *mísil*)
   missile
la olimpiada Olympiad
la orgía orgy
la ósmosis or *osmosis* osmosis

el pabilo wick (of a candle)
el parásito parasite
el/la pediatra paediatrician/
   US pediatrician
el periodo or *período* period
el/la políglota polyglot
el/la psiquiatra psychiatrist
policiaco police (adjective; see *demoniaco*
   above)
la quiromancia palmistry/hand-reading
   (see note vi)
el rádar radar
el reptil reptile
el reuma rheumatism (everyday usage
   prefers *el reúma*)
el sánscrito Sanskrit
el termostato thermostat
la tortícolis stiff neck
la utopía utopia
el zodiaco zodiac (see *demoniaco* above)

Some 'mispronunciations' are usual in speech, e.g. *el soviet* 'Soviet', *el oceano* 'ocean' (written and correctly pronounced *el océano*).

(i)   Written and pronounced *chofer* (i.e. [chofér]) in all of Latin America.
(ii) *El dínamo* in some Latin-American countries, including Argentina and Cuba.
(iii) Similarly *componte* 'compose yourself', *detente* 'stop'.
(iv) Stressed *el frijol* in Latin America.
(v)   *El futbol* is heard in some Latin-American countries.
(vi) Likewise all words ending in *-mancia* that have the meaning 'divination'.

39.2.5 Accent on interrogative forms

In the case of some words, the form used in questions carries an accent. These words are: *cómo* 'how', *cuál* 'which', *cuándo* 'when', *cuánto* 'how much', *dónde* 'where', *qué* 'what/which', *quién* ' who'. Chapter 24 gives further details.

39.2.6 Accent used to distinguish words pronounced the same

In the case of some two dozen common words, the written accent merely elimi- nates ambiguities:

	without accent	with accent
de/dé	of	present subjunctive of *dar*
el/él	the (def. article)	he/it
éste/este	see 6.3	
ése/ese	see 6.3	
aquél/aquel	see 6.3	
mas/más	but (rare)	more
mi/mí	my	me (after prepositions)
se/sé	reflexive pronoun	(i) I know, (ii) *tú* imperative of *ser*
si/sí	if	(i) yes, (ii) prepositional form of *se*
sólo/solo (see 9.15)	alone	only (*solamente*)
te/té	object form of *tú*	tea
tu/tú	your	you

(i) *Dé* 'give' ought to lose its accent if a pronoun is attached and the stress is regular: *denos*, 'give us', *deme* 'give me', etc. However, the spellings *déme*, *déles*, etc. are usual, even though the accent is not really necessary.

(ii) The Academy recommends that *o* ('or') should take an accent when it appears between two numerals so as to avoid confusion with zero, e.g. 7 *ó* 8 '7 or 8'. See 33.2.

(iii) The following words do **not** have a written accent: *da* 'gives', *di* 'I gave', *fe* 'faith', *ti* prepositional form of *tú*, *vi* 'I saw', *ve* 'sees', *vio* '(s)he saw', *fui* 'I was', *fue* (s)he was', *dio* (s)he gave'.

(iv) *Aun* 'even' [áwn] and *aún* 'still/yet' [a-ún] are in fact pronounced differently in good Spanish.

39.3 Upper- and lower-case letters

39.3.1 Upper-case letters

Capital letters are used less than in English. They are written:

(a) At the beginning of sentences, as in English.

(b) With proper nouns, but not with the adjectives derived from them: *Madrid*, *la vida madrileña* 'Madrid life'; *Colombia*, *la cocina colombiana* 'Colombian cooking'; *Shakespeare*, *el lenguaje shakespeariano* 'Shakespearean (or Shakespeare's) language'.

Adjectives that are part of an official name are capitalized, e.g. *Nueva Zeland(i)a* 'New Zealand', *el Reino Unido* 'the United Kingdom', *Los Estados Unidos* 'the United States', *El Partido Conservador* 'The Conservative Party', *Las Naciones Unidas* 'The United Nations', etc.

When a proper name includes the definite article, the latter is written with a capital letter: *El Cairo* 'Cairo', *La Haya*. But in the case of countries that appear with the definite article, the article is not part of the name so a lower-case letter is used: *la India* 'India', *la Argentina*. See 3.2.17 for discussion of this use of the article.

39.3.2 Lower-case letters

Lower-case letters are used for:

(a) Months, seasons and days of the week: *julio* 'July', *agosto* 'August', *verano* 'summer', *invierno* 'winter', *jueves* 'Thursday', *viernes* 'Friday', *martes* 'Tuesday', etc.

(b) Names of religions and their followers: *el cristianismo* 'Christianity', *el catolicismo* 'Catholicism', *el protestantismo* 'Protestantism', *el islam* 'Islam', *un testigo de Jehová* 'a Jehovah's witness', *los musulmanes* 'the Muslims', etc.

(c) Official titles, e.g. *el presidente de la República*, 'the President of the Republic', *la reina de Gran Bretaña* 'the Queen of Great Britain', *el papa Juan XXIII* 'Pope John XXIII', *los reyes de España* 'the King and Queen of Spain', *el señor García* 'Sr. Garcia', *ministro de Obras Públicas* 'the Minister for Public Works', etc.

(**d**) Book and film titles: only the first letter is in upper case, as well as the first letter of any proper name that appears in the title: *Cien años de soledad* 'One Hundred Years of Solitude', *El otoño del patriarca* 'The Autumn of the Patriarch', *El espía que surgió del frío* 'The Spy who came in from the Cold', *La guerra de las galaxias* 'Star Wars', *Vida de Manuel Rosas* 'The Life of Manuel Rosas', etc. But the titles of newspapers and magazines are capitalized: *El País, La Nación, Ordenador Personal* 'Personal Computer', etc.

(**e**) Points of the compass: *norte* 'North', *sur* 'South', *este* 'East', *oeste* 'West'. They are capitalized if they are part of a name: *América del Norte*, 'North America', etc.

39.4 Punctuation

These remarks refer only to major differences between Spanish and English. Readers who need a detailed account of Spanish punctuation should refer to specialized manuals.

39.4.1 Full stops/periods and commas

The full stop/US period (*el punto*) is used as in English, except that abbreviations are usually always written with a full stop:

English	Spanish
Dr Moreno	*Dr. Moreno*
Sr González	*Sr. González*

For the use of points and commas in writing numbers, see 10.1 note iii.

Commas (*la coma*) are used much as in English, except for writing decimals (see the preceding paragraph). Commas are not written before the conjunction *y* in a series: *pumas, coyotes y monos* 'pumas, coyotes and monkeys'. Two clauses with different subjects are separated by a comma whereas in English the comma is nowadays often omitted: *Juan es uruguayo, y Marta es chilena* 'Juan is Uruguayan and Marta is Chilean'.

39.4.2 Colons

Colons (*dos puntos*) are used as in English except that they often appear after salutations in letters: *Muy Sr. mío:* (the formula used in the Southern Cone is *De mi consideración:*) 'Dear Sir,' *Querida Ana:* 'Dear Ana.'

39.4.3 Semi-colons

Semi-colons (*punto y coma*) are used much as in English, and they are often used after a series of commas to denote a longer pause:

Tenía pan, huevos y vino; pero no tenía carne	(S)he had bread, eggs and wine, but (s)he had no meat
Miguel entró cansado, confuso; María le siguió, radiante y orgullosa.	Miguel came in, tired, confused. Maria followed him, radiant and proud

The semi-colon is also regularly used before phrases like *sin embargo/no obstante* 'nevertheless', *a pesar de esto* 'despite this', that are themselves followed by a comma:

Les escribí más de una vez; sin embargo, no
me contestaron

I wrote to them more than once.
However, they did not reply

Seco (1998), 369, notes that the semi-colon is often used before words like 'but' to separate long clauses, as in *el camino no ofrecía grandes peligros; pero no me atreví* 'the trail presented no great dangers, but I didn't have the courage'.

39.4.4 Quotations and the representation of dialogue

There is no clear agreement over the use of *comillas* or inverted commas.

(**a**) Chevrons (« »: *comillas francesas* or *comillas angulares*) may be used (at least in Spain) like our inverted commas to indicate quotations or slang, dialect or other unusual forms, and occasionally to indicate dialogue within a paragraph:

> *Un inspector de bigotillo con acento «pied noir» acompañado de un gendarme de uniforme, va recorriendo las mesas pidiendo documentación: «No pasa nada, es sólo una operación de rutina». Sin embargo, todo este impresionante montaje sorprende a todos. (Cambio16, Sp.)*

A further quotation within « » is indicated by " " .

However, the *Libro de estilo* of *El País*, 2002, 11.32, explicitly forbids the use of « » and requires use of " " for quoted material and ' ' for quotations within quotations. This convention is used in many publications.

Single quotation marks are much used to enclose isolated words: *La palabra 'esnob' viene del inglés* 'the word "snob" comes from English'.

(**b**) There are three types of dash in Spanish:

el guión	hyphen	short -
el signo de menos	minus sign	medium length –
la raya	dash	double length —

In the representation of continuous dialogue inverted commas are not used, the words spoken being introduced by a *raya*.

A *raya* marks either the beginning of dialogue, a change of speaker or a resumption of dialogue after an interruption: *—Ahora váyase —dijo— y no vuelva más hasta que yo le avise.* Dialogue is closed by a *raya* only if unspoken words follow it, as in *—¿Qué tal estás? —Angustias lo dice con una sonrisa.*

Punctuation in direct speech is disconcertingly placed after the *raya*: *—Aprovecha ahora que eres joven para sufrir todo lo que puedas —le decía—, que estas cosas no duran toda la vida* (G. García Márquez, *El amor en los tiempos del cólera*).

The following text is copied from a reputable publisher:

> *—¿Crees que es maniaco-depresiva?*
> *—¡Cristo!, qué lenguaje empleas —dijo—. No sé lo que es, es una persona rara. Más rara que la calentura —dijo, buscando otra comparación.*
> *De ahí no la pude sacar.*
> *—¿Y mi padre? ¿También era raro?*
> *—¿Raro? —repitió, como si fuera la palabra que no comprendiese, ella que la había estado empleando todo el tiempo—. No, por Dios, nada de eso. Era el hombre más normal que he conocido. ¿Es que no has leído sus obras? Normal, ¿no? Así es la vida, como la pinta él.*
> from Soledad Puértolas, *Todos mienten* (Barcelona: Anagrama)

39.4.5 Question and exclamation marks

Spanish and Galician (*el gallego*) are unique among the world's languages in that questions and exclamations are introduced by upside-down question or exclamation marks and followed by normal question and exclamation marks. The argument for this is that it prepares readers to use the correct intonation pattern, so words that are not included in the interrogatory or exclamatory intonation pattern lie outside the signs:

Oye, ¿quieres una cerveza?	Hey, d'you want a beer?
Hace calor, ¿verdad?	It's hot, isn't it?
Si te digo que no he gastado más que	If I tell you I've only spent 200 euros,
doscientos euros, ¿me vas a creer?	will you believe me?
Pero, ¡qué estupidez!	But what stupidity!
¡Lo voy a hacer! ¿Me oyes?	I'm going to do it! Do you hear me?

39.4.6 Hyphens

Hyphens (*guiones*) are used very sparingly, since compound words are usually written as single words: *latinoamericano* (not **latino-americano*), *antisubmarino* 'antisubmarine', *hispanohablante* 'Spanish-speaking', *tercermundista* 'Third-World'.

They appear between compound adjectives in which each part represents separate things or people (not the case, for example, with *latinoamericano*). Only the second of two adjectives agrees in number and gender:

las guerras árabe-israelíes	the Arab-Israeli wars
negociaciones anglo-francesas	Anglo-French negotiations
el complejo militar-industrial	the military-industrial complex

In other cases the hyphen may be used to join two nouns:

misiles superficie-aire	surface-to-air missiles
la carretera Madrid-Barcelona	the Madrid–Barcelona road

Hyphens are sometimes printed between compound nouns of the sort *mujer policía* 'policewoman', *año luz* 'light year', but this does not conform either with the Academy's recommendation or with the best editorial practice.

39.5 Division of words at end of line

A thorough knowledge of the structure of Spanish syllables is necessary for a good pronunciation, and readers should consult manuals of phonology and phonetics for precise details. As far as word division at the end of a line is concerned, the following rules apply:

(a) *Ch, ll, qu, gu* and *rr* and the following combinations of consonants are not divided at the end of a line:

br	*cr*	*fr*	*gr*	*pr*	*dr*	*tr*
bl	*cl*	*fl*	*gl*	*pl*		

(b) Bearing in mind that the combinations listed under **(a)** are never divided, a single consonant is always grouped with the following vowel:

ha-ba	*ro-ca*	*nu-do*	*a-gua*	*pe-lo*	*ra-za*	*mar-ca*
ha-cha	*ca-lle*	*pe-rro*	*ca-bra*	*co-fre*	*o-tro*	*co-pla*
sa-que	*pa-gue*	*de-sa-güe*				

and no syllable begins with more than one consonant:

cal-do	*cos-ta*	*cuan-do*	*par-te*	*can*-cha
as-ma	*hem-bra*	*em-ble-ma*	*com-bi-nar*	*in-na-to*
ex-cla-mar	*con-lle-var*	*cons-truc-ción*	*al-co-hol*	*rehén*
blan-den-gue				

(**c**) *El País, Libro de estilo*, 2002, 11.129, advises against separating vowels, and this is the easiest rule to remember:

viu-do	*cié-na-ga*	*fiel-tro*	*can-táis*	*a-ma-bais*
bue-no	*ha-cia*	*pe-río-do*	*ha-cía-mos*	*con-ti-núas*

(**d**) When a prefix ending with a vowel is added to a word beginning with *r-*, the latter consonant is doubled in writing: *contrarrevolucionario* 'counter-revolutionary', *prorrogar* 'to adjourn'. If the prefix is divided from the word at the end of a line, the single *r* reappears: *contra-revolucionario, pro-rogar*.

(i) The above rules reflect Spanish pronunciation, but the Academy states that when a word is clearly divisible on etymological grounds it may be divided accordingly. An etymological division is preferred when the usual division does not reflect the correct pronunciation: *su-brogar* for *sub-rogar* 'to substitute' looks and sounds wrong. Further examples :

de-sa-gra-da-ble or *des-a-gra-da-ble* disagreeable
sub-rep-ti-cio (better than *su-brep-t-i-cio*) subreptitious
sub-ru-ti-na (better than *su-bru-ti-na*) subroutine
*sub-ra-y*ar (better than *su-bra-yar*) to underline
sud-a-me-ri-ca-no or *su-da-me-ri-ca-no* South American
vos-o-tros or *vo-so-tros* you

(ii) Any of these rules is overridden to avoid a comic or shocking result. One does not write *sa-cerdote, cal-culo, al ser-vicio del gobierno*.

(iii) There is disagreement over the combination *tl*. The rule is that it is optionally separable, except in the words *a-tlas, a-tle-ta* and their derivatives. It should also not be separated in Mexican words like Tenochtitlán.

(iv) Foreign words should be divided according to the rules used in the language of origin.

(v) Words containing the sequence *interr-* are divided thus: *in-ter-re-la-cio-na-do*.

Sources: Macpherson (1975), *Nuevas normas* (1959), Martínez de Sousa (2001), Manuel Seco (1998), *El País, Libro de estilo* 2002.

Glossary of grammatical terms

Many terms are already defined in the text of the grammar at the section shown. Words printed in capital letters are defined elsewhere in the glossary. Some of the definitions are inspired by the glossary in Martin Durrell's *Hammer's German Grammar and Usage*, 4th edition (London: Arnold, 2002).

a personal	see PERSONAL *A*
accent	loosely used in Spanish studies to mean the sign over the letters *á, é, í, ó, ú*. See also STRESS.
active voice	the form of the verb in which the subject of the verb also really performs the action, e.g. '**Mike** painted the kitchen' as opposed to the passive 'the kitchen was painted by Mike'. See Ch. 28.
adjectival participle	defined at 19.4
adjective	a word that describes a NOUN or PRONOUN, e.g. 'a **red** book'/*un libro rojo*, 'you're **tall**'/*eres alto*.
adverb	a word or phrase that modifies a VERB or an ADJECTIVE, often giving extra information on **how, when, where** or **why**: 'she came **yesterday**'/*vino ayer*, 'I left it **here**'/*lo dejé aquí*, 'it's **totally** untrue'/*es completamente falso*, 'to work **in vain**'/*trabajar en balde*.
agreement	the rules whereby a feature of one word is repeated or echoed in other related words. In English verbs usually agree in person and number, so we must say 'he is' and not *'he are'. Spanish verbs have similar but stronger rules. Spanish ARTICLES and ADJECTIVES agree in number and gender with NOUNS and PRONOUNS: *la casa blanca* 'the white house', *él es guapo* 'he is good-looking', *ellas son guapas* 'they (females) are good-looking', etc.
antecedent	the NOUN or PRONOUN that a RELATIVE CLAUSE refers to, e.g. '**the woman** who lives over the road'/*la mujer que vive en frente*.
anterior preterite	defined at 14.10.4

apposition   the use of a phrase to extend or clarify the meaning of a NOUN PHRASE without being connected to it by a PREPOSITION: 'Paris, **the capital of France**'/*París, **capital de Francia**.* See 3.2.25.

article   the grammatical name given to the words 'the' and 'a(n)' in English, and *el/la/los/las* and *un/una/unos/unas* in Spanish, as in '**the** fox ate **a** duck'/*el zorro se comió **un** pato.* Words meaning 'the' are called 'definite articles', and words meaning 'a(n)' are 'indefinite articles'. See Chapter 3.

aspect   Regardless of *when* they occur, events can have other qualities: they may be completed or finished ('I broke my leg', 'I will have finished my exams'), or incomplete at the time ('the garden was in full bloom'), or 'continuous' ('I was smoking a cigar') or 'non-continuous' ('I smoked a cigar'). These features are described by some linguists as differences of 'aspect'. It has been claimed that the Spanish PRETERITE and IMPERFECT reflect a difference between completed and non-completed 'aspect'. However, other experts hotly deny this, and this book avoids the term 'aspect' since it is too controversial and is not very helpful to learners. See 14.4.4 for more on this point.

auxiliary verb   a VERB used in combination with the PAST PARTICIPLE of another verb to form a COMPOUND TENSE. In English the auxiliary used is 'to have' as in 'I **have** drunk it'; in Spanish it is *haber*, as in *lo **he** bebido*, or, more rarely *tener*. See 14.8.

cardinal number   the form of a number used for counting : 'one, two, three'; 'I bought **eight** novels'/*compré **ocho** novelas.* See 10.1.

clause   a part of a SENTENCE which itself contains a VERB or VERB PHRASE. A main clause can stand on its own as a separate sentence, a SUBORDINATE CLAUSE cannot. In 'my car is parked where you left it yesterday', 'my car is parked' is a main clause, 'where you left it yesterday' is a subordinate clause' dependent on the main clause. Sentences therefore consist either of a main clause alone – 'John likes classical music' – or a main clause plus one or more subordinate clauses, e.g. 'John likes listening to music **when he can't go out**'.

cleft sentence   defined at 36.2.1

collective noun   defined at 2.3.1

comment   defined at 37.5.1

comparative   the form of an ADJECTIVE or ADVERB used to express a comparison: 'faster', 'less intelligent', 'better', 'worse', *más rápido, menos inteligente, mejor, peor*, etc. See Chapter 5.

compound noun	a noun formed by joining two or more words, e.g. 'police dog'/*perro policía*, 'missile launcher'/*lanzamisiles*. See 2.1.7.
compound tense	TENSES formed by using an AUXILIARY VERB (normally *haber* in Spanish) with the PAST PARTICIPLE of another verb. See 14.8 for a list.
conditional	a form of the VERB used to express conditions, e.g. 'it would break'/*se rompería*. See 13.1.8 and 14.7.
conditional sentence	a SENTENCE which expresses a condition, i.e. 'if X, then Y'. See Chapter 25.
conjugate(d)	refers to the way a verb takes different forms to show AGREEMENT with the SUBJECT, and to indicate TENSE or MOOD. The statement *'hablar* conjugates exactly like *amar'* means that the endings of both verbs are identical: *hablo/amo, hablas/amas, hablé/amé*, etc.
conjugation	see 13.1.1
conjunction	a word or phrase (other than a RELATIVE PRONOUN) used to link words, phrases or CLAUSES within a SENTENCE, e.g. 'and', 'but', *y, pero*, etc. See Chapter 33.
continuous form	the Spanish verb form made up of *estar* + the gerund: *estoy hablando, estabas durmiendo*, etc. See 15.1.1 and 15.1.2.
count noun	defined at 2.2.1
dative	a term occasionally used in this book to refer to the third-person pronouns when they are used to indicate an INDIRECT OBJECT, i.e. *le* or *les* or 'I gave **her** five dollars'. It has wider meanings in general linguistics.
defective verb	a verb of which certain forms are not used. *Abolir* is an example: see 13.3.2.
definite article	see ARTICLE
demonstrative	an ADJECTIVE or PRONOUN which points to something specific, e.g. 'this'/*este*, 'that'/*ese/aquel*, 'those'/*esos/aquellos*. See Chapter 6.
descriptive adjective	see RELATIONAL ADJECTIVE
determiner	a word used with NOUNS and ADJECTIVES to make them definite or specific (or, in the case of adjectives, to turn them into nouns). They include the ARTICLES, DEMONSTRATIVES, and POSSESSIVES. See 4.1d and 4.10b for their effect on adjectives.
dieresis	the two dots over the *ü* in words like *lingüista*. See 39.1.3e.

diminutive suffix a SUFFIX added to a word to denote smallness, affection, etc., e.g. 'pig**let**', 'kitchen**ette**', *casita*.

direct object a NOUN, NOUN PHRASE or PRONOUN that receives the direct action of the verb. In 'Mary gave Bill a present', 'a present' is the direct object since the action is done to it; Bill is the INDIRECT OBJECT since he is the receiver.

direct speech see INDIRECT SPEECH

discourse marker words and phrases like 'nevertheless', 'on the contrary', 'incidentally', 'obviously', that are used to connect statements in continuous speech or writing. See 33.11.

dynamic a dynamic verb refers to an action done by someone or something: 'he **broke** a window', 'I **wrote** a novel'. Some verbs do not denote actions but 'states', i.e. no one is actually *doing* anything, as in 'the sky **is** overcast', 'Jill **seems** absent-minded'.

ending a SUFFIX which gives grammatical information, e.g. about the NUMBER, TENSE, MOOD, GENDER of a word. .Typical Spanish endings are *hablaron, buenos, vivas*, etc. Typical English endings are 'ship**s**', 'lik**ed**', 'walk**ing**', etc.

exclamation an expression of surprise, anger, wonder, admiration, etc., e.g. 'what a nerve!'/*¡qué cara!* See Chapter 24.

existential sentence defined at 30.1.

feminine one of the two GENDERS into which Spanish NOUNS are divided.

finite verb a form of the VERB which shows TENSE, PERSON and NUMBER. *Hablan*/'they talk' are finite verbs since they indicate when (present), who and plural. *Hablar, hablado, hablando* are non-finite form since they do not indicate tense, person or number.

fulfilled condition used in this book to refer to sentences that look like conditions but actually are not: 'if she slept all day it was because she went clubbing all night'. See 25.7.

future perfect a TENSE formed with the AUXILIARY VERB 'to have'/*haber* and a PAST PARTICIPLE used to refer to an action or event which will occur before another in the future: 'I **will have finished** it by then'/*para entonces lo* **habré terminado**. See 14.11.

future tense in Spanish this usually refers to the special tense forms like *hablaré, vendrá, irán* used to refer (among other things) to future time. See 13.1.8 and 14.6.

gender	all Spanish NOUNS (except for a few undecided ones) are divided into two classes called MASCULINE and FEMININE. These labels have nothing to do with sex when the nouns refer to plants, most wild animals, and non-living things (see Chapter 1). For neuter gender see Chapter 7.
generic	a generic noun refers to concepts, things or people in general: '**monkeys** are intelligent', 'I don't like **beer**', '**freedom** means different things'. 'Partitive' nouns refer only to a part of the whole: 'she brought **some roses**/*trajo rosas* (not roses in general).
gerund	a NON-FINITE Spanish verb form, defined at 20.1
idiom, idiomatic	an idiom is a group of words whose meaning cannot be worked out from the meaning of the individual words. The sense of 'he was hung-over' cannot be deduced from the words 'to hang' and 'over'. *Echar de menos* 'to miss (someone)' must be learned separately: it has no relation to *echar* 'to throw', or *menos* 'less'.
imperative	a MOOD of the VERB used to give commands or instructions or to make requests. See Chapter 17.
imperfect tense	an important TENSE form of Spanish verbs that refers to actions that were going on *at the time*, e.g. *hablaba, comías, eran*, etc. See 14.5 for a definition.
impersonal *se*	see *SE* IMPERSONAL
impersonal sentences	defined at 28.1
indefinite article	see ARTICLE
indefinite pronoun	see PRONOUN
indicative	the verb forms used to state facts or beliefs: 'the earth **is** round'/*la tierra **es** redonda*; 'I think Anne is away'/*creo que Ana **está** fuera*. See 16.2.5. The immense majority of verbs in English and Spanish appear in the indicative.
indirect object	in Spanish, a NOUN, NOUN PHRASE or PRONOUN that receives or loses something from the effect of a verb or adjective. In *Miguel **le** dio mil euros*, *le* receives the money and is therefore the indirect object. In Spanish, but not in English, indirect objects can also lose: ***me** robaron mil euros* = 'they stole 1000 euros off/from me'. See 11.7.2 and 12.3 for details.
indirect question	a question reported in INDIRECT SPEECH. 'When did you arrive?' is a direct question; 'I wonder when you arrived?' is an indirect question. So is 'I don't know how to do it' (direct question: 'how do I do it?'). Another definition: a sentence which has a subordinate CLAUSE beginning with an INTERROGATIVE word.

indirect speech   see REPORTED SPEECH

infinitive   the dictionary form of a VERB, always ending in *–ar, -er, ir* or *ír* in Spanish. See 18.1.

interrogative   words like 'when?', 'where?', 'who?', 'which?', 'what?', 'how?' used to ask questions. See Chapter 24 for a list.

intransitive verb   a VERB is **intransitive** if it cannot have a DIRECT OBJECT: 'I came'/*vine* is classified as intransitive since one cannot 'come something' or 'someone'.

irregular verb   a VERB which is CONJUGATED in a way that does not follow the pattern of the immense majority of Spanish verbs. See 13.1.3 and 13.3–4 for lists and comments.

masculine   one of the two GENDERS into which Spanish NOUNS are divided

mass noun   defined at 2.2.1

modal auxiliaries   defined at 21.1

mood   Spanish and English verbs have three 'moods': the INDICATIVE mood, the IMPERATIVE mood and the SUBJUNCTIVE mood, the latter being rare in English but much used in Spanish. See this glossary for definitions. English-speakers often confuse this term with the word used in 'I'm in a bad *mood*', but the grammatical term derives from a Latin word meaning 'mode'.

neuter   in Spanish, the special form of some pronouns and articles used to refer to things that are not nouns and therefore neither masculine nor feminine. See 7.1.

nominalizer   defined at 36.1.1

non-finite verb form   See FINITE VERB

noun   a type of word which refers to a person, animal, plant, lifeless object, place or abstraction: 'man', 'student', 'dog', 'oak-tree', 'book', 'New York', 'home', 'justice', 'happiness' are all nouns. In Spanish nouns have either masculine or feminine GENDER.

noun phrase   A group of connected words containing a NOUN (or a PRONOUN) and any other words accompanying it, i.e. a DETERMINER and/or an ADJECTIVE: 'bread', 'white bread', 'the shop on the corner', etc.

number   the grammatical distinction between SINGULAR and PLURAL

object pronouns	used in this book to refer to the Spanish pronouns *me/te/lo/la/les/nos/os/los/las* and *les*. See 11.1 and 11.7.
open conditions	defined at 25.2
ordinal number	a form of a numeral used as an ADJECTIVE to indicate the place something occupies in a series: 'my **first** kiss' / *mi primer beso*, 'the **sixth** chapter' / *el sexto capítulo*. See 10.12.
participle	NON-FINITE forms of the VERB. Spanish has a PAST PARTICIPLE, e.g. *hablado* and an ADJECTIVAL PARTICIPLE, e.g. *saliente, perteneciente*. See Chapter 19.
participle clause	a clause in which the FINITE VERB is replaced by a PARTICIPLE: 'having realized the truth, I left', instead of 'when I had realized the truth, I left'.
partitive	the opposite of GENERIC
passive	a verbal construction where the doer of the action is not necessarily mentioned and the SUBJECT is typically a person or thing to which something happens, e.g. '**Maurice** was elected as chairperson'. Spanish has two passive constructions, (1) passive with *ser* – *la casa fue construida* – defined at 28.2, and (2) 'passive *se*' – *la casa se construyó* – defined at 28.4. A special version of the latter construction is used when the noun or pronoun refers to a human being, e.g. *se arrestó a tres personas*. See 28.5.
past participle	a NON-FINITE form of the VERB, typically ending in *–ado* or *–ido*, e.g. *hablado, vivido, comido*. See 19.1 and 19.2 for its forms and uses.
past tense	in Spanish, any TENSE that refers to the past, e.g. PRETERITE, IMPERFECT, PERFECT, or PLUPERFECT, as opposed to PRESENT or FUTURE tenses.
perfect tense	a COMPOUND TENSE of the verb, defined at 14.9. It is called 'present perfect' in some grammar books since the AUXILIARY VERB is in the present tense.
person	a grammatical category indicating the person speaking. Spanish and English have three 'persons': the 'first' person: 'I' / 'we' / *yo* / *nosotros/as*, the second person, i.e. the person addressed, 'you' / *tú/vos/ usted/ vosotros/as/ ustedes*; and the third person, i.e. other persons or things that we are talking about: 'he' / 'she' / 'it' / 'they', *él/ella/ellos/ellas*. See 11.1 and 11.2.
personal *a*	defined at 22.1
personal pronoun	see PRONOUN

phrase	any meaningful combination of words that does not contain a FINITE VERB. So 'coffee with milk' is a phrase, whereas 'I like coffee with milk' is a SENTENCE.
pluperfect tense	a COMPOUND TENSE defined at 14.10
plural	a grammatical term referring to more than one person or thing. 'Dog' is a SINGULAR noun, 'dogs' is plural.
possessive adjective or pronoun	a word that indicates the identity of the possessor, e.g. 'my'/'your'/'his', *mi/tu/su*, 'mine'/'hers'/*mío/suyo*, etc. See 8.1–2.
predicate	the part of the sentence which says something about the SUBJECT. In this grammar the word is used only of the predicates of the verb 'to be', e.g. *Miguel es **amigo de Pedro***.
prefix	letters added to the beginning of the root form of a word so as to alter or add meaning, e.g. '**pre**conception', '**re**place'.
preposition	a word or phrase used before a noun or pronoun to relate it grammatically to another word or phrase: 'the dog's sleeping **on** the bed', *fuimos **a** Caracas*, 'I came back **with** her'/*volví **con** ella*, etc. See Chapter 34 for a list.
present participle	in Spanish studies, a rather inaccurate alternative name for the ADJECTIVAL PARTICIPLE
present tense	the simple TENSE, e.g. *hablo, comes, son*, that indicates – among other things – that an action is occurring *now*. See 14.3.
preterite tense	(American spelling 'preterit'). A TENSE of Spanish verbs that indicates actions or events in the past that are viewed as completed at the time, e.g. *habló, hizo*. See 13.1.7, 14.4.
pronominal verb	any Spanish verb whose third-person infinitive ends in *–se*, i.e. *lavarse, irse, dormirse, salirse*. The meanings of such verbs are variable. Other grammars often call these 'reflexive verbs', a term that we reject for the reasons given at 26.1.
pronoun	a word which replaces a NOUN PHRASE already mentioned, or about to be mentioned, in a sentence: 'John came in and **he** said to **me**', *¿conoces a **alguien** que pueda ayudar**me**?* Personal pronouns refer to known people or things: 'he', 'she', 'you', it', etc. Indefinite pronouns refer to unidentified persons or things: 'someone', 'anyone', 'something', *algo, alguien*, etc.
reciprocal	one possible *meaning* of plural PRONOMINAL VERBS, i.e. when the subjects perform an action on or for one another. See 26.3.
reflexive	used in this book to refer to one possible *meaning* of a Spanish PRONOMINAL VERB, i.e. when the subject performs and action upon or for himself/herself, as in 'I wash myself'/*me lavo*. See 26.2.

reflexive verb   a term replaced in this book by PRONOMINAL VERB

relational adjective   a type of Spanish ADJECTIVE that typically replaces a phrase consisting of *de* + a noun, e.g. *problemas **estudiantiles*** for *problemas de los estudiantes, industria **petrolera*** for *industria del petróleo* 'oil industry'. See 4.12 for details. Adjectives that merely describe qualities (the majority), like '**big** tree', *hombre **inteligente***, are 'descriptive' adjectives.

relative clause   a **subordinate** CLAUSE that modifies a noun or pronoun used earlier in a sentence, e.g. 'the house **that Jack built**', *el amigo **con el que fui al cine***. All Spanish relative clauses must be introduced by a RELATIVE PRONOUN. See Chapter 35.

relative pronoun   defined at 35.1

remote conditions   defined at 25.3

reported speech   a construction by which what someone said is built into a sentence rather than given in the speaker's original words. 'Bill said "I feel tired"' reports Bill's direct speech; 'Bill said that he felt tired' is an example of reported speech.

restrictive   a term applied to ADJECTIVES (see 4.11.1) and to RELATIVE CLAUSES (see 35.1.2)

se de matización   defined at 26.5

se impersonal   a name for the Spanish pronoun *se* when it has the same meaning as the French word *on*, German *man*, English 'people'/'one', as in *se entra por aquí* 'one goes in this way', *se come demasiado* 'people eat too much'. It must be distinguished from *SE PASIVO*.

se pasivo   see PASSIVE

sentence   the longest unit of grammar, ending with a full stop in writing. It must have at least one main CLAUSE, e.g. *Miguel compró un coche*, and the main clause(s) can have one or more dependent **subordinate clauses**: *Miguel compró un coche **que tiene cuatro puertas***. 'Fantastic party last night!' is not a sentence but a phrase since it has no FINITE VERB. See also PHRASE.

singular   a grammatical term referring to one person or thing. See also PLURAL.

stress   a feature of Spanish, English and many, but not all, languages whereby one syllable in a word is pronounced more energetically than the rest. The position of the stress can affect meaning in both languages, cf. 'a re**bel**' and 'they re**bel**', or the difference between *hablo* and *habló*.

subject
the person or thing that performs the action of a verb, as in '**Mike** slammed the door', '**Jill's** sleeping'. In the case of verbs like 'to be' or 'to seem' that do not refer to actions, the person or thing about which something is predicated or stated, as in '**Robert** is blond', '**bread** can go stale', '**she** looks pleased'.

subjunctive
a MOOD of the VERB. It is much used in Spanish, but attempts to give a single definition of its various different uses invariably generate confusion. See 16.2.

subordinator
defined at 16.12.1

suffix
letter(s) added to the end of the root form of a word so as to alter or add meaning, e.g. 'social**ism**', 'art**ist**', 'deep**en**'

superlative
the form of an adjective or adverb used to show that a noun or pronoun has the most or least of a quality, e.g. 'he is the **tallest**'/*él es el más alto*, 'the **least expensive**'/*el menos caro*

tense
a form of the VERB which indicates the time of an event or state. Tenses can be past, present or future, but there are more than three tense forms in English and Spanish. See Chapter 14.

topic
the element in a sentence about which we wish to say something. It usually, but by no means always, coincides with the SUBJECT of the sentence, e.g. '**Peter** won the lottery'. But it could be a DIRECT OBJECT, e.g. '**pork** I'm not eating, so there!', or some other word or phrase. See 37.5.1.

transitive verb
a VERB is transitive if it can have a DIRECT OBJECT: 'I **broke** a glass', *Ángel la criticó*. See also INTRANSITIVE VERB.

unfulfilled conditions
defined at 25.4

verb
a type of word which refers to an action, event, process or state: 'to sleep', 'to shine, 'to go', to be', *comer, brillar, estar/ser*.

verb phrase
the part of a SENTENCE containing a VERB and its DIRECT or INDIRECT OBJECT(s) if they exist. In 'Peter's girlfriend ate five kebabs'. 'Peter's girlfriend', the SUBJECT, is a NOUN PHRASE, the rest is a verb phrase.

Bibliography and sources

The following general works are useful for serious students of Spanish.

Mention must also be made of the two series *Problemas básicos del español* published by the Sociedad General Española de Librería of Madrid and *Problemas fundamentales del español*, published by the Colegio de España, Salamanca. Although uneven in quality, all these booklets contain important information for intermediate and advanced learners of Spanish.

Gerboin, P. & Leroy, C., *Grammaire d'usage de l'espagnol contemporain* (Paris: Hachette, 1994). A reference grammar useful for students who know French.

Moliner, M., *Diccionario de uso del español*, 2 vols, new edition (Madrid: Gredos, 1998). An enhanced version of an indispensable work. The CD version is useful.

Oxford Spanish Dictionary, 3rd edition, ed. B. Galimberti Jarman, R. Russell, C. Styles Carvajal, and J. Horwood (Oxford: University Press, 2003). Clear, accurate, comprehensive and rich in Latin-American vocabulary.

El País, *Libro de estilo*, 16th edition (Madrid: Ediciones *El País*, 2002). Based on the house rules of this prestigious daily newspaper. A generally uncontroversial and reliable guide to good Peninsular written usage. *Abc* and *El Mundo* also publish their house rules.

J. Pountain, C. and de Carlos, T., *Practising Spanish Grammar* (London, Arnold: 2000). A workbook based on Butt & Benjamin.

Ramsey, M. and Spaulding, J. K., *A Textbook of Modern Spanish* (New York, 1958; often reprinted). Composed by Ramsey in the 1880s and revised by Spaulding in the 1940s. Very thorough but dated.

Real Academia Española, *Gramática de la lengua española: Nueva edición* (Madrid, 1931, often reprinted). A useful but old-fashioned reference-point.

——*Esbozo de una nueva gramática de la lengua española* (Madrid: Espasa Calpe, 1973). Largely superseded by the following work.

——*Gramática descriptiva de la lengua española*, ed. I. Bosque Muñoz and V. Demonte Barreto, 3 vols (Madrid: Espasa Calpe, 1999). A collection of articles by more than seventy authors: the most comprehensive descriptive grammar available, but strictly for theoretical linguists. The bibliography is extensive.

Seco, M., *Diccionario de dudas y dificultades de la lengua española*, 10a edición revisada y puesta al día, (Madrid: Espasa Calpe, 1998). Remains indispensable amid the flood of sometimes mutually contradictory guides to good usage now available in Spain.

——, Andrés, O. and Ramos, G., *Diccionario del español actual*, 2 vols (Madrid: Aguilar, 2001). An excellent, up-to-date monolingual dictionary.

Collins Spanish-English English-Spanish Dictionary, 7th edition, ed. T. Álvarez García and C. Lilly (Glasgow & New York: HarperCollins, 2003). Clear, rich in Latin-American vocabulary and colloquial examples.

The following works are mentioned in the text:

Arjona Iglesias, M., *Estudios sintácticos sobre el español hablado de México* (Mexico: Universidad Autónoma, 1991).
Carnicer, R. *Nuevas reflexiones sobre el lenguaje* (Madrid: Prensa Española, 1972).

The numerous articles of George DeMello of the University of Iowa, based on his analyses of the Corpus of Educated Spoken Spanish from eleven cities, are especially useful in determining the geographical range of certain constructions in spontaneous speech. The following are quoted in the text:

DeMello, G, (1992, 1) *'Se los* for *se lo* in the Spoken Cultured Spanish of Eleven Cities', *Hispanic Journal* 13, 1 (1992), 165–79.
——(1992, 2) *'Les* for *Les* in the Spoken Educated Spanish of Eleven Cities', *The Canadian Journal of Linguistics*, 37, 4 (1992), 407–30.
——(1992, 3) 'El artículo definido con nombre propio de persona en el español hablado culto contemporáneo', *Studia Neophilologica* 64 (1992), 221–34.
——(1992, 4) 'Duplicación del pronombre relativo de objeto directo en el español hablado culto de once ciudades', *Lexis*, XVI, 1 (1992), 23–52.
——(1992, 5) *'Cuyo* y reemplazos por *cuyo* en el español hablado contemporáneo', *Anuario de lingüística Hispánica*, VIII (Lima, 1992), 53–71.
——(1994, 1) 'Pretérito compuesto para indicar acción con límite en el pasado: *ayer he visto a Juan'*, *Boletín de la Real Academia Española*, LXXIV, Cuaderno CCLXIII (1994), 611–33.
——(1994, 2) *'El cual* vs. *el que* en el español hablado culto; parte I: su empleo como sujeto u objeto de preposición', *Hispanic Journal*, 15, 1 (1994), 89–110.
——(1994, 3) *'El cual* vs. *el que* en el español hablado culto: parte II: su empleo como sujeto u objeto de verbo, con sustantivo propio, con "todo", con expresiones temporales', *Hispanic Journal*, 15, 2 (1994), 393–408.
——(1995, 1) 'Concordancia entre el verbo pronominal de tercera persona y su sustantivo: *se venden flores* vs. *se vende flores'*, *Anuario de letras de la Facultad de Filosofia y Letras: Centro de Lingüística Hispánica* XXXIII (Mexico: UNAM, 1995), 59–82.
——(1995, 2) Preposición + Sujeto + Infinitivo: "Para yo hacerlo" *Hispania*, 78, 4 (1995), 825–36.
——(1996, 1) [Pronombre 'sí'] vs [Pronombre no-reflexivo]: 'Juan lo compra *para sí* vs 'Juan lo compra para *él mismo'*, *Bulletin of Hispanic Studies* (Liverpool), LXXIII, 3 (1996), 297–310.
——(1992, 2) 'Indicativo por subjuntivo en cláusula regida por expresión de reacción personal', *Nueva Revista de Filología Hispánica*, XLIV, 2 (1996), 365–86.
——(2001, 1) 'A de acusativo con nombre propio geográfico', *Hispania*, 83, 2 (2000), 301–13.
——(2000, 2) '"Tú" impersonal en el habla culta', *Nueva Revista de Filología Hispánica* XLVIII, 2 (2000), 359–72.

———(2000, 3) 'Variantes en las formas de algunos determinantes delante de sustantivo femenino que empieza por "a" tónica: "un arma" vs. "una arma"', *Hispanic Journal*, 21, 1 (2000), 47–60.

——— *Estudios de lenguaje infantil* (Barcelona: Biblograf, 1972).

García, E., *The Role of Theory in Linguistic Analysis: The Spanish Pronoun System* (Amsterdam/Oxford: North-Holland, 1975).

Gili y Gaya, S., *Curso superior de sintaxis española*, 8a edición (Barcelona: Biblograf, 1958; often reprinted).

Gooch, A. L., *Diminutive, Pejorative and Augmentative Suffixes in Modern Spanish*, 2nd edition (Oxford: Pergamon, 1970).

Hammer, A. E., *German Grammar and Usage*, 1st edition (London: Edward Arnold, 1971).

Ingamells, L. & Standish, P., *Variedades del español actual* (London: Longman, 1975), a useful collection of texts from all over the Hispanic world.

Kany, C. E., *Sintaxis hispanomericana* (Madrid: Gredos, 1970, several reprints); English original published by the University of Chicago (1945). A valuable guide to the variety of Latin-American syntax. It does not reliably mark register, so many examples may be sub-standard even on their own territory.

Lope Blanch, J. M., *Estudios sobre el español de México* (Mexico City: Universidad Nacional Autónoma, 1991).

Lorenzo, E., *El español de hoy: lengua en ebullición*, 3a edición (Madrid: Gredos, 1980).

Macpherson, I. R., *Spanish Phonology: Descriptive and Historical* (Manchester & New York: Manchester University Press, 1975).

Marsá, F., *Diccionario normativo y guía práctica de la lengua española* (Barcelona: Ariel, 1986).

Martínez de Sousa, J., *Diccionario de usos y dudas del español actual*, 3rd edition (Barcelona: Vox, 2001).

Moreira Rodríguez, A. & Butt, J., *Se de matización & the Semantics of Spanish Pronominal Verbs*, King's College London Hispanic Series (London: King's College London, 1996).

Navas Ruiz, R., *El subjuntivo castellano* (Salamanca: Colegio de España, 1986).

Quirk, R., Greenbaum, S., Leech, G. & Svartvik, J., *A Grammar of Contemporary English* (London: Longman, 1972).

Santamaría, A. et al., *Diccionario de incorrecciones, particularidades y curiosidades del lenguaje* , 5th edition (Madrid: Paraninfo, 1989).

Santillana Editorial, *Diccionario de dificultades de la lengua española* (Madrid: Santillana, 1995).

Sources of examples

They are too numerous to be listed individually. Many of the examples are modified versions of extracts from printed or spoken sources; these are not attributed. Attributed quotations are often from sources chosen not for their literary qualities but because they exemplify the plain everyday Spanish that this grammar describes. Poetry and poetic prose have been excluded. The following authors and publications are quoted several times:

Argentina: Jorge Asís, Jorge Luis Borges, Julio Cortázar, *Gente*, *La Nación*, Abel Posse, Manuel Puig, Ernesto Sábato, *Río Negro*. **Bolivia**: *La Prensa*. **Chile**: Isabel

Allende, José Donoso, Luis Sepúlveda, Sergio Vodanovic, *La Época*. **Colombia**: Gabriel García Márquez, *El Tiempo, El País*. **Costa Rica**: *La Nación*. **Cuba**: Reinaldo Arenas, Antón Arrufat, Pablo Armando Fernández, Guillermo Cabrera Infante, *Cuba Internacional*, *Granma* (official organ of the Communist Party of Cuba), Lisandro Otero, *Vindicación de Cuba* (the published transcript of a show trial). **Dominican Republic**: *Hora*. **Ecuador**: *El Comercio, Hoy*. **Guatemala**: *Prensa Libre*. **Honduras**: *La Prensa*. **Mexico**: Juan José Arreola, *Excelsior*, Carlos Fuentes, Sergio Galindo, Jorge Ibargüengoitia, *La Jornada*, Ángela Mastretta, *El Nacional*, Octavio Paz, Sergio Pitol, Elena Poniatowska, *La Reforma*, Luis Spota, *UnoMásUno*, Carlos Solórzano (born in Guatemala). **Nicaragua**: *Tiempos de Mundo*. **Panama**: José de Jesús Martínez (born in Guatemala), *La Prensa*. **Paraguay**: *Abc Color*. **Peru**: Alfredo Bryce Echenique, *El Comercio*, Mario Vargas Llosa. **Puerto Rico**: Luis Rafael Sánchez. **Spain**: *Abc*, Ignacio Aldecoa, Josefina Aldecoa, Eloy Arenas, Carlos Barral, Antonio Buero Vallejo, *Cambio16*, Camilo José Cela, Miguel Delibes, *Diario16*, Antonio Gala, Federico García Pavón, Juan Goytisolo, Luis Goytisolo, Alfonso Grosso, José María Guelbenzu, Juan Madrid, Javier Marías, José Antonio Marina, Juan Marsé, Carmen Martín Gaite, Eduardo Mendoza, Terenci Moix, Rosa Montero, *El Mundo*, *El País*, Soledad Puértolas, Carmen Rico-Godoy, Alfonso Sastre, *La Vanguardia*, Manuel Vázquez Montalbán, Federico Umbral. **Uruguay**: *Hoy*, Mario Benedetti. **Venezuela**: *El Nacional, Rebelión, El Universal*.

Index of English words

The sign = should be read 'when it has the meaning of'. English words not listed should be sought in the main index under their most obvious translation, e.g. 'to beat' under *pegar*.

Index of Spanish words and grammatical points

For the conjugation of individual verbs see 13.4 (irregular) and 13.5 (regular).

A preceding interrogation mark indicates a questionable form censured by grammarians, e.g. *?contra más…, ?se los dije.*